PRAISE FOR *NAKED WORSHIP*

I am delighted to recommend this outstanding book with its provocative title. A must read for any Christian wanting to go deeper. WARNING… this is not for everybody but for true worshippers. Dr. Carmont, my beloved mentor and friend has in this tome spread a rich biblical feast before us, with systematic exposition, insightful illustration and practical application that will warm your heart, stimulate your mind and draw you to BEING a worshipper in Spirit and truth.

—**Jonathan Michael,** *Faculty, Trinity Western University, Langley, British Columbia*

Naked Worship speaks to both the mind and heart of our relationship with God. Don Carmont's writing gives a comprehensive Biblical overview of insight and truth; at the same time applies Job's narrative to the central response of our complete submission to the Lord. I commend this book for your reading and response. You will be thankful for the breadth of information and be drawn into a life of worship.

—**Rev. Stan Powers,** *Regional Director, Pacific Region, Apostolic Church of Pentecost*

If we are fortunate, every generation produces a few brilliant people who affect our thinking and ultimate behavior. For our generation, Don Carmont, my friend and mentor, is one of those men, extremely talented and deep thinking with a God given ability to get the core of nagging issues.

—**Bruce Hampson,** *Author, Entrepreneur, Philanthropist*

I have always been in awe of the gift of music God has entrusted to Don. One day as he was playing a new song that he had composed I saw his beloved piano revealed as the Old Testament altar of incense. It has always been about praise and worship for him. This book will take you on a journey from the shallows of nominal church attendance into the deeper waters of a transformed life in Christ.

—**Marcel Paul Carpenter,** *MCS, (retired) Faculty, Southern Alberta Institute of Technology*

Naked Worship is a book most urgently needed in the confusing and sometimes bitter debate about the multiplicity of worship forms presently in vogue. In an age which says, "If it feels good, do it!" the Church itself has succumbed in many ways. In a sound, biblical and theologically clear manner, Dr. Donald Carmont addresses the issues which have been contentious and divisive within the evangelical community. It is factual and fascinating. Every pastor, elder, deacon and church member should prayerfully think his way through this book. I cannot recommend it highly enough! Personally, I can't wait to see it in print and available to everyone. It has been a privilege to read it in advance of publication."

—**Rev. Cal Bombay,** *Author, Teacher, Missionary*

If you are honestly and sincerely seeking answers to questions like, "What is Worship, Why should we worship, and How should worship?" then, *Naked Worship* is must reading. Dr. Carmont's peace plan for the worship wars arises from profound Biblical insight, scholarly research, and pastoral sensitivity. Ultimately, however, Dr. Carmont provides the reader with specific principles that will help guide your church to create worship worthy of our Lord and King.

—**Rev. Albert Vantassel,** *Pastor, Bethlehem Baptist Church, Hampden, MA*

From Mongolia to Indonesia, from Korea to Nepal, all across this great continent of Asia, I have had the joy and privilege of worshipping with the Church of Jesus. Some were conducted in great cathedrals and stadiums, others were in caves, or deep in the forest. But one thing is for sure, their worship is not just a celebration before their King, but it is also a battle cry for their Lord of Hosts. Dr. Donald Carmont's latest book, *Naked Worship*, is an extraordinary insight into the true nature of worshipping the Lord.

—**Rev. Dr. David Wang,** *Director, Asian Outreach, Hong Kong*

In *Naked Worship*, Dr. Donald Carmont covers the whole spectrum of what is true worship, and what is not. While worship is expressed with emotion, he shows the difference in true worship and just emotionalism. Jesus said "true worship must be in spirit and truth." Genuine worship can be expressed toward a wrong object as in the case of the Golden calf, so it must be in truth. A performance with no heart or spirit involved is not true worship. This book will cause one to do some soul-searching, and make us aware as to whether we have or are offering acceptable worship to our God. Don illustrates that much that is called worship, is not worship at all; it is merely a religious exercise without heart.

—**Rev. E. P. Wickens (late),** *former General Superintendent, UPC, Fredericton, NB*

It was at Moose Lake Gospel Camp in Alberta that I first heard Donald Carmont speak on the Worship. I was impressed by his approach to the subject of Worship and later found out he was writing a book on the subject. I was looking forward to reading the book. Donald is a man of many talents: He is a gifted speaker and musician. He also has expertise in communication as demonstrated in his book. The book, *Naked Worship* manuscript came to me, and I am so impressed by the in-depth research he has done on the subject—more thorough than anything I have previously read. There has been a lot of talk and teaching about worship, but you will appreciate this book because it gives a balanced presentation of the subject and provides a lot of background and reference material.

—**Rev. Gillis Killam,** *former Moderator, ACOP, Calgary, AB*

Naked Worship illuminates the great moments of worship providing a rich understanding of what worship means and what it is to participate in a worshiping community. In these exciting times of renewal in worship, this book lays a strong Biblical foundation for the emerging dialogue. It points out the centrality of worship in the experience of a life of faith and, not content with an overview, it mines the Scriptures for the gems of truth on this matter of significant importance for every believer.

—**Rev. Dr. Barry Crane,** *Pastor, Northsound Church, Edmonds, Washington*

After Dr. Carmont's many years of worshiping, leading in worship, mentoring worship leaders, and studying and teaching God's Word, his book, *Naked Worship* is a theologically sound yet practical book every worshiper of Christ must read.

—**Rev. Allen Pangburn,** *Pastor, Praise Tabernacle, Cranston, Rhode Island*

In his latest book, *Naked Worship,* Dr. Donald Carmont with personal craft and pastoral care opens the windows on worship that too long have been closed. His comprehensive, compassionate and Christo-centric style not only inspects the history and mystery of worship; but also brings an invitation for us to once more enter His Presence with intimacy, integrity and heart-felt fervency.

—**Rev. Randy Leavitt,** *Pastor, Peoples Full Gospel Church, Winnipeg, Manitoba*

I found this book to be stimulating and thought-provoking. It is powerful reading and could change your life. A significant addition to my library.

—**Rev. Dr. John Lucas,** *Founder and President, Maranatha Evangelistic Association Worldwide*

Worship is neither a theological statement nor a prescribed activity. Whatever draws attention to Christ is worship; whatever diverts attention from Christ is not. Worship is participation; worship is relational. It is not something one does; it is something one exudes. Don Carmont suggests that worship is a total lifestyle. Seeking foundations in biblical, historical, and theological principles *Naked Worship* elaborates the diversity of Christian worship while distinguishing it from personal preference. The Christian worship experience centers on the communication of divine grace for salvation in the here and now. At the same time, Christian worship translates once–for–all time historical events into present realities so that the faithful might understand, participate and rejoice. Don Carmont invites Christians of all persuasions to rediscover the dimensions of worship that are authentic, total, and transparent.

—Professor Thomas A. Fudge,
Historian and Theologian, University of New England, Australia

My dear friend and mentor, Dr. Donald Carmont, skillfully created an invitation to return to the heart of Worship through thought provoking insight and wisdom. This book expertly reminds us that the writings of the Scriptures are complete and sufficient for our supplication and reverence for the most-high God; and therefore should be solely directed towards God without condition.

—Jeff Ferrey, *Deacon, Calvary Worship Centre, Surrey, British Columbia*

Dr. Don Carmont is a friend, mentor and brother. One of the few today who can expound and articulate the richness of Biblical truth. *Naked Worship* stretched my narrow and preconceived understanding about the history of authentic, Biblical worship. In a 'me-generation' of personal gratification, Dr. Carmont challenges the reader as he walks through the Biblical story and reviews recent history to see for ourselves, that we have lost living life as worshippers of God. My overwhelming sense in putting the book down was this: It's all about You—Jesus.

—**Robert Melnichuk,** *Director of Western Canada, YES TV / Crossroads Christian Communications, Calgary, Alberta*

Naked Worship

Naked Worship

TRANSCENDING STYLE TO TRANSFORM
WORSHIP THROUGH TRANSPARENCY

DONALD M. CARMONT, Ph.D.

Published by Advantage, Charleston, South Carolina.
Member of Advantage Media Group.

ADVANTAGE is a registered trademark, and the Advantage colophon is a trademark of Advantage Media Group, Inc.

Printed in the United States of America.

10 9 8 7 6 5 4 3 2 1

ISBN: 978-1-64225-093-0
LCCN: 2011000000

This publication is designed to provide accurate and authoritative information in regard to the subject matter covered. It is sold with the understanding that the publisher is not engaged in rendering legal, accounting, or other professional services. If legal advice or other expert assistance is required, the services of a competent professional person should be sought.

Advantage Media Group is proud to be a part of the Tree Neutral® program. Tree Neutral offsets the number of trees consumed in the production and printing of this book by taking proactive steps such as planting trees in direct proportion to the number of trees used to print books. To learn more about Tree Neutral, please visit **www.treeneutral.com**.

Advantage Media Group is a publisher of business, self-improvement, and professional development books and online learning. We help entrepreneurs, business leaders, and professionals share their Stories, Passion, and Knowledge to help others Learn & Grow. Do you have a manuscript or book idea that you would like us to consider for publishing? Please visit **advantagefamily.com** or call **1.866.775.1696**.

TABLE OF CONTENTS

Foreword

TO THE FIRST EDITION

There are those who can perform worship, and there are those who can proclaim concepts of worship to others. As surely as God is seeking worshippers of Himself He surely must be seeking men through whom He can proclaim concepts of worship, for our performance will never out distance our perception.

Some years ago when I shared the speaking assignment at a major convention with Don Carmont I became aware that here was a man who could form and proclaim concepts. Later, when I was a guest speaker in his church, I was thrilled to hear him expound some of his concepts of worship. I urged him to write them for a wider distribution than his local congregation. He plead the business of a growing church and magnanimously gave me a complete set of his notes on the theme of *Great Moments in Worship* and urged me to write the book. He said that he didn't even need to be credited in the book.

I took the notes and left them unread on a shelf in my study for months. Somehow I felt hesitant to touch them. When, much later, Dr. Carmont phoned me to see how the book was progressing I told him that I was convinced that he, not me, should write the book. For a period of several months I pressed him to begin writing, and I rejoiced greatly when he finally reported that the project "was underway." That project is now completed, and the body of Christ is about to be exposed to some exciting ways of viewing worship, some beautiful Biblical examples of these principles in action, and a progressive picture of worship unfolding throughout the Old Testament.

Having viewed the manuscript before it was printed I am thrilled that I obeyed the inner prompting of the Spirit to urge Pastor Carmont to do the writing. It is blessed with his style, his vocabulary, his insights, as well as his concepts.

The marvelous ability of this man to make the Word of God come alive in the pulpit now has the opportunity to do the same thing on the printed page. I urge you to do more than merely read about these great moments. Become an active participant in them by joining these great heroes of faith in their worship of Jehovah God.

—JUDSON CORNWALL, TH.D., PHOENIX, AZ. 1987

Introduction

I first met Don Carmont in the early seventies when as a young preacher he was a guest speaker at the Full Gospel Church in Halifax, Nova Scotia. Since I was also a young preacher, pastoring Christianview Church in the Halifax suburb of Spryfield, I wanted to see and hear his ministry.

The service had begun when I arrived and a tall young man was playing the piano and singing. He displayed a masterful touch on the keyboard and sang with a hearty voice in a manner that both indicated a love for God as he worshipped and an assurance that his gifting was being effectively used. He proceeded to the pulpit and delivered a message on the story of Esther in a manner that evidenced speaking skill, passion for the subject, and respect for the Word of God. As I listened and received blessing from the song and the message, I remember thinking that here was a man who at the very core of his character is a worshipper.

Within a matter of weeks, Don moved to Halifax to pastor the Full Gospel Church, and we quickly became close friends. When I moved to Vancouver to my current pastorate, Don visited our church for guest ministry, and within a couple of years became my neighbor again when he assumed the pastorate of the Peoples Church in Surrey, British Columbia. We have maintained both fellowship in ministry and a close friendship for more than thirty years. We have travelled in ministry together to different parts of the world, and when Don became pastor of Westgate Chapel in the Seattle area, he returned to bless our church with ministry on several occasions.

Don's approach to any task is thorough, comprehensive and never superficial. In this book you will be able to trace in history and in scripture the real purpose, scope and depth of what genuine worship is intended to be. You will witness that each of us has not only the command from God to worship Him with all that we are and possess, but the joy and strength that this assures us as we enter into His presence.

In our odyssey of life there are for each of us unbroken threads of character and recurring themes of expression that anchor us in the valley and on the mountains and everywhere in between. Whether accompanying Big John Hall at the Royal Albert Hall in London, England, playing and singing on his own television program, ministering in churches or composing on the piano at home, Don has consistently expressed a deep awareness of our primary purpose to love and worship God. It is with honor and joy that I recommend this book to anyone desiring to know God and find ways to express their love for Him. I am pleased to count the author as my friend: Don Carmont—worshipper.

—DR. GORDON MCDONALD

Preface

S ome of my earliest childhood memories surround the worship of God. We were taught to pray and worship not only by exhortation but also by example. The family altar in our home went beyond the "Now I lay me down to sleep…" of bedtime prayers and the postscript of "God bless the missionaries…" added to the blessing over the food. My parents were worshippers of God. My Dad loved to read the Bible in his personal and private devotions, and loved the congregational singing of hymns, gospel songs, and choruses of praise that characterized our tiny Pentecostal congregation. His exuberance in raising, clapping and swinging his hands and arms as he sang his praises to God was a remarkable sight and a source for juvenile jibing as we kids would mimic him! My mother, although more reserved in her expression of worship, spent long seasons of time in private prayer and worship. Her prayer took on Biblical proportions of worship, as she would try to contain her love and adoration of her Lord when a passage of Scripture would be illuminated to her heart. The depth of her outbursts of praise to God was evidence of her deep faith and commitment, and of the relationship that she had with God.

The Pentecostal church in which I was raised was part of a small denomination. In my small church, there was no piano or organ when I was younger. We sang to the accompaniment of an electric steel guitar (we called it a Hawaiian guitar). The music was mostly upbeat, fast-paced, and was accompanied by hand-clapping on the fast songs and hand-raising on the slower hymns. For us, this worship style and methodology was sacred. We believed that we had a leg up on the Wesleyans and Baptists who were more subdued, and we looked down our self-righteous noses at the ritualistic ups-and-downs of the Anglican/Episcopal church service. Since we were on the extreme edge of Protestantism, we had little understanding or regard for the more formal worship rituals of the Catholic faith.

It took many years for me to realize that our Pentecostal style of worship itself was a ritual. While we prided ourselves in our "freedom", we had become enslaved to a style of worship that bore little semblance to Biblical worship. During my years as a pastor, I recognized that we had developed and defined our own Pentecostal comfort zone for worship expression, and became extremely uncomfortable when we witnessed anything outside of that comfort zone. My former pastor and good friend, the late Les Burton, captured that reality in the comments he offered having reviewed part of my manuscript:

So much of what people like and don't like about worship is about their personal tastes in music…which is soulish rather than spiritual. People who think they are very spiritual attribute the chills and tears they experience when a piano flourish occurs to the anointing. However, a lead guitar riff can have the same affect on a teenager. In either case, it can be either a soulish response or a sense of the anointing. A little education in this area is greatly needed in the church since much of the entrenchment surrounds this issue: what is really spiritual? The devil is laughing all the while having perverted the mechanism designed to take us from the place of the soul to the spirit by making the mechanism the point thereby missing the point![1]

---

1   E-mail message to Don Carmont from Rev. Les Burton, February 23, 2005

I had been pastoring for about ten years when I was asked to address the subject of "Pentecostal Worship" at a cross-denominational ministerial gathering. I now shamefully remember priding myself in having faithfully expounded on the "higher level" of worship that the Pentecostal style offered than that represented by my brethren of other denominations. I recall a question that came from the father of the Baptist pastor who had invited me to speak. He asked where the "Preaching of the Word" figured in Pentecostal worship, since I had not even alluded to it in my address. I was struck by his question; we had separated the "worship" part of our congregational gathering from the "preaching" part. We had developed a very narrow view of what worship really entailed.

My interest in exploring a deeper approach to worship resulted in a series of sermons that I first preached to the congregation in Seattle where I pastored at the time. I shared a more abbreviated version as a series at various camp meetings and conferences, and taught the material as a course in Bible Colleges in Canada and the United States, and as far afield as the Far East Advanced School of Theology (FEAST) in the Philippines. Based on the response received to the message, I was persuaded to expand upon it and put it in book form. While I was seeking a publisher, circumstances in my personal life compelled me to leave the pastoral ministry, and the book was put aside. While select chapters appeared as a series of articles in several magazines, the book remained unpublished.

Meanwhile, I had no electronic copy of the text, and only one paper copy of more than 200 pages of material! After having put it aside for nearly two decades I felt a strong compulsion to dig it out and revisit the content. I later learned that this urge coincided with the death of my mentor in worship, the late Judson Cornwall, who had written the foreword to the first edition of the proposed book

Great Moments in Worship. Around the same time, an inquiry from a respected friend and colleague requesting my "work on worship" confirmed that it was time to prepare the manuscript for publication. I scanned the text, reformatted it, and after reviewing it, decided to revisit and revamp the material.

When I revisited the material and began to update my research, I was overwhelmed by the sheer volume of scholarly work that was now available on the subject of worship. When I wrote the original manuscript twenty years ago, I had built a significant library on the topic. However, I was not prepared to face the massive mountains of insightful content and commentary now available to me on the web. When I googled the word "worship" I came up with *81.5 million hits* in only two seconds. As I surfed from site to site, I found that the available information was not only profuse, but much of it was also profound. Humbled by the breadth and depth of the insightful work to which I was now exposed, I was almost dissuaded from pursuing the revision of the manuscript. What could I possibly say in the face of such scholarly work? How could I add anything of value? However, I could not put aside the prompting to finish the work.

Perhaps that urge sprang from my own discomfort in leaving tasks unfinished. Or possibly, there was some nostalgia in re-reading material that I had written two decades before. In any case, I immersed myself in the task and quickly found that although nearly twenty years had elapsed since the first writing, the central message was as relevant to today's church as it was when I first wrote it.

I discovered, however, that the church world in which I ministered when I wrote the original manuscript had changed. The lines that had been drawn around denominational and doctrinal distinctives had been redrawn around issues of worship. It had become a battleground where the army of the Lord were shooting themselves in the feet while shooting each other in the heart. How could it be, that this glorious calling to which we are summoned could become a theatre of war?

WHY *NAKED WORSHIP?*

While my original intention was to call the book, "Great Moments in Worship," much of the current controversy around the subject of worship compelled me to instead consider the title "Worship Wars". When I ran the idea by several of my pastor friends, I received various responses. One found the idea oxymoronic: how can you put the words "worship" and "war" in the same sentence? Others found it intriguing, controversial, and engaging. For several months, this remained my title of choice. And yet, I found it strangely unsettling. It just didn't seem right to me to make this the title of the book.

And while the theme of "worship wars" is one to which I devote considerable time in this book, it was while listening to a sermon by Pastor Charles Price at the Peoples Church in Toronto that I fell upon the obvious truth that I had missed. While preaching on the Old Testament character, Job, he read the passage that would become the anchor text and furnish the title for the book. "And Job rose up, and rent his mantle, and shaved his head, and fell down on the ground, and worshipped; and he said, Naked came I out of my mother's womb, and naked shall I return thither: Jehovah gave, and Jehovah hath taken away; blessed be the name of Jehovah! In all this Job sinned not, nor ascribed anything unseemly to God" (Job 1:20-22 Darby).

Ultimately, I settled on the title *Naked Worship*. It is more than coincidental that my first book was entitled *The Naked Mentor*. In that book, I write about transparency and authenticity in human relationships as I tell my own story of failures and the lessons that I learned from my experiences and the many mentors in my life. It occurred to me that what God is looking for in our relationship with Him is nakedness, honesty and authenticity.

I use the phrase *naked worship* to denote that worship which is unfeigned, transparent, real, authentic and without guile or pretense. I use the phrase to describe a worship that is pure, simple, honest and open before God. I use the word *naked* to describe the innocence of our first parents who were created to worship God, and who were unaware of their nakedness until sin invaded Eden's paradise. It is instructive to note that when Adam and Eve disobeyed God, their first impulse in His presence was to cover up.

> Then the eyes of both of them were opened, and they realized they were naked; so they sewed fig leaves together and made coverings for themselves. Then the man and his wife heard the sound of the LORD God as he was walking in the garden in the cool of the day, and they hid from the LORD God among the trees of the garden. But the LORD God called to the man, "Where are you?" He answered, "I heard you in the garden, and I was afraid because I was naked; so I hid." And he said, "Who told you that you were naked? Have you eaten from the tree that I commanded you not to eat from?" (Genesis 3:7-11 NIV).

I find it rather interesting that the third chapters of both the *first* and *last* books of the Bible address the subject of nakedness. Speaking to the church of Laodicea, Christ says,

> You say, "I am rich; I have acquired wealth and do not need a thing." But you do not realize that you are wretched, pitiful, poor, blind and naked. I counsel you to buy from me gold refined in the

fire, so you can become rich; and white clothes to wear, so you can cover your shameful nakedness… (Revelation 3:17-18 NIV).

When we attempt to cover ourselves, God will find us naked. However, when we come before Him naked, He will clothe us. In fact, He promises to clothe us with a garment of praise.

> And provide for those who grieve in Zion—to bestow on them a crown of beauty instead of ashes, the oil of gladness instead of mourning, and a garment of praise instead of a spirit of despair (Isaiah 61:3 NIV).

The glorious truth of the gospel is that through God's redemptive love, Christ became naked that we might be clothed in His righteousness. Isaiah goes on to describe how God clothes us:

> I delight greatly in the LORD; my soul rejoices in my God. For he has clothed me with garments of salvation and arrayed me in a robe of righteousness, as a bridegroom adorns his head like a priest, and as a bride adorns herself with her jewels (Isaiah 61:10 NIV).

Paul speaks of the condescension of Christ and of how He voluntarily stripped himself of all that was rightfully His,

> Who, being in very nature God, did not consider equality with God something to be grasped, but made himself nothing, taking the very nature of a servant, being made in human likeness. And being found in appearance as a man, he humbled himself and became obedient to death—even death on a cross! (Philippians 2:6-8 NIV).

In the next chapter, Paul goes on to speak of the covering of God's righteousness,

And be found in him, not having a righteousness of my own that comes from the law, but that which is through faith in Christ—the righteousness that comes from God and is by faith (Philippians 3:9 NIV).

Naked worship means that I come before God bare, stripped of any self-righteousness, works, good deeds, or any rites or rituals by which I might hope to impress Him. As the third stanza of the great hymn *Rock of Ages Cleft for Me* states,

Nothing in my hand I bring, Simply to Thy cross I cling; Naked, come to Thee for dress; Helpless, look to Thee for grace; Foul, I to the fountain fly, Wash me, Savior, or I die![2]

In fact, the Father's quest for worshippers is a search for *naked* worshippers. While we attach much ritual, rite, and religious ceremony to our worship of God, ultimately the Father seeks those who will worship in spirit and in truth. This essential theme is woven through the entirety of this book.

Of the many contemporary worship songs that we sing, one that has captured the essence of my heart's desire in this book is found in the first few words of *The Heart of Worship* by Matt Redman, "I'm coming back to the heart of worship and it's all about You, it's all about You, Jesus…"[3]

I find it difficult to move away from theologically proofreading and doctrinally editing every song and chorus that we sing in church. While I find many lyrics to be somewhat shallow, I also recognize that they represent the individual experience of the composer. Moreover, my quest is to find the Biblical root and the practical relevance in what is being sung or said. And to that quest, we begin with a panoramic

---

2   Montague, Augustus. *Rock of Ages, Cleft for Me.* Toplady, 1776.

3   Redman, Matt. *The Heart of Worship.* 1997 Kingsway's Thankyou Music.

view of the Scriptures as a worship encyclopedia, and then follow in the footsteps of those who have gone before—as worshippers of God.

1

LET'S GET BIBLICAL

ho could have anticipated that Rick Warren's book *The Purpose Driven Life* would become a best-seller—and not just among religious publications—but, on the New York Times Best-Seller's List? Warren makes the point that "We were planned for God's pleasure…bringing pleasure to God is called worship."[4]

What Warren brilliantly expounds in his book reiterates the shorter Westminster catechism's statement that "Man's chief end is to glorify God and enjoy Him forever."[5] In essence, this means that worship is the supreme purpose for man's existence. In 1543, five centuries before Warren's bestseller swept the nation, in a document to be presented by the leaders of the protestant movement to the Emperor Charles V, *On the Necessity of Reforming the Church*, John Calvin, wrote:

> If it be inquired, then, by what things chiefly the Christian religion has a standing existence amongst us, and maintains its truth, it will be found that the following two notonly occupy the principal place, but comprehend under them all the other parts, and consequently the whole substance of Christianity, viz., a

4   Warren, Rick. *The Purpose Driven Life*. Grand Rapids, MI: Zondervan, 2002., pp.63-64.

5   http://www.asa3.org/gray/westminster_standards/shorter_catechism.html

knowledge, first, of the mode in which God is duly worshipped; and, secondly, of the source from which salvation is to be obtained.[6]

Calvin's ranking of worship as first in importance over salvation might draw immediate protests from the most devout of Protestants. Certainly, evangelical Christians would tend to contend that salvation must take precedence over worship. However, Calvin's ranking is due to one very important fact: that salvation is a *means* to an end, and that worship is the *end* itself. We are *saved* to *worship* God, now and eternally, with our temporal worship being a foretaste of the eternal worship that awaits us. Calvin went on to pen these words:

> There is nothing more perilous to our salvation than a pre-posterous and perverse worship of God...Let us know and be fully persuaded, that wherever the faithful, who worship him purely and in due form, according to the appointment of his word, are assembled together to engage in the solemn acts of religious worship, he is graciously present, and presides in the midst of them.[7]

While great attention has been given to the subject of worship in recent years, much of the preoccupation has been with worship experience in "church gatherings" rather than viewing worship as encompassing the entirety of a believer's life. In the Pentecostal and Charismatic circles of the Church, to which I trace my own roots, we have witnessed a fixation on worship expression and style at the expense of and to the sad neglect of the true substance of worship.

While this recognized "worship renewal" is part and parcel of what many have dubbed a "new wave" of the Spirit of God, and has brought a breath of fresh air to the Body of Christ, the preoccupation

---

6   Calvin, John. *On the Necessity of Reforming the Church.* Dallas, TX: The Protestant Heritage Press, 1995. First published by The Calvin Translation Society, 1844, 1995.

7   Ibid.

with worship style and the neglect of worship theology has produced a somewhat narrow perspective, and a limited and less than Biblical definition for what constitutes worship.

THE WORSHIP RENEWAL

Since a principal area of focus in the worship renewal has been on worship expression and style, worship has been examined primarily as the expressive demonstration found in the corporate gathering of the Body of Christ. What might be reasonably viewed as matters of taste, background, culture and comfort zones has been championed by some as right or wrong ways to worship.

Like most areas of controversy that bring division to the Church, fanatical insistence on one way versus another, one methodology versus another, results in entrenchment and polarization in the Body of Christ, with each side appealing to obscure passages of Scripture to bolster a particular position.

While the "worship renewal" has helped the church to transcend what one writer described as "the Bible lecture hall mentality"[8], and has called the church to celebration, its overemphasis on style misses the point that true worship must be based on a solid theological foundation.

Real worship is an act of response to something God has already done, and can be expressed in a variety of methods and modes. Whether individual or congregational, worship is a response of thanksgiving to God for His creative and redeeming acts that focuses on the person and work of our Lord Jesus Christ.

---

8   Fitch, David E. *Beyond Sermons and Songs 2: Further Thoughts on Worship and Liturgy.* https://www.christiani-tytoday.com/pastors/2005/december-online-only/beyond-sermons-and-songs-2-further-thoughts-on-worship-and.html

When I use the term, "worship renewal" I refer to the emphasis in the Pentecostal/Charismatic church on some of the following features of congregational celebration of worship:

Sustained harmonious singing of verbal praise (Hallelujah, Praise You Lord, Thank You Jesus, etc.) versus the Classical Pentecostal tradition of cacophonic verbalizing of the same phrases with no attempt at musical harmony

Introduction of "dance" as an expression of worship: the deliberate engagement in dance, with form and step, whether simple or sophisticated versus the Classical Pentecostal experience of "dancing in the Spirit" (a phrase used to describe various forms of shaking, quaking, jumping, etc., when 'induced' by the Spirit)

Singing of the "Scriptures" themselves, along with new "Scripture choruses" of worship, often in replacement of Protestant hymnology, versus the Classical Pentecostal mixture of reformation and revival hymns and choruses

Those who championed the cause of "worship renewal" often did so to the disparagement of the Classical Pentecostal worship expression and experience, and in so doing, did detriment to their cause. While the entire Pentecostal ritual itself might have needed some renovation, where it was revamped, it was replaced with a new ritual: that of the "worship renewal". The advocates of the "new wave" of worship desperately sought to establish Biblical basis for their emphasis.

THE TABERNACLE OF DAVID

Some represented this "new wave" as the rebuilding of the "tabernacle of David" enunciated by Peter, *"After this I will return and will rebuild the tabernacle of David, which has fallen down; I will rebuild its ruins, and I will set it up…"* (Acts 15:16 NKJV).

From this starting point, it was an easy leap to insist upon the restoration of the worship style modeled by David in the Book of Psalms. Therefore, anything that could be proof-texted from the Book of Psalms was regarded as normative for the Christian Church. Hence, the emphasis upon external expressions of worship was of singular significance in the "worship renewal."

It ought not to come as any surprise that the Pentecostal culture would furnish the appropriate soil for this seed to take root and flourish. After all, Pentecostal worship expression and experience had itself focused on external elements. This was true not only in matters of congregational worship, but also in matters of personal holiness. Lacking a theological base and understanding for what worship entails, the Pentecostal movement gradually and eventually embraced a modern and modified style of congregational worship, without embracing the truth that worship encompasses all of the believer's life.

While the emphasis of the exponents of the Tabernacle of David theory brought a fresh breeze of worship *expression* to the corporate worship *experience*, the interpretation insisted upon for the Acts 15:16 passage lacked solid Biblical evidence. If James had intended this to mean a restoration of Davidic worship style, why is the rest of the New Testament and especially the epistolary teachings silent on the subject? Further, historical evidence indicates that since the Psalter was already in use as the "hymnal" for synagogue worship, it carried through into the worship of the early church. Clearly, James, in quoting from the prophet Amos (Amos 9:11-12) was referring to the fact that Gentile salvation was not contrary to God's plan for Israel.

God made a covenant with David and his seed. Since David had initially dwelt in tents, his house and lineage are described as a tabernacle. This tabernacle, however, was ruined and fallen down. For centuries, there had been no king from the house of David. The scepter had departed from Judah and the royal family had been buried in obscurity. But God's promise was to return, build it again, and raise it out of its ruins. This was now fulfilled in Christ, the seed of David. And, when the tabernacle of David was thus rebuilt in Christ, the church of Christ may be called the tabernacle of David. On his *Laudemont Ministries* website, in an article entitled *Davidic Worship: A Model for Renewal*, Richard C. Leonard writes:

Some twentieth-century interpreters saw a New Testament reference to Davidic worship in the words of the apostle James in Acts 15:15-18... However, James is quoting Amos 9:11-12, where the Hebrew word is *sukkah* (booth or shelter), not *ohel* (tent or tabernacle) as in the narrative of the Ark's installation in Zion (2 Sam 6:17; 2 Chron. 16:1). Amos' and James' reference is to the renewal of the dynasty of David, in Jesus the Messiah (Anointed), not specifically to the restoration of Tabernacle of David worship.[9]

It is a gigantic leap to suggest that this prophesy is referring to any kind of restoration of Davidic worship style to the church. Further, worship is neither an atmosphere to cultivate nor an experience to achieve, but rather an expression of faith that encompasses the entirety of life. Our approach to understanding what Biblical worship entails must encompass a larger view.

---

9   http://www.laudemont.org/index.html, footnote 1.

A LARGER VIEW OF WORSHIP

Worship is much larger than either the private devotional experience of the individual believer or the corporate expression of the Church assembled congregationally. Worship is more comprehensive than simply praise, prayer, adoration or any one of the individual components that are part of the congregational or corporate worship experience. Worship, for the believer, is all of life! The New Testament believer is a priest unto God and a minister of God. Therefore, not only all that we *do*, but also all that we *are* is rendered to God. This is worship!

A BIBLICAL OVERVIEW OF WORSHIP

When I first began to observe what I recognized as a "systematic theology" of worship through the Scriptures, I naively believed that I had stumbled on something that Bible Scholars had not identified. And it wasn't until twenty years after first postulating my thesis that I first came across the work of Dr. Richard Leonard. While his overview doesn't correspond exactly with my own description of the systematic and progressive development of the great themes of worship, it does offer an interesting and insightful description of what he calls *The Way of Worship Through the Scriptures*.

- On his *Laudemont Ministries* website, Richard C. Leonard states "This article originally appeared as the introductory article in the Praise and Worship Study Bible, published in 1997 by Tyndale House. It is reproduced here with the permission of the publishers."[10] In the text below, I offer only the overview, not the full article itself:

---

10   http://www.laudemont.org/index.html

- God's Covenant: the Basis for Worship

- The Pentateuch: Foundations of Worship

- The Historical Books: Setting Worship in Order

- The Poetical Books: The Worship of Our King

- The Prophetic Books: Worship's Genuine Motivation

- The Gospels and Acts: Focusing Worship on Jesus

- The Letters of Paul: Worship As Life in Christ

- Other Letters and the Revelation: The Consummation of Worship[11]

THE FOUNDATIONAL PRINCIPLES OF WORSHIP

The foundational principles of worship are found in the first few books of the Bible. In Genesis and Exodus, we discover the great tenets of worship theology. For example, from the first recorded incident of worship, where Cain and Abel bring their offerings to God, through Moses' various encounters with God in Exodus, the essential elements of worship appear in embryonic form.

THE BEGINNINGS OF CORPORATE WORSHIP

Corporate worship begins with Israel at the Passover. Throughout the rest of Exodus and on into the remainder of the Pentateuch the theological structure for worship is raised upon this foundation. A significant part of this concerns the instructions for the tabernacle in the wilderness, where God is teaching His people how to worship. The concepts of worship that emerge in New Testament theology can

---

11   Ibid.

be discovered in the worship principles that are distilled in these early books of the Bible.

WORSHIP IN THE KINGDOM BOOKS

Further, in the "kingdom" books, particularly during the time of David, we discover the life and presence of God inhabiting this (theological) structure. With David's approach to praise and worship, the proximity of the presence of God is realized in a more intimate and personal way.

The message of the prophets relative to worship is uniform and universal. It can be summarized in the Word of God articulated by the prophet Isaiah, "These people come near to me with their mouth and honor me with their lips, but their hearts are far from me. Their worship of me is made up only of rules taught by men" (Isaiah 29:13 NIV). God's complaint with His people throughout the prophetic books is that they have negated the real value and virtue of their worship by their idolatry and apostasy. He tells them that going through the motions and conducting rituals does not constitute true worship. God tells His people that all they have left is the structure. It is void and vacant of the presence and power of God. In a word, ICHABOD describes their worship, for the glory of God has departed. God does not accept ritualistic performance for worship. He is looking for a people whose hearts are honest as well as open and whose worship is more than mechanical ceremonialism.

ANNOUNCING A NEW TRANSITION

It is in such a setting that Jesus arrives upon the scene. In the most unlikely of circumstances, Jesus reveals the most profound and important truths concerning worship to a Samaritan woman—a sinner.

Understanding the context of this passage is critical to an understanding of the disclosure of Christ concerning true worship. Christ was passing through Samaria as he traveled from Jerusalem to Galilee when He stopped to rest at a well and seized the opportunity to reveal Himself to an adulterous Samaritan woman. After revealing the secrets of her heart, the discussion naturally shifted to the subject of worship. Upon her realization that Christ was a prophet, she raised the question as to the proper place of worship.

Although at first glance it might seem that the woman's question introduced a totally new topic, Christ persists in pointing the woman toward salvation. As He elaborates on the nature of true worship, he discloses that a *true knowledge* of God is necessary for *true worship* and that salvation and revelation derives from God's people, the Jews. He then proceeds to describe worship under the new covenant and to affirm the Father's desire for true worshippers.

Whether the woman's question was a sincere quest for God or simply a ploy to avoid the conviction of her own sinfulness is a matter of speculation, and is not germane to our study. It is not unusual for people under conviction of their sin to shift the topic to a religious debate.

However, her question does reveal certain assumptions concerning the roots of true worship. Her views were founded on human tradition rather than upon the clear teachings of Scripture. Rather than seeking Christ's interpretation, she focuses her attention on contrasting the traditions sacred to her Samaritan heritage to the doctrines held by the Jewish religious leaders of her day.

Christ's teachings assault the flawed foundation of the false religious system of the Samaritans to which she appealed. He directs the woman's attention to the Jewish Scriptures and to Himself as the Messiah promised in their pages. The Samaritans rejected the Old Testament (except for the Pentateuch—the first five books of the Hebrew Scriptures). Moreover, their version of the Pentateuch *erroneously* held that Mount Gerizim was the mountain that Abraham ascended to sacrifice Isaac and where he later met Melchisedec.

The Samaritans were a mixed race of Jews and pagans. They had intermarried and had consequently developed their own culture, tradition and religious systems. They were detested and disparaged by the Jews as a hybrid race who practiced a false religion. Yet Christ treated the Samaritans as a special class of people who were neither Jewish nor Gentile. Although the Jews and Samaritans shared many things in common, their religious differences were so vast that the Jewish people denigrated them as ignorant and apostate. The Jews viewed the Samaritans as absolutely alienated from God's covenant.

The false worship of the Samaritans reflected their flawed theology. They distorted the text of Scripture to support their choice of Gerizim as the sacred site, thus rejecting God's choice of Jerusalem. Their convenient denial of all Scripture except the Pentateuch allowed them to ignore the teachings of Scripture that specifically placed the Temple in Jerusalem.

The surprising nature of this disclosure is intriguing in several ways. Revelation belonged to the Jews, the chosen people of God. It was the *prophets* who heard from God. God revealed Himself to *men* whose lives were godly. To the Jews of Jesus' day, if God was going to speak, He would have spoken to the Pharisees. After all, they were the caretakers of God's revelation. Moreover, of course, God always gives His revelation to a man. However, Jesus, predictably unpredictable, delighting in shocking the hypocritical systems of His day, chooses to disclose this profound revelation to a woman, a sinner, *and* a non-Jew!

This fourth chapter of John's gospel is transitional. A new era has come! Worship will no longer be concerned with the physical, geographical, material realm. True worship is spiritual. Under the Old Covenant, conformity to ritual, observance of days, specific offerings, and particular places were all important. The whole emphasis was on the material realm, since Israel was an earthly nation. But Jesus announces that *worship is changing*.

When Christ said, "Believe Me", He used a statement that is not found elsewhere in the gospels. Rendered in the present active imperative, and similar to His "verily, verily, I say unto you", the truth He was about to disclose was both profound and new. He was about to announce that in the new covenant era there will be no more sacred sites of worship. His impending death and the accompanying rending of the veil covering the holiest of holies would result in the disappearance of sacred sites. The battle between Samaritans and Jews over worship locations would in effect become an exercise in futility.

Christ proceeds to describe the essential nature of biblical worship. He denounces and dismisses Samaritan worship as ignorant and ineffectual. By disregarding most of God's revelation and by diluting the remainder, the Samaritans ended up in a delusion that was void of any legitimate knowledge of God. Their faulty theology and flawed faith left them with false worship. In a word, they were now apostate.

Christ's statement is not only startling but also incongruent with the modern approach that sacrifices true worship and theology to the idols of tolerance and compromise. This is even more arresting when you consider that the audience to whom He makes this disclosure is a woman who had professed belief in a coming Messiah and who held the Five Books of Moses as Scripture. His statement rings with similarity to Paul's denouncement of the Athenian idolaters, "Therefore, the One whom you worship without knowing, Him I proclaim to you" (Acts 17:23 NKJV). As we will observe throughout this work, whenever people tamper with divine revelation, their departure from truth will be reflected in a declension in worship.

When Christ says, "We know what we worship for salvation is of the Jews," He is affirming the fact that Paul elaborates, "Who are Israelites, to whom pertain the adoption, the glory, the covenants, the giving of the law, the service of God, and the promises; of whom are the fathers and from whom, according to the flesh, Christ came, who is over all, the eternally blessed God. Amen." (Romans 9:4-5 NKJV).

Our Lord goes on to define the essence of true worship. "But the hour is coming and now is, when the true worshipers will worship the Father in spirit and truth". While many commentators state that the term *spirit* refers to the human spirit, others argue that the term *spirit* indicates that the worship of God must be spiritual as opposed to ceremonial or material. However, worship in the new covenant era is not *only* internal—that is, it does not take place solely in the human spirit. Since God's human creation consists of body, soul *and* spirit, every aspect is to be engaged in the worship of God.

God is looking for worshippers who will worship *in spirit*, with the innermost part of their being. New Testament worship hereafter cannot be said to have the physical, material realm as its primary emphasis. The Father is seeking for true worshippers whose worship will come from the depth and center of their beings, and whose worship will be unfeigned and genuine.

By stating that the worship that God accepts and the worship that He seeks *must* be *in spirit* and *in truth*, our Lord not only excluded the Samaritan worship, but also the lifeless worship of the Jews who drew near with their lips, but whose hearts were far from God. Christ denounced such lifeless worship, saying, "You hypocrites! Isaiah was right when he prophesied about you: 'These people honor me with their lips, but their hearts are far from me. They worship me in vain; their teachings are but rules taught by men'" (Matthew 15:7-9 NIV). Our Lord's decrying of the practice of vain worship was drawn from the words of Isaiah who said, "The Lord says: 'These people come near to me with their mouth and honor me with their lips, but their hearts are far from me. Their worship of me is made up only of rules taught by men'" (Isaiah 29:13 NIV).

What might be easily overlooked in John 4:21-24 is the two polarities of unacceptable worship represented in the conversation between Christ and the Samaritan woman. While the Jewish worship of the day was *in truth* it was not *in spirit*. And, by contrast, while the Samaritan worship was *in spirit* it was not *in truth*.

John MacArthur discusses what he describes as "The Deviations of Worship in Spirit and Truth" in his book *True Worship*, where he identifies Samaritan worship as worship constituted of *spirit without truth* and Jewish worship as worship characterized by *truth without spirit*. "Samaritan worship then was enthusiastic worship without proper information. Their worship was aggressive, enthusiastic, excited, and faithful, but they didn't have the right content. In other words, they worshiped in spirit but not in truth."[12]

It is instructive to note that while their temple was destroyed in 125 B.C., the few hundred remaining Samaritans still go to Mount Gerizim on their holy days and slice up animals exactly as

---

12   MacArthur, John F.: *True Worship*. Panorama City, CA: Word of Grace Communications, 1982, 1985., p.86.

their ancestors did under the Mosaic economy. As MacArthur notes, "They're enthusiastic, but they don't have the right information or content."[13]

As we discussed earlier, whereas the Samaritans accepted only the Pentateuch, the Jews accepted the entire Old Testament that contained the entire revelation of Christ and God's salvation. On another occasion, Christ reprimanded the Jews saying, "Nor does his word dwell in you, for you do not believe the one he sent. You diligently study the Scriptures because you think that by them you possess eternal life. These are the Scriptures that testify about me..." (John 5:38-40 NIV). This passage is powerful and pivotal. Christ acknowledges that the Pharisees searched the Scriptures in their quest for eternal life. This itself was to be applauded. They were looking to the right source. However, they mistakenly thought that the "ritual" of studying the Scriptures gave them eternal life, rather than the living Word of God to which the Scriptures pointed. Christ states that eternal life resides in and resonates from those Scriptures that point to Him. And sadly He adds, "yet you refuse to come to me to have life" (John 5:40 NIV).

In one sense, the Jews were on the opposite end of the spectrum from the Samaritans. They possessed the truth without the spirit. Jesus denounces their religious practices as being cold, legalistic, and hypocritical in Matthew 6:1-8. While some Jews of Christ's day had a genuine zeal for God, for the most part the religion they practiced was void of any life. As MacArthur observes,

> So, Jerusalem had the truth without the spirit, and Mount Gerizim had the spirit without the truth. Those are the two extreme poles of worship. On the one hand is Mount Gerizim, or enthusiastic heresy. On the other hand is Jerusalem, or barren, lifeless

---

13   Ibid.

orthodoxy. The Jews had all the accurate data, but they didn't have any heart. The Samaritans had all the heart, but they didn't have the data. What Jesus is saying is that both spirit and truth must be present in true worship. One without the other causes an imbalance. Sincere, enthusiastic, aggressive worship is great, but it must be based on truth.[14]

Christ goes on to state that the Father is *seeking* true worshippers. That is, God is actively reaching out to save souls and transform them into biblical worshipers. These words of Christ set forth the singular significance that God places on worship. While God loves the human race and redeems us through Jesus Christ, He reconciles us to Himself that we might worship and glorify Him!

A LANDMARK AND A WATERSHED

The truths disclosed in this passage establish both a landmark in worship theology as well as a watershed. Not only is there a fundamental shift in the nature and essence of Biblical worship, but everything we believe and practice concerning worship must find its source in the teachings here disclosed. If we are to render the appropriate significance to the teaching of Christ in this passage, there are several sacred principles regarding worship to which we must faithfully adhere as well as important applications and implications for Christian worship.

---

14   Ibid.

PRINCIPLES AND PRACTICES FROM JOHN 4:21-24

- To maintain perpetuity of purity in worship we must never use traditions as an authoritative standard for worship practices.

- The Scriptures must remain the sole foundation and guide for the worship of God.

- When human traditions dictate our worship, we are in danger of becoming enemies of the truth.

- Believers who refuse to participate in man-made rituals may be alienated and rejected for refusing to worship God in a non-biblical fashion.

- Worship practices must be subjected to the scrutiny of Scripture to prevent the imposition of traditions that replace the true worship of God.

- True worship of God is fundamental to the fulfillment of the Great Commission. God has redeemed us through Christ to create a "holy priesthood" who worship Him in the manner that He has divinely instituted.

The significance of this passage has not been adequately grasped in the worship renewal. God's design in worship is not to recreate or reproduce Old Testament worship style in the Church. The Church of Christ is a completely new creation! The entire emphasis of the New Covenant is upon the spiritual as opposed to the natural or material realm. While God will fulfill His promises to the *natural* nation of Israel, the Church, the Body of Jesus Christ, is a holy nation, a royal priesthood, a spiritual house, to offer up spiritual sacrifices acceptable to God by Christ Jesus. The New Covenant concerns itself with a heavenly Zion, as Hebrews 12 assures us. Circumcision is of the heart, upon which the laws of God are written, laws that are spirit and life (John 6:63).

SPIRITUAL FEATURES—NOT PHYSICAL FACETS

Jesus announces that no longer will Jerusalem or any other physical location constitute a center of worship, but rather, true worship will proceed from the hearts and spirits of redeemed humankind. New Testament worship is first and foremost a spiritual thing.

The spiritual nature of New Testament worship, however, does not negate the value of the various expressions of worship that are common to both testaments. Worship that begins in the regenerated spirit of a redeemed child of God must find its expression through the soul, and ultimately the physical body. Of paramount importance, though, is that worship expression is not seen as constituting worship in and of itself. Style does not replace substance in worship. Of equal importance is the principle that the absence of these expressions does not necessarily constitute an absence of true worship. The transitional text in John four calls us to a larger and higher definition of worship—a definition that must embrace all of the believer's life.

INTELLIGENT HOLISTIC WORSHIP

This emphasis is repeated in the second principal text in the New Testament on this subject. In Romans 12, Paul invites us, in view of the abundance of God's mercies, to present our entire beings to God as our intelligent act of worship. Much of the New Testament epistolary teaching has to do with this aspect of worship. Since for the believer, worship is all of life, then the ordering of our lives in the threefold commitment to God, each other, and God's world, constitutes a triune tribute of worship to our triune God!

The ultimate priority contained in the law and reiterated by our Lord when asked "which commandment was the most important" is thus comprehended in this larger view of worship. Put simply, **worship is loving God.** But we love God by loving our neighbors. Therefore, a loving lifestyle is worship to God. We worship God by loving His world (all of humanity) and by loving the church. Worship is not an isolated act that happens when the people of God assemble on the Lord's Day. Worship is the *entirety* of the believer's life. While there are significant passages in the New Testament epistles that relate to the dynamics of corporate worship, yet the preponderance of attention is given to the larger view of worship that Paul introduces to us in Romans 12.

THE GRAND FINALE

When we arrive at the Book of Revelation, we find worship in its perfection. Although we do not see it in Genesis, we must believe that some similar concert of worship constituted the natural atmosphere of heaven before the creation of the world. Revelation presents worship in its purest form. Man is eternally occupied in the business of celebrating God. Moreover, Christ as the Eternal Lamb of God is the center of worship for all eternity. Interestingly, the song of Moses makes its way from the early chapters of the Old Testament and travels across two testaments all the way into eternity future to be harmonized with the song of the Lamb in that great and grand finale of worship!

The worship scenes in the Revelation begin with John's own anthem of praise to the Redeemer in Revelation 1. John sings of the

Lord who loved us and washed us from our sins in His own blood and made us a kingdom of priests unto God. The other worship scenes view both the heavenly hosts of angelic beings as they worship the Creator as well as the company of the redeemed worshipping the Redeemer! We can learn much from this perfected portrait of praise.

Worship begins with God. He takes the initiative in moving toward us. We cannot worship someone we do not know. A prerequisite to worship is to know the Lord we worship, and that revelation of God comes through His Word.

In the chapters that follow, we will not view worship abstractly, but examine it in the flesh and blood context of human experience. We will probe beyond the "style" and search for the "substance" of worship. In so doing, we will discover that the Word of God is a veritable encyclopedia of worship experiences. Beginning with the upward lift of man toward God at the first altar in Genesis, and pursuing worship to the ultimate "upward lift" into God's presence, we will discover the purpose for which God created us. We will trace the systematic development of a worship theology that finds its fountainhead in Genesis and its tsunami in the grand finale of the Book of Revelation. In addition, in this exercise, we will grow in our worship of the Lord who loved us, gave Himself for us, and who is seeking for those who will worship Him.

2

NAKED WORSHIP

"Trust the past to the mercy of God, the present to His love, and the future to His providence."

—St. Augustine

To worship is to quicken the conscience by the holiness of God, to feed the mind with the truth of God, to purge the imagination with the beauty of God, to devote the will to the purpose of God.

—William Temple

And Job rose up, and rent his mantle, and shaved his head, and fell down on the ground, and worshipped; and he said, Naked came I out of my mother's womb, and naked shall I return thither: Jehovah gave, and Jehovah hath taken away; blessed be the name of Jehovah! In all this Job sinned not, nor ascribed anything unseemly to God. (Job 1:20-22 Darby)

In this passage, Job has just heard from the last of a quartet of messengers of the ultimate disaster that has befallen him. Still reeling from the news of the slaughter of his livestock and his servants, he now confronts the tragic reality that his entire family has perished in a tornado.In the face of that news, having been stripped of all that was near and dear, Job now strips himself, and falls before God in naked worship.

In the face of this loss, Job said, "Naked came I out of my mother's womb, and naked shall I return thither: the LORD gave, and the LORD hath taken away; blessed be the name of the LORD." Job *looked back to his birth*, he *looked ahead to his death*, and then he *looked up to His God*. He worshiped… naked… stripped of his past, his present and his future.

After the loss of family and finances, of both possessions and posterity, Job fell to the ground in submission and humility and worshiped. His loss reached backward into all that he had built and accumulated, and forward into all that he might hope for in a future posterity. Further, he lost his position in the community where he had known respect and reputation. But, instead of abandoning his faith and denying God, as Satan had predicted that he would, Job worshiped.

When I reflect on the minor losses and setbacks that I've experienced in life, they pale in comparison to Job. They are not even worthy to be reckoned a comparison. And, those losses were not the result of my faith or Christian witness. I'm not sure how I would react in a circumstance such as Job experienced. Would I worship God? Would you? I've known many, who in the face of great loss have all but *denied* their faith and *defied* their God. They have come dangerously close to capitulating to the advice of Job's wife who in the face of their loss told him to "curse God and die" (Job 2:9).

The Bible says, "In all this Job sinned not, nor charged God foolishly." Here in one of the earliest books of the Bible is an initial fulfillment of the promise given in the Garden of Eden: that of Satan's ultimate defeat (Genesis 3:15). Satan failed to prove that Job's worship was contingent upon God's blessing. In spite of colossal loss and great grief, Job neither shook his fist nor pointed his finger in the face of God. While Job did not understand why all these things happened to him, he recognized God's sovereignty.

While some conclude from this book that affliction is the norm for God's people, the book of Job is not a story of how God imposes suffering on mankind. It is, however, a story of Satan's assault on God's people, and the natural inclination of people to misinterpret that assault. The sovereignty of God takes preeminence over the subtleties of Satan in the Book of Job. In the first chapter, God's sovereignty is illustrated in that Satan has to seek permission to launch his attack on Job.

Satan's accusation against **Job** was an accusation against **God**. In essence Satan said, "Job worships you because you protect and prosper him. You are not worthy of worship… let me strip Job naked, and he won't worship you." Job's naked worship proved that Satan was utterly wrong. *Dedication* to God without *dividend* received in return may seem like an unpopular idea in an era when the prosperity gospel has become so popular. And yet it remains the hallmark of Biblical worship. As Paul said, "Some have erred, supposing that gain is godliness… but, godliness with contentment is great gain" (I Timothy 6:5-6).

If you listen to how the proponents of the prosperity gospel handle the book of Job, you will find that they focus only on one passage. They quote the words of Job when he said, "The thing that I feared came upon me" (Job 3:25), and meanwhile, neglect the rest of the book. I find it interesting that this particular confession of Job was *not* marked by God as a *flaw* in Job's faith nor a *fault* in his integrity. When God raised the topic of "His" servant Job to Satan, He didn't qualify that Job was mostly upright, but had this spiritual Achilles heel that would ultimately be his downfall, that he suffered from a fatal flaw in the framework of his faith. God said that he was upright and righteous. *God found no fault with Job, but Satan did.* There was nothing in Job's life that compelled God to cause him to suffer.

The fundamental reason for Job's suffering was *to silence the blasphemous accusations of Satan and prove that Job would worship God even though he had lost everything.* Satan accused God of being unworthy of worship. The purpose of God was to demonstrate the truth of "naked worship." There are specific features of Job's worship that make it significant, and profound lessons resident in this unfolding drama that instruct us in the worship of our God. Job was a "naked worshipper" long before he met with disaster. From Job's worship experience, we can glean many significant truths concerning naked worship.

I. NAKED WORSHIP DOESN'T BLAME GOD FOR LIFE'S LOSSES

During my years in pastoral ministry, I had the privilege of ministering to many people during periods of great loss. I have performed funeral services for children that died in infancy or in early childhood. I have buried young men in the prime of life whose lives were taken in freak accidents. I have watched others fall prey to cancer, heart disease, or become crippled both mentally and physically by accident. I've even buried a young man who became victim to a vicious and vindictive act of murder. In all of those vicissitudes of life I have observed the responses of people in the community of faith as they tried to make sense of the senseless losses they incurred.

For some, their grief was cloaked by their anger. Others, appealing to an exaggerated application of God's sovereignty, attempted to acquiesce to what they attributed to be the mysterious will of God.

Others abandoned their faith in the face of the storms they encountered. Some sought to rationalize as to why God had "allowed" these things to come upon them.

As with Job's so-called friends, many of the well-intentioned comments of contemporary would-be comforters stem from a flawed and faulty theology. I've shuddered as I've heard people suggest in the face of an untimely death that "God needed her more than we did," or tritely state, "He's gone to a better place."

Often when I visited the church that I pastored in the Vancouver suburb of Surrey, B.C., I would see a couple, getting on in years, who have since been promoted to His heavenly presence. The very week I was moving from Surrey to Seattle, their son was cruelly murdered. I was called back to perform the funeral service. Several years later, their beautiful younger daughter was stricken with a rare disease that took her life. I watched them as they worship. They couldn't hide the traces of sadness in their countenance, nor did they seek to do so. Yet those marks of tragedy and loss were eclipsed by the glow of God's presence as they turned their faces toward God in humble worship. The memory of the witness of their worship continues to inspire me.

I've seen this drama play out time and again the lives of devout Christians. They refused to blame God for taking their loved one. Stripped of that which was near and dear, they did not shake their fist nor point their finger in the face of their Creator. They knew the secret of naked worship.

It would be folly to ascribe to every loss in a believer's life the kind of pageantry that is recorded in the Book of Job. Suffering and loss in the believer's life is not always the result of a dialogue in the spiritual realm initiated by God who brings to the attention of Satan the integrity of one of His saints. And yet, every time a child of God maintains faith and integrity in the face of tragedy and loss, it makes the same point to all observers in the spiritual realm: the character of God's children is proven to Satan, the demons, the angels, and to humans who are observing what is transpiring.

Satan thought he could cause Job to blame God for his suffering and turn his back on the Almighty. Even Job's wife got in on the action when she told him to curse God and die. Job does not deny that he has suffered; nor does he claim to understand why he suffers. Job simply commits himself to a sovereign Creator in humble, naked worship. Faced with the sudden, crushing loss of everything—children, servants, herds—in all this Job did not sin nor charge God with wrong. Job does not blame and curse God, getting rid of the problem by getting rid of God. But neither does Job explain his suffering. He does not instruct us in how to live so that we can avoid suffering. Suffering is a mystery, and Job comes to respect the mystery.

The question as to why righteous and innocent people suffer reveals an assumption that there is a direct correlation between righteousness and innocence on the one hand and pain-free living on the other. The righteous and innocent are not exempt from the painful situations that arise in an imperfect and sinful world. Suffering sometimes *is* the direct result of sin. There is a natural cause-and-effect relationship with sin: the *direct* harvest of sin is suffering. Much suffering is self-inflicted because of sin. At other times it may be for chastening, for strengthening, (II Corinthians 12:7–10, I Peter 5:10), or even to reveal God's comfort and grace (II Corinthians 1:3–7).

There are times when we suffer because of spiritual warfare, such as in this story, where Satan is given permission by God to cause Job to suffer. But there are still other times when the compelling issue in the suffering of the saints is unknowable. It may be for a heavenly purpose that those on earth can not discern (Exodus 4:11,

John 9:1–3). People sometimes suffer for no specific reason that can be clarified. There is suffering that has no apparent redeeming value whatsoever.

2. NAKED WORSHIP DOESN'T DEMAND THAT
GOD REVERSE AND RESTORE THE LOSSES

While the end of Job's story reveals that God indeed restored Job, the restoration did not come about as the result of Job's demanding that God reverse the losses that he had incurred. Job did not *initially* engage in questioning God, although the hollow philosophizing of his friends *ultimately* compelled him to do so. Yet, Job did not assert his "rights as a believer" to the restoration of all that had been taken away from him.

We have entered an era in the Christian Church that loudly claims a restoration to New Testament faith while proclaiming the rights of the child of God to a fullness of blessing. Wrapping itself in Biblical terminology, this western warp of the Christian gospel insists that it is up to the believer to command material and financial blessings from God. This is not the proclamation of naked worship. The naked worshipper joins his voice with Job in saying, "Jehovah gave, and Jehovah hath taken away; blessed be the name of Jehovah" (Job 1:22 Darby).

Nineteenth-century pastor and author E.M. Bounds, well-known for his writings on the subject of prayer, said, "Prayer honors God; it dishonors self."[15] The narcissism of our indulgent, selfish, materialistic society has invaded Christian theology in the prosperity gospel. Although the Bible teaches that God is sovereign and man is His servant, the prosperity gospel implies the opposite. To claim

---

15   Bounds, E.M. *Prayer and Praying Men.* Grand Rapids, MI: Christian Classics Ethereal Library, 2004.

that we can demand things from God is vain justification for sinful self-indulgence. It perverts the purpose of prayer and worship, taking the Lord's name in vain. It is both unbiblical and ungodly, and is a perversion of the Holy Scriptures.

Worship begins and ends with the glory of God, not with the needs of man. It is primarily concerned with who God is, what He wants, and how He can be glorified. Those who teach otherwise fixate on fulfillment of their own selfish desires rather than the extension of Christ's kingdom. Such teaching denies the heart of Christian truth and impugns the very character of God. To represent God as a genie or a cosmic bellhop, waiting to grant our every desire, violates the clear teaching of Scripture.

Many Old Testament saints certainly had just cause to *demand* that God take them out of harrowing circumstances. Conversely, they sought to glorify God and follow His will. When Jonah recalled what happened while he was inside a great fish, he said, "I remembered the Lord; and my prayer came to Thee, into Thy holy temple… I will sacrifice to Thee with the voice of thanksgiving. That which I have vowed I will pay. Salvation is from the Lord" (Jonah 2:7, 9). While Jonah may have been justified should he have chosen to demand God to get him out of the fish, he simply extolled the character of God.

Daniel didn't demand that God deliver him from the frequent dangerous situations that he encountered because of his strategic role within the pagan Babylonian society. He began his prayer by affirming the nature and character of God. Faced with the specter of the den of lions, Daniel simply affirmed his confidence in God's ability to deliver him. The Old Testament saints knew they were to recognize God in His rightful place of sovereignty and bring their wills into conformity with His. This is precisely how Christ taught

his followers to pray in what we commonly refer to as *The Lord's Prayer.* (Matthew 6:9).

Naked worship does not demand explanations; it rests on the promises and integrity of God. Abraham knew that God's will never contradicts His promise, so he held on to the promise "in Isaac shall thy seed be called" (Genesis 21:12). Abraham believed that even if God allowed him to slay his son, He could raise Isaac from the dead (Hebrews 11:17–19).

In Psalms 57:1–3, the psalmist does not *demand* deliverance, as if he had a right to expect it: he asks it as a mercy from God. From a privileged place of conscious nearness, he cries to God Most High with the confidence that no one and nothing can hinder Him from accomplishing His purposes in the lives of His people. When the answer comes from heaven, it will be an unforgettable demonstration of God's love and dependability.

The Scriptures present us with interesting *anecdotal* evidence of God's response when His people make demands upon him. Psalm 78:17-22 recalls Israel's insolent demand for bread and meat while journeying in the wilderness. The Bible says that they began to provoke the Lord about their diet. Dissatisfied and grumbling, they presented new demands to the Most High. They insinuated that God had led them out into the wilderness to die of starvation. They doubted His ability to provide. Grudgingly admitting that He had provided water, they questioned His willingness and ability to provide bread and meat.

The Lord was infuriated that His people did not trust Him. He was understandably furious that they did not trust His saving power. He caused the fire of His anger to blaze forth against Israel. Surprisingly, God granted their request, even though He was angered by their demands. Psalm 78:23-25 goes on to describe the intervention of God. The people demanded bread in a wilderness where there was neither ovens nor the ingredients for making bread. So God opened the doors of His heavenly bakery and rained down unfailing supplies of manna. The people feasted on something better than bread; it was angels' food, the bread of heaven.

This passage is rather instructive in view of the link that modern prosperity preachers have made between God's covenant and commanding blessing. They boldly affirm that the believer has the right to *demand* healing and prosperity from God on the basis of the relationship that we enjoy in the new covenant. I have heard similar anecdotal evidence of how demanding God's blessing or commanding His healing has resulted in the supernatural intervention of God. This is then advanced as evidence and prima facie proof to support their doctrine. However, these occurrences are probably more of an exhibition of God's mercy and grace than an illustration of a Biblical precept, principle or practice to observe.

Man says, "Seeing is believing." God says, "Believing is seeing." Jesus said to Martha, "Did I not say to you that if you would believe you would see?" (John 11:40). The writer to the Hebrews noted, "By faith we understand…" (11:3). The Apostle John wrote, "I have written to you who believe…that you may know…" (I John 5:13). God is not pleased with the kind of faith that demands a prior miracle. He wants us to believe Him simply because He is God. As Jesus said to Thomas, "Blessed are those who have not seen and yet have believed" (John 20:29). In God's economy, seeing follows believing.

Despite all the miracles Jesus had performed, the scribes and Pharisees had the temerity to ask Him for a sign, implying that they would believe if He would prove Himself to be the Messiah (John 12:38). But their hypocrisy was transparent. If they had not believed as a result of so many wonders, why would they be convinced by one

more? The attitude that demands miraculous signs as a condition for belief does not please God. Later, Paul wrote that since the Jews demanded signs, God graciously condescended to give them signs (I Corinthians 1:22).

However, the Lord described this sign-demanding people as an evil and adulterous generation; evil because they were willfully blind to their own Messiah, and adulterous because they were spiritually unfaithful to their God. Their Creator-God, a unique Person combining absolute deity and perfect humanity, stood in their midst speaking to them, yet they dared to ask Him for a sign. Christ told them summarily that no sign would be given to them except the sign of the prophet Jonah, referring to His own death, burial, and resurrection.

In Mark 8:11, the gospel records that the Pharisees were awaiting Him, demanding a sign from heaven. Their blindness and boldness were enormous. Standing in front of them was the greatest Sign of all—the Lord Jesus Himself. He was truly a Sign who had come from heaven, but they had no appreciation for Him. They heard His wonderful words, saw His matchless miracles, and came in contact with an absolutely sinless Man—God manifest in the flesh—yet in their blindness asked for a sign from heaven. The worship that God accepts and which glorifies Him does *not* make demands.

Interestingly, the *demanding* in the book of Job came from God: "For I will demand of thee... where wast thou when I laid the foundations of the earth? Declare, if thou hast understanding" (Job 38:3-4). Again, in Job 40:7-9, "I will demand of thee... wilt thou condemn me, that thou mayest be justified? Or hast thou an arm like God?"

3. NAKED WORSHIP DOESN'T GUARANTEE
EXEMPTION FROM SUFFERING OR QUESTIONING

There is an interesting parallel between the claims of Satan and the accusations of Job's friends. Satan asserted that Job would sin and wouldn't worship God if God stripped him naked, and Job's friends insisted that it was because of sin in his life that he had been stripped naked. Both of these claims proved to be heretical.

Were we to attempt to construct a theology from anecdotal evidence, we might posit that becoming a naked worshipper of God may make you the target of Satanic attack. I recently heard a preacher boast that he "wanted everything in the Book of Acts." While the congregation shouted "Amen," I breathed a prayer to God, "No thanks, Lord…" I don't want the suffering, the stoning, the imprisonment and shipwreck that accompanied the earlier followers of our Lord. Nor am I anxious to submit to a martyr's death.

Just as we would be wrong to claim that worshipping God grants provision to every blessing from above, so would we err in assuming that it gives protection from every attack from below. Like Job and his friends, we may seek to analyze suffering and look for causes and solutions. And just as they, with all of their sound theological insight into the situation found only useless ideas, we too, may come up empty except for a divine rebuke (Job 42:7).

As his suffering intensified, and under the harsh judgments of his friends, Job eventually struggled to understand why God seemed unwilling to settle matters. Job questioned God. Good people question God. And the good news is that God can handle our questions.

After Job cursed the night of his conception and the night of his birth (Job 3:1–13), he closed his curse with four "why?" questions that only God could answer. While asking "why" is an easy exercise,

it is much more difficult to get the right answer. There is nothing inherently wrong with asking why, as long as we don't insist that God *owes* us an answer. Even our Lord asked, "Why hast Thou forsaken Me?" (Matt. 27:46) But even if the Lord did tell us why things happen as they do, it would not likely provide a balm to ease our pain or heal our broken hearts. The Christian lives on *promises,* not on *explanations,* and the exercise of asking God why yields at best a very modest return.

Often those who refuse to believe the gospel or who claim not to believe in God will hurl the universal question of human suffering in the face of the believer. Their taunt seems to suggest, "If you can answer this for me, then I'll believe in your God." We may at times be tempted to wonder, "Why doesn't God answer all of our questions?" This question itself assumes that if God answered all our questions, it would be easier to believe. This is simply not true. Trust transcends answers. Often questions are a means to evade God and to avoid trust. God doesn't answer all of our questions because we are incapable of understanding His answers.

The worship of Job rejects neither questioning nor answers as such. Faith is not simply "blind" faith. There is intelligent content to biblical theology. It is the secularization of answers that is rejected—answers severed from their Source, the living God, and the Word that both prunes and heals us. We cannot discover truth about God divorced from the mind and heart of God. Ultimately, we must trust God more than our capacity to understand His ways.

From Job's experience we learn that God does not forbid asking questions. These questions may or may not instruct us as to the reasons for our suffering. Job's experience also teaches us that we may not be able to understand our suffering.

Job's name is synonymous with suffering. In the midst of his suffering, he posed questions to God. He didn't merely ask, "Why?" He also asked, "Why me?" And he posed his questions before the Almighty. He prosecuted his questions persistently, passionately, and articulated them eloquently. He refused to accept silence for an answer. He refused to embrace clichés for an answer. He wouldn't let God off the hook.

Job did not take his sufferings quietly nor piously acquiesce to his plight. While he held the idea of going for a second opinion to outside physicians or philosophers in contempt, he did take a stance before God. And there he mightily and vehemently protested his suffering. Job went to the source—he went "to the top" with his questions.

It is not merely because Job suffered that he is an important example to us. It is because his suffering invaded many of the same arenas as our own suffering. Job suffered in the vital areas of family, material possessions, and personal health. Job also provides valuable instruction to us because he searchingly questioned and boldly protested his suffering.

Suffering as such doesn't trouble us as much as the occurrence of undeserved suffering. In our adolescence, we learned that discipline is connected with wrongdoing with a certain sense of justice: when we do wrong we incur punishment. One of the surprising lessons of adulthood, however, is that there is no real correlation between the amount of wrong we commit and the amount of pain we experience. We are in for an even greater surprise when we do right and get knocked down. We might find that when we do our best we are blindsided by the blows of jealousy and injustice and sent reeling in what we deem to be undeserved pain.

Unwarranted suffering first bewilders and then outrages us. This was the case with Job. Job was doing everything right when suddenly everything went wrong. And it was the occasion of Job's unwarranted suffering that birthed his voice of protest to God.

The accuracy and honesty with which Job gives voice to his suffering takes on an eloquence and intensity that enables all who suffer to hear their pain in the voice of Job. What most of us are too timid or intimidated to say, Job boldly and loudly proclaims. What we might whisper or whimper he weaves into poetic verse. What we might mutter or complain to a friend in quiet solitude, he loudly heralds before the Almighty God. He refuses to posture himself as a defeated victim.

It is in the evolving process of facing, questioning, and respecting suffering that Job encounters an even larger mystery—the mystery of God. Quite possibly, the greatest mystery about suffering is how the suffering saint enters the presence of God in a state of awe, wonder, praise, love, and worship. While suffering does not inevitably and unequivocally eventuate in that result, this ensues far more often than we might expect. This was obviously the case with Job.

In chapters nine and ten, Job's questions begin to take the form of litigation. Job's preoccupation is *the justice of God,* and the language that he employs is that of *a legal trial.* His appeal is to face God in court and have the opportunity to prove his own integrity. Even a cursory examination of the vocabulary that he uses supports this idea:

- In 9:3 and 10:2, we find the word *contend* which means to enter into litigation

- In 9:3, 16, he uses the word *answer* which is best understood as testify in court

- In 9:15, we note the word *accuser*, an opponent at law, accuser

- In 9:19, *set a time* means to summon to court

- In 9:33, the word *daysman* signifies an umpire, an arbitrator

- In 13:3, the word *reason* means to argue a case

- In 9:18, the phrase *order my cause* suggests to prepare my case

- In 9:19 and 23:6, the word *plead* means to dispute in court

- In 31:35, the phrase *hear me* means give me a legal hearing

- In 31:31, the word *adversary* means accuser in court

The trio of questions that Job poses in chapters nine and ten are intricately and integrally connected. He asks "How can I be righteous before God, How can I meet God in court," and, finally, "Why was I born?" Job is confident that he is righteous, but has a compelling need to prove it before God. Yet he faces the quandary as to how a mere mortal can achieve this. How can he take God to court? And if God doesn't step up to the stand and testify in Job's behalf, why is he suffering? And furthermore, why was he even born?

When Job asks, "How can I be righteous before God?" (Job 9:2), his question is not about salvation or justification as we understand it. Rather, his question has to due with vindication. He wants to know how he can be declared innocent. While he wants to face God in court, he knows that he would be stumped by God's questions and left speechless. There is a sense in which Job wants to do this not only for his own sake, but also as a means of clearing himself before his friends. Furthermore, how would any person dare to go to court with a God who is invincible? But this God that he wants to question

is not only invincible, He is also *invisible.* It is impossible for Job to confront him and issue Him a summons to appear in court. The quagmire of his quandary deepens as he realizes that even if he could meet God in court, he would be at a loss as to what to say.

As he entertains the "what if scenario" Job begins to imagine a variety of scenarios. He wonders what he would say if he could face God. He recognizes the impossibility of his situation when he entertains attempting to respond to God's cross-examination. He wonders how he could reason with God or present his case before Him. And, if God answered, how could he know that it was really His voice? And, if Job answered inappropriately, surely this would result in further affliction from God.

Later in the book, we discover that when this "what if" scenario actually happened, and Job finally did meet with God, he was subjected to a litany of seventy-seven questions! And all Job could do was to sit an absolute silence. He had no answers. He was compelled to bow in ignorance, repentance and worship.

As Job pursues to prosecute his case, he takes it a step further. He recognizes that declaring his innocence offered no guarantee that God would set him free. While his friends postulated that God rewards the righteous and judges the wicked, Job held that there are times when God destroys both the wicked and the righteous. When Job states that God refuses to intervene when wicked judges help the ungodly and condemn the righteous, he is actually accusing God of injustice—not only toward himself—but also toward other innocent people in the land.

Job goes on to ponder whether positive thinking might alleviate his situation. He quickly dismisses this idea as he says, "If I try to be happy, what good will it do?" Even if he were to take a more positive attitude toward his afflictions, try to forget his pain, and put on a happy face, that wouldn't change anything. God would still find him guilty, his friends would still reject him, and he would still be mired in his state of abject pain and suffering. Even taking a bath and changing his clothes as an act of public contrition would avail nothing. In his desperation and depression, Job has become convinced that God is against him and that any effort on his part will only meet with divine rebuke. Even if he puts on a brave front and smile of confidence before the judge's bench, he will still hear the verdict and judgment rendered—guilty.

The next phase of Job's remonstrance takes on a prophetic overtone as he enters his plea for a mediator. Job pleads, "If only there were someone to arbitrate between us" (Job 9:33). If God were a man, then Job could approach him and plead his case. Or if there were a "daysman" (mediator) between God and Job, he could take away the rod of judgment and bring Job and God together. But God is not man, and there is no mediator! This is where Jesus Christ enters the picture! Jesus is God and became man to reveal the Father (John 14:7–11) and to bring sinners to God (1 Tim. 2:5–6; 1 Peter 3:18). He is the "daysman" for whom Job was pleading centuries before the incarnation (Job. 16:21).

Job ponders and poses the question, "Why was I born?" (Job 10:1–22). Job's argument here is that God made him and gave him life (Job 10:3, 8–12, 18–19), but God was not treating him like one of His own creations. After putting time and effort into making Job, God was destroying him! Furthermore, God was judging Job without even telling him what the charges were against him (Job 10:2). No wonder Job was weary, bitter, and confused (Job 10:1,15). Note that in this chapter Job speaks directly to God and not to his friends.

God is not a man that He has to investigate things and fight against time (Job 10:4–6). God is eternal and can take all the time

He needs, and God is all-knowing and doesn't have to investigate like a private detective. Job had previously yearned for an umpire (9:33), but now he asks for a deliverer (Job 10:7) so he can escape judgment. God was an ever-present Guard, watching Job's every move (Job 10:14). He was stalking Job like a lion (Job 10:16) and attacking him with His army (Job 10:17). Job was hemmed in, and there was no way out.

So Job's question seems reasonable: "Why then did You bring me out of the womb?" (Job 10:18 NIV) Job's existence on the earth seemed so purposeless that he begged God to give him a few moments of peace and happiness before his life ended. He could see his life going by swiftly (Job 7:6–7; 9:25–26), and there was not a moment to waste. "Let me alone," he prays, "so that I can have a little comfort before I go to the world of darkness."

Job could not understand what God was doing, *and it was important that he not understand.* Had Job known that God was using him as a weapon to defeat Satan, he could have simply sat back and waited trustfully for the battle to end. But as Job surveyed himself and his situation, he asked the same question the disciples asked when Mary anointed the Lord Jesus: "Why this waste?" (Mark 14:4) Before we criticize Job too severely, let's recall how many times we have asked that question ourselves when a baby has died or a promising young person was killed in an accident.

Nothing that is given to Christ in faith and love is ever wasted. The fragrance of Mary's ointment faded from the scene centuries ago, but the significance of her worship has blessed Christians in every age and continues to do so. Job was bankrupt and sick, and all he could give to the Lord was his suffering by faith; *but that is just what God wanted in order to silence the devil.*

Job asked, "Why was I born?" In the light of his losses and his personal suffering, it all seemed such a waste! But God knew what He was doing *then,* and He knows what He is doing *now.* "You have heard of Job's perseverance and have seen what the Lord finally brought about," wrote James. "The Lord is full of compassion and mercy" (James 5:11, NIV). If you had told *that* to Job, he might not have believed it; but it was still *true.* It was *true* for him, and it is *true* for us today. Believe it!

4. NAKED WORSHIP MAY MAKE YOU THE TARGET OF CRITICISM AND MISUNDERSTANDING

The worship of Job is more than a witness to the dignity of suffering and God's presence in the midst of that suffering. It is also a fundamental defense against religion that has been reduced to explanations or "answers." While many of the answers offered by Job's so-called friends were technically true, it was the "technical" part that ruined them. They represent responses without relationship, intellectual rationalizing with no relational intimacy. Their answers are thrown into Job's face adding insult to injury. Job refuses to receive secular wisdom that has no contact with the living realities of God.

Without going into the arguments of Job's friends and God's remonstrance in any detail, we can simply conclude that they couldn't know why Job suffered because what happened in heaven between God and Satan was unknown to them. There are matters going on in heaven with God that believers know nothing about; yet, they affect their lives. They thought they knew all the answers, but they only intensified the dilemma by their insistent ignorance. Even the best effort at explaining the issues of life can be useless.

Every sincere believer who has experienced trouble, tragedy or trauma of any kind will be able to relate to the experience that Job had when his friends arrived on the scene. Have you ever experienced a similar visitation of so-called friends and instructors the moment you find yourself in any kind of trouble—be it illness, bereavement, job-loss, fractured relationship, depression or simply bewilderment—people surface instructing us in precisely what is wrong with us and what we need to do to get better? When I first moved to Toronto, I noticed dozens of tow-trucks positioned on the shoulder of the highway, or perched on the median, waiting for an accident to occur so they could be first on the scene. When one of my friends described them as "vultures" waiting for road-kill, the image stuck indelibly in my mind. In a similar manner, people who are in suffering often attract would-be fixers of their problems. Initially, we may be touched by the fact that they seem to care about us and be almost amazed at the ease and readiness with which they offer answers. They seem to know so much! We are compelled to wonder how they became such experts in all of the vicissitudes of life.

And what makes it more seductive, is the fact that these people use the Word of God fluently, frequently and freely. Eager to offer both spiritual diagnosis and prescription, their exhortation at first seems hopeful. But the hope turns hollow when we realize that their apparent compassion produces condemnation, and their caring results in compounding guilt. Recently while channel-surfing through the "gospel ghetto" of Christian television programs, I heard the familiar ring of the promise of Job's comforters, "If you'll just obey God and do what's right, you'll be richly blessed."

In every generation individuals arise whose boast is in their ability to provide counsel that guarantees a life where we can be "healthy, wealthy, and wise." The proponents of the modern prosperity gospel are a reincarnation of those false prophets, and their message merely a recasting of an ancient propaganda: anyone who lives right is exempt from suffering. To hear them speak, the arrogance and cockiness of their perspective should cause us to realize our good fortune: that they are now at hand to provide the answers that we so desperately need.

You have doubtlessly been subjected at times to those who prate their pious platitudes. And on your behalf, and mine, and on behalf of all who have been misled by the well-intentioned but misguided instruction of those who tell us everything will be all right if we simply and do as they say, Job becomes our mouthpiece. Job categorically rejects those theological concepts that have God all figured out and those theories that offer glib explanations for all of life's situations. Job's honest defiance remains the best defense against the clichés of prosperity preachers and the prattle of religious materialists.

How often do God's people, on the heels of immense and intense suffering, find themselves surrounded and accosted by the conventional religious wisdom of the day? Whereas for Job it came in the form of speeches by Eliphaz, Bildad, Zophar, and Elihu, for today's Christian it may come at them through religious television broadcasts or books, or by those promoting the teaching contained therein. Just as Job's counselors methodically and pedantically recited their bookish precepts to Job, today's messengers are quick to pronounce judgment on those in the midst of their trials, meanwhile exhorting them as to why it happened, and how to avoid it in the future. Although we are separated from Job by a few thousand years, Job's reality is ours: real faith can neither be reduced to spiritual tonics nor merchandised in testimonies of success. Real faith is still refined in the fiery furnace of trial and in the turbulent storms of pain.

5. NAKED WORSHIP DEFIES SATAN'S CLAIMS
AND DEFEATS THE DEVIL'S SCHEMES

It is not unusual to hear people speak of the cosmic battle between good and evil, between God and Satan, as if the two personalities were more or less equal, and the jury is out as to who will ultimately win the battle. This idea is often propagated in literature, ancient and modern, and proliferated in the media and movies of the day. It is important to recognize that while Satan may be God's sworn enemy, they are not equals. Satan is merely a creature; God is the Creator. Satan had his origin as an angel unwilling to serve in his exalted role. As a result of his rebellion against God, he was thrown out of heaven.

The Book of Job allows us to visit the throne room of heaven and hear God and Satan speak. We are given a glimpse "behind the scenes" and we know *who* caused the destruction and *why* he was allowed to cause it. Job knew *what* had happened, but he did not know *why* it had happened; and that is the crux of the matter. We have a rare glimpse into the realm of the heavenlies. In writing to the Ephesians, Paul makes it clear in the early chapters that all of our blessings have their source in the heavenlies, and in the last chapter, that our battles are also centered there.

From this scene we have early Old Testament evidence that God is sovereign in all things. God reigns on the throne of heaven and the angels do His will and report to Him. Even Satan must approach God to acquire permission before he can do anything to one of God's children. The name "The Almighty" is used thirty-one times in the Book of Job and is one of the key names for God. From the very outset the writer wants to remind us that no matter what happens in this world and in our lives, God is on the throne and has everything under control.

From this scene we also learn that Satan has access to God's throne in heaven. As a result of improper and non-Biblical teaching, many people have the mistaken idea that Satan is ruling this world from hell. However, Satan will not be cast into the lake of fire until before the final judgment (Rev. 20:10). Today, he is free to go about on the earth (Job 1:7; 1 Peter 5:8). He is referred to as "the god of this world" (II Corinthians 4:4) and "the spirit that now worketh in the children of disobedience" (Ephesians 2:2).

Satan's statement that righteous people remain faithful to God only because of what they get is an indication of the continual conflict between Satan and God. Satan's claim was that the righteous trust in God only as long as God is nice to them. Satan challenged God's claims of Job's righteousness, insisting that it had not been tested. The fact that Satan was convinced that he could destroy Job's faith in God by inflicting suffering on him is indicative that he is not ominiscient or all-knowing, and far from operating on a level playing field with God.

When Satan's initial assault did not cause Job to falter in his faith, God once more brings up the subject of His servant Job, giving us the impression that God is confident that Job will not fail the test. Satan accepts the challenge. Having failed in his initial assault, he increased the stakes. Satan demonstrates a pernicious perseverance. He returned to God's throne to accuse Job more than once. Having stripped Job of his **possessions** and his **posterity**, he then seeks permission to afflict him **physically**. "Every man has his price," said Satan. "Job can raise another family and start another business because he still has health and strength. Let me touch his body and take away his health, and You will soon hear him curse You to Your face" (Job 2:4-5).

With God's permission (Job 2: 6, I Corinthians 10:13), Satan afflicted Job with a disease we cannot identify. Whatever it was, the symptoms were terrible: severe itching (Job 2:8), insomnia (Job 2:4), running sores and scabs (Job 2:5), nightmares (Job 2:13–14), bad breath (Job 19:17), weight loss (Job 19:20), chills and fever (Job 21:6), diarrhea (Job 30:27), and blackened skin (Job 30:30). When his three friends first saw Job, they did not recognize him (Job 2:12).

Not all physical affliction comes directly from the evil one, though Satan's demons can cause (among other things) blindness (Matthew 12:22), dumbness (Matthew 9:32–33), physical deformities (Luke 13:11–17), incessant pain (II Corinthians 12:7), and insanity (Matthew 8:28–34). Sometimes physical affliction is the natural result of carelessness on our part, and we have nobody to blame but ourselves. But even then, Satan knows how to use our folly to further his cause.

The accusation of Job's friends that his suffering was because of his sin simply was not true. Many people have quoted from the words of Job's friends in efforts to establish Biblical basis for their beliefs or exhortations. However, if their statements are not verified and validated in the whole of Scripture, they are not to be taken as *Biblical* truth, but as the truthful Biblical record of their human origin. Granted, there was *partial* truth in some of their statements. For example, Elihu said that God was chastening Job to make him a better man, and that was partly true. But the fundamental reason for Job's suffering was *to silence the blasphemous accusations of Satan and prove that a man would worship God even though he had lost everything.* It represents the ultimate truth of naked worship. Job was oblivious to the fact that he was the principal protagonist and primary player in a battle that was centered "in the heavenlies" (Ephesians 6:12). The arena of Job's life became the battlefield where the forces of God and Satan were engaged in a spiritual struggle to decide the question, "Is Jehovah God worthy of man's worship?"

While unaware of the ethereal battlefield in which he was placed, and of the eternal issues at stake, Job's integrity of faith silenced the accuser of the brethren. Job was resolutely unyielding in his resistance of the advice of his friends. Had he hearkened to their advice to "repent of his sins so that God would remove the suffering and make him prosperous again", Job would have had to "invent" sin in his life and go through the motions of repentance to "earn" the blessing of God. And to do so would have meant playing right into the hands of the accuser. When Job held fast to his integrity and blessed God even though he did not understand what God was doing, this brought about a decisive defeat to the prince of darkness.

From the experience of Job's worship of God we learn not only that Satan can touch God's people *only* with God's permission, but also when he does, God turns it around and uses it for their good and His glory. In this is fulfilled the statement of Paul that "all things are working together for the good of those that love the Lord and are called according to His purpose." The purpose of God is to make us more like Jesus Christ—to transform us into the image of His Son (Romans 8:29). To achieve this purpose, God can and will use even the attacks of the devil to perfect us.

Many of the so-called tragedies in the lives of God's people have become the weapons of God to "still the enemy and the avenger" (Psalms 8:2). God's Word declares that the angels watch the church to learn from God's dealings with His people (I Corinthians 4:9; Ephesians 3:10). We may not know until eternity why God allowed certain things to happen. In the meantime, we walk by faith and say with Job, "Blessed be the name of the Lord."

Satan suffered yet another defeat as God demonstrated through the life of Job that saving faith could not be destroyed regardless of how much trouble the believer suffers or how incomprehensible and undeserved the suffering seems. When his efforts to destroy Job meet with failure, Satan disappears from the story. He remains God's defeated enemy, still raging against God's inevitable triumph.

6. NAKED WORSHIP TAKES YOU FROM IMPERSONAL TO PERSONAL KNOWLEDGE OF GOD

Once God did speak and respond to Job, Job's problem becomes at least partially clear: he confused a *relationship* with God with *familiarity* with God. The Lord did not rebuke Job's faith or sincerity; instead, God questioned Job's insistence on an answer for his difficulties. By allowing Job to hear just a little of the extent of his ignorance, God showed Job that there was a great deal he would never understand. As a creature, Job simply had no right to demand an answer from his Creator. Job's final words are filled with humility and repentance: "I have heard of You by the hearing of the ear, but now my eye sees You. Therefore I abhor myself, and repent in dust and ashes" (Job 42:5, 6).

The confession of worship in these words is powerfully moving. For Job to say that "now my eye sees You" boggles the mind and baffles the imagination. Where did Job see God? How did he see Him? Previously his confession of faith was strong. Job maintained a confident confession of faith in the midst of confounding confusion.

In 19:25–27, Job expressed confidence that, even if he died, he would still have a Redeemer who one day would exercise judgment on the earth. Furthermore, Job affirmed that he himself expected to live again and see his Redeemer! "And after my skin has been destroyed, yet in my flesh I will see God" (Job 19:26, NIV). In verse 27, he adds, "Whom I shall see for myself, and mine eyes shall behold, and not another." And in chapter 23 when he says, "But if I go to the east, he is not there; if I go to the west, I do not find him. When he is at work in the north, I do not see him; when he turns to the south, I catch no glimpse of him," he immediately follows that with this confession of faith, "But he knows the way that I take; when he has tested me, I will come forth as gold" (Job 23: 8-10 NIV).

When I first embarked on exploring the theme of *naked worship* as it related to the life and experience of Job, I wrote down the following preliminary thoughts:

- Naked worship confesses confidence in God's integrity while admitting confusion as to God's activity.

- Naked worship provides no guarantee of exemption from suffering, intensified suffering, nor against desperation, depression and despondency.

- Naked worship is often shaped in the shadows of suffering.

- Naked worship may make you the target of Satanic attack.

- Naked worship is a slap in the face of Satan as it silences the accuser of the brethren.

- Naked worship may result in your being misunderstood by your friends, and may make you the target of criticism by the self-righteous.

- Naked worship opens your heart and mind to the counsel of others, but doesn't make you gullible to swallow everything you hear.

- Naked worship rejects the fundamental premises of the "prosperity gospel."

- Naked worship may lack theological orthodoxy: God confronts Job with his ignorance.

- Naked worship is ultimately honest worship: there is no pretense.

- Naked worship bows humbly at the voice of God's reproof and rebuke and brings you to your knees in repentance.

- Naked worship brings you to a place of forgiveness: forgiveness from God and forgiveness of those who have wrongly judged you.

- Naked worship is not a religious exercise that has been reduced to explanations or "answers."

- Naked worship transforms you into a servant of God.

- Naked worship takes you from impersonal to personal knowledge of God.

- Naked worship recognizes that it is God who writes the last chapter of our lives.

The more I delve into the topic of worship, the more I am aware of how little I really know. It is an ocean of truth and I don't even know how to swim. It is a bottomless goldmine and I can only scratch the surface. It is that for which I was created, and it will be my eternal occupation in glory. I can only bow before my Lord in prostrate praise and raise my heart to Him in adoration, wonder and worship. I can begin to practice now that which I have been destined to do forever.

In my study of Job and his worship of God, I am indebted to many great Bible scholars, from whom I have drawn and adapted ideas. Since I have tried to avoid using direct quotations, I have not footnoted these sources throughout this chapter but acknowledge the following sources of inspiration and ideas for this chapter:

- The Believer's Bible Commentary[16]

- Be Patient[17]

- Wiersbe's Expository Outlines on the Old Testament[18]

- The MacArthur Study Bible[19]

- Matthew Henry's Commentary on the Whole Bible[20]

- The Preacher's Commentary Series, Volume 12: Job[21]

- Thru the Bible with J. Vernon McGee[22]

- The Word Biblical Commentary[23]

16 MacDonald, William and Farstad, Arthur: *Believer's Bible Commentary: Old and New Testaments*. Nashville, TN: Thomas Nelson, 1997.
17 Wiersbe, Warren W. *Be Patient*. Wheaton, IL: Victor Books, 1996.
18 Wiersbe, Warren W. *Wiersbe's Expository Outlines on the Old Testament*. Wheaton, IL: Victor Books, 1993
19 MacArthur, John Jr. *The MacArthur Study Bible*. electronic ed. Nashville, TN: Word Pub., 1997.
20 Henry, Matthew. *Matthew Henry's Commentary on the Whole Bible*. Peabody, MA: Hendrickson, 1996.
21 McKenna, David L. and Ogilvie, Lloyd J. *The Preacher's Commentary Series, Volume 12: Job*. Nashville, TN: Thomas Nelson Inc, 1986
22 McGee, J. Vernon. *Thru the Bible Commentary*. electronic ed. Nashville, TN: Thomas Nelson, 1997.
23 Clines, David J. A. *Word Biblical Commentary: Job 1-20*. Dallas, TX: Word, Incorporated, 1989, 2002.

THE FIRST MURDER—ON THE WAY OUT OF CHURCH

A faith is something you die for, a doctrine is something you kill for. There is all the difference in the world.

—Tony Benn

In the course of time Cain brought some of the fruits of the soil as an offering to the LORD. But Abel brought fat portions from some of the firstborn of his flock. The LORD looked with favor on Abel and his offering, but on Cain and his offering he did not look with favor. So Cain was very angry, and his face was downcast. Then the LORD said to Cain, "Why are you angry? Why is your face downcast? If you do what is right, will you not be accepted? But if you do not do what is right, sin is crouching at your door; it desires to have you, but you must master it." Now Cain said to his brother Abel, "Let's go out to the field." And while they were in the field, Cain attacked his brother Abel and killed him (Genesis 4:3-8 NIV).

n those long, cold, dark Eastern Canadian winter nights, one of our favorite pastimes was playing church. Since my older brother had already outgrown all of this, I would arrange the chairs in a

row, get out my grandmother's hymnals, and together with my two older sisters get ready to "have church." The fact that each of us had a different hymnal seemed irrelevant to this activity. Being the baby of the family, I was naturally the entertainer—or perhaps as some more accurately preferred to call it—the "show-off". I wanted to lead the singing, do the preaching, and, of course, take the offering! In her book, *Up With Worship,* Anne Ortlund describes a similar scenario from her childhood, and adds, "That generation of children has now grown up, but most of them haven't changed too much. Every Sunday they still play church. They line up in rows for the entertainment. If it's pretty good, their church may grow. If it's not too hot, eventually they'll drift off to play something else..."[24]

Ortlund goes on to propose the following questions: "Could it be that we still play church? Is it possible that when the congregation tires of the performance of the people "up front," they move on to other toys and more exciting forms of entertainment? How can we be sure that we are not "playing church"? How can we be certain that our religious activities truly constitute worship? How can we really understand what worship is?[25]

Worship is the celebration of God! When we worship, we extol Him. We celebrate Him. We sound His praises. We boast in Him and in the glorious perfections of His person and the wondrous works of His power. Worship is a response to God whereby we declare His worth. The old English word from which we derive "worship" began as "worth-ship." In our worship we declare the worthship of God, His worth and worthiness.

Worship, therefore, cannot be passive; it must be active and participative. It cannot be viewed simply as a mood; it must be seen as

---

24   Ortlund, Anne. *Up With Worship.* Nashville, TN: Broadman and Holman, 2001.

25   Ibid.

a response. It is not just a feeling; it is a declaration. It is a declaration of the worthiness of God. Worship means to attribute worth to something or someone.

When we worship God we attribute to Him the glory that is due His name. In a very real sense this is an impossible task! God is infinite in all of His attributes. We are finite in our noblest and purest efforts at worship. Therefore it is impossible for the finite to adequately glorify the infinite. And yet in the divine design of God, that is precisely what we are called to do in worship. But worship cannot be so simply defined, nor can it be understood merely by definitive statements. There is no such thing as worship in the abstract. To properly probe its profound potential, we must study it subjectively as well as objectively. Worship must be understood by the experiences and expressions of praise offered to God by real flesh and blood men and women who not only knew God, but walked with Him, and who worshipped Him.

As we journey through the Word of God we will find not only a foundation, but also a framework for worship. We will discover something of its dimensions and elements. We will view the prism of its light and see its many-splendoured beauty unfold. We begin our exploration by examining the very first worship encounter recorded in the pages of God's Word: a story of the first human family, and their worship of their creator God.

THREE DIMENSIONS OF WORSHIP—AND
HOW THE FIRST MURDER OCCURRED

1. The First Dimension of Worship—the Upward Lift of Man

One of the first lessons to be learned concerning worship is found in the first worship experience recorded in Scripture—that of Cain and Abel. Most of us remember this Bible story from our earliest days in Sunday School. The first two brothers to live on planet earth bring different offerings to the same God. One brother, Abel, invokes both the blessing of God and his brother's curse. Cain's offering is rejected. The results are history. The first murder in the human race is related to the first worship experience and happens on the way out of church.

Before we examine the dynamics of this incident, we must first recognize that the foundational dimension of worship is identified for us in this passage. Somehow, both of these men instinctively, intuitively, had a worship drive within them.

Anthropologists readily admit that the worship drive is common to all mankind, regardless of history, origin, or behavior patterns. Man is created with an elevator in his spirit—an "upward lift" in his inner being. Paul argues in Romans chapter one that this upward lift is basic to all men. In fact, his argument states that even in the absence of God's recorded Word, every human being has adequate evidence of God's existence and majesty to compel him to worship his Creator.

In Pauline theology this evidence is twofold: there is both intrinsic and extrinsic evidence of God's existence. Externally, the majesty of God's creation furnishes proof of the transcending greatness of the Creator. Internally, the sense of right and wrong encoded into man's consciousness (conscience) is proof not only of God's existence, but also of His moral perfection. When man looks around him, he knows that he is incapable of creating the surroundings in which he finds himself. Even the most primitive man knows that the lesser worships the greater.

Paul's case against man is this: that when man knew God instinctively, he did not glorify Him (worship Him) as God, but rather made God in man's own image, worshipping created things rather than the Creator. Paul states that man chose to gamble his knowledge of God away for the lie of Satan, i.e., the possibility of human godhood. Ultimate idolatry is the worship of self rather than the worship of God.

In the story of Cain and Abel we have early Old Testament evidence of the inward/upward lift of man towards God. We will discover in this passage a demonstration of both true and false worship. Essentially, we should note that both true and false worshippers appeared at the altar of God. The upward thrust of man towards God is found in every culture and is undeniable. We may be unable to define or describe it, but recognize it, we must.

There is no record that Cain and Abel were instructed in the habits of worship. However, God Himself had initiated the lessons by slaying the first animal to clothe the parents of these brothers. We can assume that at that time it was customary to approach God with an appropriate offering of worship that had been divinely prescribed. Abel's offering could not have been an obedient and acceptable response, and conversely, Cain's could not have been unacceptable, had there not been established some criteria of worship procedures.

One salient detail that provides an interesting clue can be found in the statement, "at the end of days," or as rendered in the NIV, "in the course of time." Each brother brought his offering before the Lord *in the course of time*. This phrase could suggest a specific time such as the end of a week, the conclusion of season, or perhaps a year. But whatever the element of time, it was a specifically prescribed period of worship.

Worship involves both sacrifice and offering. The offering must encompass more than the mere release of material substance. The sacrifice must deal with sin as well as with thanksgiving. But the sacrifice itself (even if it is the prescribed one) has no value, and the sacrificial act becomes immoral when the worshipper attaches merit to his own act, and does not attribute the whole worth of the sacrificial offering to God.

Both Cain and Abel brought to God those things that were representative of their respective fields of labor. Cain was a tiller of the ground, and therefore brought the fruit of the ground as an offering to God. Perhaps Cain thought that he had a better idea than God's idea. After all, bloody sacrifices are not that attractive. In fact, they are rather repulsive. Cain's offering, on the other hand, was beautiful.

When I think of Cain's offering I picture the Thanksgiving cornucopia that often adorns the altar areas of churches throughout the autumn season. The variety of color and texture, shape and size represented there speaks of the infinite variety of God's creation. Perhaps such thoughts contributed to Cain's offering. He really thought that he was improving on God's plan.

By so doing, however, Cain became the prototype and paternal progenitor of all false worshippers. This we learn in the Book of Jude, the shortest book of the Bible, and the vestibule to the Revelation that depicts the acts of the apostates. Jude, writing of contemporary heresy as he defends the faith, describes those that have gone in "the way of Cain."

But what exactly is the "way of Cain" in worship, and how does it contrast with Abel's worship that found acceptance before God? One of the clues is supplied in Hebrews eleven where Abel's name is listed in the roll call of the heroes of faith. There it is said that it was by faith that Abel offered unto God a more excellent sacrifice than Cain. In what sense was faith present and active in Abel's worship but lacking in the worship of Cain?

The answer is both obvious and simple. Faith is never passive. It is not a mental mood. Faith is reflected in what we do. Faith and obedience go hand in hand. Trust and obey are two sides of the same coin. Abel demonstrated his faith in what God had said by his obedience in bringing the offering that God had required. Perhaps he saw something of the symbolic and prophetic nature of his offering. Perhaps he saw through eyes of faith that one day *the Lamb* would come as the final fulfillment of all the lambs. But even if he was not privy to such revelation, his obedience was demonstrative of his faith in the Word of God.

Cain, on the other hand, disregarded God's requirement. The gravity of his error was found not only in his disobedience of the requirement of God, but also in the establishment of man's religion. Since Cain, multitudes of people have tried to worship God with the fruit of their labors. Millions have trusted in religious systems that place meritorious and atoning value in the works of their hands. At the very beginning, God must declare to the world that this is unacceptable worship.

Could it be that this kind of legalism is not limited to the false cults and those religious systems that insist upon faith plus an infinite variety of other additives for salvation? Is it possible that this subtle spirit may have invaded some of the worship systems of orthodox evangelical Christianity? Any approach of worship that places merit in the style, the expressions themselves, the methodology, the mechanics of the worship experience comes dangerously close to approximating the "way of Cain."

One of Protestantism's chief criticisms of Catholic tradition is the placing of meritorious value in parts of the worship ritual. Unless our worship exalts only Christ, the finished work of His cross, His blood and His victorious conquest through the cross and resurrection, we can fall into the same deception. If we see worship as being comprised of some of the forms and rituals that we have sanctified in our corporate congregational gatherings, we too may miss the mark. Colossians 2:22 describes the various restrictions, rituals and regimented regulations that some early Church Gnostics imposed upon the people of God as "worship." Paul calls it "will-worship" or "self-imposed worship" as opposed to that which God requires. He warns that such things tend to distract from Christ, rather than to direct glory to Him. Rather, they render a false sense of holiness to the participant and inflate his fleshly ego. The end result produces no God-honoring discipline in the worshipper's life, even though the religious regimen may appear wise and beautiful.

2. The Second Dimension of Worship— the Downward Look of God

Worship, however, is not a one-way street. It goes beyond the lifting of our hearts to God. Worship is a dynamic duo between God and man. Man's worship is a response to God's initiative in redemption. As man responds to God by lifting his heart to God in worship, God responds to man by receiving that act of worship.

The first criterion for Biblical worship is that it must be acceptable to God. When worship is acceptable, the up-reach of man is reciprocated by the down-reach of God. Thus the upward lift of man and the downward look of God are harmonized together in worship. Since God ultimately evaluates and judges our worship, it must first be acceptable to Him. In other words, our worship must be thoroughly Biblical. We must ascertain that there is adequate Scriptural evidence to substantiate our worship activity.

The Scriptures tell us that God had respect (Genesis 4:4 KJV) to Abel's offering. This literally means that He looked favorably upon it.

In the original text, however, the Hebrew word "sha'ah" is stronger than "a favorable look": it literally means to gaze.

This concept of God **gazing** at Abel's offering conveys the message that He cared for it. It was acceptable and delightful to Him. It captured His attention and captivated His focus. There are some important reasons why God looked at Abel's offering with favor. Those reasons have striking parallels for worshippers in every generation.

We already observed that Abel offered his worship in faith. He looked forward to the promise of God that was prefigured by His offering. He trusted in the Word of God that he had received, and in which he had been instructed. Closely related to Abel's faith was his obedience. God had required that blood be shed, and Abel had conformed to the commandment of God.

But the principal reason for God's response to Abel's worship was Abel's obedience. The only way that sinful man may approach a holy God is through the divine prerequisite of a blood sacrifice. This concept is developed throughout the Old Testament Book of Leviticus (hereinafter referred to as the Levitical system) and becomes the foundational framework for the New Testament theology of the virtue and value of Christ's Blood.

Abel's act of obedience was a giving of himself to God. When the will is surrendered to God in obedience, when the heart is given to God in faith, when the offering is brought according to God's specifications rather than our whims and wishes, God looks favorably upon our worship—He literally gazes there. It captivates His attention, and He responds to that kind of worship.

This passage reveals one of the earliest pictures of the cross. The firstborn of the flock foreshadows the Lamb of God who would come to take away the sins of the world. Abel demonstrated his faith in that promise when he came, acknowledging that he was worthy of death for his own sins, and brought the lamb as a substitutional sacrifice.

Cain, conversely, brought an offering that represented his own labors. His represents worship that does not honor God's Word. Consequently, God could not respond favorably to Cain's worship. It is vitally important to reflect upon the reasons why God could not accept the worship of Cain. **Firstly**, *Cain did not consider the importance of obedience to God's Word.* He presumed upon the Lord's mercy and overlooked His holiness. He assumed that his produce—the product of his own hands —the fruit of his own efforts—the offering of his own works would merit acceptance with God. **Secondly**, *Cain did not have faith in God's Word.* Faith is always demonstrated by obedience, as is evidenced in Abel's worship. Cain's worship was rendered from a posture of *resistance* rather than one of *reverence* for God and His Word.

These historic lessons are indispensable to contemporary worship. Our offerings, our worship must be in obedience to God and His Word. We must not bypass the cross and the resurrection of Christ by looking subjectively to our own experiences, but must look objectively to the divine sacrifice and the Savior's finished work. Cain's worship not only lacked faith and obedience, but was also a religious activity that bypassed the necessity of a blood sacrifice.

For this reason we should reconsider the songs and choruses that are intertwined in our worship expression. The power of the old hymns that were forged in the fires of the Reformation lies in their exaltation of the Person and work of Christ, His deity, His cross, His resurrection, and His power to save through His redeeming blood. Many new worship choruses have perpetuated these truths in contemporary style. But many others find a focus that is less Biblical and more experientially subjective. Our worship must maintain a balance that keeps Christ in the center and magnifies His Person and work.

The writer to the Hebrews adds an interesting detail concerning Abel's offering. He says that God testified of his offerings (Hebrews 11:4). We can only speculate as to the nature of God's testimony of acceptance, but our conjecture will be based upon patterns that emerge elsewhere in Scripture. The normal manner in which God demonstrated His acceptance (of an offering) was by fire. God would send fire down to consume the sacrifice as an indication that He was receiving the offering presented to Him. Although the passage does not state this, it is possible that God thus demonstrated His acceptance of Abel's offering. One thing is certain: in some way that was observable by physical evidence to both Cain and Abel, God demonstrated His acceptance of Abel's offering and His rejection of Cain's. The concept of fire is the most logical conclusion, based upon all proper principles of Biblical interpretation.

God's vindication of Abel's worship and His rejection of Cain's worship teach us one more important principle: our worship is ultimately to God and for God. It is God who must judge our worship and determine its acceptability. This does not distract from the fact that there are obvious and certain earmarks by which we can determine that our worship is Biblical. But beyond the essential elements of faith, the blood of Christ, and obedience, we are well advised not to impose the bias or prejudice of our particular worship style upon others. God is the judge of our worship.

When looking at the fact that worship is a dynamic duo between God and man, we are often content to limit it to these two dimensions. But there is a third dimension to worship, without which the worship experience is incomplete.

3. The Third Dimension of Worship—the Outward Life of Man

The third dimension of worship is often overlooked. While worship is certainly a vertical relationship between God and man, there are two bars in the cross: one vertical, one horizontal. These two bars have traditionally been symbolical of the twofold work of reconciliation that Christ accomplished. The vertical bar, reaching upward toward heaven and downward to earth, speaks of the reconciliation of God and man. God has brought man together with Himself through the cross of His Son. But the horizontal bar represents what may be called the "horizontal" aspect of reconciliation. The cross, according to Ephesians chapter two, is also the meeting place of man and man.

Through the cross God has reconciled the two most diametrically opposed groups of humanity in bringing Jew and Gentile together. Consequently, the horizontal dimension of worship cannot be forgotten. In fact, it is intriguing that God attached such importance to this horizontal dimension in worship that it is revealed in the very first worship experience recorded in the Scriptures. In the first human family, in the first recorded worship scene, God introduces us to the dynamics of corporate worship.

Worship is never *fully* experienced solo. Of course we can worship God when we are alone, but this is not the point. Our relationships with our spiritual family impact our fellowship with God. Since worship is not strictly between God and the individual, it is never in absolute individual isolation. It is impossible to separate our worship from our human relationships. Just as most of us believe that we sing better in the shower than anywhere else, we also sometimes speculate that we could get along fine in life except for people. I remember a pastor friend once saying to me in a moment of frustration, "Don, life would be great if it wasn't for people!" If we could live our lives in a cloistered convent, in ascetic monasticism, we would have fewer problems loving God with all of our beings.

Jesus made it clear that loving God and loving our neighbor are simply two sides of the same coin. Mother Teresa has captured that concept when she speaks of the "distressing disguise" of God in which she sees Him in the gaunt faces of starving Indian children. Tony Compolo stresses and stretches this truth to the discomfort of orthodox evangelicalism when he talks of Jesus being alive in all people.[26] But the point is well taken. God would have us to understand that our response to His crowning act of creation, the human beings we relate to, is interpreted by Him as our response to Him. In the words of our Lord, "Inasmuch as ye have done it unto one of the least of these my brethren, ye have done it unto me" (Matthew 25:40 KJV).

This emphasis of Christ is echoed and reiterated by that disciple whom Jesus loved. John, in his first epistle, talks about this dimension of Christian life as being the supreme evidence of our conversion to Christ. He states that love for God and hatred of brethren cannot coexist. Even James, who by some is perceived as the legalist opponent of Pauline theology, tells us that the validation of our faith in Christ is the demonstration of a lifestyle of love that fulfills the Royal Law of God (James 2:14-22).

From Cain and Abel there are principles that painfully parallel our own lives. Probably all of us have at times been touched with the feeling of Cain's infirmity in our response to our brothers and sisters in Christ. Cain was angry with his brother, and probably with God as well... and understandably so. There was no fire for his offering. His offering was much more attractive and appealing than that of his younger brother. His *younger* brother! That's another matter, God! If

---

26   Campolo, Tony. *Partly Right: Learning from the Critics of Christianity.* Dallas, TX: Word Publishing, 1985.

anyone should have received the blessing of God's approval it should have been the older son. After all, the firstborn is guaranteed the blessing of God!

Cain was immensely incensed at God's inconsistency and inequity. God had demonstrated favoritism towards his younger brother. In his anger Cain was blinded to his own sin of rebellion and disobedience against God. The mercy of God is demonstrated so powerfully with the first human family. God, in mercy, had provided a covering for Adam and Eve in the nakedness of their sin. And now, in mercy, God provides an alternative for Cain, even after his act of rebellion against God.

God takes the initiative to communicate with Cain. Quite simply, God tells him that if he does what is right he can also find God's acceptance. If he is willing only to obey, God will not reject him. But God also warns him that if he rebels, sin is crouching at his door, exercising its desire to master him. Somehow, Cain must master sin.

This illustration of sin crouching at Cain's door is a powerful portrait of the results of incomplete obedience. Worship cannot be genuine when sin is allowed harbor in our lives. Our communion with God is impaired. Some have thought that the word translated "sin" could mean "sin offering" since the same Hebrew word is translated that way elsewhere. Therefore, some have supposed that God was telling Cain that even if he did wrong, there was a sin offering just outside his door. While this interpretation has some interesting implications, it misses the essential point of the passage.

God offers Cain an alternative, but it seems to have very little appeal to him. Cain is not interested in being treated equally with his brother Abel. He wants the upper hand. He wants exclusive rights, executive privileges, exemption and exclusion from the requirements of God that are binding on others. Refusing God's remonstrance, he goes out and kills his brother.

What a compelling portrait this is of the reality of our worship experience! We worship with brothers and sisters, some of whom (in our opinion) are more favored of God than we are. We are prone to jealousy, envying, and strife in the body of Jesus Christ. And it impacts the quality of our worship. It impairs our ability to see God. It impedes God's ability to respond to us.

Jealousy is evil. Hatred constitutes murder by the divine standard that Jesus describes in the Sermon on the Mount. Cain leaves the presence of God and slays his own brother. Is it possible that there is murder in the heart of a "fellow-worshipper"? Can two brothers go to the same altar and leave that place of worship with hatred in their hearts toward one another? The fact that it occurred in the first recorded worship experience in Scripture is indicative of its horrible possibility.

John admonishes us, "Do not be like Cain, who belonged to the evil one and murdered his brother. And why did he murder him? Because his own actions were evil and his brother's were righteous" (I John 3:12 NIV). Earlier in his letter, John informs us, "Anyone who claims to be in the light but hates his brother is still in the darkness. Whoever loves his brother lives in the light and there is nothing in him to make him stumble. But whoever hates his brother is in the darkness and walks around in the darkness; he does not know where he is going because the darkness has blinded him" (I John 2:9-11 NIV).

Is it possible that our worship is less than what God intended because of the strife in human relationships within the Body of Christ? Have we adopted a pseudo-spirituality that has successfully (in our eyes) separated our relationship and worship of God from our relationships with people? The question is rhetorical. The answer is patently plain.

Worship must not be seen as unidirectional. The dimension of human relationships must be taken into account. Jesus tells us if we bring our gift to the altar and there remember that our brother has something against us, we are to first go and reconcile with our brother and then come and offer the gift (Matthew 5:23-24). In our worship experience we offer our praise to God through Jesus Christ. But unless our horizontal relationships are reconciled, the vertical expression of our worship is less than acceptable to God.

From the first recorded worship experience, God teaches us the fundamentals. True worshippers come before God, lifting their hearts, their spirits and beings to Him in gratitude, humility, praise and adoration. This kind of worship delights the Father's heart and He looks down upon us and views us accepted through the blood of Christ, our Savior, Substitute, and Sacrificial Lamb. Since God accepts us for Christ's sake, we then must accept one another on the same basis.

From this foundation we will be able to construct a theology of worship that will be both acceptable to God and fulfilling to us. After all, that is the purpose for which we were created! When we discover the power of worship, we are fulfilling the pattern of the divine design. And when this becomes a reality in our lives, we will say, "I was born for this! This is life at its ultimate!"

LOOK FOR THE GOLD AT THE END OF THE RAINBOW

My heart leaps up when I behold a rainbow in the sky...

— William Wordsworth

Then Noah built an altar to the LORD and, taking some of all the clean animals and clean birds, he sacrificed burnt offerings on it. The LORD smelled the pleasing aroma and said... "Never again will there be a flood to destroy the earth... this is the sign of the covenant I am making between me and you and every living creature with you, a covenant for all generations to come: I have set my rainbow in the clouds, and it will be the sign of the covenant between me and the earth... whenever the rainbow appears in the clouds, I will see it and remember the everlasting covenant between God and all living creatures of every kind on the earth" (From Genesis 8:20-21, 9:8-17 NIV).

While Hosea Ballou described a rainbow as *"God's glowing covenant"*, Henry Wadsworth Longfellow referred to it as *"God's illumined promise."* Both were far closer to the Biblical denition than any contemporary application made to this wonder of God's creation.

The proverbial "pot of gold at the end of the rainbow" has lost much of its luster since it has become symbolic of the empty promise of charlatans from Madison Avenue to Wall Street and from infomercials to televangelism. Yet, people everywhere love rainbows, and they are still used as trademarks by many business institutions. More recently, it has become the symbol of choice for those championing and advancing the social agenda of the lesbian, gay, and transgender (LGBTQ) community. And the old legend about the pot of gold at the end of the rainbow remains a fascinating concept.

Finding "gold at the end of the rainbow" may be a fitting metaphor for worship. Just as a rainbow is formed as sunlight shines through water, so the Light of God's glory is manifest in a multitude of radiant hues as it shines through the person of Jesus Christ.

It is Christ who is the centre of worship. When John the Revelator saw Christ on the throne he said, "And the one who sat there had the appearance of jasper and carnelian. A rainbow, resembling an emerald, encircled the throne" (Revelation 4:3 NIV).

The tendency and temptation is to become infatuated with the beauty of the rainbow, enamored with its exquisite colors and composition, and forget to focus on the gold. Similarly, in worship, we can so enthrall in the beauty of the experience and the thrill of the expression that we forget that worship is for God and not for ourselves.

When we examine the wide spectrum of worship encounters in the Old Testament, we find indeed that various worship experiences elicited a veritable rainbow of responses in God's people. At times, they were motivated to destroy their idols. On other occasions, they promised to obey everything that God had said. In other places, there is much music and celebration. In various circumstances, they lift their hands, bow their heads, or fall on their faces before God. They may weep, laugh, rejoice, or repent, but invariably, in worship, God's people are moved to action.

There is no substitute for the realm of worship in which we find ourselves overwhelmingly aware of God's presence. His Spirit moves upon us to release our utmost adoration from the depths of our being. As the Holy Spirit prompts and precipitates our response to God, we discover our purpose in life. We were made to worship!

What comes to your mind when you think of the word "worship"? Is it quiet prayer and meditation? Or is it joyful, exuberant praise and celebration? All of these are acceptable demonstrations of our worship to God, as well as many other forms of expression. But worship goes deeper than the external shell of either the experience or the expression.

In the second worship experience recorded in Scripture, we will discover three elements of worship that must be present, regardless of the form or style our worship takes. These elements are at the very heart of worship, and it is of these components that worship is comprised.

THE THREE ELEMENTS OF WORSHIP

1. Worship is Gratitude for Past Deliverance

The second worship experience recorded in Scripture centers around the familiar story of Noah and the Ark. As the flood waters subsided, the first item on Noah's agenda was to build an altar, and offer sacrifices to God in worship. Genesis 8:21-22 states that God smelled the aroma of Noah's offerings and said in His heart that He would never again curse the ground because of man, even though man was bent towards evil.

The birthing of God's covenant with Noah came in response to Noah's worship. God wrote the laws of the seasons into that covenant at that time, and we live in the benefits and blessings of that covenant to this day. But it was when Noah's worship ascended as a sweet aroma that God promised to bring His creation into this covenant relationship.

One aspect of worship is that of gratitude to God for His divine deliverance. Peter teaches us that the deliverance of Noah and his family dramatically portrays the deliverance that we have found in the Lord Jesus Christ (I Peter 3:20-21).

Peter is stressing the symbolic significance of water baptism in this passage. Through the waters of baptism, he suggests, we have left behind the old creation, and have entered into the new creation. There is no saving virtue in the water. Baptism is not the "putting away of the filth of the flesh." That is to say, baptism itself does not wash away our sins. Peter describes baptism as "the answer of a good conscience toward God." The conscience that has been cleansed by the blood of Christ through faith, now responds in the obedient step of baptism. This act of baptism becomes a declaration to the Lord, the Church, and the world that the former life of sin is now left behind. But the believer is saved by virtue of the fact that he is in Christ, the Ark of Salvation.

What role then, does the water have? Peter likens it to Noah and his family in the ark. The floodtides did two things. Firstly, they brought God's judgment upon the old creation that was corrupted through sin. Secondly, they buoyed or carried the ark above that condemned creation into a new creation that had been purged and cleansed by God.

Baptism serves similarly as the vehicle of declaration of God's judgment upon the former life. The old life is now buried with

Christ by baptism into His death. We rise to walk in newness of life in Christ (Romans 6:2-4).

Worship declares our thanksgiving, gratitude and praise to God for completing this deliverance! We celebrate the fact that we are in Christ, and old things are passed away. The former life is removed from us. This is the celebration of forgiveness. In forgiveness, God has literally carried our sins away.

This fact was symbolized in the Old Testament by the scapegoat. Besides the sacrificial animal burned upon the brazen altar of the tabernacle, there was another animal called the scapegoat. The priest would place his hands upon the goat's head, and confess his sins and those of the people. The scapegoat would then be sent away to wander in the wilderness.

In His sovereignty, God saw to it that the Israelites never found the scapegoat again! It never returned to the camp. There is no record of their discovering its bleaching bones protruding from the wilderness sands to remind them of their sins. Their sins were (symbolically) carried away. "As far as the east is from the west, so far hath he removed our transgressions from us" (Psalm 103:12 KJV).

Corrie Ten Boom quips that God has put our sins in His sea of forgetfulness and posted a sign, "No fishing in the sea of God's forgetfulness."[27] Worship celebrates the fact that we have been rescued from the former life. God instructed His people, however, to remember the pit from which they had been brought. God does not dangle us over the pit of hell on a shoestring, nor hold our past over our heads in horrid detail to remind us of what we once were. But there are reminders throughout the New Testament to help us appreciate and worship God for our deliverance.

---

27   http://ecclesia.org/truth/corrie.html

For example, Paul talks about the former life. "You were dead in trespasses and sins, in which you used to live when you followed the ways of this world and of the rule of the kingdom of the air, the spirit who is now at work in those who are disobedient. All of us also lived among them at one time, gratifying the cravings of our sinful nature and following its desires and thoughts. Like the rest we were by nature objects of wrath" (Ephesians 2:1-4 NIV).

Later in the same chapter, Paul continues, "Therefore, remember that formerly you who are Gentiles by birth and called 'uncircumcised' by those who call themselves 'the circumcision' (that done in the body by the hands of men)—remember that at that time you were separate from Christ, excluded from citizenship in Israel and foreigners to the covenants of the promise, without hope and without God in the world." (Ephesians 2:11-12 NIV). Again in chapter four and in many other places, believers are reminded of where they were before Christ found them.

This same pattern can be discerned in Old Testament Judaic worship. The Psalms are very reminiscent of the great works of God that wrought their deliverance. The Jewish people knew how to recall the memory of their former life as a basis of their praise to God for their present deliverance.

The anthems of praise in the New Testament celebrate God's deliverance from past bondage. John sings "unto Him that loved us and washed us from our sins in His own blood and has made us a kingdom of priests unto God" (Rev. 1:6).

We celebrate the fact that God has fully judged sin in the person of our Lord Jesus Christ. The tyranny of sin has been broken at the cross. Satan's domain has been conquered! We have been set free by the power of Christ's blood.

When Paul describes the various kinds of vice that characterize those who will not inherit the kingdom of God in I Corinthians 6:10-11, he says, "And such were some of you. But you are washed, you are sanctified, you are justified in the name of the Lord Jesus and by the Spirit of our God."

From the days of the Reformation through the present renewal, God has been at work in history. This primary lesson is learned from Noah's act of worship. True worship will always have historical roots. Whether offered in a comfortable sanctuary or at the edge of subsiding floodwaters, real worship is rooted in the past redemptive activity of God. God is the God of the living. We don't live in the past, but we don't live apart from the past. In our worship we praise God for delivering us from our previous enslavement to sin.

In Jewish worship, God gave the Passover as a perennial and perpetual reminder of God's past deliverance. The New Testament Church celebrates the Table of the Lord with its past, present and future implications. We remember the Lord's death and all it accomplished for us. We celebrate the Living Body and Presence of Christ among us. And we do it "until He comes" (I Corinthians 11:26). There is ever an upward look, a forward look, a posture of waiting for the return of our Lord.

2. Worship is Rejoicing in God's Present Provision

Worship consumed and concerned with the past, however, will never be dynamic and vital, for worship is a present reality. God is at work now. We are now in His presence. This too is illustrated in Noah's worship.

Noah stepped out of the ark into a brand new world! It was a new creation in which there was no more scoffing nor mocking. The taunting ridicule of that unbelieving and ungodly generation had been silenced. No longer would he be subjected to the surrounding sin that had grieved and angered God's heart. The taint and stains of sin were gone. The earth had been purged by the judgment of God. It was clean! It was brand new!

This is worship! We are in a new creation, and God has given to us a new nature now. Eternal life is the Christian's present possession, rather than merely the ultimate future promise.

Now, don't stretch this metaphor out of context. That is one of the dangers of interpreting the Bible typologically. Although we attempt to make every minute detail fit, it simply doesn't work. While we are in a new creation, the potentials of evil still exist. We are surrounded by a sinful world. We soon learn in Genesis 9 that Noah's world was not perfect, either. But the positive truth that can be stressed is that of the new creation.

Paul not only said that "old things had passed away." He also said that "all things become new." And "If any man be in Christ, he is a new creation" (II Corinthians 5:17). This is the reality that we celebrate in worship. The believer worships God in the "newness of the Spirit" (Romans 7:6).

The present provisions of God should be our central focus in worship. Paul tells the Ephesian believers that we have already been blessed with all spiritual blessings in the heavenlies with Christ (Ephesians 1:3), while Peter states that God has given to us all things that pertain to life and godliness (II Peter 1:3).

In Ephesians 1, Paul proceeds to describe some of those blessings. We've been chosen in Christ before the creation of the world to be holy and blameless in His sight. He predestined us to be adopted as his sons by Jesus Christ, in accordance with his pleasure and will, to the praise of His glorious grace (Ephesians 1:4-6).

If you examine this passage carefully, you will find that Paul himself is unable to suppress his praise and worship to God when he begins to contemplate the multitude of present provisions that are ours because of the grace of God.

Ephesians 1:6 is itself a brief anthem of worship. "To the praise of his glorious grace, which he has freely given us in the One he loves," expresses the worship that is prompted in Paul's spirit as he ponders the greatness of God's grace.

Paul goes on to describe other present provisions that are ours in Christ. We have "redemption through his blood, the forgiveness of sins, in accordance with the riches of his grace that he lavished on us…" (Ephesians 1:7-8). Ephesians is rich in superlatives, all of which are employed in stretching language to its extremeties in an attempt to magnify God for His monumental mercies.

Paul continues to expound the richness of our inheritance in Christ. The mystery of the will of God has been revealed to us. That mystery for ages was concealed, but to us it is made known. In the church God plans to fulfill His eternal and ultimate purpose. In this present age, we experience that fulfillment and become the recipients of the revelation of God.

We have been sealed with the Holy Spirit of promise, the sign of God's acceptance. It is not His acceptance of us in our own merit, but rather our acceptance before God in Christ. It is also a seal of ownership. We are set apart as uniquely belonging to God. He has branded us for Himself. The Holy Spirit sets His unique ensign upon us.

However, the word *earnest*, which describes another facet of the seal of the Holy Spirit, means even more. One of the Greek usages of this word means "engagement ring." The Holy Spirit's presence in the life of the church is the present proof of our betrothal to Christ, and His personal guarantee that He will return to receive us unto Himself.

The seal of the Spirit also speaks of security and preservation. We are sealed *into* Jesus Christ. In Him we are safe and secure. Christ has promised that no man shall be able to pluck us from His hand, and has guaranteed our safe passage to heaven.

We have been chosen in Christ, in accordance with God's plan that we who trust in Christ might be for the praise of His glory. This is man's ultimate purpose: "...the praise of His glory" (Ephesians 1:6, 12, 14). Our present position in Christ, as well as the provision of Calvary, is the fountainhead and watershed of our worship!

Numerous passages could be referenced to inventory the present provisions that furnish the ground of our worship. Romans 5:1-5 speaks of our justification by faith, our peace with God through the Lord Jesus Christ, our access by faith into the standing of grace, and the hope of the glory of God. It adds the contrasting element of sufferings as a ground of praise and rejoicing, since sufferings produce perseverance, perseverance produces character, character produces hope, and hope does not disappoint us.

God has poured out His love into our hearts by the Holy Spirit that He has given us. Each of these blessings is a present provision through Christ for the child of God. Worship is birthed in our hearts when these benedictions become present reality.

Worship is concerned less with petition, more with praise; less with asking, more with acknowledgment. Our spiritual understanding is opened to discern what is already ours in Christ. This is the substance of Paul's prayer for the Ephesian believers (Ephesians 1:18-19). In worship we begin to realize how great God is. The unfolding of His *provision* intensifies our awareness of the glory of His *Person*. This in turn refines the quality of our worship. When we discover the hope to which God has called us, how gloriously rich *we make Him*, and the availability of His incomparable power to us who believe, there is no other appropriate or adequate response but that of worship, rejoicing in God's present provision.

While our state of being as born-again believers enables us to worship God in "newness of spirit," our status as born-again children of God also enables us to worship Him in the "now-ness of sonship." John declares that while "now we are children of God," yet "what we will be has not yet been made known. But we know that when he appears, we shall be like him, for we shall see him as he is. Everyone who has this hope in him purifies himself, just as he is pure" (I John 3:2-3 NIV). It is in the blend and balance of present position and future promise that worship must be seen.

3. Worship is Believing in God's Future Promise

The three elements of worship also represent three tenses of worship. Our adoration must reflect its redemptive roots (the past tense) as well as focus on the present position of the believer and the provision that is ours today (present tense). However, our worship is less than Biblical, unless we focus on the future fulfillment of God's promises. This basic element of hope is essential to the true gospel of our Lord Jesus Christ.

Here is an area of theology that has come under a great deal of debate in the contemporary charismatic scene. For example, the "kingdom now" message is an extreme pendulum swing from the traditional "rescue rapture" mentality that characterized fundamental evangelicalism and especially the Pentecostal/Full Gospel movement for many years.

Although extreme doctrinal positions have been entrenched, and both sides may have gone from being dogmatic to becoming "bulldog-matic", the truth (as it usually is) is to be found somewhere in the middle. The kingdom is both present and future. It is both "now" and "then." The "rescue rapture" approach insisting that the destiny of the church is merely to "hold the fort" until Christ returns to remove us from this apostate world is woefully inadequate and theologically weak and wearisome.

Yes, Jesus Christ will return for His church. Yes, apostasy is predicted to characterize the days preceding His return. But His church is to be militant, occupying enemy territory, advancing the banner of our monarch, taking ground from the enemy, and establishing the principles in advance by which the King will rule when He returns. But there are limitations. Until the King returns to purge the earth and establish the kingdom in its fullness, our ideal Utopian spiritual nirvana will not arrive.

In response to the disciples' question as to whether He would restore the kingdom to Israel now, Jesus gave an answer that was both direct and elusive. He told them it was not for them to know the times and the seasons that the Father had reserved in His own power. Jesus used two different Greek terms in His reference to "times" and "seasons." One depicts the great epochs of God, the other, depicts the chronological development of God's plan.

In both cases, Jesus was instructing his disciples to be agnostic in attempting to ascertain the time relative to the return of Christ and the establishment of the kingdom. There are some things about which we can afford to be dogmatic. Those are non-negotiable, and are clearly taught by our Lord. There are others concerning which we can afford to be agnostic, for God has seen fit to shroud them in mystery.

It is not our purpose here to attempt to adequately treat this eschatological question. Rather, it is raised only in reference to how our positions impact our worship. For example, it seems rather obvious that the apostle Paul expected Christ to return in his generation. When speaking of the return of Christ in I Thessalonians 4:15, Paul includes himself in the company that will be alive at the translation when he says, "*We* that are alive and remain." (emphasis mine)

The Apostle John saw nothing to hinder the immediate and imminent return of Christ. In the last chapter of his Revelation, in response to Jesus' promise, "Behold I come quickly," John responded, "Even so, come, Lord Jesus" (Revelation 22:20).

Did our Lord reveal to them the timing? Obviously not, for He said that even He didn't know, only the Father did. Yet, Paul tells the Thessalonians that they need not be in darkness concerning the times and the seasons. Were Paul and Jesus talking about the same thing? It would appear that Jesus is referring to the coming kingdom in its fullness and Paul to the return of Christ and the events that must lead up to it.

Jesus' own treatment of the kingdom was both present and future. He announced that the kingdom of God had come to them, and yet He spoke of that kingdom as having futuristic fulfillment. The proper understanding of the balance between present and future was embodied in Jesus Christ. This balance is significant insofar as the manner in which it impacts our worship. To a large degree, our theology dictates our worship. At least, in evangelical Christianity, that should be the case. If we are committed to a Biblical basis for doctrine, that Biblical base will shape our worship. If, however, we are less concerned about orthodox theology, then it is possible that our worship will shape our doctrine.

While the Latin phrase "lex orandi, lex credendi"[28] has not received much treatment in Protestantism, yet it can become

---

28   http://en.wikipedia.org/wiki/Lex_orandi,_lex_credendi

axiomatic for evangelicals if our commitment to Biblical worship and theology is fuzzy. What we pray will become what we believe. We will attempt to adjust our doctrine to our experience. In fact, "lex orandi, lex credendi" is quite true in much of Protestant evangelicalism. Our doctrinal structure has been constructed to accommodate our experience. This is the proven history of denominationalism in the Protestant movement, particularly beginning with the Revival age and the Wesleyan influence. While our experience should *inform* our theology and our worship, it certainly should not *form* it.

If therefore we embrace a faulty eschatology, our worship will be faulty. If, in our worship, we become so committed to a "kingdom now" attitude that we lose the quality of hope, then our worship is less than Biblical. If we adopt the fatalistic attitude of the "rescue rapture" that denies God's people any benefits of the present kingdom, then we lose sight of the present reality of worship.

The kind of religious worship that focuses upon "Canaan's Land" as representing heaven and the age to come projects upon the worshipper the denial of God's working here and now. To project only millennial realization of God's provision is to overemphasize the element of hope. On the other hand, hope is a vital part of our worship. To stress the kingdom now at the expense of hope is equally to miss the mark.

The ultimate and logical conclusion of the "kingdom now" emphasis is to suggest that the believer has the present right to physical immortality. Such a position is very close to the teaching that the believer should not incur disease or decay in his mortal body. This, in fact, is being taught in some extreme "kingdom now" circles. But this flies in the face of one of the greatest "hope" passages in New Testament literature. Paul says in Romans 8:23- 25,

Not only so, but we ourselves, who have the firstfruits of the Spirit, groan inwardly as we wait for our adoption as sons, the redemption of our bodies. For in this hope we were saved. But hope that is seen is no hope at all. Who hopes for what he already has? But if we hope for what we do not yet have, we wait for it patiently (Romans 8: 23-25 NIV).

The believer looks for the coming of Christ. Paul talks about the crown that awaits those who love Christ's appearing. He places himself among the company of those who will be alive and remain at that coming. This posture of waiting is also confirmed in non-Pauline epistles. Peter talks about living a lifestyle that enables us to look forward to and speed the day of Christ's coming. John exhorts us to live in such a way that we will not be ashamed before Him when He comes. John says that the hope of Christ's return and of being made like Him supplies the believer with a source of purification.

One cannot have an authentic New Testament theology without this essential element of hope. James exhorts us to patience in waiting for the return of Christ. The Christian's attitude is clear. We are to occupy this earth by advancing Christ's kingdom. We are to combat the forces of evil in the power of Jesus' name and through the conquest of His cross. We are to establish God's kingdom on earth. But we are not getting this world ready to hand over to Jesus. The world will not continually improve. There will be an increase of evil. But we are not to fold our arms and succumb to it. We are to rise up and take territory in the name of our King. However, until He comes to rule and reign personally, His kingdom will be realized in a qualified and limited state.

It should be patently plain that without a future focus, our worship cannot be truly Biblical. The challenge is to balance our living in the tension between the present kingdom and future kingdom emphasis.

In the story of Noah's worship, God's covenant of promise introduces the futuristic element into the worship. God responded to Noah's expression of gratitude by giving what we now recognize as the Noahic covenant. The giving of the covenant is thus symbolically linked to the cross, as this passage contains the first mention of a whole burnt offering, an entire animal offered to God. Christ is powerfully foreshadowed in this sacrifice, since Noah offered only clean animals to God. Our Lord Jesus Christ fulfilled this when through the eternal spirit He offered Himself without spot unto God (see Heb. 9:14).

God covenants to never again destroy the earth by a flood, and to never again smite all living things as He had done in this judgment. He also promises that both the laws of the seasons and of day and night will not cease as long as the earth stands. These laws, written into creation, govern our world to this day, the evidence that God can be depended upon to keep His Word.

As a sign of the covenant, God places a rainbow in the sky. When clouds cover the earth, God sees the rainbow serving as a reminder to HIM of His covenant to never again destroy all life upon the earth.

It is worthy of note that the rainbow appears elsewhere in Scripture. The rainbow makes it all the way across both testaments to appear around the throne of God in the Book of Revelation. It represents to us the glory of God surrounding His throne in heaven. But it also points us to the future when the Redeemed of the Lord will gather around the throne to worship both God the Father and God the Lamb with perfected praise!

Noah's act of worship was an expression of his confidence in God for the future, but God's response to Noah was based upon what

He (GOD) would do in the future. God's response required Christ. It was Christ whom God saw prefigured in the offerings of Noah. Thus the cross, both in symbol and in shadow, became the basis of God's promise of future hope.

Noah had built the ark with his own hands. He might have taken credit himself for the preservation of his family and of the animals. Instead, Noah gave God the glory. His first priority when he entered the new creation was to worship God.

We too have been brought out of the old creation through Jesus Christ, the Ark of our salvation. Christ is the altar of our sacrifice. He is our hope for the future. He will return to set up His kingdom in its fullness upon this earth.

Our eternal occupation will be that of worshipping Him. With that future destiny before us, let us worship Him now! Worship Him for His past deliverances, His present provisions, and the future fulfillment of His precious promises.

ARE YOU SURE GOD TOLD YOU TO KILL YOUR SON?

It is so hard to believe because it is so hard to obey.

— **Søren Kierkegaard**

Then God said, "Take your son, your only son, Isaac, whom you love…sacrifice him as a burnt offering on one of the mountains I will tell you about." Abraham…set out for the place God had told him about…looked up and saw the place…said to his servants, "Stay here with the donkey while I and the boy go over there. We will worship and then we will come back to you." When they reached the place God had told him about, Abraham built an altar there and arranged the wood on it. He bound his son Isaac and laid him on the altar, on top of the wood. Then he reached out his hand and took the knife to slay his son. But the angel of the LORD called out to him from heaven, "Abraham! Abraham!" "Here I am," he replied. "Do not lay a hand on the boy," he said. "Do not do anything to him. Now I know that you fear God, because you have not withheld from me your son, your only son." Abraham looked up and there in a thicket he saw a ram caught by its horns. He went over and took the ram and sacrificed it as a burnt offering instead of his son. So Abraham called that place The LORD Will Provide. And to this day it is said, "On the mountain of the LORD it will be provided" (Genesis 22:2-14 NIV).

The Genesis account of God's instructions to Abraham to take his only son, the son of promise, and offer him as a sacrifice, could cause one to question the credulity of the Scriptures and the credibility of a God who would make such a demand—if you were to take part of the narrative, and fail to read the story in its entirety. For those who choose *not* to believe in God and His Word, this story adds great fuel to the fire of skepticism.

Entire websites have been devoted to the idol of infidelity in which God is made the villain by empowering the Israelites to slay and defeat their enemies in battle. In this day of Jihad, killing in the name of God is not limited to those who purport to worship Allah. Those of us who call ourselves Christians must be careful that we don't become modern-day "crusaders" by so believing in the justice of our cause that indiscriminate killing is legitimized when done in the name of the Lord. When the president of the most powerful nation in the free world claims that God has told him to strike the enemy, the line becomes very fine: difficult to draw and easy to cross.

However, when individuals claim that God has instructed them to kill another person, their claims are rightly taken as immediate and incontrovertible proof of their insanity. Newspaper headlines bring such stories to our attention from time to time. The following are two cases in point.

A Texas psychiatrist recently testified that a mother who crushed her sons' skulls with rocks was suffering from delusions and did not know right from wrong. Dr. Park Dietz said Deanna Laney believed God ordered her to kill her children on a Mother's Day weekend. "She struggled over whether to obey God or to selfishly keep her children," Dietz testified.

Laney, a 39-year-old stay-at-home mother who home-schooled her children, pleaded innocent by reason of insanity to charges of capital murder and serious injury to a child in the deaths of 8-year-old Joshua and 6-year-old Luke and severe injury to then-14-month-old Aaron. This murdering mother, who is deeply religious, had a series of delusions on the day of the killings. She said she saw Aaron with a spear, then throwing a rock, then squeezing a frog and believed God was suggesting she should stab, stone or strangle her children. She at first resisted, but she felt she had to do what she perceived to be God's will to prove her faith. She felt as if the Lord were saying, "If you keep rejecting, it's going to keep getting worse".

Laney had delusions in which she would read everyday events or objects as messages from God. When her baby had abnormal bowel movements, for example, she thought it was a message from God that she was not properly "digesting" God's word.Laney had at least one other psychotic experience several years earlier in which she had hallucinations of smelling sulfur she believed was God's way of alerting her the devil was near, he said. Laney's husband testified that he saw no change in his wife's mood before the attack and no clue that she was capable of killing the boys. "I don't understand it," said Keith Laney, who has stood by his wife in court. Keith Laney, 47, smiled at his wife when prosecutors asked what year they were married but briefly lost his composure at the sight of a poster-sized photograph of the three smiling boys, taken months before the killings.

The jury also saw a crime-scene video of 8-year-old Joshua and 6-year-old Luke, lying dead in a yard, near garden signs that read, "Mom's Love Grows Here" and "Thank God for Mothers." The boys were found in their underwear with heavy rocks on their chests. The video also showed a large spot of blood in a baby bed, where Deanna Laney severely injured the couple's youngest son, Aaron, 14 months old at the time. Laney lowered her head during the testimony and wept as graphic autopsy photos were shown to the jury of eight men and four women.

Dr. Park Dietz has worked on other high-profile cases, including those of child killers Andrea Yates and Susan Smith, serial killer Jeffrey Dahmer and "Unabomber" Ted Kaczynski. In Yates' case, the Houston mother contended that Satan ordered her to kill her five children to save them from eternal damnation. Dietz concluded that Yates must have known murder was wrong if Satan ordered her to do it. He also saw Yates' attempts to conceal her murder plans as a sign that she knew they were wrong.

In another recent case, a college student who confessed to shooting his parents and then breaking a chain saw trying to cut up their bodies said, "God told me to" in a interview with police. He was then charged with the deaths of his 47-year-old father and 46-year-old mother, who were killed after returning from a mission trip to Haiti.

Investigators found their dismembered bodies in a locked bedroom when they went to their home to check on them after they failed to show up for work. Handcuffed and shackled as he was escorted into the courtroom, the 22-year-old showed no emotion and at times looked at television cameras as several officers testified and the District Attorney played the recorded interview.

He said the killings were "spur of the moment" after his parents scolded him when they returned from a weeklong mission trip to Haiti, where they drilled wells. He told police he used a rifle to first shoot his father and then struggled with his mother and struck her with the gun before also shooting her in the head. He said he was using a chain saw to cut up the bodies before it broke and that he planned to burn the remains in a beer keg with a hole cut in it.

The Biblical narrative before us recounts an intriguing story. No, it doesn't end in the tragic slaughter of a child by his parent. However, Abraham was fully committed to that act of sacrifice, had it been required of him. Even more intriguing is that Abraham describes this sacrificial act to which he has committed as an act of worship. Fully intent upon placing his son on the altar and offering him as a sacrifice to God, he says, "I and the lad will go yonder and worship" (Genesis 22:5). Apart from spiritual enlightenment on this act of obedience, the only appropriate judgment would be to render this an act of insanity. And yet, this story recalls one of the noblest acts of worship and conveys to us deeper spiritual truths about what worship really is. Worship is fundamental to our being. It is not only part of, but also central to, the divine design.

If we don't experience what it means to worship God in a true and Biblical manner, then we will worship in some other way. That is why God spoke so strongly against idolatry. Worship of any other being other than Himself was the greatest sin in the Old Testament. God described that sin as spiritual fornication and harlotry. It brought a breach in God's relationship with His people time and again.

Once I embarked upon the journey to study the many faces of worship, I began to see evidence of the universal phenomena of worship everywhere I looked. Decades ago, I watched with interest and intrigue as hundreds of people boarded buses for a commune in Oregon. These street people hoped to find a new way of life in a religion headed up by a self-proclaimed Indian guru, who only a few months later fled the country proclaiming the death of his religion. It was impressive while it lasted. What a strange sensation to witness them throng the roadsides as the guru rode by in one of his dozens of Rolls-Royces.[29] It seemed rather ironic to this preacher, raised in

---

29   www.apologeticsindex.org/b40.html

an old-fashioned Pentecostal environment, to watch them with their hands raised in song and their bodies swaying. I thought to myself, "This is worship."

In Romans one, Paul describes man's rebellion against God. When mankind had an adequate enough knowledge of God through both creation and conscience to constitute him a worshipper of the true God, he willfully chose not to retain God in his knowledge. He inverted the order and worshipped the creature more than the Creator. He made idols of man, beasts, and creeping things that represented to him the gods of his own fabrication. He made God in his own image instead of accepting the fact that he, man, was made in God's image.

Man still wants to manufacture a God that he can control. Some of the doctrines that are popular in the church today flirt dangerously with this same kind of idolatry. A teaching that makes man a 'god' and empowers man to control and manipulate God is a false teaching. If I can command God, He ceases to be sovereign. And when God ceases to be sovereign, He ceases to be God.

Paul's description of the depravity of man at his worst indicates that one of the results of *inversion* of the divine order in worship was a *perversion* in sexual sin. Once man has inverted that divine order, it is a short step to inverting the divine order in the sexes. The result is homosexuality, men with men and women with women. This connection between perverse sin and wrong worship must not be overlooked.

In our enlightened age, it seems inconceivable that the kind of false worship that Paul describes could occur. Yet, in India, where animals are considered sacred, even rats are revered and worshipped. In India the "reverend rodents" outnumber India's 600 million people by nearly five to one. It seems like they are capitalizing on the

Hindu belief in the sanctity of animal life. While India fights famine in many of the impoverished states, rats have been quietly gnawing their way into granaries and emerging with full stomachs. According to the Indian Institute of Socioeconomic Studies, there are more than 2.5 billion rats in India. Scientists and statisticians believe the losses from rats in the country exceed $240 million a year. In India rats are considered holy since the Hindu mythology holds that they are the "divine mouths of prosperity." In the heart of the West Indian desert state of Rajasthan, an ancient temple, Deshnok, is dedicated to rats. Here many thousands of dollars worth of precious food grains annually go to feed the sacred species. Not only do the holy rats of Deshnok have a good deal, but the temple coffers continue to fill up too. Any pilgrim who happens to trample a rat to death accidentally must pay a fine. The fine is a golden statue of the dead rodent costing $450.00! For every one of India's 600 million people there are five rats. The country loses one and one quarter million tons of grain each year to the revered rodents.

This, too, is worship, to be sure, but how tragic it is! How great is the darkness! It hardly seems conceivable to those of us who have had our consciousnesses awakened to the reality of true worship. While we are sure this could never happen in "enlightened" America, yet there does exist in this country, worship efforts that are as meaningless to God, and as unfulfilling to the unenlightened worshipper.

A few years ago a New Mexico woman was frying tortillas when she noticed that the skillet burns on one of her tortillas resembled the face of Jesus. Excited, she went to her priest to have the tortilla blessed. The priest, not accustomed to blessing tortillas, was somewhat reluctant but agreed to do it.

The woman took the tortilla home, put it in a glass with piles of cotton to make it look like it was floating on clouds, built a special altar to it, and opened the little shrine to visitors. Within a few months, more than eight thousand people visited the "shrine of the face of Jesus of the tortilla," and all of them agreed that the face in the burn marks on the tortilla was the face of Jesus.[30]

It seems incredible that so many people would worship a tortilla, but such a distorted concept of worship is not really unusual in contemporary society. Tragically, although the Bible is clear about how, whom, and when we are to worship, much false worship still takes place today.

Man was created to worship God. Therefore worship is his most important priority. It is our supreme duty in time and will be our glorious occupation throughout eternity. This concept dominates the Bible. The Word of God is clear concerning the right and wrong way to worship, since some worship forms are totally unacceptable to God.

FORMS OF WORSHIP UNACCEPTABLE TO GOD

1. God will not tolerate the worship of any other gods. He makes this clear in such passages as Isaiah 48:11; Exodus 34:14; Romans 1:23. We must recognize that even an atheist worships. He worships himself, which is the ultimate form of idolatry. But God is a jealous God, and equally rejects the worship of material objects, mythical gods, supernatural beings, or anything other than **himself**, the **one true God**.

2. God also rejects worship directed to Him that is in the wrong form. This was discovered by the children of Israel when they built

---

30   www.roadsideamerica.com/attract/NMLAKtortilla.html

the golden calf, and said, "This is the god that brought us out of Egypt" (Exodus 32:4).

3. Nor will God receive worship that is done in a "self-styled manner" that does not recognize the requirements of His Word. This was illustrated by the offering of Cain, and again by Nadab and Abihu in Leviticus 10:1-2. Their offering was that of strange fire. God had required that **only** the fire from the brazen altar (that HE had ignited) be used to ignite the burnt offering. Nadab and Abihu brought their own fire to God. What a lesson there is here! Only worship that is kindled by the coals of Calvary, only worship that is precipitated by the fire of God can ignite incense of praise that will cause a sweet-smelling savor and fragrance in His nostrils!

4. One more form of worship that God finds totally unacceptable is the worship of the true God in the right way, but with the wrong attitude. The prophets are filled with God's call to correct His people from worship that is nothing more than outward conformity to ritual. Such passages as Malachi 1:7-10; Amos 5:21; Hosea 6:4-6; Isaiah 1:11-20 reiterate this message over and again.

From both the message of the prophets and the teaching of Jesus in the gospels, it is clear that God's primary concern for worshippers is their possession of a right attitude. God cannot stand hypocrisy in any form, and Jesus' most scathing words are directed at the pretence of the Pharisees, whose worship conformed to outward standards, but whose hearts were not right with God. Stephen Charnock wrote, "To pretend a homage to God, and intend only the advantage of self, is rather to mock him than to worship him. When we believe that we ought to be satisfied, rather than God glorified, we set God below ourselves, imagine that he should submit his honor to our advantage; we make ourselves more glorious than God."[31]

We don't worship God for what we can receive from Him. We worship Him because He is God! In the story of Cain and Abel, we learned about the three dimensions of worship. From Noah, we discovered the three tenses, or elements, of worship. From Abraham, we will learn the three attitudes of worship.

THE THREE ATTITUDES OF WORSHIP

1. Submission to God's Sovereignty

Abraham was no stranger to the sovereignty of God. It was God who took the initiative to become involved with the human family. It was God who called Abraham (when he was still Abram) out of Ur of the Chaldees. It was God who had sovereignly given him a promise. It was God who had sovereignly fulfilled this promise late in Abraham's life.

For Abraham, worship was not an isolated act of obedience. For him, worship pervaded the entirety of his life. His relationship with God made him cognizant that worship could not be relegated to just one place, time, or segment of life.

Worship is much larger than either our private devotional life or the corporate gathering of believers. It involves all of life. Abraham knew this. His entire lifestyle was one of obedience and surrender to the sovereignty of God.

There can be no true worship when we resist God's sovereignty. When we refuse to submit to God, we cannot worship Him. Here again, our theology is very important, for it impacts how we worship. I am not suggesting a subscription to hyper-Calvinistic fatalism when

---

31   Charnock, Stephen. *The Existence and Attributes of God*. Grand Rapids, MI: Baker Book House, 2000.

acknowledging God's sovereignty. But if we challenge His supreme authority, our worship is hollow and worthless.

God's sovereignty is challenged in various ways. One principal concept is an exaggerated view of the power of man's volition as a free moral agent. The Scriptures assuredly teach that "whosoever will may come," and that man is created with the capacity of choice. However, transcending the sovereignty of God by the projection of man's volition is a violation of scriptural principles.

If by my "faith," my "confession," my "prayers," or any other methodology, I can coerce God, then He is no longer sovereign. The prayers of Christ did not challenge the sovereignty of God, but rather acknowledged it. He prayed, "My Father, if it is possible, may this cup be taken from me. Yet, not as I will, but as You will" (Matthew 26:39).

When we lose the marvel of God's sovereignty our worship becomes manipulative and materially motivated. Worship requires a vision of God "high and lifted up". When we see His transcending sovereignty, we are at His feet, and He makes this place glorious when we discover the reality of this attitude of worship.

Abraham's pilgrimage of faith continuously submitted to God's sovereignty of purpose. In Genesis 13, when a quarrel arose between his herdsmen and those of his nephew Lot, Abraham submitted to God by submitting to Lot. In essence, Abraham said, "Lot can take the left, Lot can take the right, or Lot can take the lot!" Abraham knew who was really in control of his life. In chapter 15, when the Lord appeared to him and gave him the promise and covenant, Abraham believed God. He said, "O Sovereign LORD (Jehovah), how can I know that I will gain possession of it?" Abraham not only acknowledged God's sovereignty, but also submitted to it. Fourteen years later, when Abraham was 99 years old, God appeared to him and required him to be circumcised. God told him that his name was being changed from Abram (father) to Abraham (father of many nations). At 99 years of age, Abraham not only submitted to God's sovereign command to be circumcised, but he also changed his name. Imagine the mockery and scoffing this created among his associates.

The name Abram was ridiculous enough for a man who couldn't live up to it. After all, he had no children! But now, he had gone mad! He was changing his name to Abraham, "father of many nations"!

These experiences were vital to the development of Abraham's faith. This faith in God was not static. The Bible says that "he was strengthened in his faith" (Romans 4:20 NIV). And his faith grew, for all of these experiences were preliminary to and preparatory for the great testing of his faith, that of his ability to submit to the sovereignty of God. When God called upon Abraham to offer his son as a burnt offering, Abraham obeyed. He told the servants, "Stay here with the donkey while I and the boy go over there. We will worship and then we will come back to you" (Genesis 22:5 NIV).

We will WORSHIP! What does Abraham mean by this? For him, what constituted worship? Were they going to sing? dance? preach? pray? NO! Abraham had purposed in his heart to offer, in obedience, his only son Isaac, as an act of submission to the Lord's sovereignty. While some scholars have suggested that since child sacrifice was common among the Canaanites where Abraham had sojourned for many years, that he had adjusted to this mindset and was therefore pre-conditioned to the idea of killing his son. However, this flies in the face of the fact that Isaac represented the summation of his past, his present and his potential future posterity.

Isaac, precious Isaac! His name meant laughter. And he had brought laughter to their home. Such joy and fulfillment he and Sarah had come to know since Isaac had been born. But beyond those paternal joys, Isaac represented the embodiment of 100 years of living by faith. He was the incarnation of all of the promises that God had made to Abraham. He was the summation of his entire life. He was the supreme evidence that God kept His Word.

But Isaac was more than the essence of all that Abraham had lived for up until this time. He was also the embodiment of God's promises for the entire future. The redemption of humanity hung on the shoulders of this boy.

The integrity of God rested upon his survival. Without Isaac, Abraham's life was meaningless. Laughter, indeed! Without Isaac, his life was a joke. Who can estimate the pathos in the heart of Abraham at this juncture?

It was in Isaac that all of the nations of the earth were to be blessed. This was more than a personal matter, although it was cutting through the heart of a father in the deepest and most intimate of personal concerns. This had universal consequences. It is impossible for us to imagine the magnitude of this matter of Isaac's sacrifice.

God called Abraham to part with that which represented the totality of his life, the purpose for which he had lived, the sum and substance of all that he was, and yet he obeyed. This is the ultimate in worship. Submission to God! Obedience and surrender to His sovereignty!

And this ultimately is the essence of humility. Humility is demonstrated in worship by our absolute capitulation to the will of God. Our total acquiescence to His Word and His ways means death, both to self and to the pride that stands between us and God.

The greatest hindrance to worship is self. The greatest obstacle to true communion with God is our pride. Pride rears its ugly head when we insist on projecting our plans and programs upon God. Regardless of our so-called spirituality, we present only pride when we approach the presence of God and yet lack an attitude of surrender and submission to His sovereignty.

This problem of submission to God is a very real one in the church today. When we have problems submitting to God, we demonstrate it by our refusal to submit to one another. Stubbornness and rebellion are tantamount to witchcraft and idolatry according to God's definition. "For rebellion is as the sin of witchcraft, and stubbornness is as iniquity and idolatry" (I Samuel 15:23 KJV). We cannot serve God and ourselves simultaneously. God says, "Worship the Lord your God and serve Him only" (Matthew 4:10 NIV).

Worship and service go hand in hand. Whoever or whatever we worship will become our master. Conversely, the equation works also. Whoever or whatever we serve, we also worship. It becomes our god, whether we want to recognize it or not. Submission is the incarnation of humility and a primary attitude of Biblical worship. It is not just something we do in certain relationships, but rather, a disposition and a lifestyle. It is recognition that God is sovereign.

Submission and manipulation cannot compatibly co-exist. We can't submit to God's sovereignty and "play God" at the same time. That is a major problem with the extreme excess of the hyper-faith message. This attitude presumes to "play God," and strips Him of the prerogative of His sovereignty. It generates a worship that is hollow, mechanical and shallow.

2. Trust in God's Might

While Abraham's worship involved submitting to God's sovereignty, there is a "flip side" to this concept. Without trust, submission may be the mere external expression of intimidation or fear. True submission is birthed out of a heartfelt trust. It is so in human relationships, and it is certainly true in our relationship with God.

When we submit to God, we are capitulating control and management to Him. We are saying, "God knows better than I do. He is well able to handle this situation." We are affirming our trust in God's divine ability.

Abraham had cultivated a lifestyle of trust. His faith was an active response, stepping out and standing upon God's promises when there was no natural possibility of their fulfillment. He accepted God at His Word, obeyed that Word, and then he trusted.

This is the most difficult exercise of faith, resting our case in the hands of God when we have done all we know to do and yet nothing has happened. It is the calm confidence of knowing that He is in control.

However, we should pause for a moment and analyze the faith of Abraham. What was it that made his faith great? What was it that earned him the title, "Father of the Faithful?"

We hear a lot of talk about "faith" today. The possession of *great faith* is applauded. The need for *more faith* is often expressed. People of *strong faith* are placed on a pedestal and revered. But all of these phrases have in common one basic misconception. It is the object, the foundation of our faith that is most important.

For example, some people with "strong faith" in thin ice have gone to a chilling, watery grave. Others have had weak faith in "thick ice" and have been as secure as if they were walking on concrete. So the issue is not the intensity, but the foundation and grounds of the faith. Through the years people with faith in faulty systems have been deceived while being blissfully blind to their deception.

Abraham's faith was integrally related to his knowledge of God. He knew two things about his God in whom he trusted. "He believed in the God who gives life to the dead and calls things that are not as though they are" (Romans 4:17 NIV). When circumstances were hopeless he believed in hope, because he knew the power of God in whom he trusted.

His God was the God who specializes in breathing life into deadness and speaking the creative word that brings into existence things that previously were nonexistent. He had no natural basis for believing that in his old age he would become the father of many nations. Yet he believed, because God had promised!

Abraham's faith was ***conversant with the problems.*** He did not ignore the fact that his body was as good as dead. I realize there are some textual problems with Romans 4:19 in this respect, but as the NIV renders it, "Without weakening in his faith, he faced the fact that his body was as good as dead—since he was about a hundred years old-and that Sarah's womb was also dead." This kind of faith is not mind over matter, mental gymnastics, or the kind of positive confession that refuses to recognize the reality of the problem. Rather, this kind of faith faces up to the facts, investing its confidence in the supernatural God Who is not confined by the limitations of physical laws.

His faith was also ***consistent in its progress.*** Some people, when faced with delay or discouragement, waver in their faith; but not Abraham. Abraham's human tendency to waver, to vacillate between the despair of reality and the euphoria of God's promise was great! Yet his faith continued to grow and develop. He fed his faith by giving glory to God: "Yet he did not waver through unbelief regarding the promise of God, but was strengthened in his faith and gave God the glory" (Romans 4:20 NIV). He glorified God in the dryness, the emptiness of his wilderness, believing God when all evidence would indicate that nothing is going to happen: this is worship!

Abraham believed that God not only had the authority to promise, but the power to perform that Word: "Being fully persuaded that God had power to do what he had promised" (Romans 4:21 NIV).

According to Romans four, this is why God credited Abraham's faith to him as righteousness. Paul then makes the leap to New Testament theology by saying,

> The words, "it was credited to him" were written not for him alone, but also for us, to whom God will credit righteousness—for us who believe in Him who raised up Jesus our Lord from the dead. He was delivered over to death for our sins and was raised for our justification (Romans 4:23-25 NIV).

The significance of this New Testament passage must not be overlooked in connection with Abraham's trust in God. Abraham became the father of the faithful, and the father of all who believe in Christ. His faith was the first to be reckoned as righteousness, according to the divine record. He was justified by faith in God, just as we are. His faith became the prototype of all believers. God has never had any other plan of salvation other than that of faith, as Romans four asserts. Therefore, true worship is very much centered in an attitude of trust in God's provision, as well as faith in Christ and the finished work of His cross.

It would be inaccurate to impute infallibility to Abraham. While we recognize that his faith produced works (as James so aptly points out), yet it was not those works by which he was justified. The works were simply the justification, the validation of his faith, just as his circumcision demonstrated that he believed God. But Abraham's justification was based not upon his circumcision, his good works, his offering of Isaac, or anything else, other than his trust in God and His might. Abraham was not sinless. Abraham's faith did not make him faultless.

He tried to help God out. He took Sarah's handmaiden, Hagar, and through her fathered Ishmael. When you realize that Ishmael became the progenitor of most of the Arab world, you immediately recognize the problems that this impetuous act created. Ishmael was as surely his son as was Isaac, but he was not the son of promise in the same sense as was Isaac. And while God's promises to the progeny of Ishmael are rich, he does not enjoy the same place of blessing or destiny that God had purposed for Isaac. Ishmael represents the works of the flesh in worship, as Paul points out to us in Galatians 4:21-31. Much of the conflict in the Middle East today surrounds the respective claims of the descendants of Isaac and Ishmael, and their interpretation of God's intent for them and their offspring.

Trusting God is no guarantee of perfection. For example, Abraham lied about Sarah's identity. He did this twice, both in Egypt and also with Abimilech (Genesis 12:11-20 and Genesis 20:1-12). It is difficult to reconcile this kind of deception, carelessness and ambiguity with the kind of faith and trust that Abraham exemplified elsewhere. Could he not trust God for his life if he were to tell the truth concerning Sarah's identity? This enigma is an eternal reminder of the frailty, the finiteness, the fallibility of man, even a man of faith.

We are so prone to make heroes of the Old Testament saints that we are willing to blind our eyes to their faults. These shortcomings are not set before us so that we might follow the example of their failures, but for two reasons: The first is that we might learn from their mistakes, but the second is that when we fail, we might realize that we also are in good company! But when Abraham came to the ultimate test of his faith, he didn't fumble or fail. He trusted in the might of God, the divine ability of God to raise the dead, if necessary. In fact, the writer to the Hebrews suggests to us that Abraham received Isaac from the dead. "Abraham reasoned that God could raise the dead, and figuratively speaking, he did receive Isaac back from death" (Hebrews 11:19 NIV).

His unflinching faith when faced with the ultimate test demonstrates his trust in the might of God. This was the culmination of many years of walking with God by faith. Now he would see God perform a miracle of His power! There was not a question in His mind as to God's ability to fulfill His promise. Abraham obeyed. This is the essence of worship.

3. Rejoicing in God's Grace

Trust and submission are always adequately rewarded. They do not exist alone. Whenever there is submission to God's sovereignty and trust in His might, these will be rewarded by rejoicing in God's grace. Abraham's trust in the Almighty was vindicated when God "saw to it" on the mountain.

Abraham called the place, "Jehovah-jireh," which means, "The LORD will provide." This word "jireh" is an interesting word. It comes from the verb root "to see." It literally means that "God will see to it." But for God to "see to it" is to foresee, or to go beforehand, to provide in advance. So it is God's "pre-vision" that becomes God's "pro-vision"! In the mount of the Lord it will be seen! God will see to it! (Genesis 22:14).

Our Lord Jesus makes an interesting comment when He says, "Your father Abraham rejoiced at the thought of seeing my day; he saw it and was glad" (John 8:56 NIV). When did Abraham see the day of Jesus? It had to be no other place but here on Mount Moriah, as he was offering up his son. It was there that Calvary was prefigured. When Abraham said, "The LORD will provide himself a lamb," he was looking forward to Calvary.

We can only speculate as to the nature and manner of the revelation. Perhaps as he raised the knife in the air and looked up to heaven, then down at his son, God gave him a vision. Perhaps he realized that God was the FATHER, who would also send HIS SON into the world, and who would require His death as a substitute for the sins of the world. Perhaps as he saw the ram caught in the thicket, God showed him the cross and the Lamb of God who would come to take away the sins of the world. We do not know, but somehow, on that mountain, Abraham saw Christ!

He saw it! He saw the provision of God's grace! This is the grace of God! God's unmerited favor—His gift of love—His divine provision is portrayed for us on that mountain! And Abraham rejoiced! Of course he rejoiced that his son was spared and that a sacrifice was given as a substitute. But he also rejoiced in the promise of God. One day, that promise, Abraham's seed, would be born, and that fulfilled promise would be the great sacrifice for the sins of the world. His rejoicing was demonstrated in a sacrifice of worship.

This brings us again to the truth that our worship must be centered in the provision of Calvary's cross. We can revel only in God's grace. We can make our boast only in the Lord. There is no other basis for boasting than the work of our Savior on the cross.

Paul in Philippians identifies this as being characteristic of true worship: "For it is we who are the circumcision, we who worship by the Spirit of God, who glory in Christ Jesus, and who put no confidence in the flesh" (Philippians 3:3 NIV).

When we come to the Revelation, this is the worship scene that surrounds the throne of God. It is "Worthy is the Lamb, who was slain to receive power and wealth and wisdom and strength and honor and glory and praise!" (Revelation 5:12 NIV). Redemption is the theme of our worship, and the LAMB of God is the object of our adoration for all eternity.

May we learn from Abraham that true worship involves a life surrendered and submitted to the sovereignty of God, a lifestyle of trust in God's power and might, and the reality of rejoicing in the glorious provision of God's grace.

LOVE, ROMANCE AND AN ARRANGED MARRIAGE

Love is not weakness. It is strong. Only the sacrament of marriage can contain it.

—Boris Pasternak

Abraham… said to the chief servant in his household… "Go to my country and my own relatives and get a wife for my son Isaac…" Then the servant… made his way… then he prayed, "May it be that when I say to a girl, 'Please let down your jar that I may have a drink,' and she says, 'Drink, and I'll water your camels too'—let her be the one you have chosen for your servant Isaac. By this I will know that you have shown kindness to my master." Before he had finished praying, Rebekah came out with her jar on her shoulder… she went down to the spring, filled her jar and came up again. "Drink, my lord," she said, and quickly lowered the jar to her hands and gave him a drink. After she had given him a drink, she said, "I'll draw water for your camels too, until they have finished drinking." Then the man bowed down and worshiped the LORD, saying, "Praise be to the LORD, the God of my master Abraham, who has not abandoned his kindness and faithfulness to my master. As for me, the LORD has led me on the journey to the house of my master's relatives" (Genesis 24: 1-26 NIV).

Years ago, a young man in a church that I pastored wanted to make his proposal to his girlfriend very special. He hired a private plane and convinced his girlfriend to go up in the air with him for an aerial view of the city. Before long (the pilot having been previously instructed) they flew over the house where he lived. On the roof she read the message in giant letters, "I love you… please marry me." When her eyes caught the message, he produced the engagement ring. Theirs was a beautiful wedding.

I still get tears in my eyes when I read this story. And this beautiful thing called "romance" is repeated thousands of times over in the lives of multitudes of people all over the world. It is neither peculiar to any particular age, nor exclusive to any particular race.

Romance is a universal phenomenon that has been with the human family since the beginning of time. Early in the Bible, we are introduced to its reality and beauty. It is an eternal quality that should not just be part of courtship leading up to the marriage relationship. Romance is an important part of marriage. Romantic love is not an adequate basis for a marriage in and of itself, but it is a vital part to the ongoing success and fulfillment of a marriage relationship.

The idea of romance began in the heart of God. The divine design for marriage in the human family is based upon a pattern that was in God's mind for His Son before the foundations of the earth. "For he chose us in him before the creation of the world to be holy and blameless in his sight" (Ephesians 1:4).

This principle holds true in the whole scheme of contrast between the natural order and spiritual order. Jesus is the true vine, the original. The heavenly tabernacle is the true, the original. God introduces into the material realm that which is a copy or replica of the spiritual. We will discover this to be true in the romance of redemption.

There are many great romance stories in the Scriptures. From Ruth and Boaz to the Song of Solomon, the Bible does not attempt to make romance a cheap subject to be secretly discussed in hushed terms. The Scriptures present romance without apology as one of the great, wonderful aspects of the beauty of God's creative design.

We must however, guard against *romanticizing* the stories of the Bible. Often, in romanticizing the heroes of faith, we forget their peccadilloes. But God doesn't sugarcoat their lives. Their histories are held up honestly in all the horrid detail, regardless how heinous their sins. This is the power of the absolute integrity of the Scriptures. We must not assume that every family in the Scriptures enjoyed the ideal family life. In fact, from the very first human family we learn the opposite is precisely the truth. Were we to take the first few families in the Genesis account as models for today's family, we would be in deep trouble.

This was certainly true in Abraham's family. There was a perennial competition between Isaac and Ishmael which has been perpetuated in their respective progeny to this day. Isaac and Rebekah, in spite of the beauty of this story of their romance, had less than the ideal family. They each had a favorite son. They fostered favoritism and deceit with their own children. Their own communication deteriorated until the wife was willing to deceive her husband to secure the blessing for her favorite son. I point these things out, only to remind us of the imperfections and frailty of those whose lives we look to, lest we should idolize them and cherish an unrealistic image of their behavior and walk with God.

We last saw Isaac when he was offered upon the altar of sacrifice, and we saw Abraham receive him (figuratively) from the dead. His next appearance in Scripture occurs when he rides out to meet his bride, who is presented to him. It hardly seems necessary to comment on how closely this parallels the story of Redemption. We have our Lord Jesus Christ offered upon the cross of Calvary, and then rising from the dead. The next we see of our Lord is in the Revelation, where He appears with His bride, the Church!

In the intervening time, however, something happens. The narrative in Genesis 24:1-27 unfolds sequentially and symbolically what God has been doing since the resurrection of our Lord. The next act of God, following the resurrection, is to send the Holy Spirit, the faithful servant, into the world to select a bride for His Son. Our position in appropriating this passage of Scripture will be the classical allegorical approach that sees Abraham as representing God the Father, Isaac portraying Christ, the Son of God, the servant symbolizing the Holy Spirit, and Rebekah typifying the Church, the Bride of Christ.

In verse 26 of Genesis 24 (NIV) we read, "Then the man bowed down and worshipped the LORD, saying 'Praise be to the LORD, the God of my master Abraham, who has not abandoned his kindness and faithfulness to my master.'" This act of worship was rendered to God when it became apparent to the servant that his mission was successful. He had found not only the right family, but also the right woman, the bride for his master's son. This is truly one of the great moments in worship, and the theme that is represented here gives us another glimpse of this many-faceted jewel. From this powerful and moving narrative, we can learn several lessons about the romance of worship.

I. WORSHIP IS THE AFFIRMATION
OF A LOVE RELATIONSHIP

Have you ever wondered what you would do if you were raised in a culture in which marriages were arranged by the parents? Surprising as it may seem, *arranged* marriages in a culture where that is the norm are often more successful than those in the Western world. Although Western societies tend to deride arranged marriages as backward, uncivilized and primitive, there are some positive aspects. The Western focus on the physical aspect of relationships obsesses with love, sex, beauty, etc. As a result, people get married based on these factors and often become very quickly disenchanted with one another.

In contrast, Eastern cultures that practice arranged marriages place far more emphasis on pragmatic elements such as integrity, diligence, ambition, humility, generosity, etc. People get married based on practical reasons, and work on building affection later. Strong characteristics like the ones described above are very conducive to building love and affection in Eastern marriages. As a result, these marriages are much longer-lasting than many Western marriages. It's because the primary emphasis is not on love, sex, and physical beauty that arranged marriages are usually so successful, because the spouses get to know one another on a practical level first, looking beyond trivial issues such as beauty or lack thereof. In fact, though, the advantages and drawbacks of arranged marriages can't be so easily appraised. And, of course, it can go both ways: there are many arranged marriages that don't work, and there are marriages that started out based only on infatuation that grew stronger as time passed.

The marriage in Genesis 24 was an Eastern marriage, and it was an arranged marriage. Abraham was adamant that his son would not marry a Canaanite, so he sent his servant, Eliezer, to find a bride for his son from among Abraham's own people.

Here is a beautiful portrait of the Father sending the Holy Spirit into the world to take out a bride for Christ. This bride will also be God's people. For in selecting the bride of Christ, He forms the Church, His holy nation, His peculiar people, His chosen generation, and His royal priesthood.

There is little question that the New Testament presents the concept that we have been espoused to Christ. Paul, in Romans seven, tells us that we have "become dead to the law by the body of Christ; that ye should be married to another, even to him who is raised from the dead, that we should bring forth fruit unto God" (Romans 7:4 KJV).

Paul tells the Corinthian believers, "I am jealous for you with a godly jealousy. I promised you to one husband, to Christ, so that I might present you as a pure virgin to Him" (II Corinthians 11:2 NIV). The analogy is made even more emphatic in Ephesians 5:22-32. The entire passage compares the marriage relationship to that mystical union that exists between Christ and His Church.

In the Book of Revelation, the New Jerusalem appears as a bride adorned for her husband. One of the great themes of Revelation is the marriage of the Lamb. The bride can be no other than the Church of our Lord Jesus Christ.

It is imperative to understand, that in the Romance of Redemption, GOD took the initiative. It was God who sent His Son to pay the price of redemption for us. It was in obedience to His Father's will that the Son of God came into the world, ascended the mountain of Calvary (possibly the same mountain range upon which Isaac had been offered) and became the sacrificial Lamb to take away the sins of the world.

Worship does not begin with us. It begins with GOD. He moves towards us. This principle will appear over and again in the worship experiences recorded in the Old Testament Scriptures. It is portrayed for us in symbol and shadow in this story. Abraham took the first steps. He offered his son. He sent his servant to select the bride. Her response was the response to a love that existed and extended towards her before she knew her lover!

It is in love that the Father has sent the Spirit into the world to select a bride for His Son. The Spirit does not try to establish His own Person. He comes to reveal the Father and the Son. The servant in this story does not establish his own identity. He introduces his master and his master's son, but his own person is incidental. Jesus said the Spirit, when He comes, will not speak of Himself. He will glorify Christ! The Holy Spirit never seeks to establish His own identity, nor does He precipitate worship that is directed towards Himself. He empowers worship that is rendered to the Father through Christ!

The servant brought gifts to the bride, which she was privileged to enjoy before she met the bridegroom face to face. What a beautiful portrait of the Holy Spirit's ministry! We are given the gracious gifts of God, salvation, eternal life, forgiveness of sins, and the full complement of the Holy Spirit's gifts and graces, which reveal to us something of the heart of our bridegroom, although we have never seen His face!

An interesting sidelight is that Laban was attracted by the gifts, even though he was not the chosen bride. There will always be those who are drawn to the gifts and demonstrations of God, but whose hearts do not bring them to worship and surrender to His claims. The faithful servant looks for the characteristics that will benefit the master's son. There must be the proper grace and beauty, as well as submissiveness and willingness to serve. He had asked God for some confirmation to signify that he had found God's choice.

The first thing God looks for is that simple surrender to His Lordship. Unless we are willing to humble ourselves and become like little children, we will not be part of His bride. We must demonstrate the willingness to leave behind our world, our most prized possessions, country, family, surroundings and lifestyle to follow Him (Matthew 10:37-39).

There is an interesting passage in the Psalms that confirms this. "Hearken, O daughter, and consider, and incline thine ear; forget also thine own people, and thy father's house; so shall the king greatly desire thy beauty: for he is thy Lord; and worship thou him" (Psalm 45:10-11 KJV).

For Rebekah, all she knew about the bridegroom was what the servant had told her. And all we know about our bridegroom is that which the Holy Spirit has revealed to us through the Word of God. Peter phrases it so succinctly and so majestically, "Though you have not seen him, you love him; and even though you do not see him now, you believe in him and are filled with inexpressible and glorious joy" (I Peter 1:8 NIV).

For us, worship is the affirmation of a love relationship. In a very real sense, it is returning to God the love wherewith He loved us. The most marvelous aspect of worship is not expressing our love toward God, for worship begins with the realization that God has extended HIS love toward us! Paul affirms this in Romans 5:8, "But God demonstrates His own love toward us, in that while we were still sinners, Christ died for us." John reiterates this, "We love him, because he first loved us" (1 John 4:19).

Dr. Karl Barth, the great Swiss theologian was interviewed by journalists when he came to America. They asked him about the most profound thing he had ever discovered in his study of the Bible. He responded, "Jesus loves me this I know, for the Bible tells me so." Astounded, the journalists responded, "You mean to say that the most profound thing you have discovered is that Jesus loves you?" The man of God replied, "Yes, but not only that Jesus loves me; Jesus loves me, THIS I KNOW." The journalists then queried, "Oh, you mean, that you can know that Jesus loves you?" Again he responded, "Yes, but not only that I can know that Jesus loves me, but the BIBLE tells me so!"

This, indeed, is the most profound revelation and realization that any person can come to. And worship begins when we are aware of God's love. The overwhelming magnitude of this realization births worship in our hearts. We are reduced before Him to unfathomable gratitude and adoration. It is here that worship begins, as the affirmation of a love relationship.

Our pilgrimage as worshippers may begin with an approach to God that sings, "Oh how I love Jesus,"[32] but as our worship matures, the song will become, "Oh how He loves you and me."[33] In the beginning of our walk with God, we are filled with enthusiasm to tell God how much we love Him.

But as we grow in Him, and in worship, we discover the greater truth that He loves us! John the beloved disciple, put it best: "Herein is love, not that we loved God, but that he loved us, and sent his Son to be the propitiation for our sins" (I John 4:10 KJV). This is worship! For this we were born!

When my interest was first ignited to purse the study of worship, I had the privilege of being exposed to the ministry of John Wimber. Since I was in the Pasadena, California area in a summer school

---

32   Whitfield, Frederick. *Oh How I Love Jesus*. London: Primitive Methodist Publishing House, 1889.
33   Kaiser, Kurt. *Oh, How He Loves You and Me*. Tarzana, CA: Fred Bock Publications, 1979.

session completing studies for my Ph.D., I drove to the Anaheim Hills Vineyard in Yorba Linda to hear Wimber. As I sat in the high school auditorium and witnessed the worship, it was an unforgettable experience—and one that differed dramatically from what I was accustomed to in my classical Pentecostal tradition. In an article entitled *Worship: Intimacy with God*, John Wimber, who with his wife Carol are founding leaders of the Vineyard Christian Fellowships around the world, including Vineyard Christian Fellowships in Australia, stated

Probably the most significant lesson that the early Vineyard Fellowship learned was that "worship is the act of freely giving love to God." Based on this principle, Vineyard developed a well-thought-out worship philosophy that closely follows the stages of romance. Those five phases are invitation, engagement, exaltation, adoration and intimacy. As we experience these phases of worship we experience intimacy with God, the highest and most fulfilling calling men and women may know.[34]

2. WORSHIP IS THE ANTICIPATION OF A LOVER'S REUNION

Rebekah's heart was filled with anticipation as she looked forward to meeting her bridegroom. All she knew about him was what the servant had revealed, but it was enough to cause her to fall in love. Once she had made her decision to go, she readied herself, and her journey seemed as nothing. How long the journey took, we are not sure. It was many days journey across a wilderness that was inhabited by warring tribes. This journey was first made by the faithful servant

---

34   https://renewaljournal.blog/2011/05/19/worship-intimacy-with-god-by-john-carol-wimber/

in finding the bride, and then by the bride who accompanied the servant back to Isaac.

We have here a twofold picture of the Spirit of God and the Bride of Christ. For two thousand years, the Holy Spirit has been walking through the wilderness of this world, touching the hearts of those who would trust the Savior. His faithful ministry for these two thousand years has been continuous and untiring.

Also, for those same two thousand years, the Church in every generation has been on a journey through the wilderness of this world. The Bride of Christ lives with the awareness that this world is not our home. The spirit of pilgrimage belongs to the people of God. Although Abraham knew the land God had promised was his, he never really settled there. "By faith he made his home in the Promised Land like a stranger in a foreign country; he lived in tents, as did Isaac and Jacob, who were heirs with him of the same promise. For he was looking forward to the city with foundations, whose architect and builder is God" (Hebrews 11:9-10 NIV). Abraham knew that material blessings were only the partial fulfillment of God's promises, for the primary focus of these promises is spiritual.

This same spirit of pilgrimage portrays the posture of the worshipper in love with Christ. This world is not our home, we are just passing through. As Paul says to the Colossians,

> Since, then, you have been raised with Christ, set your hearts on things above, where Christ is seated at the right hand of God. Set your minds on things above, not on earthly things; for you died, and your life is now hidden with Christ in God. When Christ, who is your life, appears, then you also will appear with him in glory (Colossians 3:1-4 NIV).

Paul again addressed this subject to the Philippian church by stating,

But our citizenship is in heaven. And we eagerly await a Savior from there, the Lord Jesus Christ, who by the power that enables him to bring everything under his control, will transform our lowly bodies so that they will be like his glorious body (Philippians 3:20 NIV).

In the same vein of thought, Peter implored,

Dear friends, I urge you, as aliens and strangers in the world, to abstain from sinful desires which war against your soul. Live such good lives among the pagans that, though they accuse you of doing wrong, they may see your good deeds and glorify God on the day he visits us (I Peter 2:11-12 NIV).

This spirit of pilgrimage is part and parcel of the New Testament faith. Jesus pronounces a benediction upon those servants whom the Lord shall find watching when He comes. There is a special crown promised to all those who love his appearing.

We have talked in an earlier chapter about the need for operating in a healthy tension between the "kingdom now" and the "kingdom then" extremes. This is vitally important to our worship. If our theology does not require and look for the return of the Savior, then our worship will be less than it should be.

That doesn't mean that we ought to capitulate to the "rescue rapture" thinking that projects God's entire blessing only in a post-rapture/translation setting. God doesn't want us to live today in a vacuum that is void of the dynamic of His power and presence. The early church knew the power of God. They knew what it was for God to meet with them. So should we! God has never changed.

But the early church also lived in anticipation of our Lord's return. Even though they were inaccurate concerning the timing of the Lord's return, our Lord structured the entire eschatological question in such a way that His people in every age could believe in and expect His imminent return.

The possibility of the imminent return of Christ is a necessary part of worship. Not in a legalistic sense, but in that our hearts stretch toward the day when we will see Him as He is, and be like Him as we behold Him! As David said, "As for me, I will behold thy face in righteousness: I shall be satisfied when I awake, with thy likeness" (Psalm 17:15 KJV).

I remember an old country song I used to hear on the radio when I was a teenager. It went something like this: "Delta Dawn, what's that flower you have on? Could it be a faded rose from days gone by? And did I hear you say that he's meeting you here today, to take you to his mansion in the sky?"[35]

It is a sad song. It is the story of a jilted, jaded lover who was left waiting at the altar. The groom never showed up. And she never recovered from it. For years she kept the wedding dress on, and waited with the wilted flowers and with the blush and bloom long since gone from her cheeks. She was the laughingstock of the town.

I sometimes wonder if this isn't a picture of the way the Church sometimes appears, as if our Lover Lord would not return. We have heard the jeering of the world hurled at us as Peter predicted they would, "Where is this 'coming' he promised? Ever since our fathers died, everything goes on as it has since the beginning of creation. But they deliberately forget that long ago by God's word the heavens existed and the earth was formed... But do not forget this one thing,

---

35   *Delta Dawn* was first recorded by Tanya Tucker in 1972, then popularized by Helen Reddy in 1973. It was written by Alex Harvey and Larry Collins.

dear friends: With the Lord a day is like a thousand years, and a thousand years are like a day. The Lord is not slow in keeping a promise, as some understand slowness. He is patient with you, not wanting anyone to perish, but everyone to come to repentance" (II Peter 3:4-9 NIV).

But what assurance do we really have that Christ will return physically to this earth? We have the overwhelming evidence of fulfilled prophecy around us, especially in our generation. But even more important, we have the Holy Spirit's seal. That seal is God's guarantee of the redemption of the purchased possession. It is more than earnest money that He has deposited.

The word "earnest" in the Ephesians 1:14 passage also means "engagement ring." The presence of the Holy Spirit in the Church is our Bridegroom's "diamond" on the finger of His espoused, His pledge of betrothal, and His guarantee that He will return to receive His bride unto Himself.

3. WORSHIP IS THE ADORATION OF A LOVING REDEEMER

Worship reaches its crescendo in the grand finale of the Book of Revelation. It is there we find the culmination of the entire history of man's redemption. The Lamb of God is enthroned and surrounded by both the Church and all the hosts of heaven. The worship and praise that is rendered unto the LAMB can be described only as adoration.

In chapter four of Revelation it is the Father that is worshipped. The theme of the heavenly anthem of praise is His creative power.

The twenty-four elders fall down before him who sits on the throne, and worship him who lives for ever and ever. They lay their crowns before the throne and say, "You are worthy, our Lord and

God, to receive glory and honor and power, for you created all things, and by your will they were created and have their being" (Revelation 4:10-11 NIV).

The fifth chapter presents a different scene. The Lion/Lamb has appeared to take the book of redemption from the hand of Him who sits upon the throne, loose its seals, and institute the redemption of the earth in restoration to redeemed humanity. This precipitates a slightly different anthem of praise.

> And they sang a new song: "You are worthy to take the scroll and to open its seals, because you were slain, and with your blood you purchased men for God from every tribe and language and people and nation. You have made them to be a kingdom and priests to serve our God, and they will reign on the earth.... Worthy is the Lamb, who was slain to receive power and wealth and wisdom and strength and honor and glory and praise!" (Revelation 5:9-12 NIV).

This is the nature of the unending anthem of adoration that fills heaven's courts as an incense of sweet fragrance for all eternity. John establishes that same theme in chapter one, "To him who loves us and has freed us from our sins by his blood, and has made us to be a kingdom and priests to serve his God and Father—to him be glory and power for ever and ever! Amen" (Revelation 1:6 NIV). The anthem of adoration and praise is the response of the redeemed to the love of God in Christ. This love began with God, as has been pointed out earlier in this chapter. Our worship is a response to that love.

There is another feature to this aspect of adoration that we must not ignore. As the Bride of Christ, His Church is precious and beautiful to Him, and He finds her desirable. He is in love with His bride, and she is arrayed in royal righteousness. "Hallelujah! For our Lord God Almighty reigns. Let us rejoice and be glad and give him glory! For the wedding of the Lamb has come, and his bride has made herself ready. Fine linen, bright and clean, was given her to wear" (Revelation 19:6-8 NIV).

The desirability of the bride to the bridegroom is portrayed prophetically in the Psalms, "So shall the king greatly desire thy beauty: for he is thy Lord; and worship thou him" (Psalm 45:11 KJV). Our Lord Jesus is in love with His bride. He has pledged "to present her to himself as a radiant church, without stain or wrinkle or any other blemish, but holy and blameless" (Eph. 5:27 NIV).

Some people are of the opinion that the present condition of the church doesn't measure up to this, therefore Christ cannot return. But this rather legalistic perspective overlooks the fact that our righteousness is imputed and imparted, it is not our own. Christ is in love with us! He sees us in His perfect provision.

Although the metaphor breaks down in some areas, yet the comparison conveys a truth. When two people fall in love, they are blind to the faults of each other. Call it "rose-colored glasses" or the "love is blind" syndrome, but that mystical phenomenon that we call "in love" has that magical effect. Now I am not suggesting that Christ is so much in love with us that He can't see our shortcomings. However, in a very real sense, it is because of His love, that He already sees us "in love" and "accepted in the Beloved." He has provided the cloak of His blood and righteousness that covers us and, in effect, eliminates our spots and blemishes in His sight.

It is only the awareness of His love that enables us to return that adoration in worship. For this reason, Paul's prayer for the Ephesian saints is vitally important.

And I pray that you, being rooted and established in love, may have power, together with all saints, to grasp how wide and long and high and deep is the love of Christ, and to know this love that surpasses knowledge—that you may be filled to the measure of all the fullness of God (Eph. 3:17-19 NIV).

Paul equates the fullness of God in our lives with the realization of the love of God. Each of these phrases contributes to the goal of being filled with God's fullness. Firstly, the foundation of our spiritual lives is to be "rooted and grounded" in love. Using mixed metaphors, Paul uses both the language of nature (rooted) and that of construction (founded, established). He does this to emphasize the importance of the awareness of God's love. This cognizance is foundational to our faith. It is important to be established in doctrine, but more important to be established in God's love. Similarly, the writer to the Hebrews instructs us to have our hearts established in grace rather than meats (do's and don'ts). "For it is a good thing that the heart be established with grace; not with meats" (Hebrews 13:9 KJV).

After being established in this love, we are then able to explore its expanse. Paul attributes four dimensions to God's love, demonstrating that it is bigger than life, and cannot be grasped in mere material terms or mental mechanism. We live in a three-dimensional world. But God's love transcends that. Various attempts have been made to describe the four dimensions of God's love. One of my favorites is a breakdown of John 3:16: "For God so loved the world (the width) that He gave His only begotten Son (the length) that whosoever (the depth) believeth on Him should not perish, but have everlasting life (the height)."

This astonishing projection of this passage is that even after being established in God's love and knowing its four dimensions, there is yet more. Paul prays further "to know this love that surpasses knowledge…" Paul is praying for the child of God to discover that which defies mere mental awareness.

Experientially, one can know that which is unknowable in the natural realm. This, after all, is the paradox of our faith. We see the invisible, touch the intangible, hear the inaudible, and know the unknowable. This is the essence, then, of being filled with all the fullness of God. Worship flows from the experiential awareness of God's love for us. It is the response to and returning of that love to God. It is beautifully illustrated for us in the following New Testament passages.

Luke 7:36-49 records the story of a Pharisee who invited Jesus to his house for dinner. While the Lord was reclining at the table, a woman, whose sinful reputation in that town had made her notorious, came into the house. She brought an alabaster jar of expensive perfume, stood behind Him at His feet weeping, and washed His feet with her tears. Then she wiped His feet with her hair, kissed them, and poured perfume upon them.

At this the Pharisee reasoned to himself, "If this man were a prophet, he would have known who is touching him and what kind of a woman she is." Jesus, discerning his thoughts, said, "Simon, I have something to tell you." When the Pharisee replied, "Tell me, teacher," Jesus shared a simple story with him. It concerned two men who owed money to a moneylender. One owed ten times what the other owed. The moneylender cancelled the debt of both, so that neither had to pay back the loan. Jesus then asked Simon, "Which of them will love more?' Simon replied, "I suppose the one who had the bigger debt cancelled." Jesus told him he had judged correctly. The Lord then turned toward the woman and said to Simon,

> Do you see this woman? I came into your house. You did
> not give me any water for my feet, but she wet my feet with her

tears and wiped them with her hair. You did not give me a kiss, but this woman, from the time I entered, has not stopped kissing my feet. You did not put oil on my head, but she has poured perfume on my feet. Therefore, I tell you, her many sins have been forgiven—for she loved much. But he who has been forgiven little loves little." Then Jesus said to her, "Your sins are forgiven" (Luke 7:44-48 NIV).

This is a story about worship, containing priceless lessons about what worship really is to the believer who knows that he is a forgiven sinner. First, we need to look at Simon, the "saint." Obviously, he asked Jesus to his house from some ulterior motivation. He did not extend to Jesus any of the common courtesies of the day or culture that would be normally given to any ordinary houseguest. In their culture, any guest received into the home was offered water to wash his feet after walking in the hot climate along dirt roads. It was common to offer a cleansing, refreshing oil to wash and anoint the head, and to cool the brow. The normal greeting was a kiss of welcome. But Simon extended none of these courtesies to Christ. Whatever his motivation, it was not worship. It was not love for the Savior that prompted his invitation. Perhaps there was political pressure that he needed to accommodate. Perhaps he wanted to look good, so that he wouldn't appear to be a biased bigot in his rejection of Christ's claims.

Perhaps he needed to be able to boast, "Well, I even had Him in my home to eat, and look at the way He talks about us Pharisees." We know for sure that there was no demonstration of love for Christ; hence, there was nothing that even remotely resembled worship. Whatever his motivation, there is ample evidence that he considered himself better than Christ, and Christ unworthy of his hospitality.

The second person we look at is the woman. Perhaps she was a prostitute. In all probability, this was her occupation. She knew she was a sinner. Under normal circumstances, she would never have dared to enter this house. In fact, under any other set of circumstances, she would not have been given entrance, nor would she have found any welcome there. But somehow, the fact that Jesus was there gave her the courage to cross the threshold into this Pharisee's home.

It is quite possible the jar of perfume that she brought represented her entire life's savings. At any rate, it was very costly. It was doubtless the most valuable thing that she had. She did not presume to anoint the head of Christ, for she saw herself unworthy of that privilege. She did not presume to kiss His cheek or His hands, but knelt instead at His feet. In His presence she wept at the awareness of her sin in the light of His holiness. She washed His feet with her tears and dried them with her hair. Then she broke open the jar of perfume and anointed the blessed feet of the Savior.

In so doing, this woman captured the essence of worship. Worship begins in the awareness of God's transcending holiness and undying love. She could sense Christ's love and acceptance of her, even before she heard His words of forgiveness. There was something about the bearing and demeanor of Christ that invited sinners to come to Him. A Pharisee once criticized Christ, not realizing that he was complimenting Him when he said, "This man welcomes sinners and eats with them" (Luke 15:2 NIV).

Jesus did not make sinners feel uncomfortable. The only ones who were uncomfortable in His presence were those who were masquerading behind a cloak of self-righteousness. They knew He could see through their masks. They were terribly uncomfortable in His presence, but sinners came to Him and sensed the warmth of His love and welcome.

Worship is not the legalistic observance of the laws of God. Worship flows from forgiveness, and the awareness of God's love.

Jesus said, "For she loved much. But he who has been forgiven little loves little" (Luke 7:47 NIV). Our Lord received the extravagant demonstration of worship that this woman brought to Him. Adoration that flows from humility of heart and freedom of forgiveness is always acceptable worship to Christ.

It is interesting that one of the most common words used in the Bible for worship is the Greek word "proskuneo" which means "to kiss" or "to prostrate oneself before." It also means "adoration." The intimate expression of love and adoration informs our worship. Even extravagance is appropriate when it flows from a heart of humility and love.

The second story is recorded in the gospel of John. There at the home of His friends, Mary, Martha, and Lazarus (whom He had raised from the dead), our Lord was enjoying a dinner that was given in His honor. While Martha was serving, Lazarus was among those reclining at the table. Mary took a pint of pure nard, an expensive perfume, poured it on Jesus' feet and wiped His feet with her hair. The house was filled with the fragrance of the perfume. One of the disciples, Judas, saw this and objected. "Why wasn't this perfume sold and the money given to the poor? It was worth a year's wages." John adds that Judas' comments were not given because he cared for the poor, but because he was a thief and used to help himself to the money that was put in the bag. Jesus said, "Leave her alone. It was meant that she should save this perfume for the day of my burial. You will always have the poor among you, but you will not always have me" (John 12:1-8 NIV). This is a very interesting passage, and provides us with many insights concerning the value of worship to our Lord Jesus Christ.

Mary had already learned this posture of worship at the feet of Christ. On an earlier occasion, she sat at His feet and listened to every word He had to say while Martha served. When Lazarus had died, we find Mary weeping at the feet of Jesus. The feet of Jesus are a glorious place to be! Mary had already learned this early in her relationship with her Lord.

When I was in Copenhagen years ago, I was taken into a large historic cathedral where there is a unique and beautiful statue of Christ. One of the interesting features of that work of art is that in order to see the eyes of Christ, you have to kneel at His feet. This sculptor knew something about worship.

Another important truth to be gleaned from this story is that worship is sometimes costly. That is not to commercialize or materialize worship. The value is not in monetary currency. But David put it well when he said that he would not offer to the Lord that which cost him nothing. The worship that will fill the house of God with a sweet fragrance is that worship which has behind it a life that is sold out and surrendered to God. That is what I mean by worship being costly. When we have given our lives to God in abject surrender, there is a beautiful aroma that fills the nostrils of God.

This kind of worship is often accompanied by brokenness. In order for the fragrance of the perfume to escape, the box had to be broken. It is often through the brokenness in our lives that our worship becomes fragrant to God.

There will always be those standing by who, like Judas, feel that such extravagance in worship is altogether unnecessary, and that the energies invested there would be better spent in feeding the poor. We must not disparage the value of feeding the poor as an acceptable act of worship to God. We have already discovered that dimension in chapter two. But the pouring out of our beings in adoration to Christ must always take precedence over any other priorities that we have set in our lives. This "pouring out" is of absolute essence.

Those who criticize such worship fail to understand it because their motivation in following Christ is not to love Him. Many are like Judas, following Christ saying, "What can I get out of it?" That is never the posture of the true worshipper. The worshipper is concerned about what GOD will get out of it! What can I do with my life that will release the fragrance of His love in the world, the incense of His praise and glory in His Church?

We are His bride. We love Him because He first loved us. When we knew Him not, He sought us, bought and brought us to His side. We will never cease to be the Bride of Christ eternally. We eagerly await the day when He will return to present us in all the glory of His righteousness to reign forever at His side. Eternally, the occupation of the Bride of Christ will be to reflect His glory. "In the coming ages he might show the incomparable riches of his grace, expressed in his kindness to us in Christ Jesus" (Eph. 2:7 NIV). As Paul so beautifully said, "Unto him be glory in the church and in Christ Jesus throughout all generations, for ever and ever! Amen" (Eph. 3:21 NIV).

WORSHIP—A TOTALLY AWESOME ENCOUNTER!

When Moses was alive, these pyramids were a thousand years old. Here began the history of architecture. Here people learned to measure time by a calendar, to plot the stars by astronomy and chart the earth by geometry. And here they developed that most awesome of all ideas - the idea of eternity.

—Walter Cronkite

Jacob… stopped for the night because the sun had set. Taking one of the stones there, he put it under his head and lay down to sleep. He had a dream in which he saw a stairway resting on the earth, with its top reaching to heaven, and the angels of God were ascending and descending on it. There above it stood the LORD, and he said: "I am the LORD, the God of your father Abraham and the God of Isaac… I am with you and will watch over you wherever you go, and I will bring you back to this land. I will not leave you until I have done what I have promised you." When Jacob awoke from his sleep, he thought, "Surely the LORD is in this place, and I was not aware of it." He was afraid and said, "How awesome is this place! This is none other than the house of God; this is the gate of heaven." Early the next morning Jacob took the stone he had placed under his head and set it up as a pillar and poured oil on top of it. He called that place Bethel (Genesis 28:10-19 NIV).

The word "awesome" has become so hackneyed, cliché and overworked, that I am hesitant to use it. When Walter Cronkite in the above quote said, "And here they developed that most awesome of all ideas—the idea of eternity,"[36] he came closer than most to capturing its meaning. When Arthur Conan Doyle stated, "There was something awesome in the thought of the solitary mortal standing by the open window and summoning in from the gloom outside the spirits of the nether world,"[37] he too used the word with approximate appropriateness.

The dictionary defines awesome as *inspiring awe* as in *an awesome thunderstorm,* or as *expressing awe* as in *stood in awesome silence before the ancient ruins.* The thesaurus offers these words as substitutes: *amazing, alarming, astonishing, awe-inspiring, awful, beautiful, breathtaking, daunting, dreadful, exalted, fearful, fearsome, formidable, frantic, frightening, grand, horrible, horrifying, imposing, impressive, intimidating, magnificent, majestic, mind-blowing, moving, overwhelming, shocking, striking, stunning, stupefying, terrible, terrifying, wonderful, and wondrous.*

The Hebrew word used here was *yare.* Most commonly it was used to mean: to fear, revere, to be afraid, to stand in awe of, be awed, to reverence, honor, respect, to be dreadful, to cause astonishment and awe, be held in awe, to inspire reverence or godly fear or awe, to make afraid, or to terrify.

---

36   http://en.thinkexist.com/quotes/with/keyword/awesome/
37   http://en.thinkexist.com/quotes/with/keyword/awesome/2.html

Many hundreds of years ago when tyrants ruled over China, a summons to appear in the emperor's court in Peking's Forbidden City made even strong men tremble. Any visitor was expected to perform the required complicated kneeling and prostrations faultlessly as he came into the presence of the tyrant. The slightest violation could bring a sentence of instant death. To gaze at the emperor was forbidden. To speak out hastily was fatal. It meant absolute and instantaneous death. Upon receiving a summons to appear before the emperor, Chinese officials frequently would say their last farewells to their friends and their families, so slim were their chances of surviving the royal audience.[38]

And yet, when we worship our Lord and Savior, we are summoned into the presence of the King of kings. How awesome! We are assured in Scripture that the God whom we are invited to approach in worship is "God, the blessed and only ruler, the King of Kings and Lord of Lords, who alone is immortal, and who lives in unapproachable light, whom no one has seen or can see. To him be honor and might forever. Amen" (I Timothy 6:15-16 NIV).

Dr. V.R. Edman, then chancellor of Wheaton College, was addressing chapel in 1967 on the subject of worship. He illustrated his message by describing how he had followed the proper protocol many years before when he had been granted an audience with the King of Ethiopia. He compared the worship service in chapel to a meeting between the King of Kings and each individual student. While offering to the students in chapel various ways they could make their worship encounter more meaningful, Dr. Edman's speech suddenly stopped as he slumped to the floor, suffering a fatal heart

---

38   Menzies, Gavin. *1421: The Year China Discovered America.* New York, NY: William Morrow and Company, 2003.

attack. He had been summoned into the presence of the King of Kings.[39]

I wonder if we really comprehend what it means to be in the presence of God. I greatly cherish my own Pentecostal extraction and roots. But often as I have pondered this question, I have reflected upon the casualness that we have cultivated in our tradition in an effort to encourage the "freedom of the Spirit."

Signs posted on the front lawns of two different churches in one neighborhood announced, "Casual worship." While the intention is to attract people by letting them know they can be comfortable, the sign's message poses a perturbing question. Can any meeting between mankind and the creator of the universe be casual? The Lord of Heaven invites us to offer praise and worship and be transformed by His redemptive grace. Can one be casual about this without falling into a reduced view of God? And when worship succumbs to scratching the consumer' itch—so they get what they want—doesn't it risk placing human wishes and comfort at the center of worship—where God belongs?

In attempting to appeal to a cross-section of the community, one church posted a sign that read, "We are traditional at 8 a.m. We are contemporary at 9 a.m. We are blended at 11 a.m." Another ran an advertisement in the newspaper: "We are charismatic in our worship, Baptist in our preaching, and Episcopal at the table."

In today's technologically sophisticated society many church leaders have felt constrained to try to offer up a more contemporary Sunday fare, and have succumbed to the seduction of creating a form of Christian entertainment. Partly as a result of the Church Growth Movement, and to appeal to the media-maddened masses, many

---

39   Cairns Earle E., and Graham, Billy. *V. Raymond Edman: In the Presence of the King*. Chicago, IL : Moody Press, 1972.

churches have developed a market-driven obsession with meeting the felt needs of religious consumers.

In many such instances, it seems that the gospel has been diluted to a religious commodity marketed to semi-spiritual-seekers on some vaguely spiritual quest. Welcome to prime-time worship! It's snappy, it has a beat, and you can dance to it. Samuele Bacchiocchi, Professor of Theology at Andrews University states in an article entitled, *Worship Wars,* in Endtime Issues No. 48, 23 June 2000, "The outcome is that the church becomes a place where people can experience physical stimulation and worship becomes an exercise to experience personal gratification rather than divine glorification." In an essay distributed by the Alliance of Confessing Evangelicals, and published on the website, *Get Religion,* church musician Leonard Payton states, "In the most extreme cases, some worship services are merely sanitized rock concerts, i.e., no foul language and no cloud of marijuana smoke up at the ceiling."[40]

"The whole world of mainstream evangelicalism is turning into an FM radio dial packed with consumer niches"[41] according to Terry Mattingly. Mattingly, in an article entitled, *Worship for Sale, Worship for Sale,* and posted on his internet column, *On Religion,* quotes pollster George Barna who talked with Protestant pastors, worship leaders and other church professionals and discovered that 90 percent of the conflicts reporting in their congregations were rooted in worship music.

What we know about Americans is that we view ourselves first and foremost as consumers," said Barna. "Even when we walk in the doors of our churches what we tend to do is to wonder how can I get a good transaction out of this experience. So, what

---

40   http://www.getreligion.org/?p=171

41   http://www.getreligion.org/?p=172

we know from our research is that Americans have made worship something that primarily that we do for ourselves. Worship is successful when we feel good.[42]

Some critics of the most contemporary form of church music have referred to it as a new erotic-worship genre. Writing in Touchstone magazine, senior editor S.M. Hutchens sees all sorts of dangers in contemporary church services that emphasize performers and ego-centric lyrics. Hutchens begins his essay, "Please Me, O Lord," by describing what he witnessed during his return to an evangelical congregation:

> On a recent visit to a fairly typical Evangelical church, we were treated to one of its regular features. A handsome young woman, attractively dressed, stood before the congregation with an eight-inch microphone, the head of which she held gently to her lips while she writhed and cooed a song in which she, with closed eyes and beckoning gestures, begged Jesus, as she worked her way toward its climax, to come fill her emptiness. The crowd liked it.[43]

The joy of the Lord is of prime value in our worship, but sometimes our joviality can produce a jocularity, levity and lightness that is not conducive to the awesome seriousness of the worship encounter. Is it possible that God is offended and the Holy Spirit grieved by our less than serious approach to an encounter with God? Isaiah tells us the story of his rather awesome worship encounter:

> In the year that King Uzziah died, I saw the Lord seated on a throne, high and exalted, and the train of his robe filled the temple. Above him were seraphs, each with six wings: With two wings they covered their faces, with two they covered their feet, and with two

---

42   http://www.tmatt.net/columns/2002/11/worship-for-sale-worship-for-sale
43   http://www.touchstonemag.com/archives/article.php?id=17-04-013-v

they were flying. And they were calling to one another: "Holy, holy, holy is the LORD Almighty; the whole earth is full of his glory." At the sound of their voices the doorposts and thresholds shook and the temple was filled with smoke (Isaiah 6:1-4 NIV).

A totally awesome experience indeed! Even those angels that have never sinned cover their faces and feet in His presence! He is the thrice-holy One. It is that attribute of God that we must not negate in our emphasis upon His love and grace. To be summoned into His presence to worship before His throne is an awesome privilege.

In *Worship: The Missing Jewel of the Evangelical Church*, Dr. A.W. Tozer said, "Far too many believers hold a superficial view of God, resulting in emasculated worship through failure to ascribe to Him His proper magnificence."[44]

What does it mean for God to be "awful" or "awesome?" Leslie Flynn in *Worship: Together We Celebrate,* writes: "Awe is essential in true worship. Transcendent wonder at God's majesty gives a sense of inadequacy on the part of the worshipper whose weakness stands in vivid contrast to the infinite might of God."[45]

One thousand years ago the word "awful" was used almost exclusively of God. Through common usage, the graphic term gradually degenerated until it was applied to any situation causing awe. By 1800, with the spelling modified, it came to mean "exceedingly great." But the once potently powerful word for holy reverence is now debased to such phrases as "awful weather" or "awful pain." The Septuagint translated "awful" as "fearful, terrible and dreadful." In its verb form, to "awe" means to fear reverently.

---

44 Tozer, A. W. *Worship: The Missing Jewel of the Evangelical Church*. Camp Hill, PA: Christian Publications, 1961.

45 Flynn, Leslie. *Worship: Together We Celebrate*. Wheaton: Victor Books. 1983.

Awe characterized the worship of the Old Testament saints of
God. Abraham fell on his face in holy wonderment when God spoke
to him. The morning after Jacob's "ladder experience" he exclaimed,
"How awesome is this place" (Genesis 28:17 NIV), When Moses
met with God at the burning bush, he was told to remove his shoes
because of the holiness of the place. This scene is repeated over and
again throughout the Bible, and is not limited to Old Testament worshippers. People who recognized Christ fell before Him in the same
manner. This same spirit characterizes the worship of the Revelation,
when we in redeemed and glorified bodies surround the throne of the
Lord God and the Lamb.

I. THE PICTURE OF WORSHIP

What can we learn from Jacob's ladder experience that will make us
better worshippers of God? In this passage there is infinitely more
than what was contained in the chorus we used to sing in Sunday
School, "We are climbing Jacob's ladder"[46]! Rather, this passage gives
us a very vivid portrait of worship.

Jacob had a dream in which he saw a stairway resting on earth
with its top reaching into heaven. There were angels climbing up
and down the ladder. This two-way escalator illustrates for us that
worship is a dynamic duet rather than a one-way street. It is a
two-way dialogue. God designed worship to be two-way. He desires
to communicate with us more than we do with Him. In the rhythm
of God, it is God Himself who takes the initiative towards us. He
reveals something of His attributes and actions, and then the believer
responds to the revelation of God. Worship is dialogue. God acts and
speaks, and we respond to Him.

---

46   *We Are Climbing Jacob's Ladder*, Words and Music: African-American spiritual, a campfire song 19th century or
     earlier.

In Jacob's ladder, God initiates the process by giving Jacob a promise. Jacob responds with a vow. This is the dynamic flow of *revelation* and *response*. There is *proclamation* and *dedication*. God *gives* a promise, and Jacob *makes* a promise. There is heaven and earth entering into dialogue in this worship encounter.

Whether in our corporate gatherings or our individual devotional time alone with God, worship is a divine, dynamic dialogue that happens between God and us. This dialogue is dramatically portrayed for us, and illustrates the awesome power of worship.

Have you ever wondered why we call it "Jacob's ladder"? It wasn't really *Jacob's* ladder! It was **God's** ladder! It did not originate with Jacob. Jacob did not construct it. As clever and conniving as he was, Jacob could not build a ladder or a staircase that would reach into heaven. Earlier in the book of Genesis, mankind had tried to do this and had fallen under the judgment of God (Genesis 11: 1-9).

The tower of Babel and Jacob's ladder are one more illustration of the contrast between man's way and God's way in worship. Man's way is attempting to reach up into heaven. It may be by a regimented lifestyle of good works. It may be by a systematized religious structure of ceremony and ritual. Or it may be by certain symbols and formalism. It may be by the wrong use of legitimate forms of worship. But if we see any of our activities, even though they may be Biblically based, as being able to bring us into the presence of God, we have missed the mark.

In some pockets of the charismatic and worship renewal, there has been an invalid interpretation of what it means to "enter his gates with thanksgiving and his courts with praise." Praise and thanksgiving are *not* the vehicles that take us into the presence of God. Rather, they are the attitudinal responses by which we affirm that God HAS brought us into His presence. It is the blood of Jesus that has brought us in. We are in the presence of God by a new and living way. This way has been consecrated for us by our Lord Jesus Christ through the giving of His body on the cross. In that sacrifice He not only opened the way to God, but He has brought us into the presence of God.

Since we are now in His presence, we draw near with full assurance of faith. We are in the holy of holies by virtue of the finished work of Calvary. We celebrate that fact when we praise and worship God! But we must never think that it is our praise or our worship that brings us in. Our praise enables us to sense, to realize, to experience, to appreciate, to recognize, and even to feel that presence. But in no sense of the word, do the works of our hands or the fruit of our lips convey us into the presence of God. Such teaching is legalism in one of its more subtle forms.

Unfortunately, many times our efforts at worship are nothing more than our attempts to somehow engineer an escalator that can get us earthbound creatures off the ground and into the heavenlies! But God never intended that worship would be something that would originate in our efforts, begin in us, and through our abilities, enable us to build a ladder to reach into heaven. That is why He has already seated us in the heavenlies in Christ. Worship enables us to comprehend this and enjoy the glory of its realization. God hasn't decreed our release from earthboundness through our own efforts in worship. It is to be His provision and His initiative!

Worship, on our part, is our response to a loving God who, in the incarnation let down a ladder from heaven that reaches all the way to the lowest depth of this earth, and even into the depths of hell itself. That ladder is Jesus Christ. The rungs of that ladder were rooted in the soil of this earth. Jesus became "earthy" when God came down to man in the person of His Son. Not only did God come down to man, but through Jesus Christ we are able to ascend into the heavenlies in worship as we glorify and praise Him!

God not only let down the ladder from heaven, but also constructed the staircase to heaven. Too often our worship is centered in our efforts to fabricate a staircase to reach into the heavens. As long as this is our focus, we will never discover the power of true worship.

In the words of our Lord to Nathanael, there is the possible hint of a connection between His person and Jacob's ladder when He said, I tell you the truth, you shall see heaven open, and the angels of God ascending and descending on the Son of Man (John 1:51 NIV). Christ is Jacob's ladder! He is our access to heaven! God has descended to us in Christ, and through Christ we are able to transcend our earthboundness in worship.

In Christ we have heaven and earth met together. Just as Jacob's ladder joined heaven and earth, so does Christ. It is as if He grasps the throne of God with one hand, and reaches down to the depths of hell with the other. And when we worship Christ, we can rise from the depths of our earthboundness and soar into heaven itself. Christ is our stairway to heaven, our median of worship. It is only through Him that our worship is acceptable to God. The writer to the Hebrews tells us, "Through Jesus therefore, let us continually offer to God a sacrifice of praise, the fruit of our lips that confess His name" (Hebrews 13:15 NIV). It is through Christ alone that we ascend into the heavenlies in our worship.

Worship is an "**up**-lifting" experience. God has come down in the person of His Son. He has let down His ladder from heaven. As we gather around Jesus and lift Him up in worship, somehow, wonderfully, mysteriously, we also are lifted up with Him. This is the uplift of worship.

Jacob's ladder portrays this powerfully for us. When I was a little boy, I frequently dreamed that I could fly. Most people have probably had that same dream. Sometimes the dream seemed so real that I wanted to try it! Deep within each of us there is that urge to rid ourselves of our earthboundness.

Worship can facilitate that. Worship is that which lifts us and launches us beyond the limitations of our physical realm. Everything looks so different when you fly. I probably fly over one hundred thousand miles every year. Frequently I leave for the airport when it's dark, rainy, miserable, depressing! There's bumper-to-bumper traffic, glaring headlights, wet pavement and irate drivers on the freeway. But when I get on that airplane and it soars up above all of that, I look out and see the city and all of its lights.

I always find that when I board an aircraft and get a little distance between me and my day-to-day circumstances, everything looks different. All of my colossal problems somehow seem to diminish in their significance and are no longer so important.

Worship can be such a transcending experience. God has designed it to be an awesome encounter with Himself wherein we are lifted above the confines of this world.

2. THE PERSON OF WORSHIP

In this passage we discover more than just a picture of what worship can be. We not only soar above the limitations of earthboundness, nor do we merely behold God's staircase. God is standing at the head of the stairs! Just as Jacob saw more than angels ascending and descending, worship is more than the ups and downs, more than the highs and lows of our finite experiences. When we ascend the staircase in worship we have an encounter with the Person of worship. It is God Himself. This revelation of God is both enlightening and instructive.

He says "I am Jehovah, the God of your father Abraham and the God of Isaac." This, then, is the purpose of worship—the revelation of God to us. He revealed Himself to Jacob as a **covenant-keeping God** as well as by His name Jehovah, the personal name of God that has to do with salvation. He revealed Himself as the **giving God**. He said, "I will give you and your descendants the land upon which you are lying." He revealed Himself as the **blessing God**, "All peoples of the earth will be blessed because of you." He revealed Himself as the **personal, ever-present God**, "I am with you and will watch over you wherever you go, and I will bring you back to this land. I will not leave you until I have done what I have promised you" (Genesis 28:13-15).

True worship not only draws us *near* to God's heart, but also discovers the *essence* of His heart. True worship is meeting with God and getting to know His person, His character. For this reason He grants us an audience. He wants us to know Him.

This is why He let down the ladder from heaven. In that ladder, called Jesus, we discover the Person of God, the Person of our worship. "No one has ever seen God, but God the only Son, who is at the Father's side, has made him known" (John 1:18 NIV).

Jesus said, "Anyone who has seen me has seen the Father… Don't you believe that I am in the Father, and that the Father is in Me? The words I say to you are not just my own. Rather, it is the Father living in me, who is doing his work. Believe me when I say that I am in the Father and the Father is in me" (John 14:9- 11 NIV).

The writer to the Hebrews tells us that Jesus is the express image of God's person. He is the precise and exact impress of His character. We have had revealed to us the very person of God in Christ. He is the brightness of God's glory. In Him all of the divine fullness was manifested!

Worship is more than the stirring of emotions. It is more than the creation of a nice feeling. It is not the liberation of the psyche. Worship is preoccupation with God. Jacob was so caught up in this experience that he described it as being awesome.

Jacob describes this as being the house of God and the gate of heaven. Worship is meeting God and becoming involved and preoccupied with His person and presence. Unfortunately, the concept of God's majesty has almost disappeared from our worship. In the Psalms, God is worshipped for His person in descriptive praise and for His work in declarative praise.

There are **three factors** that animate the psalms of descriptive praise. They include *His names, His incomparability, and His attributes*. His power is seen in **nature**, so we worship Him. We see Him in **creation**, so we worship Him. We worship Him for His **knowledge**, for His **wisdom**, for His **omnipresence**, for His **eternity**, for His **trinity**, for His **righteousness**, for His **faithfulness**, for His **grace**, for His **mercy**, for His **lovingkindness**. It is the study of the **character** of God that readies and enables us to worship Him.

We not only worship Him for His *attributes*, but also for His *activities*. He *forgives* us sinners, He *answers our prayers*, He *grants us guidance*, He *loads us with benefits*, He *protects us, heals us*, and He *enlightens us*.

Worship requires awareness of God's person and awe in His presence. We adore Him because of His excellent acts. In worship we give Him affirmation and praise for all He is and all that He does. We cannot worship someone that we do not know. The glorious attributes of His person, when drawing upon our hearts, prompts and precipitates praise and adoration of His Being.

3. THE PLACE OF WORSHIP

Jacob's ladder introduces us not only to a picture of worship and to the Person of worship, but also to the place of worship.

> When Jacob awoke from his sleep, he thought, "Surely the LORD is in this place and I was not aware of it." He was afraid and said, "How awesome is this place! This is none other than the house of God; this is the gate of heaven" (Genesis 28:16-17 NIV).

This experience preceded tabernacle and temple worship. It was long before Hebron, Zion, Jerusalem or any other location had been declared a place of worship. But for Jacob, it was the house of God, the place of worship, for he met God there. This place had great significance in Jacob's own life and experience. Once when Jacob was in trouble and fleeing from Laban, the angel of the Lord appeared to him and said, "I am the God of Bethel, where you anointed a pillar and where you made a vow to me" (Genesis 31:13 NIV). It is significant that the name Bethel is best translated "house of God."

> God called Jacob back to this place again, when He wanted to change his name from Jacob to Israel. It was when Jacob returned to this place of worship, he instructed his household and company to get rid of all the foreign gods, and built an altar again to the Lord, that God appeared to Him again.

> God appeared to him again and blessed him. God said to Him, "Your name is Jacob, but you will no longer be called Jacob; your name will be Israel." So he named him Israel. And God said to him, "I am God Almighty; be fruitful and increase in number. A nation and a community of nations will come from you, and kings will come from your body. The land I gave to Abraham and Isaac I also give to you, and I will give this land to your descendants after you." Then God went up from him at the place where he had

talked with him. Jacob set up a stone pillar at the place where God had talked with him, and he poured out a drink offering on it; he also poured oil on it. Jacob named the place where God had talked with him Bethel (Genesis 35:9-14 NIV).

It was at the place of worship that God renewed the covenant and promise that He had given to Abraham and Isaac. At the place of worship God talked with him, and confirmed His prophetic Word.

In the Old Testament, the places of worship became very significant. God told Moses that He would commune with him between the cherubim. "There, above the cover between the two cherubim that are over the ark of the testimony, I will meet with you and give you all my commands for the Israelites" (Exodus 25:22 NIV). When Solomon dedicated his temple to the Lord, God responded to his prayer,

I have heard your prayer and have chosen this place for myself as a temple for sacrifices… Now my eyes will be open and my ears attentive to the prayers offered in this place. I have chosen and consecrated this temple so that my Name may be there forever. My eyes and my heart will always be there (II Chronicles 7:12-16 NIV).

But when we enter the New Testament era, something changes. For in the New Testament, Jesus Christ is God "tabernacled among us." He is the "temple of God." He is "Emmanuel," God with us. And after His death and victorious resurrection, He builds a new tabernacle, which is His spiritual Body of believers. He is the head, the cornerstone, and we are His building. But the **place** of worship changes in the New Testament. It is no longer a physical building; it is Jesus Christ in the midst of His people, wherever they are gathered together.

Jesus confirms this transition in His teaching on worship in the fourth chapter of John's gospel. In John 4:19, the woman at the well says to Christ, "'Sir,' the woman said, 'I can see that you are a prophet. Our fathers worshipped on this mountain, but you Jews claim that the place where we must worship is Jerusalem.' Jesus declared,

> Believe me, woman, a time is coming when you will worship the Father neither on this mountain nor in Jerusalem… we worship what we do know, for salvation is from the Jews. Yet a time is coming and has now come when the true worshippers will worship the Father in spirit and in truth, for they are the kind of worshippers the Father seeks. God is spirit, and his worshippers must worship in spirit and in truth (John 4:19-24 NIV).

The place of worship on the individual level is the heart that is open to God, worshipping "in spirit and in truth." This means, simply, in sincerity, honesty, and with the whole heart, and with the revealed knowledge of the true God. Corporately, the temple of God is described for us by Paul the Apostle in his letter to the Ephesians:

> Consequently, you are no longer foreigners and aliens, but fellow citizens with God's people and members of God's household, built on the foundation of the apostles and prophets, with Christ Jesus himself as the chief cornerstone. In him the whole building is joined together and rises to become a holy temple in the Lord. And in him you too are being built together to become a dwelling in which God lives by his spirit (Ephesians 2:19-22 NIV).

There are two words that are the key to understanding the place of worship: "in Him." It is IN HIM that we are being built together. It is IN HIM that the temple grows together. It is IN HIM that the building becomes the habitation of God for the Holy Spirit to indwell. Since "IN HIM" is the place of worship, it is possible that one can be "IN HIM" and enjoy individual worship. While individual worship is certainly valid and meaningful, in each of these phrases in Ephesians, the emphasis is on the forming of the people of God. In fact, that formation of one man (or one new people) by the bringing together of Jew and Gentile is central to what Paul is describing. It is possible to enjoy worship as an individual, but God has designed that the place of worship be His people in a corporate sense. We lift up one another when we worship together. Individually our bodies are the temples of the Holy Spirit, and collectively we together become the dwelling place of God. We enjoy a fuller measure of God's blessing and presence in our lives when we celebrate God's life and love together with His people.

A pastor once noticed that a member of his congregation had not been attending church regularly, so he dropped by to visit him. The man was sitting in his rocking chair by the fireplace. He told the pastor, "I can worship God just as effectively sitting here alone by the fire." Taking the tongs, the pastor knelt down, removed a coal off the fire and set it over to one side, asking the man to watch it for five minutes. In a few moments, of course, the life and the fire in that solitary coal died out while those that were on the fire were still glowing. There are times when the fire in my soul may get a little dim and I need to be ignited and warmed and encouraged by the people of God. This is the power of corporate worship.

Jesus Christ with His people will be the eternal place of worship. John said, "I did not see a temple in the city because the Lord God Almighty and the Lamb are its temple" (Revelation 21:22 NIV). What a day that will be, when loosed eternally from our earthboundness, we will ascend into His presence, behold the glory of His person, and be forever in the place He has prepared for those that love Him!

WRESTLING WITH GOD COULD GIVE YOU A LIMP

Wrestling with God is a sign of intimacy. You can't wrestle with someone you're far away from.

—Jon Acuff

So Jacob was left alone, and a man wrestled with him till daybreak. When the man saw that he could not overpower him, he touched the socket of Jacob's hip so that his hip was wrenched as he wrestled with the man. Then the man said, "Let me go, for it is daybreak." But Jacob replied, "I will not let you go unless you bless me." Then the man said, "Your name will no longer be Jacob, but Israel, because you have struggled with God and with men and have overcome." Then he blessed him there. So Jacob called the place Peniel, saying, "It is because I saw God face to face, and yet my life was spared." The sun rose above him as he passed Peniel, and he was limping because of his hip (Genesis 32:24-31 NIV).

By faith Jacob, when he was dying, blessed each of Joseph's sons, and worshiped as he leaned on the top of his staff (Hebrews 11:21NIV).

've never really been a fan of wrestling. Especially of the type featured on television that appears to be more entertainment than actual sport. Although, I must say that as a teenager I gained an appreciation for some wrestling holds that my brother taught me. Courtesy of those lessons I was able to permanently fend of the schoolyard bully that found his daily entertainment in beating me up after class. As I went from adolescence into adulthood, I quickly learned that the demons with which I wrestled in my youth were more powerful than the schoolyard bully. And conquering them would require a different strategy than that learned from my older brother.

The passage before us introduces us to a wrestling match of a different genre. It gives us a closer look at the man we met in the previous chapter—a man called Jacob.

In the last book of the Old Testament, we discover a very interesting statement concerning Jacob and his brother Esau. "Yet I have loved Jacob, but Esau I have hated" (Malachi 1:2-3 NIV). Paul quotes this passage in Romans nine,

> Yet, before the twins were born or had done anything good or bad—in order that God's purpose in election might stand: not by works but by him who calls—she was told, "The older will serve the younger.' Just as it is written, "Jacob I loved, but Esau I hated" (Romans 9:11-13 NIV).

This passage poses a conundrum. God's love for Jacob and hatred for Esau baffles us. We cannot attribute it solely to their responses to God, for as Paul indicates, it is really an affirmation of God's election (Romans 9:11). But, putting the doctrine of election aside, we can learn some valuable lessons by looking at the respective lives of each individual.

When we examine the life of Esau, it is not so difficult to understand why his choices would incur God's displeasure. He despised his birthright. He had no appreciation for the value of spiritual things. He exchanged the blessing of God for a single meal, a mess of pottage, a bowl of stew. To Esau, the immediate gratification of his natural, carnal, human appetite was more important than spiritual blessing. Spiritual posterity was virtually meaningless to him.

> See that no one is sexually immoral, or is godless like Esau, who for a single meal sold his inheritance rights as the oldest son. Afterward, as you know, when he wanted to inherit this blessing, he was rejected. He could bring about no change of mind, though he sought the blessing with tears (Hebrews 12:16-17 NIV).

The Word of God describes Esau as a "fornicator." When the King James Version states that Esau could find no place of repentance, it is not talking about repentance before God. It literally means that he was unable to get his father to change his mind about the blessing. Once the blessing had been given to Jacob, Esau could do nothing that would bring about a change of God's mind (repentance). Isaac could not reverse the blessing once it had been given. Esau sought that with tears. This passage does not teach that there is some mystical line people may cross where repentance from their sins is no longer available to them from God. Those who render it such wrest the Scriptures to their own destruction (II Peter 3:16).

Equally difficult to fathom is that statement of God that says, "Jacob have I loved." That obviously had to be a statement of grace, for Jacob was a real rascal! He lied and cheated. He deceived his father and cheated his brother out of the blessing. He was a conniver and a manipulator. He was a con artist par excellence. He was twisted and deceptive in all of his thinking. He lived much of his life as a fugitive, running from one scam and con to another. But in spite of all of this, Jacob had learned what it meant to become a worshipper.

It was to Jacob that God let down the ladder from heaven. He was one of the first to see a picture of the incarnation of Christ. Not only had this mama's boy hoodwinked his father into giving him the blessing (and this was irreversible), but he had played upon his brother's weakness to get the birthright. Surely this was wrong! God did not put his stamp of approval and approbation upon the wrong that Jacob committed. But behind the human conniving and deception, God saw his deep desire for the divine blessing upon his life. It was **the** blessing. It was **God's best** that Jacob wanted. He went about it the wrong way, and God had a lot of work to do in his life, but his heart longed for God and God's best.

He had the heart of a worshiper. It was to this man that God opened heaven. It was to this supplanter that God opened His heart. God gave him promises. And Jacob learned to recognize and revere the presence of God. He said, "Surely the LORD is in this place. This is the house of God and the gate of heaven." He called the name of the place "Bethel," the house of God (Genesis 28:16-19).

But God does not ignore our sinfulness and frailty, even though that is not the basis of his mercy in our lives. He is a God of grace. His lovingkindness is everlasting. His mercies endure forever. But He is equally intent upon bringing about our transformation. He will not allow the heart of the worshipper to cloak his own perversion. God will deal with that perversion, and produce His change in our lives. When God sets His love upon us, He has a plan for our lives. That plan includes our being changed and transformed into His likeness and image. This is a championship challenge as there are many elements that must be overcome. This is the challenge of worship.

One worship experience, one encounter with God will not be enough. There must be others. God had already changed Jacob's *name*. Now He must change his *nature*. There is a championship match where we see more than ladders into heaven and angels climbing up and down.

There is a more "heavyweight" kind of experience with God. Jacob must learn this lesson as well. "By faith Jacob, when he was dying, blessed each of Joseph's sons, and worshipped as he leaned on the top of his staff" (Hebrews 11:21 NIV). What does worship have to do with Joseph's leaning on his staff? Our examination of the challenge of worship should provide the answer to this question.

I. WORSHIP INVOLVES WARFARE

The concept of warfare is usually not considered to be an essential element in the worship experience. We prefer to focus on the peace of God, His presence, our rest in His finished work, and on the ability of worship to enable us to transcend the limitations and distractions of life's vicissitudes.

But we must recognize that our worship, in being directed Godward, is also directed upward. That is not to minimize in any way either the reality of God's presence among us, or the fact that the Church corporate is His holy habitation. We know that God inhabits the praises of His people. Yet the upward lift of our hearts to God is common to all of mankind. We lift our hearts to God in worship and our hands to Him in praise. This vertical dimension of worship is axiomatic to the nature of worship itself.

God is in our midst when we worship Him. But while the Spirit of God is among us, God is also enthroned in heaven. Heaven is His throne, and earth His footstool. When our Lord Jesus Christ was upon earth, He was a visible manifestation of God in human form, but He is now exalted in the heavenly realm.

> Therefore God exalted him to the highest place and gave him the name that is above every name, that at the name of Jesus every knee should bow, in heaven and on earth, and under the earth, and every tongue confess that Jesus Christ is Lord, to the glory of the Father (Philippians 2:9-11 NIV).

Paul also writes of the exaltation of Christ in his letter to the Ephesian believers.

> He raised him from the dead and seated him at his own right hand in the heavenly realms, far above all rule and authority, power and dominion, and every title that can be given, not only in the present age but also in the one to come. And God placed all things under his feet and appointed him to be head over everything for the church (Ephesians 1:20-22 NIV).

The believer in Christ also shares this exalted position since "the God and Father of our Lord Jesus Christ… has blessed us in the heavenly realms with every spiritual blessing in Christ" (Ephesians 1:3 NIV). This same idea is conveyed again in the next chapter when Paul says that God… made us alive with Christ… and God raised us up with Christ and seated us with him in the heavenly realms in Christ Jesus" (Ephesians 2:5-6 NIV).

In marked contrast to Christ's exaltation and the believer's position in the heavenlies in Him, is the description of the forces of evil which are also at work in the heavenly realm, "…the ruler of the kingdom of the air, the spirit who is now at work in those who are disobedient" (Ephesians 2:2 NIV). Perhaps the most familiar passage, and the classic text on spiritual warfare, is found in the sixth chapter of Ephesians, where Paul states, "For our struggle is not against flesh and blood, but against the rulers, against the authorities, against the powers of this dark world and against the spiritual forces of evil in the heavenly realms" (Ephesians 6:12 NIV).

Whether we want to recognize it or not, we are involved in a spiritual warfare. While we may dislike war, we are already engaged in battle. The war is waging and the conflict is raging. We prefer to see Christ as our Prince of Peace, and that He is, but before peace is ultimately realized, He is also the One who will come to make war. The Bible describes God as a "man of war" (Exodus 15:13).

Jesus is not only the Captain of our salvation, but He is also the Commander-in-Chief of the Army of the Almighty. There is a perpetual conflict between the Kingdom of Light and the kingdom of darkness. Satan has allied his forces and arrayed his troops in inveterate opposition to the kingdom and work of God. Satan is intent upon destroying the Church of Jesus Christ. His declared purpose is to deceive, to rob, to kill and to destroy (John 10:10). He lays waste God's flock, and takes a spoil of God's family, and is doing everything within his diabolical power to thwart the progress and advance of God's kingdom upon his territory.

Spiritual warfare is too intense and comprehensive a subject to investigate here, except as it applies to worship. Our worship involves warfare, because we are involved in a spiritual realm. Our worship must ascend to God, reaching the heavenlies to fill His throne room with its sweet incense. Satan would attempt to hinder that from happening by keeping God's people from discovering the power of the weapon of worship.

If Satan could, he would construct an umbrella, a shield that would hinder the believers' praises and prayers from ascending to the throne of God. There is an indication in the Scripture that at times, the prayers of God's people are taken into His presence by angels, although this may not always be the case (Revelation 5:8, 8:3-4). If it were, and if Satan could, he would construct a defense system to wrestle those prayers and praises from the angels before they reached heaven. However, there is no evidence that his power includes such ability, so Satan attempts to blind God's people, rendering their worship impotent so that it will not ascend to God.

A passage in Daniel indicates that the prayers of God's people get through to Him, when those prayers are effectual and fervent, and are offered by righteous men.

> Since the first day that you set your mind to gain understanding, and to humble yourself before your God, your words were heard, and I have come in response to them. But the prince of the Persian kingdom resisted me twenty-one days. Then Michael, one of the chief princes, came to help me, because I was detained there with the king of Persia. Now I have come to explain to you what will happen to your people in the future (Daniel 10:12-14 NIV).

The influence of Satan was to prevent the angel whom God had dispatched from delivering his message. We dare not suggest that Satan also has the power to hinder our worship or prayers from reaching God, but we can safely conclude that he will do everything possible to prevent God's people from discovering the power of the weapon of worship. Spirit-empowered worship not only breaks through the enemy's shield, piercing and penetrating any defense system erected to keep us from contacting God, but worship moves God's heart! This, however, does not mean that we are to worship with the motivation of getting God to do something for us, for the moment we reduce worship to mere mechanics and methodology, it ceases to be worship. True worship is rendered to God with no expectations, except that of honoring and glorifying Him.

Worship is a powerful weapon in spiritual warfare. Consequently, it is a weapon that will not go unopposed by Satan. He will endeavor to hinder God's people from discovering the power of worship, attempting to deceive the people of God by reducing worship to mere formality, by removing it from its central redemptive theme, by making it mechanical, or by any other method he can devise to negate its impact upon his kingdom.

But what is it that makes worship such a powerful weapon in our spiritual warfare? I believe that there are three principal things. These three things God has given to us as believers, and in them we have authority and power. They are: the **Word of God**, the **Name of Jesus**, and the **Blood of our Lord Jesus Christ**. Worship is powerful when it *exalts the name of Jesus*, comes *through the power of the blood*, and is *thoroughly Biblical* in its base and content. These elements comprise the real power of worship. We ascribe God the glory due His name by worshipping Him in this way.

Paul talks about worship that is empowered by the Spirit when he writes, "We who worship by the Spirit of God, who glory in Jesus Christ" (Philippians 3:3 NIV). He talks of praying in which the Spirit takes over and helps our weakness, "The Spirit helps us in our weakness. We do not know what we ought to pray, but the Spirit himself intercedes for us" (Romans 8:26 NIV). When our worship, praise, and prayers are energized by the Spirit of God, they become a powerful weapon in waging spiritual warfare against the enemy of our souls.

After reviewing an earlier version of this manuscript, Dr. David Wang, a veteran missionary leader and statesman, and president of Asian Outreach wrote the following:

> From Mongolia to Indonesia, from Korea to Nepal, all across
> this great continent of Asia, I have had the joy and privilege of

worshipping with the Church of Jesus. Some were conducted in great cathedrals and stadiums, others were in caves, or deep in the forest. But one thing is for sure, their worship is not just a celebration before their King, but it is also a battle cry for their Lord of Hosts.[47]

2. WORSHIP INVOLVES WRESTLING

If it is difficult for us to conceive how worship has anything to do with warfare, it may be equally difficult to imagine what it could possibly have to do with wrestling! But, after all, the passage we are considering has to do with Jacob's wrestling with the Lord. From Jacob's experience, many truths are applicable to our own worship experiences.

Whereas warfare deals with battling in the spiritual realm against the forces of evil, wrestling involves another realm, that of the battle against the flesh. We often confuse the two in our Christian walk. It is easier, like television comedian Flip Wilson's character, Geraldine[48], to say, "The devil made me do it," than to accept the divine discipline that is necessary for us to live overcoming lives as we walk with God. This truth could be taken one step farther. In our Pentecostal/Full Gospel/Charismatic culture, we have become far too accustomed to seeking "God's deliverance" for problems of the flesh. By that I mean, we want "inner healing," or "exorcism," or "deliverance," or immediate help by some other spiritual nomenclature for problems that God wants to eliminate from our lives by the discipline of His Word. It would certainly be much more convenient to simply get "zapped" by God than to have to internalize, inculcate, and obey

---

47   Wang, Dr. David, in an e-mail message to Don Carmont, March 31, 2005.

48   In 1972, The Flip Wilson Show was rated the most popular variety show, and the second most popular show overall in the United States.

the Word of God, submit to His disciplinary process in our lives, and accept the verdict of the cross. A life of obedience, surrender and discipleship is unpopular in an era of instant solutions. We want immediate results and relief from any problems we experience, and somehow believe that we are so entitled as the children of God.

The Scriptures are clarion clear about the flesh. Paul tells us in Romans eight, "The mind of sinful man is death, but the mind controlled by the Spirit is life and peace; the sinful mind is hostile to God. It does not submit to God's law, nor can it do so. Those controlled by the sinful nature cannot please God" (Romans 8:6-8 NIV).

Paul also teaches us in Galatians that there is a perennial warfare that exists between the flesh and the spirit. "For the sinful nature desires what is contrary to the Spirit, and the Spirit what is contrary to the sinful nature. They are in conflict with each other, so that you do not do what you want" (Galatians 5:17 NIV).

What implications does this have for worship? Simply this: that if worship is to be what God intended it to be, the flesh must be subdued. The old nature must be conquered by God. Certainly worship to God will flow through these human bodies of ours, but the real "flesh" nature is something more deeply rooted than our physical beings. The flesh exerts its influence and exhibits its character through our earthly bodies, for the sin principle is deeply embedded within us. The flesh will inhibit our worship to God. The flesh will vaunt itself in the presence of God. The flesh must be "wrestled" and conquered for our worship to be what God intends it to be.

Our flesh desires to have supremacy and control of our lives. We will awaken to this awareness some time after we have been born again. Unfortunately, the flesh is alive and well! It will gladly accept regimen, regulation, religion, rules and ritual, rather than God's verdict of the cross, where it was crucified with Christ.

It is the flesh that resists and impedes the flow of the Spirit in worship. True worship begins in our spirit, travels to our soul, (mind, will, and emotion) and then finds expression through the body. The flesh will resist and protest the release of worship to God. Although our spirit has been regenerated by God in the new birth, the flesh life has not been changed. It cannot be. It must be neutralized and mortified if worship is to flow unhindered to God.

It is the nature of the flesh to resist both the flow and the control of God's Spirit. It is the flesh that grieves the Spirit by the carnal demonstrations Paul mentions in Ephesians 4:29-31. It is the flesh that quenches the Spirit. Deeply ingrained in the flesh is this inveterate resistance to the Spirit of God. It must therefore be conquered!

Positionally, the flesh has been crucified with Christ. This is abundantly evident in Paul's teachings in Romans chapter six. It becomes reality in our lives, however, when we refuse to yield our members as the instruments of sin, disallowing reign and control by the flesh in daily situations. Our refusal is based on God's verdict—what He says about the flesh having gone to the cross is true! We resist rendering our bodies as the instruments of sin by instead surrendering them unto God as our reasonable, intelligent act of worship.

Paul, in fact, tells us that this is "spiritual worship." In Romans twelve, he says, "Therefore, I urge you, brothers, in view of God's mercy, to offer your bodies as living sacrifices, holy and pleasing to God—which is your spiritual worship" (Romans 12:1 NIV). Paul also tells us how he managed to maintain control over the compulsions of the flesh in his daily life. "I do not fight like a man beating the air. No, I beat my body and make it my slave" (I Corinthians 9:26-27 NIV). Although the metaphor is boxing, rather than wrestling, the truth is evident. As we subdue the flesh we are released to properly worship God.

But there is an element in this wrestling that must not be ignored. We are not able to subdue the flesh by the flesh. An old pastor friend of mine used to say, "After you have nailed one hand to the cross, how will you nail the other one there?" No, it has to be a work of the Spirit of God. And this is beautifully illustrated for us with Jacob.

Jacob's *name* had already been changed. Now, he needed to have his *nature* changed as well. God had given him His promises, but God wanted to make Jacob into a new person. Jacob resisted that. He was crooked by nature. He wanted to run his own life, even though it meant running for his life. He, like all of us, resisted being conquered by God. But, ultimately, in his wrestling with the Lord, he learned that only those touched and conquered by God really become champions.

This wrestling brought about a deep transformational change in Jacob's life. This is most important for us to recognize, for God wants to change us when we worship Him. Unless our lives are transformed, our worship will never mature into what God intends it to become.

As we discovered in our consideration of Romans 12:1, the surrendering of our bodies and total beings to God has a great deal to do with worship. Worshipping with our physical bodies, as they are presented "living sacrifices, holy and pleasing to God" is "spiritual worship." This may seem incongruous to us, but GOD says it is so.

The extent to which our bodies are the temples of the Holy Ghost in every day living is the true measure of spiritual worship, even more so than the physical expressions that we render to God when we are assembled with the corporate Body of Christ.

It seems that far too much has been made of the physical expressions of the body in the contemporary worship renewal. We clap our hands, we raise our hands, we move our bodies, and we dance with our feet. But are these same bodies given to God in daily worship by being the holy temples that God has sanctified and set them apart to be? If not, then God needs to wrestle the flesh until we are touched by Him, conquered by Him, and He has control over every aspect of our lives.

The sacredness and sanctity of these temples is expounded by Paul in his letter to the Corinthian church. "The body is not meant for sexual immorality, but for the Lord, and the Lord for the body. By his power God raised the Lord from the dead, and he will raise us also. Do you not know that your bodies are members of Christ himself?" (I Corinthians 6:13-14). Paul then goes on to say,

> Shall I then take the members of Christ and unite them with a prostitute? Never! Do you not know that he who unites himself with a prostitute is one with her in body? For it is said, 'The two will become one flesh.' But he who unites himself with the Lord is one with him in spirit. Flee from sexual immorality. All other sins a man commits are outside his body, but he who sins sexually sins against his own body. Do you not know that your body is a temple of the Holy Spirit, who is in you, whom you have received from God? You are not your own; you were bought at a price. Therefore honor God with your body (I Corinthians 6:15-20 NIV).

What does this have to do with worship? Everything! In this day when sexual immorality is rampant in the Church and even in Christian ministry, we need to be made aware that worship is not how we present our bodies in performance in church, but how we present our bodies in consecration to God in daily living.

We live continually in a battle with the flesh. We *war* against the spiritual forces, but we *wrestle* with these fleshly natures. Our bodies are now the temples in which worship takes place. Our bodies must be surrendered to and inhabited by the Spirit of God. In this wrestling match, the Spirit longs to prevail over the flesh, producing a flow of worship that is pure and holy, ascending to God as a sweet-smelling savour.

3. WORSHIP INVOLVES WINNING

Now, how can this possibly be? Perhaps we can concede that in worship there is warfare against the forces of evil and wrestling with the foe of the flesh, but how does worship involve winning? Jacob won—by losing! He prevailed with God, and secured the blessing, although the blessing was already his. The truth is, in the final analysis, that nobody outwrestles God. In this wrestling match, Jacob got a new name. In that sense he won. But his name also meant that he lost. Sound confusing? Sorry! You see, the name Israel, not only means "power with God" or "prince of God" but also "conquered by God." We have power with God and we are princes of God only insofar as we have been conquered by God.

Winning in worship has nothing to do with manipulating God by selfish motivation. When we learn to worship, God often does what we want Him to do, BUT not as we would think. When we discover what it means to worship our "want Him to do" gets changed! The more time we spend in the presence of God, the more likely we are to understand the purposes of God, the greater the possibility of His mind being infused into our minds. Our perspective changes in His presence. Our desires are altered. We are melted down and made over. And so worship often results in God doing what we want Him to do, but it happens as we begin to want the same things that God wants, as the Psalms illustrate.

Psalms 120 through 134 are known as the Psalms of Degrees or the Psalms of Ascents. There is no real agreement among Bible scholars as to how these Psalms were used. Some believe they were sung on the steps leading up to the temple. Others believe they were sung as Israel came out of Babylonian captivity. Others believe they were sung by the pilgrims as they came to Jerusalem to worship at the feasts. But whether any or all of the above are true or not is not really germane to the purpose of our illustration.

Most commentators will agree, however, that there is a definite progression from one Psalm to the other, portraying for us different stages or levels of spiritual development. Psalm 132, for example, gives us a beautiful illustration of what occurs as we move towards the ideal of union with the Lord, portrayed in Psalm 134. In verse nine, David prays, "May your priests be clothed with *righteousness*; may your saints sing for *joy*." God answers this in verse sixteen, "I will clothe her priests with **salvation**, and her saints will **ever** sing for **joy**." (emphasis mine)

In this passage, David is so attuned to God's heartbeat, that he prays the will of God! So much so, that when God answers, He not only *agrees* to what David has asked, but He *eclipses* it! David asked for the priests to be clothed with *righteousness*; God says He will clothe them with **salvation**! David prays for the saints to *sing for joy*; God says they will **ever sing for joy**!

When we draw near to God in worship and our hearts are attuned to Him, God meets us, answers our prayers, and gives us the desires of our hearts. The secret is in our will melting and molding to His will. That is why Christ could dare to make the magnificent promise, "If you remain in me and my words remain in you, ask whatever you wish, and it will be given you" (John 15:7 NIV). Our Lord has taken no risk with this promise! If we abide in Him and His Word abides in us, we will never ask anything that He cannot honor.

This changing of our nature is fundamental to worship. God wants more for us than the mere sight of seeing angels ascending and descending. He wants us to know that we have met Him face to face, and have been changed by His touch.

God said to Jacob, "Your name will no longer be Jacob, but Israel, because you have struggled with God and with men and have overcome." Jacob said, "Please tell me your name." But the angel said to Jacob, "Why do you ask my name?" Then he blessed him there (Genesis 32:28-29 NIV).

As a result of this meeting with God, Jacob called the name of that place Peniel, because he said, "It is because I saw God face to face, and yet my life was spared" (Genesis 32:30 NIV). It is impossible to see God face to face and not be changed. From this moment onward, Jacob's life was changed. This is the worship that wins! This is the worship that produces champions!

One other thing that happened here made Jacob a worshipper. "When the man saw that he could not overpower him, he touched the socket of Jacob's hip so that his hip was wrenched as he wrestled with the man" (Genesis 32:25 NIV). *There was something about this touch that was of a **permanent nature**.* "The sun rose above him as he passed Peniel, and he was limping because of his hip. Therefore to this day the Israelites do not eat the tendon attached to the socket of the hip, because the socket of Jacob's hip was touched near the tendon (Genesis 32:31-32 NIV).

The writer to the Hebrews adds a salient detail that conveys a powerful truth. "By faith Jacob, when he was dying, blessed each of Joseph's sons, and worshiped as he leaned on the top of his staff" (Hebrews 11:21 NIV). What possible connection is there between worship and leaning on the top of his staff? A very obvious one, if we remember that Jacob's lameness was of a permanent nature. Jacob's limp was a perpetual reminder of his meeting with God in which he had become a championship worshipper, being championed by God. He probably traded his walking stick for a staff to support him, due to his crippled condition. But he had learned to glorify God in this divinely inflicted infirmity, because it was the very thing that brought him into right relationship with his God.

Here we learn what it is to "win" in worship. When we have such a meeting with God that we are changed, there will usually be some area of our lives upon which God will see fit to put his finger. There will also be a permanent remembrance of that touch that will never leave us. We will be marked for life in our spirits where God's touch has left its impress. Every time he limped, Jacob worshipped. He remembered his encounter with God. He remembered how God changed his name and changed his nature. That caused him to thank God and to remember where he met Him face to face in a life-transforming experience.

If, when we meet with God in worship, we can see the face of our Lord, we too will not remain the same. "And we, who with unveiled faces all reflecting the Lord's glory, are being transformed into his likeness with ever-increasing glory, which comes from the Lord, who is the Spirit" (II Corinthians 3:18). This is a powerful promise! As we behold the face of Jesus Christ in His Word, and gaze upon that face, we become transformed into His likeness, in ever-increasing measure and splendor! The change is progressive and continual. Little by little He changes us into His own likeness!

It was actually at this place that "Israel" began. It was here that God gave the name by which the nation would be known. At this point of transformation in Jacob's life, the prophetic potential of his posterity was confirmed to him by God. We cannot estimate what God will do in us, for us, and through us when we discover the challenge of worship. This kind of worship enables us to break through the forces of Satan as well as conquer the confines of our fleshly nature. And when we meet with God, we become winners by surrendering to His claims, and receiving His touch that changes our lives.

A BAREFOOT BRIEFING
BY A BURNING BUSH

The fire which enlightens is the same fire which consumes.

—Henri Frederic Amiel

The angel of the LORD appeared to him in flames of fire from within a bush... though the bush was on fire it did not burn up... God said. "Take off your sandals, for the place where you are standing is holy ground... I am sending you to Pharaoh to bring my people the Israelites out of Egypt." But Moses said to God, "Who am I that I should go to Pharaoh and bring the Israelites out of Egypt?" And God said, "I will be with you. And this will be the sign to you that it is I who have sent you: When you have brought the people out of Egypt, you will worship God on this mountain... I am who I am. This is what you are to say to the Israelites: 'I AM has sent me to you'" (Exodus 3:2-14 NIV).

There's something about a fire that captivates people's attention. One of the more vivid memories from my childhood is watching the grass fires that marked the end of summer in my small Eastern Canadian town.

I've witnessed the spectacular New Year's Eve show of fireworks at Disneyworld with fascination and awe. I've been both amused and amazed as I've watched performers "eat" fire and jump through "rings of fire" at so-called magic shows.

The passage before us describes the encounter of Moses with God at the burning bush—a most unusual fire. While the bush was on fire and continued to burn it was never consumed. It would be easy to get caught up in the *figurative fire* of this story and miss the real *flame of truth* that it contains. It's about worship.

We have already stressed the redemptive roots of worship as they are foreshadowed in the experiences of the patriarchs. But when we come to Moses and the Exodus, the theme of redemption is much more pronounced. What was foreshadowed in symbol in the Book of Genesis becomes the theme in Exodus. Moses' calling had to do with redemption. God proposed to bring His people out of Egyptian bondage so that they might worship Him.

God had spoken to Moses, "I will be with you. And this will be the sign to you that it is I who have brought the people out of Egypt, you will worship God on this mountain" (Exodus 3:12 NIV). He told Moses to say to Pharaoh, "This is what the Lord says: Israel is my firstborn son, and I told you 'Let my son go, so he may worship me'" (Exodus 4:22-23 NIV). "When Moses had assembled the people together to tell them all that God had said… they believed; and when they heard that the Lord was concerned about them and had seen their misery, they bowed down and worshipped" (Exodus 4:31 NIV).

Not only does God state that the purpose for redeeming His people is to bring them out so that they can worship Him, but when they heard that word and believed His promise, their immediate response was to worship God as their affirmation of faith in His purpose.

But before the people of God could become worshippers on the level that God desired and designed for them, Moses, their leader, had to learn about worship. In subsequent chapters we will follow the development of worship in Moses' life and ministry, and see how he became a worshipper par excellence. Moses' experience at the burning bush becomes one of the preliminary experiences that presents to us a paradigm of worship for the people of God. What Moses would experience as an individual is a microcosm, a miniature, of what the people of God must learn corporately.

In the Scriptures, worship is never viewed as optional. In both testaments, worship is recognized as a mandate from God. In fact, Jesus responded to Satan's temptation in the wilderness to fall down and worship him, quoting from the commandment of God, "You shall worship the Lord your God and serve Him only" (Deuteronomy 6:13, Matthew 4:10).

By His repetition and reiteration of that command, our Lord acknowledged its all-embracing and comprehensive nature. Every created being is included in its injunction. The Book of Revelation portrays the time in eternity future when the entirety of creation will join in worship to God. Paul states to the Philippians, "That at the name of Jesus every knee should bow, of things in heaven, and things in earth, and things under the earth; And that every tongue should confess that Jesus Christ is Lord, to the glory of God the Father" (Philippians 2:9-10).

We have already adequately stressed that the purpose of the creation of man involved worship. God made man in His own likeness, and created man to mirror that impress back to God, thus glorifying Him. There is a sacred and sanctified sense in which God is egocentric. I hesitate to use the term because of its obvious connotation in relation to man. Egocentricity in man is wrong. It is the essence of sinfulness. Pride in its ultimate form is egocentricity.

And yet with God, ultimately everything must redound to His glory. God is the center of the universe: man is not. And when we lose that perspective, we lose sight of the quintessential nature of worship.

Paul's indictment against humanity in Romans one is that mankind lost sight of that fact. The knowledge of God with which man was born insists upon the glorification and exaltation of God. Innate to man's mentality and spiritual awareness is the sense of God's transcendence. God is most important; He is over all. This awareness insists upon worship, and worship requires surrender to the God who is above all. Basic rebellion against that imperative constitutes sin. Man did not find it desirable to retain knowledge of God, because this knowledge of God required that he become a worshipper. Human rationalization willingly accepts some other substitute, and hence the knowledge and worship of God is bartered off for something inferior.

The first two and one half chapters of Romans are devoted to the discussion of man's ruin. The rest of the letter discloses his redemption and the results of that redemption, and the appropriate response of the redeemed believer to the Lord who has bought him from sin and brought him into resurrected life in Christ. Chapter twelve summarizes what that response should be when it tells us to "offer our bodies as living sacrifices, holy and pleasing to God, which is your spiritual worship" (Romans 12:1 NIV).

Worship is the purpose for which God created mankind, and therefore, is also the reason for redemption. God did not send His Son into the world just to provide us with a fire escape from hell.

That is not to depreciate, devalue or disparage His compassion and the love with which He loved us, for this love brought the Savior to the world. But in the eternal economy of God, once love had been satisfied, there was another overarching and under-girding purpose of God. That purpose is His ultimate glory. He is not glorified by sin and rebellion. There is a sense in which His holiness and justice are glorified when He executes judgment upon sin. But God desires for His grace to triumph, that His purpose of enjoying His creation and of His creation enjoying Him might be fulfilled. Only by this could He be glorified.

Of course the angels sang when Christ came down to earth. They had worshipped Him in heaven for ages! But now, He came to earth to bring creation back into harmony with the Creator. So they could sing, "Glory to God in the highest." Thus the cross became the **triumph of God**, rather than the **tragedy of the ages**. Calvary was not an afterthought of God, for Christ is the Lamb slain from the foundation of the world (Revelation 13:18). In the work of the cross and resurrection, the plan and purpose of God is fulfilled, thus bringing man back into harmony with Him, and resulting in His glorification.

So, from God's perspective, the objective of redemption is to make worshippers. Escaping hell and being destined for heaven are incidental by comparison. They are blessed benefits, indeed, but God wants to make us worshippers.

Ultimately His purpose is that He must be honored, magnified, worshipped and glorified. It may be difficult for us to comprehend and receive, but the supreme purpose of redemption is not for *us*, it is for **God**. We've been redeemed to become worshippers. We've been bought with a price, so that we might glorify God with our bodies and our spirits which now belong to God (I Corinthians 6:20).

The experience of Moses at the burning bush is rich in many truths and applications for the child of God. Many have seen the bush itself as representing the people of God, first Israel, and later the Church. Both the nation of Israel and the Church of Christ have proven to be inextinguishable through the fiery flames of the furnace of persecution. Although there are many applications of this passage for the nation of Israel, with parallels for the Church, our focus will be upon that which relates directly to worship. As such, we will view Moses as representing the people of God, and try to discern the preliminary, prerequisite elements that must characterize our worship.

I. AWARENESS OF THE UNAPPROACHABLE HOLINESS OF GOD

It is important to keep in mind that Moses was a highly educated man. Reared in the courts of Pharaoh, he had been thoroughly indoctrinated in the most sophisticated schooling of his day. He had learned the disciplines of science, art, and mathematics at the feet of Egypt's most learned scholars. Moses had been groomed to be Pharaoh's successor, having been raised as the son of Pharaoh's daughter. I never contemplate this fact without smiling in reflection upon the ironic humor of God. He delights in demonstrating His sovereignty in the affairs of man in ways that we would never imagine!

Egypt was at the apex and pinnacle of her glory when Moses grew up in the palace of the mightiest emperor of his time. But Moses was also schooled in another discipline of which Egypt had no knowledge. Moses was trained (again by the irony of God's intervention) by his own mother, who knew the God of Abraham, Isaac, and Jacob. Bearing in mind that Moses gave us the first five books of the Bible, it is obvious that he knew the plan of God. He knew the destiny of the people of God. He knew the promise of God to Abraham, that through his seed all nations of the earth would be blessed. From his own experience some forty years earlier, he knew that the deliverance of God's people was something close to his own heart and the heart of God. He refused the splendor of Egypt because there pulsated through his veins the awareness that God was greater, and that somehow, he had a place to fill in the divine scheme of God for His people.

Forty years had passed—forty long years in which Moses got to know the wilderness in which he would spend another forty years with the people of God. Those forty years of tending sheep for his father-in-law, Jethro, were also years of frustration. This is evidenced by the name he gave to his son, "Gershom, saying, 'I have become an alien in a foreign land'" (Exodus 2:22 NIV).

It was after this painful experience of waiting for God's timing that the Lord appeared to Moses when he was tending his father-in-law's sheep on the far side of desert. He had come to Horeb, the mountain of God. It was there that the angel of the Lord appeared to him in flames of fire from within a bush. Moses saw that though the bush was on fire it was not consumed. So Moses thought, "I will go over and see this strange sight—why the bush does not burn up." God had succeeded in getting Moses' attention. When the Lord saw that he had gone over to look, God called to him from within the bush, "Moses, Moses!" And Moses said, "Here I am." "Do not come any closer," God said. "Take off your sandals, for the place where you are standing is holy ground." Then he said, "I am the God of your father, the God of Abraham, the God of Isaac and the God of Jacob." At this, Moses hid his face, because he was afraid to look at God. The Lord said,

> I have indeed seen the misery of my people in Egypt. I have heard them crying out because of their slave drivers, and I am concerned about their suffering. So I have come down to rescue them from the hand of the Egyptians and to bring them up out of that land into a good and spacious land, a land flowing with milk and honey (Exodus 3:1-8 NIV).

A closer look at this passage reveals that "the angel of the Lord" appeared in a flame of fire. This Old Testament phrase is both interesting and important. Since the Hebrew word for *angel* and *son* are often used interchangeably, many scholars believe that this term refers to what they describe as a "theophany." A theophany is a pre-incarnate appearing of the Lord Jesus Christ. That is, an Old Testament appearing of Christ, before He came to this earth in the form of man, incarnate in flesh. At any rate, whether or not the phrase "the angel of the Lord" refers to Christ specifically, one thing is certain. Whenever the angel of the Lord appears, God is on the scene!

Now there was something of a magnetic quality about the presence of Christ when He was upon the earth. Sinners came to Him. They were mysteriously and magnetically drawn into His presence. Something about His person drew them to Him. But after His glorification, there is an enigmatic change. He is gloriously awful! When John beholds Him in the Revelation, he falls at His feet as though dead (Rev. 1:17). We catch a glimpse of this occasionally in the gospels. The transfiguration is one obvious example. "When the disciples heard this, they fell face down to the ground, terrified" (Matthew 17:6 NIV). Another occasion is when the Roman soldiers came to arrest Jesus. Jesus asked them whom they were seeking. When they said, "Jesus of Nazareth," our Lord replied, "I am he." The word he" is in italics, indicative that it was inserted by the translators. In, fact, what Christ said is, "I AM." The disclosure of His person was so powerful that they fell down before him. "They drew back and fell to the ground" (John 17:4-6 NIV).

There is an awesomeness associated with drawing near to the presence of God. Moses must learn this as a prerequisite to worship. The unapproachable holiness of God would be taught to the people through the law. Moses would learn this lesson over and over again.

When the law was given, God wrapped the mountain in a mantle of smoke. He dictated that if so much as a beast drew near the mountain it was to be thrust through with a sword. The unapproachable holiness of God was evident in the construction of the tabernacle in the wilderness. This was to become the pattern for worship, the model for approaching God. The necessity of bloodshed, sacrifice, and a complex system of ceremonial cleansing demonstrated the unapproachable holiness of God.

The holiness of God is symbolized for us by the fire. The writer to the Hebrews, after contrasting the glory of the heavenly Zion to the burning fire of Sinai, states, "Let us be thankful, and so worship God acceptably with reverence and awe, for our God is a consuming fire" (Hebrews 12:28-29 NIV).

There are not many definitive statements given to us as to the nature of God. We are told that God is *light*, God is *love*, and God is a *consuming fire*. Light and fire have much in common. These two essential aspects of God's character can be described as His holiness and His love. Mercy, grace, kindness, longsuffering, etc., are related to His love. Justice, truth, righteousness, judgment are related to His holiness.

We would prefer to forget about the "fire" of God and focus instead upon His mercy. We don't want to be reminded of Sodom and Gomorrah and of the fire that consumed them for their wickedness. If a preacher is spoken of disparagingly, he is referred to as a "fire and brimstone" preacher. That says it all! It speaks volumes of our attitude towards the judgment and holiness of God.

But the Scriptures present both facets of God's nature. Paul tells us to" Behold the goodness and the severity of God" (Romans 11:22). Without an awareness of His holiness, there can be no understanding of nor appreciation for His love, mercy and grace that brings us salvation.

Only the awareness of God's holiness enables us to understand the severity of sin, and a realization of the severity of sin is imperative to appreciation for forgiveness. If our theology of sin is inadequate, then our appreciation of forgiveness will also be inadequate. When sin is treated as casual, forgiveness is seen as a shrugging of the divine shoulders, a closing of one eye to sin. But an awareness of the heinous nature of sin, that it is a clenched fist in the face of God, enables us to worship a God of forgiveness.

The cross is as much a triumph of holiness and justice as it is of mercy and love. Sin had never been adequately punished before. Never before had justice been absolutely satisfied. Only in the sacrifice of the perfect, sinless substitute of the Son of God was the justice of God fully met. Only then were the exacting demands of holiness fully executed.

Thus, the cross is a triumph of holiness as well as a victory of grace. Mercy and truth met together in the Christ of the cross; righteousness and peace there kissed each other (Psalm 85:10). But without an awareness of God's holiness, the cross becomes sentimental symbolism. It stirs our emotions. It moves our hearts.

But when we see the holiness of God *requiring* it, and the grace of God *providing* it, then the cross is not only the meeting place of God and man, but of God's justice and grace!

Worship begins with an awareness of the holiness of God. It is interesting to observe that the holiness of God constitutes the theme of the angels in Isaiah's vision. The angels don't chant, "Eternal, eternal, eternal," nor do they say, "Wise, wise, wise," nor is it the omnipotence, the might, the power, the grace, the mercy, the love, the kindness, the longsuffering of God that they praise. Rather, they sing to the thrice-Holy One, and cover their faces and their feet in the awfulness of His Presence. "Holy, holy, holy is the Lord God Almighty." Exodus 15:11 asks the question, "Who is like unto thee among the gods, O LORD? Who is like Thee, majestic in holiness, awesome in praises, working wonders?"

God doesn't *conform* to a holy standard because He **is** the standard of holiness. He never errs, never does anything wrong. He never makes a misjudgment, never causes something to happen that isn't right. There are no degrees in His Holiness: He is absolutely impeccable. He is without flaw, and fully righteous.

The Word of God teaches us that unholiness will not be admitted to His presence. He commands us to be holy even as He is holy. This is a requirement that is beyond our reach, except in and through the imputed and imparted holiness of Jesus Christ. But, without holiness, no man will see the Lord.

God's holiness can be seen in His holy hatred for sin. He expelled Satan and the angels that sinned from His presence in heaven. But the holiness of God is also discernible in the creation of mankind. Man intuitively has within him the moral code of God, the conscience and consciousness of right and wrong, the function of God's holiness coded intrinsically within him. The holiness of God is further reflected in the moral code of the law that was given to Moses in its exacting legal standards. But God's holiness is evident as well in the sacrificial and ceremonial law that required such elaborate preparation in coming to God when the moral law had been offended.

The holiness of God can be witnessed in the outpourings of His judgment upon sin. In the Garden of Eden, in the flood, in the tower of Babel, and in Sodom and Gomorrah, God was demonstrating His holiness when He executed punishment upon the sins of men.

But the ultimate testimony to God's holiness is the cross of Jesus Christ. For there we actually behold the great lengths to which God is willing to go to ensure that His holiness is protected and His justice fulfilled. The holiness of God required a holy sinless substitute to die in the place of man. The grace of God provided it in Christ. Holiness was willing to break the heart of Father God in giving up His Son to die on the cross! What higher testimony could there be to the awesome holiness of our God?

2. AWARENESS OF THE UNSEARCHABLE IDENTITY OF GOD

When Moses met with God at the burning bush, it was a rather overwhelming experience. The holiness of God was firmly established in his mind as he removed his shoes in the presence of God on holy ground. But Moses learned a second prerequisite to worship as he responded to the calling of God upon his life and the task that God laid upon his shoulders.

As Moses conversed with God, he speculated as to how the Israelites would respond to the idea of his being sent to them as their deliverer. No doubt there were lingering memories of his last encounter forty years earlier when his reputation had been spread abroad as a one-man revolutionary! His own brethren had not looked too favorably upon him at that time. Would forty years really make a difference?

Moses, in contemplating the various implications and ramifications of going to his people as their "deliverer", realized that he would require an identity larger than his own. He needed to have some authority behind him. He needed to be sent by someone with greater credibility. His credentials must validate his person and verify his calling. He must have some sense of identity by which Israel would receive him. And so he asked God, "Who am I, that I should go to Pharaoh and bring the Israelites out of Egypt?" And God said, "I will be with you. And this will be the sign to you that it is I who have sent you: When you have brought the people out of Egypt, you will worship God on this mountain" (Exodus 3:11-12 NIV).

At first, that looks pretty good! God is going to go with him. And God is going to give him a sign. But wait a minute! The sign won't be given until he gets the people out of Egypt and into the land and they find themselves worshipping on the same mountain where God first appeared to him. This is hardly an adequate credential to convince either the Israelites or Pharaoh. Moses continued his remonstrance with God:

> Suppose I go to the Israelites and say to them, "The God of your fathers has sent me to you," and they ask me, "What is his name?" Then what shall I tell them? God said, "I am who I am. This is what you are to say to the Israelites: 'I AM has sent me to you.'" God also said to Moses, "Say to the Israelites, 'The Lord, the God of your fathers—the God of Abraham, the God of Isaac, and the God of Jacob—has sent me to you.' This is my name forever, the name by which I am to be remembered from generation to generation" (Exodus 3:13-15 NIV).

This name "**I AM**" is a statement of God's Being. "**I AM WHO I AM**." God is the **Self-Existent One**. He is the **Eternally Present One**. "**I AM**" is the summary of His Being. Without attempting an exhaustive exegesis of the meaning of this name, let us consider some aspects of it that are germane to the concept of God's unsearchable identity.

God is the **Incomprehensible One**. Since He is infinite and we are finite, we can never hope to fully comprehend His Being and His character. Paul in Romans one introduces to us an interesting phrase, "what may be known about God, when he says:

> What may be known about God is plain to them, because God has made it plain to them. For since the creation of the world God's invisible qualities—his eternal power and divine nature— have been clearly seen, being understood from what has been made, so that men are without excuse (Romans 1:19-20 NIV).

Paul speaks of "what may be known about God." Implicit in this text is the idea that full disclosure is not possible. *That which can be known about God* is already revealed to us in the creation. We can perceive His eternal power and His divine nature.

Paradoxically, the heartbeat of God is to reveal Himself to men in His intercourse with us. God has revealed Himself to us in Christ. In the gospels, Jesus identified Himself as the "**I AM**." He said, "Before Abraham was, **I AM**" (John 8:58).

The writer to the Hebrews indicates that Christ is the full and final revelation of God to us (Hebrews 1:1-4). In times past, God parceled out His revelation piecemeal. He gave to one prophet or patriarch one part and to another a different facet of His person. But in Christ, we have heard all that God has to say. Christ is God's final word to man. And yet we stand before Christ and marvel for we cannot fully comprehend the incarnation. That God could become a man. That the infinite could become an infant! That He could exchange the ethereal for the earthly. We not only marvel, but we bow our knees before this great and glorious truth of the incarnation. In Philippians two Paul describes the condescension and incarnation of Christ and His subsequent exaltation and glorification. He then brings the entire created world to its knees before the glory of Christ incarnate, exalted and glorified.

The **I AM** is also the **Independent** and **Absolute One.** As the self-existent God, He is not dependent upon man for anything. He is the absolute One. He created all things. He upholds all things by the Word of His power. He is the master creative mind behind the entire universe. His Word is the glue that holds it together. His Word was the force that birthed it into existence. He is absolute and independent. And yet, again enigmatically, He enters into covenant and relationships with men. He is the God of Abraham, Isaac and Jacob. While He is self-existent, He is not content to exist alone. His glory He will not give to another, and yet He creates mankind in His likeness and image. We bow before this. We cannot fathom the enigma of this seeming contradiction. We cannot hope to fully comprehend it. The only appropriate response is to humbly acknowledge the unsearchable identity of God.

God is the **Eternal One**, and yet He is the God of dying men. Abraham, Isaac, and Jacob will go to their grave, and God, the Eternal Father will live on. From everlasting to everlasting He is God. But he also gives to His creation the possibility of eternal life, sharing His essence and being with those who will believe. How can we fathom this marvelous provision!

He is the **Unchangeable One** and yet the God of men who are of different dispositions and changing temperaments. He is the Lord who changes not, whose ways are irrevocable. He is the Father of lights, with whom there is no variableness nor shadow of turning. Unlike the sun, itself His creation, which causes varying effects upon the earth in different places and at various times, **His** character and nature is constant. And to men who vacillate and fluctuate from one opinion and direction to another, He remains the unchangeable God (Malachi 3:6, James 1:17).

The **I AM** is the **permanent** name! We bow before **Him** who is the same yesterday, today, and forever. Jesus is the **One** who is the same and does not change (Hebrews 13:8). We cannot hope to fully fathom His being. Worship is the awareness of this truth. Prerequisite to worship is knowing that God is transcendent and unsearchable, that His ways are past finding out.

The **I AM** includes the past, present, and future of all that God has been, is and ever will be! We bow our knees before this reality and realization. We stand in His presence with the three inner-circle disciples on the Mount of Transfiguration, and worship as we see the glory of God in the face of Jesus Christ. With Peter we acknowledge that we are "eyewitnesses of His Majesty." With John we "behold His glory, the glory as of the only begotten of the Father, full of grace and truth" (John 1:14).

Unless our God is **bigger** than our *understanding*, **larger** than our *faith*, **greater** than our *comprehension*, we cannot begin to worship. Worship insists upon the "otherness" of God: His *separateness*, His *exaltedness*, His *holiness* and His *worthiness*. Moses will get to know God better. He will press into God's presence, and in subsequent worship experiences discover more of God's person, but God will ever remain infinitely unsearchable. It is precisely this attribute that compels us to know Him more! No matter how high the heaven of revelation, nor how profound the depth of understanding, nor how broad the scope of knowledge, nor how long the lifetime of study,

God will remain more than our finite beings can contain. Until, of course, our beings are transformed into His likeness, and we pass through the veil of death, and share in His resurrection glory. Then shall we know no more in part, but then shall we know even as we are known (I Corinthians 13:12).

3. AWARENESS OF THE UNCHANGEABLE PURPOSE OF GOD

The third prerequisite of worship that Moses must learn is another foundational principle that will become central to his life. God will expand upon this, and it will become central to his whole existence. But now it must be given in embryonic form. It must be instilled and inculcated into Moses' being. His worship will relate fundamentally to this aspect of God's revelation. The commandments, the law, the tabernacle, the whole Mosaic economy, the entire Levitical system will appertain to this principle. Moses must learn of the unswerving purpose of God.

There was an immediate as well as an ultimate aspect to the purpose of God. The immediate is comprehended in His love and compassionate concern for His people. He has seen their misery and heard their cries for deliverance. He is intent upon delivering them out of the bondage of Egypt.

But God's purpose was infinitely more than to merely release them from the bondage of Egypt. He proposed to take them into the blessing of Canaan, giving them a land of promise that would be theirs forever. This was the perpetration of the promise that He had made to Abraham. Abraham grasped that. He never fully settled down in this world. He looked for a city that had foundations, whose builder and maker was God (Hebrews 11:10). When God made His covenant with Abraham, He told him to look up to heaven and try to count the stars (Genesis 15:5). He told him that his seed would be as numberless as the stars and as the sand of the seashore. God's ultimate purpose always transcends the immediate circumstance, although it takes that circumstance into account.

God not only said the land would be theirs; He led Abraham out to a land that he would show him. This purpose is now being restated. But the redemptive plan of God was not fully comprehended in the land or in the nation. This was the physical, natural representation of God's greater purpose of redemption for the human race. God's purpose is not totally seen in the nation, nor is it fully fulfilled in the land. God is bigger than that! But God must preserve a seed to bring forth a Savior to redeem the world.

In the third chapter of Galatians, the apostle Paul gives an eloquent exposition of the purpose of God in Abraham and in the nation of Israel.

> Understand, then, that those who believe are children of Abraham. The Scripture foresaw that God would justify the Gentiles by faith, and announced the gospel to Abraham: "All nations will be blessed through you." So those who have faith are blessed along with Abraham, the man of faith. He redeemed us in order that the blessing of Abraham might come to the Gentiles through Christ Jesus, so that by faith we might receive the promise of the Spirit… The promises were spoken to Abraham and to his seed. The Scripture does not say "and to seeds," meaning many people, but "and to your seed," meaning one person, who is Christ. If you belong to Christ, then you are Abraham's seed and heirs according to the promise (Galatians 3:8-29 NIV).

So the redemptive purpose of God was much greater than the immediate provision of deliverance for Israel from the bondage of

Egypt. Yet that was the crucible of redemption, and the cradle of Israel's birth. But the unswerving, unchangeable, unalterable purpose of God was more far-reaching and universal than the nation of Israel.

Moses laid hold of that purpose. He recognized that the destiny of God's people had greater implications than the immediate concerns. Moses wrote of Christ, in both the law and in the typology of the tabernacle. Jesus could say, "Had you believed Moses, you would have believed me, for Moses wrote of me" (John 5:46).

God's redemptive activity was surrounded in a glorious pageantry of miracles in the exodus from Egypt. The great epochs of God are always attended by an unusual demonstration of the supernatural. The effecting of redemption through the coming of Christ and His death upon the cross was also attested by the miracle-working power of God.

Prerequisite to worship is the awareness of God's unswerving purpose. God has created us to worship and glorify Him. He has redeemed us to glorify and to worship Him forever.

When we arrive at the grand finale in the Book of Revelation, it is worship based on the redemptive theme that fills the chambers and courts of heaven. In fact the songs of Moses and of the Lamb (both redemptive songs) harmonize to become the anthem of praise that is rendered unto God eternally.

Our worship here and now is obviously something less than what it will be when we enjoy the full freedom of our glorified state in God's presence eternally. But we can begin to prepare ourselves for worship by focusing on these prerequisites. The reason for redemption is to transform us into worshippers of God. Worship is impossible unless there is first an awareness of God's Holiness, the recognition of His unfathomable Person, and the realization of His eternal purpose.

10

FAST FOOD, BLOODY DOORS AND RAPID TRANSIT

For Christ, our Passover lamb has been sacrificed.

—**St. Paul, I Corinthians 5:7 (NIV)**

They have washed their robes and made them white in the blood of the Lamb. Therefore, they are before the throne of God and serve him day and night in his temple

—**St. John, Revelation 7:14 (NIV)**

The LORD said to Moses, "…each man is to take a lamb for his family… take some of the blood and put it on the sides and tops of the doorframes of the houses where they eat the lambs… I will pass through Egypt and strike down every firstborn—both men and animals—and I will bring judgment on all the gods of Egypt. I am the LORD. The blood will be a sign for you on the houses where you are; and when I see the blood, I will pass over you… This is a day you are to commemorate; for the generations to come you shall celebrate it as a festival to the LORD… When you enter the land that the LORD will give you as he promised, observe this ceremony…" Then the people bowed down and worshiped (Exodus 12:1-27 NIV).

By the time we reach Exodus 12, Pharaoh and the Egyptians are effectively exhausted from the plagues that God has visited upon them. In urging Pharaoh to let His people go from Egypt, God had intensified the pressure through a series of ten plagues. When bloody water, frogs, lice, boils, hail, locusts, and darkness failed to soften Pharaoh's heart, the next plague would be death of the Egyptian's firstborn sons. More weary than the Egyptians, however, were the Israelites, who had suffered as slaves under the tyranny of Egypt during their 200 years of exile. As God prepared them for their exodus, He gave them a plan whereby their firstborn would be spared on the eve of their departure.

The term that we use for the commemoration of this event is "Passover" or as it is in Hebrew, the word "Pesach" (pronounced PAY-sakh). Pesach is the holiday that commemorates the Hebrews' rapid departure from ancient Egypt. The Jews had just endured over 200 years of exile, including several decades of torturous slave labor, and now God was going to fulfill His promise to Abraham—the promise to redeem the Jews and do justice to their slave-masters. Right before the Exodus, God commands the Jews to sacrifice one lamb per family and mark the Jewish doorposts with its blood. This would be a sign for God to "pass over" the Jewish homes as He slew the Egyptian firstborn—the last of ten supernatural attacks on the Egyptians. This is the origin of the name "Passover."

One of the highlights of my four years serving as pastor of the Full Gospel Church in Halifax, Nova Scotia, was the visiting ministry of speakers from what was then known as the American Board of Missions to the Jews, now renamed *Chosen People Ministries*. Their ministry served as a reminder of our shared heritage of faith, and of God's unwavering purpose to redeem His people,

Israel. On several occasions, we experienced a live demonstration of the Jewish Passover, conducted by a blind Jewish-Christian minister, the late Rev. Dr. Alexander Marks. The vidid representation of the symbolism of the Passover eternally affirmed the redemptive work of God in Christ, foreshadowed in the first Passover revorded in Exodus 12.

Passover is observed today much the same way the Jews did on the first 15th of Nissan in Egypt. Pesach is observed by sacrificing a lamb, eating "bitter herbs", and Matzah, and purging one's house of any grain-based leavened items. The lamb is not slaughtered and sacrified today, but every other Passover element is present: the mad, meticulous scrubbing and cleaning of every nook and cranny, the Seders on the first two nights, and the Shabbat-like services on the first and last days. While the Jewish position is that the absence of the lamb is due to the Temple's absence, could it be that there is no lamb because "Christ our Passover Lamb has been sacrificed for us"? (I Corinthians 5:7)

In the Jewish commentary on Pesach we gain further illumination into its meaning for Israel. "The lesson of Pesach is that you have unlimited potential. In Hebrew, Egypt is Mitzrayim—etymologically related to meitzarim, or borders. The moral of the Exodus story is that we all can escape our personal Egypts. And the seek-and-destroy-any-leavened-particle part of Passover teaches us to eradicate our puffed-up, inflated, doughy egos and be simple, flat, unleavened matzot."[49] While this is a worthy lesson, and one that we as Christians should also embrace, there is a much more significant lesson for us in the Passover—and it's all about how worship is centered in Christ, the Lamb of God, who takes away the sins of the world.

---

49   http://www.askmoses.com/article.html?h=107&o=148

1. WORSHIP PRINCIPLES FROM THE PASSOVER

One of the most central and significant events in the life of the nation of Israel is that of the Passover. On the eve of their departure from Egypt, God instituted this feast, and it is still celebrated to this day wherever the Jewish people live and worship. The Passover gives divine perspective to the deliverance from Egypt. It provides not only the historical background, but also the theological framework for Israel's birth as a nation.

An awareness of the Passover and its significance is imperative for the Christian Church to adequately understand worship. We cannot rightly appreciate the cross of Christ nor appropriate the provision of His Blood until we understand something of the theology of the Lamb of God and the economy of the Passover in Israel.

Paul tells us that "Christ our Passover" has been sacrificed for us. He is the Pascal Lamb that was offered to God without spot or blemish. Only when we appreciate what this entails can we truly comprehend the fact that Christ as the precious Lamb of God occupies the center of worship for all of eternity.

Jesus never ceases to be the Lamb of God. He *was* the Lamb of God in eternity past, slain from the foundation of the world. And throughout the ages to come He *will continue to be* worshipped as God's Lamb. The throne is the throne of the Lord God and of the Lamb (Revelation 22:3). The heavenly Jerusalem is the city where there is no need of light, for the Lord God and the Lamb are the light thereof (Revelation 21:23). The bride of Christ is presented as the Lamb's wife, and has readied herself for the marriage by washing her robes and making them white in the blood of the Lamb (Revelation 19:7). Blessed are those who are called to the marriage supper of the Lamb (Revelation 19:9).

If, the LAMB is the central theme in Revelation, where we have the culmination of worship in its most perfected form, then it is patently plain that God has something to teach us concerning this most significant aspect of our worship.

The blood of Jesus Christ is central to our worship experience and expression. It is Christ's blood that has given us access into God's presence. We draw near to God, the path having been paved for us through the new and living way, according to Hebrews 10:20. This new and living way is through His blood. We must emphasize the blood of Christ in our worship for this blood not only cleanses us from sin, but also causes our consciences to be purged so that we can worship God. The blood satisfied God's holiness so that we could be admitted into His presence, and that same blood causes Satan to tremble and flee. Also, our entrance into heaven is purchased by the precious blood of Christ. It must figure predominantly in our worship, if our worship is to be found acceptable to God.

2. WORSHIP INVOLVES FAITH IN CHRIST'S BLOOD

Certainly one of the great moments in worship in the life of God's people, Israel, is recorded in the twelfth chapter of Exodus. The Passover is a story of salvation, deliverance, and victory that came through the sacrifice of a lamb. Not only did the lamb die and shed its blood, but that blood had to be applied in a specific way in order to ensure the people's salvation.

Many aspects of the Passover represent a perfect portrait of Christ. The Lamb of God gave His life and shed His blood, not only for our deliverance from sin's bondage, but from sin's penalty, death. Initially, we are confronted with the fact that this Passover lamb had to be without blemish and without spot. Peter tells us that Christ is this Lamb (I Peter 1:7). My heart never ceases to be thrilled when I contemplate this truth concerning Christ.

Not only was He without blemish, He was also without spot. He had no blemish in His birth, the result of the Holy Spirit over-shadowing the Virgin Mary, who conceived and brought forth the Son of God. There was no sin in Him, for He was sinlessly conceived. Christ was peerlessly pure in His birth. Furthermore, He committed no sin. The prince of this world came to tempt Him, but found nothing in Him (John 14:3).

But just as the Savior was without blemish in His birth, so was He also without spot in His life. He lived upon this earth, walked among sinful men, and yet was not contaminated with their sin. In fact, He so identified with and associated with sinners, that He was considered one of them. The religious leaders of His day accused Him of eating with sinners and called Him a winebibber, and yet Christ never repelled sinners from His presence. Rather, He drew them to Him. And yet, when He died upon Calvary's cross, He offered Himself sinless and spotless to God. "How much more, then, will the blood of Christ, who through the eternal Spirit offered himself unblemished to God, cleanse our consciences from acts that lead to death, so that we may serve the living God" (Hebrews 9:14 N IV).

Had Jesus not offered Himself spotless, He could not have been made our sin offering. His sinlessness enabled Him who knew no sin to be made sin for us. "God made him who had no sin to be sin for us, so that in him we might become the righteousness of God" (II Corinthians 5:21 NIV). Not only did Christ suffer the punishment of our sin and take its penalty upon Him, but also He partook of our sin. It was not merely sin's punishment, death that Christ endured. He was made sin for us. I can't comprehend how this is possible, but somehow, the sinless Son of God, on the cross of Calvary so identified with our sin that He became sin for us. The same sense in which His righteousness can now indwell, pervade, and enclothe us is the sense in which He was made sin. The extent to which Christ identified with our sin is the degree to which we identify with His righteousness.

It is the blood of Christ, the Lamb of God, which every Old Testament offering anticipated and prefigured. It was only insofar as those offerings symbolized the ultimate offering of Christ upon the cross that they procured any atoning value. In fact, Paul teaches us that God delayed judgment upon sin through these offerings until Christ came. "God presented him (Christ) as a sacrifice of atonement, through faith in his blood. He did this to demonstrate his justice, because in his forbearance he had left the sins committed beforehand unpunished—he did it to demonstrate his justice at the present time, so as to be just and the one who justifies the man who has faith in Jesus" (Romans 3:25-26 NIV).

It is faith in Christ's blood that brings salvation. Although we have redemption and are justified through His blood, and although He has made peace through the blood of His cross, none of these blessings become ours apart from an act of faith by which Christ's blood is appropriated to our lives.

This is portrayed for us in the Passover lamb. It was not enough for them to kill the lamb and spill its blood. That same blood had to be taken and sprinkled upon the doors, on both sides and on the top. It was the blood which God saw, and which offered the provision of His protection from the death angel.

The blood was primarily for God, not for the Israelites. Of course, it was for their protection, but it was GOD who must see the blood. As we learned in Abel's worship, God had respect, or gazed, looked favorably at the sacrifice that he brought—one that involved bloodshed. The blood is for God. The life of the flesh is in the blood (Leviticus 17:11), God said, and the soul that sinneth it shall die (Ezekiel 18:20). God required the blood. His holiness and justice demanded it. "When I see the blood, I will pass over you" (Exodus 12:13 NIV).

There are two possible meanings for the word "Passover." One is to "skip" over. That is to say, when God came through to smite the Egyptians, He would *skip* over the houses where the blood had been applied and not kill the firstborn who dwelt there. Another possible translation for the word is to "hover over" or to "hesitate." This could mean that God's presence would *hover* over those houses where the blood was applied, preventing the death angel from taking the lives of the firstborn. Both ideas are Biblically sound.

But the blood was not ONLY for God. It was also for them. God said, "The blood will be a sign for you on the houses where you are… (Exodus 12:13 NIV). The blood is also a sign for the believer. We cannot "see" the blood, but it is the covering that separates us from the world, and the blanket, the umbrella or canopy under which we find fellowship with Christ and with the family of God.

Only those who were under the blood were safe from the destroyer. That is part of the glorious provision of the blood of Christ for the believer. We are saved from wrath through Him (Romans 5:9). His blood has guaranteed our salvation from the wrath of God and has taken care of our guilt. Only under the protective canopy of Christ's blood is there any refuge from the judgment of God. Christ has taken that judgment for us, and beneath the covering of His blood we are safe.

Of course, every symbol and shadow in the Old Testament is fundamentally imperfect. And such is the case with the Passover lamb. The Passover lamb was killed every year, whereas Christ was only offered once for us.

> The law is only a shadow of the good things that are coming—not the realities themselves. For this reason it can never, by the same sacrifices repeated endlessly year after year, make perfect those who draw near to worship. If it could, would they not have stopped being offered? For the worshippers would have been cleansed once for all, and would no longer have felt guilty for their sins. But those sacrifices are an annual reminder of sins, because it is impossible for the blood of bulls and goats to take away sins (Hebrews 10:1-4 NIV).

The writer to the Hebrews tells us,

> He did not enter by means of the blood of goats and calves; but he entered the Most Holy Place once for all by his own blood, having obtained eternal redemption... For Christ did not enter a man-made sanctuary that was only a copy of the true one; he entered heaven itself, now to appear for us in God's presence. Nor did he enter heaven to offer himself again and again... with blood not his own. Then Christ would have had to suffer many times since the creation of the world. But now he has appeared once for all at the end of the ages to do away with sin by the sacrifice of himself... Christ was sacrificed once to take away the sins of many people (Hebrews 9:12; 24-28 NIV).

The "once-for-all-ness" of Christ's sacrifice is reiterated over and again in the letter to the Hebrews. "We have been made holy through the sacrifice of the body of Jesus Christ once for all... when this priest had offered for all time one sacrifice for sins, he sat down at the right hand of God" (Hebrews 10:10-12 NIV).

Peter describes the blood of Christ as being *precious* when he says, "For you know that it was not with perishable things such as silver or gold that you were redeemed from the empty way of life handed down to you from your forefathers, but with the precious blood of Christ, a lamb without blemish and without spot" (I Peter 1:18-19 NIV). Christ's blood is precious, because it has purchased our redemption. There was no human resource or natural commodity that was valuable enough to purchase redemption.

The Psalmist once said, "Who can by any means redeem his brother, for the redemption of their souls is precious and ceaseth forever" (Psalm 49:7). There never was a man rich enough to purchase the human race out of the slave market of sin. But the blood of Christ has done exactly that. He has redeemed us by His blood!

In worship, we celebrate this redemptive aspect of Christ's blood. Acts 20:28 tells us that the flock of God was purchased with **His** own blood. The blood of Christ was the only blood that God ever had. While hereditary factors are carried in the blood of both mother and father, since Christ had no earthly father, this is the *only* blood that God ever had. To whatever extent the bloodline comes from the father, Christ's blood is divine blood. It is precious blood, for it is the only blood that God ever had.

I Peter 1:18-19 implicitly suggests that the blood of Christ is also *incorruptible*, unlike silver or gold. This would seem to indicate that somehow, mysteriously, the blood of Christ still exists today. We dare not become too fanatical and insist upon its existence in liquid form somewhere in heaven, but there is obviously a sense in which the blood of Christ is eternal, immortal, and incorruptible. Eternity has been described as "an ever-present now." Since Jesus offered His blood through the eternal spirit, it was offered to God, and also presently exists in an ever-present "now".

From God's perspective, that which is "everlasting" or "eternal" is that which is birthed in the Father's heart from eternity, finds its expression in time, and then returns to God. We have been bought back from sin's slave-market by that blood. Not only that, but also that blood has purchased back for us the entire inheritance that we lost in the fall of Adam. Revelation 5 celebrates the victory of the Lamb in opening the book, which is the title-deed, not only to the earth, but also to all of God's inheritance that was lost due to sin. The blood of Christ has purchased this for us as well. That is not to suggest for one moment that God was doing business with Satan when He bought us back, or when He redeemed the earth. We were temporarily sold into sin's slave-market, but it was from death that we have been redeemed. God's holiness had imprisoned us to death. The law had enslaved us (holy as it was) and we were imprisoned by the judgment of God. It was GOD who released us when Christ paid the ransom price, not Satan. And it was God who held the mortgage on the earth when man defaulted by sin. Consequently, it was God who restored to us all that Adam lost, and this God did through the blood of Christ's cross.

Christ made peace through the blood of His cross, according to Colossians 1:20. We are reconciled to God through His blood. The sin that caused the enmity between God and man has been eliminated. So, He made peace. All that we have in Christ, our reconciliation, redemption, forgiveness, justification, sanctification, peace and every other blessing is secured for us through the blood of Christ. His blood ushers us into heaven's throne room and gives us the confidence to worship God!

When we come to the book of Revelation we find several worship scenes portrayed for us. One of these is found in chapter seven:

After this I looked and there before me was a great multitude that no one could count, from every nation, tribe, people and language, standing before the throne and in front of the Lamb. They were wearing white robes and holding palm branches in their hands. And they cried out in a loud voice: "Salvation belongs to our God, who sits on the throne, and to the Lamb." All the angels were standing around the throne and around the elders and the four living creatures. They fell down on their faces before the throne and worshipped God, saying, 'Amen! Praise and glory and wisdom and thanks and honor and power and strength be to our God for ever and ever. Amen!" Then one of the elders asked me, "These in white robes—who are they and where did they come from?" I answered, "Sir, you know." And he said, "These are they who have come out of the great tribulation; they have washed their robes and made them white in the blood of the Lamb. Therefore, they are before the throne of God and serve him day and night in his temple; and he who sits on the throne will spread his tent over them. Never again will they hunger; never gain will they thirst. The sun will not beat upon them, nor any scorching heat. For the Lamb at the center of the throne will be their shepherd; he will lead them to springs of living water. And God will wipe away every tear from their eyes (Revelation 7:9-17 NIV).

I won't even attempt to consider the eschatological implications of the identity of those who have come through the great tribulation! It is not germane to the point I wish to make from the passage. It is impossible to view this worship scene without seeing the centrality of the Lamb of God. The worshippers have received salvation through the Lamb. They have washed their robes in His blood, and their garments of worship are made white. The Lamb of God is in the center of the throne before which they worship, and He is also their Shepherd who will lead them to springs of living water.

Our worship in heaven will be centered in the Lamb of God. We will ever behold Him whom John the Baptist saw and described as the One who came to take away the sin of the world (John 1:29, 36). Faith in His blood brings us into His presence, and there we are eternally reminded that the blood of the Lamb is the basis of our redemption.

3. WORSHIP INVOLVES FREEDOM FROM THE POWER OF SIN

Part of the preparation for the Passover involved the cleansing of the house from leaven. God was very specific in the command He gave to the Israelites in this regard.

> Celebrate the Feast of Unleavened Bread, because it was on this very day that I brought your divisions out of Egypt. Celebrate this day as a lasting ordinance for the generations to come. In the first month you are to eat bread made without yeast, from the evening of the fourteenth day until the evening of the twenty-first day. For seven days no yeast is to be found in your houses. And whoever eats anything with yeast in it must be cut off from the community of Israel, whether he is an alien or native born. Eat nothing with yeast. Wherever you live, you must eat unleavened bread (Exodus 12:17-20 NIV).

Leaven symbolizes sin, according to Paul's application of this concept found in the letter to the Corinthian church.

> Your boasting is not good. Don't you know that a little yeast works through the whole batch of dough? Get rid of the old yeast that you may be a new batch without yeast—as you really are. For Christ, our Passover lamb has been sacrificed. Therefore let us keep

the Festival, not with the old yeast, the yeast of malice and wicked-ness, but with bread without yeast, the bread of sincerity and truth (I Corinthians 5:6-8 NIV).

Paul makes a very strong case for leaven representing sin, and for the importance of cleansing our lives from that leaven of sin in order that we might truly celebrate Christ our Passover Lamb. It is in worship that we celebrate Christ. A very important part of worship is that cleansing that purges our lives before God.

This passage is sandwiched between two sections that deal spe-cifically with sexual sins in the church. "It is actually reported that there is sexual immorality among you, and such sexual immorality as is not even named among the Gentiles—that a man has his father's wife! And you are puffed up, and have not rather mourned, that he who has done this deed might be taken away from among you"(I Corinthains 5:1-2 NKJV)

Paul continues,

Even though I am not physically present, I am with you in spirit. And I have already passed judgment on the one who did this, just as it I were present. When you are assembled in the name of our Lord Jesus and I am with you in spirit, and the power of our Lord Jesus is present, band this man over to Satan, so that the sinful nature may be destroyed and his spirit saved on the day of the Lord (I Corinthians 5:1-5 NIV).

After Paul gives the exhortation concerning leaven that is found in verses six through eight, he continues:

I have written you in my letter not to associate with sexually immoral people—not at all meaning the people of this world who are immoral, or the greedy or swindlers, or idolaters. In that case you would have to leave this world. But now I am writing you that you must not associate with anyone who calls himself a brother but is sexually immoral or greedy, an idolater or a slanderer, a drunkard or a swindler. With such a man do not even eat. What business is it of mine to judge those outside the church? Are you not to judge those inside? God will judge those outside. Expel the wicked man from among you (I Corinthians 5:9-13 NIV).

It is important to keep in mind that the first epistle to the Corinthians deals with correcting many aspects of worship in the Corinthian church. Part of their problem in worship was the closing of their eyes to the sinful practices of members of their fellowship. This case is singled out by Paul as a prototype, a hallmark case that demonstrates God's attitude towards unrighteousness in the body of believers. God does this kind of thing early in the Book of Acts when he brought His judgment upon Ananias and Sapphira because they lied to the Holy Ghost, misrepresenting themselves in their financial giving. It seemed a rather severe punishment for something that we might consider so incidental, but again, God was presenting a flagship case so that we might understand that the church is to be pure.

The Corinthian passage teaches us that sexual uncleanness renders the worshipper spiritually impotent before God. This is true of all kinds of sin when it is allowed to go unconfessed, and unforsaken in the life of the believer. When our lives are cleansed from habitual sin, our worship is powerful and fulfilling, both to us and to God. But God focuses upon the sexual sins in this passage, and again in the next chapter:

Flee from sexual immorality. All other sins a man commits are outside his body, but he who sins sexually sins against his own body. Do you not know that your body is the temple of the Holy Spirit, who is in you, whom you have received from God? You are not your own; you were bought with a price. Therefore honor God with your body (I Corinthians 6:18-20 NIV).

In addressing this sin that Paul identifies as being one of the most serious, he summarily includes the whole scope of immorality as that which defiles the worshipper. In chapter six, he continues,

> Do you not know that the wicked will not inherit the kingdom of God? Do not be deceived: Neither the sexually immoral nor idolaters nor adulterers nor male prostitutes nor homosexual offenders nor thieves nor the greedy nor drunkards nor slanderers nor swindlers will inherit the kingdom of God (I Corinthians 6:9 NIV).

Paul goes on to remind them, "And this is what some of you were. But you were sanctified; you were justified in the name of the Lord Jesus Christ and by the Spirit of our God." (I Corinthians 6:11 NIV).

The leaven must be cleansed if our worship is to be pleasing to God. Paul again exhorts the Romans,

> Therefore, I urge you, brothers, in view of God's mercy, to offer your bodies as living sacrifices, holy and pleasing to God—which is your spiritual worship. Do not conform any longer to the pattern of this world, but be transformed by the renewing of your mind. Then you will be able to test and approve what God's will is—his good, pleasing, and perfect will (Romans 12:1-2 NIV).

It is the presentation of our bodies and beings to God as **holy** that **pleases Him**. This is the ridding of the leaven.

Paul develops for us in Romans the possibility of living free from the dominating power of sin in our lives. He assures us that this is God's will for us, and that it is possible as a result of the cross and resurrection. But he also insists that is takes place experientially only as we surrender our lives to the control of the indwelling Spirit of God.

It is only through the Spirit that we are enabled to mortify, or to put to death, the works of the flesh. We are powerless in the flesh to deal with the flesh! It must be the Holy Spirit's application of the provision of the cross that makes this a reality in our lives.

In fact, this particular aspect of worship is the principal emphasis of the New Testament epistles. When we embrace a larger theology of worship, we understand the significance of the Romans 12:1 passage cited above. It is one of the key and transitional texts. It distils into a few words what the entirety of the Christian life is. Our lives are to be rendered to God as worship. And as such, our lives must experience the transforming and cleansing power of God.

We can journey from one epistle to another and find this theme reiterated. In both chapters six and eight of Romans we are given the secret of living a life that is acceptable to God. Romans six presents the theological foundation, the cross of Christ, and the argument from the position of the believer in Christ. "For we know that our old self was crucified with him so that the body of sin might be rendered powerless, that we should no loner be slaves to sin—because anyone who has died has been freed from sin" (Romans 6:6-7 NIV). This is our position in Christ! Romans eight adds the dimension of the Holy Spirit as the enabler in our lives to make this happen. This presents the other practical aspect that goes beyond the positional aspect— the enabling capacity of the Holy Spirit.

But if Christ is in you, your body is dead because of sin, yet your spirit is alive because of righteousness. And if the Spirit of him who raised Jesus from the dead is living in you, he who raised Christ from the dead will also give life to your mortal bodies through his Spirit, who lives in you (Romans 8:10-11 NIV).

We have already noticed several of the Corinthian passages that deal with this aspect of our worship. To the church at Galatia, Paul continues this same theme,

> So I say, live by the Spirit and you will not gratify the sinful nature. For the sinful nature desires what is contrary to the Spirit, and the Spirit what is contrary to the sinful nature… Those who belong to Christ Jesus have crucified the sinful nature with its passions and desires. Since we live by the Spirit, let us keep in step with the Spirit (Galatians 5:16-17, 24-25 NIV).

Even in the Ephesian epistle, which ascends to loftier themes, Paul pursues this same truth.

> You, however, did not come to know Christ that way. Surely you heard of him and were taught in him in accordance with the truth that is in Jesus. You were taught, with regard to your former way of life, to put off your old self, which is being corrupted by its deceitful desires, to be made new in the attitude of your minds; and to put on the new self, created to be like God in true righteousness and holiness. Therefore each of you must put off falsehood and speak truthfully to his neighbor, for we are all members of one body. In your anger do not sin. Do not let the sun go down while you are still angry, and do not give the devil a foothold. He who has been stealing must steal no longer, but must work, doing something with his own hands, that he may have something to share with those in need. Do not let any unwholesome talk come out of your mouths, but only what is helpful to building others up according to their needs, that it may benefit those who listen. And do not grieve the Holy Spirit of God, with whom you were sealed for the day of redemption. Get rid of all bitterness, rage and anger, brawling and slander, along with every kind of malice. Be kind

and compassionate to one another, forgiving each other, just as in
Christ God forgave you (Ephesians 4:20-32 NIV).

God wants our worship to be an approach to Him that is characterized by "hearts sprinkled to cleanse us from a guilty conscience and
having our bodies washed with pure water" (Hebrews 10:22 NIV).
He not only forgives our sins, but also cleanses us from all unrighteousness. There flowed from the side of our Lord, both blood and
water, a "double cure" for the "double curse" of sin in heart and in
deed.

True worship must combine this element of freedom from the
world and the taint and tarnish of sin in our lives. This is further
illustrated by the fact that they could not properly celebrate the
Passover until they were out of Egypt and into the land that God
had promised. As long as we are living a worldly lifestyle, one that is
characterized by sin, we cannot properly worship God.

4. WORSHIP INVOLVES FEASTING ON THE LAMB OF GOD

When we look more closely at the Passover, we discover that the lamb
not only had to be killed, and its blood applied to the homes, but its
flesh must also be eaten by the Israelites. God commanded them to
roast the lamb over the fire, and to consume it in its entirety. No part
of the lamb was to be left uneaten.

The roasted lamb portrays to us the sufferings of Christ. He
endured the very horrors of hell in all of their terrible and torrid
torment. Jesus could not avoid the drinking of the cup whose bitter
dregs were the punishment for our sins.

Jesus suffered in spirit, soul and in body. There are several passages
in the narrative describing His passion and death that address the
psychological and emotional suffering that He endured for us. He

suffered the spiritual isolation from His Father. His physical body underwent the cruelest form of death known to man. Jesus was totally consumed in the sufferings of the cross.

The Israelites were required to eat all of the lamb. They could not elect to eat one portion and leave another. And so it is in our approach to feasting upon Christ, the Lamb of God. We cannot discriminate arbitrarily as to that portion of Christ that we may find most palatable to our taste. We are to feast upon the entire Lamb of God and be filled with all the goodness of God!

God told them to eat the lamb along with bitter herbs, a perpetual reminder of the bitterness of Egypt from which He had delivered them. For the believer, the herbs speak to the fact that feasting upon Christ involves repentance, confession, cleansing, purging. These may not always be sweet to our taste. "No discipline seems pleasant at the time, but painful. Later on, however, it produces a harvest of righteousness and peace for those who have been trained by it" (Hebrews 12:11 NIV).

God further instructed the Israelites to eat the Passover meal with their loins girt, and standing upon their feet. Theirs was to be a posture of pilgrimage, for they didn't know at what moment they might have to leave! May we learn from this, that while experiencing the joyous privilege of feasting upon Christ, God doesn't intend us to become too comfortable in the present moment. We are to eat having our loins girt with truth, and having on the whole armor of God But, most importantly, we are to have our feet shod with the preparation of the gospel of peace (Ephesians 6:10-17). Ours must also be a posture of pilgrimage, as we await the trumpet call, in the continual conviction that we are strangers upon this earth (Hebrews 11:13, I Peter 2:11).

We are to be feasting upon Christ, ready to go at any time, prepared for exodus, ready to move at His command, and never allowing our roots to become too firmly planted in this world.

God gave some further restrictions on the eating of the Passover meal that have interesting implications for our lives. No slave could eat of it. This teaches us that only when one is free from the bondage of sin, can he truly enjoy feasting upon Christ. A foreigner or stranger could not partake unless circumcised and proselytized to the Jewish faith. Only those who have come into the family of God by being born again can truly feast upon Christ. And finally, it was to be eaten inside of the house. Feasting upon the Lamb of God is a privilege that belongs uniquely to the household of faith.

Those New Testament passages that deal with the eating of Christ's flesh and drinking of His blood are difficult to understand. We do know that when we partake of the Lord's Table there is nothing mystical that takes place. The bread and wine do not mysteriously become the body and blood of Christ. When we partake of the table of the Lord, we declare the efficacy of His death and anticipate His return. Yet, feasting on the Lamb of God is something that happens to us by another dynamic. Jesus said,

> I tell you the truth, unless you eat the flesh of the Son of Man and drink his blood, you have no life in you. Whoever eats my flesh and drinks my blood has eternal life, and I will raise him up at the last day; for my flesh is real food and my blood is real drink. Whoever eats my flesh and drinks my blood remains in me, and I in him. Just as the living Father sent me and I live because of the Father, so the one who feeds on me will live because of me. This is the bread that came down from heaven. Our forefathers ate manna and died, but he who feeds on this bread will live forever (John 6:53-58 NIV).

It was at this point that many of his disciples said, "This is a hard teaching. Who can accept it" (John 6:60 NIV)? "From this time many of his disciples turned back and no longer followed him (John 6:66 NIV). Jesus continued, "The Spirit gives life; the flesh counts for nothing. The words I have spoken to you are spirit and they are life" (John 6:63 NIV).

Jesus is teaching us that just as He lived on the Father's words, so we are to live on His words. When we feast upon the Word of God, we are feasting upon the Lamb of God. When we partake of the living Word, we are partaking of the living Lamb. We are to assimilate His life and nature into our beings as we feast upon the Lamb of God.

The Lamb of God is central to our worship now and will be throughout all eternity. It is the Lamb who has redeemed us and we are saved by faith in His Blood. It is the Lamb who frees us from the power of sin by His own indwelling Presence. And it is the Lamb upon whom we feast as we worship around the Word of God. Cleansed and redeemed by the blood, filled with the Lamb of God, we await His return. When we are united with Him finally in glory, we will become the "Lamb's wife" and live forever with Him in the "city where the Lamb is the light."

Worship Him, for worthy is the Lamb that was slain. Our song in heaven will be, "You are worthy to take the scroll and to open its seals, because you were slain, and with your blood you purchased men for God from every tribe and language and people and nation. You have made them to be a kingdom and priests to serve our God, and they will reign on the earth" (Revelation 5:9-10 NIV).

11

A SONG AND DANCE ON THE RED SEA BANKS

When natural music is sharpened and polished by art, then one begins to see with amazement the great and perfect wisdom of God in His wonderful work of music.

—Martin Luther

Then Moses and the Israelites sang this song to the LORD: "I will sing to the LORD, for he is highly exalted... The horse and its rider he has hurled into the sea. The LORD is my strength and my song; he has become my salvation. He is my God, and I will praise him, my father's God, and I will exalt him... Your right hand, O LORD, was majestic in power. Your right hand, O LORD, shattered the enemy... Who among the gods is like you, O LORD? Who is like you—majestic in holiness, awesome in glory, working wonders? In your unfailing love you will lead the people you have redeemed. In your strength you will guide them to your holy dwelling... You will bring them in and plant them on the mountain of your inheritance" (Exodus 15:1-18 NIV).

n *Doxology,* Geoffrey Wainwright writes, "Singing is the most genuinely popular element in Christian worship. Familiar words and music, whether they are repeated response to biddings in a litany or the well-known phrases of a hymn, unite the whole assembly in active participation to a degree which is hardly true of any other component in the liturgy."[50]

1600 years ago Augustine remarked that prior to his conversion the most impressive element of the Christian service that left an indelible impression upon his memory was the hymn-singing of the congregation that was assembled together.[51] Augustine eloquently stated, "How greatly did I weep in Thy hymns and canticles, deeply moved by the voices of Thy sweet-speaking Church! The voices flowed into mine ears, and the truth poured forth into my heart, whence the agitation of my piety overflowed, and blessed was I therein."[52]

Hymns were not always used to convey the "orthodox" message of Christianity, however. Often, aberrational views from traditional interpretation were propagated through singing as well. Yet, the great truths of the Reformation were not only preached, but also sung by Martin Luther, who was not only an exceptional theologian, but also a gifted hymnist.[53] As well, the Methodist movement was born in song, and who can match the 6,500 songs written by Charles Wesley[54], or the 750 anthems composed by one of Spurgeon's favorite hymnists, Isaac Watts[55]?

The passage before us, the song of Moses recorded in Exodus fifteen, is the earliest of sacred songs in the history of Israel, and also

---

50 Wainwright, Geoffrey. *Doxology: The Praise of God in Worship, Doctrine and Life.* Oxford: Oxford University Press, 1984.

51 St. Augustine, *A Select Library of the Nicene and Post-Nicene Fathers of the Christian Church, Volume VI, The Confessions and Letters of St. Augustine,* Edited by Philip Schaff, D.D., L.L. D, Grand Rapids: Eerdmans Publishing Company.

52 ibid

53 Pick, Bernard. *Luther as a Hymnist.* Philadelphia, 1875: Publisher Unknown, Public Domain.

54 www.songsandhymns.com/Brix?pageID=7130

55 https://hymnary.org/person/Watts_Isaac

the foremost in their worship. In fact, for the Jewish people them-selves, this song came to be known as "**The Song**." It must have been one of God's favorites as well, for when we arrive at the grand finale in Revelation, this song re-appears. The Song of Moses is harmonized with that of the Lamb as the great anthem of the people of God in the ages to come! (see Revelation 15:3)

This song of Moses is a great proto-type for all music in Christian worship. But before we look at it from this perspective, we need to consider some aspects of the song itself.

1. Firstly, the song of Moses was Israel's natal or "birth" song. It was in the crossing of the Red Sea, that they passed through the birth throes of their national existence. From this epoch, a new chronology in their calendar was begun. While it is true that the nation of Israel existed when they were still in Egypt, the divine purpose was not realized until they came through the "birth of the water" as they left Egypt and its bondage behind.

2. But it was more than their birth song. It was also their eman-cipation song, their song of liberty. It signals a triple deliverance. It marked the supreme moment of their rescue from the evils of domestic slavery, political bondage, and religious enslavement. Finally, they were free! And freedom is one of the things that belongs to Abraham's children. It is a freedom song!

3. Thirdly, the song of Moses was Israel's first National Anthem. For Israel, the song of Moses was their National Anthem! How their hearts would thrill when it was lifted by the voices of their fellow Isra-elites. Although they could not yet appreciate that what was about to happen to them would become a mighty religious movement, yet they recognized that this was a repetition on a larger scale of the migration of Abram from Ur of the Chaldees. It was a larger re-enactment of his breaking away from the idolatrous and superstitious worship of pagans to find a home for the free development of a higher creed and true worship.

But it was more than a national anthem. For the Exodus was not a mere effort on the part of the Hebrew race to achieve their independence. It was not just their idea to realize their aspirations of being a separate nationality. The spirit of this idea had yet to be created in them. But everything depended upon their being delivered from the corrupting influences of Egyptian idolatry and bondage. So it had to be an act of **God**.

4. Therefore, this song become Israel's "Te Deum," or song of praise to God! It is not just a war-song, or a song of patriotic triumph! It is not a shriek of insult over a fallen foe. It is an anthem of blessing and gratitude for a great deliverance by the hand of God. It does not have a strain of vindictiveness or vainglory within it.

Therefore, it became Israel's "Church-song," the prototype of all songs of redemption and salvation. In fact, these very words are first introduced in connection with this event. "I will **redeem** you with an outstretched arm; stand still and see the **salvation** of the Lord" (Exodus 14:13). It was through this event, and in this song, that the people became unified into a worshipping assembly.

But it is also the forerunner to the final and glorious epilogue of praise and worship at the end of the ages, when the spiritual Israel, which no man can number, from every people, tribe, and language, "having got the victory over the beast, and over his image, and over his mark, and over the number of his name," (Revelation 15:2) shall take up their position, not on the shores of the Red Sea, but by the sea of glass mingled with fire. This choir will not be led by Miriam and her chorus, but all of them with the harp of God will be singing the song of Moses and of the Lamb" (Revelation 15:3). This will be the ultimate worship experience, for which God is now preparing us!

As we look at the Song of Moses as a worship experience, we will discover how our singing can be worship to God. It was Augustine who said that a hymn is "a song with praise to God."[56] With this as a beginning, we shall discover that singing is worship when the song is **to** the Lord, **of** the Lord, and **for** the Lord.

I. WORSHIP IS SINGING TO THE LORD

Moses' song begins with the words, "I will sing to the Lord." We could interpret the words of Moses as saying, "I will bring myself into the immediate and felt presence of Jehovah, and sing my song directly to Him!" Moses has sensed the nearness of God throughout the night. The presence of God that was promised to Moses has accompanied him through the long night of the Red Sea crossing. The awareness of God's presence and nearness is a pre-requisite for this kind of worship. If God is afar off, remotely removed in His heaven, while we are struggling down here on earth, then it is difficult to sing to Him in this way. But when His presence is recognized, when His nearness is acknowledged, you can sing to Him.

The Church needs to realize and practice this when we assemble in the Lord's house. God is in our hearts, as well as in the particular location. Therefore, even inaudibly, we can be "making melody in our hearts" unto the Lord, and He will hear us! It is not the loudness or shrillness of our singing that comprises worship, but rather the

---

56   St. Augustine, *A Select Library of the Nicene and Post-Nicene Fathers of the Christian Church, Volume IX, The Confessions and Letters of St. Augustine*, Edited by Philip Schaff, D.D., L.L. D, Grand Rapids: Eerdmans Publishing Company.

cognizance of His presence, which enables us to render the song to Him.

If our singing is to the Lord, then it is a sacrifice, an oblation to Him. Since our worship is poured out to Him, it cannot be a mere self-pleasing exercise of our gifts, abilities and talents. Paul instructs us, "Speak to one another with psalms, hymns, and spiritual songs. Sing and make music in your heart to the Lord, always giving thanks to God the Father for everything, in the name of our Lord Jesus Christ" (Ephesians 5:19-20 NIV). This same direction of worship is reiterated in another passage, "Let the word of Christ dwell in you richly as you teach and admonish one another with all wisdom, and as you sing psalms, hymns and spiritual songs with gratitude in your hearts to God (Colossians 3:16 NIV).

Worship is **multilingual**! **Prayer** is the *language of desire* in worship. **Singing** is the *language of joy*! It is the worship of joy, just as fasting is the worship of repentance. When singing becomes worship to God, it will be more than *descriptive*. It will be *ascriptive* as well. Exodus 15:6-8 ceases to talk about God, and directs the worship to God. In the first part of the song, Moses is talking about what God has done, and what God means to him. Moses says,

> He is highly exalted. The horse and its rider he has hurled into the sea. The LORD is my strength and my song; he has become my salvation. He is my God, and I will praise him, my father's God, I will exalt him. The LORD is a warrior; the LORD is his name. Pharaoh's chariots and his army he has hurled into the sea. The best of Pharaoh's officers are drowned in the Red Sea. The deep waters have covered them; they sank to the depths like a stone (Exodus 15:1-5 NIV).

The details of this deliverance are important to Israel. This heritage of their salvation will be passed on to future generations through this song of Moses. But in the next passage, Moses begins to address God directly,

> Your right hand, O Lord, was majestic in power. Your right hand, O Lord, shattered the enemy. In the greatness of your majesty you threw down those who opposed you. You unleashed your burning anger; it consumed them like stubble. By the blast of your nostrils the waters piled up. The surging waters stood firm like a wall; the deep waters congealed in the heart of the sea (Exodus 15:6-8 NIV).

There is something about the exercise of rehearsing the goodness of God in descriptive terms that prompts us to direct our worship to God. As we reflect upon His mercies, His kindness, His grace, His goodness and His provision in our lives, we are suddenly aware of His presence! Praise makes us aware of God's presence. I cannot say that praise takes us into God's presence. Experientially, this is so. But theologically, it is not! Let me explain. When we begin to praise God, we suddenly sense that we have "entered" His presence. And as far as we are concerned, we have. But, in fact, what has happened is that we are now more acutely aware of His presence. Our eyes have been opened, our ears have been loosed, and our beings have become attentively attuned to Him.

But we have already been in the presence of God, for the blood of Christ brought us in. So, theoretically, we don't enter God's presence *by* our praise, but **with** our praise. There is a difference. And I believe it is infinitely more than a moot point or mere semantics for this reason. If we could enter the presence of God *by* our praise, then our praise would have meritorious value, resulting in a subtle form of legalism. We are already seated in the heavenlies in Christ. We have been brought into the holiest of all by the blood of Jesus. Our praise is a drink offering that is poured out to God in appreciation of this fact, and in adoration of and to the God who in His grace has redeemed us. Through praise and worship we become increasingly aware that we are in His presence. Consequently, we no longer merely speak or sing about Him. We begin to speak or sing to Him! This is what worship is all about. It is communion with the Infinite. It is enjoying the presence of the Divine.

This dynamic of worship is extremely important. Have you ever noticed that those songs or choruses, which are in the first person to God, seem to bring a much greater awareness of His nearness? For example, when you sing, "Thou art worthy,"[57] or "I love you Lord, and I lift my voice,"[58] you sense that God is right there with you. Although there are times when our worship needs to be descriptive, or even instructive, this level of worship in singing creates a sense of intimacy with God that is very powerful.

Our singing becomes worship when it is directed to God! When we become so caught up in His majesty, His magnificence, His wonder, His glory, His greatness and His grace, it is no longer adequate to sing *about* Him. We find that we must address our song **to** the Lord.

I first stumbled on this truth years ago when I was preaching from Psalm 45, where the Psalmist writes, "My heart is stirred by a noble theme as I recite my verses for the king; my tongue is the pen of a skilful writer" (Psalm 45:1 NIV). Immediately, the Psalmist does not speak about the King, but to the King,

> You are the most excellent of men and your lips have been anointed with grace, since God has blessed you forever. Gird your sword upon your side, O mighty one; clothe yourself with splendor and majesty. In your majesty ride forth victoriously in

---

57   Mills, Pauline M. *Thou Art Worthy.* Tarzana, CA: Fred Bock Music Co., 1963,1965.

58   Klein, Laurie. *I Love You Lord and I Lift My Voice.* Costa Mesa, CA: Maranatha Music, 1978, 1980.

behalf of truth, humility and righteousness; let your right hand display awesome deeds. Let your sharp arrows pierce the hearts of the king's enemies; let the nations fall beneath your feet. Your throne, O God, will last for ever and ever; a scepter of justice will be the scepter of your kingdom. You love righteousness and hate wickedness; therefore God, your God, has set you above your companions by anointing you with the oil of joy. All your robes are fragrant with myrrh and aloes and cassia; from palaces adorned with ivory the music of the strings makes you glad (Psalm 45:2-9 NIV).

The Psalmist begins writing about the King, but soon is addressing the King Himself. Later in the Psalm, he instructs the daughter to worship the King, for the King desires her beauty. This Psalm is a powerful worship expression, both in its ascriptive praise, as well as in the symbolism of Christ and the Church. Worship is singing praise to the Lord!

Moses continues his song to the Lord in verse 11 of Exodus 15,

Who among the gods is like you, O LORD? Who is like you—majestic in holiness, awesome in glory, working wonders? You stretched out your right hand and the earth swallowed them. In your unfailing love you will lead the people you have redeemed. In your strength you will guide them to your holy dwelling. The nations will hear and tremble; anguish will grip the people of Philistia. The chiefs of Edom will be terrified, the leaders of Moab will be seized with trembling, the people of Canaan will melt away; terror and dread will fall upon them. By the power of your arm they will be as still as a stone—until your people pass by, O LORD, until the people you bought pass by. You will bring them in and plant them on the mountain of your inheritance——the place, O Lord you made for your dwelling, the sanctuary, O Lord, your hands established (Exodus 15:11-17 NIV).

In this passage Moses advances the promises of God in a very personal way for His people. He is affirming God's stated and intended purpose, reiterating in worship both what God *has done* and *will do* in the future.

There is a school of thought that distinguishes between praise and worship by saying that praise describes the deeds of God while worship is our response to His character. That character is demonstrated by His deeds. We worship God in the adoration of His person as well as in the praise of His deeds. To apply the term "worship" strictly to the adoration of God's person, and the term "praise" to His works is to reduce "worship" to far too small a minimum and to a much narrower understanding than what worship is by Biblical definition. Worship is much more all-encompassing than this concept would allow.

The exhortation to sing to the Lord is repeated over and again throughout the Scriptures. When David brought the ark back, his declaration of praise was, "Sing **to** the LORD, all the earth; proclaim his salvation day after day" (I Chronicles 16:23 NIV). Psalm 30:4 commands us, "Sing **to** the Lord, you saints of his; praise his holy name." Throughout the Psalms we read such instructions as, "Come, let us sing for joy **to** the Lord…Sing **to** the LORD a new song; sing to the LORD, all the earth, sing **to** the LORD, praise His name…Sing **to** the LORD with thanksgiving; make music to our God on the harp…(Psalms 30:4; 5:1; 96:1-2; 147:1, **emphasis** mine).

Psalm 33:1-3 tells us, "Sing joyfully **to** the LORD, you righteous; it is fitting for the upright to praise him. Praise the

LORD with the harp; make music to him on the ten-stringed lyre. Sing to him a new song; play skillfully, and shout for joy." Psalm 68:32 encourages us, "Sing **to** God, O kingdoms of the earth, sing praise to the LORD." In Psalm 71:22-23, the Psalmist writes, "I will sing praise **to** you with the lyre, O Holy One of Israel. My lips will shout for joy when I sing praise **to** you...I, whom you have redeemed." Psalm 98:4-6 tells us, "Shout for joy **to** the LORD, all the earth, burst into jubilant song with music; make music **to** the LORD with the harp, with the harp and the sound of singing, with trumpets and the blast of the ram's horn—shout for joy before the LORD, the King." (**emphasis** mine)

David's heart, the heart of a worshipper, is expressed powerfully in his exclamation, "I will sing **to** the LORD all my life; I will sing praise **to** my God as long as I live. May my meditation be pleasing to him, as I rejoice **in** the LORD" (Psalm 104:33 NIV **emphasis** mine).

The song of Moses acknowledges the whole person and character of God. It does not exaggerate any one aspect of His character at the expense of another. Moses' God is "majestic in holiness." The holiness of God is described. He details and delineates the execution of God's righteousness and equity. And at the same time, God's unfailing love is described by Moses. "In your unfailing love you will lead your people you have redeemed; and in your strength you will guide them to your holy dwelling." God is not only holy and loving, He is powerfully strong!

The theme of redemption causes worship to be released from the depth of my being. When I contemplate the grace and mercy of Christ, and focus upon the work of His cross, I have no problem directing my worship to Him. Sing to the Lord, He is worthy of praise!

2. WORSHIP IS SINGING OF (ABOUT) THE LORD

While most people will agree that singing to the Lord constitutes worship, some will argue that singing of the Lord is not worship, but merely "praise." As I pointed out earlier, for me, that definition of worship is much too small. I believe that praise is very much a part of worship, but that worship is much larger than any one aspect of our Christian devotion and discipline. Worship, for the believer, is all of life. Even our labors, when done "unto the Lord" are an act of worship to God. The realization of this truth is tremendously liberating to the child of God!

The LORD is not only the **object** of our song of worship, but He is also the **subject**. One of the interesting things about this song is its title—the "Song of Moses." Moses is not mentioned in the song! His name doesn't appear at all, and Moses neither explicitly nor implicitly refers to himself. Not a word about Moses. The song is totally about the LORD, and His faithfulness in His dealings with His people! "The LORD is my strength and my song." Forget men, forget time, forget earth, forget this mortal life, and think only of Him! Let your heart and mind and total being become absorbed in the glorious reality of His person.

The song dwells upon what God has done! God has thrown the horse and rider into the sea. Moses didn't do it. The children of Israel didn't do it. God did it! Moses talks about God in metaphorical language, "The LORD is a warrior." The whole song is filled with the mighty deeds of God.

Worship becomes abstract if it is not incarnationally related. What do we mean by that? For some people, worship is a mystical something that happens somewhere beyond praise. To them, praise is the preliminary in which you focus upon what God has done. In this concept, praise is a kind of "warm-up" for worship. It suggests that after you move beyond His deeds, somehow, mysteriously, you come into that indefinable thing that they call "worship." But this is not Biblical worship.

Biblical worship is not mysticism! Jesus said, "You Samaritans worship what you do not know; we worship what we do know, for salvation is from the Jews" (John 4:22 NIV). On Mars Hill, when Paul saw the image erected to the unknown God, he said, "Now what you worship as something unknown I am going to proclaim to you" (Acts 17:23 NIV).

Closely related to the worship of the Jewish people was the intervention of God in their history. God is not abstract. God is incarnate. The whole purpose of the incarnation is to bring God down to us. And we worship Christ in the glory of what He has done. To say that ascriptive or descriptive praise is less than worship is missing the mark. We worship God as we adore Him for the wonderful Person that He is. We worship Him for the redemptive love that He has exhibited to us in His incarnational involvement. It is this feature that was celebrated by Israel in their special festivals and celebrations of worship. Worship must have that incarnational aspect, or it will be too abstract to be real.

Don't buy the idea that worship happens when you move beyond the concentration upon God's deeds. His person and character are demonstrated and illustrated to us in His deeds. This is neither narcissistic nor man-centered worship. Rather, it is exalting God for all that He is and all that He has done for us, the object of His love and grace.

Moses not only worships God for what **He** *has done*. He also worships God for what **He** *will yet do*! I love this part of the song, for it says something of Moses' relationship with God. His terms with God were intimate enough to know the details of God's plan, character and being well enough to predict what God would do in the preservation of His people. God does not weary of our rehearsing His promise and covenant with us in His presence. He loves for us to affirm this when we worship Him. In fact, this is what the word "confess" in the New Testament actually means. Profession in the King James Version is the Greek word "homologia," meaning to say the same thing as God is saying, or to agree with God.

When, in our worship time before the Lord, we affirm and reiterate His promises, we are agreeing with God. What God will do is dictated by what and who He is. It is out of His character that His acts will flow. He will not fail us, for He is God! One could take this one stanza of Moses' song, and develop a whole *repertoire* of praise and worship to God. "He will lead us because of His unfailing love." Therefore, *He will not leave us*, because of His unfailing love. *He will not cast us off*, because of His unfailing love. *He will not withhold His blessing* from us, because of His unfailing love.

The LORD is my strength. Now I usually sing that when I am weak! But Moses sang it upon the heels of a great victory. We need to remind ourselves of God's strength, in not only the moments of our weakness, but also when we have just triumphed victoriously in Him. When things are going well, we tend to take much of the credit ourselves, and fail to acknowledge that God did it all for us. Moses would not allow the people to give him the credit. He made sure that God was declared to be strong, and Jehovah received the glory for the victory!

The LORD is also my song. Literally, this means, the LORD is the giver of song. He breathes music into the hearts of HIS people. He is the Creator of joy. He is the subject of our songs. He is the object of our songs. He is the author of our songs. We sing of Him and all that He has done for us. The LORD is my song!

The chapter starts off by saying, "*Then* sang Moses..."(*emphasis mine*) The moment of realized salvation was after a great deliverance. Moses sang initially then Miriam led the whole congregation in a song of praise to God. Our worship experience needs to be like this. It is personal and individual, but it also shared. We are not prima donnas. Worship is not a solo act. We join our hearts and our voices in praise to God. It is both personal and corporate. Moses says, "I will sing," and "MY strength," but the whole of the congregation must share in this experience. David employs this same technique when in Psalm 124 he says, "If the LORD had not been on our side—let Israel say—if the Lord had not been on our side…" (Psalm 124:1-2 NIV).

There are striking parallels between the experience of Israel in the Red Sea crossing, and our redemption and deliverance from sin. In both cases, there was a deliverance from the terrible danger of death. It was an inevitable danger, universal and terrifying. In each case, the deliverance was by glorious and miraculous intervention. With Israel, as well as with us, the deliverance was accomplished, notwithstanding the sin of the people. While we were yet sinners, Christ died for us (Romans 5:8). In each case, deliverance was accomplished by the power of God alone without any room for human merit or boasting. And with Israel and the believer in Christ, the deliverance grants great promises for the future. May our song of worship be of the LORD and of His greatness!

3. WORSHIP IS SINGING FOR THE LORD

Singing **to** the Lord and **of** the Lord are not mutually exclusive. The song of praise can be both *of* and *to* the Lord. For Augustine, one of the qualifying factors to constitute a song a "hymn" was "a song of praise to God."[59] God is the center of worship. The words of Isaac Watts have been considered to be the greatest single sentence in any hymn: "God is a name my soul adores."[60] Ralph Martin says "Watts is perpetuating and enlarging the tradition that goes back to the period of the Greek-speaking church whose 'most remarkable characteristic of... hymnody is its objectiveness."[61] In his "Dictionary of Hymnology," Julian wrote,

> Whether the theme be the mystery of the Triune Godhead or the Incarnation, or the mighty periods of Christ's incarnate work in earth or heaven; or whether some life or narrative of Holy Writ, considered in its doctrinal or typical reference—the attitude of the poet is always one of self-forgetful, rapt, or ecstatic contemplation.[62]

This factor is extremely important in our worship. Worship is for God. The music must not be enjoyed as an end in itself; its function is to bring the worshipper to an awareness of God's divine presence. The fear of pre-occupation with music in and of itself has caused some groups to remove instrumental music from their worship.

The song of Moses was to exalt and glorify the Lord. It was for Him. In singing, we are able to express our praise to God in a manner not possible in ordinary speech. And we do this to glorify God.

Certainly, there is a dynamic of fellowship that is present when we sing together. The sense of harmony is singing helps to promote the *koinonia*, which we are to experience when we assemble together to worship. But the primary focus of our worship is for God. We are singing, praising, and glorifying Him in our worship. If our singing

---

59   St. Augustine, *A Select Library of the Nicene and Post-Nicene Fathers of the Christian Church, Volume IX, The Confessions and Letters of St. Augustine*, Edited by Philip Schaff, D.D., L.L. D, Grand Rapids: Eerdmans Publishing Company.

60   Watts, Isaac. *God Is the Name My Soul Adores*. 1706. Melody, *Janes*, Wolfgang A. Mozart.

61   Martin, Ralph P. *Worship in the Early Church*. London: Marshall, Morgan and Scott. 1964.

62   Julian, John. *Dictionary of Hymnology*. London: John Murray, 1892.

is to be worthy, it must have the same objective as that of Moses, not to entertain, but to exalt and glorify the Lord.

As believers, we do not sing for entertainment. The American Heritage Dictionary defines entertainment as, "Something that amuses, pleases, or diverts, especially a performance or show."[63] As the people of God, this is not our purpose for singing. We sing for the Lord.

In fact, we don't even sing to lift people up, to excite them, to edify them, to build them up or even to inspire them. This may indeed happen in the process of singing worship to God, but this is not the goal. It happens as the by-product of lifting up Christ in our singing.

If we exalt Christ, and lift Him up, He has promised that He will draw people to Him. We are lifted up, when we lift Him up. When He is exalted, we are lifted up, edified, and drawn up into Him!

To extol and to exalt the LORD is declared to be the ultimate end and aim of this song of Moses. This is the highest reach and the final purpose of all praise. Singing is worship when its goal is to manifest and express the Divine character, the Divine working and ways and the Divine glory and honor of God.

Glorifying God is the purpose for which we exist, and is declared to be the occupation of redeemed humanity and angelic beings for all of eternity. We magnify the Lord. Mary said, "My soul magnifies the Lord" (Luke 1:46). To magnify is to make larger! Christ is magnified, made larger in our praise and worship, when our song it **to, of** or **for Him.**

This approach to worship doesn't ask the question, "What will I get out of worship?" but rather "What will God get out of this act of

63 *The American Heritage® Dictionary of the English Language, Fourth Edition*, Boston, MA: Copyright ©2000 by Houghton Mifflin Company.

worship?" Worship is for God. Our singing is for God. All that we do in word and deed is to be done in the name of the Lord Jesus, giving thanks unto God and the Father by Him.

4. WHAT SHOULD WE SING

The song of Moses teaches us a number of lessons concerning the role of singing in worship, and demonstrates the prerequisites that cause our singing to truly constitute worship. It establishes both a pattern and precedent for music that is more fully developed in the kingdom age of the Old Testament. Moses' song is the first recorded song in the Scriptures, although it is commonly held that on the morning of creation the morning stars sang together (Job 38:7).

At the dedication of Solomon's temple there was much music. There were choirs and other instrumental musical contributions.

> All the priests who were musicians… stood on the east side of the altar, dressed in fine linen and playing cymbals, harps and lyres. They were accompanied by 120 priests sounding trumpets. The trumpeters and singers joined in unison, as with one voice, to give praise and thanks to the LORD. Accompanied by trumpets, cymbals and other instruments, they raised their voices in praise to the LORD and sang: "He is good; his love endures forever." Then the temple of the LORD was filled with a cloud, and the priests could not perform their service because of the cloud, for the glory of the LORD filled the temple of God (II Chronicles 5:12-14 NIV).

It is difficult to determine the precise era of time in which the Psalms were used as the Psalter or songbook of Israel. Most scholars believe that there were different timeframes for different psalms. For example, such psalms as 24, 118, and 136 are thought by some to belong to the period of Solomon's temple, while others have seen these as part of the hymnbook of the second Jewish temple. Attempts have been made to assign specific time periods to most of the Psalms. But one thing is certain, these were sung by the people of God as representative of their experiences, reflecting their praise and worship of God in the normality of their lives.

Although many of the Psalms do not have a specific situation attached to them, they do represent the full spectrum of human experience with its highs and lows. At times they are individual expressions, and at other times they represent corporate experiences. It is sometimes difficult to ascertain where the two interface or overlap. Obviously, the psalms of thanksgiving and praise are both timely and timeless. And the songs of ascent and pilgrimage are also timely and timeless, doubtlessly relating the journeys of God's people up to the temple for the special festivals and celebrations of worship.

However, woven into the fabric of the Psalms is one common thread. It is the strand and strain of the revelation of Jehovah in all of the events in Israel's history. God is seen in all that happens, and Jehovah's redemptive power is acclaimed and proclaimed. It is a record of man in his every day human experience interacting with God. It is God's involvement, the Divine interest, the Sovereign intervention and compassionate concern of God in the normal experiences of life.

Perhaps the majesty of the Psalms is this incarnational aspect. God is involved in the daily routine of their living. No lid is placed upon the honesty of human expression: doubt, guilt, and grief are there—but at the same time, God enables humankind to triumphantly transcend all of life's vicissitudes, because He is involved with His creation.

5. PSALMS, HYMNS, AND SPIRITUAL SONGS

It seems obvious that singing was an integral part of the worship of the New Testament church. Paul, in two separate passages, speaks of the use of "psalms, hymns, and spiritual songs." Many different possibilities have been offered as to the distinction of each of these three. Although it is difficult to definitely ascertain the precise boundaries between each, it may be helpful to look at each in the context of where the New Testament church was.

It doesn't require a great deal of insight to interpret what is meant by "psalms." We have already considered the Psalter in brief, but it needs to be taken into the context of Christian worship. An interesting feature in this regard is the usage of the writer to the Hebrews of the passage in Psalm 22:22 in application to Christ, "So Jesus is not ashamed to call them brothers. He says, 'I will declare your name to my brothers; in the presence of the congregation I will sing your praises'" (Hebrews 2:12 NIV). In this passage Christ is seen as leading the singing of worship to God. We will later discover that the New Testament writers will also see Jesus as the celebrated theme of song, as well as the ultimate celebrant of praise! Christ becomes the celebrated and the celebrant in New Testament singing.

Very early in the history of the New Testament church, passages from the Psalms were used both apologetically and theologically, as we discover in the preaching of Peter on the day of Pentecost. But they also found the Psalms useful as a means of spiritual strength and sustenance in their normal, everyday Christian experience. James exhorts them, "Is any one of you in trouble? He should pray. Is anyone happy? Let him sing songs of praise" (James 5:13 NIV). It is interesting to note that the Greek form of the verb "sing" used by James in this passage means to play the harp! Many of the Psalms were Messianic, as well as life-situational, and thus the doctrine of Christianity was conveyed in their use in singing.

"Hymns" probably referred to those songs of worship that were tributes directed to God. Some prime examples are the canticles of praise found in the scenes surrounding the birth of Christ as recorded by Luke in the first two chapters of his gospel. Mary's "Magnificat," Zachariah's "Benedictus," the angels' "Gloria," and Simeon's "Nunc Dimittis" are examples of worship ascribed to God in sacred song. These four are powerful Scriptural examples of true worship in singing. The magnificence and majesty of God expressed in these songs is powerful!

I am awed by the overwhelming grace of God in how He gives us song. It was during a period of my life when I was at my lowest spiritual ebb that God put song in my heart. Although pastoring at the time, I was wrestling with personal issues in my life when the first worship song came to me. I was in an early morning prayer meeting with our pastoral staff. I had opened the Bible to Psalm 63, and began to pray the prayer of the Psalmist, "O God, you are my God, earnestly I seek you; my soul thirsts for you, my body longs for you, in a dry and weary land where there is no water" (Psalm 63:1). Something was sparked within me that caused me to pray the Psalmist's prayer. Later, as I sat at the piano with my Bible open, the Lord gave the music. This is a chorus of desire and prayer, of petition and supplication that is directed TO GOD. And it represented the cry of my heart in a very desperate time and place.

Around this same time I often found it difficult to pray. However, when I couldn't pray, I could praise and worship God. And through the vehicle of song I could communicate my heart to God, and sense the presence of God as He ministered to me. One of the earlier Scripture choruses that I wrote was based on the words of Christ:

My house shall be called a house of prayer for all the nations
My house shall be a pure and holy place
My house shall be called a house of power, grace and healing
My house shall be filled with my children's praise[64]

While studying the experience of Moses when summoned to the mountain by God in Exodus 33, I was struck by his dual requests to God, first to show him God's way, and then to behold God's glory. In comtemplation of the blessedness of his experience with God in the mountain, I wrote:

Show me Your glory, Lord,
Shine your blessed presence on my face;
Hide me in the cleft of the rock,
Come and show your glory in this place.[65]

Other choruses came to me as I prepared a sermon series on the songs of Christmas. Beginning with Mary's song, and including the songs of Zechariah, the angels, and Simeon, I brought a series of messages of the music of Christmas. For each of them, the Lord put a song in my heart. Again, the most amazing aspect of this experience for me was that God had birthed song in my life during the darkest night of my soul.

It was several years later that God gave me a song of deliverance. I had left the pastorate, had suffered significant losses in life and in business. My wife and I were going through a divorce, and I was driving to New Brunswick to be with my mother who had suffered a stroke. As my heart cried out to God, this song was born in my heart:

---

64   Words and music© by Donald M. Carmont
65   Ibid.

The God that I serve will deliver me;
Yes the God that I serve will deliver me
Heat the furnace seven times
Throw me to the hungry lions
For the God that I serve will deliver me.
The God that I serve will deliver me;
Yes the God that I serve will deliver me
To thy gods I won't bow down
For Jehovah wears the crown
And the God that I serve will deliver me.
The God that I serve will deliver me;
Yes the God that I serve will deliver me
I'll refuse the devil's meat
At God's table I will eat
For the God that I serve will deliver me.[66]

Several months later I settled in Toronto and began to rebuild my life. The business plan that I had hoped to materialize had fallen through. I had no income, and was living in borrowed accommodations, with very few possessions. As I was reading the New Testament out loud a new song was born in my heart:

Father knows, Father knows,
I'm so glad I know my heavenly Father knows,
Father knows what's best, so I'll leave the rest to him,
I'm so glad I know my heavenly Father knows.
See the lilies of the field and how he clothes them,
Earthly kings in all their glory can't compare
See the sparrows in the sky and how he feeds them

---

66   ibid

How much more for me my heavenly Father cares.
Every hair upon my head He said was numbered;
And He sees when even one falls to the ground
So when burdens of this life have me encumbered
With His arms of love and grace He'll me surround.
So I won't worry what I'll eat or wear tomorrow
All these things my heavenly Father knows I need
And sufficient to each day is its own sorrow
So I'll follow gladly where my Father leads.[67]

Truly, God gives a song in the night. And whether in congregational gathering or private praise, one way that God has chosen for us to render our worship is through song.

Mary was and is a perfect example of a worshipper of God. Though she was very young, she was mature in faith. Her devotion to God, her willing consecration to His purpose, and her unconditional surrender to His plan qualified her as a worshipper of God. She was the third woman in the Bible whose lips burst forth in praise to God. It is interesting that the first female singer in the Old Testament had the same name. Miriam is the Hebrew form for Mary! But Mary's song is about Mary's God! She sings of her God who is magnificent. She magnified the Lord, saw Him as exalted and lifted up (Luke 1:46-55). Mary sang of a God who is **magnificent, mighty, mindful and merciful.**

Our singing must reflect this posture of humility before Him who is **magnificent**. Mary's God is also **mindful**. She realized that God knew all abut her, and in spite of her weakness, found her and reached down to her where she was. She knew that her God was mindful of her humility, of her submission, of her purity, but mostly,

---

67   ibid

of her unworthiness. Mary's God is also **mighty**. He is the "mighty one" who has done great things! Only the Mighty God could impregnate her with Divine Seed. Only the Almighty could cause her to conceive when she had not known a man. But Mary's God is also **merciful**. God has remembered to be merciful to Abraham and his descendants forever! Mary caught a glimpse of the mercy of God.

This is a powerful pattern of worship in singing! God is praised! God is magnified! God is exalted! There is one other feature of Mary's song that is worthy of our notice. Mary said, "My soul praises (present tense) the Lord, and my spirit has (past tense) rejoiced in God my Savior." Worship begins in the spirit and then travels to the soul, and is ultimately expressed through the body. This is an important point.

Jesus emphasized that the Father was seeking "true worshippers," who would worship in "spirit" and in "truth." To worship in spirit, is for our spirit being to be touched by God's spirit and respond to Him. Then the spirit seeks expression through the soul (our mind, will, and emotions) and ultimately the soul gives expression through the vehicle of the body. So it is impossible to worship God without our bodies, but worship neither begins nor ends with the physical expressions!

Worship begins in the spirit, and is ultimately expressed through the body. If we emphasize the physical out of proportion, we will have people attempting to worship God with their physical being, without that worship being prompted and precipitated by the Spirit of God working within.

When I began to study Mary's song, I wanted to sing it! And God put these words into my heart, and also gave me the melody. It was an exciting experience for our congregation to be able to sing this together.

My soul praises the Lord and my spirit rejoices in God my
Savior
For He has regarded my lowly estate
My soul praises the Lord and my spirit rejoices in God my
Savior
For the things He's done for me are mighty and great![68]

The Christocentricity of the Lucan songs is amazing! It is interesting that Zechariah's son, John, is not the theme of his song of praise to God. Now, the entire song could be entitled "John," because the name "John" means the grace of God, and that is what the song is all about! The song actually becomes a justification, an explanation of Zechariah's choice of the name "John" for his son! Zechariah's name means "God remembers," and his wife Elizabeth's name means "The oath of God," but John means "God is gracious" or "Jehovah's gift."

When meditating upon the son of Zechariah, I recognized that there is much there that is vital to our Christian conviction. But the Holy Spirit impressed upon me the significance of the phrase "because of the tender mercy of our God, by which the rising sun will come to us from heaven to shine on those living in darkness and in the shadow of death, to guide our feet into the path of peace" (Luke 1:68-69). A song of tender mercies was born with the following words:

The dayspring from on high has come to us
To reveal the tender mercies of our God
To bring light to all who dwell in darkness
And with peace to guide our feet in the path we trod[69]

---

68   ibid
69   ibid

The song of the angels, "The Gloria," has been sung in the church for ages. It is another powerful hymn of worship to God. The purity of the praise is obvious. It comes from heaven itself, from angels who have never sinned. It is true that the angels cannot sing the song of the Redeemed (as we discover in the Book of Revelation) but the redeemed can sing the song of the angels! The song of the angels includes a **prescription of divine praise**, a **proclamation of divine peace**, and a **pronouncement of divine pleasure** (Luke 2:14). I looked at the words, and knew it was impossible to improve upon them, but I wanted to sing them to God in my own expression of praise. This is what flowed from my spirit as I waited upon the Lord:

> *Glory to God in the highest, Rejoice in Messiah's birth*
> *Glory to God in the highest, He brings peace and good will*
> *to the earth*
> *Glory to God in the highest, Sing of the dear Savior's worth*
> *Glory to God in the highest For the Highest has come down*
> *to earth![70]*

There is one more song in the gospel of Luke that is associated with the Christmas story. Although it doesn't immediately surround the birth of Christ, this song is the first significant subsequent event. Simeon, a just and devout man, was a worshipper of God. He looked forward to the consolation of Israel. He was waiting and looking for the Messiah. His heart was possessed by hope. I believe that this is a vital ingredient in the life of the worshipper in any age.

The coming of the Lord's Christ is the hope that possesses the being of the worshipper. His anticipation rested upon both the logos and the rhema of God. Simeon's hope was based upon the written

---

70   ibid

Word of God's promise, as well as upon the revealed Word of God to him personally. When Simeon was drawn to the temple courts on a particular day by the Spirit of God, he had the unique privilege of taking Christ into his arms and blessing Him (Luke 2:27-32).

It is fitting that this song is the fourth hymn in this quartet for its primary emphasis is upon the heart's preparation for its final meeting with God as a result of having seen Christ. For Simeon, this song was personal, for in Christ he beheld the realization of his life's longings. When Simeon embraced Christ he also embraced a promised salvation. Christ is history's long-awaited desire! But receiving Christ, embracing the Son of God, is also preparatory. It produces a readiness for passing into eternity.

I was sitting at the piano with my Bible open when the Spirit of God brought to my heart the words to this song. I still weep, as I did almost uncontrollably then, when I think upon them:

> *With my eyes I've beheld God's salvation*
> *In my arms I've held God's revelation*
> *I have waited for this blessed consolation*
> *I am ready Lord to meet you face to face*
> *I am ready Lord to see you face to face*
> *I've beheld the wonders of your saving grace*
> *As you promised you have brought me to this place*
> *And Your Son, my God and Savior, I embrace*[71]

One cannot possibly look at these songs without recognizing the Christological theme. They are so powerful because they exalt God. They are *personal* as well as *participatory*. The whole of God's people can celebrate His praise together in singing such songs. When this is

---

71   ibid

done, there is a *koinonia* that is experienced in worship. We share in common the hope, the revelation of God, the realization of salvation, the wonder, the majesty, the might, the mercy of our God!

These four hymns from Luke's gospel are not the only hymns in the New Testament, however. Those that are contained in other passages are still Christological, but become more didactic. The New Testament teaching on the person of Christ can be found in such passages as John 1:1-18; Philippians 2:6-11; Colossians 1:15-20 and I Timothy 3:16. Found in each of these is an emphasis upon the eternality of Christ, His pre-existence, His pre-incarnate existence, His incarnation, His essential Godhood or Deity. These hymns were sung in the early Church, and the message of Christ's essential Deity was heralded and perpetuated before the gospels or epistles were actually written! They were not only hymns of worship to God, but also a means of conveying the central message of the Christian faith. When the early Church would sing these hymns, Christ was exalted among them, and His absolute Lordship was continually affirmed in their worship and fellowship.

Although we will not take the time to examine each of these four hymns from the passages mentioned above, we will attempt to summarize their message. First, Christ pre-existed as God. He was the Word that was with God and was God. He is the creator of all things. He holds the universe together by the power of His Word even now. The entire created world owns Christ as its originator. He existed in the very form, or impress, of God, and was by nature God. He is before everything that is created. He existed before anything else came into existence. All thrones, dominions, authorities, rulers, etc., were made by Him and for Him. He is the matrix of all! In everything He has supremacy.

The Father has been pleased to indwell Christ in all of His divine fullness. He is God manifested in the flesh. Yet, this God became a man. He humbled Himself. He became obedient to the death of the cross. He took upon Him the form and likeness of sinful flesh. The Word of God tabernacled among us. We beheld the glory of God in the face of Jesus Christ! He suffered the shame and disgrace of the cruelest death known to man. He laid aside the glory and splendor of heaven. He cast aside His reputation, and laid down His life for us. As a result of His voluntary self-humiliation, God has highly exalted Him. He has been given "the name that is above every name." This was a phrase used by the Jewish scholars when they referred to the unspeakable, unpronounceable name of God. Every knee will ultimately bow before Him, every tongue will confess His Lordship, and this will bring glory to the Father. God's purpose is to make Christ the center of the reconciliation of all things back to Himself.

Working through these passages one cannot help but be overwhelmed with the powerful doctrinal declarations concerning the person of Christ. In fact, there is enough theology contained in these passages to give an adequate system of Christological teaching. Ralph Martin says, "The New Testament hymns tremble on the verge of a cosmic Jubilee when God will be 'all in all' (I Corinthians 15:28) as all things are brought under the sole headship of the reigning Christ (Eph. 1:10).[72]

The third classification mentioned in Pauline teaching is "spiritual songs" or "sacred songs." Whether it means spiritual as opposed to sacred, or spiritual as to the origin of the inspiration is difficult to ascertain, although the latter is more probable. This group of worship songs probably refers to those that were prompted by the immediate inspiration of praise in the form of improvised compositions, Paul is

---

72   Martin, Ralph P. *Worship in the Early Church*. London: Marshall, Morgan and Scott. 1964.

probably referring to such when he said, "When you come together, everyone has a hymn, or a word of instruction, a revelation, a tongue or an interpretation. All of these must be done for the strengthening of the church" (I Corinthians 14:26 NIV).

Clearly, it is inspired utterance that is the subject of discussion. That utterance may be by word or song. Consequently, this is probably an impromptu prophetic type of song, or at least one that has been born by the Spirit of God in the heart of the worshipper, and meant to bless the entire body of Christ. Paul suggests in I Corinthians 14:15 that this kind of song may or may not include *glossolalia*. There will be times when he will sing with the spirit, and other times he will sing with the understanding. Both are acceptable expressions of worship to God.

In his confessions, as quoted earlier in this chapter, Augustine acknowledged the important role of music when he testified of his own conversion, "I wept at the beauty of your hymns and canticles, and was powerfully moved at the sweet sound of your Church singing. These sounds flowed into my ears, and the truth streamed into my heart."[73]

Martin Luther, himself a great composer of sacred song wrote, "When natural music is sharpened and polished by art, then one begins to see with amazement the great and perfect wisdom of God in His wonderful work of music. It is an inexpressible miracle of the Lord... it is no invention of ours; it is the gift of God. I place it next to the Word of God itself."[74]

Heaven will be filled with singing! Worship in its most perfected form will be constituted of sacred song: And they sang a new song:

---

73   St. Augustine, *A Select Library of the Nicene and Post-Nicene Fathers of the Christian Church, Volume IX, The Confessions and Letters of St. Augustine*, Edited by Philip Schaff, D.D., L.L. D, Grand Rapids: Eerdmans Publishing Company.

74   Martin Luther's preface to a musical collection by his friend Walther, printed in 1538.

You are worthy to take the scroll and to open its seals, because you were slain, and with your blood you purchased men for God from every tribe and language and people and nation. You have made them to be a kingdom of priests to serve our God, and they will reign on the earth. Worthy is the Lamb, who was slain, to receive power and wealth and wisdom and strength and honor and glory and praise. To him who sits on the throne and to the Lamb be praise and honor and glory and power, for ever and ever. The four living creatures said, "Amen," and the elders fell down and worshipped (Revelation 5:9-14 NIV).

12

A FAMILY CELEBRATION
WITH THE IN-LAWS

If we want to bring up a godly family, who shall be a seed to serve God when are heads are under the clods of the valley, let us seek to train them up in the fear of God by meeting together as a family for worship.

—Charles Haddon Spurgeon

Jethro was delighted to hear about all the good things the LORD had done for Israel in rescuing them from the hand of the Egyptians. He said, "Praise be to the LORD, who rescued you from the hand of the Egyptians and of Pharaoh, and who rescued the people from the hand of the Egyptians. Now I know that the LORD is greater than all other gods, for he did this to those who had treated Israel arrogantly." Then Jethro brought a burnt offering and other sacrifices to God, and Aaron came with all the elders of Israel to eat bread with Moses' father-in-law in the presence of God (From Exodus 18:9-12 NIV).

M ost of my early memories of worship experiences are recollections of going to church with my family. My mother and father were God-fearing, God-loving people, and they loved to worship God! My dad used to lead the singing quite often, and in our small Pentecostal congregation, he poured a lot of fire and fervor into the worship service. Mom was always a little quieter than my dad in church, but there were occasions when she would be so intense in her concentration upon God's goodness that she would lose a bit of her inhibitions of propriety and become quite expressive in her praise to the Lord. But I also remember Mother as a worshipper of God at home. It was not at all unusual to find her weeping or rejoicing in the presence of God, hands raised, knees bowed, blessing the Lord. And many times as a family we would gather around the old piano, and with my Dad leading the singing, lift our voices in praise to God.

Those early worship experiences—both in our home, and in our little church— indelibly imprinted upon my soul the fact that worship was a family affair. I cherish that heritage today, even though it had its moments of frustration when I was growing up. As a young teenager, I was playing the piano, leading the singing, and even preaching occasionally in church. We were very much into exuberant, exhilarating praise, and placed a high priority upon experiencing the presence of God in our worship gatherings. Few of the pastors or people in the church were well educated. Consequently, their interpretation of the Scripture often missed the mark. But most of them knew God! And they knew how to pray, how to praise, and how to enjoy the family gathering in worship to the Lord.

When we look into the Word of God, we discover that the very first recorded worship experience in the Scriptures is a "family worship" experience. We dealt at length with Cain and Abel in chapter four, so will only touch upon it here. Two brothers go to the same altar to worship the same God, but each brings a different offering, and each comes with a different attitude towards God. One is rejected of the Lord, and the other is accepted. They leave that altar of worship estranged, separated, with one brother bearing hatred in his heart for the other. As a result of that hatred, brother kills brother. The righteous brother, a true worshipper, becomes the first man to enter heaven. The writer to the Hebrews tell us that "By faith Abel offered God a better sacrifice than Cain did. By faith he was commended as a righteous man, when God spoke well of his offerings. And by faith he still speaks, even though he is dead" (Hebrews 11:4 NIV). His brother became the pioneer of apostasy, and he wandered as a fugitive, a marked man, and a vagabond on the earth. Jude tells us that there are false worshippers in the church who have gone in the way of Cain, the worship of a faithless and bloodless religion (Jude 11).

This is hardly a perfect portrait of what family worship should be! In fact, until we come to the exodus of God's people from the bondage of Egypt, we do not possess a truly clear focus upon corporate worship. The people of God had to be redeemed and leave the bondage of Egyptian paganism behind before they could become worshippers of God. Most of the worship encounters in Genesis focus upon the worshipper's individual life. But worship is more than individual. It is also corporate. And there is a sense in which worship is incomplete and less than God designed it to be, until we discover this element.

God has designed us for fellowship. Because God saw that it was not good for man to be alone, he made a wife for him. God created mankind for fellowship with himself. The whole foundation of our existence insists upon the fact that man was created for fellowship and communion. And it is not enough for us to have communion with God; we must also learn to worship with the family of God. There is something about the jostle and joy of fellowship that tends to bring balance to our lives. The "body of Christ" motif that Paul uses requires this. No member can exist in isolation from the other. God has designed worship to be enjoyed by the body of Christ in assembly together.

The Scriptures employ a number of different metaphors and motifs by which to represent the people of God. In fact, when both testaments are taken into account, there are nearly one hundred different figures utilized to portray the people of God. But in the New Testament, the Church of Jesus Christ is primarily in focus. At least seven metaphors are used to describe the Church, beyond our Lord's description of His people as the salt of the earth and the light of the world.

The Church appears as the **Body of Christ**. Paul tells the Ephesians, "God appointed him (Christ) to be head over everything for the church, which is his body, the fullness of him who fills everything in every way" (Ephesians 1:22-23 NIV). To the Colossians he reiterates this, "For the sake of his body, which is the church" (Colossians 1:24 NIV). Again to the Ephesians, Paul writes, "Christ is the head of the church, his body, of which he is the Savior" (Ephesians 5:23 NIV). The Church as Christ's body is Paul's emphasis to the Corinthians, "Now you are the body of Christ, and each one of you is a part of it" (I Corinthians 12:27 NIV).

The Church is also the **Building of God**. Christ said, "I will build my church, and the gates of Hades will not overcome it" (Matthew 16:18 NIV). Paul picks up this strain and writes,

> Consequently, you are no longer foreigners and aliens, but fellow citizens with God's people and members of God's household,

built upon the foundation of the apostles and prophets, with Christ Jesus himself as the chief cornerstone. In him the whole building is joined together and rises to become a holy temple in the Lord. And in him you too are being built together to become a dwelling in which God lives by his Spirit (Ephesians 2:19-22 NIV).

Peter echoes this theme when he writes, "You also, like living stones, are being built into a spiritual house to be a holy priesthood, offering spiritual sacrifices acceptable to God through Jesus Christ" (I Peter 2:5 NIV).

The Church is also the **Bride of Christ**, as we previously discovered in our discussions on the romance of worship. "Christ loved the church and gave himself up for her to make her holy, cleansing her with the washing of water through the word, and to present her to himself as a radiant church, without stain or wrinkle or any other blemish, but holy and blameless" (Ephesians 5:25-27 NIV). In the Book of Revelation the Church appears as a bride adorned for her husband (Revelation 21:2). We have been espoused as a chaste virgin to Christ, according to Paul's writing to the Corinthians (II Corinthians 11:2).

The Church is also the **Flock of God**. Christ is the *Good Shepherd* who gave Himself for the sheep (John 10:14-15). He is the *Great Shepherd* in His resurrection from the dead (Hebrews 13:20). He is the *Chief Shepherd* who will one day appear to reward His undershepherds for caring for the flock (I Peter 5:4). We are His flock, His fold, purchased by the blood of Christ. "Keep watch over yourselves and all the flock of which the Holy Spirit has made you overseers. Be shepherds of the church of God, which he bought with his own blood" (Acts 20:28). It took the Blood of the Lamb to redeem all of the little lambs!

The Church is also the **Field of God**. John records the words of Christ who said, "I am the true vine and my Father is the gardener" (John 15:1 NIV). Paul says, "You are God's field, God's building" (I Corinthians 3:9 NIV). The Church is the field of God's planting, the vineyard of God. He plants the seed of His Word, and we are to bear fruit unto Him. The Church is God's cultivated field!

The Church is also the **Priesthood of God**. Peter describes the church as "A holy priesthood, offering spiritual sacrifices acceptable to God...a chosen people, a royal priesthood, a holy nation, a people belonging to God, that you may declare the praises of him" (I Peter 2:5, 9 NIV). According to Hebrews, "We have an altar from which those who minister at the tabernacle have no right to eat… Through Jesus, therefore, let us continually offer to God a sacrifice of praise—the fruit of our lips that confess his name" (Hebrews 13:10, 15 NIV).

But the Church is also the **Family of God**! Paul tells the Ephesians that we are "the members of God's household" (Ephesians 2:19 NIV). As the family of God, we derive our sense of belonging from one Father, and we have one Family name. "For this reason I kneel before the Father, from whom his whole family in heaven and on earth derives its name" (Ephesians 3:14-15 NIV).

We belong to the same family as Jesus Christ! In fact, He became our brother when He entered the human family, and made us His brethren! "Both the one who makes men holy and those who are made holy are of the same family. So Jesus is not ashamed to call them brothers" (Hebrews 2:11 NIV). Belonging to God's Family makes us God's children. "You received the Spirit of sonship. And by him we cry, 'Abba, Father.' The Spirit himself testifies with our Spirit that we are God's children. Now if we are children, then we are heirs—heirs of God and co-heirs with Christ" (Romans 8:15-17 NIV). "Because you are sons, God sent the Spirit of his Son into our hearts, the Spirit who calls out, 'Abba, Father.' So you are no longer a slave, but a son; and since you are a son, God has made you also an heir" (Galatians 4:6-7 NIV).

The Family of God is both "in heaven" and "in earth." As we discovered in our examination of Cain and Abel in Chapter Three, worship has both a vertical and a horizontal dimension. The dynamic of worship that is comprehended in the concept of the family of God is marvelous! We are part of a universal family.

The bread that we break in celebrating the Lord's Table represents the body of Christ universal. And we are not limited to the generation that is alive in the world today! Part of the family is already in heaven! When we worship, we participate in that which is the occupation of those that have already been promoted to the Lord's presence.

I. WORSHIP INVOLVES A FAMILY RELATIONSHIP

The story recorded in the first twelve verses of Exodus eighteen is another great moment in worship. Verse 12 states, "Then Jethro, Moses' father-in-law, brought a burnt offering and other sacrifices to God, and Aaron came with all the elders of Israel to eat bread with Moses' father-in-law in the presence of God." The significance of this event cannot be grasped unless we see it as happening on the very verge of Sinai. On the eve of the giving of the law, itself another great moment in the saga of worship, the worship of grace is prefigured! God causes the lines to be crossed, for people to gather in His name, declare His worth, unite in praise, sacrifice unto Him, and worship Him for His faithfulness.

Some scholars are not sure that Jethro was Moses' father-in-law. The reason for this is that according to Exodus 2:18, Reuel was the father of Zipporah, Moses' wife. Many scholars believe that Jethro, therefore, was the brother-in-law to Moses, a brother of Moses' wife, Zipporah. It is a moot point, but one over which scholarship might stumble!

When Moses decided to go back to Egypt to fulfill the calling of God upon His life in bringing the Israelites out of bondage, he sent his wife back to her father (or brother) with the two sons that she had borne Moses. Moses had appropriately named the sons Gershom (I have become an alien in a foreign land) and Eliezer (my Father's God was my helper). Jethro gave protection to Moses' wife and two sons during the process of the Exodus and the passing through the Red Sea. When he heard about this great triumph, he set out to meet Moses.

Now Jethro was a Midianite, so his ancestry also went back to Abraham (Genesis 25:2). It is quite possible that the worship of Abraham's God had stayed with him through the centuries that had passed. The land of Midian was not far from Sinai, where Moses had now taken the children of Israel after the Red Sea crossing. Jethro sent word ahead that he was coming to meet Moses, since he had heard of the great things that God had done for Israel.

It is important to understand some of the human dynamics, even if we must use some element of conjecture here. Moses had at one time been the servant of Jethro. Once he had tended Jethro's sheep. He marries Jethro's daughter (or sister), and follows this "religious call" leaving behind his wife, family, and his in-laws with the sheep! Jethro probably viewed the whole situation with some distaste, to say the least. More than likely, he looked upon Moses with some disdain. Moses, who had been his shepherd, is now the shepherd of Jehovah, and of Jehovah's people. Jethro, having had to care for Moses' family while Moses is off on this "ministry" was not likely in sympathy with Moses' mission.

After the mutual exchange of the common courtesies of the eastern world, Moses told Jethro all that the LORD had done to Pharaoh and the Egyptians for Israel's sake, and about the hardships they had met along the way and how the Lord had saved them from them all.

Part of the worship experience is sharing with the family of God both the victories and the hardships. This is one of the reasons the Book of Psalms is so popular. It pulsates with the passion of life as we know it. It reflects the doubts and dreams, the ups and downs, the mountains and valleys, the pain and the pleasure, the joy and the sorrow of real life. To celebrate God, we must celebrate Him in the context of His involvement with us in daily life and experience. God is not an abstract God. He is not mystically worshipped. God is interested in us. The name Immanuel means "God is with us", and this is the purpose for which Christ came into the world, to bring God down to earth where we could experience His intimate involvement with us in both the anguish and anxiety of life.

When we are unable to share this dimension in worship, we miss something. We need to share our lives with one another in a manner that recognizes God's involvement. We must not emphasize the hardships at the expense of neglecting to point out God's salvation. Moses shared with Jethro "how the Lord had saved them (Exodus 18:8)."

This prompts worship in the hearts of people. When people share with me their difficulties, I can empathize with them. Sometimes, I can even sympathize with them. But when they share how God has helped them, how God has brought them through and showed them His salvation, then I can worship with them.

This conversation was one of gladness not of gloom. It was a time of rejoicing in the victories that God had given. This is a part of our worship. We celebrate together the life and the presence of God. Together we celebrate. Together we rejoice. Together we worship.

Worship is the gathering of the family of God. All members of the family are not alike. In fact, we are all quite different. Our backgrounds are different. Our interests are different. Our preferences are different. But in the melting-pot of worship, we are molded together as one. Jethro and Moses came from different backgrounds. Jethro had spent his life in the desert of Midian looking after sheep.

Moses had put in his time at the same occupation, but he came from the courts of Pharaoh, where he enjoyed the highest education his world could offer. He had a special calling of God upon his life, a very special mission to accomplish. Yet, he and Jethro could sit down and worship together. And they had more in common than the fact that Moses' wife was related to Jethro! They worshipped the same God.

Worship will do this. The family of God transcends national, ethnic, educational, cultural, social, political and even religious barriers. God, in Christ, has reconciled and united the two most diametrically opposed groups in the world, Jew and Gentile. In worship, we celebrate that reconciliation. In worship, we celebrate our togetherness in Christ. In worship, we flow together as one body, one people, and one family!

When Moses and Jethro meet for this reunion, they reflect upon the many years that they have shared together. There is no jealousy on the part of Jethro when he hears of how God has used Moses. He recognized the honor that had been put upon Moses. He honors the man that once had been dependant upon him. This is a beautiful spirit of humility, and one that is conducive to the kind of worship that the family of God has been called to enjoy. We have here a beautiful picture of wholesome and healthy friendship. There is a kindred spirit that is cultured between them, and Jethro is anxious to hear of what God had done for the children of Israel in their divine deliverance from the hand of Pharaoh.

If this kind of atmosphere could be cultivated in our churches, our worship would be much more wholesome. The family of God should take more seriously the "one another" passages that appear 58 times in the New Testament, excluding the gospels. Paul the apostle uses the phrase some 40 times in his writings! Paul tells the Romans that we are "members one of another" (Romans 12:5 NASB). In verse ten of the same chapter, he tells us to be "devoted to one another in brotherly love," and to "honor one another above yourselves." He exhorts them again in Romans 15:5, "Be of the same mind with one another," and in the seventh verse of the same chapter, "Accept one another, then, just as Christ accepted you, in order to bring praise to God." The fourteenth verse of the same chapter exhorts us to "Admonish one another," while in chapter 16, we are told to "Greet one another." To another church, Paul writes, "Serve one another in love" (Galatians 5:13). Writing again to the Galatians, Paul says, "Bear one another's burdens," while to the Ephesians he writes, "Bearing with one another in love" (Ephesians 4:2). Again to the Ephesians, he writes, "Submit to one another out of reverence for Christ" (Ephesians 5:2 1). To the Thessalonian church, Paul writes, "Encourage one another and build each other up" (I Thessalonians 5:11).

When we discover and put into practice what it means to be the Family of God, our worship will be more than collective. It will be corporate! There is a dynamic to the worship of God's people as a family that is more than collective. The whole becomes more than the sum total of the parts when worship is corporate as the Family of God. There is an interaction, a flow of life that is enhanced by the life of God among us when we discover this togetherness in worship.

2. WORSHIP INVITES A PERSONAL RESPONSE

Worship can be simultaneously corporate and personal. We can have both intimacy with God, as well as a shared experience with the people of God at the same time in worship. This is vividly illustrated for us in this passage. When Jethro had heard of all that God had done for Israel, his heart was prompted with a desire to respond to God.

There are many substitutes for corporate worship that totally overlook the necessity of personal intimacy with God. It is possible to rejoice in what God has done for others, to exult in what God has done for His people, without ever entering into a worship experience. For example, many nominal Christians identify with the Zionist cause and support the development and defense of the state of Israel, while they have never known what it is to personally worship God. We cannot experience worship vicariously. We must know God for ourselves. And this is part of the promise of the New Covenant. Each man will know God for himself, and sit under his own vine and fig tree and personally rejoice in God! (Micah 4:4)

Taking this into the context of the local congregation of believers, we can rejoice in what God has done in the lives of others in the church, but we must also develop an intimacy with God in our worship. Worship is also between God and each individual. It is the response of the individual heart to Him. We worship in the congregation, but we also worship individually. We blend our hearts and voices to the Lord, but we must personally experience intimacy with God before our expressions of praise actually constitute worship.

Although Jethro was probably a believer in the one true God, it is hard to determine whether or not he was actually a worshipper prior to this time. But when he heard the things that God had done for Israel, something happened in his life. He said, "Now I know that Jehovah is greater than all other gods" (Exodus 18:11). There came a point in time when he confessed his knowledge of the greatness of Jehovah, and his desire to respond to that in worship. He said, "Praise be to JEHOVAH, who rescued you from the hand of the Egyptians" (Exodus 18:10). Jethro expressed his praise to the God who had redeemed Israel, but he followed it with the "now I know!" confession of his own faith in God. His worship was precipitated by his revelation of God, and of God's power on behalf of Israel.

In reflecting on this passage, I recall a sermon preached by my dear friend, Rev. Bill Fullerton, who was my early mentor in preaching. I was just a teenager at the time (so it was more than fifty years ago), but it is impressed indelibly on my mind. He preached from the text in John 18:33-38 where Christ is before Pilate and Pilate asks Christ if He is King of the Jews, Christ answered, "Sayest thou this thing of thyself, or did others tell it thee of me?" Entitling his message, "First-hand faith or second-hand religion," his focus on the necessity of a personal encounter with God rather than a hand-me-down faith deeply penetrated my adolescent heart and mind.

Jethro says that God has overthrown the Egyptians in the area of their strength! God conquered them in the very thing at which they were most skilled. The nation of Egypt was well known for its abilities in combat, for its strength in warfare. God has triumphed over them and over their arrogance. Jethro recognized what God had done on behalf of His people. He accepted that report and rehearsed his own perception of God's intervention. But, characteristic of true worship, Jethro was not satisfied to merely give lip service and mental acquiescence to what God had done. His worship must give individual expression to Jehovah.

It is instructive to note that Jethro's worship was rendered to God within the parameters of God's prescribed pattern. Jehovah cannot be appropriately approached with some Gentile, heathen song and dance! Jehovah must be approached in conformity with the pattern that He has already laid down.

Jethro brought a burnt offering and other sacrifices to God. Once again, we have established that the only way to God is through the cross of our Lord Jesus Christ. We need offer no other sacrifice; in fact, we must offer no other sacrifice. We come solely through the blood of the cross of the Savior. True worship is always centered in the cross of Christ. True worship celebrates the Lamb of God and His resurrection from the dead. We have already discovered that Christ is the eternal Lamb of God whose worship will be the celebration of eternity in heaven. But until each individual realizes that Christ is not only the Lamb of God, but that He is also *my* Lamb, true worship cannot take place.

This is illustrated for us in the gospel narrative that describes one of the post-resurrection appearances of our Lord Jesus. Thomas was having trouble believing the report of the other disciples that Christ had actually risen from the dead. He said, "Unless I see the nail marks in his hands and put my finger where the nails were, and put my hand into his side, I will not believe it."

A week later the disciples were in the house again, and Thomas was with them. Though the doors were locked, Jesus came and stood among them and said,

"Peace be with you." Then he said to Thomas, "Put your finger here; see my hands. Reach out your hand and put it into my side. Stop doubting and believe." Thomas said to him, "My Lord and my God." Then Jesus told him, "Because you have seen me, you have believed; blessed are those who have not seen and yet have believed" (John 20:25-29 NIV).

The revelation of the wounds of Christ caused Thomas to cry out, "My Lord and My God." I believe that it is a glimpse of the crucified and risen Lord, who still bears in His body those wondrous wounds, that becomes the most powerful precipitator of praise and worship. Thomas had seen the miracles of Christ, but had not been totally convinced. Yet a glimpse of Him and a vision of those wounds caused him to fall before Christ in the posture of worship. The prophet Zechariah points forward to a time when Christ will reveal Himself as Messiah to His people, Israel, when he says, "And one shall say unto him, 'What are these wounds in thine hands?' Then he shall answer, 'Those with which I was wounded in the house of my friends'" (Zechariah 13:6).

When we worship corporately with the Body of Christ, we are able to rejoice in all that God has done in the lives of people. We are able also to celebrate the redemptive work of God for all of His people. But there is something about the quality of individual, intimate expression of worship to God, prompted by the revelation that Jesus died for me that cannot be fully fathomed or described!

Paul describes the post-resurrection appearances of Christ in his apologetic defense and description of the gospel.

He appeared to the Twelve. After that, he appeared to more than five hundred of the brothers at the same time, most of whom are still living, though some have fallen asleep. Then he appeared to James, then to all the apostles, and last of all he appeared to me also, as to one abnormally born. For I am the least of the apostles and do not deserve to be called an apostle, because I persecuted the church of God. But by the grace of God I am what I am, and his grace to me was not without effect (I Corinthians 15:5-10 NIV).

The appearance of Christ to Paul produced within him the humility of heart by which he was able to see himself in a proper light. This posture of humility is the essence of worship. It characterized Paul's surrender to Christ as the act of His lifelong worship of God.

Worship is nothing, if it is not personal. There must be that individual intimacy with God such as Moses himself had developed. Abraham knew that kind of relationship with God. The Psalms of David are so powerful because they reflect the kind of personal intimacy that David knew with God. In the Psalms there are approximately one hundred references to God as "my God" or "our God." It is interesting that over two thirds of these speak of "My God," or the "God of my Salvation," or some similar expression!

For Jethro, Moses' God was being owned as his God as well! His worship was reflective of more than rejoicing in the victory of God's people. It was more than reunion with his brother-in-law! It was a statement of his newfound relationship with God, his acknowledgment of who God was in his own life.

3. WORSHIP INVOKES THE DIVINE PRESENCE

"Aaron came with all the elders of Israel to eat bread with Moses' father-in-law in the presence of God" (Exodus 18:12). This verse conveys to us a third dynamic of worship as a family gathering, when this kind of worship takes place, the presence of God is there. We share the fellowship of breaking bread in the presence of God!

To truly appreciate the particular significance of this event, we need to be remember that Jethro was not an Israelite. Although related to Abraham, he was a Gentile. What happens in this experience of breaking bread together is a coming together of Jew and Gentile in worship. And what makes it even more interesting, is that it happened at the brink of the Sinai event of the giving of the law.

It is as though God has portrayed and prefigured for us, in this pre-Sinai event, the glory of the Church. Jew and Gentile are eating together. Such a thing was not possible under the Mosaic Law. But here it happens, and both Moses and Aaron are participants in this fellowship! The sovereign hand of God must be seen in this rather enigmatic encounter. God is demonstrating the fact that worship has the power to transcend all of the barriers that we might erect.

This particular feature and facet of the cross-work of Christ is vital to our worship.

But now in Christ Jesus you who once were far away have been brought near through the blood of Christ. For he himself is our peace, who has made the two one and has destroyed the barrier, the dividing wall of hostility, by abolishing in his flesh the law with its commandments and regulations... to create in himself one new man out of the two, thus making peace, and in this one body to reconcile both of them to God through the cross (Ephesians 2:13-16 NIV).

Paul goes on to say that it was through the cross that Christ "put to death their hostility, and He came and preached peace to you who were far away and peace to those who were near. For through him we both have access to the Father by one Spirit" (Ephesians 2:16-18 NIV). The hostility Paul is describing is that which separated Jew from Gentile. It is this that the cross of Christ has bridged.

This work of reconciliation is prefigured in the worship of Jethro and Moses, when they broke bread together with Aaron and all the elders of Israel. God has proven that He can reconcile the two most irreconcilable groups in the world, Jew and Gentile. And yet, we allow factions to fracture our fellowship in the Church today. Fellowship cannot be fractured without worship being affected. The two are very closely related.

The Church has always had trouble learning this lesson. Peter had trouble learning it in the early Church. When God sent him to the household of the Italian, Cornelius, God had to give Peter the message three times before it got through to him. It has always intrigued me that Cornelius got God's message the first time, while it took three attempts before it got through to Peter! Sometimes the Church is last to catch on to what God is saying and doing in the world. The battle with acceptance plagued the early church. The Judaizers, the legalizers, the cult of the circumcision were a continuous threat to the liberty of the gospel of grace. Much of Paul's writing is given to correct and balance this problem.

But it is not a problem that was unique to the early church. We wrestle with it as well. We have our exclusive attitude about our particular fanciful franchise on truth. We fight the feeling of being on the cutting edge, of being "one-up" on other churches. And any sense of spiritual superiority colors our worship. In fact, it is a fly in the ointment and incense of our praise. It causes it to send forth a "stinking odor" in the words of the preacher in Ecclesiastes 10:1. Worship cannot be what God has designed it to be when we allow disharmony to prevail in the body of Christ.

The presence of God's spirit is invoked by the unity of God's people! Psalm 133 declares this.

How good and pleasant it is when brothers live together in unity! It is like precious oil poured on the head, running down on Aaron's beard, down upon the collar of his robes. It is as if the dew of Hermon were falling on Mount Zion. For there the Lord bestows his blessing, even life forevermore (Psalm 133:1-3 NIV).

God's people dwelling together in unity is both good and pleasant. The word "good" is the same word that God used to describe His own work of creation. Each day He looked at what He had done and saw that it was good (Genesis 1:3-24). This is how God views His people when they are together in worship. When their hearts are blended together in one purpose, God says it is GOOD! But it is also "pleasant". This is a word that connotes harmony. It is not the same as unison, or unanimity. Rather, it suggests the blending of different parts that harmonize. The "pleasant" nature of a choir is the blending of the different parts, each in harmony with the other. This is how the Body of Christ is to function.

The whole body cannot be "eyes" or "ears" but each part has its particular function. This is harmony and this is "pleasant." What is it like? It is like the precious anointing oil! This was a special secret recipe that God had given to Moses, and it was secretly and sacredly guarded. No one was to attempt to simulate or duplicate this concoction. It was God's recipe, and there was to be no substitute for it. And this is like the anointing of the Holy Spirit. There is no substitute. No imitation, simulation, or attempted duplication will be acceptable to God. But brethren dwelling together in unity will produce an atmosphere, an essence, like the anointing oil.

It is also like the dew of Hermon. This was a very copious dew that settled upon the sides of Hermon that produced a very lush form of vegetation that was highly unusual to its area. David says that God's people dwelling together in unity will produce a similar result. There will be extraordinary life and growth. The fruitfulness of the Holy Spirit will be sensed by all of those around. And it will be obvious that God is at work.

But the Psalmist adds one further comment. It is there that the Lord bestows or "commands" His blessing, even life forevermore! Where brethren are worshipping in unity, God commands His blessing to rain upon them! If we could capture the significance of this, we would realize what really counts with God in our worship is our willingness to open our hearts and receive other people. For as we do that, we are actually opening our hearts to God!

When the Body of Christ is truly united in purpose as well as in praise, we don't have to beg God to pour out His Spirit. He did it on the day of Pentecost, and He will do it again. Someone has said that the greatest miracle on the day of Pentecost was not the tongues of fire, nor the speaking with tongues, nor the mighty rushing wind. The greatest miracle was the one hundred and twenty were in one place, at one time, with one accord. The miracle of their togetherness, their unity, after such competition in their ranks was the most outstanding feature! Perhaps, during those days of waiting, one by one they confessed their doubts, their fears, their sins, their jealousies, and sought and received each other's forgiveness. And, quite possibly, by the time they had spent those many days in prayer, they had each been reduced to the lowest common denominator, and thus were candidates for the infilling and infusion of the life of God's Spirit.

What a sight it must have been on that eve of Sinai. There was Aaron, the expert in worship in Israel. He was the guardian of the worship code. There was Moses, who would become the custodian of the law. There were the elders, the spiritual leaders of Israel; and Jethro. Perhaps it's the "Beverly Hillbillies"[75] connotation of his name

---

75 Jethro Bodine, played by Max Baer Jr., was a character in the popular television series *The Beverly Hillbillies* which originally ran from 1962-1971.

that makes me feel like he was out of place, but surely he was! He was a Midianite. Israel would have lots of trouble with Midianites in the future. The Midianites would try to hire Baalam to prophesy against God's people. They will war with them. But now, in celebrating the victory that God has given to His people Israel, Jethro, a Midianite, worships with Moses, Aaron and the elders of the Jewish community.

Oh, the triumph of God's grace! Worship is designed by God to loose the limitations and horizons of our smallness. We must look up to see that God is bigger than we could ever imagine! God is magnified in our worship! God is larger than we can comprehend. In worship we acknowledge His transcendence. And if we can see that God is bigger than we are, surely our horizons can be broadened to include in worship those that will respond to God and to His grace!

There is at least one other aspect of breaking bread in the presence of God that needs to be considered. The breaking of bread in the Hebrew custom was always a symbol of peace, forgiveness, friendship and fellowship. In chapter twenty-one of John's gospel, Jesus illustrates this for us when, after His resurrection, He sought out Peter and the other disheartened disciples who had returned to their occupation of fishing. Fishing all night, they caught nothing. Jesus stood upon the shore, but they didn't recognize Him. He called out to them, "Friends, haven't you any fish?" They answered that they hadn't caught anything. Jesus told them to throw their net on the right side of the boat and they would find some. Now they did this, still not knowing that it was Christ. Why would they do this, if they didn't know it was Jesus? For one simple reason: because the vantage point of any person standing on the higher elevation of the shore in the early morning would enable him to see where the fish were. He could tell by the shadows on the water where the fish were. So the Galilean fishermen were accustomed to listening to someone on the shore who told them where to cast their nets. It was only when they caught such a large catch that they couldn't haul them into the boat, that John woke up and said, "It is the Lord" (John 21:7).

I've always been both amused and intrigued by Peter's response. He wraps his coat around him and jumps into the water! The other disciples followed him in the boat, and towed the net full of fish, for they were only a hundred yards from shore. When they landed, they saw a fire of burning coals there with fish on it, and some bread. Jesus said, "Bring some of the fish you have just caught." Peter climbed aboard and dragged the net ashore. The net contained 153 large fish, but it hadn't broken! Jesus said, "Come and have breakfast." None of the disciples dared ask him, "Who are you?" They knew it was the Lord. Jesus came, took the bread and gave it to them, and did the same with the fish. This was now the third time Jesus appeared to his disciples after he was raised from the dead" (John 21:2-14 NIV).

There are so many details of this story that are powerful, but only a few are apropos to our discussions here. Jesus had already provided bread and fish upon the fire. Where did he get the bread? Perhaps he turned stones to bread on this occasion just to prove to Satan that He could do it when He wanted to! That is, of course, only conjecture. But Christ provided the bread. He also provided the fish. I don't think He went fishing! I don't think he bought it at the market! But He provided it. But still he asked the disciples to bring some of the fish that they had caught. He could have provided enough for all of them. But He invites them to participate with Him in this fellowship.

Christ says nothing to Peter about his failures. He never mentions the crowing of the rooster! He never brings up his denial. He simply invites him to have fellowship with Him. Peace has been made through the blood of His cross. And so, He is our peace, and

He comes and preaches peace. He gives to His disciples the peace meal. They are forgiven. They are accepted. They are loved.

There has been much debate through the centuries around the concept of the "presence of Christ" as it relates to the table of the Lord. In some theology, the bread and wine become the body and blood of Christ. In other theology, the real presence of Christ is seen in the emblems. But for the worshipper, it is important to recognize that the real presence of Christ is *at* the table, not *on* the table. We experience the presence of Christ when we celebrate His broken body and shed blood in a Scriptural way.

The discerning of the body of Christ has to do with recognition of the Church as the community of the redeemed. In I Corinthians 10, Paul's emphasis is more upon the *shared* blood and body than it is upon the *shed* blood of Christ.

> Is not the cup of thanksgiving for which we give thanks a participation in the blood of Christ? And is not the bread that we break a participation in the body of Christ? Because there is one loaf, we, who are many, are one body, for we all partake of the one loaf (I Corinthians 10:16-17 NIV).

When this truth is recognized in worship, we can anticipate the divine presence as being with us. Paul said that we declare or proclaim the Lord's death when we celebrate the Lord's Table. And we do it in anticipation of His return. So we live between the Lord's redeeming work on the cross of Calvary, the climax of His ministry upon earth, and His return from heaven, when He will come to set up His kingdom upon this earth. Between the tension of those two points, we recognize the personal, physical, absence of Christ. So it is Christ's **absence** that makes possible His **presence**! He has left this world, ascended into heaven, received from the Father the promised Holy Spirit, and sent forth His Spirit into the world, which Spirit is present with us in worship when we remember His death and proclaim His coming!

It is the presence of Christ through the Holy Spirit that sets Christian worship apart. No other religion can offer the presence of its founder in the midst wherever believers assemble! Because He was **bodily** absent, He could be **spiritually** present! The fellowship meal, the love or agape feast, became the outward declaration of the uniting force of His Spirit in their hearts. The *last* supper became the *Lord's* Supper, for it was fellowship with Him that was both commemorated and perpetuated through this memorial. Christ was the very center of all the worship of the early Church. They prayed in His name. They proclaimed His Lordship. They echoed His words. They remembered His death. They heralded His resurrection. They anticipated His return.

But the force of all of the Christocentric elements of their worship was the unifying power of the Holy Spirit. As Professor W.C. van Unnik says, the worship of the New Testament church "stands within the magnetic field of the Holy Spirit."[76] It is the Spirit of God that leads men to accept and confess Christ. The Spirit inspires prayer and praise. The Spirit opens the minds and hearts of believers to receive the Word.

The Spirit distributes and imparts the various giftings for ministry. The presence of the Spirit of God in worship is so important that Paul writes to the Philippians, "We worship by the Spirit of God" (Philippians 3:3).

---

76 van Unnik, W.C. *Luke-Acts, a Strom Center in Contemporary Scholarship, Studies in Luke-Acts.* edited by L. Keck and J. Martyn. Philadelphia: Fortress, 1966.

4. THE DYNAMIC OF CORPORATE WORSHIP

God has so created us that the dynamic of corporate worship eclipses that of individual devotion. Corporate worship is more intense than private communion with God. Martin Luther acknowledged that when he said, "At home in my own house there is no warmth or vigor in me, but in the church when the multitude is gathered together, a fire is kindled in my heart, and it breaks its way through."[77]

We bless and encourage each other by fellowship, but we are strengthened and lifted up by united worship. In fact, Christ promises His presence "where two or three are gathered together in my name, there am I in the midst of them" (Matthew 18:20). That does not suggest that Christ is not with us individually, but the promise of His presence in a more intensified realization is ours when the people of God are gathered in assembly to worship Him.

The presence of Christ among the people of God is not something that we can work up or bring down! It is the result of the promise of Christ Himself when His people gather in His name. Another aspect that we have already mentioned is that of the Body of Christ. Each member of the Body of Christ is not merely an individual, but can function properly only in relationship. If this is not true, then the analogy of the Body is inappropriate. No one member constitutes the Body of Christ. To each of us is assigned a specific gift and function. And those gifts comprise a great variety. And the Body of Christ is the Body of Christ only when the members find and fulfill the function that God has assigned.

God has given to us a divine design. Worship must be personal and intimate. But it must be infinitely more. We are designed to worship with the Family of God. We have not been created or called to worship in isolation. God's people are called to corporately be the

77 cited in http://www.watton.org/riverministries/believe/03_foundational.htm

temple of God! While our individual bodies are the temples of the Holy Spirit, yet it is the Church *corporate* that becomes the habitation of God through the Spirit.

> Consequently, you are no longer foreigners and aliens, but fellow citizens with God's people and members of God's household, built on the foundation of the apostles and prophets, with Christ Jesus himself as the chief cornerstone. In him the whole building is joined together and rises to become a holy temple in the Lord. And in him you too are being built together to become a dwelling in which God lives by his Spirit (Ephesians 2:19-22 NIV).

We have alluded to this passage a number of times because of its paramount importance. It is exciting to know that we are no longer strangers to God. We are no longer outside the economy of His grace and provision. Christ has brought us into the presence of God. We have become fellow citizens with the people of God (the Jewish nation) for God has made of Jew and Gentile one new man, one new nation, a holy nation, the Church. Therefore, we are the family of God. We are the household of God. But the household is also a house. The family becomes the dwelling place of God, but only insofar as we are being built together. Twice in this passage Paul says that we are "joined together" and "being built together." Only in the corporate dimension do the people of God become the habitation of God, His holy temple and dwelling place.

This realization must pervade and permeate our worship experience. We must recognize the dynamic of family relationship. Worship is a great family gathering. Our response to God is individual, and intimate, but it is not what God intended it to be until we blend our hearts, voices, and spirits together with the people of God in worship to the Lord who loved and redeemed us.

In the Book of Revelation, the people of God are represented in the four and twenty elders who share the common song of praise to God. Then there is a multitude that no man can number. Worship in its final perfected form will be the common, corporate, and collective expression of all of God's family! All who have been redeemed, from Old and New Testament times, throughout the ages will be assembled on that great day!

When we gather as the family of God today in worship, we are united with the universal church. Our worship enables us to join with the multitudes around the world who acknowledge the Lordship of Jesus Christ. We are one with all of God's people. But more than that, the whole family, in heaven and in earth, who bear the family name, are joined together. Those redeemed saints of God who have gone into the presence of Jesus Christ are already worshipping around the throne! The assembled Church of Jesus Christ on earth declares its oneness with the Church in heaven when we worship.

The writer to the Hebrews captures this vision when he says "But you have come to Mount Zion, to the heavenly Jerusalem, to the city of the living God. You have come to thousands upon thousands of angels in joyful assembly, to the church of the firstborn, whose names are written in heaven" (Hebrews 12:22-23 NIV). These are the cloud of witnesses who are also a company of worshippers.

When John saw them surrounding the throne, there was no indication that worship would be an occupation that they would *eventually* enter into when all of the people of God were finally gathered home! The assembled host in heaven are *already occupied* in the glorious business of worshipping the Lamb. Worship, for which we have been created and redeemed, becomes the corporate expression of God's people when they reach the other side. And every believer that is promoted to God's presence immediately becomes a part of that worshipping throng.

The closest foretaste that we can have today of that heavenly experience is when the people of God gather in glad and joyful assembly. And there should be an increased enthusiasm and anticipation as we draw closer to the coming of the Lord. The sense of celebration and exhilaration accelerates as the Lord's coming draws near. The writer to the Hebrews says,

> Therefore, brothers, since we have confidence to enter the Most Holy Place by the blood of Jesus, by a new and living way opened for us through the curtain, that is, his body, and since we have a great high priest over the house of God, let us draw near to God with a sincere heart in full assurance of faith, having our hearts sprinkled to cleanse us from a guilty conscience and having our bodies washed with pure water. Let us hold unswervingly to the hope we profess, for he who promised is faithful. And let us consider how we may spur one another on toward love and good deeds. Let us not give up meeting together, as some are in the habit of doing, but let us encourage one another—and all the more as you see the Day approaching (Hebrews 10:19-25 NIV).

In this classical passage that speaks at length about the various elements of Christian worship, the word "together" appears along with the phrase "one another" a total of three times. Worship is not only entering the holiest by the blood of Christ, although it is that. Worship is more than drawing near to God with cleansed hearts and pure minds. Worship is more than steadfastly holding our hope and profession of faith, although all of these things are important.

Worship involves the mutuality of ministry, as we positively impact the lives of others towards more productive Christian service. And the "bottom line" of all of these things is assembling together to facilitate all of the aforementioned dynamics. It is in the context of corporate worship that we experience the blessings and benefits of the Cross of Christ. It is in the crucible of corporate worship that mutuality of ministry takes place. And we are instructed to continually accelerate our gathering together as the coming of the Lord draws near.

There is one more meeting together that will be summoned by Christ Himself prior to our assembly in heaven, but after the last corporate worship service upon earth has ever been held.

> We believe that Jesus died and rose again and so we believe that God will bring with Jesus those who have fallen asleep in him. According to the Lord's own word, we tell you that we who are still alive, who are left to the coming of the Lord, will certainly not precede those who have fallen asleep. For the Lord himself will come down from heaven, with a loud command, with the voice of the archangel and with the trumpet call of God, and the dead in Christ will rise first. After that, we who are still alive and are left will be caught up with them in the clouds to meet the Lord in the air. And so we will be with the Lord forever (I Thessalonians 4:14-17 NIV).

That will be the greatest corporate worship service that the Church will experience between earth and glory! When we gather together in the clouds at the feet of our Lord, we will worship Him. This will be a great "family gathering" eclipsed only by the celebrations to follow in heaven, when all the family gathers around the throne of the Lord God and the Lamb, and commence our eternal occupation of worshiping the Savior who loved us and redeemed us by His precious blood.

TREMBLING MOUNTAIN, TREMBLING HEARTS

It is not light that we need, but fire; it is not the gentle shower, but thunder. We need the storm, the whirlwind, and the earthquake.

—Frederick Douglass

Oh God, how do the world and heavens confine themselves, when our hearts tremble in their own barriers!

—Johann Wolfgang von Goethe

I am made to tremble and I fear!

—Pope John XXIII

The LORD said to Moses, "I am going to come to you in a dense cloud, so that the people will hear me speaking with you and will always put their trust in you." On the morning of the third day there was thunder and lightning, with a thick cloud over the mountain, and a very loud trumpet blast. Everyone in the camp trembled. Then Moses led the people out of the camp to meet with God, and they stood at the foot of the mountain. Mount Sinai was covered with smoke, because the LORD descended on it in fire. The smoke billowed up from it like smoke from a furnace, the whole mountain trembled violently, and the sound of the trumpet grew louder and louder. Then Moses spoke and the voice of God answered him. The LORD descended to the top of Mount Sinai and called Moses to the top of the mountain (Exodus 19:9-20 NIV).

B y the time we arrive at the Sinai event in the Book of Exodus, we are already aware of the fact that worship involves a meeting with God. But this event is of singular significance, in that the meeting was convoked by God. It was when Moses met with God at the burning bush, that God told him, "I will be with you. And this will be the sign to you that it is I who have sent you: When you have brought the people out of Egypt, you will worship God on this mountain" (Exodus 3:12 NIV).

Moses learned something of the holiness and "otherness" of God in this encounter in which he received his calling from God. It was at that time that God also revealed to him His name and His purpose for His people. So, when Moses, in obedience to God, assembled the people at Sinai, it was with a sense of divine design and destiny that he convened the meeting that God had called.

This divine appointment was the reason that God had brought them out of Egypt. He proposed to make worshippers of them. He brought them out to worship Him at this place. We will discover in the passage in Exodus 19 that it was here at Sinai that God renewed the covenant He had made with their fathers. He had called them to be a kingdom of priests unto Him. This meant that His purpose was for the entire nation to consist of priests. Every Israelite would possess and exercise the privileges of priesthood, according to God's plan.

But this was too awesome and overwhelming for them. When God descended upon them at Sinai, they not only fled from His presence, but from the privilege of priesthood. It was their own consciousness of sin that caused them to realize they were not ready for this kind of priesthood. At their insistence, God allowed Moses to become their mediator.

God called the meeting, appointed the time, and pre-arranged and ordained the place. At Sinai there is a natural amphitheatre[78] that is created by two converging valleys confronted by an enormous perpendicular cliff. This forms a natural altar, before which the people had room to congregate. It was an awesome sight to behold, and God used this site to create a sense of the elevation and transcendence of His holiness. The surrounding scenes produce an ambience of loneliness, a fitting environment for the unparalleled revelation that awaited the people of God.

The Scripture is careful to give us the exact day of this meeting. It was in the third month, five or six weeks, bringing us to the same time frame as the Day of Pentecost. In fact, later on, the nation would celebrate Pentecost as the date of the giving of the law, although it cannot be absolutely documented to be the exact day. Nevertheless, it is a fitting observance, because of the similarity and the contrast of the two events.

At Sinai, God came down and wrote His laws in tables of stone. At Pentecost, by the Holy Spirit, He wrote those laws in the fleshly tables of the heart. Pentecost launched a new era, the age of the Church. One does not have to be a hyper-dispensationalist to

---

78   http://www.geographia.com/egypt/sinai/mtsinai.htm

recognize the new thing that God began with the birthing of the Church on the day of Pentecost!

It is impossible for us to grasp the significance of this meeting unless we recognize the magnitude of what transpired at Sinai. God is about to give the law that would govern the life and worship of His people. God is not merely giving a list of rules and regulations, for all of this is based upon His holiness, and is, in fact, a revelation of that holiness.

The whole Levitical system is based upon the premise, "I the LORD your God am holy" (Leviticus 19:2). When God gives them commandments regarding the civil responsibilities as well as the moral and ethical implications of being His people, it is always predicated upon the "I the LORD your God am holy" premise. Sinai is the first major disclosure of the holiness of God as it relates to man's response to God. God will divulge in awful detail the requirements of man in response to God's holiness.

But what God will give at Sinai is much more than the law. He will also give to Moses the pattern for worship. When God's holiness is delineated and man's sinfulness is understood, how can man then worship God? It is preposterous and presumptuous to think that sinful man can approach such a holy God as this! No wonder the Israelites shrunk away in horror and refused the call to priesthood! The awfulness of God's holiness impressed them with God's "otherness" and with the fact that they could not approach Him in their sinful condition. Therefore, God gives to Moses the plans for the tabernacle, showing the people how it is possible for them to approach a holy God, and showing them how He proposed to deal with the sin that separated them from Himself.

None of the previous worship encounters can be viewed as totally prototypical of Christian worship in the same sense as in the Sinai-event. Although there was an awareness of sin, and the bringing of sacrifices in faith, until the law there was not the same sense of transgression, as Paul points out in Romans 5:13. The exact and exacting character of God must be proclaimed by the law in order to instill an adequate measure for sin. While the moral component of the law prohibits man from coming into the presence of God, yet its ceremonial element makes it possible for man to come through the sacrifice and substitutionary work of another.

It is on the eve of Sinai, on the very edge of this awesome event that is about to transpire, that God assembles His people and establishes communion with them. He enters into covenant with them. He knows that they are going to be frightened by the demonstration of His power and holiness, so He reassures them of His love and of His care. In this meeting with God, there are three principal elements that are part of every worship encounter when God and His people meet in communion.

I. THE RECOGNITION OF GOD'S PROVISION

Communion is a wonderful experience. The American Heritage Dictionary defines it as "the act or an instance of sharing, as of thoughts or feelings, and as religious or spiritual fellowship."[79] The idea of communion with God is an awesome thought when we recognize His holiness and our sin, when we reflect upon the fact that He is Almighty and we are weak and frail. The sense of awe at God's desire to commune with us is something we must never lose if true worship is to take place. But on the other hand, we must never allow our sense of our own *finiteness* to intimidate or inhibit us from enjoying communion with the *infinite* God.

---

79 *The American Heritage® Dictionary of the English Language, Fourth Edition*, Boston, MA: Copyright © 2000 by Houghton Mifflin Company.

God begins the dialogue with a threefold reminder of His involvement and interaction with them. God is a master communicator! We would do well to learn from Him. The people were aware of the distance and separation between them and their God. The giving of the law will intensify that sense of separation. God desires to reassure them of His involvement with them and of His desire to maintain intimacy and communion with them.

There is a threefold recognition that He wants to instill upon them. He therefore reminds them of several facts:

A. What He did to Egypt

B. What He did for them

C. Why He did it

God prefaces His appeal to Israel with respect to the future by reminding them of what He had done for them in the past. The phrase "what I did to Egypt" serves to recollect the whole series of supernatural signs and wonders from the plagues to the drowning of Pharaoh in the Red Sea. God didn't have to say any more than "what I did to Egypt." That phrase was adequate to awaken memories of God's divine deliverance in a multitude of ways. It was also reminiscent of God's personal involvement in each of their lives. Their experience was both corporate and individual. Each of them was part of the company God had rescued.

A. What He did to Egypt

God's statement through Moses, "You yourselves have seen what I did to Egypt, and how I carried you on eagles' wings and brought you to myself" (Exodus 19:4 NIV), must have caused His people to reflect His marvelous works of judgment and grace. Possibly one man suppressed a smile as he remembered the frogs. Others thought of the lice, the plagues on the livestock, and the boils that came upon the Egyptians. Others may have recalled the hail or the locusts. The younger children may have relived the darkness and the terror they felt. Mothers may have recalled the plague on the firstborn, and their mourning for the Egyptian mothers who lost their infant boys. They remembered the plagues… how could they forget? The men among them who had thought they would have to defend their families in the face of Pharaoh's army may have pictured the opening of the Red Sea, and the drowning of the most sophisticated military machine in the world. The shrieks of soldiers and the cursing of the Pharaoh as he went down for the last time were still ringing in their ears. They remembered. They remembered what God did to Egypt.

The parallel for Christian worship is obvious. God wants us to know that **He** has taken care of Satan. When the disciples came back rejoicing because even the devils were subject unto them in the name of Jesus, our Lord said, "I beheld Satan as lightning falling from heaven" (Luke 10:18). Christ wants us to know that He has conquered the enemy for us. He told His disciples, "In the world you will have tribulation, but be of good cheer, I have overcome the world" (John 16:33). Paul assures us that God has put all things under the feet of Christ, including every principality, power, kingdom, might, and name that can be named. Christ is head over all of those to the church. (I Corinthians 15:27, Ephesians 1:22, Hebrews 2:8)

God has taken care of the enemies. He took our sins to the cross. He took our sin nature to the cross. In the cross he triumphed over Satan. By the cross the world is crucified unto us and us unto the world. Potentially, every enemy has been defeated by Christ in Calvary's provision. Even death, the last enemy to be destroyed, has already been conquered by Christ through His death and resurrection. The Christian is given a victorious position, and we need to be reminded of this that we might celebrate Christ's victory and our participation in that victory in our worship.

B. What He did for Israel

God also reminds the Israelites of His providential care for them. The tenderness and personal nature of that caring is portrayed in the figurative language that God employs to describe His watchfulness over them. "How I carried you on eagles' wings", (Exodus 19:4) metaphorically depicts what God had done. Eagles are unlike other birds, which take their young in their claws. Eagles bear their young upon their wings. The little eaglet may wriggle uneasily, wondering about the speed at which the parent flies. It may tremble with anxiety in the unfamiliar scenes through which it is passing.

But the little eagle is safe and secure. God is describing the strong, sustaining and powerful help by which He delivered them. He had borne them upon His wings. Just as the eagle flies under its young to catch them should they fall in flight, so God protects His children. In contrast to Egypt, whom He drowned in the Sea, He watches over the nation of His special grace and favor.

Again it must be emphasized that God gives them this reminder in the context of Sinai. God never deals with His people solely on the basis of the law. The hyper-dispensationalist misses the fact that even under law people were saved only by grace through faith. At the threshold of Sinai we witness the most gracious provision and promise of God! God is emphasizing His gracious dealings with the Israelites. Those dealings in grace formed the prelude both to the relationship He is about to form and the covenant He is about to forge with His people, Israel.

C. Why He did it

That brings us to the third recognition as to *why God did it*. Why did God see fit to do such things to Egypt and to graciously confer such privileges upon Israel? The phrase "Brought you to myself" (Exodus 19:4) provides insight as to the "why". The destination of God's people was not merely Sinai, or yet, the land of Canaan. The divinely appointed destination was "to God." If they had known their destiny and had been asked during the exodus, "Where are you going?' they would have had to reply, "To meet with God." In fact, Moses' remonstrance with Pharaoh was to let God's people go *that they might worship Him* (Exodus 5:1, 7:16, 8:1, 8:8, 8:20, 9:1, 9:13, 10:3).

This desire of God to be with His people and for His people to be with Him has never changed. He told Moses, "Then have them make a sanctuary for me, and I will dwell among them" (Exodus 25:8 NIV). Jesus chose the twelve to be with Him. God still calls His people to be with Him, to meet with Him, and to live in the awareness of His presence.

2. THE REALIZATION OF GOD'S PROMISE

The promise of God is realized in the covenant God makes with His people at Sinai. This is not the first covenant God has made. For example, the Abrahamic covenant was essentially an aid to Abraham's faith, for God bound Himself to be faithful to His Word. With *this* covenant, however, the people of God bind themselves to be faithful to Him. The Israelites take an oath of allegiance to their invisible King and pledge themselves to obedience.

The condition that God put upon this agreement was "If you obey me fully and keep my covenant." And yet, in the midst of this covenant of law, there was ample evidence of grace. Some of the factors demonstrating the modifying power of grace include:

1. There was grace preceding the law, as we discover in God's reminders of their deliverance from Egypt.

2. There was the employment of a mediator, Moses, to stand between God and the people.

3. There was the blood of sprinkling involved in the ratification of the covenant, indicating God's propitious plan.

4. The system of sacrifices and offerings was instituted to afford God's gracious dealing with them.

5. The actual facts of Israel's history reveal that God showed them mercy and grace time and again.

Although the covenant was made upon conditions, God did not default when Israel defaulted. Law was superseded by grace, while grace saw to it that the law was not ignored. It was grace that fulfilled the law in providing Jesus Christ as the fulfillment of the law's requirements both morally and ceremonially. The righteousness of Christ satisfied the moral demands of the law. The sacrifice of Christ fulfilled the need for a perfect substitute to take the place of the people and to bear their sins.

However, another area needs to be considered when we confront the law. Was if fair for God to bind upon the people a legislation to righteousness that He knew they could not fulfill? It was unfair, if the keeping of the law was to actually comprise the basis upon which He kept His covenant with them. In the giving of the law at Sinai, two impressive elements are inescapable:

1. God promises to award life to the obedient

2. God promises penalties upon the breaker of even the least of its commandments

It is difficult to conceive of God imposing such a strict behavioral code upon people as a means of attaining life, if He did not also impart to them the ability to measure up to it. Apart from an understanding of the role of the law, this covenant and God's subsequent dealings with His people cannot be rightly understood.

The imposition of a moral code beyond their capability as a means to life would be a mockery. God was not, however, mocking their weakness. Nor was He asking them to attain righteousness by a means beyond their capability. God had a purpose *beyond* having the Israelites to live righteously as a light among the other nations.

His purpose in the law went far beyond that. God designed the law in such a way that the sincere seeker after righteousness would *not* become proud of his own virtues, but rather *humbled by his inability* to produce righteousness. God's plan was to cause man to turn back to faith as the only means of salvation. The law was introduced to exclude boasting, to stop every mouth before God, to show that all are guilty, and to cause man to look instead to God for His righteousness and His salvation (Romans 3:18-20, Galatians 3:15-22).

So as Paul tells us, the law had an end beyond itself. It was the schoolmaster to bring us to Christ (Galatians 3:24). The later Jews who clung to its letter in unbending tenacity missed the entire purpose of the law, as Jesus pointed out to them many times in His Sermon on the Mount.

The honest Jew was quick to learn that what mattered to God was an obedient will, and that "He that feareth God and worketh righteousness is accepted of Him" (Acts 10:35). Such a man knew that there was forgiveness with God that He may be feared. They knew that if God was quick to mark iniquities no person could stand before Him. The law itself recognized its own offerings. So, while the covenant God gave had conditions, while externally it appeared as a covenant of law, internally it was a covenant of grace.

Having viewed the conditions upon which the covenant was given, we will consider what God promised and proposed to do for His people Israel. First, God says, Israel will be to Him a peculiar treasure, His treasured possession (Exodus 19:5). The Hebrew word, *segullah*, describes a precious possession to be esteemed highly and carefully guarded from all that might injure it. Out of all the nations of the earth (and they all belong to God) God had chosen Israel to whom and through whom He would reveal Himself. Theirs would be His laws and judgments, and He would be their King, their Defender, and their Benefactor!

God goes on to say that although the whole earth is His, they will be a "kingdom of priests" (Exodus 19:6). They will be both kings and priests simultaneously. What are the implications of their kingship? Spiritually, they would be lords over hell, death, the devil, and all evil. They would also be a theocracy under God, never having an earthly king over them! They would also rule over the heathen.

Whereas most men are enslaved to Satan, sold out to sin, servants of their evil passions, the children of God are to call no man master, for God's intention is that we live as kings. This He promised to His people Israel. They were to enjoy royalty and dignity, and rule as the special people of God.

But they were also priests. Each of them would be able to draw near to God Himself directly in prayer and praise, though not in sacrifice. They would also serve as intermediaries between God and the heathen world to whom they were to be examples. They would enjoy the privilege of acceptable approach to Him and would be especially consecrated to this service.

For the believer in Jesus Christ, all of these promises are realized. Peter, employing the precise language of this covenant, tells us that we are a royal priesthood and that we are to offer up spiritual sacrifices acceptable to God by Christ Jesus (I Peter 2:9). This is very much part of our worship. Knowing that we are kings appointed by Christ to reign in life, and knowing that we are priests, anointed by Christ to worship and serve Him, we are motivated to worship God acceptably with holiness and godly fear (Hebrews 12:28).

God tells His people both what they will be to Him, and what they will be to the world. To Him, His people are a precious treasure. He has purchased us at infinite cost. He bought the Church with His own precious blood. To the world, we are to be a kingdom of priests, and a holy nation. When God said that Israel was to be a holy nation, He meant quite simply that Israel was to be a nation unlike other nations. Israel was to be consecrated to God's service. They would be outwardly marked by the symbol of circumcision and inwardly marked by purity and holiness.

The missional design of God in making Israel a kingdom of priests is the principal thrust of this passage. Although they were priests to God and living under His reign, the primary emphasis is God's design to make them the vehicle of His message in the world. They were to stand between the other nations and God as His intermediary. Their kingship was more than spiritual. Their priesthood was more than their relationship to God. The ultimate end of their calling was to stand between God and the nations, just as a priest stands between God and the people.

For the Christian, this truth has a very obvious application. We must not separate our worship of God from our mission in the world.

Worship and mission are closely associated. We are priests to God, but also to the world. Our priesthood enables us to worship, but it also enables us to represent God in this world. As God's representatives, we take the message of His love from His presence in worship into the world.

3. THE RESPONSE OF THE GOD'S PEOPLE

In this entire passage, God has not spoken to the people directly. He has given His Word to Moses, who was charged simply, "This is what you are to say to the house of Jacob and what you are to tell the people of Israel… these are the words you are to speak to the Israelites" (Exodus 19:3, 6 NIV). Moses, in strict obedience to God's command, "went back and summoned the elders of the people and set before them all the words the Lord had commanded him to speak" (Exodus 19:7 NIV).

The initial response of the people is a rather naive statement that they proved they could not fulfill. "We will do everything the Lord has said," they replied (Exodus 19:8 NIV). A simple and singular response it was! And yet, while this commitment was commendable, the unfolding saga of Israel's history would prove that it was made rather rashly and broken repeatedly. D. L. Moody comments:

> "All that the Lord has spoken we will do." Bold and self–confident language. The golden calf, the broken tablets, the neglected ordinances, the stoned messengers, the rejected and crucified Christ, are overwhelming evidences of man's dishonored vows.[80]

There is no doubt that the people were sincere in their response. At long last their liberated minds arose to the challenge of the nobility

---

[80]   Moody, D. L. *Notes From My Bible*. Amsterdam, NL: Fredonia, 2002.

of their new relationship with God. How they longed to be what He called them to be! But the response was inadequate, as we will soon discover.

1. Firstly, this response was made without much knowledge of the law. The Ten Commandments had yet to be given. They had yet to comprehend the breadth and the depth of the law of God. They knew practically nothing of the spirituality of its requirements. But part of Israel's role would be to grow increasingly in the knowledge of this law so that they might have knowledge of sin (Romans 7:7-25).

2. Secondly, this response was given with very little knowledge of themselves. They didn't doubt their ability to keep God's commandments. They thought that all they had to do was to try it. Here again, God's purpose in putting them under the law, was to prove to them their own spiritual impotence.

3. Thirdly, it was a response made without any true heart-conversion, given in a burst of exuberance and excitement. It was merely an emotional response, and consequently it lacked depth. This response was not given from hearts transformed by God.

Commenting on the rash and rapid response of the Israelites to God's command, J. Vernon McGee notes,

> They said, "Bring it on; we'll keep it" before they even knew what it was! Then they demonstrated for fifteen hundred years that they could not keep the Law. This is the attitude of a great many people today—they think the natural man can please God. The natural man cannot keep the Law and he fails terribly in the attempt. The Law was given to control the old nature but it

cannot, because the old nature is a revolutionary which cannot be controlled… There is nothing that makes a greater hypocrite out of a person than for him to say, "I keep the Law!" No one can measure up to God's standards. Look at Israel. God is going to give them the Law and they say, "Bring it on, we are ready to keep it." What a display of self-confidence and arrogance. Yet there are multitudes of men and women today that claim they keep the Law even after God clearly demonstrated that no one can be saved by the Law—because no one can keep the Law. It was tried out under ideal conditions by the nation Israel.[81]

Worship is a response that is much more intelligent than the trite, emotional, naive and rash reply to God's Word that we find here. Is it possible that much of what passes for worship today is emasculated by these same faults? Do we attempt to worship without knowledge of God's Word and of our own hearts? Do we attempt to worship God without a transformed spirit? Jesus zeroes in upon these areas in His conversation with the woman at the well, when He insists that the Father is seeking true worshippers, whose worship will be birthed in sincerity, honesty, and from the depth of a being that has been touched by God (John 4:21-24).

But we discover in this passage that God did not stop with the verbal response of the people. Although made in naiveté, God proceeded to teach them something about worship, and about His person and character. When Moses brought their response back to the Lord, God told Moses, "I am going to come to you in a dense cloud, so that the people will hear me speaking with you and will always put their trust in you' (Exodus 19:9 NIV).

When Moses told God what the people had said, the Lord instructed Moses how to prepare the people for meeting with Him.

---

81   McGee, J. Vernon. Thru the Bible Commentary. electronic ed. Nashville, TN: Thomas Nelson, 1997.

What happens in this passage as the people are readied for their meeting with God becomes a fitting preface to the stricter and more sophisticated plan for worship that God will give to Moses later in Exodus. God was preparing to reveal to the people something of Who He is, and the people must be readied for this revelation. The people were required to wash their clothes, and to get ready for the third day in which the LORD would appear. Limits were to be placed around the mountain so that the people were not to go near it or touch it. God told Moses that if any touched the mountain they were to be stoned to death. They were also to abstain from sexual relations in preparation for their appointment with God.

On the morning of the third day there was thunder and lightning with a thick cloud over the mountain, and a very loud trumpet blast. Moses led the people out of the camp to meet with God, and they stood at the foot of the mountain. Mount Sinai was covered with smoke, because the Lord descended upon it in fire. The smoke billowed up from it like smoke from a furnace, and the whole mountain trembled violently, as the sound of the trumpet grew louder and louder. When Moses spoke, the voice of the Lord answered him!

The Lord descended to the top of the mountain and called Moses up to Himself. When Moses went up, God told him to warn the people not to try to force their way through to see the Lord for they would perish if they did. Moses told God that the limits they had imposed according to His instructions would keep the people out. God then told Moses to go down and bring Aaron up, but the rest of the priests and the people must not force their way up to the Lord, or He would break out against them and they would die.

The spectacle and specter of Sinai was awesome! After the people responded with the words "We will do everything the Lord has said," it was necessary for God to awaken them to an awareness of what they had covenanted to do. God must impress upon them His holiness, and the holiness of His law. God communicated directly to Moses so that the people as witnesses would preserve "Moses'" law forever as the oracles of God. God wanted them to fear His majesty. They were not to draw near. Even the priests, whose calling was to approach God, could not do so in this awful revelation of Himself. They must be aware of the unapproachable holiness of Jehovah and cognizant of their own unholiness.

New Testament worship is obviously different in some areas, but there are similar features that must not be overlooked. We cannot properly worship God without an awareness of His holiness. It is not that God is less holy and we are more holy, as believers in Christ, for God's holiness has not changed, nor has the fact of man's sinfulness. It is not the experience of our regeneration that enables us to approach God, but the blood and righteousness of Christ in which we stand. We are transformed by the power of God in regeneration, but we still have a nature that has a propensity to sin. We are holy "in Christ." We have put on His righteousness and are clothed in true holiness, being renewed in the image of Christ (Eph. 4:23-24).

The cross of Christ and the grace of God are exalted when the holiness of God is exalted. The holier that we see God to be, the greater will we see the grace of God that made a way into His presence, and the more powerful the blood of Christ that gained us access to God. Thus, we must embrace the God who revealed Himself on Sinai in the law and recognize His absolute holiness and majesty if we are to adequately appreciate Calvary and the provision of God's Lamb.

There is no real evidence in Scripture to support how many of the commandments were written upon each tablet, although much has been made of this by Bible scholars throughout the years. There are some who believe that the first four commandments, relating to our relationship with God, were engraved upon the first table, and that the last six, relating to our relationships with others, were written upon the second table. This view sees the words of Christ relative to the "first and great commandment" as embracing the first four (or the first table of the law), and the "second which is like it" embracing the other six (the second table of the law). At any rate, Christ has summarized the law in the two statements relative to loving God and loving our neighbor as ourselves.

Although an interesting study, it is not pertinent to our consideration of the law as it relates to worship. There can be no question that the Ten Commandments were God's instruction to His people as to how they were to worship Him in daily life. Worship for Israel was much more than the ceremonies and rituals they performed in approaching God. It involved the inculcating of these Ten Commandments into the fabric of their lives. Thus, they were to become the kingdom of priests that God ordained them to be. He had called them to be worshippers. Now He gives them the guidelines by which to live their lives as worshippers of God in the world.

The response of the people was quite different after the giving of the law from their initial naive response. When they saw the thunder and lightning, and the mountain in smoke, and heard the trumpet, they trembled with fear. They stayed at a distance and said to Moses, "Speak to us yourself and we will listen. But do not have God speak to us or we will die" (Exodus 20:19 NIV). Moses told them not to be afraid, saying, "God has come to test you, so that the fear of God will be with you to keep you from sinning" (Exodus 20:20 NIV). But the people remained at a distance while Moses approached the Lord in the thick darkness.

Before God proceeds to give them further laws concerning servants, personal injuries, protection of property, social responsibility, laws of justice and mercy, laws governing the Sabbaths and feasts, He introduces to them the sacrificial plan by which they are to approach Him. This will be more fully developed in the subsequent revelations, but now He tells them, "You have seen for yourselves that I have spoken to you from heaven. Do not make any gods to be alongside me; do not make for yourselves gods of silver or gods of gold. Make an altar of earth for me and sacrifice on it your burnt offerings and your fellowship offerings, your sheep and goats and your cattle. Wherever I cause my name to be honored I will come to you and bless you" (Exodus 20:22-24 NIV).

The response of the people has vacillated from the exuberant, excited, enthusiastic promise to do all that God has said, to a fearful intimidation and cowering away from His presence. God takes this response and now gives it some direction. He does not dilute His holiness, but gives them a plan and a pattern by which they can representatively approach His presence, and receive covering and forgiveness for their sins. This we will discover when we look more closely at the tabernacle in the wilderness. The writer to the Hebrews has the Sinai event in focus when he writes,

> You have not come to a mountain that can be touched and that is burning with fire; to darkness, gloom and storm; to a trumpet blast or to such a voice speaking words, so that those who heard it begged that no further word be spoken to them, because they could not bear what was commanded: "If even an animal touches the mountain, it must be stoned." The sight was so terrifying that Moses said, "I am trembling with fear." But you have come to Mount Zion, to the heavenly Jerusalem, the city of the living God. You have come to thousands upon thousands of angels in joyful assembly, to the church of the firstborn, whose names are written in heaven. You have come to God, the judge of all men, to the

spirits of righteous men made perfect, to Jesus the mediator of a new covenant, and to the sprinkled blood that speaks a better word than the blood of Abel. See to it that you do not refuse him who speaks. If they did not escape when they refused him who warned them on earth, how much less will we, if we turn away from him who warns us from heaven? At that time his voice shook the earth, but now he has promised, "Once more I will shake not only the earth but also the heavens." The words "once more" indicate the removing of what can be shaken—that is, the created things—so that what cannot be shaken may remain. Therefore, since we are receiving a kingdom that cannot be shaken, let us be thankful, and so worship God acceptably with reverence and awe, for our God is a consuming fire (Hebrews 12:18-29 NIV).

The bottom line of this entire passage is **worship God acceptably with reverence and awe.** The contrast for the New Testament believer between Sinai and Zion is powerful! We have come to the holy habitation of God! It is not to a mountain wrapped in a mantle of thunder nor a message carved by lightning! We are introduced to a new covenant, through Christ's blood, and are part of the Church of the firstborn. Our names are written in heaven! We have come to the heavenly Jerusalem! Each line of this passage warrants careful exegesis, and is rich in its significance for the Christian. But the essential point is that the bottom line has not changed. As I mediated on this passage, the lyrics and melody of an old chorus, the source of which I have yet to identify began to go through my mind: "Not to Sinai, not to Sinai, but to Zion we've arrived;Not to broken law, not to broken law, but to Christ who is alive. John Newton more eloquently captures this glorious truth:

Not to Sinai's dreadful blaze, But to Zion's throne of grace,

By a way marked out with blood, Sinners now approach to
God.

Not to hear the fiery Law, But with humble joy to draw

Water, by that well supplied, JESUS opened when he died.

LORD, there are no streams but thine, Can assuage a thirst
like mine!

'Tis a thirst thyself didst give, Let me therefore drink and
live.[82]

How precious is this truth! However, we do not become careless
in our worship because of the fact that our place of privilege and
position in Christ eclipses that of the Old Testament worshiper. In
fact, to whom more is given, more is required. And "to whom much is
given, much is required" (Luke 12:48). The New Testament believer
has no excuse for carefree, careless worship that is not rendered to
God intelligently.

The only appropriate and adequate response to what the
Christian has received in Christ is to say "I will do everything the
LORD has said." This consecration and dedication is the heart of
worship. Worship is the response of our hearts to God. It is the most
glorious and significant action that can take place in human life. It is
too urgent a priority for us to take lightly.

The writer to the Hebrews is concerned about worship. He is
concerned about the Christocentric nature of worship that must
characterize the worship of the Church. He is also concerned that
worship be taken outside the sanctuary where we gather to honor the
Lord's name.

Let us, then, go to him outside the camp, bearing the disgrace
he bore. For here we do not have an enduring city, but we are

---

82   Newton, John., *Not to Sinai's Dreadful Blaze*. http://www.ccel.org/ccel/newton/olneyhymns.h3_94.html

looking for the city that is to come. Through Jesus, therefore, let us continually offer to God a sacrifice of praise—the fruit of lips that confess his name. And do not forget to do good and to share with others, for with such sacrifices God is pleased (Hebrews 13:13-17 NIV).

This entire paragraph is concerned with worship. The passage talks about the altar that we have in Christ (v. 10). The writer then proceeds to describe to us where we gather unto Christ. Christ is "outside the camp." We offer the sacrifice of our livelihood in sharing our financial substance with others. We offer the sacrifice of our lives in submission to God and our leaders as we serve God in this world. No other response is an adequate response of worship to the God who has redeemed us at such a cost.

14

AN EXCLUSIVE INVITATION
TO DIVINE INTIMACY

*I've never been on good terms with God, but now I'm becoming
His intimate, for He is truly absolute and extremely legitimate.*

—Franz Grillparzer

*Nearer, my God, to Thee, nearer to Thee! Still all
my song shall be, nearer, my God, to Thee.*

—Sarah F. Adams

Then he said to Moses, "Come up to the LORD, you and
Aaron, Nadab and Abihu, and seventy of the elders of Israel. You
are to worship at a distance, but Moses alone is to approach the
LORD; the others must not come near. And the people may not
come up with him"…Moses and Aaron, Nadab and Abihu, and
the seventy elders of Israel went up and saw the God of Israel.
Under his feet was something like a pavement made of sapphire,
clear as the sky itself… they saw God, and they ate and drank.
The LORD said to Moses, "Come up to me on the mountain and
stay here, and I will give you the tablets of stone, with the law
and commands I have written for their instruction." When Moses
went up on the mountain, the cloud covered it, and the glory of

the LORD settled on Mount Sinai. For six days the cloud covered the mountain, and on the seventh day the LORD called to Moses from within the cloud. To the Israelites the glory of the LORD looked like a consuming fire on top of the mountain. Then Moses entered the cloud as he went on up the mountain. (From Exodus 24:1-18 NIV).

A s I watched the epic film *Titanic*,[83] winner of the Academy Award for best picture of 1997, I fought back the tears when I heard the refrain being played by the ship's band. But this was not the first for Hollywood: the 1936 movie *San Francisco*[84] was nominated for several Academy Awards. At the end of the movie you hear the refrain "Nearer, My God, to Thee" being sung.

There are other inspiring true life stories associated with this hymn. While some *Titanic* survivors said it was played by the ship's orchestra as the ocean liner went down, other survivors said it was a different song. When American president William McKinley, assassinated in 1901, lay on his death bed, Dr. Mann, the attending physician, reported that among McKinley's last words were the words from this hymn.[85] On September 13, 1901, bands in New York City played the hymn in memory of the fallen president. It was played again in Westminster Abbey, London at a memorial service held for him. The hymn was also played as the body of assassinated American President James Garfield was interred at Lakeview Cemetery in Cleveland, Ohio.[86]

83   *Titanic*, 1997, directed by James Cameron
84   *San Francisco*. (MGM, 1936), directed by WS Van Dyke
85   http://articles.latimes.com/2002/mar/24/news/mn-34488
86   http://berbc.org/hymns/Nearer%20My%20God%20to%20Thee.shtml

Fanny Crosby, the blind hymn-writer, was visiting Mr. W. H. Doane in his home in Cincinnati, Ohio. They were talking together about the nearness of God as the sun was setting and evening shadows were gathering around them. The subject so impressed the well-known hymn-writer that before retiring she had written the words to this hymn, which has become one of the most useful she has ever written. The music by Mr. Doane so well fitted the words that the hymn has become a special favorite wherever the Gospel Hymns are known.[87]

> I am Thine, O Lord, I have heard Thy voice, and it told Thy love to me;
>
> But I long to rise in the arms of faith and be closer drawn to Thee.
>
> *Draw me nearer, nearer blessed Lord, to the cross where Thou hast died.*
> *Draw me nearer, nearer, nearer blessed Lord, to Thy precious, bleeding side.*
>
> Consecrate me now to Thy service, Lord, by the power of grace divine;
> Let my soul look up with a steadfast hope, and my will be lost in Thine.
>
> O the pure delight of a single hour that before Thy throne I spend,
> When I kneel in prayer, and with Thee, my God I commune as friend with friend!
>
> There are depths of love that I cannot know till I cross the narrow sea;
> There are heights of joy that I may not reach till I rest in peace with Thee.[88]

The twenty-fourth chapter of Exodus portrays a picture of intimacy with God as it unfolds the story of the conclusion of the covenant that God made with Israel. Chapter twenty-five begins the instructions relative to the construction and worship of the tabernacle. At first glance, the beginning of chapter twenty-four reads like a repeat of the nineteenth chapter. But a close look will reveal that there are distinct differences that indicate to us that it is indeed a separate

---

87   http://www.hymntime.com/tch/htm/i/a/m/t/iamthine.htm

88   Crosby, Fanny J. *Nearer My God to Thee*, 1841

event. Some scholars believe that the first two verses reflect back to chapter nineteen and twenty, and cover what God said and did from chapters twenty through twenty-three. For our considerations, however, it is the remainder of the chapter, itself an event of singular importance, that reveals to us *three distinct levels of worship*.

Before I attempt to describe the **three levels of worship** that are outlined for us in this passage, and prior to suggesting any parallels that they might have for Christian worship, it is imperative to point out that in the Body of Jesus Christ there are no degrees or levels of importance. The entire Pauline theology on the Body of Christ insists upon the fact that we are all one body, and as such, there is no room for pride or pity. We have all been made to drink into one Spirit. We have all been baptized into one Body (I Corinthians 12:13).

In fact, this theme of unity in diversity becomes Paul's argument in Ephesians four to encourage the believers to make every effort to maintain the unity of the Spirit in the bond of peace. We serve the same Lord, are part of the same Body, have received the one and same Spirit, have been participants in the same calling, and embrace a common faith. Notwithstanding this common heritage, God gives us distinct giftings and callings in the Body, but we are all equal. Paul devotes a large segment of his letter to the Corinthian church to develop the motif of the Body, primarily to emphasize the equality of importance that is shared commonly by all the members of the body (I Corinthians 12:12-27).

Therefore, when we speak of **levels of worship** we are not referring to distinct orders of favor or grace that are based upon our position in Christ. It is a given fact that our position in Christ is on the basis of grace, and that we share that commonly with all Christians. The levels of worship, however, are determined by our response to God. We worship at the level of our discipleship and obedience.

The degree of our devotion and dedication will determine the degree of our discovery of God's presence. We will not worship beyond the level of our surrender to Christ's lordship. Excelling in the mechanics of worship style and expressions will not enhance the level of our worship, if we attempt to worship beyond our walk with God. The holistic nature of worship that we have emphasized throughout this book must be taken into account very seriously when we address the levels of worship.

I. LEVEL ONE: INVITATION

When we consider the meeting convened by God between Himself and His people at Sinai, we must readily concede that the meeting was by divine initiative. God called the meeting. He issued the summons, the invitation to assemble in His presence and to meet with Him. It was God who had called the people out of Egypt and brought them to Himself at Mount Sinai. It was here at the foot of this mountain that they became the "Q'hal Yahweh" or the assembly of God. This invitation by God is a prerequisite to worship. God calls His people to meet with Him.

In the previous chapter we examined the elements that provide evidence that the covenant was a covenant of grace. Those same features serve to identify the invitation as an invitation of grace. The mere fact that a holy God was willing to meet with an unholy people is in itself evidence of the great grace of God.

But what emerges in chapter twenty-four that we don't find in chapter nineteen are the sacrifices and offerings and the sprinkling of the blood upon the altar. The blood was not only sprinkled by Moses on the altar, but the blood was also sprinkled upon the people. Here again we have confirmed what we learned earlier, that the blood is first for God, and then for the people.

At this *first level of worship*, the people are assembled in response to the divine invitation. They are also assembled in a specific order with structure of responsibility. Although the role of leadership was given to Moses, other parts of the drama were played by Aaron, Nadab, Abihu, the seventy elders, the young Israelite men, and the people.

The picture portrayed is not that of the leaders and an audience, but of full participation on the part of those congregated. Each person was involved in this worship gathering. The full orchestration brought the entire congregation together in a harmonious whole. This illustrates for us the very important element of participation as a fundamental aspect of worship.

A *further* aspect in which this worship encounter typifies our gathering to Christ is that it was characterized by the **proclamation of the Word**. God spoke and made His will known to them. Worship is never complete without hearing from the Word of God. Unfortunately, in too many churches, the Word is not seen as being part of the worship experience. In other churches, the Word constitutes the entirety of the worship experience. We must hear from God through His Word, but worship also involves more than the hearing of the Word. There must be a response to God and to His Word on our part in order for worship to be the dynamic duo that God intends.

The meeting at Sinai was climaxed by a dramatic symbol of ratification, a sealing of the agreement by blood sacrifice, sealing God's relationship with His people. This, of course, points to the once-for-all sacrifice of our Lord Jesus Christ. If our worship fails to center around the celebration of Christ as the Lamb, it will miss the mark of what God wants it to be.

Thus in this event at Sinai, we have most of the basic elements that constitute Christian worship:

1. We are invited by God to gather together around Jesus Christ.

2. We hear His Word.

3. We respond in obedience.

4. We recognize that we are distanced from God by the law.

5. We draw near through the blood.

Invitation is the *first level of worship*, to which every child of God is brought by the blood of Jesus Christ. We are given a relationship with God. We have heard the divine summons to draw near to Him. We know that our sins are forgiven us and that we are accepted through the blood of Jesus Christ. We know that we have eternal life. We are in a covenant relationship with God through Christ. We are arranged in our particular structured roles of responsibility in His Church.

Certainly we rejoice in the fact that we are saved, that we have received the invitation of grace, and have responded to His call. But there is more to worship than responding to the call of salvation.

The phrase in Exodus 24:1 that says, "You are to worship at a distance," describes the worship of far too many of God's people. Although they know that they are saved and know how to praise God for the full and free forgiveness that they have received, they have never learned to worship God except "at a distance."

But it is not God's will for us to be distanced from Him. He doesn't want us to be numbered among those who, like Peter, prior to the cross, "followed him at a distance" (Matthew 26:58 NIV). Our summons is to "draw near to God with a sincere heart in full assurance of faith" (Hebrews 10:22 NIV). What separated Moses from other worshippers was his daring to press into the presence of God. He dared to ask God, "I beseech you, show me your glory" (Exodus 33:18).

The promise of God is that if we will draw nigh to Him that He will draw nigh to us (James 4:8). But the first level of worship becomes a plateau for many of God's people, because they are too easily satisfied to have forgiveness of sins and assurance of eternal life. But once you have tasted of the glory of worship beyond this first level, you can never be satisfied with that plane of experience in God!

2. LEVEL TWO: ILLUMINATION

Once we have heard the divine invitation to draw near, we recognize that God does not desire to distance Himself from us. It is paradoxical that the Holy One who is high and lifted up will grant us audience with Him. God desires to reveal Himself, to relate to us, to draw us closer to Himself. After coming to the knowledge of God's salvation through the blood of Christ, we hear the summons to "draw near." The second level of worship is a level of illumination where God is revealed to us in a greater way than just our Savior, as great and glorious as that is.

The writer to the Hebrews phrases it this way, "Therefore, brothers, since we have confidence to enter the Most Holy Place by the blood of Jesus, by a new and living way opened for us through the curtain, that is, his body... let us draw near" (Hebrews 10:19-22 NIV). This passage teaches us that the rending of the body of Christ has opened for us the way to God.

We partially grasp that truth when we come to God for salvation. We readily recognize that it is through the cross and the finished work of Jesus that we have access to God. When Jesus' body was broken and torn in the crucifixion, the penalty of sin was paid, and the way to God was opened for us.

But to fully comprehend the significance of the language employed in this passage, we need to understand the role of the "veil." The veil was one of several curtains in the tabernacle. It was the curtain that separated the holiest of all from the holy place. It guarded the glory of God's presence. The veil forbade entrance to God's presence by any except the high priest, and that only once a year, and not without blood. It was the veil that "veiled" the glory of God from the people of God. In a very real sense, the body of Jesus Christ was the fulfillment of that veil. God was at once both revealed *to* us and yet veiled *from* us in Christ. In Christ we behold the glory of God (John 1:14; II Corinthians 4:6) in as intense a manifestation as our finite beings are able to withstand. So the physical body of Christ served to simultaneously "veil" God from us and to "reveal" God *to* us. Therefore, the rending of the body of Christ released the glory of God to man, and granted mankind permission to enter into the presence of God.

Therefore, when we worship Christ, we are granted the glorious privilege of beholding the glory of God. That happened partially and figuratively on the Mount of Transfiguration. While Jesus prayed, He was transfigured before them. His face shone like the sun, and his clothes became as white as the light. What happened in that moment? The disciples were permitted a glimpse of the glory of God. It was probably this of which John wrote in John 1:14. It was this of which Peter spoke when he said, "We were eyewitnesses of His Majesty" (II Peter 1:16). For a brief moment in time, the physical body of Christ became mysteriously translucent, or transparent, and the glory of God radiated through Him.

This represents to us that **second level of worship**, that of **illumination**, where God opens our eyes and reveals Himself to us in His splendor and in His glory. This is what happened to Moses and the seventy elders on the mountain!

It is interesting to note that God gave permission only to Moses to draw closer, and yet He did not kill those that dared to press into His presence, as long as they had made the proper preparation. "Moses and Aaron, Nadab and Abihu, and the seventy elders of Israel went up and saw the God of Israel. Under his feet was something like a pavement of sapphire, clear as the sky itself. But God did not raise his hand against these leaders of the Israelites; they saw God, and they ate and drank" (Exodus 24:9-11 NIV). "They saw the God of Israel." A simple statement is made, without any indication of the form and shape. We would do well not to speculate as to the nature of what they saw, beyond what is told us! All we know is that they saw with their physical eyes some representation and manifestation of the Divine Being that had summoned them to His presence. There are several important truths for us to consider at this level of illumination:

1. A vision of God is possible

2. The vision of God is at the place of His feet

3. The vision of God invites us to feast in His presence

4. The vision of God provides a prophetic glimpse of the gospel

1. First, a vision of God is possible. Moses saw a similitude of God. Isaiah saw the Lord high and lifted up (Isaiah 6:1). Ezekiel saw upon the throne "the appearance of a man" (Ezekiel 1:5). These men had a vision of God. John said, "No one has ever seen God, but God the only Son, who is at the Father's side, has made him known" (John 1:18 NIV). Jesus told us, "Anyone who has seen me has seen the Father" (John 14:9 NIV).

The apostle Paul talks about beholding Christ when he says, "Now the Lord is the Spirit, and where the Spirit of the Lord is, there is freedom. And we, who with unveiled faces all reflecting the Lord's glory, and being transformed into his likeness with ever-increasing glory, which comes from the Lord, who is the Spirit" (II Corinthians 3:17-18 NIV). Is it possible for us to behold Christ? Yes! Not with natural eyes, nor by the use of "imaging" or "imagining," but we behold Him in the pages of the Word. The Holy Spirit reveals Christ to us through the Word, and we, with John, behold His glory. Like Moses, we "see Him who is invisible." We behold Him by faith, for faith is the substance of things hoped for, the evidence of things not seen. Images or impressions of Christ are impressed upon our spirit from the Word of God, and we behold Him through eyes of the Spirit. God wants to open our eyes to see Jesus in ever-increasing glory and splendor.

2. Secondly, the vision of God is at the place of His feet. There is no mention of any physical form. Perhaps they were so enveloped in haze that they couldn't distinguish any form. We do not know. But what we do know is that they beheld the place of His feet. Actually, they saw what was *under* His feet! They saw, beneath His feet, a pavement like sapphire. This certainly declares that the God of heaven is enthroned above the heaven in super-terrestrial glory. Even the most glorious of the heavens are beneath His feet!

The Place of His Feet

But the place of His feet has even richer implications when studied in the Word of God. Isaiah 60:13 says that God will "make the place of His feet glorious." In this passage, the context refers to the rebuilding of the temple of God in Jerusalem. That is significant, because the temple became known as "the place of God's feet," or "Jehovah's footstool." In I Chronicles 28:2, David said, "I had it in my heart to build a house as a place of rest for the ark of the covenant of the Lord, for the footstool of our God." Solomon's temple became the dwelling place of God, or the place of His feet.

a. A Place of Revelation or Illumination

The *place of His feet* is glorious as a *place of revelation or illumination*. Technically, revelation is complete in Christ. What we now receive is illumination upon God's revelation in Christ. David discovered this joy as we learn in Psalm 27:4, "One thing I ask of the Lord, this is what I seek; that I may dwell in the house of the Lord all the days of my life, to gaze upon the beauty of the Lord and to seek Him in His temple."

Nowhere is this better illustrated than in Luke 10:39 where Mary sat at the Lord's feet listening to what He said. Martha was busily engaged in serving Jesus, but missed out on revelation by not sitting at His feet. Mary had found the place of His feet to be glorious for revelation, and listened intently to every word that He spoke. Too many of us are "Martha" Christians. We are so preoccupied with "serving" Christ that we have not discovered the glory of the place of His feet in worship.

b. A Place of Supplication and Intercession

The *place of His feet* is also glorious as a *place of supplication and intercession*. Many times in the gospels we read of those who came and fell at the feet of Christ pleading earnestly for His intervention in their problems.

In Mark 5:22, Jairus falls at the feet of Christ, pleading for mercy for his dying daughter. In Mark 7:25, the woman whose daughter was demonized falls at the feet of Christ begging for His help. Mary, in John 11, falls at the feet of Christ and weeps over the loss of her brother Lazarus. The power of intercession is discovered at the place of His feet. This is illustrated for us in the two books of the Bible that are named for women.

In the Book of Ruth, when Naomi and Ruth had returned to Bethlehem in Judah, they had need of a kinsman who would be able and willing to buy back their land of which their family had been dispossessed. When Ruth lay at Boaz' feet, his heart was moved to respond to their need, and he consequently became her kinsman-redeemer. Ruth had discovered the power of intercession at the place of Boaz' feet (Ruth 3:7).

In the story of Esther, we find another beautiful picture of intercession at the feet of a king (Esther 7:3-4, 8:3). When Esther discovered that her people, the Jews, faced annihilation, she was persuaded by her uncle Mordecai to step in and intercede for her people. She fell at the feet of the king, weeping and pleading for the life of her people. The king responded favorably to her, and her people were spared.

The place of God's feet is glorious as a place of intercession and supplication. In each of the above cases, intercession was achieved by virtue of establishing a favorable relationship with the one in power. We cannot discover the power of intercession unless we have spent enough time at the feet of Christ to develop a relationship with Him by which we dare to intercede.

c. A Place of Worship, Inspiration and Adoration

But beyond illumination and intercession, the place of His feet is also a *place of worship and inspiration, or a place of adoration.* In Matthew 28:9 we read, "Suddenly Jesus met them. 'Greetings,' He said. They came to Him, clasped His feet and worshipped." When Thomas saw Jesus' hands and feet, he worshipped Him, saying, "My Lord and my God" (John 20:28).

In an earlier chapter we described the twin stories of the women who came and washed the feet of Jesus with their tears, anointing them with precious perfume. What a picture of worship! Mary was one of those women. She, who had found the place of His feet to be a place of **waiting** and **weeping**, also found it to be a place of **worship**. Worship at the feet of Jesus will always fill the house with the fragrance of the incense of praise and adoration!

For the Christian, we know that God has put all things under the feet of our Savior, and given Him to be head over all things to the Church. All things are put under those feet. Suppose that our place in the body of Christ is to be the bottom of the feet, still, all things are under us!

The **place of His feet** shows us that He is exalted over all. When Moses and the seventy elders saw the place of His feet, they knew that nothing was above Him. True worship sees God enthroned over all.

Every vision of God in Old or New Testament sees Him exalted! John the Revelator saw Him in exalted form in his vision. God wants to open our eyes until we behold Him high and lifted up, until we know that He is truly God, King of kings and Lord of lords.

3. The vision of God invites us to feast in His presence

The third aspect of this level of illumination is that *we can feast in the presence of God.* "They saw God, and they ate and drank." There are two things we need to learn from this passage. Worship is not the mysterious, mystical, metaphysical, esoteric, surreal thing that some people want to make it. As great and as glorious as a vision of God may be, you don't have to be out of your body or out of your mind to receive it! We are still human beings, with human appetites, and we can eat and drink in the presence of God.

Not only so, but to be in the presence of God is to "have meat to eat that you know not of" (John 4:32). Being in the presence of God is indeed food and drink in a very beautiful way as we learn what it is to feast upon Him. The old song we used to sing went something like this, "Since my soul is saved and sanctified; feasting, I'm feasting; on the hidden manna I'll abide; feasting with my Lord."[89] How I remember singing that in church as a child! Even at a young age I recall how precious those moments of worship were in the presence of God when I sensed that I truly was feasting upon Him!

4. The vision of God provides a prophetic glimpse of the gospel

The fourth thing that we observe on this second level of illumination is *a prophetic glimpse of the gospel.* The act of eating and drinking is a sign of reconciliation. Offering food in Biblical times was an indication of peace and friendship. That is why Jesus had prepared breakfast on the beach for Peter and the disciples after His death and resurrection. Although they had abandoned Him, and Peter especially had denied Him, He was offering them the peace meal. Moses and the seventy elders on that mountain with God prefigured both

---

89   Brown, John S. (Words) and Brown, L. O.(Music). Indianapolis, IN: 1899.

the feast of the gospel and the marriage supper of the Lamb, when we will sit down in the kingdom with the redeemed of the ages and partake of that meal with our Lord!

3. LEVEL THREE: INTIMACY

Although it hardly seems possible, there was yet a *higher level of worship* than that of seeing God. It was reserved for Moses alone, to whom God called out of the cloud to come up into the cloud with Him. The glory of the Lord had settled upon Mount Sinai! To Israel it looked like a consuming fire, but Moses was not harmed.

Seeing God is illumination, but not necessarily intimacy. But being one with Him, and being with Him for forty days is a different matter! Moses discovered something of God's person and character, and God said that He spoke to Moses face to face. He made known His acts to Israel, but His ways to Moses (Psalm 103:7). Moses was privileged to develop an intimacy with God that enabled him to approach God with boldness and confidence.

Moses was alone with God when he received the plan for Israel's pattern of worship. For somewhere between thirty-four and forty days he stayed alone in the presence of God on that mountain, receiving the plan and pattern for true worship in the nation of Israel.

There is a *place of intimacy in worship* that defies description! You may be in church when you experience this, but you know that it is just "you and the Lord." You may be surrounded by people, but when you step up into the cloud and enjoy this kind of intimacy with God, you know that this is the purpose for which you were born.

The heart of the worshipper will be ever seeking to go higher and deeper with God. Even after this experience, Moses dared to advance further and even asked God to show him His glory. The worshipper will always be satisfied with the quality of what God does, but never with the quantity! Moses pressed in for more of God. This characterizes all of God's saints. David was the same way. He wanted a deeper realization of God's presence than he had ever experienced.

The apostle Paul in the New Testament demonstrates this same quest for the divine presence. After having been caught up into the third heaven of revelation, he still prayed to know Christ in the power of His resurrection, the fellowship of His suffering, and to be made conformable unto His death (Philippians 3:10). Paul wanted yet more and more of God!

When we are magnetically drawn into His presence, the fire of His presence causes us to be melted before Him until His life is fused into ours and we become one with Him. This is the highest level of worship possible, when we are so united with Him in spirit and heart, that we become one with Him.

John, the beloved disciple, knew such intimacy with Christ. He was that disciple whom Jesus loved. He leaned upon the bosom of our Lord. He knew Christ in an intimate way. When he wrote his epistle, John expressed the desire to pass on to his readers that same experience of intimacy. "We proclaim to you what we have seen and heard, so that you may also have fellowship with us" (I John 1:3 NIV). John is describing the dynamic of Jesus' life and presence in his life many years after Christ had died, been buried, risen and ascended. John was saying, "I can still hear His voice ringing in my ears. I can still sense the touch of His hand. I can still see him with my eyes. And now I want to pass on to you that same sense of intimacy of fellowship that I still enjoy with my Lord" (I John 1:1-3).

This is possible for every worshipper. It is not a place of privilege that is assigned or foreordained by divine election! We choose at what level we will worship. We decide whether we will enjoy the fullness of fellowship or whether we will be content to worship at a distance.

SUMMARY

At what level are you worshipping God? Are you content to "worship at a distance," knowing that you have been redeemed by His blood and are in a covenant relationship with Him? Are you satisfied to know that your sins are forgiven and you have eternal life? Or do you long for the illumination of His Spirit and the revelation of His Person?

Have you seen the Lord? Have you caught such a vision of His exalted holiness and His transcending power that your mind has been filled with the vision of His Lordship? Have you been an "eyewitness of His Majesty"? Have you "beheld His glory"? Have you seen Christ the risen, reigning Lord with the eyes of your spirit?

Have you dared to step beyond the rank and file and step up into the cloud with the Lord where you have experienced the glorious divine intercourse of intimacy with Him? Have you felt His heartbeat? Have you sensed Him breathe upon you the breath of divine life? Is your will welded and wedded to His? Have you known intimacy with God?

Wherever you are in your worship experience, at whatever level you may be, it is not the will of God for you to plateau at that plane. God has higher heights to be scaled and deeper depths to be plummeted for the worshipper that will not be satisfied with the status quo, but will seek to draw near to God.

FURNISHINGS OF GOLD IN
A PORTABLE CHURCH

And see to it that you make them according to the
pattern which was shown you on the mountain.

—Exodus 25:40 NKJV

The LORD said to Moses, "Tell the Israelites to bring me an offering... Then have them make a sanctuary for me, and I will dwell among them. Make this tabernacle and all its furnishings exactly like the pattern I will show you. Have them make a chest... overlay it with pure gold... the ark the Testimony... make an atonement cover of pure gold... make two cherubim out of hammered gold at the ends of the cover... over the ark of the Testimony... I will meet with you and give you all my commands for the Israelites. Make a table... overlay it with pure gold... put the bread of the Presence on this table to be before me at all times. Make a lamp stand of pure gold and hammer it out, base and shaft; its flowerlike cups, buds and blossoms shall be of one piece with it... then make its seven lamps and set them up on it so that they light the space in front of it. See that you make them according to the pattern shown you on the mountain. (Exodus 25:1-40 NIV)

The year that Israel spent at Sinai was one of tremendous significance for the Hebrew race and for the entire world. The events that happened during this period of time occupy the latter half of Exodus, all of Leviticus and a large portion of Numbers. That's over eighty pages of my Bible, constituting over six percent of the entire Scriptures! And in all of this section, God is teaching His people how to worship. The amount of copy that God gives to this should impress upon us that God is laying down a permanent pattern for worship. Not only are fifty chapters of the Old Testament devoted to this subject, but over forty percent of the Book of Hebrews is given to its explanation!

Central to the corporate worship of God's people was the tabernacle that God told Moses to have them build so that He might dwell among them. "Then have them make a sanctuary for me, and I will dwell among them. Make this tabernacle and all its furnishings exactly like the pattern I will show you" (Exodus 25:8-9 NIV).

When God descended upon the mountain in Sinai with His presence and gave the Ten Commandments to Moses, He was revealing His holiness to His people. Before the Israelites could appreciate God's plan of access, they first must realize that His holiness makes Him unapproachable. Only when we have an awareness of the holiness of God do we have an understanding of the sinfulness of sin. And only by this two-fold realization can we appreciate the magnanimous nature of the privilege of drawing near to God in worship.

The tabernacle in the wilderness was divinely designed, down to the most minute detail. Apparently Moses "saw" something in the mountain. He probably saw the tabernacle in vision in the form in which it was ultimately constructed. It is doubtful that he saw the "heavenly" tabernacle, for "heavenly" things are not discerned with physical faculties. But Moses was instructed repeatedly to ascertain that the tabernacle's construction conformed precisely to the divine pattern he had received.

This tabernacle was a perfect replica of something that already existed in heaven. It is difficult to determine whether or not there actually exists in heaven a physical structure after which the tabernacle of God on earth was patterned. However, we do know that the tabernacle is a picture, a shadow and a type of the Lord Jesus Christ. "The point of what we are saying is this: We do have such a high priest, who sat down at the right hand of the throne of the Majesty in heaven, and who serves in the sanctuary, the true tabernacle set up by the Lord, not by man" (Hebrews 8:1-2 NIV).

Our Lord Jesus Christ is God tabernacled among us. John writes "And the Word became flesh, and did tabernacle among us, and we beheld his glory, glory as of an only begotten of a father, full of grace and truth" (John 1:14, Young's Literal Translation). The Amplified Bible renders it like this, "And the Word [Christ] became flesh (human, incarnate) and tabernacled—fixed His tent of flesh, lived awhile—among us; and we [actually] saw His glory—His honor, His majesty; such glory as an only begotten son receives from his father, full of grace (favor, loving kindness) and truth." In this verse, the Greek word "skenoo" means to tent or to encamp, so the idea of "tabernacling" is conveyed in the original language.

This concept is theologically sound. Christ is certainly God with us. The name *Immanuel* which the prophet said He would receive (but by which He was never literally known) intends the same truth. Christ is God tabernacled among us. This truth must also inform our worship. We worship God when we worship Christ. The whole message of the tabernacle insofar as its applications and implications for Christian worship are concerned has to do with the Christocentric nature of Christian worship.

The study of the tabernacle can be approached from many different angles. Some see the tabernacle as representing the individual believer as well as portraying Christ. Some view the tabernacle as a dispensational portrait of church history. It is our intention to approach the tabernacle as a representation of Christ. I believe we are on shaky ground hermeneutically when we attempt to take it any further than this.

Many wonderful works have been written on the tabernacle itself as it portrays to us the beauty and the glory of our Lord and Savior Jesus Christ. In some writings the minutest of details of the furnishings are developed to rather dubious conclusions. A lot of speculation goes into many of the interpretations that are made. Obviously, my approach to the tabernacle will be much sketchier, and I will merely attempt to hit the high points and the highlights as it relates to our worship of Christ.

The worship of Christ will therefore prejudice our view of the tabernacle. Since the tabernacle worship of Israel prefigures Christian worship then the tabernacle itself must be viewed Christologically.

When God gave the instructions to Moses, He began with the contents of the Holiest of all and moved out from there. That is the way it should be when revelation comes down from heaven! We should begin with that which is most critical and which represents to us the presence of God in its most immediate sense. But the approach to the tabernacle begins from man's level. Therefore, we will begin at the outer court, and gradually work our way into the holiest of all.

I. THE PROVISION OF CHRIST

1. The Outer Court

With its gate pointing to the east, the outer court stretched one hundred fifty feet in length and seventy-five feet in width, enclosed by a seven and one-half foot high fence covered in white linen. The linen hung on rods of silver suspended by sixty posts.

It served to assure the people of God that God would not "burst forth" upon them, as He had warned when He descended upon Sinai. It also separated the people from God, and gave a sense of privacy to the priests who carried on their duties within the tabernacle. White linen always represents the righteousness of God, and here it demonstrates that it is His righteousness that shuts Him in and shuts man out. It also pointed forward to the Messiah by whose righteous covering we would gain access to the presence of God, and by whose provision we could become worshippers of God.

God gave the name "tent of the congregation" to this particular enclosure, because none but the priests could come any closer to Him. What a striking contrast this white fence would be to the blackness of the goats hair of which most tents were made in that part of the world.

But there was a door through this fence into the presence of God! The door was made of curtains of blue, purple, scarlet and fine-twined linen—the work of an embroiderer—and were hung of four posts on four bases.

Some scholars have seen this four-fold curtain as representing the gospels. For instance, Matthew presents Christ as the King, corresponding to the purple or royal color. Mark presents Jesus as the suffering servant, suggested by the scarlet. Luke presents Christ as the righteous one, depicted by the white or fine-twined linen. John presents Christ as the heavenly Savior, answering to the blue. It is interesting that this was all embroidered together. So the gospels present the harmonious woven work of the life and ministry of Jesus Christ.

The curtains themselves hung upon posts of wood, over bases of brass, with sockets of silver. What a combination! But a perfect picture of Christ, the door to salvation. The wood speaks of our Lord's humanity; the brass always speaks of judgment, and silver of redemption. Through the cross of Christ, where Jesus gave up His life, God judged sin, but in the same moment redeemed humanity.

Even the placing of each element is important. Judgment (brass) is under us. We are crowned with the helmet of salvation (silver). The silver hooks joined the curtains to the posts. It is the redemption of our Lord Jesus Christ that joins us to His righteousness as well! As seemingly minor a detail as the order of the colors remains constant throughout the tabernacle instructions. This is not only true for the other hangings, but also for the garments of the High Priest. Blue always comes first, purple second, scarlet next, and white is last. Jesus is first of all the heavenly Son of God. He is next the King of Kings, then the suffering Savior, and finally the sinless son of God as proved in His resurrection.

2. The Brazen Altar

If it were possible to have an aerial view of the tabernacle, or to look at it as God saw it from heaven, there was the definite formation of a cross in the arrangement of the furniture. By drawing a straight line from east to west, and also one from south to north, passing through each article of furniture, the shadow of the cross appears! The top part of the cross, where Christ's head was crowned with thorns, would correspond to the Ark of the Covenant. At the foot of the cross, where His feet were pierced, would be the brazen altar, the place of judgment. How thrilling to know that Christ's sacrifice is now complete and He has put all things under His feet in the triumph of the cross.

Our pilgrimage of worship will begin at the foot of the cross and take us into the presence of God's glory! The brazen altar was rather large and imposing. In fact it was large enough that every other piece of furniture in the tabernacle could have been placed inside of it.

How beautifully this describes the completed work of Christ upon the cross! From the fountainhead of the cross every other blessing flows into our lives. The altar was a perfect cube, seven and one-half feet each direction. It was made of wood overlaid with brass. Wood was very practical, since the actual form of the construction was wooden planks overlaid with brass. No gold or silver was to be used on this altar, because it was primarily a place of judgment. Only when the worshipper moved beyond this point could he know the significance of redemption and of God's glory.

The altar also had horns on each of the four corners and a grate-work around the base of it. The sacrificial offerings were brought to and placed upon this altar where they were burned. The fire, which ignited the sacrifices, was to find its source in the pillar of fire that hovered over the holy place. Any other fire that originated with man was considered to be "strange fire."

This indicates to us that the judgment of God upon the sins of man took Christ's life, not merely the cruelty of His executioners. It also reveals that the sacrifice must ultimately be accepted before God. The fire in the holy place, which ignited the incense, had to come from the brazen altar. Our worship must be ignited by Calvary, and even that fire doesn't begin with us. It begins with God!

The sacrifice had to be lifted up and placed upon the altar, just as our Lord was lifted up on the cross. The brazen altar was the place of substitutionary atonement, and pointed forward to the cross where Jesus Christ would be offered as the final sacrifice for the sins of the world. There He who knew no sin was made sin for us. He suffered the judgment of God for our sins. He experienced the wrath of God for our transgressions that we might go free.

All true worship begins here! We cannot hope to come to God for salvation apart from the cross of our Lord Jesus Christ. The cross alone is the basis of our salvation, and the gateway to worship. There is no true worship of God that is not ignited by the coals of Calvary. The Lamb of God is the eternal theme of worship. The blood shed at the brazen altar is taken all the way into the holiest place, so the entirety of our worship and service to God is colored by the scarlet sacrifice of the Savior.

For many years skeptics criticized the construction of the brazen altar in particular as being ridiculous, stating that anything made of wood and overlaid with bronze (or copper, as this brass probably was) would eventually be destroyed by such intense heat. An interesting development in London, England during the Second World War brought an answer to this criticism. When incendiary bombs were wreaking havoc, the London County Council Fire Brigade was faced with the challenge of creating a fire-proof door while conserving metals. After many unsuccessful efforts, they opened it to the public and offered a reward for the best door. The type of door that went through every test perfectly—even in the worst of fires—was a wooden door, overlaid with copper. It became heralded as a late scientific discovery as they found that beaten copper allows no air to penetrate, thus preventing fire. God used this principle centuries before man discovered it.

3. The Brazen Laver

The second piece of furniture encountered in the outer court, the laver of brass, represents another important aspect of Christ's provision, and another important element in our worship. There are no particulars given in Scripture as to the size or shape of the laver. It was a large bronze vase of basin, which stood between the altar and the holy place.

Since the priests were required to wash both their hands and feet at the laver, it probably had a base on the bottom upon which they could put their feet for cleansing, and a larger bowl at the top, from which they could take water for the washing of their hands.

This giant bowl also served as a sort of concave mirror, which, when filled with water would produce an effect of magnification. In fact, it was made from the mirrors of bronze, which the Israelite women brought with them out of Egypt.

Both the laver and the altar are made of brass. Both, in a sense, speak of judgment, although each in a different way. However, there are more differences between these two articles of furniture than similarities. While the altar is square, the laver is round. The altar is wood overlaid with brass, while the laver is solid brass. Whereas the altar had prescribed coverings for its transit, the laver had none. Only the priests could wash at the laver, but the altar was for all the people. Perhaps the most obvious contrast is the fact that there was water in the laver, and fire on the altar.

Most scholars see the laver as representing to us the "washing of the water by the Word" (Ephesians 5:26), or the practical cleansing, whereas the altar presents God's positional and provisional cleansing in the cross, where God has judged our sins in Christ. He has secured our salvation. Faith in God's Word, however, makes this a pragmatic experience in our lives.

Some see the altar dealing with the sin principle within us, while the laver provides for acts of sin that we commit. I believe that the laver represents to us the more comprehensive cleansing that God has provided by the blood, but which is made efficacious by His Word. In the life of a sinner who comes under conviction, it is the WORD of God, which effects the cleansing of Christ's blood when that person believes in Jesus. Likewise for the Christian who commits an act of sin after he is saved, it is still to the Word that we go to receive cleansing. We cannot, in fact we dare not, isolate, differentiate between the cleansing of the blood and that of the water. From the side of Jesus there flowed both blood and water when He died upon the cross. The Bible sees fit to record this because of its special significance to the believer.

Upon the hearing of the Word, faith is born. The hearing of the Word simultaneously cleanses our lives and gives birth to faith. The blood of Christ purges our consciences from dead works to serve the living God, and yet the Word is the divine agency that God uses to convey the power that is resident in that blood (Hebrews 9:14, Hebrews 4:12, I Peter 1:23, James 1:18).

While it is difficult to develop a theology on this point, a careful study will determine that there is life in the blood that we don't understand. When the breath of life leaves the individual, the blood dies. When oxygen is no longer supplied, the blood cannot live. Mysteriously, the blood is linked to the spirit. When the spirit leaves a man his blood dies. What does this have to do with Christ? Jesus said, "The *words* that I speak unto you they are spirit and they are life" (John 6:63, *emphasis* mine). God's Spirit cannot operate separate from His Word. His Word and Spirit are of the same essence. God is Word, and God is Spirit. God's life indwells both. The only vehicle that can convey the Life of God into the life of mankind is the Spirit of God through His Word. And the only means by which the blood of Christ can be appropriated to the life of the believer is through the eternal Word of God. The efficacy of the blood is made effective through the Word.

Thus the provision of the laver is predicated upon the provision of the brazen altar. That which was secured provisionally at the cross is applied pragmatically through the Word of God. Whether for initial salvation, or for continuous cleansing, these two articles constitute the provision of God on our behalf for sin. As it relates to our worship, we come to God by way of the cross. By faith in His blood we receive the promised provision of His Word and are cleansed. There is a perennial cleansing that the believer enjoys as he walks with God that is an extremely vital part of our worship.

The laver served as a mirror. The priest could see his reflection in it. The Word of God serves similarly. When we come to God's Word we see not only our sin, but also our need of cleansing. However, it is not enough to see ourselves. James tells us that the man who looks in the mirror and goes away unchanged is an unwise man (James 1:22-25).

Jesus demonstrated to us the significance of the laver when at the last supper, He took a towel, and a basin of water and began to wash His disciples' feet. When He came to Peter, Peter said, "Lord, you'll never wash my feet" (John 13:8). Upon hearing that he could have no part with Jesus if he didn't let the Lord wash his feet, Peter said, "Not just my feet, but also my hands and my head" (John 13:9). Jesus reassured Peter that once he was clean, he needed only to have his feet washed. Later Jesus told them that they were clean through the Word that He had spoken unto them (John 15:3). I believe that Jesus' command concerning the washing of each other's feet, was not necessarily a reference to the literal act of foot-washing, so much as to the washing of each other's lives with the water of God's Word (John 13:14-15). He certainly was telling Peter that once he had been cleansed from sin, he needed not to get saved over and again, he needed only to have his walk washed by the Word of God.

We must never remove God's Word from our worship. We often think of the worship service being divided into "worship" and "word" as if the two were separate. In truth, the hearing of the Word of God is a vital part of our worship encounter, for it is that hearing that brings the cleansing of Christ's blood into effect in our daily lives. But it is not only the hearing of the Word that we need. We must apply it! Merely looking into the laver didn't bring any cleansing! And just listening to the Word won't cleanse from sin. We must apply it to our lives in every-day situations.

We need to be careful in the distinction between inward and outward sin. While it is obvious that the altar is the place where God has dealt with the judgment of inherent sin, and the laver is the place for cleansing from the outward acts of sin, the distinction may be debatable. *What we do* is caused by *what we are*, and we need the cleansing of the Word of God *internally*, not merely in an *external* way. We do, however, need to recognize the difference between the *cleansing of daily defilement* and the *once-for-all work* of the cross of Christ. We don't have to get born again over and again! We don't need to get saved every time we commit an act of sin. But we must never forget that only the blood of Christ can cleanse from sin, and the cleansing **provided** by the Word is **procured** by the blood. The New Testament is "in Jesus' blood" (Luke 22:20, I Corinthians 11:25). He sealed and ratified the new covenant with His blood, and the only way the blood can be conveyed into our lives is through the Word of God acting in the power of the Holy Spirit.

It is interesting that there was no floor in the tabernacle! The priests, performing the daily service in the tabernacle, continued to get their hands and feet dirty as they did God's service. This speaks of the daily defilement and contamination that even the most holiness-minded child of God cannot avoid in this world. Even in the occupation of serving God, we need provision for the cleansing of our deeds and of our walk!

Perhaps it is significant that there were no dimensions given for the laver. Who can estimate the power of God's Word? The writer to the Hebrews has exhorted us to "draw near with a true heart in full assurance of faith, having our hearts sprinkled from an evil conscience, and our bodies washed with pure water" (Hebrews 10:22).

II. THE PERSON OF CHRIST

In the outer court we have come into contact with the provision of Christ. The worshipper, looking to the cross and the blood of Christ, has found salvation and cleansing from sin. He has been washed with the water of the Word and separated unto God. Having laid hold of God's provision in Christ, he is now ready to discover something of the person of Christ.

The worshipper must pass through another entrance into the holy place. Once again it was a curtain of blue, purple, scarlet and fine-twined linen. This time it had cherubim worked into the curtain by skilled craftsmen. It also was hung upon four posts of acacia wood, but these posts were overlaid with gold. The posts for the gate at the entrance of our courtyard were made of wood with brass bases, silver crowns and hooks. But these were different! They were overlaid with gold, set upon bases of brass, with crowns of gold. What was the difference? There was no vision of the person of Christ in the outer court. We have seen His provision, but His person has yet to be revealed. The common foundation of brass tells us that we never get away from the fact of the cross and of God's judgment upon our sins, which was executed there. Yet the addition of gold in overlaying and crowning the posts reveals to us that Christ is more than a man. Gold speaks of deity. Christ is also God. The posts also tell us that we are crowned not only with redemption (silver) but also with glory (gold).

1. The Lampstand

The golden lampstand was one of the most difficult pieces of furniture to construct. It was hammered out of one solid piece of gold and had very elaborate and intricate artwork in its design. It weighed about 125 pounds. Pricing gold at its current rate of more than $1,200 an ounce, that makes it worth 2.4 million dollars! According to Sheffield of England, it would be impossible to duplicate today. Not only was the gold of which it was made beaten, but also the olives from which the oil came to light the lamps had to be beaten. Every utensil, including the tongs and snuffers that were used with the lampstand had to be a beaten work.

The word that is used in the Hebrew for the "shaft" is elsewhere used in connection with living things, translated as "thigh, body or side." This shaft was the central stem including the base with the branches issuing out from the side of the shaft.

The entire lampstand had not been forged in the fire, but was one solid beaten work. There were no seams. The artwork on the branches was that of the almond in its three stages of bud, blossom and bloom. Each branch had three of these, making a total of nine on each branch. The central shaft had four sets of the almonds. Here we have depicted the nine-fold fruit of the Spirit on the branches, and the number of divine government on the shaft! God makes no mistakes. The almond is especially significant, because it is the first tree to spring to life after the winter. Thus it speaks to us of the resurrection life of our Lord Jesus Christ.

When the authority of Moses and Aaron was questioned by Korah and company, God attested to the authority and leadership that He had placed in Israel by causing Aaron's rod, that representing the house of Levi, to bud, blossom and produce almonds! So the almond pattern was also a portrait of spiritual authority. The resurrection of Jesus Christ corresponds to this as well.

Jesus is declared to be the Son of God with power by the resurrection from the dead. His place and position of authority is established by this act of God. The lampstand itself did not produce light apart from the oil that burned within its bowls. The concept of a candlestick misleads us, for it was not a candlestick that held waxen candles as we would envision it. The oil was placed in the bowls and it burned directly, providing light for the ministry within the tabernacle. The other furnishings in the Holy Place were illuminated by the brilliance of the lampstand.

It is the person of our Lord Jesus Christ, who Himself is the Light of the world (John 9:5), and who "lightens every man that comes into the world" (John 1:9). "In him was life, and that life was the light of men" (John 1:4 NIV). The anointing of the Holy Spirit, which was given to Christ without measure, made His life the light of the world.

And so it is in worship! Jesus Christ Himself is the light, he is the one who "has the seven spirits of God" (Revelation 3:1, 4:5). It is the ministry of the Holy Spirit to illuminate and reveal the person of Jesus Christ to us in worship. We don't have to worship the Holy Spirit to do that. When we glorify Jesus, the light of the Spirit will illuminate Him to our hearts.

As to the seven branches of the candlestick, some scholars believe that this reflects the seven-fold Spirit of God that was prophesied by Isaiah concerning Christ. "The Spirit of the Lord will rest on him—the Spirit of wisdom and of understanding, the Spirit of counsel and of power, the Spirit of knowledge and of the fear of the Lord" (Isaiah 11:2 NIV). There is a possible connection between the general description "the Spirit of the Lord" and the main stem of the candlestick. Since the remaining titles are given in three pairs, the correspondence to the three branches on either side suggests an obvious parallel.

It is possible to even develop this concept further to show how each of those three divisions parallel the division of the nine gifts that are enumerated by Paul in I Corinthians 12. For example, corresponding to the Spirit of wisdom and understanding, are the gifts of the word of knowledge, the word of wisdom, and the discerning of spirits. These are those gifts that enable us to *know* as God knows. Paralleling the Spirit of counsel and power are the gifts of faith, healing and miracles that enable us to *act* or *do* as God acts or do. The third pair described as the Spirit of knowledge and the fear of the Lord relates to the gifts of tongues, interpretation, and prophecy that enable us to *speak* as God speaks and to communicate with Him.

The Holy Spirit helps our infirmities and enables us to worship. We do not worship with the oldness of the letter, but with the newness of the Spirit (Romans 7:6). We worship God empowered by the Spirit, as Paul says in Philippians 3:3. Our worship would be dead and dull without the life of the Spirit of God. According to God's Word, one of the ministries of the Holy Spirit is to reveal Jesus to us (John 14:15-26, 16:7-15). This is what happens in worship. The Holy Spirit never attempts to establish a separate identity from that of Christ. Rather, He always lifts up Jesus. When we worship

God by the Spirit, Christ will become more real and precious to us. The golden lampstand represents our Lord who was bruised, beaten, battered and broken for us. The oil symbolizes the Holy Spirit by which Jesus was anointed for ministry.

The fact that no dimensions were given for the lampstand is indicative of the fact that we cannot measure the impact of the illumination of the Savior as the light of the world. The centrality of the lampstand in the tabernacle teaches us that Christ in all of His fullness must be central to our worship.

We know that there are seven distinct colors that make up pure light. Seven is the number of divine perfection, and speaks of the perfection of Christ. The Jesus that we worship must be seen in all of His divine fullness. True worship does not take place when we are not willing to accept Him as the one who has the seven spirits of God! We dare not tamper with the fullness of His revelation. The golden lampstand still burns brightly, and the illumination that flows from Christ in the world today flows through the burning ministry of the Spirit of God!

The Holy Spirit is vital to our worship. There is no illumination apart from the Holy Spirit's ministry. Without the Holy Spirit's fuelling, there is no illumination in the Holy Place. If we attempt to worship without the Holy Spirit, we will be in darkness and never fully discover the greatness of God and the completeness of the Savior.

The light of the lampstand also revealed its beauty. The ministry of the Holy Spirit reveals the beauty of Christ. As the result of His beatings and brokenness, we are able to behold His beauty. "He will bring glory to me by taking from what is mine and making it known to you" (John 16:14 NIV). The flame of the lampstand would reflect upon the beaten gold and shine forth in rare and radiant beauty.

The Holy Spirit reveals to us the deity, the divinity (gold) of Christ. We behold His glory through Spirit-enabled worship. As long as we stay outside the Holy Place, we can enjoy forgiveness from our sins through the Lamb of God, but we will not adequately grasp the glorious truth of who Jesus really is!

The lampstand also shed light upon the table of shewbread. "He placed the lampstand in the Tent of Meeting opposite the table" (Exodus 40:24 NIV). This table represents Christ, the Bread of Life, as well as the Word of God. The Holy Spirit illuminates the Word to our hearts. Through the power of the Holy Spirit we can fellowship with Christ, partaking of the Bread of Life through His Word (Ephesians 1:17).

One more piece of furniture was illuminated by the lampstand—the golden altar of incense, representing prayer and praise. "Aaron must burn fragrant incense on the altar every morning when he tends the lamps" (Exodus 30:7 NIV). While it is certainly possible to offer prayer and praise apart from the help of the Holy Spirit, yet it is Spirit-empowered prayer and praise that ascends into the very presence of God in heaven. Effective ministry in prayer and praise is ministry that is bathed in, empowered by and rendered with the Holy Spirit's anointing (Romans 8:26).

2. *The Table*

Directly across from the lampstand was the Table of Shewbread. Three feet long, a foot and a half wide, and two feet three inches high (the same height as the Ark of the Covenant), it faced the priests on the right-hand side as they entered the Holy Place. It was made of acacia wood, overlaid with gold. Its surface was surrounded by an edging or border, with rings on each corner, through which staves were placed for carrying. The table had a crown of gold around the top, which would hold the bread upon the table when Israel was on the move.

Placed upon this table were twelve loaves of special bread that was made of fine flour. This bread was known as the "bread of face" or the "bread of presence," because it was set before the face or presence of God. Around this table the priests were to gather daily. This was the only food placed upon the table for the priests to eat. It would remain before God for seven days after which it would be eaten by the priests and then replaced.

It is not difficult to see how this table and its contents represent our Lord Jesus Christ. The wood overlaid with gold symbolizes His dual nature, His humanity and His divinity. The crown of gold speak of Christ's glory, for He is the King of kings and Lord of lords. The bread itself represents to us our Lord Jesus who is the bread that came down from heaven. He is the Bread of Life (John 6:35, 48, 51). The bread was pierced or perforated, speaking again of Christ who was pierced for our sins. It was sprinkled with frankincense, itself a symbol of suffering, pointing to the sufferings of Christ.

The table was a place of communion with God. The wood overlaid with gold speaks to us of God's desire to relate to us. Communion with God is symbolized in the union of wood and gold in the table. The fact that it was the same height as the ark indicates that there is no higher revelation of God than that which we receive in communion with Him in His Word. While we cannot fully comprehend God's person this side of the veil, yet we do behold Him crowned in glory. We will discover more of His depth and breadth, but at the table of communion we are able to ascend into the heights of revelation as we behold Him exalted and crowned King of kings.

While both the table and the bread represent Christ, they also represent the Word of God. We must not forget that Jesus is the Word of God. We partake of the life of Christ through His Word. Jesus talked about partaking of His flesh and blood, and then proceeded to say, "The Spirit gives life; the flesh counts for nothing. The words I have spoken to you are spirit and they are life" (John 6:63 NIV). We partake of the life of Christ when we feast upon the Word of God.

The worshipper will discover that the Word is not only useful in cleansing from sin, but also as the basis of our spiritual sustenance. God's Word is described as being milk to spiritual babies, and meat to the spiritually mature (I Corinthians 3:2, I Peter 2:2, Hebrews 5:12-14) . But it is the bread of life, the staple of spiritual existence to all.

When we feast upon the Word, the person of Christ is revealed to us. Christ is to be found on every page. He is foreshadowed and prophesied in the Old Testament and revealed in the New Testament. Fellowship with God is a vital part of our worship. We worship God when we feast upon the Word and the person of Christ is revealed to our hearts.

Communion with God is the message of the table. God has called us to Himself for personal fellowship. Throughout the Word, God called people to communion with Him, and permitted them to share fellowship by eating with Him. Abraham celebrated fellowship with Melchizedek, the King of Salem (a type of Christ) by sharing bread and wine (Genesis 14:18). Moses, Aaron and the seventy elders ate food in the presence of God (Exodus 24:11).

Jesus called His disciples together at the last supper and shared intimate final moments with them in sweet communion (Matthew 26:26-27). Our Lord has instructed us to celebrate His table in communion with Him and with one another (I Corinthians 11:23-26). Paul, referring to this aspect of our worship, said, "Is not the cup of thanksgiving for which we give thanks a participation in the blood of Christ? And is not the bread that we break a participation in the body of Christ? Because there is one loaf, we who are many, are one body, for we all partake of the one loaf" (I Corinthians 10:16-17 NIV).

Jesus told us to do this often in remembrance of Him. He told us to do it as a proclamation of His death, as well as an anticipation of His coming. But we don't have to wait until we celebrate the communion service to enjoy communion with Christ. Communion with Jesus is possible on an ongoing basis. He invites us to "come and dine," to feast upon Him and to feast with Him. The invitation of Revelation 3:20 is "Here I am! I stand at the door and knock. If anyone hears my voice and opens the door, I will come in and eat with him, and he with me" (Revelation 3:20 NIV).

3. The Altar of Incense

The golden altar was both the smallest and the tallest piece of furniture within the Holy Place. Standing three feet high and one and one-half feet square, it was made of acacia wood, and overlaid with gold. It had a crown of gold around its edge with horns on each corner. Upon this altar, incense was to burn perpetually in the presence of God.

The golden altar was as close to the glory of God as was possible to attain without going beyond the veil, and was the last piece of the furniture the priest would pass before entering into the holiest of holies. Whereas the brazen altar was the place where the animal sacrifices were brought for the sins of the people, there was no involvement with sin in the incense offerings at the golden altar. Whereas the brazen altar had to do with God's provision for sin, the golden altar was the place of worship. From here the incense ascended to God, and wafts of its fragrance would filter through the veil into the holiest of all and hover over the mercy seat where God dwelt.

God gave very strict requirements as to the kind of incense and the nature of the fire that ignited it. The recipe for the incense was sacredly guarded, and available only to Moses and Aaron, the high priest. It could not be simulated or duplicated by anyone else. Its ingredients all had medicinal qualities or healing properties. The fire that was used to ignite the incense must be taken from the brazen altar into the holy place, and must be the fire that God Himself had ignited.

There are implications for our worship that powerfully parallel God's guidelines for the altar! Our worship must be worship that is empowered by the Spirit of God. Both fire and oil are symbolic of the Holy Spirit. It is the Spirit of God that ignites the incense of our praise and worship and makes it acceptable to God. We can pray and praise with the limitations and restrictions that our finiteness imposes, or we can worship God with the enablement of the Holy Spirit. Paul talks about *praying with the Spirit* (I Corinthians 14:15, Ephesians 6:18). He tells the Philippians that "we worship God by the Spirit" (Philippians 3:3).

All of our praise and worship must be ignited by the coals of Calvary! Here is where the anointing of God truly is. The Holy Spirit answers to the blood. When the blood of Jesus was taken into heaven, the Holy Spirit was released into the world. The Holy Spirit's anointing follows the atonement of the blood of Christ. So it is the cross of Jesus, His triumph, His conquest of sin and Satan that ignites the incense of our worship to God.

We do not dare to attempt to simulate the Holy Spirit! Only Christ, our High Priest has the recipe! It is Jesus who baptizes with the Holy Spirit. The anointing flows from the head of the body to its outer perimeters (Psalm 133:2). God will not tolerate our own incense, and He will not accept "strange fire," or fire that He has not ignited. He demonstrated this when Nadab and Abihu were slain for offering strange fire before His presence.

Our praise and worship must be offered to God through Jesus Christ. He is the altar of incense. The wood overlaid with gold speaks to us of His perfect humanity and His deity, which were fused, but not confused. Christ is the perfect God-man. It is His dual nature that qualifies Him to be our great high priest. As our high priest, our prayers, praises, and worship are rendered to God through Him.

The writer to the Hebrews put it like this, "We have an altar... through Jesus, therefore, let us continually offer to God a sacrifice of praise—the fruit of lips that confess his name" (Hebrews 13:10, 15 NIV). Our praise must be directed to God through Christ. Peter picks up the same theme when he writes, "You also, like living stones, are being built into a spiritual house to be a holy priesthood, offering up spiritual sacrifices acceptable to God through Christ Jesus" (I Peter 2:5 NIV).

Much attention is given in the Book of Hebrews to the discussion and description of Jesus Christ as our great high priest. It is this priestly function that is portrayed for us in the altar of incense. Not only do we direct our prayers to God through Christ, but also Christ represents us to God. He takes our worship and directs it to God. He is the altar of our worship!

It is clear in the Book of Revelation that the golden bowls full of incense presented by the elders and the angels in the presence of God are the prayers of the saints (Revelation 5:8; 8:3-4). Since God has taken care of our need for salvation at the brazen altar, the prayers represented by the golden altar are the prayers of adoration and worship. Worship will be the perpetual incense! Worship has been going on since the beginning of God's creation! In eternity past, the angels worshipped God in heaven. In eternity future, worship will continue endlessly. Long after every prayer of intercession and supplication has been answered, the perpetual prayers of praise and adoration will continue to fill heaven with their fragrance!

David asked, "Let my prayer be set forth as incense" (Psalm 141:2). The prayer of adoration yields great power for God's people. When we worship God, that incense ascends into His presence, hovers over the mercy seat, and God responds to us in a powerful way. The horns on the altar speak of the power and authority of Christ our altar, and also of the power that is represented in the ministry of praise and worship to God. Paul and Silas discovered the power of praising God when in the midst of their worship God shook the prison and opened its doors (Acts 16:25-26).

It is interesting that the writer to the Hebrews places the altar of incense not in the holy place, but in the most holy place.

> Now the first covenant had regulations for worship and also an earthly sanctuary. A tabernacle was set up. In its first room were the lampstand, the table and the consecrated bread; this was called the Holy Place. Behind the second curtain was a room called the Most Holy Place, which had the golden altar of incense and the gold-covered ark of the covenant (Hebrews 9:1-4 NIV).

What is the significance of this change? One can only speculate, but possibly to elevate the place of worship and demonstrate that it moves us into the very presence of God Himself! The Book of Revelation portrays a similar scene. The altar of incense is before the throne after the opening of the seventh seal. There is an increase, rather than a decrease in praise and worship! As God's program for the ages marches on, He prepares heaven for an eternity of praise and worship!

III. THE PRESENCE OF CHRIST

As we approach the ark, the final piece of furniture, there is a sense of having arrived, for when God gave Moses the commandment to build a tabernacle, the very first piece of furniture God mentioned was the ark. It was obviously the most important piece of furniture in the entire tabernacle, and it presents the most complete picture of Christ to be found in the Old Testament.

It was the only piece of furniture within the most holy place, a room that was a fifteen foot cube. The ark itself was an oblong box or chest three and three-fourths feet long, two and one-fourth feet wide, and two and one-fourth feet high. It was made of acacia wood, covered with pure gold, both within and without. It, too, had a crown of gold around its edge, and was covered by a slab of gold with cherubim, known as the mercy seat.

The mercy seat was a slab of beaten gold with two cherubim of beaten gold all in one piece. It formed a lid or a covering for the ark. The two cherubim that were part of the beaten work faced one another and looked downward where the blood would have been applied, when once a year the priest entered the most holy place. Their outstretched wings formed a shield of covering over the ark.

To gain entrance into this holiest of all, the priest must pass through the veil. The veil was almost identical to the other two hangings, found at the gate before the brazen altar, and before the door leading into the holy place. The one difference in the veil was the addition of the cherubim. It is interesting that the square footage of each entrance was identical, but the entrance to the court is lower and wider, while the entrance into the holy place and holiest of all is higher and narrower. The route to higher experiences in God always requires a narrower path!

The veil was cunningly made, upheld by four pillars of wood that were overlaid with gold and had gold hooks, set on sockets of silver. Once again, the redemptive foundation is accentuated, and the heights of glory suggested by the golden crown. The wood overlaid with gold in these posts, as well as in the Ark of the Covenant, speaks to us of the dual nature of our Lord.

The cherubim on the veil and the mercy seat teach us that we have entered the very presence of God! The first mention of cherubim was in Genesis 3:24 where God placed them at the entrances of the garden to keep sinful man from re-entering God's paradise. Their presence may also indicate the protection of the immediate presence of God from access by sinful man.

God stated that He dwelt between the cherubim. It was from this place that He would commune with Moses. His presence came down here in an intense manifestation of light. While the priests could enter only once a year, Moses could enter here at any time to commune with God.

The contents of the ark also reveal to us the reality of the presence of Jesus Christ. It contained the two tables of stone on which God's commandments were written, a golden pot of manna, and Aaron's rod that budded. Aaron's rod represents to us the authority and rule of the resurrected Christ, who, although He was cut off, was proved to be the Son of God with power when God raised Him from the dead.

The golden pot of manna (which along with Aaron's rod would be removed when they built a permanent house for God) was a reminder of God's providence and provision during their wilderness wanderings. But it also represented God's presence among them. The provision of God reveals His presence. Christ is the bread that came down from heaven. "Your forefathers ate the manna in the desert, yet they died. But here is the bread that comes down from heaven, which a man may eat and not die. I am the living bread that came down from heaven. If a man eats of this bread, he will live forever. This bread is my flesh, which I will give for the life of the world" (John 6:49-51 NIV).

The unbroken tablets of the law represent Christ who Himself fulfilled the law. He is the only person who ever lived without breaking those commandments. It was by His obedience that many have been made righteous.

When the law was contained and confined in the ark, it could not reach out to kill or destroy those that offended it. As long as it was covered by the mercy seat where the blood was applied, it could not condemn. It is the blood of our Lord Jesus Christ that provides the covering for the law, so that its condemnation cannot touch the child of God.

In the Ark of the Covenant, with its contents and coverings, there is a perfect picture of the fullness of Christ. He is the manifestation of God's glory. We behold the glory of God in the face of Jesus Christ. He is crowned with glory and honor. He has fulfilled the law's requirements by both His righteous life and His vicarious death. He Himself is our mercy seat, our propitiation, our covering before God, and His blood has provided that covering for our sins (see Romans 3:25). Just as the mercy seat was made of beaten gold, Christ became our mercy seat by His sufferings for us.

Not only has Christ entered into the holiest of all for us, but the worshipper also enters the very presence of God through Christ.

When Christ came as high priest of the good things that are already here, he went through the greater and more perfect tabernacle that is not man-made, that is to say, not a part of this creation. He did not enter by means of the blood of goats and calves; but he entered the Most Holy Place once for all by his own blood, having obtained eternal redemption (Hebrews 9:11-12 NIV).

Therefore, brothers, since we have confidence to enter the Most Holy Place by the blood of Jesus, by a new and living way opened for us through the curtain, that is, his body, and since we have a great priest over the house of God, let us draw near to God with a sincere heart in full assurance of faith, having our hearts sprinkled to cleanse us from a guilty conscience and having our bodies washed with pure water (Hebrews 10:19-22 NIV).

The pattern of worship that God presented in the tabernacle is laid out for the believer in Christ. We look to the provision of the cross. We are cleansed by the Word of God and then enlightened to behold the person of Christ, who gives us the full assurance of faith. We partake of the bread of presence that continually cleanses us from a guilty conscience. We enter the holiest of all, knowing that the veil, the body of Christ has been rent for us, and the blood has paved the way to God.

When Christ died upon the cross of Calvary, the veil of the temple was rent in two from top to bottom. God was showing that they way into His presence was now possible through the rending of the body of His Son. The glory of the Lord was now accessible to any person who would come by faith in Jesus Christ. And the believer can enter the very midst of God's presence, since the veil was torn in the middle! The rending of our Lord's physical body made possible the release of His presence into the world, and gave access to the presence of God to any person who would come to Him by Christ.

The ark was the place where God dwelt. It was a *place of government.* This was His throne among His people. It was also a *place of communication,* where Moses would meet with God and receive His instructions concerning how to lead His people. It also became the *place of God's guidance*, and would precede them when they would journey.

Over the Ark of the Covenant in the holiest of all dwelt the pillar of cloud by day and the pillar of fire by night. It was the place of God's presence among His people. The place and privilege of God's presence—which was once reserved for only a representative priest and that once a year—was now perpetually available to the people of God. It is in worship that the presence of God is realized. Although we know that He is with us always, the realization of that presence is not always a present reality unless we discover the power of worship. The pattern that God gave Moses is the way to His presence. We must first come by way of God's provision in Christ. We then have revealed to us His glorious person as we worship Him. And ultimately, the revelation of His person will usher us into His glorious presence.

As we have seen in this chapter, every aspect of the Tabernacle of Moses points to our Lord Jesus Christ in some way. In its layout, design, and furnishings it prefigures some aspect of His atoning work. Further, it definitively depicts for us God's pattern for worship. We are taken from celebration to adoration in this Old Testament model for worship. And we have that, while the Holy of Holies was off limits to all but the high priest (and that only once yearly) during Old Testament times, the rent veil of Christ's Body has signaled the change that the way into God's presence is now accessible to all.

IV. THE PROGRESSION OF WORSHIP

As I began to seriously study the subject of worship, I was blessed and inspired by both the teaching and writings of the late Judson

Cornwall, who graciously wrote the foreword to this book back in 1987. Having the privilege of sharing conference speaking assignments, and entertaining him as a guest speaker in the church that I pastored at the time, I was also privileged to spend time with him in fellowship over the Word of God. He was a worshipper of God in all of his life. As I look back on Dr. Cornwall's writings, I note that he recognized a sequential order and progression to the tabernacle arrangement that can be mirrored in the worship service.

1. Outside the Gates in the Camp

Before entering God's presence, people tend to preoccupied with their own needs and concerns, and have limited God-consciousness. Since the congregational preoccupation is self-centered, they can be brought into community of thought and soul by singing songs of testimony. The common thread of personal experience and struggle and of finding God's intervention through that experience will bring the people of God into a more concerted focus on God's faithfulness in their lives. That awareness should bring them to the next phase.[90]

2. Through the Gates with Thanksgiving

Just as ancient Israel marched in joyful procession through the eastern gate into the outer court of the temple, so should God's children joyfully unite their hearts and voices in thanksgiving and praise to Him. Their reflections at phase one have paved the way for them to begin offering sacrifices of praise and thanksgiving, even though these expressions remain highly subjective in nature: that is, they focus on what "God has done for me".[91]

---

90   Adapted from *Let Us Worship* by Judson Cornwall, South Plainfield, NJ: Bridge Publishing, 1983
91   Ibid.

3. Into His Courts with Praise

At this phase, the focus shifts somewhat from what God has done to who He is. The balance of emphasis shifts from the first and second phases. Those were centered on self and God; now self is less a focus and God becomes more and more the subject of our praise. We are not necessarily done with *soulish* expression at this stage. Since the soul is the seat of the mind, will and emotions, are emotions may be significantly stirred to motivate us to pursue the heart of God in a more concentrated and consecrated manner.[92]

4. Solemn Worship inside the Holy Place and Holy of Holies

As God becomes the sole focus of our worship and adoration, our spirit connects and communes with God. This phase is less likely to be noisy; we are more likely to be solemn or silent in the overwhelming and awesome awareness of His presence. It is a mistake to disrupt this by breaking the silence with an up-tempo chorus or some inappropriate clever comment. God's people should be free to abide at His feet and revel in the glory of His presence. As we saw, once inside the Holy of Holies, everything speaks of Christ and glorifies God. There is no presence or reminder of sin.[93]

IV. THE PATTERN OF WORSHIP

Many scholars have suggested that an aerial view of the arrangement of the furniture of tabernacle would portray the form of a cross. Perhaps it would be more accurate to say that when viewed from heaven, the shape of the cross would be evident. Another possible

---

92   Ibid.

93   Ibid.

approach is to view the profile of the tabernacle furnishings horizontally in its Old Testament shadow and vertically in its New Testament substance.

The illustration below is intended to illustrate the ministry of the priests within the tabernacle. The *two* arrows represent that their ministry was *twofold*. One aspect was to represent the Lord to his people which occurred when they pronounced a blessing upon Israel and when they proclaimed God's ordinances to His people. The second part of their ministry was in the opposite direction: to represent the people before the Lord.[94] This was performed as the priests brought the sacrifices and sprinkled the blood, and when they burned incense on the altar built before God. They brought the prayers of the covenant people to their God.[95]

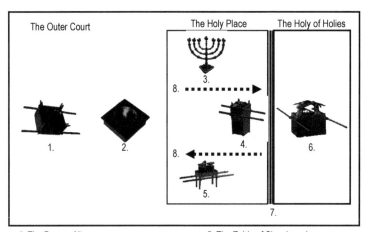

1. The Brazen Altar
2. The Brazen Laver
3. The Golden Candlestick
4. The Golden Alter of Incense
5. The Table of Shewbread
6. The Ark of the Covenant
7. The Veil of Separation
8. Ministry of priests

The two arrows are intended to represent that the ministry of the priests was twofold. One aspect was to represent the Lord to his people

94   VanDooren, G. Adapted from *The Beauty of Reformed Liturgy.* Winnipeg, MB: Premier, 1980.
95   ibid

which occurred when they pronounced a blessing upon Israel and when they proclaimed God's ordinances to His people.[96] The second part of their ministry was in the opposite direction: to represent the people before the Lord. This was performed as the priests brought the sacrifices and sprinkled the blood, and when they burned incense on the altar built before God. They brought the prayers of the covenant people to their God.[97]

This *pattern* was shown to Moses in the mount when he received divine and explicit instructions for the precise layout and construction of the tabernacle, and a repeated injunction to build it exactly as he was commanded by God. The book of Hebrews makes it crystal clear that this pattern did not stand on top of Mount Horeb, but that it stood in heaven itself. Yet, while this was built according to divine instructions, and was the meeting place for God and His people, it was still an earthly sanctuary. As such, it remained horizontal where the mercy seat stood on this earth, on the ground.[98]

Having already explored the significance of the tabernacle furnishings that were built according to the heavenly pattern, we are reminded that every object, every action—the sacrifices, the incense, etc.—spoke of Christ Jesus. Still, it remained merely a shadow of the heavenly tabernacle—provisional, preparatory and prophetic—pointing to Christ who would reveal the heavenly tabernacle.

Hebrews 8:5 (NIV) quotes Exodus 25:40 when it states, "See to it that you make everything according to the pattern shown you on the mountain." However, this is prefaced by the comment "They (the Old Testament priests) serve at a sanctuary that is a copy and shadow of what is in heaven" (parenthesis mine). It was because the earthly

---

96   VanDooren, G. Adapted from *The Beauty of Reformed Liturgy.* Winnipeg, MB: Premier, 1980.
97   Ibid.
98   Ibid.

tabernacle was a copy and not the original, that Moses was warned to strictly adhere to the pattern that God had given him.

The tent, or tabernacle, however, belongs to the past. "But the ministry Jesus has received is as superior to theirs as the covenant of which he is mediator is superior to the old one, and it is founded on better promises" (Hebrews 8:6 NIV). The whole letter to the Hebrews proclaims the superiority of the "true tent", which is set up, not by man, but by God. "…the true tabernacle set up by the Lord, not by man" (Hebrews 8:2 NIV).

Jesus Christ, the high priest according to the order of Melchizedek, has fulfilled all shadows and entered the real, the heavenly sanctuary where he now ministers as our high priest. Through His blood we have free access to the Most Holy Place. "Therefore, since we have a great high priest who has gone through the heavens, Jesus the Son of God… Let us then approach the throne of grace with confidence, so that we may receive mercy and find grace to help us in our time of need" (Hebrews 4:14, 16 NIV).

Therefore we could say that Jesus Christ, by the perfect sacrifice, with which He entered the heavenly sanctuary has set the Old Testament horizontal tabernacle on its end. And when He died, God's hand tore the curtains apart. There are no longer three partitions, divided by heavy curtains. The congregation is no longer kept outside the tabernacle proper. The tabernacle is no longer horizontal, but vertical.[99]

The vertical pattern, if rendered appropriately (void of the furnishings), would seem empty in comparison with the tabernacle that Moses built. I have left the graphics of the furnishings in the following illustration to convey the manifold manifestation of Christ as the fulfillment of all the furnishings of the tabernacle. In actual

---

99 ibid

fact, there are no longer any altars, or golden ark, or any of the other objects and utensils. Yet in fact the tabernacle in Christ is more *full* because it is the completion of all that preceded it.

The new covenant pattern reaches through the clouds up to highest heaven, where Jesus Christ himself is ministering at the heavenly mercy seat. Hebrews 4:16 along with Hebrews 10:19-22 instruct us that we may draw near with confidence. In the new covenant, we live under an open heaven! The curtains were torn apart! The congregation, now a royal priesthood are ushered into the presence of Jesus Christ. Our risen and exalted Lord poured out his Spirit, who came down and filled the church. While Christ is our Paraclete (Advocate) in heaven, the Spirit is our Paraclete (Advocate) here on earth.

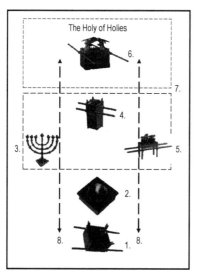

The Holy of Holies

1. We come through Christ our sacrifice
2. Christ washes us by His Word
3. Christ enlightens us
4. Christ prays for us and we pray through Him
5. Christ is our Bread of Life
6. Christ is our Mercy Seat
7. The Veil is removed
8. We can enter the Holy of Holies through Him

We enter God's presence through the blood of Christ our perfect sacrifice

Christ cleanses us with the washing of His Word

Christ enlightens and illuminates us through the Holy Spirit

Christ our High Priest prays for us and we offer prayers to God through Him

Christ is our Bread of Life that came down from heaven

Christ is our Mercy Seat

The Veil is rent and removed

We can enter the Holy of Holies through Him

All this is the glorious reality of worship, when we as his people meet with him. According to his promise, Christ himself is among us. And he has made us "to sit with him in the heavenly places" (Ephesians 2:6). All those glorious expressions that we heard in the previous passages are true and real in worship. "But you have come to Mount Zion, to the heavenly Jerusalem, the city of the living God. You have come to thousands upon thousands of angels in joyful assembly, to the church of the firstborn, whose names are written in heaven. (Hebrews 12:22, 23 NIV). On the great and final day of the Lord, God will consummate his covenant, and the heavenly Jerusalem will descend. God will dwell with men, and no temple or church building will be needed any longer on the new earth (Revelation 21:1-4).[100]

In His presence there is fullness of joy. The fragrance of the incense lingers long and abides upon us long after the glorious moments when we are before Him in worship. The blessedness of discovery of His presence is the highest joy that mankind can experience here upon earth, for it is indeed a taste of the glory of heaven yet to come.

---

100   Ibid.

16

A MAN-MADE GOD AND
A GOD-MADE MAN

Mankind are an incorrigible race. Give them but
bugbears and idols—it is all that they ask; the distinctions
of right and wrong, of truth and falsehood, of good
and evil, are worse than indifferent to them.

—William Hazlitt

One is proud to worship when he cannot be an idol.

—Friedrich Nietzsche

When the people saw that Moses was so long in coming down from the mountain, they gathered around Aaron and said, "Come, make us gods who will go before us. As for this fellow Moses who brought us up out of Egypt, we don't know what has happened to him." Aaron… made… an idol cast in the shape of a calf… built an altar in front of the calf… the people sacrificed burnt offerings and… sat down to eat and drink and got up to indulge in revelry. Then the LORD said to Moses, "Go down, because your people, whom you brought up out of Egypt, have become corrupt and have made themselves an idol cast in the shape of a calf… Now leave me alone so that my anger may burn against them and that I may destroy them. Then I will make you into a great nation." But Moses sought the favor of the LORD his God. "O LORD," he said, Turn from your fierce anger; relent and do not bring disaster on your people… Then the LORD relented and did not bring on his people the disaster he had threatened… When Moses approached the camp and saw the calf and the dancing, his anger burned and he threw the tablets out of his hands, breaking them to pieces at the foot of the mountain. And he took the calf they had made and burned it in the fire; then he ground it to powder, scattered it on the water and made the Israelites drink it… So Moses went back to the LORD and said, "Oh, what a great sin these people have committed! They have made themselves gods of gold. But now, please forgive their sin—but if not, then blot me out of the book you have written." The LORD replied to Moses, "Whoever has sinned against me I will blot out of my book… And the LORD struck the people with a plague because of what they did with the calf Aaron had made (Exodus 32:1-35 NIV).

I. THE PERIL OF IDOLATRY

Forty days is a long time, if you are waiting for your leader to show up and direct the worship. Moses had been gone for forty days and forty nights, alone with God in the mountain, and the natives grew restless as they waited for Moses to reappear. I don't even want to think about how restless modern worshippers would become if their leader were late by merely forty minutes. And, if every modern worship leader was as committed as was Moses to proper preparation for the role, church services might be a bit different today!

One of the qualities that made Moses the great man of God that he was stemmed from his desire to know God—a desire reflected in his own pursuit of God. This is documented in the events recorded in Exodus chapter thirty-three. But before we examine Moses' encounter with his God, it will be instructive to look at the events of Exodus chapter thirty-two—where God's people first fell into idolatry. From this passage we will learn:

1. The dangers of losing patience in the pursuit of God

2. The perils of theological ignorance

3. The devastating influence of the world upon the worship of God's people

The Israelites gathered around Aaron and said, "Come, make us gods who will go before us. As for this fellow Moses who brought us up out of Egypt, we don't know what has happened to him" (Exodus 32:1 NIV).

This event in and of itself is incredible. No people in the course of human history had seen a greater pageantry of the miracle-working power of God than these Israelites. Plagues upon Egypt, the opening of the Red Sea, water from the rock, manna and quail from heaven—you name it—they had seen it. But yet, their knowledge of God was inadequate to keep them from false worship.

What does this teach us? Put simply, we don't really know God by witnessing His miracles. Oh, we certainly know His power. But it is possible to be surrounded by the miracles of God and never truly know Him. That is no fault of God. It is not a criticism of miracles. It is simply illustrative of the fact that it is possible to be acquainted with God's power and not with His person. The Psalmist records, "He made known his ways to Moses, his deeds to the people of Israel" (Psalm 103:7 NIV). It is possible to know God's deeds and not His ways. Israel knew God's acts. Moses knew God's ways.

The verses that follow in Exodus thirty-two are equally interesting. Aaron, the man who will lead the worship of Israel, leads the people into idolatry. Aaron tells them, "Take off the gold earrings that your wives, your sons and your daughters are wearing, and bring them to me." The Bible records, "So all the people took off their earrings and brought them to Aaron. He took what they handed him and made it into an idol cast in the shape of a calf, fashioning it with a tool" (Exodus 32:2-4 NIV). The passage goes on to record:

> Then they said, "These are your gods, O Israel, who brought you up out of Egypt." When Aaron saw this, he built an altar in front of the calf and announced, "Tomorrow there will be a festival to the Lord." So the next day the people rose up early and sacrificed burnt offerings and presented fellowship offerings. Afterward they sat down to eat and drink and got up to indulge in revelry (Exodus 32:4-6 NIV).

Although previously they had been adequately instructed in the worship of the one true God, they quickly fell into idolatry because they couldn't wait for God to show up. From the surface, it looked like a great worship gathering! Moses said, "It is not the sound of victory, it is not the sound of defeat; it is the sound of singing that I hear" (Exodus 32:18). Moses was angered when he saw the people running wild and that Aaron had let them get out of control. God noticed the worship of Israel. He said to Moses,

> Go down, because your people, whom you brought up out of Egypt, have become corrupt. They have been quick to turn away from what I commanded them and have made themselves an idol cast in the shape of a calf. They have bowed down to it and sac-

rificed to it and have said, "These are your gods, O Israel, who brought you up out of Egypt." "I have seen these people," the Lord said to Moses, 'and they are a stiff-necked people. Now leave me alone so that my anger may burn against them and that I may destroy them. Then I will make you into a great nation" (Exodus 32:7-10 NIV).

It is interesting in this passage that God refers to Israel in His conversation as your people and not as my people. God has, at this point, disowned them and is ready to annihilate them. This points to us the gravity of false worship.

The peril of idolatry today lies in our impatience and refusal to wait for the Lord. If God doesn't show up, we will worship anyway. We are ready to "have church" and to get on with our "program" whether or not God is present. The peril of idolatry must always be kept in perspective in our pursuit of God. In the pursuit of God there will be many idols that will present themselves and vie for our allegiance and worship. Perhaps more than anything else, the flesh will compete for the place of pre-eminence in our lives and in our worship that belongs only to Christ.

Ultimately, idolatry is anything that takes the place of God Himself. This has vast implications for us in the worship of God. Taken in the context of viewing worship as all of life then, anything that pre-empts God Himself in our lives is an idol. We may give lip service to certain priorities, but our values and priorities are ultimately indicated by what consumes our time and our interest. For example, I can say that I love God. But if I would rather be in front of the television than in His presence, I love television more than I love God. Our priorities are those things that get our time and attention.

Paul identifies "covetousness" as the essential idolatry in the life of the Christian. It is interesting that in Romans chapter seven, covetousness is the only specific sin that Paul identifies as being part of his own personal struggle (Romans 7:7-9).

All of the other sins identified by the Ten Commandments are overt and obvious. Covetousness is inward, the heart of all other sin. And yet it can be so subtly concealed and camouflaged that we may not even be aware of it. Covetousness is the cardinal sin of our age of materialism. Covetousness is the spirit of the age, especially in the western world. In today's church, the spirit of covetousness has wrapped itself in the "prosperity gospel", which is not gospel, but greed. The Apostle Paul repeatedly warned against its insidious and pernicious danger (I Tmothy 6:5-10). The desire to have, the inordinate drive for personal gain and success that some so glibly regard as being spiritual can be idolatrous.

We are quick to give our worship and allegiance to things that we can see rather than to wait upon God whom we cannot see. We want to be able to experience our gods with our senses. Anything that comes between God and me is an idol. Whatever *diminishes my service* to God, *dulls my appetite* for His Word, *deadens my desire* for His presence, or *dwarfs my drive* to witness is tantamount to idolatry.

God's people were going through the motions. They had sacrifices, offerings, singing, dancing and all the accoutrements of worship. But at the center of all this commotion was a god that they had created—a material god. A god they could look upon. A god they didn't have to submit to—a god of their own making.

Today, the greatest act of idolatry in the church is the making of God in our own image. We have created a god that can be accommodated to our fleshly and material desires. This god is only "good." This god is interested more in our happiness than in our holiness. This god wills our success in worldly things. This god guarantees a problem-free life of ease. This god is a great god. But this god is not the God of the Bible.

Intimacy with God means waiting upon Him. The Scriptures are filled with instruction relative to waiting upon the Lord. "Be still before the Lord and wait patiently for him" (Psalm 37:7 NIV). "Let none that wait on thee be ashamed" (Psalm 25:3). "I will wait on thy name" (Psalm 52:9). "Because of His strength will I wait" (Psalm 59:9). "Wait only on God" (Psalm 62:5). "So our eyes wait on the Lord" (Psalm 123:2). "I wait for the Lord, my soul doth wait" (Psalm 130:5). "But they that wait upon the Lord shall renew their strength" (Isaiah 40:31) "I waited patiently for the Lord" (Psalm 40:1).

If in our worship services the program we have planned and prepared takes precedence over waiting for God, then we may be as guilty of idolatry as were the ancient Israelites in erecting the golden calf. The veneration of the Scriptures themselves, the elevation of theological orthodoxy out of proportion can also become idolatry *if* is placed higher than the worship of God Himself. We can worship our faith, our doctrine, our miracles, our music, our polity, and thus be guilty of idolatry. It is the pursuit of God's presence, of God Himself that must take priority over everything else. All else is subservient to this greater value.

Why do we wait for God? If it is to "see what God will do," then we are worshipping His power and not His person. What if God shows up and does nothing? (Although this is highly unlikely!)

Would it be enough for us to be in God's presence even if there were no healings, no miracles, nor evidences of the supernatural? Would we be satisfied just to be with Him? If not, I wonder if we are really worshipping. God is looking for those who will be satisfied just to be in His presence. He is looking for those who are content just to enjoy Him, to embrace Him and to be embraced by Him. This is the worship that He longs for.

Idolatry is man's substitute for God. Much of our religion is idolatry. Much of what passes for worship in our churches is idolatry by that definition. Anything that replaces God's presence can become idolatry. The pitfall and peril is ever before us. Let us follow so hard after God Himself that we will never be satisfied with anything less.

2. THE PRIVILEGE OF INTERCESSION

Moses wasn't the only one angry at the idolatry of Israel! Moses' anger was a mere reflection of the anger of God. God told Moses, "I have seen these people, and they are a stiff-necked people. Now leave me alone so that my anger may burn against them and that I may destroy them. Then I will make you into a great nation" (Exodus 32:9-10 NIV). I wonder what might have happened if Moses had said, "All right Lord! That sounds like a super idea. I rather like the sound of 'the children of Moses' instead of 'the children of Abraham.'" It is obvious that God was testing Moses. But God was not playing games. His anger was genuinely aroused by the idolatry of Israel. And He was prepared to disown them.

What follows can be comprehended only by the awareness that Moses was a worshipper of God. Had he not been a worshipper, he would not have known God's heart. Consequently, he might have been sufficiently self-centered to allow God to wipe out the Israelites. Only the worshipper of God who has some knowledge of God's heart and character dares to draw near to the Lord and ask God to change His mind! Moses began his remonstrance with God,

O Lord, why should your anger burn against your people, whom you brought out of Egypt with great power and a mighty hand? Why should the Egyptians say, "It was with evil intent that he brought them out, to kill them in the mountains and to wipe them off the face of the earth?" Turn from your fierce anger; relent and do not bring disaster on your people. Remember your servants Abraham, Isaac and Israel, to whom you swore by your own self: "I will make your descendants as numerous as the stars in the sky and I will give your descendants all this land I promised them, and it will be their inheritance forever" (Exodus 32:11-13 NIV).

It is interesting that God had spoken to Moses of the people as *his* (Moses') people. God says to Moses, "*Your* people, whom *you* brought up out of Egypt" (Exodus 32:7). Moses says to God, "**Your** people, whom **You** brought out of Egypt with great power and a mighty hand" (Exodus 32:11—**emphasis** *mine*). This is a dialogue between friends. This conversation cannot be conducted apart from a basis of friendship. Moses had such a relationship with God that He was able to draw near to God in intercession.

Only the worshipper can know the power of intercession. Intercession is based upon friendship and relationship. Whenever intercession occurs in the Bible or in human life, it presupposes relationship. We approach someone that is our friend to approach his friend to obtain a favor for us. When Queen Esther interceded for her people Israel, it was because of her special relationship with the king (Esther 7:3-4). When Ruth obtained favor for her mother-in-law and herself from Boaz, it was because of relationship. Intercession requires relationship (Ruth 3, 4). And the kind of relationship that can effect intercession with God is the relationship of the worshipper.

When Abraham interceded for Lot and for the cities of Sodom and Gomorrah, he was able to "draw near" to God because he was a friend of God (Genesis 18:20-32). Only those who spend time in the presence of God will discover the power of intercession. Only worshippers of God become intercessors. And intercessors are by necessity worshippers.

In intercession, the party being entreated responds favorably for the sake of the party with whom they are in relationship. The merits of the party in trouble are not necessarily considered. It is not how thoroughly the case is presented. Response is not made because of any qualities or virtues of the party for whom intercession is made. It is based solely upon one thing—the relationship of the intercessor with the one in authority.

We utilize this principle in life every day. Because of our friendships and relationships we will intercede on behalf of others with those in authority when their decisions impact the lives of our friends. And this is a principle that is foundational to the gospel of our Lord. God has forgiven us for Christ's sake. We are accepted in the beloved. Our sins are forgiven us for His name's sake.

Moses continued His intercession with God by reminding God of His acts and of His attributes. Moses said, "Remember that it was by Your power and Your might that You brought them out of Egypt" (Exodus 32:11). Moses further reflected that if God wiped out Israel, God's name would be reproached among the heathen. Moses said, "God, it is Your own name and reputation that is at stake here. Please consider what the other nations will say about You. They will accuse You of being evil in your intentions concerning Your people" (Exodus 32:12). Then Moses reminded God of His friends. "For the sake of Your friends, Your servants, those who followed You, don't do this" (Exodus 32:13). Then Moses brought to God's attention the promise of His own Word, "Remember, God, You swore to give them this land and to make their descendants numberless! You cannot go back on your own word" (Exodus 32:13). The Scriptures simply say, "Then the Lord relented and did not bring on his people the disaster he had threatened" (Exodus 32:14 NIV).

There is no record of God deliberating, vacillating from one opinion to the other, but with Moses' intercession, God "repented" (KJV) and changed His mind about His intentions toward His people.

This is the power of intercession that the worshipper enjoys! In our efforts to get things from God, we would like to reduce everything to pat little formulae, employed with a money-refundable guarantee, to always get the desired results! How crass we have become in our approach to God! "Follow these simple steps, and you can get from God anything you want," we are told. "If you will do these things, your prayers will be answered." Wait a minute, please! Is God nothing more than a Santa Claus? Is He just a benign benefactor? Is He a cosmic bell-hop? This kind of approach to God reduces prayer to magic. Magic employs incantations and formulae to produce guaranteed results. Getting results from God requires drawing near to Him in worship; in short, intercession.

We have created in our age an attitude towards worship that reduces worship to the same kind of "magical" formula. We are told that if we will praise God, that God will respond to our "praises" with the goodies that we desire of Him. The teaching goes something like this: worship and praise coupled with faith and confession practically guarantee the child of God a vouch-proofed means of getting our desires from God. Intercession must never be prostituted in this way. Intercession is not another quick gimmick that shortcuts the necessity of walking with God, or short-circuits the channels of faith and obedience.

Yes, God responds to us when we worship, but if our "worship" is rendered to God with the ulterior motive of "getting" from God, then it is not worship. Moses enjoyed the privilege of intercession because He had become a friend of God. God listened to Moses, because Moses listened to God. There was a mutual relationship that was based upon reciprocal desire. When God spoke, Moses listened and obeyed. When Moses spoke, God listened, and considered what he said. But we must understand that the power of intercession of the worshipper is the result and not the cause of worship. We don't worship because it gains us proximity to God that eventuates in a place and position of influence. We don't worship because God will listen to us about our desires. But because we are worshippers, we become the friends of God. And because we are His friends, we enjoy the benefits of friendship, one of which is the place of intercession.

In a technical theological sense, it borders on blasphemy to intimate that it is possible for our "worship" to curry favor with God and to gain us entrance into His presence. This is the whole system of legalism re-introduced in another guise. And we are idolatrous if we attempt to manipulate God by our worship and praise. Our praise must be rendered to Him, for Him, and our worship must be directed only to the glory of His person and name.

But with this privilege of intercession came awesome responsibility. Moses did not glibly run down the mountain and proclaim that he had received from God what he had asked for. He did not take the forgiveness for granted. He recognized that sin must be duly punished. When he found the people running wild, his anger was aroused.

> When Moses approached the camp and saw the calf and the dancing, his anger burned and he threw the tablets out of his hands, breaking them to pieces at the foot of the mountain. And he took the calf they had made and burned it in the fire; then he ground it to powder, scattered it on the water and made the Israel-

ites drink it. He said to Aaron, "What did these people do to you, that you led them into such great sin?" (Exodus 32:10-21 NIV)

Moses held the people responsible and accountable for their sin, and although his angry reaction cost him dearly, he was sensitive enough to God and godliness not to ignore their sin. He held Aaron responsible for leading them into the sin. The record shows that the people led Aaron into it, but as a leader, he could have influenced them otherwise. Rather, he went along with the crowd. Aaron answered,

> Do not be angry, my Lord… You know how prone these people are to evil. They said to me, "Make us gods who will go before us. As for this fellow Moses who brought us up out of Egypt, we don't know what has happened to him." So I told them, "Whoever has any gold jewelry, take it off;" then they gave me the gold, and I threw it into the fire, and out came this calf" (Exodus 32:22-24 NIV).

This story might seem funny, were it not so tragic! Aaron told the truth for the most part. But the part where he said, "Out came the calf"! It is difficult not to chuckle when you see him twisting the truth, rather than assuming the responsibility for his role in leading the people into sin.

Moses knew that part and parcel of his privilege of intercession was the place of sanctifying the people.

> So he stood at the entrance to the camp and said, "Whoever is for the Lord, come to me." And all the Levites rallied to him. Then he said to them, "This is what the Lord, the God of Israel, says: 'Each man strap a sword to his side. Go back and forth through the camp from one end to the other, each killing his brother and friend and neighbor.'" The Levites did as Moses commanded, and that day about three thousand of the people died. Then Moses

said, "You have been set apart to the Lord today, for you were against your own sons and brothers, and he has blessed you this day" (Exodus 32:26-29 NIV).

Along with the privilege of intercession comes the accompanying responsibility of sanctification. When we would draw near to God, we must through the Spirit be willing to cut off the works of the flesh. We must be willing to put to death those things that are not of God. We must be wiling to separate that which does not respond to God in our lives, and be sanctified, set apart to Him. This cannot happen without paying a price. It cost Israel dearly. It cost Moses dearly to see the people slain that he loved. But Moses had already laid his life on the line, and having done so, there was no holding back from God.

Abraham also knew this same kind of relationship with God. When it came to offering up Isaac, he had already crossed that bridge long ago when he had given himself to God. When he was tested on that mountain side, he could lift the knife and was ready to plunge it into the bosom of his son whom he loved. Abraham had proven his fidelity to God. This is the heart of the worshipper.

But Moses' intercession was not yet complete. The following day he appeared before the people and said, "You have committed a great sin. But now I will go up to the Lord; perhaps I can make atonement for your sin" (Exodus 32:32 NIV). So when Moses went back to the Lord, he said, "Oh, what a great sin these people have committed! They have made themselves gods of gold. But now, please forgive their sin—but if not, then blot me out of the book you have written" (Exodus 32:31-32 NIV).

This step on the part of Moses was incredibly bold. What a risk he was taking. What if the sin was of such serious gravity that God did not see fit to forgive it? Moses was laying his life on the line for his people. And this is the ultimate act of intercession. This, in fact, is what Christ has done for us. Moses wasn't dictating to God what to do. He wasn't trying to strike some bargain with God. He didn't prate or parrot some formula to God. He didn't parade his own merit. He simply pressed the relationship with the God that he knew and tested the strength of their friendship. His was the ultimate act of intercession to the point of laying down his life. Moses did not view his place as a worshipper as enabling him to coerce God or guarantee that God would deliver. His approach to God was tentative, "But now I will go up to the Lord; *perhaps* (emphasis mine) I can make atonement for your sin." There was neither presumption nor assumption on the part of Moses. Was the tentative character of his statement an indication of unbelief or wavering? I rather think not! It was a submission to God's sovereignty. Even though he knew the God whom he approached as few have, he was not about to presume upon God, nor put words in the mouth of God. He allowed God the essential prerogative that is rightly His, that is, His sovereignty.

When God responded to Moses' petition, He said, "Whoever has sinned against me I will blot out of my book. Now go, lead the people to the place I spoke of and my angel will go before you. However, when the time comes for me to punish, I will punish them for their sin" (Exodus 32:33-34 NIV). The chapter closes saying, "And the Lord struck the people with a plague because of what they did with the calf Aaron had made" (Exodus 32:35 NIV).

The privilege of intercession that belongs to the worshipper is not an exclusive membership into an elite elect where all privileges are free! Unrighteousness cannot be ignored. We dare not assume that this place of intercession affords us charge privileges with no credit limit. It is not some kind of spiritual American Express card that is paid by a rich relative. The power of intercession is awesome.

The privilege and the potential are far reaching. But so are the responsibilities.

I fear that we have overplayed our position as Sons of God to the point where we have lost the sense of reverence. We misinterpret the New Testament word "boldness" and instead use "brazenness." Moses, in spite of His relationship with God drew near to Him softly. When Abraham drew near to God on behalf of Lot, it was reverentially. We are children of the King, but He is still the King of kings and Lord of lords.

There is one more act of intercession that takes place at the beginning of chapter thirty-three. God told Moses,

> Leave this place, you and the people you brought up out of Egypt, and go up to the land I promised on oath to Abraham, Isaac and Jacob, saying, "I will give it to your descendants. I will send an angel before you… but I will not go with you, because you are a stiff-necked people and I might destroy you on the way" (Exodus 33:1-3 NIV).

Once again we are back to God describing the people to Moses as "you and the people you brought up out of Egypt." But this time, God seems to have numbered Moses with this "stiff-necked people." When the people mourned because of God's Word to Moses, Moses again entered the tent and went into the presence of the Lord, while the people stood at a distance and watched, waiting for him to return.

But when Moses approaches God this time, there seems to be a different agenda. He has made intercession for the people. But now he wants to be with God. He wants to know God. His intense desire for the knowledge of God becomes the theme of the next passage.

3. THE PLACE OF INTIMACY

The name that Moses put on the tent where he would go to commune with God is instructive.

> Now Moses used to take a tent and pitch it outside the camp some distance away, calling it the "tent of meeting." Anyone inquiring of the Lord would go into the tent of meeting outside the camp. And whenever Moses went out to the tent, all the people rose and stood at the entrances to their tents, watching Moses until he entered the tent. As Moses went into the tent, the pillar of cloud would come down and stay at the entrance, while the Lord spoke with Moses. Whenever the people saw the pillar of cloud standing at the entrance to the tent, they all stood and worshipped each at the entrance to his tent. The Lord would speak to Moses face to face, as a man speaks with his friend. Then Moses would return to the camp (Exodus 33:7-11 NIV).

This tent was the place where Moses went to meet with God and to talk with God. Already Moses enjoyed a level of communion with God that few have ever known. Yet Moses had a desire to know God more intimately. "Moses said to the Lord, 'You have been telling me, *Lead these people*, but you have not let me know whom you will send with me. *If* I have found favor in your eyes, teach me your ways (emphasis mine) so I may know you and continue to find favor with you'" (Exodus 33:12-13 NIV).

This is an awesome passage! Here is the man whom God accosted at the burning bush. He is the man whose rod turned to a serpent, brought plagues upon Egypt, divided the Red Sea, and brought water from the rock. This is the man that has been on the mountain with God, alone for forty days. This is the man who received the Ten Commandments, the plans and pattern for the tabernacle. This is the man who asked God to reverse His judgment upon His people, and he is asking God, "Show me your ways"?

How too, too easily are we satisfied with our revelation of God! How near the entrance we are willing to stop on our way into God's presence. How little we are content to settle for when there are oceans of revelation for us to swim in. The pursuit of God will never be satisfied with miracles, signs, wonders, or even with dialogue with the divine. The pursuit of God will be satisfied with nothing less than intimacy, enjoying oneness with the God of glory and in the glory of God.

Do you want to know the ways of God? You don't discover His ways by merely reading about them. One discovers God's ways by being with God. Intimacy enables us to predict the actions of the one with whom we are intimate. When we know the ways of God, we are able to anticipate His actions. He still loves to surprise us, but when He does, it is like being pleasantly surprised by the one you love! It is exciting, exhilarating, and enjoyable!

The God whose ways are "past finding out" (Romans 11:33) revealed those ways to Moses, the worshipper of God. God simply said, "My Presence will go with you, and I will give you rest" (Exodus 33:14 NIV). Moses responded,

> If your Presence does not go with us, do not send us up from here, How will anyone know that you are pleased with me and with your people unless you go with us? What else will distinguish me and your people from all the other people on the face of the earth? (Exodus 33:15-16 NIV)

This passage is powerful! First of all, God's ways have never changed. His way is still the winning combination of His presence and His peace (rest). His promise to go with us remains the same. Secondly, His presence is still the only quality that distinguishes the man of

God and the people of God from the rest of the world. We can attempt all kinds of external distinctives, but those are so superficial. It is the "presence" of God upon His people that marks us and makes us different from the world. The Book of Acts records that the people took knowledge of the disciples of our Lord that "they had been with Jesus" (Acts 4:13).

We need the accompanying anointing of God's presence upon our lives. We need to purpose with Moses, "If your Presence does not go I am not going!" How different would the Church be if we determined to stay out of everything in which God was not involved? How different would our world be if we didn't go anywhere that His presence did not go? And how different would our lives be if we made His presence the mandatory accompaniment everywhere we went?

God's way is always to give us His rest, His peace. He does not will for us to be so flustered, frustrated and fragmented with striving, stressing and straining, that we are worn out in our frenetic, frantic and frenzied efforts to serve Him. He wants to give us rest. We are assured in Hebrews 4 that there remains a rest for the people of God. When we enter into God's rest, we cease from our own works, even as God did from His when He rested on the seventh day (Hebrews 4:1-11).

The accompanying presence of God in Israel not only went "with them," it also went "before them." God's presence among His people became associated with and represented by the Ark of the Covenant. The ark went before the people, searching out the place God had for them (Numbers 10:33). When they crossed the Jordan this was the case (Joshua 3:3-17), as it was when they circled the walls of Jericho (Joshua 6:12-14). The entire book of Joshua chronicles the accompaniment of the ark as they entered and conquered Canaan, in obedience to God's command that the ark was to go ahead of them a three-days journey (Numbers 10:33).

It is interesting to note that the presence of God (the ark) was borne upon the shoulders of the priests (Numbers 7:9). As long as the ark was among the people, God was there. The removal of the ark from Israel resulted in the departure of God's glorious presence from among them, as illustrated in the naming of Ichabod, which means "the glory is departed" (I Samuel 4:21).

God responded again to Moses, "I will do the very thing you have asked, because I am pleased with you and I know you by name" (Exodus 33:17 NIV). For most worshippers, the level of intimacy attained at this point would be adequate. But not for Moses. He wanted more. He pressed further, "Now show me your glory" (Exodus 33:18 NIV).

Now this request was another matter. Without doing violence to the sacredness of this moment, stop and consider the most intimate of human relationships that you enjoy—that with your spouse. Has there ever been a moment of intimacy when your spouse has asked you some very special favor? Have you ever felt that you couldn't say "No!" to that request? Have you ever been in a place where you would do anything possible in this world for the one you love? If so, that is perhaps the closest you can ever humanly come to the position of God with Moses in this moment of spiritual intimacy.

Did Moses really know what he was asking? After all, what is the glory of God? And is it really possible to see God's glory? Regardless of the answers to these questions, Moses was pressing closer, advancing nearer to God than he had ever before. Moses knew enough of God's holiness to not take His glory lightly. But yet, the sense of intimacy that he was experiencing enabled him to wax bold with God.

What is the glory of God? I am not sure that it can be adequately defined. I rather believe that it is the rainbow of all of God's attributes. God's glory is all that He is. It is more than the sum-total of His attributes, although it is certainly that. Could you answer the question, "What color is the rainbow?" I compare God's glory to the rainbow. The glory of God cannot be comprehended in any one of His attributes.

Nor can it be comprehended in their collective whole. But in God's response to Moses, He reveals to us as much of His glory as it is humanly possible to comprehend.

God says, "I will cause all my goodness to pass in front of you, and I will proclaim my name, the LORD (JEHOVAH), in your presence. I will have mercy on whom I will have mercy, and I will have compassion on whom I will have compassion" (Exodus 33:19 NIV). This is the glory of God. His Name, "Jehovah," the Savior. His mercy, His compassion that is free, full and sovereign. In this we begin to catch a glimpse of what constitutes the glory of God. The Hebrew word translated "goodness" means constancy or consistency. This refers to the unchangeable, reliable and dependable nature of the God who is the same, yesterday, today and forever. In a world of change, He does not change. He will not fluctuate. He is unchangeable, and His name reveals His character. Jehovah speaks of His power to save. But He also says, "I will be gracious upon whom I will be gracious." No merit is involved in God's grace in either testament. It is in the character of God to be gracious upon whom He will be gracious. We do not deserve and can never earn that grace. God loves us because His nature is love. God is love.

God continues His revelation to Moses, "But you cannot see my face, for no one may see me and live… There is a place near me where you may stand on a rock. When my glory passes by, I will put you in a cleft in the rock and cover you with my hand until I have passed by. Then I will, remove my hand and you will see my back; but my face must not be seen" (Exodus 33:20-23 NIV).

We must not construe from the language employed that God has a literal face or back. The words are transferred anthropomorphically from man to God because human language and thought can only conceive of the nature of God in the analogy of the human form. As the inward nature of man is expressed in his face and his back gives only an outward and imperfect view of him, so Moses saw only the back of Jehovah. It was not possible for him to have a complete revelation of God's glory.

No mortal man can see the absolute glory of God and live because God is a consuming fire. Just as the eye is dazzled and its power of vision destroyed by gazing into the sun, so would our entire nature be destroyed by an unveiled vision of the brilliancy of the glory of God. The limitations that we experience now, however, will be done away when we are changed into the likeness of Christ and receive our glorified bodies.

It is difficult for us to comprehend the experience of Moses on that mountain. For forty days, with no physical sustenance, he pursued the vision of God. He was absorbed with an eternal passion, that of drawing near to God. He talked with God as a man talks face to face with his friend. Moses was oblivious to the fact that his face was shining as a result of this experience.

When Moses came down from Mount Sinai with the two tablets of the Testimony in his hands, he was not aware that his face was radiant because he had spoken with the Lord. When Aaron and all the Israelites saw Moses, his face was radiant, and they were afraid to come near him… when Moses finished speaking to them, he put a veil over his face. But whenever he entered the

Lord's presence, he removed the veil until he came out. And when he came out and told the Israelites what he had been commanded, they saw that his face was radiant. Then Moses would put the veil back over his face until he went in to speak with the Lord (Exodus 34:29-35 NIV).

The worshipper becomes so engrossed in God's glory that he is not focusing upon his own radiance or reflection of that glory. The apostle Paul picks up this theme in II Corinthians, where he contrasts the glory that was associated with the giving of the law to Moses with the glory that is ours in Christ.

Now if the ministry that brought death, which was engraved in letters on stone, came with glory, so that the Israelites could not look steadily at the face of Moses because of its glory, fading though it was, will not the ministry of the Spirit be even more glorious? If the ministry that condemns men is glorious, how much more glorious is the ministry that brings righteousness! For what was glorious has no glory now in comparison with the surpassing glory. And if what was fading away came with glory, how much greater is the glory of that which lasts! Therefore, since we have such a hope, we are very bold. We are not like Moses, who would put a veil over his face to keep the Israelites from gazing at it while the radiance was fading away. But their minds were made dull, for to this day the same veil remains when the old covenant is read. It has not been removed, because only in Christ is it taken away. Even to this day when Moses is read, a veil covers their hearts. But whenever anyone turns to the Lord, the veil is taken away. Now the Lord is the Spirit, and where the Spirit of the Lord is there is freedom. And we, who with unveiled faces all reflecting the Lord's glory, are being transformed into his likeness with ever-increasing glory, which comes from the Lord, who is the Spirit (II Corinthians 3:7-18 NIV).

If we can grasp the significance of what Paul is saying, we will understand that for the New Testament believer, there is a glory that eclipses the glory that Moses experienced. We have seen "the light of the gospel of the glory of Christ, who is the image of God… For God, who said, 'Let light shine out of darkness,' made his light shine in our hearts to give us the light of the knowledge of the glory of God in the face of Jesus Christ" (II Corinthians 4:4-6 NIV).

When Jesus took the three disciples who were in the inner circle upon the mountain of transfiguration, they were the first to truly behold His glory. While Jesus prayed, "There he was transfigured before them. His face shone like the sun, and his clothes became as white as the light. Just then there appeared before them Moses and Elijah, talking with Jesus" (Matthew 17:1-3 NIV). This incident took place some two thousand years after Moses had prayed, "Show me thy glory." But it was here, upon the unnamed mountain, that Moses first saw the glory of God in its most full and final revelation.

John wrote of it and said, "The Word became flesh and lived for a while among us. We have seen his glory, the glory of the one and only Son, who came from the Father, full of grace and truth" (John 1:14 NIV). Peter said, "…we were eyewitnesses of his majesty. For he received honor and glory from God the Father when the voice came to him from the Majestic Glory, saying, 'This is my Son, whom I love: with him I am well pleased.' We ourselves heard this voice that came from heaven when we were with him on the sacred mountain" (II Peter 1:16-18 NIV). The writer to the Hebrews tells us that "The Son is the radiance of God's glory and the exact representation of his being" (Hebrews 1:3 NIV).

There can be no question that Christ is the revelation of the glory of God! And the human flesh of Christ, His earthly body, served as a veil to shield the full manifestation of God's glory. Now that His body has been glorified, when we are glorified, we too will be able to witness God's glorious manifestation in a more complete manner.

The lessons from all of this for the worshipper are significant. The pursuit of God will bring us into proximity with Christ. Intimacy with God is intimacy with Christ. We know God only through our Lord Jesus Christ. And as we behold Him, we become like Him. When we catch a glimpse of His glory, we will begin to reflect it. And yet it will not be our radiance but His resplendence that will capture our attention.

What Moses longed for and sought after is now ours in the gracious provision of Christ. We can behold the glory of God in His face. When we cultivate communion with Him, we are permitted to behold His glory, and that glory will continually change us into ever-increasing glory. And this experience comes from the Lord, who is the Spirit.

God's design is that the worshipper reflects and radiates Christ. That in turn will cause others to behold Christ in us. And as they do, they will be drawn to Him, and He will be worshipped and glorified. And as they reflect Christ, others will be drawn to His person. In this can be seen the plan of God that merges worship and evangelism. By worshipping God, we draw near enough to receive and then reflect His glory. When unbelievers behold Christ in us, they will be drawn to Him. This is evangelism. And as they turn to Him, they will glorify God. This is worship! And God's plan is that this perpetual process would continue to repeat itself until all men everywhere are drawn to His glory and He is lifted up and exalted by all!

4. THE PURSUIT OF THE INFINITE

The divine desire for God's presence has been encoded within each human being by our Designer. God has created us with the capacity to know Him, to experience His presence and to enjoy communion with Him. It is this basic characteristic that furnishes the worship drive within man.

This upward lift of man that we discovered in *Chapter Three* can be found in people of every culture. The created world without and the conscience within are a two-fold witness to every person that there is a being superior to himself that is responsible for his existence and worthy of his worship.

This quest for God that is native to every human being finds its initial fulfillment when a person trusts Christ as Savior. When Christ comes to live within the heart by faith, the believer becomes a partaker of God's divine nature. Christ is now resident in the life through the indwelling presence of the Holy Spirit. This experience is an initiation into an eternal relationship with God. This relationship will be progressive in this lifetime and culminate in the ultimate union with Christ at His coming.

It is the progressive nature of this pursuit of God that propels the believer from an initial encounter with Christ to an ever-increasing desire for more of Him. The apostle Paul captured this concept in His letter to the Philippians,

> What is more, I consider everything a loss compared to the surpassing greatness of knowing Christ Jesus my Lord, for whose sake I have lost all things. I consider them rubbish that I may gain Christ… I want to know Christ and the power of his resurrection and the fellowship of sharing in his sufferings, becoming like him in his death… not that I have already attained all this, or have

already been made perfect, but I press on to take hold of that for which Christ Jesus took hold of me (Philippians 3:8-12 NIV).

The longer one follows Christ, the more intense this desire becomes. The pursuit of God becomes the preoccupation of the Christian life. Knowing God, discovering and developing intimacy with Him is the highest occupation that one can pursue. Knowing God is much more than knowing about God. The academic pursuit of knowing about God is eclipsed by the fulfillment of knowing God. In fact, all academic pursuit of theology needs to be balanced by the pursuit of God, or else it will become empty and meaningless.

While it is true that we know God through His Word, as we search the Scriptures, we need to invoke the presence of the Holy Spirit to bring illumination to our hearts. Jesus gave us one of the keys in this matter when He said, "Search the scriptures; for in them ye think ye have eternal life: and they are they which testify of me" (John 6:39). The knowledge of Christ is the key to Scriptural knowledge. The pursuit of His person and presence is that to which we have been called as Christians. J.I. Packer writes,

> For this very reason we need, before we start to ascend our mountain, to stop and ask ourselves a very fundamental question—a question, indeed, that we always ought to put to ourselves whenever we embark on any line of study in God's holy Book. The question concerns our own motives and intentions as students. We need to ask ourselves: what is my ultimate aim and object in occupying my mind with these things? What do I intend to do with my knowledge about God, once I have got it? For the fact that we have to face is this: that if we pursue theological knowledge for its own sake, it is bound to go bad on us. It will make us proud and conceited. The very greatness of the subject-matter will intoxicate us, and we shall come to think of ourselves as a cut above

other Christians because of our interest in and grasp of it… Our aim in studying the Godhead must be to know God Himself the better. Our concern must be to enlarge our acquaintance, not simply with the doctrine of God's attributes, but with the living God whose attributes they are. As He is the subject of our study, and our helper in it, so He must Himself be the end of it. We must seek, in studying God, to be led to God. It was for this purpose that revelation was given, and it is to this use that we must put it.[101]

It was this desire for God that characterized the Psalmist David, and constituted him a man after God's own heart. Psalm 42 is typical of that desire that runs through the Psalms. "As the deer pants for streams of water, so my soul pants for you O God; my soul thirsts for God, for the living God. When can I go and meet with God?" (Psalm 42:1-2 NIV). In Psalm 63, David prays,

O God, you are my God' earnestly I seek you; my soul thirsts for you, in a dry and weary land where there is no water. I have seen you in the sanctuary and beheld your power and your glory. Because your love is better than life, my lips will glorify you. I will praise you as long as I live, and in your name I will lift up my hands. My soul will be satisfied as with the richest of foods; with singing lips my mouth will praise you. On my bed I remember you; I think of you through the watches of the night. Because you are my help, I sing in the shadow of your wings. I stay close to you; your right hand upholds me (Psalm 63:1-8 NIV).

This craving for God is something that springs from the depth of the being. it is the quintessential quest of life. The metaphors that David employs in Psalm 63 are descriptive of the satisfying nature of knowing God. Once having tasted of God's presence, there is an

---

101   Packer, James I. *Knowing God.* Downers Grove, IL: Intervarsity Press, 1993.

insatiable desire for more of God. And the closer one draws to God, the more intense the desire for intimacy.

One of the glorious facets of the Christian experience is that there are depths in God that we will never fathom, neither in this life nor in that which is to come. "No eye has seen, no ear has heard, no mind has conceived what God has prepared for those who love him" (I Corinthians 2:9 NIV). The text goes on to say, "But God has revealed it to us by his Spirit." The Holy Spirit enables us to have revelation on the riches of God's resources, on the surpassing greatness of His person, but we can never fully fathom the greatness of God's glory. The paradox with which the Christian lives is that we have found God and still we are seeking Him. As the hymn-writer expressed it, "We taste Thee, O Thou Living Bread, and long to feast upon Thee still: We drink of Thee, the Fountainhead and thirst our souls from Thee to fill."[102]

The Psalmist said, "Deep calls to deep in the roar of your water-falls" (Psalm 42:7 NIV). There is a depth in us that searches for the depth in God. And there is a depth in God that calls unto the depth of our being. It is this pursuit of God that is at the very heart of worship. Knowing God is the purpose for which we were created. Knowing God is the essence of eternal life. Jesus said, "Now this is eternal life: that they may know you, the only true God, and Jesus Christ, whom you have sent" (John 17:3 NIV). The greatest value in life is not in material possessions, human wisdom, success, pleasure, or even human relationships. The greatest value in life is to know God.

This is what the Lord says: "Let not the wise man boast of his wisdom or the strong man boast of his strength or the rich man

---

102 Words by Bernard of Clairvaux, 12th Century (Jesu dulcis memori); translated from Latin to English by Ray Palmer, 1858, in his Poetical Works (New York: 1876). *Hymns of the Christian Church*. Vol. XLV, Part 2. The Harvard Classics. New York: P.F. Collier & Son, 1909–14.

boast of his riches, but let him who boasts boast about this: that he understands and knows me, that I am the Lord, who exercises kindness, justice and righteousness on earth, for in these I delight," declares the Lord (Jeremiah 9:22-24 NIV).

Charles Spurgeon considered the pursuit of God "the highest science, the loftiest speculation, the mightiest philosophy, which can ever engage the attention of a child of God… a subject so vast, that all our thoughts are lost in its immensity; so deep, that our pride is drowned in its infinity."[103] The King James translates Psalm 63:8, "My soul followeth hard after thee: thy right hand upholdeth me." The impulse to pursue God originates in God, not in us. He plants the desire within us by divine design. Yet the outworking of that impulse must be an active reciprocation of God's drawing us to Himself. Our created capacity to know God is in the area of our conscious awareness. When we have been born again by the Spirit of God, our senses become alive to the fact that we now have relationship with God. The pursuit of God begins only at this point, and becomes the career of the Christian for time and for eternity. A.W. Tozer in his great classic, The Pursuit of God, writes,

> I want deliberately to encourage this mighty longing after God. The lack of it has brought us to our present low estate. The stiff and wooden quality about our religious lives is a result of our lack of holy desire. Complacency is a deadly foe of all spiritual growth. Acute desire must be present or there will be no manifestation of Christ to His people. He waits to be wanted; too bad that with many of us He waits so long, so very long, in vain."[104]

103   https://www.spurgeon.org/resource-library/sermons/the-immutability-of-god#flipbook/
104   Tozer, A.W. The Pursuit of God. Camp Hill, PA: Christian Publications, 1993.

That God made us for Himself is fundamental to even an elementary understanding of the Scriptures. Augustine captured this when he said, "Thou has formed us for Thyself, and our hearts are restless till they find rest in Thee."[105]

---

105   Saint Augustine, Confessions, Book One, Chapter One, 397 A.D. http://www.ccel.org/a/augustine/confessions/confessions.html

DON'T FOLLOW THE CROWD—FOLLOW THE CLOUD

Numerous have been the manifestations of God's providence in sustaining us. In the gloomy period of adversity, we have had 'our cloud by day and pillar of fire by night.' We have been reduced to distress, and the arm of Omnipotence has raised us up.

— Samuel Adams

Then the LORD said to Moses: "Set up the tabernacle, the Tent of Meeting... Moses did everything just as the LORD commanded him... so Moses finished the work. Then the cloud covered the Tent of Meeting, and the glory of the LORD filled the tabernacle. Moses could not enter the Tent of Meeting because the cloud had settled upon it, and the glory of the LORD filled the tabernacle. In all the travels of the Israelites, whenever the cloud lifted from above the tabernacle, they would set out; but if the cloud did not lift, they did not set out—until the day it lifted. So the cloud of the LORD was over the tabernacle by day, and fire was in the cloud by night, in the sight of all the house of Israel during all their travels (Exodus 40:1-38 NIV).

n the passage above, the Israelites have advanced a long way from the worship of the golden calf that we discussed in our last chapter. They've put their golden jewelry to better use than making a false god. It has been melted down into the furnishings for the tabernacle. And although all the furnishings were now in place, and the *human* work was done, it was incomplete apart from the presence of God. God's glory is indispensable to our worship. We can have all of the other components in place, but if God doesn't show up, we have not experienced true worship. We can follow the pattern, have the liturgy ever so orthodox, but until the glory of God descends in the midst of God's people, our worship experience will be inadequate, incomplete, and unsatisfying to God and to us.

This lesson in and of itself will occupy most of our attention in this chapter. However, another principle surfaces in this chapter that is critical to the life of Israel and the people of God in any generation. As they began their journey through the wilderness, they learned not to move until God was ready to move with them.

> In all the travels of the Israelites, whenever the cloud lifted from above the tabernacle, they would set out; but if the cloud did not lift, they did not set out—until the day it lifted. So the cloud of the LORD was over the tabernacle by day, and fire was in the cloud by night, in the sight of all the house of Israel during all their travels (Exodus 40:36-38 NIV).

In essence, they had learned an invaluable lesson for every child of God and every church, "If the Lord isn't going ahead of us or if God isn't moving with us, we're staying put—we're not going anywhere." In chapter forty of Exodus we read,

> Then Moses set up the courtyard around the tabernacle and altar and put up the curtain at the entrance to the courtyard. And

so Moses finished the work. Then the cloud covered the Tent of Meeting, and the glory of the Lord filled the tabernacle. Moses could not enter the Tent of Meeting because the cloud had settled upon it, and the glory of the Lord filled the tabernacle (Exodus 40:33-35 NIV).

That which Moses tasted in his pursuit of the glory of God becomes available to every New Testament believer who will cultivate communion with Christ in worship. The glory of God's presence is not some esoteric, abstract, mystical experience in the ethereal realm. That is not to say that God's glory is to be regarded without reverence. But the veil has been taken away, and in the Lord Jesus Christ we have beheld the glory of God.

The crux of the matter is the attitude of the worshipper. Do we really want to experience God's glory? Do we truly desire to be in His presence? Or are we satisfied to go through our ritual and liturgy, and never enter to the place of intimacy with God? Spiritual intimacy is the end (if there is an end) of worship. God has designed the worship encounter to result in intimacy with Christ. Intimacy with Christ involves both the beholding of His glory and the experience of His presence.

When we speak of the presence of God, we are not speaking of His omnipresence. For we know that there is a sense in which God is everywhere present and nowhere absent. His "omni" presence fills the heavens and the earth (Psalms 139:7-12, Acts 17:27-28). But His Personal Presence is another thing, as is illustrated for us in the tabernacle of worship.

As we have already discovered in our examination of the pattern of worship, when the priest entered the tabernacle, he did not actually enter the "presence" of God until he went beyond the veil into the holiest of all. He could sacrifice at the brazen altar, wash at the brazen layer, eat at the table of shewbread, offer incense on the golden altar in the light of the golden lampstand, but until and unless he went through the veil, he had not experienced the glory of God's presence.

This same principle is paralleled in the New Testament Church and in the individual life of the believer. It is possible to come to the cross of Christ, receive forgiveness through His sacrifice and blood, be washed and sanctified by the Word of God, offer prayer and praise, feast on God's Word, enjoy the illumination of the Spirit upon the Word, and yet not truly experience the glory of God's presence.

As we discovered in the last chapter, the glory of God's presence is available to every New Testament believer. The veil is done away in Christ. He has made a new and living way through the veil of His flesh by which we can enter with boldness into the holiest of all. Yet, sadly, too many of God's people stop short of experiencing the glory of His presence. There is no reason for the Christian to be hesitant or afraid of entering the holy of holies. God has provided and planned for us to enter His presence and for us to live our lives in the awareness of His presence in a conscious experiential walk with God.

As we examine the subject of the glory of God's presence in worship, we will look at it from three perspectives.

1. First, from the Old Testament, where God dwelt among His people in the tabernacle and the temple.

2. Then we will move to the New Testament era, where God indwelt Christ and now indwells His Body, the Church.

3. Finally, we will focus upon the future where the people of God will enjoy the fullness of His presence and glory

throughout eternity as we surround His throne in our worship of the Lamb.

1. GOD'S PRESENCE IN THE PAST

When God first gave Moses the command to build the tabernacle it was because God desired to dwell among His people. "Then have them make a sanctuary for me, and I will dwell among them" (Exodus 25:8 NIV). It was the flame of God's presence that formed the heartbeat of the entire tabernacle worship.

Without the presence of God, the tabernacle furnishings were meaningless. The greatest feature of the tabernacle was that Jehovah was dwelling among them, and His presence was within the veil.

As important as it was for Moses to follow the specifications to precision (and it was of vital importance) having done so would have proved incomplete, had not the presence of God's glory descended upon the tabernacle when Moses had completed the work.

God's glory became that which marked the people, and His presence among them was the principal purpose of the tabernacle. The glory of God's presence among them became that which led them.

> In all the travels of the Israelites, whenever the cloud lifted from above the tabernacle, they would set out; but if the cloud did not lift, they did not set out—until the day it lifted. So the cloud of the Lord was over the tabernacle by day and fire was in the cloud by night, in the sight of all the house of Israel during their travels (Exodus 40:36-38 NIV).

But the glory of God dwelt more specifically between the cherubim, over the mercy seat, on the Ark of the Covenant. It was this that was behind the veil, and it was here that God's glory dwelt. Consequently, the ark was more than a symbolical representation of God's presence. God's glory actually was manifest there, and His presence was upon the ark.

For this reason, the ark always went before them as they journeyed. "The ark of the covenant of the Lord went before them during those three days to find them a place to rest. The cloud of the Lord was over them by day when they set out from the camp. Whenever the ark set out, Moses said, 'Rise up, O Lord! May your enemies be scattered; may your foes flee before you.' Whenever it came to rest, he said, 'Return, O Lord, to the countless thousands of Israel'" (Numbers 10:35-36 NIV). Moses was cognizant of the fact that it was the ark of God in the midst of His people that guaranteed His presence.

When Moses recounts the history of their idolatry to Israel and talks of his intercession for them, he also talks about the special role of the Levites, "At that time the Lord set apart the tribe of Levi to carry the ark of the covenant of the Lord, to stand before the Lord to minister and to pronounce blessings in his name" (Deuteronomy 10:8 NIV). When Joshua was leading God's people through the Jordan,

> The priests carrying the Ark of the Covenant went ahead of them. Now the Jordan is at flood stage during harvest. Yet as soon as the priests who carried the ark reached the Jordan and their feet touched the water's edge, the water from upstream stopped flowing. It piled up in a heap a great distance away… while the water flowing down to the Sea… was completely cut off. The priests who carried the ark of the covenant of the Lord stood firm on dry ground in the middle of the Jordan (Joshua 3:14-17 NIV).

When the Israelites came to take Jericho, Joshua "had the ark of the Lord carried around the city, circling it once. The seven priests carrying the seven trumpets went forward, marching before the ark of the Lord and blowing the trumpets" (Joshua 6:11-14 NIV).

This procedure was followed for six days, then seven times on the seventh day, and the walls of Jericho fell before the ark of the Lord. Also, when Joshua discovered that Achan had sinned by not completely obeying the Lord, he "tore his clothes and fell face down before the ark of the Lord, remaining there till evening. The elders of Israel did the same" (Joshua 7:6 NIV). When they were faced with the question as to whether to fight against the Benjamites,

> Then the Israelites, all the people, went up to Bethel, and there they sat weeping before the Lord. They fasted that day until evening and presented burnt offerings and fellowship offerings to the Lord. And the Israelites inquired of the Lord. [In those days the ark of the covenant of God was there, with Phinehas son of Eleazar, the son of Aaron, ministering before it] (Judges 20:26-28 NIV).

The ark of God's presence continued to be the center for seeking the will of God as they carried out His plan for the conquest of the land He had given them.

One of the greatest calamities that befell the people of Israel is recorded in I Samuel 4, and surrounds one of their perennial conflicts with the Philistines. Israel has just suffered defeat by the Philistines.

> When the soldiers returned to camp, the elders of Israel asked, "Why did the LORD bring defeat upon us today before the Philistines? Let us bring the ark of the LORD's covenant from Shiloh, so that it may go with us and save us from the hand of our enemies." So the people sent men to Shiloh, and they brought back the ark of

the covenant of the LORD Almighty, who is enthroned between the cherubim. And Eli's two sons, Hophni and Phinehas, were there with the ark of the covenant of God. When the ark of the LORD's covenant came into the camp, all Israel raised such a great shout that the ground shook. Hearing the uproar, the Philistines asked, "What's all this shouting in the Hebrew camp?" When they learned that the ark of the LORD had come into the camp, the Philistines were afraid. "A god has come into the camp," they said. "We're in trouble! Nothing like this has happened before. Woe to us! Who will deliver us from the hand of these mighty gods? They are the gods who struck the Egyptians with all kinds of plagues in the desert. Be strong, Philistines! Be men, or you will be subject to the Hebrews, as they have been to you. Be men, and fight!" So the Philistines fought, and the Israelites were defeated and every man fled to his tent. The slaughter was very great; Israel lost thirty thousand foot soldiers. The ark of God was captured, and Eli's two sons, Hophni and Phinehas, died. That same day a Benjamite ran from the battle line and went to Shiloh, his clothes torn and dust on his head. When he arrived, there was Eli sitting on his chair by the side of the road, watching, because his heart feared for the ark of God. When the man entered the town and told what had happened, the whole town sent up a cry. Eli heard the outcry and asked, "What is the meaning of this uproar?" The man hurried over to Eli, who was ninety-eight years old and whose eyes were set so that he could not see. He told Eli, "I have just come from the battle line; I fled from it this very day." Eli asked, "What happened, my son?" The man who brought the news replied, "Israel fled before the Philistines, and the army has suffered heavy losses. Also your two sons, Hophni and Phinehas, are dead, and the ark of God has been captured." When he mentioned the ark of God, Eli fell backward off his chair by the side of the gate. His neck was broken and he died, for he was an old man and heavy. He had led Israel forty years. His daughter-in-law, the wife of Phinehas, was pregnant and near the time of delivery. When she heard the news that the ark of God had been captured and that her father-in-law and her husband were dead, she went into labor and gave birth, but was overcome by her labor pains. As she was dying, the women attending her said, "Don't despair; you have given birth to a son." But she did not respond or pay any attention. She named the boy Ichabod, "The glory has departed from Israel"—because of the capture of the ark of God and the deaths of her father-in-law and her husband. She said, "The glory has departed from Israel, for the ark of God has been captured" (I Samuel 4:4-22 NIV).

This is one of the saddest chapters in the history of Israel. It will be instructive for us to learn what had transpired among God's people that led up to the loss of God's glory and presence from among them. First, they had lost the value of the *presence* of God, and viewed the ark as representing only the *power* of God. They had seen what happened when the ark of God was around. The Jordan opened and the walls of Jericho fell down. They began to *presume upon the presence of God*. When they got in trouble, they would send for the ark.

Not only that, but "Eli's Sons were wicked men; they had no regard for the Lord... the sin of the young men was very great in the Lord's sight for they were treating the Lord's offering with contempt" (I Samuel 2:12, 17 NIV). Eli tried to correct them, but to no avail.

So he said to them, "Why do you do such things? I hear from all the people about these wicked deeds of yours. No, my Sons; it is not a good report that I hear spreading among the Lord's people. If a man sins against another man, God may mediate for him; but if a man sins against the Lord, who will intercede for him?" His sons, however, did not listen to their father's rebuke, for it was the Lord's will to put them to death (I Samuel 2:23-25 NIV).

Worship does not focus on the *power* of God's presence. It focuses upon the *person* of the presence, the *personal presence* of God Himself. If our exercise in worship is to create an atmosphere in which God will manifest His power through supernatural acts, then we tend to treat His presence lightly and presumptuously. God wants His people to value His presence because they love Him, not because they love what he does. There is no question that where God is, there is power, but we don't worship God merely to experience His power.

I have talked to people of wealth and power who have experienced the same kind of exploitation that God was receiving from Israel at this time. They grow to feel that their friends come to them only because of what they can receive from them. Wealthy individuals often become recluses for this very reason. They grow lonely and experience severe emotional pain because they can never be sure that people want to be with them just to be with them.

The ark of God continued to demonstrate the same kind of power when it left Israel. "After the Philistines captured the ark of God, they took it from Ebenezer to Ashdod. Then they carried the ark into Dagon's temple and set it beside Dagon. When the people of Ashdod rose early the next day, there was Dagon fallen on his face…"

> After the Philistines had captured the ark of God, they took it from Ebenezer to Ashdod. Then they carried the ark into Dagon's temple and set it beside Dagon. When the people of Ashdod rose early the next day, there was Dagon, fallen on his face on the ground before the ark of the LORD! They took Dagon and put him back in his place. But the following morning when they rose, there was Dagon, fallen on his face on the ground before the ark of the Lord! His head and hands had been broken off and were

lying on the threshold; only his body remained… The Lord's hand was heavy upon the people of Ashdod and its vicinity; he brought devastation upon them and afflicted them with tumors. When the men of Ashdod saw what was happening, they said, "The ark of the God of Israel must not stay here with us, because his hand is heavy upon us and upon Dagon our god." So they called together all the rulers of the Philistines and asked them, "What shall we do with the ark of the god of Israel?" They answered, "Have the ark of the god of Israel moved to Gath." So they moved the ark of the God of Israel. But after they had moved it, the Lord's hand was against that city… So they sent the ark of God to Ekron. As the ark of God was entering Ekron, the people of Ekron cried out, "They have brought the ark of the God of Israel around to us to kill us and our people." So they called together all the rulers of the Philistines and said, "Send the ark of the God of Israel away; let it go back to its own place, or it will kill us and our people." For death had filled the city with panic (I Samuel 5:1-11 NIV).

The Philistines were quick to observe the power of the presence of God among them. For them it spelled death and destruction. In I Samuel chapter six we read of the return of the ark to Israel. Having learned an expensive lesson concerning its power, they were quite intent upon returning it properly. Upon consultation with their priests and diviners, they were told to make gold tumors and rats and to get a new cart ready for the ark. The cart was to be pulled by two cows that had never calved and had never been yoked.

They took the ark and put it on the cart next to a chest in which they placed the gold objects that they were sending as a guilt offering. They were very careful not to turn to their right or left as they took the cart up to Beth Shemesh. When the people of Beth Shemesh who were harvesting their wheat in the valley looked up and saw the ark, they rejoiced at the sight. When it stopped beside a large rock, the people chopped up the wood of the cart and sacrificed the cows as a burnt offering to the Lord. "The Levites took down the ark of the Lord… and on that day the people of Beth Shemesh offered burnt offerings and made sacrifices to the Lord" (I Samuel 6:15 NIV).

But God struck down some of the men of Beth Shemesh, putting seventy of them to death because they had looked into the ark of the Lord. The people mourned because of the heavy blow the Lord had dealt them, and the men of Beth Shemesh asked, "Who can stand in the presence of the Lord, this holy God? To whom will the ark go up from here?" Then they sent messengers to the people of Kiriath Jearim saying, "The Philistines have returned the ark of the Lord. Come down and take it up to your place" (I Samuel 6:19-21).

The saga of the journey of the ark continues in the chapter seven of I Samuel, where we read:

So the men of Kiriath Jearim came and took up the ark of the LORD. They took it to Abinadab's house on the hill and con-secrated Eleazar his son to guard the ark of the LORD. It was a long time, twenty years in all, that the ark remained at Kiriath Jearim, and all the people of Israel mourned and sought after the LORD. And Samuel said to the whole house of Israel, "If you are returning to the LORD with all your hearts, then rid yourselves of the foreign gods and the Ashtoreths and commit yourselves to the LORD and serve him only, and he will deliver you out of the hand of the Philistines." So the Israelites put away their Baals and Ashtoreths, and served the LORD only (I Samuel 7:1-4 NIV).

When the ark of God was returned and the presence of God given its rightful place, the people repented and spiritual revival came to

Israel. Samuel came into leadership with the anointing of God upon Him, and the blessing of God was on His people. Unfortunately, their consecration to God was short-lived. The influence of the other nations around them began to take its toll, and they asked Samuel to give them a king like the other nations.

Although Saul began well, it was not long before his disregard for God was obvious. He grew impatient when he was waiting for Samuel, and intruded into the office of the priest by offering burnt offerings and fellowship offerings to God.

> "You acted foolishly," Samuel said. "You have not kept the command the Lord your God gave you; if you had, he would have established your kingdom over Israel for all time. But now your kingdom will not endure; the Lord has sought out a man after his own heart and appointed him leader of his people, because you have not kept the Lord's command" (I Samuel 13:13-15 NIV).

It was not until Saul found himself out of God's favor that he sought the ark of God. "Saul said to Abijah, 'Bring the ark of God.' (At that time it was with the Israelites)" (I Samuel 14:18 NIV). Saul's disregard for the glory of God's presence and for the holiness of God was demonstrated by his presumption upon God. Later, when he sought guidance from hell that he couldn't get from heaven by going to the witch of Endor, he confirmed that his heart was not that of a worshipper (I Samuel 28:6-20).

The saga of God's presence among His people follows the Ark of the Covenant to its next mention in Scripture, which is found in II Samuel 6, after David had been anointed as King of Judah and Israel.

> Again, David gathered together all the chosen men of Israel, thirty thousand. And David arose, and went with all the people that were with him from Baale of Judah, to bring up from thence

the ark of God, whose name is called by the name of the LORD of hosts that dwelleth between the cherubims. And they set the ark of God upon a new cart, and brought it out of the house of Abinadab that was in Gibeah: and Uzzah and Ahio, the sons of Abinadab, drave the new cart. And they brought it out of the house of Abinadab which was at Gibeah, accompanying the ark of God: and Ahio went before the ark. And David and all the house of Israel played before the LORD on all manner of instruments made of fir wood, even on harps, and on psalteries, and on timbrels, and on cornets, and on cymbals. And when they came to Nachon's threshingfloor, Uzzah put forth his hand to the ark of God, and took hold of it; for the oxen shook it. And the anger of the LORD was kindled against Uzzah; and God smote him there for his error; and there he died by the ark of God. And David was displeased, because the LORD had made a breach upon Uzzah: and he called the name of the place Perezuzzah to this day. And David was afraid of the LORD that day, and said, How shall the ark of the LORD come to me? So David would not remove the ark of the LORD unto him into the city of David: but David carried it aside into the house of Obededom the Gittite. And the ark of the LORD continued in the house of Obededom the Gittite three months: and the LORD blessed Obededom, and all his household. And it was told king David, saying, The LORD hath blessed the house of Obededom, and all that pertaineth unto him, because of the ark of God. So David went and brought up the ark of God from the house of Obededom into the city of David with gladness. And it was so, that when they that bare the ark of the LORD had gone six paces, he sacrificed oxen and fatlings. And David danced before the LORD with all his might; and David was girded with a linen ephod. So David and all the house of Israel brought up the ark of the LORD with shouting, and with the sound of the trumpet. And as the ark of the LORD came into the city of David, Michal Saul's daughter looked through a window, and saw king David leaping and dancing before the LORD; and she despised him in her heart. And they brought in the ark of the LORD, and set it in his place, in the midst of the tabernacle that David had pitched for it: and David offered burnt offerings and peace offerings before the LORD. And as soon as David had made an end of offering burnt offerings and peace offerings, he blessed the people in the name of the LORD of hosts (II Samuel 6:1-18 NIV).

David had failed to search the Scriptures adequately to determine how the ark was to be carried. It is interesting to note that God's people quickly adopted the same method of carrying the ark as the Philistines had. They built a new cart. God had determined that the ark was to be carried only on the shoulders of the priests. When David was more careful to see that the ark was carried as God had required, there was great rejoicing among God's people.

It is apparent that Saul's daughter was of the same spirit as her father. She had no appreciation for the presence of God among His people. She could not understand David's exuberance and excitement at the return of the ark. Because of her despising of David for his act of worship to God, she was barren till the day of her death. We must be careful in our criticism of those who demonstrate physically their response to the divine presence. Those who know the glory of God's presence may exhibit their worship to God in ways that we may consider to be unorthodox. Yet, in the eyes of God, it is the heart that counts. And the worshipper who was dancing before the ark was a man after the heart of God!

It was the same passionate pursuit of and high regard for God's presence that birthed a desire in David to build God a house, a permanent dwelling place for the ark of God's covenant.

After the king was settled in his palace and the Lord had given him rest from all his enemies, he said to Nathan the prophet, "Here I am, living in a palace of cedar, while the ark of God remains in a tent." Nathan replied to the king, "Whatever you have in mind, go ahead and do it, for the Lord is with you." That night the word of the Lord came to Nathan, saying: "Go and tell my servant David, 'This is what the Lord says: Are you the one to build me a house to dwell in? I have not dwelt in a house from the day I brought the Israelites up out of Egypt to this day. I have been moving from place to place with a tent as my dwelling. Wherever I have moved with all the Israelites, did I ever say to any of their rulers whom I commanded to shepherd my people Israel, "Why have you not built me house of cedar?" Now then, tell my servant David, "This is what the Lord Almighty says: I took you from the pasture and from following the flock to be ruler over my people Israel. I have been with you wherever you have gone, and I have cut off all your enemies from before you. Now I will make your name great, like the names of the greatest men of the earth. And I will provide a place for my people Israel and will plant them so that they can have a home of their own and no longer be disturbed. Wicked people will not oppress them anymore, as they did at the beginning and have done ever since the time I appointed leaders over my people Israel, I will also give you rest from all your enemies. The Lord declares to you that the Lord himself will establish a house for you: When your days are over and you rest with your fathers, I will raise up your offspring to succeed you, who will come from your own body, and I will establish his kingdom. He is the one who will build a house for my Name, and I will establish the throne of his kingdom forever'" (II Samuel 7:1-13 NIV).

When Nathan gave this message to David, he accepted it humbly and gratefully, revealing the heart of the worshipper that motivated his life. When David went into the presence of God, he prayed,

> Who am I, O Sovereign Lord, and what is my family that you have brought me this far? And as if this were not enough in your sight, O Sovereign Lord, you have also spoken about the future of the house of your servant. Is this your usual way of dealing with man, O Sovereign Lord? What more can David say to you? For you know your servant, O Sovereign Lord... How great you are, O Sovereign Lord! There is no one like you, and there is no God but you, as we have heard with our own ears, And who is like your people Israel—the one nation on earth that God went out to redeem as a people for himself, and to make a name for himself, and to perform great and awesome wonders by driving out nations and their gods from before your people, whom you redeemed out of Egypt? You have established your people Israel as very own forever, and you, O Lord, have become their God. And now, Lord God, keep forever the promise you have made concerning your servant and his house. Do as you promised, so that your name will be great forever. Then men will say, 'The Lord Almighty is God over Israel!' And the house of your servant David will be established before you. O Lord Almighty, God of Israel, you have revealed this to your servant saying; 'I will build a house for you. So your servant has found courage to offer you this prayer. O Sovereign Lord, you are God! Your words are trustworthy, and you have given this good promise to your servant. Now be pleased to bless the house of your servant, that it may continue forever in your sight; for you, O Sovereign Lord, have spoken, and with

your blessing the house of your servant will be blessed forever (II Samuel 7:18-29 NIV).

David's career becomes sullied by his sin with Bathsheba, and he begins to reap the bitter harvest of his sin in his own family. His own son, Absolom raised up a conspiracy against him, and David finds himself fleeing from the presence of his own son. Yet, in the midst of David's dangerous departure from the kingdom, he cherished the presence of God.

> The whole countryside wept aloud as all the people passed by. The king also crossed the Kidron Valley, and all the people moved on towards the desert. Zadok was there, too, and all the Levites who were with him were carrying the ark of the covenant of God. They sat down the ark of God, and Abiathar offered sacrifices until all the people had finished leaving the city. Then the king said to Zadok, "Take the ark of God back into the city. If I find favor in the Lord's eyes, he will bring me back and let me see it and his dwelling place again. But if he says, 'I am not pleased with you,' then I am ready; let him do to me whatever seems good to him" (II Samuel 15:23-26 NIV).

David prized the Presence of God. And yet, he would not selfishly keep the ark to himself, knowing that it belonged in the midst of God's people. But paramount in David's interest was not the throne, but the ark! God's *presence* meant more to him than his *throne* in God's kingdom. David was not concerned about whether or not he would return to the palace. It wasn't the rule that concerned him. It was the presence of God that he cherished more than life itself. This is the heart of the worshipper that he demonstrates over and again.

> God's promise to David was fulfilled in his son, Solomon. David was not permitted by God to build the house, but his son, Solomon,

built a magnificent temple to the Lord. In its construction, only blocks dressed at the quarry were used, so that no hammer, chisel or any other iron tool was heard at the temple site while it was being built. It had three floors, and inside the stone was covered with cedar. He covered the inside of the temple with pure gold, and he extended gold chains across the front of the inner sanctuary, which was overlaid with gold. He overlaid the whole interior with gold. The furnishings were elaborate beyond description! It took seven years to complete its construction. There were ten bronze basins, ten golden lamp stands, a golden altar of incense, a golden table of the presence, but there was one piece of furniture that he did not reconstruct.

> Then King Solomon summoned into his presence at Jerusalem the elders of Israel, all the heads of the tribes and the chiefs of the Israelite families, to bring up the ark of the Lord's covenant from Zion, the city of David… and they brought up the ark of the Lord and the Tent of Meeting and all the sacred furnishings of it. The priests and Levites carried them up and King Solomon and, with him, the entire assembly of Israel that had gathered about him were before the ark, sacrificing so many sheep and cattle that they could not be recorded or counted. The priests then brought the ark of the Lord's covenant to its place in the inner sanctuary of the temple, the Most Holy Place, and put it beneath the wings of the cherubim… there was nothing in the ark except the two stone tablets that Moses had placed in it at Horeb where the Lord made a covenant with the Israelites after they came out of Egypt. When the priests withdrew from the Holy Place, the cloud filled the temple of the Lord. And the priests could not perform their service because of the cloud, for the glory of the Lord filled his temple (I Kings 8:1-11 NIV).

This was truly one of the great moments in worship! Solomon's message to the people was majestic! He talked about his father's desire to build God a house, and how God had graciously permitted Solomon to fulfill that desire. "I have built the temple for the Name of the Lord, the God of Israel, I have provided a place for the ark, in which is the covenant of the Lord" (I Kings 8:20-21 NIV). His message is eclipsed by his prayer to God in which he glorifies God for His faithfulness, and entreats Him to fulfill His promise. Then he dedicates the house,

> But will God really dwell on earth? The heavens, even the highest heaven cannot contain you. How much less this temple I have built… may your eyes be open toward this temple night and day, this place of which you said, "My name shall be there,' so that you will hear the prayer your servant prays toward this place" (I Kings 8:27-29 NIV).

Solomon's prayer is *more* than a prayer of *dedication* for the temple. It is an *affirmation* of **God's purpose** to make the temple, where the ark was housed, and the center of **His dwelling** among the people. Solomon asked God to hear the prayers that were offered in that place. After Solomon dedicated the temple by offering twenty-two thousand cattle and one hundred twenty thousand sheep and goats, God appeared to him, assuring him that his prayer was heard. "I have heard the prayer and plea you have made before me; I have consecrated this temple, which you have built, by putting my name there forever. My eyes and my heart will always be there" (I Kings 9:3 NIV).

It is interesting to discover that in the revival that came under Josiah's administration (nearly 300 years after Solomon), the ark of God was once more given its place of pre-eminence among the people of God. This came about when the Book of the Law was found.

Then the king called together all the elders of Judah and Jerusalem. He went up to the temple of the Lord with the men of Judah, the people of Jerusalem, the priests and the Levites—all the people from the least to the greatest. He read in their hearing all the words of the Book of the Covenant, which had been found in the temple of the Lord. The king stood by his pillar and renewed the covenant in the presence of the Lord; to follow the Lord and keep his commands, regulations and decrees with all his heart and all his soul, and to obey the words of the covenant written in this book. Then he had everyone in Jerusalem and in Benjamin pledge to do it; the people of Jerusalem did this in accordance with the covenant of God, the God of their fathers. Josiah removed all the detestable idols from all the territory belonging to the Israelites, and he had all who were present in Israel serve the Lord their God. As long as he lived, they did not fail to follow the Lord, the God of their fathers. Josiah celebrated the Passover to the Lord in Jerusalem, and the Passover lamb was slaughtered on the fourteenth day of the first month. He appointed the priests to their duties and encouraged them in the service of the Lord's temple. He said to the Levites, who instructed all Israel and who had been consecrated to the Lord: "Put the sacred ark in the temple that Solomon son of David king of Israel built. It is not to be carried about on your shoulders. Now serve the Lord your God and his people Israel. Prepare yourselves by families in your divisions according to the directions written by David king of Israel and by his son Solomon. Stand in the holy place with a group of Levites for each subdivision of the families of your fellow countrymen, the lay people. Slaughter the Passover lambs, consecrate yourselves and prepare the lambs for your fellow countrymen, doing what the Lord commanded through Moses" (II Chronicles 34:29-35:6 NIV).

The passage that follows describes a powerful worship service with sacrifice, offerings, music, praise, feasts and celebration! The acknowledgment of God's presence where His glory is given pre-eminence creates cause for worship and celebration.

To continue the pursuit of God's glory in the past, we move from the scenes of temple worship recorded in the Chronicles, across the prophets, and into the New Testament. The voice of God through His prophets continually called His people to repentance because they had forgotten the priority of His presence and His glory in their midst.

"O, that one of you would shut the temple doors, so that you would not light useless fires on my altar! I am not pleased with you," says the Lord Almighty, "and I will accept no offering from your hands. My name will be great among the nations, from the rising to the setting of the sun. In very place incense and pure offerings will be brought to my name, because my name will be great among the nations,' says the Lord Almighty" (Malachi 1:10—11 NIV).

2. GOD'S PRESENCE IN THE PRESENT

When we move into the New Testament narrative and look at the scenes surrounding the birth of our Lord, we are aware of a brand new manifestation of the glory of God that has come into the world. When His birth was announced to the shepherds by the angels, they sang this song of praise, "Glory to God in the highest and on earth peace to men on whom his favor rests" (Luke 2:14 NIV). John writes in his gospel concerning Christ, "The Word became flesh and lived for a while among us. We have seen his glory, the glory of the one and only Son, who came from the Father, full of grace and truth" (John 1:14 NIV). Paul tells us "For God, who said, 'Let light shine out of darkness,' made his light shine in our hearts to give us the light of the knowledge of the glory of God in the face of Christ" (II Corinthians 4:6 NIV). Hebrews 1:3 states that "The Son is the radiance of God's glory and the exact representation of his being, sustaining all things by his powerful word."

While Jesus Christ was upon this earth, He was the manifestation of the glory of God. He was the incarnation of the presence of God. Although somewhat veiled through His flesh, since the glory of God is too intense for human eyes to behold, yet He was the most powerful manifestation of God's glory that humankind has ever been privileged to witness! But when Jesus left this world and was glorified, He sent His Holy Spirit to indwell His body, the Church. The glory of God is now resident in the Church of Jesus Christ, His Body, and His People. The Church as the building of God becomes His dwelling place (Eph. 2:21-22).

The Bible clearly states that God will not share His glory (Isaiah 48:11). But it also states, "To him be glory in the church and in Christ Jesus throughout all generations, for ever and ever! Amen" (Ephesians 3:21 NIV). When God invests His Church with His glory, He is not sharing His glory. Why? because His church is "His body, the fullness of him who fills everything in every way" (Ephesians 1:23).

Without the Church, His Body, Christ is somehow incomplete. It is the Body, which is His complement, and therefore, when the glory of God is invested in that Body, it is not a sharing of the glory, but a matter of the glory of God flowing from the Head of the Body through the remainder of the Body!

The glory of God's presence today is to be found among His people. God desires to manifest that glory through the development of the character and graces of Jesus Christ, and through the power of His working among His people in transforming love. He still wants the cloud of glory to abide over His tabernacle.

The experience of God's glory is not restricted to some exhilarating experience that we share when we gather with the people of God in a corporate worship setting. Certainly, the awareness of the glory of God, of His surpassing and transcending greatness should be native to that environment. But the glory of God is more acutely witnessed when the kind of harmony and oneness that is shared by the Father and the Son is realized by the people of God. When Jesus talks abut glory, He does so in the context of community.

> "I have brought you glory on earth by completing the work you gave me to do. And now, Father, glorify me in your presence with the glory I had with you before the world began... I have given them the glory that you gave me, that they may be one as we are one... I in them and you in me. May they be brought to complete unity to let the world know that you sent me and have loved them even as you have loved me. Father, I want those you have given me to be with me where I am, and to see my glory, the glory you have given me because you loved me before the creation of the world" (John 17:4-5; 22-24 NIV).

God's glory today is revealed through His Church, and when the Body of Christ is united, forged together with the force of love, the glory of God can be released and revealed to a dying world.

In Isaiah's vision, he saw and heard the angels singing, "The whole earth is full of His glory" (Isaiah 6:3). The prophets looked forward to a time when the knowledge of the glory of the Lord would cover the earth as the waters cover the sea (Habakkuk 2:14). In our worship today we can anticipate the worship of heaven, when we will in glorified bodies and beings celebrate the eternal glory of God for all eternity!

3. GOD'S PRESENCE IN THE FUTURE

When the apostle Paul tasted of what the writer to the Hebrews describes as the "glories of the world to come," (Hebrews 6:4-5, I Corinthians 2:9-10, II Corinthians 12:2-4, Philippians 1:21-23) he found it difficult to finish his term upon planet earth. For him, to depart and be with Christ would be far better. One taste of the things that God has prepared for them that love Him was enough to spoil his appetite for any earthly substitutes.

And this should be the case with any worshipper of God. What God permits us to enjoy while we are yet in our mortal, finite, beings will be so incredibly eclipsed by that which He has reserved for us in the ages to come, that there is no worthy comparison!

In the future, following the return of Christ and our resurrection, or translation, we will be clothed in immortality, and these bodies will be glorified. There will no longer be any limitations as to the intensity of God's presence that we will be able to withstand! Once sin is removed forever, we will have the capacity for experiencing the full revelation of the glory of God.

Have you ever tried to look at the brightness of the sun with shielded eyes? You know that it is impossible to look into the sun without going blind. This is a striking parallel to our relative inability to behold the glory of God in our mortal bodies. But there will come a time when death is swallowed up in victory, when mortal puts on immortality, when we will in glorified beings behold the glory of our God eternally!

Throughout this book we have pointed forward to the grand finale of worship, which incidentally, is not a finale at all, for it will never end! The scene surrounding the throne in Revelation chapters four and five represents the unending occupation of the redeemed. We will forever worship and celebrate the glory of our God!

There will come a time when there will be no physical separation between Christ, the Head, and the rest of His Body. While we are truly joined spiritually today, when we are finally united with Him in glorified bodies, the electrifying power of His presence and glory will radiate through that body in incredible splendor and majesty!

The New Jerusalem that John saw is a picture of the Church of Jesus Christ. John was instructed that he would see the "bride, the wife of the Lamb." And what he was shown was the New Jerusalem. "It shone with the glory of God, and its brilliance was like that of a very precious jewel, like a jasper, clear as crystal" (Revelation 21:11-12 NIV).

The writer to the Hebrews tells us that this heavenly city is "the church of the first-born, whose names are written in heaven" (Hebrews 12:23 NIV). The splendor and glory of God manifest through His people eternally can only be communicated to us in figurative, pictorial language. But one of the most important features is found in this, "I did not see a temple in the city, because the Lord God Almighty and the Lamb are its temple. The City does not need the sun or the moon to shine, on it, for the glory of God gives it light, and the Lamb is its lamp" (Revelation 22:22-23 NIV).

The glory of God's presence is the ultimate destiny for which God has divinely designed His creation. The chief end of man is to glorify God and to enjoy Him forever. This is worship. And for this we were created. Amen.

18

SEEKING SEEKER-
SENSITIVE SEEKERS

*To gather with God's people in united adoration of the
Father is as necessary to the Christian life as prayer.*

—Martin Luther

*Father in heaven! When the thought of thee awakes in our hearts
let it not awaken like a frightened bird that flies about in dismay
but like a child waking from its sleep with a heavenly smile.*

—Sören Kierkegaard

"Yet a time is coming and has now come when the true worshippers will worship the Father in spirit and in truth, for they are
the kind of worshippers the Father seeks. God is spirit, and his
worshippers must worship in spirit and in truth" (John 4:23-24
NIV).

Because you are sons, God has sent the Spirit of his Son into
our hearts crying, "Abba! Father". Therefore you are no longer a
slave, but a son: and if a son, then an heir through God. (Galatians
4:6 NASV)

For all who are being led by the Spirit of God, these are sons
of God. For you have not received a spirit of slavery leading to

fear again, but you have received a spirit of adoption as sons by which we cry out, "Abba! Father!" The Spirit Himself bears witness with our spirit that we are children of God, and if children, heirs also, heirs of God and fellow-heirs with Christ. (Romans 8:14-17 NASV)

See how great a love the Father has bestowed on us, that we should be called the sons of God; and such we are. (I John 3:1)

Had I told my first congregation back in 1968 that we were going to design a "seeker-sensitive" worship service, they would have looked at me with countenances of perplexity. In fact, had I used the term with the last congregation where I pastored twenty years later, I would likely have met with the identical response. Yet, while we didn't call it that, over the years the ministry teams that I led in several churches sought to design a philosophy of ministry that could well be defined as "seeker-sensitive".

The phrase itself simply describes a philosophy of ministry that strives carefully not to offend or "turn off" a "seeker". The term "seeker" usually refers to a non-churched person, a non-believer who may be curious about Christ and Christianity. To be "seeker-sensitive" is to design ministries, programs, and facilities that are sensitive to the needs of the seeker, and understandable to the seeker.

SEEKER-SENSITIVE PHILOSOPHY

The proliferation of the "seeker-sensitive" model has fostered much debate and controversy. Flagship churches of the "seeker-sensitive" motif such as Willow Creek[106] and Saddleback[107] have become the brunt of much criticism and attack. I have no interest in rehashing those arguments or becoming embroiled in this dispute. A quick search on the web for "seeker-sensitive" will produce reams of pages aimed at condemning any pastor or church that identifies with the "seeker-sensitive" ideology.

In an article entitled, *Seeker-Sensitive Silliness*, Frank Patrick, a Canadian Pentecostal pastor writes:

> We are called to seeker sensitivity as a kingdom function. To be seeker sensitive does not mean we dilute the Gospel. Paul did not compromise the Gospel message in any way, yet he did accommodate his message to his audience… When writing to Jewish believers, he used a different approach than he normally did when he spoke to Gentiles. When he addressed the Stoic and Epicurean philosophers on Mars Hill he changed his approach yet again. In essence, Paul always tried to start his discussion at some common point of interest or question. Jesus did the same. He was always telling relevant stories, raising questions, and using current illustrations in His effort to communicate with those who listened. According to the plain teaching of Paul in I Corinthians 14, through the power of the Holy Spirit we have the ability to simultaneously evangelize, edify, and bring glory to God in a Christ-centered way. While remaining sensitive to the needs of those who are already found, let us also develop a sensitivity to those who are lost, for lost people matter to God. And let us get over the silliness of refusing to meet people where they are and get on with the work of the kingdom.[108]

---

106 www.willowcreek.org
107 www.saddleback.com
108 https://www.christianity.ca/page.aspx?pid=11648

SEEKER-SENSITIVE SENSITIVITIES

Many of the articles that I read thundered with denunciation in their diatribe against the "seeker-sensitive" approach. In many cases they were written by church leaders who hold that the seeker-sensitive worship service is a shallow worship experience. This seems based on the premise that deep, life-changing, God-honoring worship must somehow be insensitive to the seeker. Also, they often equate worship and music as being synonymous, when in fact, they are not. As Rick Muchow from Saddleback Community Church points out, music is a method, and worship is a purpose. He adds, "The role of music in the seeker service is to magnify God in a way that the seeker will not feel threatened and can understand what is being said."[109]

While driving in my car, I frequently tune into Christian broadcasters, influding "The Bible Answer Man,"[110] Over the years, I often found it instructive to tune in to the opinions of Walter Martin, and in recent years, those of his successor, Hank Hanegraaff. The Christian Research Institute is the self-proclaimed bastion of historical conservative Christianity, and describes itself as a "parachurch organization committed to defending historic Christianity against theological heresy". Suspicious of any "aberrant teachings in the church", Hanegraaff's CRI Internet site, www.equip.org, includes not only daily and archived *Bible Answer Man* radio programs but also articles and debates on cults and aberrant Christian practices. Never one to be on the fringes of any issues in the Christian community, Hank Hanegraaff conducted extensive research on the Saddleback Community Church culminating in his historic interview with Rick Warren.

---

109   www.saddleback.com

110   www.equip.org

SEEKER-SENSITIVE SOUNDNESS

Hanegraaff said he "literally was stunned by a message that is altogether biblically correct"[111] after listening to Warren's audiotapes *The Purpose Driven Church: Growth Without Compromising Your Message and Your Mission.*[112] Hanegraaff said he found Warren's principles to be not only "biblical but also revolutionary... dynamic... sound... and exhilarating." He said the principles will "not only revolutionize your church if applied... they'll revolutionize your life as an individual." Hanegraaff introduced Warren as "a guy with a vision and most of all a guy with a passion... a passion not to empty out other churches to fill his mega-church but to reach the lost to take the message of the gospel that transforms hearts... and make that message adaptable to the culture without ever compromising the message itself."[113]

Hanegraaff said he has come to see that the seeker-sensitive strategy is "not about [church] size not about classes and masses. It's about changed lives." He said Warren's purpose-driven church principles are "so important in an age when we desperately need healthy well-balanced churches and called Warren's materials a roadmap to help churches be what they ought to be."[114]

Rick Warren states, "The idea that a seeker-sensitive approach is light on doctrine is one of the greatest misunderstandings about the church. God expects us to be sensitive to the fears and the hang-ups and the needs of unbelievers when they're present in our worship services." Warren noted I Corinthians 14:23 and Colossians 4:5 in which the apostle Paul says Christians ought to be tactful with those who are not Christians. "A worship service doesn't have to be shallow

---

111   http://www.sbclife.net/article/556/orthodox-evangelistic-and-seeker-sensitive
112   Warren, Rick. *The Purpose Driven Church: Growth Without Compromising Your Message and Your Mission.* Grand Rapids, MI: Zondervan, 1995.
113   http://www.sbclife.net/article/556/orthodox-evangelistic-and-seeker-sensitive
114   Ibid.

to be seeker-sensitive," Warren said. "The message doesn't have to be compromised. It just has to be understandable."[115]

WHEN THE FATHER IS THE SEEKER

While I readily accept the proposition that it is Biblical to design ministries and worship experiences that are "seeker-sensitive" as described in the preceding discussion, as I reflected on this, it occurred to me that there is another "seeker" to whom we want to be sensitive as well. Jesus said, "…true worshippers will worship the Father in spirit and in truth, for they are the kind of worshippers the Father seeks." (John 4:23-24 NIV). From this passage we can conclude several truths:

1. The ministry and work of Christ would bring about a transition in worship

2. That transition would be from the physical and material to the spiritual dimension

3. True worshippers are those who worship from the heart in honest response to God

4. Worship is for God, and the Father is seeking for true worshippers

5. True worship is directed to the Father, and is about a relationship with God as Father

TRANSITION: KNOWING THE FATHER

If we miss this truth, we miss the weight and intent of what Christ was saying. While Old Testament worship was directed to God,

115   Warren, Rick. *The Purpose Driven Church: Growth Without Compromising Your Message and Your Mission.* Grand Rapids, MI: Zondervan, 1995.

and to the one true God, we are not brought into the full awareness of what it means to know God as Father. This is primarily a New Testament truth.

While passages in the Old Testament hint at the concept of God as Father, it is not until we cross the threshold into the New Testament that this idea fully materializes and matures. Quite apart from God's revelation in redemptive history, there is a natural knowledge of God based on creation that leads us to recognize him as the origin and transcendent cause of the world and of man, and in this sense to perceive his fatherhood. God can be known as father at various levels, depending on the perspective from which we look at him and the aspect of the mystery considered.

This knowledge is deepened in the progressive light of Revelation, that is, on the basis of God's words and his interventions in salvation history. In the Old Testament, knowing God as father means returning to the origins of the people of the covenant: "Is he not your father, who created you, who made you and established you?" (Deuteronomy 32:6). The reference to God as father guarantees and maintains the unity of those who belong to the same family: "Have we not all the one Father? Has not the one God created us?" (Malachi 2:10). God is recognized as father even when he rebukes the son for his own good: "For the Lord reproves him whom he loves, as a father the son in whom he delights" (Proverbs 3:12).

In all these forms, the values experienced in human fatherhood are applied pre-eminently to God. We immediately realize that it is impossible to know the full meaning of this fatherhood except to the extent that God himself reveals it. We also must acknowledge that the Hebrew Scriptures sometimes speak of God acting toward us like a gentle mother (Isaiah. 49:14-15) as well as responding to us as a tender father (Psalm 103:13; Hosea. 11:1-4).

While the passages cited above introduce to us the "universal fatherhood of God" they do not reveal to us the "unique" fatherhood of God. In the unfolding saga of salvation history there is a gradual revelation of God the Father in greater fullness. Inasmuch as the person of Christ as the Eternal Son of God is not revealed in the Old Testament, neither is the full revelation of God as Eternal Father made manifest until we arrive at the New Testament. When Mary is informed that she has been chosen to mother the Son of the Highest, a new era has dawned, and God is about to reveal Himself to us in a new dimension.

In Chapter Four we explored the significance of the Latin phrase "lex orandi, lex credendi"[116] in the context of the relationship between worship and theology. While our earlier examination of this principle, which states, "What we pray will become what we believe," addressed our natural inclination to adjust our doctrine to our experience, there is another application that is equally true. What we pray or "how we worship" will also issue from our belief system—or more specifically, what we believe about God. Therefore, in this chapter we will explore:

I. Theological and doctrinal limitations that impede our worship of the Father

II. Psychological projections that distort and hinder our worship of the Father

III. Inclusive language and feminist views that prevent proper worship of the Father

Therefore, our view of God as Father will not only dramatically impact our relationship with God on a daily basis; it will also shape

---

116　http://www.catholic.org/featured/headline.php?ID=2367

our worship expression and experience. While experience and anecdotal evidence are never adequate to establish a theory, they can serve to illustrate, support and confirm a concept that has already been established.

I. THEOLOGICAL LIMITATIONS THAT IMPEDE OUR WORSHIP OF THE FATHER

A. A Non-Trinitarian View of God

In this context, I am compelled to examine my own theological roots and their contribution to my appreciation for the knowledge of the Father. I was raised in the Oneness Pentecostal tradition, often disparagingly referred to as "Jesus only" by the mainstream Pentecostal body, and other evangelical groups aware of their existence. Oneness teaching categorically rejects the doctrine of the Trinity, or at least their perception of the doctrine of the Trinity. One key Scripture appealed to by proponents of Oneness doctrine states, "For in Him dwelleth all the fullness of the godhead bodily" (Colossians 2:9). While the word "godhead" eventually came to be used as a description of the existence of God in three persons, in its strict New Testament use, it referred simply to the Deity (Acts 17:29, Romans 1:20). Harper's Bible Dictionary defines it thus, "the divine quality that distinguishes God from other entities."[117] Similarly, Easton's Bible Dictionary states that the word means "the essential being or the nature of God."[118] In fact, the word *godhead* is an old (Middle English) English term that is simply synonymous with the word *God*.[119] The

---

117 Achtemeier, Paul J. *Harper's Bible Dictionary, 1st ed.* San Francisco: Harper & Row, 1985.

118 Easton, M.G. *Easton's Bible Dictionary.* Oak Harbor, WA: Logos Research Systems, Inc., 1996.

119 Youngblood, Ronald F., Bruce, F. F., Harrison, R. K. *Nelson's New Illustrated Bible Dictionary.* Nashville: TN: Thomas Nelson Publishers, 1995.

Oneness interpretation therefore took the term "godhead" which in the New Testament described the essence and uniqueness of God and applied a more modern interpretation to it to insist that Christ is Father, Son and Holy Spirit. In short, Oneness doctrine teaches the following major concepts:

- God is Spirit, and is one in absolute eternal essence as both Father and Holy Spirit. Any distinction of Father and Holy Spirit is a distinction in manifestation and not in person.

- Jesus is **not** the **eternal** son of God. The two terms "son" and "eternal" are self-contradictory. Jesus as the Son of God had His beginning at Bethlehem. Therefore, the term "Son of God" or "Son of Man" both refer strictly and solely to the **humanity** of Christ.

- The "deity" of Christ is purely the indwelling nature of the Father in the Son. Jesus Christ is God in the flesh, because the Father indwells the Son. (passages that allude to seeing the Father when you see Christ, etc., are interpreted in an exclusive sense)

- Since God is Spirit, He did not cease to exist outside of Christ, because, after all, He fills all things. *However,* God incarnate in Christ is God in a more concentrated embodiment: the fullness of God indwelling His son.

- Hence, there a "duality" referred to as the "dual nature" of Christ. God the Father is the "deity" and the "Son of God" is the humanity: in one person.

- When Jesus prays it is "humanity" praying to "divinity" because God doesn't need to pray.

- When Christ died on the cross, the Father (divine nature) vacated the Son (human nature).

- When Christ rose from the grave, the divine nature (God/Father/Spirit) re-entered the human body of Christ (Son) and in His resurrected form He is now glorified in heaven, and is God.

- The "right hand of the Father" is only a figurative term referring to a position of power, because He can't be at His own right hand.

It is neither my objective nor my intent to dispute or disprove Oneness doctrine in this work. At this juncture I allude to its teaching as part of my upbringing for a totally different reason. The primary emphasis of the Oneness in its early genesis was to exalt the person of Jesus Christ. While I will join the ranks of all Trinitarians who will insist that it operates from a flawed and faulty framework, I can testify that the spirit and purpose of its first focus was the uplifting of our dear Lord Jesus.

And, in most circles today, those who adhere to Oneness teaching do so in their well-intentioned efforts to preserve the exaltation and centrality of Christ. In their zeal to do this, they fail to see that not only is it possible to exalt Christ adequately and properly within the Trinitarian understanding of God, but they also fail to see that it is impossible to rightly honor and worship Him apart from that understanding.

As I reflect on my own upbringing in the Oneness tradition, I consider not only my childhood and adolescence when I was reared in this teaching, but also the first years of my preaching ministry when I championed the Oneness message. I was barely twenty years of age when I went to Newfoundland to establish the first Oneness

Pentecostal churches in a Canadian province where the Trinitarian Pentecostal movement was well established. In fact, nearly forty percent of the population of Newfoundland were numbered among the Pentecostal movement. Since this was the "classical" Pentecostal denomination, it was solidly Trinitarian.

Laboring in this vineyard, I was compelled to master the "Oneness" doctrine, and did so masterfully. I could debate the most devout Trinitarian, and never have to back down from an argument. I didn't realize that I was using a form of "circular logic" and that I was shaping the Scriptures to accommodate my doctrine, rather than letting the Scriptures speak for themselves. When I left Newfoundland, having established a couple of small Oneness congregations, I was still holding to the doctrine, albeit, not as tenaciously.

In reflecting on my preaching in those days, and the worship in our churches, there is no question that Jesus Christ was exalted, proclaimed and lifted up. However, in our "Oneness" efforts to glorify Christ, we moved dangerously close to a very subtle form of idolatry. We elevated the doctrine and made it sacred. The teaching that we held to be the "truth" became the ultimate benchmark by which we stood in judgment on the rest of Christendom.

But perhaps most significantly, we missed the purpose of why Jesus came. Yes, He came to destroy the works of the enemy. We know that for that purpose the Son of Man was manifested. Yes, He came to seek and to save that which is lost. Yes, He came that we might have life and have it more abundantly. He came not to condemn the world, but that world through Him might be saved. Yes, He came to reveal the Father, to reveal the heart of God. But in reconciling us to God through His death on the cross, He came to bring us into right relationship with the Father.

Oneness doctrine dare not allow us to enter into the relationship with God as Father that God intended. And therein is found the fundamental flaw of its impact on our relationship with God. Granted, the doctrine is fraught with flaws, but this one is one that impairs and impedes our primary relationship with God. It should come as no surprise, therefore, that most Oneness systems of teaching are accompanied by a legalistic approach to salvation with burdensome works beyond simple faith in Christ.

Jesus is obsessed with the Father. He talks about the Father incessantly. He promises us relationship with the Father. He wants us to enjoy the Father and the Father's love in the same manner in which He enjoys fellowship with the Father. "I'm not saying I will ask the Father on your behalf, for the Father himself loves you dearly because you love me and believe that I came from God" (John 16:26-27 NLT).

B. An Inadequate Understanding of God as Father

Dan Hammer served with me in the church that I pastored when I first preached a series on worship. When I spoke with him recently, he still had the notes from my sermons twenty years ago. Dan has always been a man who walks with God. He is a man of prayer. He is a godly man. And God has greatly blessed his life and ministry. After reading my manuscript, Dan said that the one thing that I might consider adding had to do with knowing and worshipping God as Father.

Dan told me that in prayer one day, God spoke to his heart, saying, "Do you know why I hate sin?" When Dan offered all the conventional answers about how it offends God's holiness, etc., he said that he felt God speak to his heart and say, "I hate sin because of how it keeps my children from having fellowship with me as their heavenly Father."

While it was my intention in this work to primarily examine the worship encounters recorded in Genesis and Exodus, I must leap forward to the gospels and consider the teachings of Christ to provide a foundation for understanding and worshipping God as Father. And the passage to which I allude, although a familiar one, may seem an unlikely passage from which to attempt to illustrate the Fatherhood of God and what that means for us in worship.

Even those with the most limited exposure to Bible Stories from the New Testament have heard the story of "the prodigal son" as told by Jesus in Luke 15. Those of us that have been to church with any degree of frequency have heard it preached time and again. We will be familiar with the fact that it is the third in a trilogy of stories that Christ tells in his series of "Lost and Found" short stories.

We will also recognize that what prompted our Lord to share these stories was the grumbling of the religious leaders that complained that "This man receives sinners and eats with them." While they stated this in contempt and condemnation, in fact, it represented one of the highest compliments that could have been paid to our Lord.

The first "Lost and Found" narrative is the story of the lost sheep; it is a one percent loss. Yet the shepherd leaves the ninety-and-nine to seek that lost sheep, and when he finds it, rejoices, and calls his friends to share in his celebration, saying, "Rejoice with me, for I have found my sheep which was lost." Christ nails the point, "I tell you that in the same way, there will be more joy in heaven over one sinner who repents, than over nine-nine righteous persons who need no repentance" (Luke 15:6-7 NASV).

The second "Lost and Found" story is that of the woman with ten coins who loses one; it is a ten percent loss. The imagery hints at the gospel with greater implication as she "lights a lamp, sweeps the house and searches carefully until she finds it". And, like the shepherd in the story before her, "When she has found it, she calls together her friends and neighbors, saying 'Rejoice with me, for I have found the coin which I had lost.'" And again, Jesus comments, "In the same way, I tell you, there is joy in the presence of the angels of God over one sinner who repents."

While each of these stories is grand and glorious in its own right, you can't help but sense that Jesus is setting us up for a greater revelation. These are but a prelude, preliminary to the main message. These are appetizers to whet our appetite. He now has these religious leaders thinking: they can't contradict the logic of what He has just proclaimed. However, they don't really know what's coming next. In fact, the real teaching behind the story that Christ is about to share may be lost on most Christians, even though we've gleaned significant truth from its message.

With His parables of the lost sheep and the lost coin, Jesus has them sitting on the edges of their seats, mouths open, bated breath, waiting for what's coming next. Christ continues with his third story in the "Lost and Found" trilogy:

> A certain man had two sons; and the younger of them said to his father, "Father, give me the share of the estate that falls to me." And he divided his wealth between them. And not many days later, the younger son gathered everything together and went on a journey into a distant country, and there he squandered his estate with loose living. Now when he had spent everything, a severe famine occurred in that country, and he began to be in need. And he went and attached himself to one of the citizens of that country,

and he sent him into his fields to feed swine. And he was longing to fill his stomach with the pods that the swine were eating, and no one was giving anything to him. But when he came to his senses, he said, "How many of my father's hired men have more than enough bread, but I am dying here with hunger? I will get up and go to my father, and will say to him, 'Father, I have sinned against heaven, and in your sight; I am no longer worthy to be called your son: make me as one of your hired men.'" And he got up and came to his father. But while he was still a long way off, his father saw him, and felt compassion for him, and ran and embraced him, and kissed him. And the son said to him, "Father, I have sinned against heaven and in your sight; I am no longer worthy to be called your son." But the father said to his slaves, "Quickly bring out the best robe and put it on him, and put a ring on his hand and sandals on his feet: and bring the fattened calf, kill it, and let us eat and be merry; for this son of mine was dead, and has come to life again; he was lost, and has been found." And they began to be merry. Now his older son was in the field, and when he came and approached the house, he heard music and dancing. And he summoned one of the servants and began inquiring what these things might be. And he said to him, "Your brother has come, and your father has killed the fattened calf, because he has received him back safe and sound." And he became angry, and was not willing to go in; and his father came out and began entreating him. But he answered and said to his father, "Look! For so many years I have been serving you, and I have never neglected a command of yours; and yet you have never given me a kid, that I might be merry with my friends; but when this son of yours came, who has devoured your wealth with harlots, you killed the fattened calf for him." And he said to him, "My child, you have always been with me, and all that is mine is yours. But we had to be merry and rejoice, for this brother of yours was dead and has begun to live, and was lost and has been found" (Luke 15:11-32 NASV).

What most casual students of the Scripture fail to appreciate is that this story, apart from the ending that Jesus gave it, was *not* a new story in the Jewish tradition. The Pharisees had heard the main body of the story before. While this story wasn't exactly folklore, it was common fodder for rabbinical teachers of the day. However, they told the story with a different ending than did Christ. The rabbinical ending did not lead to a full restoration to sonship in the manner in which our Lord declared it.

Because of the richness and reach of this parable, it is easy to get caught up in the nuance of its nuggets and miss the gold that lies beneath the surface. We will first examine some of the general gems in the story, and then delve more deeply into the vein of its truth. Jesus has upped the ante. This is not a one percent, nor is it a ten percent loss. This is a fifty percent loss. And it's not just a coin or a sheep: it's a son.

If we can assume that Christ is speaking primarily to a male audience (the Pharisees) we can also assume that many of them were fathers. They could relate. Behind their parade of righteousness they had to parent their own children. And in all probability they had understood the rebellious and relentless demands of sons that refused to follow in their father's footsteps. But these Pharisees were not quite ready for what follows in the narrative of Jesus.

Christ wastes no time getting into the meat of the story. The younger son makes his demands, which apparently meet with no resistance from the father. He takes his inheritance, hits the road and squanders it on riotous living. You can't help but chuckle at the humor of Jesus when he has this Jewish lad feeding the pigs and wanting to eat what the pigs are eating.

When Jesus has the young man coming to his senses and realizing that he has blown it, the Pharisees are right there with him. Jesus plays the story into their hands. They would agree that the son has forfeited his relationship and the best he can hope for is a servile position when he comes back on bended knee.

But then Christ zaps them with a different twist. He offers a different ending than they had heard before. And it's not an ending that sits well with them. It doesn't fit their picture of God. Jesus has the father spotting the son from a distance, running out to meet him, embracing him, and throwing a party to welcome him home.

Much has been said and written of the "elder brother syndrome." It is often held up as the example of the religious self-righteousness of those that fail to understand the purpose of the evangel. And a fitting picture it is of those who pride themselves in their obedience to God's commands, and who resent the attention given to the sinner who comes to Christ. But here again there is a deeper truth that we need to see.

This parable is really about **two erroneous views of God the Father**, representing two different philosophies that people tend to have about God.

1. The first erroneous view, held by the prodigal son, goes something like this: God is a stern strict Father who doesn't want you to be fulfilled. And, once you fail Him, you've blown it; you can't be restored to sonship. He'll be angry with you, but if you come on bended knee, and humbly beg Him, He might admit you back as a servant.

2.   The second erroneous view, held by the elder brother, is that God is a stern strict Father, and if you are faithful to keep the commandments, while you may never enjoy your relationship with the Father, eventually, you will gain the inheritance. And, God shouldn't receive back those that have disobeyed him. They have no right to his favor and blessing.

Christ wants to teach the Pharisees, and wants to settle for all time, that neither of these views are accurate or adequate pictures of God the Father. He shows us the Father heart of God, towards both those who serve Him faithfully, and those who return to Him.

From this story we can glean the following truths Christ wants us to know about the Father:

- The Father will never impose His will on us against our own; even though it may break His heart when we rebel and insist on our rights, He will allow us the latitude and freedom to "do our thing" and "go our way".

- The Father is ever vigilant in His "lookout" for us; He is ever watchful, and sees us "afar off" long before we are even in proximity.

- The Father doesn't wait for us to make it all the way home: He has compassion on us, runs out to greet us, embraces and kisses us. (You have to picture this pious Jewish father, who would typically walk slowly in his long flowing robes, now running out to greet his son to catch the imagery).

- The Father doesn't receive us with condemnation, but with compassion when we come to our senses and come back to Him.

- He embraces us while we are yet in the stench and stink of our "pig poop" and kisses us before he cleanses us.

- He doesn't merely clothe us, He puts the "best robe" on us; He robes us in His own righteousness, and puts the shoes of salvation on our feet.

- He doesn't put us on probation, but immediately puts the ring of authority on our finger (this was the signet ring, the family seal—the equivalent of the checkbook).

- The Father throws a party: "Kill Spotty" was the command given the servants. They were instructed to prepare a feast.

- God the Father celebrates the return of His children, because above all, He delights in having fellowship and seeing relationship restored.

- His rebuke of the "elder son" is soft, not stern; the Father reassures the elder son of his relationship and his heritage.

The real and deeper meaning of the parable is all about understanding God as our Father. Yes, it speaks to us of His redemptive grace in salvation. Yes, it is rich in implication and application at many levels. But primarily, it shouts to us "This is what God is like. This is how the Father wants you to relate to Him."

In going back to my Oneness roots, this is a level of intimacy with the Father that the Oneness doctrine could not allow. While the doctrine gave lip service to the idea that to know Christ is to know the Father, it denied its followers the very thing that it sought to proclaim: the opportunity to know the **Father**. The fear of admitting the "personhood" of the Father and the "personhood" of the Son thus reduced the knowledge of God to something less than God intended.

In reducing our vision and view of God, the relationship with God was dwarfed and diminished as well.

It is by knowing Jesus, we are able to know the Father, as Jesus himself teaches in reply to Thomas: "If you had known me, you would have known my Father" (John 14:7-10). This makes it possible to know the Father and to become capable of worshiping him "in spirit and truth" (John 4:23). This living knowledge is inseparable from love. It is communicated by Jesus, as he said in his priestly prayer: "O righteous Father... I made known to them your name, and I will make it known, that the love with which you have loved me may be in them" (John 17:25-26). To know the Father means to find in him the source of our being and our unity as members of one family and thus to be immersed in a "supernatural" life, the very life of God.

C. An Inadequate Grasp of Grace and Emphasis on Conditional Salvation

Here again I hearken back to my upbringing. The branch of Pentecostalism in which I was raised, like most of the Pentecostal movement, traces its roots to the Holiness traditions. In those traditions, the Arminian view of conditional salvation held sway over the eternal security position of Calvinism.

My upbringing in such a legalistic setting caused me to embrace a view of a distant and angry God as He was portrayed in many of the Renaissance paintings—resulting in a wrong "mental picture" of God as Father. This image was reinforced by the multitude of things necessary to secure and maintain salvation. Furthermore, the threat of losing one's salvation was predicated on failure to fulfill those requirements. This resulted in living in fear, and seeing God as an angry Father, reluctant to let you into heaven, and ready to abandon you to hell for the slightest violation of His code of holiness.

During my teenage years, I began preaching on a regular basis in my small-town church and in neighboring communities. I purchased a Bible Dictionary, Bible Commentary and a Thompson Chain[120] Reference Study Bible. As I searched the Scriptures for sermon material, I began to read things that I hadn't heard preached. When I stumbled on the teaching of "justification by faith" my heart was enraptured with its truth. I thought I was Martin Luther! I read in Paul's writings, "For it is by grace you have been saved, through faith—and this is not from yourselves, it is the gift of God—not by works, so that no one can boast" (Ephesians 2:8-9 NIV). Even the faith by which I am saved is God-given! It is all of grace! When this awesome truth dawns upon your soul, all you can do is bow your heart in worship and raise your voice in praise.

Theologians for centuries have debated the issue of unconditional eternal security vs. conditional salvation. It is not my intent to engage in that debate in any depth. Those who seek a compromise suggest that the river of God's grace runs between those two banks of teaching. Others suggest that the Bible teaches *both* of these doctrines. While there are passages that pose difficulty for either side, my understanding of the Scriptures is that God is a God of *grace*. His holiness and justice have been totally satisfied by the sacrifice of His Son on Calvary. Salvation is the gift of God. "In whom we have redemption through His blood, even the forgiveness of sins." (Ephesians 1:7) The NLT renders it, "He is so rich in kindness that he purchased our freedom through the blood of his Son, and our sins are forgiven."

---

120   Thompson, Frank C. *The Thompson Chain-Reference Bible.* Dobbs Ferry, NY: 1908.

Paul got carried away with this theme over and again. In Romans 5:20-21, he writes, "Where sin abounded, grace has more abounded; and so, just as sin reigned wherever there was death, so grace will reign to bring eternal life thanks to the righteousness that comes through Jesus Christ our Lord." Paul's fascination, preoccupation and obsession with God's grace is abundantly evident:

- It is totally and entirely by the grace of God that we are made righteous (Romans 3:24; Titus 3:7)

- There is a plenitude of grace to which we now have access through Christ (Romans 5:2)

- Our standing before God is based solely on the grace of God (Romans 5:2)

- Grace supersedes and replaces works as a means of salvation (Romans 11:5; Ephesians 2:5; II Timothy 1:9)

- Grace eclipses and surpasses the law as the basis of salvation, and to hold to the law is to nullify the grace of God (Galatians 2:21, 5:4)

- To be in Christ is to no longer be under law but to under the domain of grace (Romans 6:14)

- Grace does not and cannot impose a debt (Romans 4:4)

As an aged servant of God exiled on Patmos, John writes richly of the love of the Father and of our relationship with Him. What a contrast this passage presents to the legalistic rigor in which I lived for many years, "Such love has no fear because perfect love expels all fear. If we are afraid, it is for fear of judgment, and this shows that his love has not been perfected in us." (I John 4:18) When we view the Father as a disciplinarian, judge and punisher, our worship is hampered by this warped view of God. Paul extols this glorious gospel of grace when he says,

> What this means is that those who become Christians become new persons. They are not the same anymore, for the old life is gone. A new life has begun. All this newness of life is from God, who brought us back to himself through what Christ did… God was in Christ reconciling the world to himself, no longer counting people's sins against them… for God made Christ, who never sinned, to be the offering for our sin, so that we could be made right with God through Christ (II Corinthians 5:17-21 NLT).

Awareness of the awesome provision of God's grace informs our approach to the Father in worship.

> That is why we have a great High Priest who has gone to heaven, Jesus the Son of God. Let us cling to him and never stop trusting him. This High Priest of ours understands our weaknesses, for he faced all of the same temptations we do, ye he did not sin. So let us come boldly to the throne of our gracious God. There we will receive his mercy, and we will find grace to help us when we need it (Hebrews 4:14-16 NLT).

And yet, we are reluctant to trust our Father God, and haltingly hesitate to enter the embrace of His outstretched arms, fearful that He may yet condemn us. Anticipating the reticent reluctance of the Roman Christians to experience the warmth of the divine embrace, Paul entreats them with great remonstrance:

> What can we say about such wonderful things as these? If God is for us, who can ever be against us? Since God did not spare even his own Son but gave him up for us all, won't God, who gave us Christ, also give us everything else? Who dares accuse us whom God has chosen for his own? Will God? No! He is the one who

has given us right standing with himself. Who then will condemn us? Will Christ Jesus? No, for he is the one who died for us and was raised to life for us and is sitting at the place of highest honor next to God, pleading for us. Can anything ever separate us from Christ's love? Does it mean he no longer loves us if we have trouble or calamity, or are persecuted, or are hungry or cold or in danger or threatened with death? No, despite all these things, overwhelming victory is ours through Christ, who loved us. And I am convinced that nothing can separate us from his love. Death can't and life can't. The angels can't, and the demons can't. Our fears for today, our worries about tomorrow, and even the powers of hell can't keep God's love away. Whether we are high above the sky or in the deepest ocean, nothing in all creation will ever be able to separate us from the love of God that is revealed in Christ Jesus our Lord (Romans 8:31-39 NLT).

When the truth of these and scores of other passages first shone the light of liberty upon a soul long imprisoned by legalism, I simply reveled in the glorious grace of God, and was freed to worship the Father in a way that I had never known. I had not *yet* become a "Calvinist" although I was brashly branded as such by some of my contemporaries. In fact, I didn't know what it meant to be a "Calvinist". When I was first taunted about the "tulip" doctrine, I didn't even know what it meant. When I researched its meaning, I found that it stood for:

- Total Depravity of Man
- Unconditional Election
- Limited Atonement
- Irresistible Grace

- Perseverance of the Saints

In embracing the essence of the gospel as championed by Spurgeon, that our salvation is "All of Grace,' I began to be taunted and teased about holding to the "TULIP" doctrine by some of my pastor friends who subscribed and adhered to the conditional salvation viewpoint of Arminianism. When this occured, I readily responded, "Better the 'tulip' doctrine than the 'daisy' doctrine." When asked what I meant by the "daisy" doctrine, I replied: "He loves me, he loves me not; he loves me, he loves me not." While this rejoinder was offered more in jovial jest than in seriousness, it does capture the opposite extreme of those who fail to embrace the grace of God.

In the glorious passage where Christ describes the relationship of the Good Shepherd with His sheep, He says,

> My sheep recognize my voice; I know them, and they follow me. I give them eternal life, and they will never perish. No one will snatch them away from me, for my Father has given them to me, and he is more powerful than anyone else. So no one can take them from me. The Father and I are one (John 10:27-30 NLT).

In posing the question, "What do we mean when we say that a *saved* person has become *forever lost?*" my friend and mentor John Kennington[121] prefaces his comments by stating, "It is important to understand that the focus here is on someone who has truly been born of God and not merely professed salvation, and that at times under emotional duress." Kennington goes on to postulate what we are saying when we take the position of conditional salvation:

- Someone with Eternal Life has died, not physically but spiritually (John 5:24).

---

121 Kennington, John D. http://www.theoed.org/

- Jesus' Promise, "shall never perish" (John 3:16) is broken. (It seems there was some fine print under that promise.)

- The Good Shepherd has lost a sheep (John 10:28). The explanation—that the sheep didn't want to be a sheep any more—doesn't make sense. It is the nature of sheep to go astray"(Isaiah. 53:6). If a shepherd doesn't keep those who want to wander, who then will be saved? Just what is it that shepherds do?

- The Gift that the Father gave to His Son has to be retrieved. At least six times in John 17 believers are said to be a gift from the Father to the Son.

- What He promised to keep has been lost so a promise is broken (John 17:11).

- A Member of His Body has either been amputated or fallen off (I Corinthians 12:13).

- Jesus' triumph has ended in defeat (Colossians 2:15).

- Angels were too hasty in rejoicing over this one's repentance, for the one they rejoiced over is now lost (Luke 15:10).

- The gift of righteousness has had to be forfeited because it wasn't deserved (Romans 5:17).

- The intercessory prayers of the High Priest have failed (Hebrews 7:25).

- The one who was to be kept from falling and presented to the Father has fallen out of Christ and is on his way to hell (Jude 24).

- The one sealed until his redemption has broken the seal (Ephesians 1:14).

- One whom God foreknew and predestined has ended up with another destiny and God knew something that wasn't true (Ephesians 1:11).

- One who was seated in heavenly places ended up in Hell (Ephesians 2:6).

- One who was born again had his new birth undone by a late term abortion (John 3:5). You can't blame God since He won't have crippled kids.

- What God knew was in fact not true: it wasn't a "seal" after all (II Timothy 2:19).

- The finished work of Christ was not finished because the person for whom it was done ended up in Hell (John 19:30): Maybe Christ sat down too soon (Hebrews 1:13).

- Jesus will not see one born by the travail of his soul on the cross because that one will end up lost (Isaiah 53:10,11).

- Love will end up failing for the one He loved will end up lost and separated forever from His love. (Romans 8:38, 39).

- A New Creation in Christ has reverted into an old creation in Adam (II Corinthians 5:17).

- The foundation upon which one is built and upon which one depends for salvation will itself burn and not just that which is built upon it (I Corinthians 3:10, 12).

- The unchangeable God Himself has changed, for the Jacob He loved has become the object of His wrath (Revelation 6:16).

- The New Covenant has become like the Old Covenant (Galatians 3:10) and its blessing is conditioned on the believer's continuing behavior (Galatians. 3:10; Hebrews 10:18).

- The anchor of hope which was firm and secure has now slipped or the cable to that anchor broken since the one once anchored is lost forever (Hebrews 6:19).

- The Reward which, according to Jesus' promise, would not be lost, is lost forever since the person was once saved is now lost and won't be there to receive the reward (Mark 9:41).

- The "eternals" and the "everlastings" of the New Testament are all turned into "temporals" by the little word if.

- The one who was married to the Lord has now been divorced.

- All the passages that speak of things being done once and for all need to be done again and again.[122]

As one who was raised and reared in the climate and culture of conditional salvation, I have first-hand knowledge of the terror of being hung over hell on a shoestring, frantically fretting that I might have done something to jeopardize my standing with God. In a recent conversation with a pastor and his wife, I heard the age-old fear resurface in the comment, "Yeah, but if people think they have 'eternal security', what will cause them to want to obey God? They'll just live like the devil and not obey the Lord."

In reality, this is so far from the true experience of the child of God who has discovered the joy of knowing and serving a kind and

122 ibid

loving Heavenly Father. It is only in the embrace of grace that I am motivated and mobilized to live a life that is pleasing to Him.

The revelation of God as a loving Father is a difficult concept for many people to embrace personally and pragmatically, although we may subscribe to it philosophically, theologically, and positionally.

Another impediment to intimately knowing God as Father is psychological:

II. PSYCHOLOGICAL PROJECTIONS THAT DISTORT OUR WORSHIP OF THE FATHER

Your concept of God is determined to a significant degree by your relationship with your earthly father. And, God the Father has been misrepresented to us by legalistic religious leaders and angry earthly fathers, who, by their lifestyles have distorted His true image.

While this concept may serve helpful in behavioral analysis, it should not apply for a Christian who is growing in the Lord. It may seem normal for our fathers to determine our view of God since both are authority figures. The meaning that we bring to the word "father" is drawn from our own experience. This can severely limit and distort our view of and relationship with God as our heavenly Father. If our view of God is formed or even informed by an earthly relationship, our wrong view of God will result in a warped relationship with the father.

If we are not grounded in a proper understanding of the fatherhood of God our faith and our worship will be adversely affected. If our understanding of God and His dealings are dictated or even influenced by past paternal relationships, disastrous conclusions and results will ensue. For example, the concept of God as a heavenly Father is very difficult for those who had a distant or abusive earthly father. There is the tendency to see the Heavenly Father through the filter of these experiences as a person who is distant and ready to judge.

If we can transcend this limited view, and not project our view of an earthly father on God as Father, we can enter into a deeper relationship with the Father. Rather than eternally seeking an earthly father's approval, we are free to discover that God accepts us in Jesus (Ephesians 1:6). Instead of wallowing in self-pity about having been abandoned by an earthly father, we are freed to turn to the One who will never leave or forsake us (Hebrews 13:5) in a relationship that supersedes anything humanly possible.

Our knowledge of God must begin with God's revelation of Himself as a loving heavenly Father. "Behold, what manner of love the Father has bestowed upon us that se should be called the children of God" (I John 3:1). Learning the truth concerning God and His will concerning us provides the proper foundation for relationship with Him, and enables us to appreciate that God wants to be in relationship with us.

When we recognize that God's desire toward us is not because we deserve it but purely because He made us and loves us, we can begin to appreciate the kind of Father that He is, and the nature of the relationship to which He calls us. God provides an eternal illustration of the kind of Father He is in His provision, pleasure, and exaltation of His Son. It boggles the mind and staggers the imagination to consider that Jesus says that everything that He enjoys from His relationship with the Father, the Father wants us to enjoy as well. For instance, John's gospel reveals the Fatherhood of God in relation to Christ when it inventories several of the prerogatives that the Father gives the Son:

- Authority (John 6:38, 17:4, 5:19, 4:34)

- Affection (John 5:20, 15:9-10)

- Fellowship (John 16:32, 8:29)

- Honor (John 17:1, 5:22-23)

As Christ begins to disclose the nature of His relationship with the Father, and informs His disciples that this same relationship is available to them, the implications of this teaching are beyond their grasp in their un-enlightened state. Jesus begins to prepare them for what must precede the realization of this relationship on their part. Only by virtue of His death and resurrection could they enter into this glorious relationship.

> It is to your advantage that I go away; for if I do not go away, the Helper shall not come to you; but if I go, I will send Him to you… But when He, The Spirit of truth, comes, He will guide you into all the truth; for He will not speak on His own initiative, but whatever He hears, He will speak; and He will disclose to you what is to come. He shall glorify Me; for He shall take of Mine, and shall disclose it to you. All things that the Father has are Mine; therefore I said, that He takes of Mine, and will disclose it to you. (John 16:7-15 NASV).

Our Lord prepares His disciples to recognize that this relationship will be predicated upon His death and resurrection from the dead. The writer to the Hebrews states that this signaled the victory that would allow "many sons and daughters to come into glory".

> But we do see Him who was made for a little while lower than the angels, namely, Jesus, because of the suffering of death crowned with glory and honor, so that by the grace of God He might taste death for everyone. For it was fitting for Him, for whom are all

things, and through whom are all things, in bringing many sons to glory, to perfect the author of their salvation through sufferings." (Hebrews 2:9-10 NASV).

Our access to the Father is through Jesus alone, since His sacrifice was the one and only price that could be paid for our redemption, reconciliation and restoration of relationship with the Father. Jesus says, "I am the way, the truth and the life, no man comes to the Father except through me". (John 14:6)

> He who sanctifies and those who are sanctified are all from one Father; for which reason He is not ashamed to call them brethren, saying, "I will proclaim Thy name to my brethren, in the midst of the congregation I will sing thy praise" (Hebrews 2:11-12 NASV).

The whole Christian life is a hymn of worship in three-part harmony. Everyone who glorifies the Father does so through the Son in the Holy Spirit; everyone who follows Christ does so because the Father draws him and the Spirit moves him (John 6:44; Rom 8:14). Jesus said, "If you know Me, you will know My Father also. From now on you do know Him and have seen Him" (John. 14:6-7). To know God the Father, we can only achieve this by the illumination of the Holy Spirit by walking in the truth through Jesus Christ Himself.

III. INCLUSIVE LANGUAGE AND FEMINIST VIEWS THAT PREVENT WORSHIP OF THE FATHER

Because of God's great and glorious intent to bring us into relationship with the Father through Christ, the enemy has crafted many obstacles that prevent this from happening. We have examined several of them above. Yet another obstacle has to do with the sensitivity to language that is construed as too masculine and patriarchal by those who honestly and innocently seek to protect the equality of women and avoid making the gospel sexist or chauvinistic.

In writing to the Galatians, Paul said, "Because you are sons, God has sent the Spirit of his Son into our hearts crying, 'Abba! Father' (Galatians 4:6). While we have little problem adjusting the language from "sons" to "sons and daughters" or "children" only those who allow a very liberal view would accordingly edit the second part of the passage to read "Abba, Father, Imma, Mother".

Some with strong feminist views and others who have suffered neglect or abuse from men often refuse to employ masculine words and especially the name "Father" in referring to God. Still others feel that language of this kind fosters a second-class status for women, and that reluctance to edit all masculine references to God stems from sexism or from dependence on father figures. And while this may be the case in some instances, the call to inclusive language poses yet another threat to knowing God as Father.

To enter into a proper relationship with God as Father, and to enjoy the fellowship that the Father has intended for us, we must develop a deeper understanding and experience of God precisely as Jesus' Father, and therefore as our Father. To do so, it is imperative that we explore the meaning of "Abba" in the experience of Jesus.

As we have already noted, our own personal experience defines what the name "father" comes to mean to us. For some of us the very word opens wounds of abandonment and betrayal, while for others it evokes a sense of unconditional love and unselfish giving.

But what did the word "father" mean to Jesus? Biblical scholars point out that the sacred Hebrew word "Yahweh" signified a God so transcendent that no devout Jew would dare even to pronounce this name. All the more, then, no Jew would have dared to address

God with the startling intimacy that springs spontaneously from the lips of Jesus himself: "Abba," "Papa," "Daddy." The Creator of the universe who dwells "in inaccessible light," whose name no one can speak, Jesus dares to call "Father."

Jesus' experience of God as "Abba" defined his entire identity. The amazing fact is that Jesus gives to us that which he uniquely enjoyed: a unique, one-of-a-kind relationship with His Father. This relationship was defined by the most intimate and personal name which Jesus *alone* used of God. It's absolutely mind-boggling that the name "Abba, Father," is now to be the one by which we are to commune with God—as familiarly as a child snuggles safe and secure in its fathers arms. Jesus invites us into such intimacy with himself that his own experience of his Father's extraordinary closeness becomes ours as well. "When you pray, say 'Father'... (Luke 11:2). Wow!

In so doing, Jesus takes a word of tender familiarity, a word little children used of their own fathers, and, applying it to the God who utterly surpasses the limitations of male gender, gives it a radically transcendent meaning. The God of Jesus is certainly "Creator of the Universe" and "Source of All Being." But far more importantly—and precisely because of all possible names Jesus himself has given us this one alone—God is our "Father."

In giving to us his own name for God, Jesus does not take an ordinary word and use it simply as a metaphor, as if to say, "God is like a father," just as God is also in some way like a shepherd and like a rock. No, it is God as "Abba" who defines the meaning of true fatherhood and not the other way around. The very best of human parenting gives only a minuscule hint of what it means that God is our Father.

The feminists fear that Jesus' use of the name "Father" for God fosters a patriarchy that subjugates women to men. In fact, it does quite the opposite. Jesus says, "Do not call anyone on earth your father. Only one is your father, the One in heaven". (Matthew 23:9) By so doing, Jesus neutralizes the patriarchal system that enslaved his disciples and prevented them from knowing God as their Father. Far from furthering male domination, the name "Father" signifies the God whose love calls us into a new kind of family relationship, based not on the ties of kinship but of love and grace.

When feminists interpret the name "Abba" out of context to present a male god who secures the primacy of the male, they not only reject God as Father, but also impose damaging stereotypical roles. They relegate the capacity for tenderness and faithful care to women alone. Yet our need for a faithful and caring father is too deep a component of our human existence to abandon this vision of God. It is far more helpful to dismiss distortions linking the concept of "Father God" with domination by embracing the Scriptural truth of the Father's love.

Entering into this love relationship with the Father makes us aware the He knows and loves each one of us so intimately, that every single hair on our head is counted (Matthew 10:30). This is the Father who refuses to give up on us, who searches for us when we sin because his own heart feels such tenderness for us. He throws his arms around our neck, kisses and embraces us in our weakness.

This is the Father, who having found us insists that all of heaven and earth must celebrate because his lost child has been found, his dead child has come back to life (Luke 15:18-23). This Father desires us to trust him without reserve and yearns to lavish his care upon us in our every need (Matthew 7:11; Luke 11:13).

These and other Gospel passages can only hint at the unbelievable tenderness that Jesus unveils to us in the one He calls "Father." But by recovering precisely this content of Jesus' own experience, we can open ourselves to the Father's extraordinary tenderness in our lives. And as our hearts become more open to the possibility of the intimacy that God offers, we become more and more cognizant that this is the primary and supreme purpose of God in the work that He accomplished through our Lord Jesus Christ.

We catch a glimpse of this at the dramatic moment when he was preparing to face death. In full view of the cross, Jesus ends his great farewell discourse (John 13-17) with a wonderful prayer to the Father. It documents a spiritual testament in which Jesus returns to the Father's hands the mandate he had received: to make His love known to the world, through the gift of eternal life (John 17:2). The life He offers is significantly explained as a gift of intimate knowledge, a gift of relationship: "This is eternal life, that they know You the only true God, and Jesus Christ whom you have sent" (John 17:3).

Knowledge, in the biblical sense of the word, is not only intellectual, but more precisely describes a living experience that involves the whole human person—including his capacity to love. This knowledge leads to an "encounter" with God, which takes place through the transforming power of God's Spirit. As we reflect on the words of Jesus, we are introduced to what it means to have a living knowledge of God the Father. This provides us with the most personal way of relating to God—as a Father.

To know God as Father requires that we have a solid foundation of understanding of the nature and character of God. And herein we encounter the danger faced by the professional theologian. Many students and scholars of the Scripture have made the mistake of thinking that, when we know a lot about God, we know him; of thinking that, when we have mastered the fine points of doctrine and can exegete His Word with skill, we have achieved intimacy with God.

It is not my purpose to attempt to provide an exhaustive theological study of God. Rather, we will review some of the highlights of His essence and His attributes as it relates to His person as our Father. This understanding should enable us to worship Him more meaningfully, and to enter into a deeper relationship with Him as our heavenly Father.

We will look at God's essence, and at His attributes. We will examine His non-moral attributes, as well as the moral attributes, then the elements that relate to His goodness.

THE ESSENCE AND ATTRIBUTES OF GOD

- When we speak of God's essence we speak of the fact that God is **spiritual** in nature. Except for the glorified body of Christ, He does not have material substance. As Infinite Spirit, He has no limitations. He is inexhaustible in every aspect of His nature. He has given to each of us a spiritual part to our nature for the purpose of uniting with Him and having a personal relationship with Him.

- God is **personal**. He has self-consciousness, self-determination, intellect, emotions and will on a level of perfection, which dwarfs our finite abilities. And yet, unbelievably, God desires an ongoing personal relationship with each of us. Even though He is our creator, He also wants to fulfill our lives as a Father, Redeemer and Provider.

- God is **self-existent**, and yet He has chosen to move beyond the sufficiency He has and share Himself with His creation.

- God is **infinite**. All that exists depends upon Him. All of creation is held in place by His power.

God's Non-Moral Attributes

- God is **Omnipresent**—God rules transcendent in the heavens and also dwells immanently in our lives.

- God is **Omniscient**—God knows everything. He not only sees every action, but He is aware of every motive and desire of our hearts. God also knows the future, because He is not restricted by time. Every desire and action of the enemy is known to God as well.

- God is **Omnipotent**—God is able to do whatever He wills; but His will is always in concert with His perfect nature. Everything He does is in harmony with His perfections.

- God is **Immutable**—God is unchangeable in regard to His essence, will, attributes, and consciousness.

God's Moral Attributes

- God is **Holy**—God is separate from all moral evil that we call sin.

- God is **Righteous and Just**—God's righteousness and justice issue out of His holiness and are demonstrated in His treatment of His creatures.

God's Goodness

- The **Love** of God moves God to share Himself. Love is an expression of His nature. His love is always unconditional to all.

- The **Grace** of God is His disposition to show favor, His unmerited goodness extended to those who do not deserve it.

- The **Mercy** of God is God's goodness shown to those in misery and distress, even though they do not deserve it.

- The **Long-suffering** of God is that aspect of His virtue that bears with the wicked in spite of their continued disobedience.

- The **Truth** of God is the foundation of all knowledge. He is the source of all true understanding. God is truth in that He is perfectly genuine.

- The **Freedom** God Allows—God has given man freedom to exercise his will. Without freedom, we are not truly unique individuals.

When we examine what the Scriptures have to say about the nature of God as Father we conclude that:

- We have a **secure and unchanging** Father. He has no limitations, so He never becomes defensive in His relationship with us. He is always truthful and does what He says He will do.

- We have a **concerned** Father. He is looking for His child to come to Him. Every issue is important to Him and He is **always** there for us even though it may appear otherwise.

- We have a **loving** Father. He loves us as we are, on the basis of who He is, not on the basis of how we perform. He desires the very best for each of our lives, according to His will and wisdom. He wants to provide us with those things that will help build us up spiritually and strengthen our relationship with Him.

- We have a **protective** Father. He watches over us and will not let us be tempted beyond our ability to bear it. He has provided a Comforter to help us get through the difficult times in life.

- We have a **committed** Father. Once we do come to Him, He disciplines us and works with us to bring us even closer to Him.

When we get to the back of the Book, we find this theme of relationship reverberating in the Revelation. "He who overcomes shall inherit these things, and I will be his God and he will be my son" (Revelation 21:7). We "overcome" by faith in "the blood of the Lamb" not by any effort on our parts. The language here is almost identical to that of II Samuel 7:14, in which the Lord says of the son of David, ultimately Christ: "I will be a father to him, and he will be a son to me." As Christ the eternal Son enjoys and intimate relationship with the Father, so do we because we are in Christ.

For this supreme purpose Christ Jesus come to earth. "And we know that the Son of God is come, and has given us an understanding, that we may know him that is true..." (I John 5:20). "And this is eternal life, that they may know You, the only true God, and Jesus Christ whom You have sent" (John 17:3).

What matters first is not that I know God but that God knows me. All my knowledge of Him depends on His initiative in knowing me. I know Him, because He first knew me, and continues to know me. "Nevertheless the solid foundation of God stands, having this seal: 'The Lord knows those who are His,' and 'Let everyone who names the name of Christ depart from iniquity'" (II Timothy 2:19). J.I. Packer, in his best-selling and practical book, Knowing God writes:

> What matters supremely therefore is not in the last analysis the fact that I know God, but the larger fact which underlies it—

the fact that he knows me. I am graven on the palms of his hands. I am never out of his mind. All my knowledge of him depends on his sustained initiative in knowing me. I know him because he first knew me, and continues to know me. He knows me as a friend, one who loves me; and there is no moment when his eye is off me, or his attention distracted from me, and no moment therefore when his care falters.[123]

This is momentous knowledge. There is unspeakable comfort in knowing that God is constantly taking knowledge of me in love and watching over me for my good. There is tremendous relief in knowing that his love for me is utterly realistic, based at every point on prior knowledge of the worst about me, so that no discovery now can disillusion him about me, in the way I am so often disillusioned about myself, and quench his determination to bless me.

Is it possible that the alpha and omega of God's redemptive purpose can be so simply stated and comprehended? The Scriptures are clear: "For God so loved the world, that he gave his one and only Son, that whoever believes in him shall not perish but have eternal life" (John 3:16). "Yet to all who received him, to those who believed in his name, he gave the right to become children of God—children born not of natural descent, nor of human decision or a husband's will, but born of God" (John 1:12-13). "How great is the love the Father has lavished on us, that we should be called the children of God! And that is what we are!" (I John 3:1-2).

Of all the theological postulations and Biblical expositions that so eloquently and majestically present to us our Father God, none do it more beautifully than the following, a simple but compelling compilation of Scripture:

---

123   Packer, James I. *Knowing God*. Downers Grove, IL: Intervarsity Press, 1993.

An Introduction to Your Heavenly Father

You may not know me, but I know everything about you I know when you sit down and when you rise up. I am familiar with all your ways. Even the very hairs on your head are numbered. For you were made in my image. In me you live and move and have your being. For you are my offspring I knew you even before you were conceived I chose you when I planned creation. You were not a mistake. For all your days are written in my book. I determined the exact time of your birth and where you would live. You are fearfully and wonderfully made. I knit you together in your mother's womb and brought you forth on the day you were born. I have been misrepresented by those who don't know me. I am not distant and angry, but am the complete expression of love. And it is my desire to lavish my love on you simply because you are my child and I am your Father. I offer you more than your earthly father ever could, for I am the perfect Father. Every good gift that you receive comes from my hand. For I am your provider and I meet all your needs. My plan for your future has always been filled with hope because I love you with an everlasting love. My thoughts toward you are countless as the sand on the seashore and I rejoice over you with singing. I will never stop doing good to you for you are my treasured possession. I desire to establish you with all my heart and all my soul and I want to show you great and marvelous things. If you seek me with all your heart, you will find me. Delight in me and I will give you the desires of your heart for it is I who gave you those desires. I am able to do more for you than you could possibly imagine for I am your greatest encourager. I am also the Father who comforts you in all your troubles. When you are broken-hearted, I am close to you. As a shepherd carries a lamb, I have carried you close to my heart. One day I will wipe away every tear from your eyes and I'll take away all the pain you have suffered on this earth. I am your Father and I love you even as I love my son, Jesus, for in Jesus my love for you is revealed. He is the exact representation of my being and He came to demonstrate that I am for you, not against you and to tell you that I am not counting your sins. Jesus died so that you and I could be reconciled His death was the ultimate expression of my love for you. I gave up everything I loved that I might gain your love. If you receive the gift of my son Jesus, you receive me, and nothing will ever separate you from my love again. Come home and I'll throw the biggest party heaven has ever seen. I have always been Father and will always be Father. My question is… Will you be my child? I am waiting for you.[124]

You are God's child (John 1:12-13). God loves you (I John 3:1). You have the assurance of eternal life (John 3:16). He put His Holy Spirit in you (II Corinthians 1:21-21). You can talk directly to God (Matthew 7:7-11) Nothing will ever separate you from His love (Romans 8:38). As God's child, you have the privilege of getting to know Him as your Father. For this you were born!

As John concludes his account of the works of Christ, he said, "Many other signs therefore Jesus also performed in the presence of the disciples, which are not written in this book. But these have been written that you may believe that Jesus is the Christ, the Son of God: and that believing you may have life in His name" (John 20:30-31).

My purpose in writing this book is to expound on the glorious privilege of knowing and worshipping God. My purpose in this chapter is to explore the wonderful prospect of entering into a deeper relationship with God as our Father. And, my assumption has been

---

124 *Father's Love Letter* used by permission Father Heart Communications Copyright 1999-2006 www.FathersLoveLetter.com

that my readers are those who already have embraced this Christ of whom I write, and have come into relationship with the Father. And yet, on the possibility that *you* have not yet entered into that relationship, the Father anxiously waits for you to come home.

19

EVERYDAY WORSHIP
AND SUNDAY BEST

*To gather with God's people in united adoration of the
Father is as necessary to the Christian life as prayer.*

— **Martin Luther**

*Worship is the dramatic celebration of God in his
supreme worth in such a manner that his "worthiness"
becomes the norm and inspiration of human living.*

— **Ralph Martin,** *The Worship of God*

"Oh, the depth of the riches of the wisdom and knowledge
of God! How unsearchable his judgments, and his paths beyond
tracing out! 'Who has known the mind of the Lord? Or who has
been his counselor? Who has ever given to God, that God should
repay him?' For from him and through him and to him are all
things. To him be the glory forever! Amen. Therefore, I urge you,
brothers, in view of God's mercy, to offer your bodies as living
sacrifices, holy and pleasing to God—this is your spiritual act of
worship. Do not conform any longer to the pattern of this world,
but be transformed by the renewing of your mind. Then you will

be able to test and approve what God's will is—his good, pleasing and perfect will (Romans 11: 33-36, 12:1-2 NIV).

Through Jesus, therefore, let us continually offer to God a sacrifice of praise—the fruit of lips that confess his name. And do not forget to do good and to share with others, for with such sacrifices God is pleased (Hebrews 13:15-16).

MEMORIES OF EVERYDAY WORSHIP

Growing up in a Christian home, my memory redounds with recollections of worship as an every day experience culminating with Sunday worship. By early childhood, I was already accustomed to going to church twice on Sunday, and once or twice through the week. This was the era when you "dressed up" to go to church. We had our "everyday" clothes, which we wore from Monday through Saturday. And we had our "Sunday best" which were reserved for the house of God and would only be worn otherwise for a very special occasion.

While we children never left home in the morning without family devotions, or went to bed at night without "saying our prayers" it was not these experiences alone that marked our home as one where the worship of God figured predominantly. I would come home from school to hear my grandmother listening to the *Back to the Bible*[125] broadcast on the radio. My mother would be humming or singing the old hymns of the faith as she performed her maternal duties. And I would often find my father with his Bible open, diving and delving into the Word of God and devouring its precious truth at every opportunity. He kept a Bible in his store,

---

125 Back to the Bible was first broadcast on May 1, 1939, with founder Theodore Epp as the speaker.

and could frequently be found scouring through its pages between customers. These hallmarks of my rearing left an indelible impression on my life, and undoubtedly contributed to my own desire to follow Christ and to become a student of His Word when I was very young. Long before I became aware of the classic book by Brother Lawrence, *The Practice of the Presence of God*,[126] I was aware of both principle and practice as evidenced in my childhood home. Our home was a home where we were taught to be always mindful of the presence of God, and where worship was a *way of life* even though we had never heard the phrase *lifestyle worship*.

I often joke about how I became an "international preacher" by age twelve. Since I was never bashful about standing up in public, I had been initiated into "preaching" by being asked to speak in our mid-week youth services and occasionally on a Sunday. The highlight of my summer was going off to church camp, and the two weeks of camp seemed to rush by so quickly because I found it so enjoyable. I remember on one particular summer, when I was only twelve, the two weeks at Harvey Lake had proved insufficient to satiate my appetite for summer bible camp. I had heard that across the border, near Old Town, Maine, another camp was occurring late in August. Together with my childhood and lifelong pal, Randy Leavitt, we concocted a scheme for getting to the camp meeting at Pea Cove. My father drove us to Campobello Island, and we took the ferry over to Eastport, Maine, where we were met by Rev. Henry Crocker who had agreed to take us with him to the camp at Pea Cove. Rev. Crocker pastored a small church in Eastport, and when Randy and I disembarked from the ferry, he immediately informed us that we would be singing and preaching in the Sunday morning service.

---

126   Lawrence, Brother (Nicholas Herman, c. 1605-1691) *The Practice of the Presence of God: The Best Rule of Holy Life*. Grand Rapids, MI: Christian Classics Ethereal Library.

Randy and I were well practiced and prepared to sing. We spent long hours listening to the old 78s of the first recorded gospel music and memorizing the melodies and lyrics, then rendering our versions of the songs to the accompaniment of a guitar or old upright piano. We both entered Christian ministry around the same time, and many years later Randy succeeded me in the pastorate of the Full Gospel Church in Halifax when I resigned its charge and moved to the west coast to pastor in the late 1970s. Whenever I visit Randy in the church in Winnipeg where he currently pastors, I revel in his anointed and insightful exposition of the Scriptures as I hear him preach. However, before he takes the pulpit, we invariably move into a time warp of several decades past, subjecting his parishioners to our two-part harmony rendition of "I've never loved Him better than today… "[127]

I have no recollection of what Randy and I sang that Sunday in Eastport, Maine, but I *vividly* recall the text that I selected for that Sunday morning service. I chose I Thessalonians 5:17 that simply states, "Pray without ceasing." I *vaguely* recall talking about always living in an attitude of prayer. I can't help but wonder how my life might have been different if I had truly learned to *practice* what I so vigorously *preached.* In reflecting on this memory, however, I am reminded that I could only have chosen that passage if the idea of living in an awareness of God—practicing God's presence in *lifestyle worship*—was a concept with which I was already familiar at the tender age of twelve.

I don't want to give the impression that my absorption in spiritual things insulated me from the mischief of adolescent behavior or isolated me from every-day living. But those early adolescent years were marked by a pursuit of God's presence and a sincere desire to

---

127   Slaughter, Henry ©1965

incorporate His life into daily existence. When Randy and I were not in church or making music in his home or mine, we spent a lot of time, together with his late brother, Allison, above the St. George bakery in worship and Bible Study with the late Ted and Inez Holmes. Ted and Inez were both zealous Christians, and were the youth leaders in our tiny church for a short period of time. I would strap on Ted's giant piano accordion, and we would sing our hearts out and with our limited understanding, explore the great truths of the Word of God.

Due to my deep immersion in spiritual things as a child, when I first encountered the phrase *lifestyle worship* itrequired little definition. And yet, it seems almost trite to trivialize worship with the phrase *lifestyle worship*. Still, almost every significant book on the subject of worship that has appeared in recent years will devote a substantial amount of discussion to this topic. In fact, there are probably more than a dozen books that speak specifically to the subject of *lifestyle worship*. When I "googled" the phrase *lifestyle worship*, I came up with 111 million hits in less than one second.

In a sermon entitled *Worship as a Lifestyle*, Doug Goins states,

Both the Old Testament and New Testament vocabulary gives us a more comprehensive understanding of worship. They combine a sense of moral and ethical behavior. This is worship that does something, it is active. It is the picture we see in Isaiah 6 where the prophet worships God on his face in humility. But then God lifts him up, puts him on his feet, and sends him out to speak and serve and minister. These are expressions of worship.

This definition affirms that all of life—every thought, every choice, every action—is worship.[128]

THE MOTIVATION FOR *EVERYDAY* WORSHIP

When I pastored the Peoples Full Gospel Church in Surrey, British Columbia, I served as faculty and chairman of the board of Jubilee Bible College. The late Rev. Lorne Pritchard, principal of the college, was famous for saying, "Whenever you see the word *therefore* look to see what it's *there for.*" Romans 12: 1-2 follows on the heels of Paul's doxology in Romans 11:33-36,

> Oh, the depth of the riches of the wisdom and knowledge of God! How unsearchable his judgments, and his paths beyond tracing out! 'Who has known the mind of the Lord? Or who has been his counselor? Who has ever given to God, that God should repay him?' For from him and through him and to him are all things. To him be the glory forever! Amen (Romans 11:33-36 KJV).

A lifestyle of worship practiced in every day living is the intelligent response to God's mercy and grace. The distinction between God's mercy and His grace has often been described as "mercy is God withholding from me that which I do deserve and grace is God bestowing on me that which I don't deserve." While not a particularly theological definition, it is an apt description of the woven cord of two glorious aspects of God's redeeming love.

Paul's appeal in this passage is more of an invitation than a command. Since God in mercy has extended His love toward us in our sinfulness and helplessness, our response is one of grateful appre-

128 https://www.pbc.org/messages/worship-as-a-lifestyle/

ciation, rather than one that is rendered from fear or obligation. The translation offered for Romans 12:2 in The Message is particularly pragmatic, "Take your everyday, ordinary life—your sleeping, eating, going-to-work, and walking-around life—and place it before God as an offering."[129]

THE MEANING OF *EVERYDAY* WORSHIP

Paul goes on to state that our *everyday* worship is to be rendered to God as a sacrificial offering: "Offer your bodies as living sacrifices, holy and pleasing to God—this is your spiritual act of worship." I find it a staggering and sobering thought that the giving of ourselves to God on a daily basis is here described as a "spiritual act of worship." When Paul speaks of our bodies, he is not merely referring to the physical, corporeal aspect of our being. He uses the term to describe all that we are: the sum total of our physical, emotional, intellectual, volitional, and spiritual being. This offering, or sacrifice to God, is merely giving back to God what is His. Paul later reminds the Corinthians, "What? Know ye not that your body is the temple of the Holy Ghost which is in you, which ye have of God, and ye are not your own? For ye are bought with a price: therefore glorify God in your body, and in your spirit, which are God's" (I Corinthians 6:19-20 KJV).

Paul further states that this rational, intelligent act of spiritual worship is to give ourselves as a *living sacrifice*. Unlike the Old Testament sacrifices that were comprised of slain animals, we are to offer to God a *living sacrifice*. Having been made *spiritually* alive in Christ, our *physical* lives are to reflect *His* life in and through us. Paul elaborates on this to the Galatians when he writes, "For through

---

129 Peterson, Eugene H. *The Message.* Colorado Springs, CO: Navpress 1993.

the law I died to the law so that I might live for God. I have been crucified with Christ and I no longer live, but Christ lives in me. The life I live in the body, I live by faith in the Son of God, who loved me and gave himself for me (Galatians 2:19-20 NIV).

Since the physical aspect of our redemption will only be consummated in the future resurrection, we still reside in sinful, carnal, physical bodies with all of their implicit limitations. However, we have a "treasure in earthen vessels" (II Corinthians 4:7), and are capable of expressing the life of God because of the indwelling presence of Christ. *Everyday worship,* therefore, becomes the very practical living out of God's life within. This is further exhorted by Paul to the Romans when he says,

> In the same way, count yourselves dead to sin but alive to God in Christ Jesus. Therefore do not let sin reign in your mortal body so that you obey its evil desires. Do not offer the parts of your body to sin, as instruments of wickedness, but rather offer yourselves to God, as those who have been brought from death to life; and offer the parts of your body to him as instruments of righteousness (Romans 6:11-13 NIV).

Our intelligent act of *everyday worship* is not only to be a *living* sacrifice, but also a *holy* sacrifice. Having been raised in the *holiness* wing of the evangelical church, my view and version of holiness as a youth consisted of a *tablet of taboos*. I was recently reminded of the narrowness of that approach when a pastor on a Sunday morning announced, "Today I'm going to preach to you on how to be holy." For the next forty minutes he enumerated a list of forbidden practices, without one single reference to living out the life of God on a daily basis through the enabling power of the Holy Spirit who produces His fruit in our lives.

While it is impossible to understand holiness apart from the awareness that it involves the "putting off" of the works of the fleshly sinful nature, this in itself does not constitute what it means to be holy. The word holy refers to the fact that we are set apart to God, and are totally dedicated completely for His ownership and purpose in our lives. Paul admonishes the Ephesian believers,

> Surely you heard of him and were taught in him in accordance with the truth that is in Jesus. You were taught, with regard to your former way of life, to put off your old self, which is being corrupted by its deceitful desires; to be made new in the attitude of your minds; and to put on the new self, created to be like God in true righteousness and holiness (Ephesians 4:21-24 NIV).

In a parallel passage to the Colossian believers, Paul joins together the "putting off" of sinful works with the "putting on" of Christ when he writes:

> Do not lie to each other, since you have taken off your old self with its practices and have put on the new self, which is being renewed in knowledge in the image of its Creator... Therefore, as God's chosen people, holy and dearly loved, clothe yourselves with compassion, kindness, humility, gentleness and patience. Bear with each other and forgive whatever grievances you may have against one another. Forgive as the Lord forgave you. And over all these virtues put on love, which binds them all together in perfect unity (Colossians 2:9-14 NIV).

THE MANIFESTATION OF *EVERYDAY* WORSHIP

The manifestation of *everyday worship* will result in a resistance to being shaped by the mold of the contemporary culture. This can only happen when we experience the transforming power of God's Spirit in a renewed mind that provides a different paradigm of the world and of life.

In my holiness upbringing, this was a favorite and familiar passage to which preachers appealed to condemn anything from movies to ice-skating. Most of the emphasis was on the *do not be conformed to this world* with very little understanding of what it meant to be *transformed by the renewing of your mind*. We were further instructed that there were three successive and graduated levels of God's will: acceptable, good and perfect, not understanding that God's *singular* will for our lives comprises all three. Sincere believers would desperately seek the rather mysterious *will of God*, since it was held to be something esoteric and ethereal that would most likely be foreign to your own desires. J. B. Phillips offers an enlightening paraphrase when he says, "Don't let the world around you squeeze you into its own mould, but let God re-mould your minds from within, so that you may prove in practice that the plan of God for you is good, meets all his demands and moves towards the goal of true maturity."[130] The Amplified Bible offers an equally compelling rendition,

> Do not be conformed to this world (this age), [fashioned after and adapted to its external, superficial customs], but be transformed (changed) by the [entire] renewal of your mind [by its new ideals and its new attitude], so that you may prove [for yourselves] what is the good and acceptable and perfect will of God, even the thing which is good and acceptable and perfect [in His sight for you]"[131] (Romans 12:2 Amplified Bible).

As we practice *everyday worship* we become agents of change in our world. Simultaneously, God is continually transforming us.

---

130   Phillips, J.B. *The J.B. Phillips New Testament*. London: HarperCollins, 1958.
131   The Amplified Bible, © The Lockman Foundation, 1958, 1962, 1964, 1965.

One rendition of the language employed by Paul in this passage is to suggest that he is saying, "Be continuously being transformed." The Greek derivative for transformed, metamorphosis, describes the same process that occurs for a caterpillar in becoming a butterfly. The metamorphosis or transformation for the child of God involves a change from the inside out that takes place through the power of the indwelling Holy Spirit. Dr. Harry Rimmer elegantly expounds this truth in his 1943 publication, *Flying Worms,* where he compares the transformation to that of the caterpillar becoming a butterfly.[132] This is an ongoing process as God works out His redeeming grace and transforming power in our lives. As Paul states to the Corinthian church, "Now the Lord is the Spirit, and where the Spirit of the Lord is, there is freedom. And we, who with unveiled faces all reflect the Lord's glory, are being transformed into his likeness with ever-increasing glory, which comes from the Lord, who is the Spirit (II Corinthians 3:17-18 NIV).

A chorus we used to sing in church conveyed this glorious truth:

> Little by little He's changing me
> Line upon line He's teaching me
> Precept on precept until I'm free
> Jesus is changing me
>
> Day by day He's changing me
> In every way He's changing me
> When I am yielded He sets me free
> Jesus is changing me

As Christ becomes more and more real to us through God's Word, and as we through prayer deepen the intimacy in our relationship to him, we are gradually transformed into His likeness. This is a trans-

---

132 Rimmer, Harry. *Flying Worms.* Grand Rapids, MI: Wm. B. Eerdmans Publishing Co., 1943.

formation that will be reflected in our emotions, attitudes, values and behavior—in *everyday* life. The values of the world are progressively and eventually displaced by the values of God.

THE MINISTRY OF EVERYDAY WORSHIP

I've often said that by doing my doctoral dissertation on lay ministry[133] I had painted myself into an ecclesiastical corner. In my upbringing, the *ministry* belonged to the *clergy*. The concept of the priesthood of all believers, and all of God's people as ministers was one with which I was totally unfamiliar.

Similarly, my Pentecostal roots viewed the inventory of spiritual gifts that were normative for today's church as being the list described by Paul in I Corinthians 12.

> There are different kinds of gifts, but the same Spirit. There are different kinds of service, but the same Lord. There are different kinds of working, but the same God works all of them in all men. Now to each one the manifestation of the Spirit is given for the common good. To one there is given through the Spirit the message of wisdom, to another the message of knowledge by means of the same Spirit, to another faith by the same Spirit, to another gifts of healing by that one Spirit, to another miraculous powers, to another prophecy, to another distinguishing between spirits, to another speaking in different kinds of tongues, and to still another the interpretation of tongues. All these are the work of one and the same Spirit, and he gives them to each one, just as he determines (I Corinthians 12:4-11 NIV).

---

133 Carmont, Donald M. *Harnessed for Harvest: The Forgotten Force of the Laity.* Glendale, CA: California Graduate School of Theology, 1984.

We seemed oblivious to the fact that Romans 12:6-8 *also* offered instructions on spiritual gifts, as did Ephesians 4: 11-12, and I Peter 4:10-11. With such a limited view of what ministry entailed, and of God's gifting for ministry, we missed the fact that Paul's injunction in Romans 12:1-2 to present ourselves to God is fulfilled in *everyday worship* through the deployment of the gifts that God has given us, and through living a life of grace among our fellow believers in our everyday world.

It would be preposterous to suggest that Paul's instruction in three separate passages concerning spiritual gifts is strictly for a select group of professional ministers known as the clergy. In fact, Paul's teaching in Ephesians 4:11-12 is that the role and function of the apostles, prophets, evangelists, pastors and teachers is precisely to equip all of God's people to do the work of the ministry so that the Body of Christ might come to a place of maturity.

> It was he who gave some to be apostles, some to be prophets, some to be evangelists, and some to be pastors and teachers, to prepare God's people for works of service, so that the body of Christ may be built up until we all reach unity in the faith and in the knowledge of the Son of God and become mature, attaining to the whole measure of the fullness of Christ. Then we will no longer be infants, tossed back and forth by the waves, and blown here and there by every wind of teaching and by the cunning and craftiness of men in their deceitful scheming. Instead, speaking the truth in love, we will in all things grow up into him who is the Head, that is, Christ. From him the whole body, joined and held together by every supporting ligament, grows and builds itself up in love, as each part does its work (Ephesians 4:11-12 NIV).

I reluctantly resist the urge to expound on this passage in any depth and detail. Suffice it to say that the purpose of God, designed in the distribution of His gifts to the church, is to equip, enable, and empower believers to experience and express *everyday worship.* Thus will Christ's church become mature and edified, and thus will God be ultimately glorified. The passage is crystal clear, and while thousands of pages have been skillfully crafted by commentators to elucidate on its meaning, the simplicity of its language makes it readily understandable. In fact, this section of Scripture may qualify for the description offered by a preacher whose lack of formal education left him deprived of translation tools and of any hermeneutic for Biblical interpretation. He simply stated, "The Bible sure does shed a lot of light on them there commentaries."

In our preoccupation with the first two verses of Romans 12, we can easily become oblivious to the obvious: that the injunction of Paul's invitation to *spiritual worship* is followed by a formula in the remainder of the chapter on precisely how to achieve and experience its reality.

For by the grace given me I say to every one of you: Do not think of yourself more highly than you ought, but rather think of yourself with sober judgment, in accordance with the measure of faith God has given you. Just as each of us has one body with many members, and these members do not all have the same function, so in Christ we who are many form one body, and each member belongs to all the others. We have different gifts, according to the grace given us. If a man's gift is prophesying, let him use it in proportion to his faith. If it is serving, let him serve; if it is teaching, let him teach; if it is encouraging, let him encourage; if it is contributing to the needs of others, let him give generously; if it is leadership, let him govern diligently; if it is showing mercy, let him do it cheerfully. Love must be sincere. Hate what is evil; cling to what is good. Be devoted to one another in brotherly love. Honor one another above yourselves. Never be lacking in zeal, but keep your spiritual fervor, serving the Lord. Be joyful in hope, patient in affliction, faithful in prayer. Share with God's people who are in need. Practice hospitality. Bless those who persecute you; bless and do not curse. Rejoice with those who rejoice; mourn with those who mourn. Live in harmony with one another. Do not be proud, but be willing to associate with people of low position. Do not be conceited. Do not repay anyone evil for evil. Be careful to do what is right in the eyes of everybody. If it is possible, as far as it depends on you, live at peace with everyone. Do not take revenge, my friends, but leave room for God's wrath, for it is written: "It is mine to avenge; I will repay," says the Lord. On the contrary: "if your enemy is hungry, feed him; if he is thirsty, give him something to drink. In doing this, you will heap burning coals on his head." Do not be overcome by evil, but overcome evil with good (Romans 12:3-21 NIV).

Without engaging in an exhaustive expository commentary on this passage, we will observe that *everyday worship* therefore is fulfilled and realized in a number of practical principles.

1. *Everyday worship* begins with the humble awareness that regardless of our giftings, we have received them from God, just as He has given us the faith whereby we are saved. (See also Ephesians 2:8-9)

2. *Everyday worship* recognizes that while some gifts may seem more prominent than others by virtue of their visibility, each is equally important, just as the members of the human body are vital to its function, regardless of their placement. (See also I Corinthians 12:14-31)

3.   *Everyday worship* is achieved through the exercise of those gifts, recognizing that they are resident in us through the grace of God, and active in us through the faith He imparts.

4.   *Everyday worship* realizes that whether it is through prophesying, serving, teaching, encouraging, contributing to the needs of others, leading, or showing mercy, all of these are *equal* and *legitimate* expressions of ministry, and the means by which we fulfill the will of God and offer spiritual worship.

5.   *Everyday worship* means practicing sincere and genuine love towards all people, abhorring that which is evil while clinging to that what is good.

6.   *Everyday worship* means being devoted to one another in brotherly love, and honoring one another above ourselves.

7.   *Everyday worship* is to maintain zeal and spiritual fervor in daily serving the Lord.

8.   *Everyday worship* is revealed when we are joyful in hope, patient in affliction, and faithful in prayer.

9.   *Everyday worship* is exemplified when we share with God's people who are in need and when we practice hospitality.

10.   *Everyday worship* will cause us to bless those who persecute us, to rejoice with those who rejoice, and mourn with those who mourn.

11.   *Everyday worship* will cause us to strive to live in harmony with one another.

12. *Everyday worship* will prevent us from becoming proud, and cause us to be willing to associate with people of low position. It will keep us from becoming conceited.

13. *Everyday worship* means that we refuse to repay anyone evil for evil, and that we will be careful to do what is right in the eyes of everybody.

14. *Everyday worship* will result in a life where we will, if at all possible, live at peace with everyone.

MEDITATIONS AND MUSINGS ON EVERYDAY WORSHIP

Ron Carlson clearly articulates that worship extends beyond the experience of Sunday gatherings, and spills over into our every day lives when he states,

> Authentic worship displays a life-style consistent with the discipleship demands of Jesus' Sermon on the Mount. Worship is more, much more, than the Sunday morning designated hour when saints and pseudo-saints gather together to do church. Though the assembly time is of critical import, it is only a component of a life-style characterized by service. Our Sunday morning worship is only as good as our Monday morning life sacrifice. We are unique and holy as Christian disciples, not because we show up in suits and ties and silk finery on Sunday mornings with contemporaries of similar ilk, but because we reject the evil of this world in favor of the righteousness and justice advocated by our Holy God and proclaimed by true prophets of every age.[134]

---

134 www.gracecentered.com/worship_as_lifestyle.htm

Everyday worship is not, however, a concept that is entirely New Testament. Lifestyle worship is part of God's earliest instructions to his chosen people: "Hear, O Israel: The Lord our God, the Lord is one. Love the Lord your God with all your heart and with all your soul and with all your strength" (Deut. 6:4-5 NIV). In an article entitled, *Live Out Loud*, Paul Guffey states,

> This lifestyle worship is what our Lord is looking for. Not just a musical moment designed to impress someone, or a tender moment when the heart flutters and tears run, but rather a consistent life of worship, rooted in deep convictions of righteousness and holiness that affect every area of our lives.[135]

A contributor who simply identifies himself as "Brother Maynard" offered these comments on the CG blog,

> Back in the early 90s in the charismatic movement we were all about worship conferences. And I think every worship conference had a session or workshop titled "Worship as a Lifestyle." We had all realized that "worship" is not just the singing of songs (with guitars and drums, of course) on Sunday mornings. Worship had to be something that could affect one's entire life, something one could live out day-to-day. Problem was it never sunk in that way. The presentations were often incomplete or unconvincing... or sometimes just that in a context where all the other seminars were about songwriting or musicianship or some facet of worship leading, the one workshop for which one didn't need to be able to sing tended to look like the add-on bit that the organizers threw in for the people who weren't really worshippers...[136]

135   Guffey, Paul. *Live Out Loud*. www.worshipHim.com
136   http://subversiveinfluence.com/2005/02/worship-as-a-lifestyle/

In a Christianity Today article entitled *9.5 Theses on Worship,* published in February 2005, Gary A. Parrett notes,

> Worship is the 24-hours-a-day, seven-days-a-week, vocation of all believers… Any discussion of worship, then, must begin with the biblical concern for worship as lifestyle, not merely as a formal gathering that features specifically "religious" actions… Religious actions at religious gatherings of the community were not intended to be substitutes for a life devoted to the true worship of God but, rather, were to be its celebratory overflow.[137]

Rick Warren, whose *Purpose Driven Life* has received international acclaim, states,

> Worship is knowingly living in the sight of God. It is so much more than a Sunday church event or a set of prayers or the singing of some songs… Worship as a lifestyle is seeing God's fingerprints in the everyday things of life, hearing the Holy One's voice in the people you spend time with during the day, listening to the quiet voice that directs you when the noise of life's demands threaten to drown your integrity out… Worship is that which happens when the stuff of earth collide with the stuff of heaven in the arena of your soul.[138]

Noel Due writes of *worship in the day-to-day,*

> There can be no doubt that worship is conducted in the day-to-day events of life. The deeds of love done in the service of the Lord are the authentic, bodily manifestations of our devotion to God the Father… These are not only our expression of worship

---

137 Parrett, Gary A. *9.5 Theses on Worship.* Carol Stream, IL: Christianity Today, February 2005, Vol. 49, No. 2, Page 38.

138 Warren, Rick ©2004. Reprinted from the website www.purposedriven.com. Used by permission. All rights reserved.

TO God, but they lead to the worship OF God, as others see his love in action and glorify him on account of it.[139]

In his book, *Lifestyle Worship: How to Bring Worship into Your Daily Life,* John Garmo writes,

> Lifestyle worship will benefit us, but it is not primarily for our benefit. If our focus is ultimately on ourselves, then we fall into the witless trap of worshiping a compromised creation instead of our incomparable Creator. Such truncated vision will produce personal barrenness. Lifestyle worship is sacrificial. A sacrifice is a gift of the essence or the product of our lives. It may be a gift of our time, a gift of our talent, or a gift of our treasure. Whatever shape it takes, it is a sacrifice given with no regard for a return on the investment.[140]

In his book, *The Air I Breathe: Worship as a Way of Life,* Louie Giglio offers some insightful thoughts on the word *continually* used in Hebrews 13:15.

> Continually gets our worship outside the walls of the church building. Continually gets our worship outside of our devotional times. Continually gets worship outside of our Christian conferences, our worship events, our MP3 players, our headphones. Continually gets worship into the marketplace, into our hangout places, into our conversations with friends, into our Starbucks moments… God wants our lives to be a seamless cord of worship. God wants our worship to be a way of life.[141]

In *Worshipping God: Rediscovering the Full Dimension of Worship,* R. T. Kendall writes,

---

139   Due, Noel. *Created for Worship: From Genesis to Revelation to You.* Scotland: Mentor Imprints, 2005, pp. 232-33. www.christianfocus.com

140   Garmo, John. *Lifestyle Worship: How to Bring Worship into Your Daily Life.* Nashville, TN: Thomas Nelson Publishers, 1993.

141   Giglio, Louie. *The Air I Breathe: Worship as a Way of Life.* Sisters, OR: Multnomah, 2003.

What we are individually, twenty-four hours a day, is more important than what happens in church once a week. The secret of acceptable worship lies in how we are at home, or at work, and when we are alone and nobody knows what we are doing. It lies in our total lifestyle… If we don't get our act together before we come to church, we can't expect to worship at church. We can't expect something magical to happen once we're inside the church doors.[142]

MANDATE FOR EVERYDAY WORSHIP

In previous chapters we have seen that New Testament worship places little value on either location or external form. Christ said,

Believe me, woman, a time is coming when you will worship the Father neither on this mountain nor in Jerusalem… Yet a time is coming and has now come when the true worshipers will worship the Father in spirit and truth, for they are the kind of worshipers the Father seeks. God is spirit, and his worshipers must worship in spirit and in truth (John 4:21-24 NIV).

Christ also clearly differentiated between worship as form and worship as substance, emphasizing that worship is an inner experience when He said, "These people honor me with their lips, but their hearts are far from me" (Matthew 15:8 NIV).

In his book, *True Worship,* John MacArthur writes,

Worship doesn't occur in a vacuum, nor is it stimulated by artificial gimmickry. If you have to be in a church building or hear a certain kind of mood music to worship, what you're doing isn't worship. You should be able to worship God on the freeway during

---

142   Kendall, R. T. *Worshipping God: Rediscovering the Full Dimension of Worship.* London: Hodder & Stoughton, 1999.

rush hour. But to do so, your heart must be right... Worship must be a way of life![143]

As John Piper states in his article, *All of Life as Worship,* "Worship is the real, authentic experience in the heart with God, or it is nothing."[144] Piper goes on to state,

> If the vital essence of that inner experience we call worship is a being satisfied in God or cherishing Christ as gain above all things, this accounts for why Romans 12:1-2 portrays all of life as worship... we get up in the morning and we get our hearts fixed on Christ. We go to him and renew our satisfaction in him through his word. And then we enter the day seeking to express and increase that satisfaction in all that God is for us in Jesus.[145]

MANIFESTO FOR EVERYDAY WORSHIP

The writer to the Hebrews summarizes the essence of a worshiping life when he says, "Through Jesus, therefore, let us continually offer to God a sacrifice of praise—the fruit of lips that confess his name. And do not forget to do good and to share with others, for with such sacrifices God is pleased" (Hebrews 13: 15-16 NIV). The praise that we offer to God in corporate worship has no value unless it is accompanied by loving action in *everyday worship.*

In the final verses of the previous chapter, the writer to the Hebrews enjoins us, "Therefore, since we are receiving a kingdom that cannot be shaken, let us be thankful, and so worship God acceptably with reverence and awe, for our 'God is a consuming fire'" (Hebrews 12:28 NIV). As we saw in the closing verses of Romans

---

143   MacArthur, John F. *True Worship.* Panorama City, CA: Word of Grace Communications, 1982, 1985.

144   https://www.desiringgod.org/messages/all-of-life-as-worship

145   Ibid.

11 and the opening verses of chapter 12, here again the verses that follow in Hebrews 13 are linked to the closing verses of Hebrews 12. The writer continues,

> Keep on loving each other as brothers. Do not forget to entertain strangers, for by so doing some people have entertained angels without knowing it. Remember those in prison as if you were their fellow prisoners, and those who are mistreated as if you yourselves were suffering. Marriage should be honored by all, and the marriage bed kept pure, for God will judge the adulterer and all the sexually immoral. Keep your lives free from the love of money and be content with what you have... Remember your leaders, who spoke the word of God to you. Consider the outcome of their way of life and imitate their faith... Do not be carried away by all kinds of strange teachings. It is good for our hearts to be strengthened by grace, not by ceremonial foods, which are of no value to those who eat them (Hebrews 13:1-9 NIV).

All of these injunctions are part and parcel of our calling to practice *everyday worship*. Again, without excessive commentary, we can observe the clear and evident principles that are contained within the text.

1. *Everyday worship* involves the continuous act offering to God a sacrifice of praise—the fruit of our lips in confessing the glory of his name.

2. *Everyday worship* engages the believer in the practice of doing good by sharing of our material substance with others—a sacrifice with which God is pleased.

3. *Everyday worship* is evidenced in the continuance of expressing and extending love to our fellow believers, regarding them as family members.

4. *Everyday worship* may result in our oblivious "entertaining" of angels when we extend the grace and kindness extolled in the previous statement.

5. *Everyday worship* remembers those imprisoned as if you were chained to their sides, and empathizes with those who are mistreated as if you were experiencing the same degree of suffering in your own life.

6. *Everyday worship* is reflected in marital fidelity and in sexual purity.

7. *Everyday worship* is marked by the absence of materialism and the presence of contentment.

8. *Everyday worship* demonstrates respect for those in leadership who speak the word of God, and whose lives warrant imitation.

9. *Everyday worship* resists the winds of strange teachings and refuses the trap of legalism.

The significance of these instructions as they relate to *everyday worship* is illuminated by an understanding of the word "serve" that is found in the text in Hebrews 12:28. The word that is used for "serve" is the Greek verb *latreuo* which when properly translated simply means "worship." It is the same derivative used in Hebrews 10:2 as a noun where it is translated "worshipers." As John MacArthur points out, what the writer is saying is simply that, "Since we have received the kingdom which cannot be moved, and since we have become worshipers of God, then let us have the graciousness to respond to God who has made us worshipers, by worshiping God acceptably."[146]

---

146   MacArthur, John F. *True Worship.* Panorama City, CA: Word of Grace Communications, 1982, 1985.

IF WORSHIP IS AN *EVERYDAY* EVENT,
WHAT'S SO SPECIAL ABOUT SUNDAY?

While throughout my pre-adolescence and into my teenage years I loved the experience of going to church, I can remember in earlier childhood that this was not necessarily the case. We used to raise our voices and clap our hands as we would lustily sing, "Every day will be Sunday by and by; there'll be no blue Mondays in the sky." I can remember thinking, "Hmm…really? Is that something I *truly* look forward to?" I remember hearing a story of a young boy who began attending church with his mother when she returned to her childhood roots after having been away from the church for a long period of time. He was very inquisitive about every part of the service, and would poke his mother's side, continually asking questions as to the significance of every activity and all of the furnishings. He saw two flags mounted on the platform: one was the American flag, and the other was the Christian flag. Having asked his mother what they represented, she replied, "The Christian flag represents our faith as Christians, and the American flag is in memory of the 'boys that died in the service.'" The little guy immediately posed this innocent but interesting question: "Which service did they die in, Mom, the morning or the evening service?"

Clearly, worship is an *everyday* demonstration of the life of the believer. And it is this *everyday* practice that gives life and vitality to the corporate gathering of believers when the church comes together in community on the Lord's Day. Even though our worship is to be a way of life, it is our corporate worship that equips us for service, and stimulates us to worship during the rest of the week. Once again the writer to the Hebrews enlightens us when he says,

> Therefore, brothers, since we have confidence to enter the
> Most Holy Place by the blood of Jesus, by a new and living way

opened for us through the curtain, that is, his body, and since we have a great priest over the house of God, let us draw near to God with a sincere heart in full assurance of faith, having our hearts sprinkled to cleanse us from a guilty conscience and having our bodies washed with pure water. Let us hold unswervingly to the hope we profess, for he who promised is faithful. And let us consider how we may spur one another on toward love and good deeds. Let us not give up meeting together, as some are in the habit of doing, but let us encourage one another—and all the more as you see the Day approaching (Hebrews 10:19-25 NIV).

These two facets that I have described as *Everyday Worship* and *Sunday Best* are intricately and inexorably woven together. It is by living a sharing and righteous life beyond the walls of the church that we are able to worship with integrity when we assemble with the congregation of God. The cycle is then complete when having been stimulated while in the fellowship of the church we go about our everyday lives sharing and doing good, and then return to the assembly of the saints, overflowing in praise and worshipful giving of thanks to God. The worship that we have individually enjoyed is enriched and enhanced in the joy of the assembly of the redeemed. This results in a life of worship that becomes even more glorious.

And while we are encouraged to approach God with boldness and confidence, we are not to do so with arrogance or pride. Our worship must never be rushed, rash nor brash; it is to be characterized by brokenness, contrition, confession and repentance of sin, and the appropriation of God's provision of forgiveness. As a Holy God, and as our Heavenly Father, God reserves the prerogative of chastening us to produce holiness in our lives (Hebrews 12:4-11).

A TALE OF THREE TEMPLES

1. The temple of our individual bodies

The truth of *everyday worship* recognizes that our bodies are the "temples of the Holy Spirit" as Paul taught in 1 Corinthians 6:19, "Do you not know that your body is a temple of the Holy Spirit, who is in you, whom you have received from God? You are not your own; you were bought at a price. Therefore honor God with your body" (I Corinthians 6:19-20 NIV).

Clearly, we can worship God anywhere, under any kind of circumstance or condition, since in redemption Christ has re-created us as living, breathing temples in whom the life and Spirit of God dwells.

2. The temple of God in Christ

In a sermon preached in Athens, Paul declared, "The God who made the world and everything in it is the Lord of heaven and earth and does not live in temples built by hands" (Acts 17:21 NIV). Upon careful scrutiny of the Bible, we will find that in actual fact, there are no gatherings that are called *worship services* in the entirety of the New Testament.

The attitude of our Lord towards the Temple, which was the centre for Jewish worship, offended and angered the religious leaders of His day. Interestingly, His description of that temple was *not* as a place to offer sacrifices for sins, but as a place of prayer. In Mark 11:17, He declares, "Is it not written: 'My house will be called a house of prayer for all nations? But you have made it 'a den of robbers'" (Mark 11:17 NIV). Two other statements of Christ concerning the temple indicate a dramatically different perspective on worship. Referring to Himself, He said, "I tell you that one greater than the temple is here" (Matthew 12:6 NIV). Again in reference to Himself, He states, "Destroy this temple, and I will raise it again in three days" (John 2:19 NIV). It was this attitude towards the temple that aroused adequate resentment and anger among the Jewish leaders to conspire to put Him to death. When Stephen reflected and reiterated the identical attitude towards the centre of Jewish worship, the religious leaders responded in hateful anger and stoned him to death (Acts 6:8-15).

By identifying himself as the true Temple, Christ was indicating that in Himself he would fulfill everything the Temple stood for, *including* the place where believers meet God. He diverts attention away from worship as having either a geographical centre or being associated with outward ritual. He makes it a personal, spiritual experience with himself at the center. True worship requires neither a building, priesthood nor a sacrificial system—all of these have been fulfilled in Christ—true worship requires the glorious presence of the risen Christ.

3. The temple of our collective assembly

While in the New Testament there is very little instruction that deals explicitly with corporate worship, the Scriptures refer to the followers of Christ gathering together for the purpose of worship. Paul peaks of "the whole church gathering together" in I Corinthians 14:23 and Acts 2:46 records that the early church engaged in "attending the temple together and breaking bread in their homes." And in Hebrews we are exhorted to "not give up meeting together, as some are in the habit of doing, but let us encourage one another" (Hebrews 10:25 NIV).

It is important to note that while these gatherings are spoken of by the apostles, they are not *explicitly* referred to as "worship gatherings." However, since they continued in the pattern of synagogue worship, the assumption is that worship was a primary purpose for their assembly.

While Christ Himself is our Temple, and there is no central location prescribed as the place of worship in the New Testament, there is, however, a *place* of worship today. And it is a *building* where God uniquely meets with His people—but it is not a physical building with any human architect responsible for its design. It is the building of God.

In writing to the Ephesians, Paul describes believers *collectively*, rather than as disconnected, individual temples.

> Consequently, you are no longer foreigners and aliens, but fellow citizens with God's people and members of God's household, built on the foundation of the apostles and prophets, with Christ Jesus himself as the chief cornerstone. In him the whole building is joined together and rises to become a holy temple in the Lord. And in him you too are being built together to become a dwelling in which God lives by his Spirit (Ephesians 2:19-22 NIV).

This passage paints several graphic descriptions that portray the collective assembly of Christian believers:

1. We are fellow citizens—not foreigners, strangers, sojourners, or aliens—but fellow citizens with the people of god.

2. We all belong to "the household of God". In other words, having been born of the Spirit and received the *adoption of sons* we are now linked by common blood as the family of God.

3. We are also linked together as a *living* building. We are secure on the firm foundation of the apostles and prophets,

and Jesus Christ himself is the chief cornerstone of this building.

4. This building of God is not only *firmly founded*, but is also *fitly framed*. Further, as a *living* building, it continues to grow together and creates a holy temple in and for the Lord.

5. This *living* building has been divinely designed to become God's special dwelling place, a "habitation of God through the Spirit."

God's special building, therefore, is the visible, living assembly of the redeemed saints. When we assemble together, we constitute the temple of God in a very unique way. So, not only are we individually temples of God; collectively we are one great temple in which God dwells.

Peter picks up this same theme when he writes, "You also, like living stones, are being built into a spiritual house to be a holy priesthood, offering spiritual sacrifices acceptable to God through Jesus Christ" (I Peter 2:5 NIV). While we can worship God in isolation and privacy, and do worship Him in everyday life, we must also worship God in the assembly of His redeemed people to "stimulate one another to love and good deeds" (Heb. 10:24 NASB).[147] And although worshiping God is *not* a geographical issue, we do come together as God's redeemed people in corporate worship. As a living priesthood of believers, we don't require special priests or a sacrificial system, since Christ our lamb has been offered once for all, and we have immediate access to God through His blood.

---

147   The Lockman Foundation, *New American Standard Bible (NASB)*, © 1960, 1962, 1963, 1968, 1971, 1972, 1973, 1975, 1977, 1995.

CHRIST OUR MEETING PLACE

Our Lord affirmed, "For where two or three come together in my name, there am I with them" (Matthew 18:20 NIV). I remember that passage being cited from the pulpit many times in my childhood as an effort to justify the scant handful of believers that had gathered to worship. We must note that what Christ referred to here was a *plurality in unity*. It spoke to a gathering in the unity of faith in Jesus and in obedience to his promise. He was not speaking of the *detached individualism* that is so common in many church gatherings today. Upon closer examination, we discover several important principles that pertain to our gathering together corporately as the Body of Christ.

1. It is on the authority of Christ that we assemble to worship Him. We don't gather any given Sunday from the sheer herd instinct or for social reasons. We do so in obedience to the mandate of our Lord.

2. It is in union with Christ and His followers that we congregate. We gather in "His Name." To do so declares our faith in Him. It is our unity in Christ that compels us to come together.

3. It is in a unity of our faith, the confession that Jesus is the Son of God that we assemble with believers of like mind.

4. It is to ultimately meet with Christ and not merely with one another that we assemble in His Name. We do so in anticipation of the fulfillment of His promise, "There am I in the midst of them." Our expectation is that in our assembly as believers we will experience the unique and special presence of our Lord.

The Tabernacle of Moses in the Old Testament was called the tent of *meeting*. Implicit in this statement is that it was where God's chosen people met with Him (Exodus 29:42). Since Christ is now the tabernacle, he has fulfilled that to which the tabernacle in Israel pointed symbolically and with anticipation. We meet with God in Christ. **He** is our Meeting Place! Paul stresses this truth when he writes to the Ephesian believers,

> But now in Christ Jesus you who once were far away have been brought near through the blood of Christ. For he himself is our peace, who has made the two one and has destroyed the barrier, the dividing wall of hostility, by abolishing in his flesh the law with its commandments and regulations. His purpose was to create in himself one new man out of the two, thus making peace, and in this one body to reconcile both of them to God through the cross, by which he put to death their hostility. He came and preached peace to you who were far away and peace to those who were near. For through him we both have access to the Father by one Spirit (Ephesians 2: 13-18 NIV).

Again, when writing to the Galatians Paul emphasizes the fact of our becoming one in Christ when he writes,

> You are all sons of God through faith in Christ Jesus, for all of you who were baptized into Christ have clothed yourselves with Christ. There is neither Jew nor Greek, slave nor free, male nor female, for you are all one in Christ Jesus. If you belong to Christ, then you are Abraham's seed, and heirs according to the promise (Galatians 3:26-29 NIV).

ARE THERE BIBLICAL *BEST PRACTICES* AGAINST
WHICH TO BENCHMARK OUR SUNDAY BEST?

Most scholars assume that early Christian worship was patterned after synagogue worship. From a website on Jewish liturgics, we learn:

The origin of liturgical worship in Judaism is clearly grounded, according to the Bible and Tradition, in the revelation of God... A clear form of worship and the atmosphere within which it was to take place was part of the revelation of God to the Children of Israel... Equally important to understand is that the worship form revealed by God to the Children of Israel was not 'just ceremonial and centered around sacrifice. According to the very same revelation, it was to reflect worship in heaven. The Torah has many instances (Isaiah chapter 6 and Daniel chapter 7) which describe worship in heaven... During the exile, however, a new form of worship had developed in the absence of the Temple: the synagogue. Originally conceived as a meeting of the faithful to pray, to hear the Torah read, and to receive instruction, over time synagogue worship flourished... The synagogue became the local house of worship... Synagogue worship, in contrast to the sacrificial forms of the Temple, was characterized by recitation of prayer, chant of the Psalms, reading from The Torah and instruction... The rise of the synagogue tradition during the exile was principally didactic (focused on teaching) rather than the sacrificial worship of the Temple, and it developed its own chant traditions. Many of these traditions were brought back to Israel after the exile and found their way into Temple worship. After the destruction of the Second Temple by the Romans in 70 A.D., synagogue worship and its liturgical form became the central aspect of Jewish worship.[148]

---

148 http://liturgica.com/home/litJLit

THE SYNAGOGUE MODEL

We know from historical sources that synagogue worship was comprised of four essential components: prayer, praise, the reading of Scripture and the preaching of Scripture. And we also know from the Biblical record in the book of Acts, that the first apostles of our Lord followed in that same tradition.

> Besides the structure or order of worship that came from Judaism into Christianity, one can also find the cycles of liturgy— the daily, weekly and yearly cycles of worship-coming from the Old Testament as well. Acts 2:46 says that 'day by day, continuing steadfastly with one accord in the temple, and breaking bread at home, they took their food with gladness and singleness of heart'. On a daily basis the Apostles continued their Jewish worship practices in the temple, and on a daily basis broke the bread of communion. This regularity of time is further confirmed in Acts 3:1 where Peter and John were going to the temple because it was the hour of prayer. Not only did they continue in Jewish worship practice, but they kept the liturgical cycle of daily prayers at set hours of the day as well as the major feast days. Christian worship, then, was a Christ-centered pattern that continued and preserved the traditional structure of synagogue worship and the meaning of temple worship that the Lord had established in Israel.[149]

The New Testament offers additional insight into early Christian worship. Acts 2:42 mentions that the disciples gathered daily for "the apostles' teaching and to the fellowship, to the breaking of bread and to prayer." The "breaking of bread" mentioned may have been the Lord's Supper, or it could also have simply referred to a fellowship meal. Paul provided instructions for worship to the Corinthian

---

149   ibid

church in I Corinthians chapters 11 through 14. These instructions dealt with matters of prayer, the Lord's Supper and spiritual gifts. Because of Paul's mention of charismatic gifts, many today have formed the impression that worship in the early church was totally free-flowing and without structure. However, Paul's instructions concerning the Lord's Supper would seem to indicate that their worship included some elements of structure.

WHY WE OBSERVE SUNDAY

It is also important to note that whereas the Jews observed the seventh day, the Sabbath, as God had commanded, the Christians broke with that tradition by meeting on Sunday, the first day of the week. The Book of Acts describes such a gathering, "On the first day of the week we came together to break bread. Paul spoke to the people and, because he intended to leave the next day, kept on talking until midnight" (Acts 20:7 NIV). I remember as a child when our church services would go on and on, that I sometimes thought this passage must be the one upon which the preacher was basing his long-winded sermon!

Paul implies that the first day of the week was the day set aside for corporate worship when he wrote, "The first day of every week, each one of you should set aside a sum of money in keeping with his income, saving it up, so that when I come no collections will have to be made" (I Corinthians 16:2 NIV). And, it was on "the Lord's Day" that John was in the spirit, "On the Lord's Day I was in the Spirit" (Revelation 1:10 NIV).

Clearly, as Christian believers, we are to worship God the first day of the week in celebration of the fact that our Lord rose from the dead on that day, and a fundamental purpose of our gathering is to praise God, lift up the cross and resurrection, and celebrate His redemptive love. However, I believe there is another important principle behind the observation of the first day of the week that goes largely unnoticed. The Sabbath principle was instituted by God for man. God said, "Six days thou shalt do thy work, and on the seventh day thou shalt rest" (Exodus 20:9, Exodus 23:12, Exodus 34:21, Deuteronomy 5:13). Implicit in this, is that man was *required* to work for six days before he was *entitled* to a day of rest. Resident in this is the concept of works *first*, reward *second*. However, the economy of grace has turned this concept on its head. When Christ uttered, "It is finished," the work of redemption was complete, and He sat down on the right hand of God. The writer to the Hebrews states, "After he had provided purification for sins, he sat down at the right hand of the Majesty in heaven" (Hebrews 1:3 NIV) and "He entered the Most Holy Place once for all by his own blood, having obtained eternal redemption" (Hebrews 9:12 NIV). Just as God rested on the seventh day in a perfect work of creation, so Christ sat down having completed a perfect work of redemption.

Paul extols this truth of the exaltation of Christ to a position of supremacy in his letter to the Ephesian church when he says,

> That power is like the working of his mighty strength, which he exerted in Christ when he raised him from the dead and seated him at his right hand in the heavenly realms, far above all rule and authority, power and dominion, and every title that can be given, not only in the present age but also in the one to come. And God placed all things under his feet and appointed him to be head over everything for the church, which is his body, the fullness of him who fills everything in every way (Ephesians 1:19-23 NIV).

Having eloquently described the exaltation of our Lord, in the very next chapter, Paul writes of the believer's status as being seated together with Christ when he states, "And God raised us up with Christ and seated us with him in the heavenly realms in Christ Jesus" (Ephesians 2:6 NIV).

Enthroned in heaven, He has seated us together with Him, and now invites us to enter into the rest provided by His perfected work of redemption. The writer to Hebrews speaks of this rest, "There remains, then, a Sabbath-rest for the people of God; for anyone who enters God's rest also rests from his own work, just as God did from his" (Hebrews 4:0-10 NIV). In the economy of grace, God gives us the rest first, and then we go forth to serve Him!

Clearly, the New Testament Scriptures teach us by practice, precedent and principle that it is God-honoring and Biblical to observe the first day of the week as the day on which we gather for congregational worship. If, then, the Scriptures are clear concerning the primary day for corporate worship, are they also clear as to the pattern of worship to be observed when we assemble in the name of the Lord?

IS THERE A BIBLICAL PATTERN FOR WORSHIP?

In an article entitled, *God's Pattern for Worship: The History of 'Doing Church' through the Centuries,* Richard Joseph Krejcir states:

> The principle pattern of worship has existed from the beginning; it has been refined as humanity grew in understanding of God and as He revealed Himself to us. The standard church meeting we have today still has the original pattern that God instituted. We gather to worship through singing, prayer, liturgy, the reading of the Word, and a message/sermon/homily. Each denomination and individual church has added traditions of man in the mix. Hence, the various worship styles, orders, preaching, and building architectures. These

minor differences need not be debated, as there are many ways to express our devotion and love to the Lord. The important thing is to honor Him in the proper pattern and essentials. The intention of doing church remains steadfast for the most part. There are churches that are apostate and forget God and do their own thing. As a community of believers, a part of the universal Church, and the bride of Christ, we are to follow the pattern that the Bible lays out. And, it should be the same through all denominations that acknowledge Christ as LORD.[150]

WHAT DO WE MEAN BY *SOLA SCIPTURA?*

The Reformers applied *sola scriptura* to worship in a tenet they described as the regulative principle. It was John Calvin who first articulated it succinctly:

> We may not adopt any device [in our worship] which seems fit to ourselves, but look to the injunctions of him who alone is entitled to prescribe. Therefore, if we would have Him approve our worship, this rule, which he everywhere enforces with the utmost strictness, must be carefully observed… God disapproves of all modes of worship not expressly sanctioned by his word. [151]

John Hooper, an English contemporary of Calvin, expressed the same principle in these words: "Nothing should be used in the Church which has not either the express Word of God to support it, or otherwise is a thing indifferent in itself, which brings no profit when done or used, but no harm when not done or omitted."[152]

---

150   Krejcir, Richard Joseph. *God's Pattern for Worship: The History of 'Doing Church' through the Centuries.* http://www.intothyword.org/apps/articles/default.asp?articleid=32875

151   Calvin, John. *The Necessity of Reforming the Church* (Dallas: Protestant Heritage Press, 1995 reprint), 17-18.

152   Hooper, John. *The Regulative Principle and Things Indifferent.* Found in Iain H. Murray, *The Reformation of the Church* (Edinburgh: Banner of Truth, 1965), 55.

While the intent of the Reformers and Puritans in applying the regulative principle was to guard against formal ritual, priestly vestments, church hierarchy, and other remnants of medieval Roman Catholic worship, its commitment to *sola scriptura* is a principle, which if adhered to, would leave many churches bereft of many of their current practices. The simplicity of worship in Presbyterian, Baptist, Congregational, and other evangelical traditions today is a legacy of the regulative principle. John MacArthur notes:

> Evangelicals today would do well to recover their spiritual ancestors' confidence in sola Scriptura as it applies to worship and church leadership… there is, as we have noted, almost a circus atmosphere in some churches where pragmatic methods that trivialize what is holy are being employed to boost attendance… Meanwhile, some churches have simply abandoned virtually all objectivity, opting for a worship style that is turbulent, emotional, and devoid of any rational sense… None of these trends are being advanced for solid biblical reasons. Instead, their advocates cite pragmatic arguments, or seek support from misinterpreted proof texts, revisionist history, or ancient tradition. This is precisely the mindset the Reformers fought against. A new understanding of sola Scriptura—the sufficiency of Scripture—ought to spur us to keep reforming our churches, to regulate our worship according to biblical guidelines, and to desire passionately to be those who worship God in spirit and truth.[153]

MacArthur goes on to indicate *four biblical guidelines for worship* that would result if the contemporary church took sola Scriptura seriously, and suggests that their recovery then would give birth to a new Reformation in the modern church's worship:

---

153   MacArthur, John F. *True Worship*. Panorama City, CA: Word of Grace Communications, 1982, 1985.

1.   Preach the Word. In corporate worship, the preaching of the Word should take first place.

2.   Edify the flock. Scripture tells us that the purpose of spiritual gifts is for the edification of the whole church (Ephesians 4:12; I Corinthians 14:12). Therefore all ministry in the context of the church should somehow be edifying—building up the flock, not just stirring emotions.

3.   Honor the Lord. Hebrews 12:28 says, "Let us show gratitude, by which we may offer to God an acceptable service with reverence and awe." That verse speaks of the attitude in which we should worship… reverently, in a way that honors God.

4.   Put no confidence in the flesh. In Philippians 3:3 the apostle Paul characterizes Christian worship this way: "We are the true circumcision, who worship in the Spirit of God and glory in Christ Jesus and put no confidence in the flesh."[154]

In 1970, I planted a new church in the town of Stephenville on the west coast of Newfoundland. The US Air Force had just vacated Harmon Field, and one of the many buildings left standing on the base was a beautiful chapel, which I rented to begin our ministry there. I recall when taking up residence in the premises that the pulpit was to the left of the congregation when they faced the altar area. Since I was not able to alter the layout of the sanctuary, one of my first priorities was to place a temporary pulpit in the center of the platform.

When the pulpit was moved to the centre of the house of worship it was done so as a declaration of the centrality of the preaching of

---

154   Ibid.

God's Word to our New Testament worship. The entire church service should revolve around the ministry of God's Word with all else being viewed as either preparatory for or responsive to the message from the Scriptures. As MacArthur boldly states, "When drama, music, comedy, or other activities are allowed to usurp the preaching of the Word, true worship inevitably suffers."[155] In his excellent book *Between Two Worlds*, John Stott says it well:

> Word and worship belong indissolubly to each other. All worship is an intelligent and loving response to the revelation of God, because it is the adoration of his Name. Therefore acceptable worship is impossible without preaching. For preaching is making known the Name of the Lord, and worship is praising the Name of the Lord made known. Far from being an alien intrusion into worship, the reading and preaching of the word are actually indispensable to it. The two cannot be divorced.[156]

IS THERE A BIBLICAL ORDER FOR THE ELEMENTS OF A WORSHIP SERVICE?

It is not unusual for churches to publish an "order of worship" in their Sunday bulletin. This practice might cause us to ponder whether there is actually any Biblical order for a worship service. To the Corinthian church, Paul wrote, "But everything should be done in a fitting and orderly way" (I Corinthians 14:40 NIV).

While he gives clear instructions to Timothy concerning certain elements of order in the church, his writings lack any clear instruction regarding the order for a congregational gathering.

---

155   Ibid.

156   Stott, John R. W. *Between Two Worlds*. Grand Rapids, MI: Eerdmans Publishing Company, 1982.

Paul instructs, "I urge, then, first of all, that requests, prayers, intercession and thanksgiving be made for everyone— for kings and all those in authority, that we may live peaceful and quiet lives in all godliness and holiness" (I Timothy 2:1 NIV) and "I want men every-where to lift up holy hands in prayer, without anger or disputing" (I Timothy 1:8 NIV).

In I Timothy 3, he offers clear guidelines for the qualifications of both bishops and deacons, and offers instructions for the care of widows in the congregation in I Timothy 5. In his second letter to Timothy, he continues his instructions regarding Timothy's respon-sibility in preaching and teaching of the Word of God. But nowhere, does he offer guidelines for the order of a congregational gathering in worship.

In *Worship & Worship Services, Biblical Studies in Worship & Worship Services*, Gregg Strawbridge notes:

> If there were ever days when the Church worshiped with one voice in a unison cadence, those days are gone, for now. After the Protestant Reformation in the sixteenth century, the tapestry of Christian worship disintegrated. The seventeenth century became the fountain head for Protestant thought… with the Westminster Confession… though no clear unity of worship practice had been reached. Then, riding the waves of revival and revivalism, eigh-teenth and nineteenth century evangelicals followed many threads of the tapestry of Christian worship. The culmination of this has apexes in a quite sermon-centered, evangelism-centered worship service. Songs and a few necessary items, like offerings are to give way to the pastor's 'message.' In this century, the impact of the Pentecostal and Charismatic movement alone accounts for a full facelift of traditional worship. While liturgical patterns drone on, 'world without end,' the ecstatic expressions of 'praise and worship'

have revitalized the worship of virtually every church, in every communion. There are deeper influences which contribute to an often unhealthy diversity in worship: the emphasis on individualism and the increased role of the psychology of self. We live in a frightfully unique time in the history of the church where the concept of sin is publicly repudiated (even from some pulpits). It is a sin to talk of sin. Salvation is dangerously connected to self-esteem. It seems that all the factors that make up the American mind significantly contribute to the modern kaleidoscope of American worship. With the diversity of church traditions, modern technological influences, and fundamental theological and psychological perspectives intersecting on Sunday morning, there is no end to the array of contemporary approaches to worship.[157]

Clearly, no Biblical precept or precedent can be advanced to establish a structure for the elements of worship in the corporate gathering of believers. However, the essential elements can be identified, and those will include:

1. Honoring God with reverence and awe as we assemble to worship Him

2. Praising His Name in congregational singing of hymns, psalms and spiritual songs

3. Confessing of our sin to God and receiving the cleansing of His forgiveness

4. Offering of prayers, with intercession, and thanksgiving, as well as supplication.

---

157 Strawbridge, Gregg. *Worship & Worship Services, Biblical Studies in Worship & Worship Services.* http://www.wordmp3.com/gs/wws.htm

5.   Reading of the Word of God and responding to the same

6.   Applying of the Word of God by the leader or pastor in the sermon or homily

7.   Fellowshipping with fellow believers to build up one another and the church

Richard Joseph Krejcir states,

> Our understanding of what a church worship service is must reflect the precepts of Scripture. This includes our influence, and the format of our worship services. Our influence must not be just trends or data from surveys. It must be from His Word, period! We can mix in new ideas, such as songs, prayers, ways of delivering the sermon, but not the fundamentals; nothing we do in doing church can contradict God's Word![158]

In his article, entitled, *Why We Worship the Way We Do*, Andrew James Webb lists and describes in some depth what he holds to be the essential elements of Christian worship in the corporate gathering of believers.

1.   Prayer

2.   The Reading of Scriptures

3.   The Sound Preaching of the Word

4.   The Attentive Hearing of the Word

5.   The Singing of Psalms, Hymns, and Spiritual Songs with Grace in the Heart

6.   The Public Confession of Our Faith

Krejcir, Richard Joseph, *God's Pattern for Worship: The History of 'Doing Church' through the Centuries.* http://www.intothyword.org/apps/articles/default.asp?articleid=32875

7. The Collection

8. The Due Administration and Right Receiving of the Sacraments[159]

In *Engaging With God: A Biblical Theology of Worship*, David Peterson wrote, "Church meetings should not be regarded simply as a means to an end—a preparation for worship and witness in everyday life—but as 'the focus-point of that whole wider worship which is the continually repeated self-surrender of the Christian in obedience of life.'" [160]

When we gather, therefore, on any given Sunday, it is not to find an escape from the world, but to worship our Lord, affirm our faith in His redemptive work and to receive encouragement to demonstrate our confidence in Christ in an unbelieving world. Our Lord is worthy of worship, not only when we gather, but at every moment of time, by every creature in creation, for all eternity. That mindset must be the goal not only of our corporate worship but also of our entire lives.

DIVERSITY, RELEVANCE AND INCLUSIVENESS IN WORSHIP

Since I am no longer pastoring nor involved in church leadership, I don't have to grapple with the challenge of planning and structuring the Sunday worship services to meet the diverse tastes of the various palettes that will be represented in a congregation on any given Lord's Day. While I don't want to fall into the trap of becoming an ecclesiastical "armchair quarterback" this does afford me the opportunity

159   https://www.sermonaudio.com/search.asp?seriesOnly=true&currSection=sermonstopic&sourceid=providence pca&keyword=Why+We+Worship+the+Way+We+Do&keyworddesc=Why+We+Worship+the+Way+We+Do

160   Peterson, David. *Engaging With God: A Biblical Theology of Worship*. Downers Grove, IL: InterVarsity Press, 2002.

to objectively reflect on the disparate styles of worship that I observe in Sunday gatherings. Furthermore, since my current vocation is engaging managers and leaders of companies in an effort to increase the effectiveness of their organizations, I am immersed in a multitude of theories and practices that will undoubtedly inform my approach on how to engage a congregation of believers in responding to the claims of Christ in their worship encounter. My challenge, therefore, is to remain faithful to God's Word as I attempt to address this sensitive and controversial concern.

The question before us then, is to what degree should a congregation be sensitized to the issues of diversity, relevance and inclusiveness in planning the worship service? If we exercise a hermeneutic that seeks to interpret Scriptures in the context of their culture in which they were written, should it not follow that we should exercise the same consideration in the application of the Scriptures as they relate to the most important business of the church—that of worship?

While I am not recommending that we dilute the gospel, or depart from the clear teachings of Scripture, I am suggesting that we give some consideration to the mix, makeup and mosaic of the congregation that has assembled to worship our Lord.

HOW DIFFERENT GENERATIONS APPROACH WORSHIP

One of the courses that I conduct for managers and leaders in organization is called *Generational Management*. In that program we talk about the differences in values, learning styles, approach to work and life that distinguish the various generations. In a similar sense, the manner in which Baby Boomers, Generation X and the Millennial worship God may significantly differ. In *A Church for the 21st*

Century[161], Leith Anderson quotes Gary McIntosh[162] in showing how those distinctions in worship preference are manifest in the various generations.

Whereas the pre-boomer generation (also referred to as the Veterans or the "great generation") prefer an atmosphere of reverence and quietness, baby-boomers and subsequent generations prefer one where people can be heard talking. The musical preference of the pre-boomers is for hymns with organ and piano. Baby boomers and baby busters (also known as "Generation X") both prefer praise songs, and while boomers prefer guitars and drums, the baby buster generations might prefer a jazz ensemble. Pre-boomers are accustomed to a pastoral prayer, whereas both boomers and busters prefer to see various people led in prayer. Pre-boomers have a preference for expository sermons, baby boomers for "how-to" sermons, and baby busters for sermons related to specific issues. Interestingly, when it comes to participation, the baby busters have returned to the taste of the pre-boomers in preferring lower audience participation, while baby boomers have a preference for a higher level of participation.

The preferences of the various generations and the differences in taste that are thereby reflected are at the core of much of the conflict in today's church that surrounds the subject of worship. In every generation, parents struggle with the style of music that their children want to listen to, while their children love to laugh and poke fun at the music their parents in enjoy.

In his book, *The Spectacle of Worship in a Wired World,* Tex Sample describes how the electronic culture has changed the way in

---

161 Anderson,Leith. *A Church for the 21st Century.* Bloomington, MN: Bethany House, 1992.
162 McIntosh, Gary L. *One Size Doesn't Fit All.* Grand Rapids, MI: Revell, 1999.

which the various generations engage with their world and states that our worship will need to adapt. Specifically, Sample asserts that the church must ensure that worship for this electronic era is based on images, sound as beat, and visualization. He describes why different generations approach worship so differently.[163] In Chapter Seven of his *Worship Leader's Manual*, Mark Tittley, Director of Sonlife Africa offers this summary of Sample's comments:

> Earlier generations grew up in an oral world where they engaged the world through proverbs, story and relationships thinking. Issues were dealt with in terms of their effect on their kin, neighbors and the relationships they had. After this there came a literate world where people thought in terms of propositional claims, in theory and conceptualization, and where they developed ideas in linear discourse. But the Boomers, Xers and Millennials grew up in a post-literate, electronic world. They think in terms of images, sound and visualization. It is significant to note that those who have been most influenced by electronic culture participate in church at far lower levels than those of previous generations.[164]

WHAT DO WE MEAN BY CONTEMPORARY WORSHIP?

One of the traps that my generation must avoid is holding contemporary worship in contempt due to our own tastes and preferences while attempting to cloak those preferences with fancy theological footwork and proof-texts. Our challenge is to maintain honesty about our alleged commitment to the *sola scriptura* principle while remaining objective about trends that may not be to our particular

163 Sample, Tex. *The Spectacle of Worship in a Wired World: Electronic Culture and the Gathered People of God.* Nashville, TN: Abingdon Press, 1998.

164 Tittley, Mark. *The Worship Leader's Manual.* Sonlife Africa, 2003.

taste or preference. In his book, *Soul Tsunami,* [165] Leonard Sweet uses the acronym "EPIC" to describe the essential elements of contemporary worship. EPIC stands for worship that is Experiential, Participatory, Interactive and Communal. In his *Worship Leader's Manual,*[166] Mark Tittley suggests that the following represents the characteristics of contemporary worship:

- Worship that connects with everyday life

- Worship that is sensory—people are encouraged to bring their senses into worship

- Worship that is experiential—the worship is an experience more than a discourse

- Worship that is filled with movement—people are allowed and encouraged to move about

- Opportunity to express intimate love and worship to God—participatory not spectatory

- A structure that is dramatic—it moves one from unawareness of God to awareness of God

- Music that is similar to the genre that music worshippers would naturally chose to listen to at home

- Using a large percentage of music written in the current or last decade

- Music that has lots of instrumentation—drums, lead guitars, bass guitar, synthesizer

- Songs that express intimacy (immanence) more that 'distance' (transcendence)

---

165   Sweet, Leonard. *Soultsunami.* Grand Rapids, MI: Zondervan, 2001.

166   Tittley, Mark. The *Worship Leaders Manual.* Sonlife Africa, 2003.

- Songs that use metaphor—especially metaphors that are sensory-orientated

- A smooth flow—i.e. songs that flow into one another with minimal sermonizing

- A large percentage of songs that address God directly and not indirectly

Bill Easum in *Growing Spiritual Redwoods*,[167] offers this analysis of contemporary worship:

- Aims at the heart rather than at the mind

- Builds harmony rather than mere ascent

- Communicates joy rather than mere contentment

- Celebrates lifetime covenants, rather than financial commitments

- Sends people into spiritual disciplines rather than committees

- Leads people towards freedom rather than bondage.

WHAT WORSHIP LANGUAGE DO YOU SPEAK?

In *Forging a Real World Faith*,[168] Gordon MacDonald writes about six different languages that worshippers speak. The following is a summary of MacDonald's analysis of those six languages:

1. **The Aesthetic Instinct**—their agenda is majesty: David is a biblical example. Aesthetics enter into worship with great

---

167 Easum, William M. and Thomas G. Bandy. *Growing Spiritual Redwoods*. Nashville, TN: Abingdon Press, 1997.

168 MacDonald, Gordon. *Forging a Real World Faith*. Suffolk: Highland, 1989.

solemnity and they love to kneel in the presence of a God of majesty.

2. **The Experiential Instinct**—their agenda is joy: Simon Peter is a biblical example. Experientialists are big-hearted and generous—they seize any opportunity to meet with God.

3. **The Activist Instinct**—their agenda is achievement: Moses is a biblical example. Activists like to experience exhaustion as they mobilize people to do something constructive.

4. **The Contemplative Instinct**—their agenda is listening: John the Baptist is a biblical example. Contemplatives love to withdraw to meet with God.

5. **The Student Instinct**—their agenda is truth: St. Paul is a biblical example is. Students see heaven as an eternal Bible study with God as the discussion leader.

6. **The Relational Instinct**—their agenda is love: Barnabas is a biblical example. They believe God is most heard when people are engaged in good relationships with each other.[169]

POSTMODERN WORSHIP

Perhaps one of the greatest areas of controversy in today's church is the influence of postmodern thinking and how it informs ministry and worship today. Essentially, postmodernism describes the disenchantment, disillusionment, and skepticism of today's world in their disappointment with the so-called "advancements" of a modern age. Embracing the *reality* of the postmodern world is not subscribing to

---

169   Ibid.

its tenets. It is simply acknowledging that its pervasive influence will permeate the thinking of a generation that we are trying to reach and therefore we would be prudent to reflect on if and how this should inform our approach to the gospel and to our worship experiences.

The transition within society from modernism to postmodernism has major implications for worship. In his *Worship Leader's Manual*,[170] Mark Tittley quotes John Hoyland's posting of the of characteristics of postmodern worship from June 1995:

1. **Culturally relevant**—rejects cultural barriers that are not part of the gospel, aims to be accessible

2. **Participative**—encourages (not forces) people to participate in worship, rather than being passive receivers—also encourages people to participate in creating and running the worship events

3. **Recognition of importance of community**—the worship is based in a community, and builds up that community

4. **No "figurehead"**—worship proceeds without a leader, or many people are involved in leading

5. **Wholeness**—rejects notion of body/mind/soul split, expects that worship should involve the whole person

6. **Recognizes that both experience and understanding are essential**—creates opportunities in worship for both

7. **Eclectic**—willing to use all kinds of ideas, music, texts, etc. from a wide range of traditions

---

170   Tittley, Mark. The *Worship Leader's Manual.* Sonlife Africa, 2003.

8. **Sense of past and present**—aware of being part of a long tradition, aware of its history, but combined with an awareness of future, of its destiny

9. **Rejects the notion of a split between "sacred" and "secular"**—willing to use ideas, forms, materials, etc. from the "secular" world in worship

10. **Willing to use non-linearity and/or concurrency**

11. **Multi-media**—willing to use all available media in worship, for communication, and to create atmosphere

12. **Provisional**—recognizes that it is not perfect, and will need to change—always experimenting with new ideas

13. **Tolerant**—recognizes that other forms of worship are valid

14. **Local**—recognizes that worship is tightly related to the worshipping community— each community must find its own style of worship, rather than following some "cookbook" approach

15. **Anti-independent**—determined to remain part of existing churches rather than form new denomination[171]

In the maddening maze of a rapidly changing world, and in a cultural mosaic with multifarious tastes, preferences and interests, the challenge to today's church is to be relevant without losing reverence, to embrace diversity without diluting the gospel, and to be inclusive without compromising our commitment to the claims of Christ and while maintaining integrity in our interpretation of the Scriptures. We must not become so fascinated with the differences in stylistic preferences that we lose sight of the substance of worship.

---

171 Ibid.

In an article entitled, *Beyond Style Wars: Recovering the Substance of Worship*, Michael S. Horton writes of the direction he has taken in the church he serves:

> In a fast-paced, consumeristic, and entertainment-saturated age… people yearn for something different—a strange Father's voice from another place, calling for them… They are weary of what one secular artist calls "novocaine for the soul." They are weary of having their "felt needs" met. They have realized that their real needs are far more significant—and that they've never really known what those needs are… Absent from our services are market-driven entertainment elements… Instead, we focus on God himself telling his story of redemption through the lips of the minister. We are evangelistic because we are convinced that this kind of worship is where the heart of evangelism lies… Those who come to our church not yet certain meet believers who can explain the gospel to them. They keep coming, and some of them arrive, by God's grace, at faith. Those who profess faith join the baptized community. This is how we evangelize. In our worship, then, we are not seeker-oriented. We try to be God-oriented, expecting God to do the seeking. We expect God to find his own through a worship style in which, primarily, we do not testify to each other, but God testifies to us.[172]

A FRESH VIEW OF CONTEMPORARY WORSHIP

Dan Wilt is the Director of the newly born *Institute Of Contemporary and Emerging Worship Studies* in partnership with St. Stephen's University in St. Stephen, New Brunswick, and is an internationally respected worship leader, songwriter, author and trainer. He is also

---

172   Horton, Michael S. *Beyond Style Wars: Recovering the Substance of Worship.* The Banner, June 9, 1997.

the Director of Vineyard Worship Resources, which creates media-based training tools for the contemporary and emerging Church. In his article, *You, You Are God,* he offers a timeless and timely perspective to current and contemporary trends:

> In a season where the Spirit of God seems to be emphasizing God's holiness, the Church responds with worship movements related to purity. In a season where the Spirit of God seems to be emphasizing separation from the world's systems of thought, the Church responds with worship movements aiding believers in removing themselves from the idolatries of their age. In a season where the Spirit of God seems to be emphasizing a return to intimate and passionate adoration, the Church responds with a fresh wealth of musical expression—to give wings to the worship of a generation. For all of these great gifts and responses, however, each age of believers can become myopic, translating the whole of the Scriptures, and God's activity in the world, through the lens of their particular revelation. Revelation is meant, as Matt Redman has said, to lead us to a response. Our response leads to greater self-revealing from God, and the circle of intimate communion progresses and deepens over the course of a lifetime. However, revelation is always meant to lead us into a bigger picture of what worship is all about—never to an increasingly smaller one.[173]

THE THREE KISSES OF WORSHIP

Throughout this book I have focused on the fact that God desires communion and intimacy with His creation. This has been His desire since He first fashioned our parents in Eden. He made us for communion and intimacy with Himself. One of the most powerful

---

173   Link to this article is no longer active. For more of Dan Wilt's work go to https://www.danwilt.com/

metaphors for conveying intimacy is that of the kiss. Having looked at contemporary thought on worship, we will now reach back a full millennium to reflect on the kiss as a metaphor for our worship experience.

Bernard of Clairvaux (1090-1153) in his classic work on the Song of Songs, speaks of three kisses as representative of three stages of growth in the life of the believer: the kiss of the feet, the kiss of the hand and the kiss of the mouth. In a sermon entitled, *The Kiss of the Lord's Feet, Hands and Mouth,* he states:

> These kisses were given to the feet, the hand and the mouth, in that order. The first is the sign of a genuine conversion of life, the second is accorded to those making progress, the third is the experience of only a few of the more perfect... There is first the forgiveness of sins, then the grace that follows on good deeds, and finally that contemplative gift by which a kind and beneficent Lord shows himself to the soul with as much clarity as bodily frailty can endure... We all know that the kiss is a sign of peace. If what Scripture says is true: 'Our iniquities have made a gulf between us and God,' then peace can be at attained only when the intervening gulf is bridged. When therefore we make satisfaction and become reconciled by the re-joining of the cleavage caused by sin, in what better way can I describe the favor we receive than as a kiss of peace? Nor is there a more becoming place for this kiss than at the feet; the amends we make for the pride of our transgressions ought to be humble and diffident. But when God endows us with the more ample grace of a sweet friendship with him, in order to enable us to live with a virtue that is worthy of such a relationship, we tend to raise our heads from the dust with a greater confidence for the purpose of kissing, as is the custom, the hand of our benefactor... The heartfelt desire to admit one's guilt brings a man down in

lowliness before God, as it were to his feet; the heartfelt devotion of a worshiper finds in God renewal and refreshment, the touch, as it were, of his hand, and the delights of contemplation lead on to that ecstatic repose that is the fruit of the kiss of his mouth.[174]

IS THERE A DIVINE ORDER OR PROGRESSION IN THE THREE KISSES OF WORSHIP?

While St. Bernard of Clairvaux views the three kisses that he describes as a progression in the life of the believer, is it possible that the progression that we experience in macro over the lifetime of our walk with God might be mirrored in micro when we approach Him in worship? In sermon three, on the same theme, and preceding the one cited above, St. Bernard commented:

This is the way; this is the order. First we cast ourselves at his feet and deplore before God who made us the evil we have done. Secondly, we reach out for the hand which will lift us up, which will strengthen our trembling knees. Last, when we have obtained that, with many prayers and tears, then perhaps we shall dare to lift our faces to the mouth which is so divinely beautiful, fearing and trembling, not only to gaze on it, but even to kiss it. When we are joined with him in a holy kiss we are made one with him in spirit through his kindness.[175]

My friend, Dr. Peter Fitch, pastor of the St. Croix Vineyard in St. Stephen, New Brunswick and Dean of Ministry Studies at St. Stephen's University suggests that the order may be duplicated in our worship of God when he writes:

---

174 St. Bernard of Clairvaux. *Commentary on the Song of Songs by Sermon 4*, http://ww55.glorifyhisname.com/

175 St. Bernard of Clairvaux, *Commentary on the Song of Songs Sermon 3*. http://ww55.glorifyhisname.com/

I don't consciously go through these steps every Sunday morning, but something like this often happens to me. My head is full of the busyness of the week, of thoughts about what I will teach later in the service, and of concerns for many of the people around me. Then suddenly I notice the music, and I feel affection for the worship team because of all of their hard work. I enjoy their efforts. I laugh at the new hat the bass player has found. I wonder if the whole thing's too loud. I give a signal to the sound person at the back; then relax a little. And that's the last thought I'm aware of before I'm swept into joy: remembering God, loving God, remembering my need, receiving His answers, singing from the heart, singing in the spirit, awakening, awakening, alive.[176]

THE CALL TO WORSHIP

On many occasions, I have attended congregation gatherings of believers where the service began with a formal "call to worship." When a church begins with a "call to worship," it is an invitation and injunction to people to focus all their energies on declaring, magnifying, and savoring the riches of God in Christ through song, prayer, and the Word. However, Harold Best makes this insightful observation, in his book *Music Through the Eyes of Faith*:

> There can only be one call to worship, and this comes at conversion, when in complete repentance we admit to worshiping falsely, trapped by the inversion and enslaved to false gods before whom we have been dying sacrifices. This call to true worship comes but once, not every Sunday, in spite of the repeated calls to worship that begin most liturgies and orders of worship. These

---

176 Fitch, Peter. *The Supreme Value of Worship,* https://vineyarddigitalmembership.com/item/inside-worship-45-building-the-local-worship-experince/

should not be labeled calls to worship but calls to continuation of worship. We do not go to church to worship, but, already at worship, we join our brothers and sisters in continuing those actions that should have been going on – privately, [as families], or even corporately – all week long.[177]

The call to worship is a wellspring in the human spirit. It is the voice of the angel of God recorded in the final chapter of the final book of the Bible, "Worship God!" *To* this we are called. *For* this we were created. And for this purpose we have been redeemed. May we today and every day hear that call and hearken to its summons. In the words of St. Augustine, "And this is the happy life, to rejoice to Thee, of Thee, for Thee; this is it, and there is no other."[178]

177 Best, Harold, *Music Through the Eyes of Faith*. New York, NY: HarperCollins, 1993.

178 St. Augustine, *A Select Library of the Nicene and Post-Nicene Fathers of the Christian Church, Volume I, The Confessions and Letters of St. Augustine*, Edited by Philip Schaff, D.D., L.L. D, Grand Rapids: Eerdmans Publishing Company.

DESIGNER WORSHIP:
IT'S IN YOUR GENES

*Yet, if he would, man cannot live all to this world. If
not religious, he will be superstitious. IF he worship
not the true God, he will have his idols.*

—Theodore Parker

*So long as man remains free he strives for nothing so
incessantly and painfully as to find someone to worship.*

—Fyodor Dostoyevsky

*A person will worship something, have no doubt about that.
We may think our tribute is paid in secret in the dark recesses
of our hearts, but it will out. That which dominates our
imaginations and our thoughts will determine our lives, and
our character. Therefore, it behooves us to be careful what we
worship, for what we are worshipping we are becoming.*

—Ralph Waldo Emerson

*Our thoughts ought by instinct to fly upwards from animals,
men and natural objects to their creator. If created things are*

so utterly lovely, how gloriously beautiful must he be who made them! The wisdom of the worker is revealed in his handiwork.

—Anthony of Padua (1195-1231) Franciscan

"He has made everything beautiful in its time. He has also set eternity in the hearts of men; yet they cannot fathom what God has done from beginning to end" (Ecclesiastes 3:11 NIV).

"God did this so that men would seek him and perhaps reach out for him and find him, though he is not far from each one of us" (Acts 17:27 NIV).

T his chapter brings us full circle to where we began the study of the worship encounters in the books of Genesis and Exodus. In Chapter Three, *Why the First Murder Happened on the Way out of Church,* I briefly alluded to the innate instinct of man to worship. In this chapter, I will develop that theme more fully, citing both anthropological and historical evidence of this phenomenon, as well as selected notations from scholars through the ages who attest to its validity.

PHILOSOPHICAL AND EXPERIENTIAL TESTIMONY
TO THE DIVINE DESIGN OF WORSHIP

There is probably no more primal or basic instinct in the human being than the innate instinct to worship. Anthropological evidence abounds in both primitive and advanced cultures of man's innate need to worship and its expression is found in many and diverse forms. This inner drive, this upward urge, this elevator in the spirit of humankind was described by French mathematician and philosopher Blaise Pascal when he said, "There is a God-shaped vacuum, a God-hewn blank, in every human heart." [179]

When Pascal wrote of his experience of faith, he differentiated between *believing that* and *believing in*. He sates that his experience was neither the God of the philosophers, nor the God that is a conclusion of an intellectual argument. He distinguished between the mere conviction that God exists, and an absolute trust in the God of Abraham and Isaac and Jacob, the God of people whose trust compelled them to take radical action that sprang from that trust.

This same principle is echoed in what is perhaps the most famous quote of Augustine's Confessions when he said, "O Lord, Thou hast made us for Thyself, and our spirits are restless until they rest in Thee."[180]

Within the core of every human being, imparted and implanted by divine design, resides this deeply-rooted and supernatural instinct that compels us to pursue something beyond our earthly realm. The fact that this is a uniquely human drive not found in any other creatures should of itself be sufficient argument for the existence of a creator who has fashioned us in His own image and likeness. From the very most ancient annals of recorded history, evidence exists for this uniquely human need to worship. In *Origin*, L.J. White writes:

> The argument that religion is indeed 'Inborn' in the human race is very strong. Since religion itself is 'Spiritual' in nature and said spiritual part of human existence is widely accepted by all of us, therefore, religion can be said to be 'Inborn' into the human race or Man… As of today we cannot say or prove through any

179   Even consultations with experts on Pascal have failed to turn up the original source of the citation for Pascal's "God-shaped vacuum" quote

180   Saint Augustine, *Confessions, Book One, Chapter One*, 397 A.D., http://www.ccel.org/a/augustine/confessions/confessions.html

method that any other species living on the planet possesses the 'Religious Instinct'... One very significant similarity present in almost all religions is turning into the "Heavens", or better put, the subconscious conviction that our creator or creators do not reside on Earth. From the Aztecs and Incas in the Southern Hemisphere to the ancient Egyptians, the skies, planets and stars have been the home of our "Creator". Even obscure and very primitive groups and tribes have the same tendency to look outside the Earth for our origin... Religious Instinct is a Spiritual phenomenon that has been present in the human race from the very beginning and to date little understood... Furthermore, we know, at this point, of no other species on the planet possessing such an instinct or behavior, only man.[181]

SCIENTIFIC AND MEDICAL TESTIMONY TO THE DIVINE DESIGN OF WORSHIP

If this urge to worship something or someone greater than self indeed were innate and instinctive within the entire human race, it would seem that some medical or scientific evidence should exist to support the anecdotal evidence. In recent years, such evidence may in fact have surfaced. In one carefully designed experiment, the researchers ascertained that one effect of patients' seizures was to strengthen their brain's involuntary response to religious words, leading the scientists to suggest a portion of the brain is naturally attuned to ideas about a supreme being. While the research team had no explanation for the existence of what they described as *dedicated neural machinery for*

---

181   White, L.J. *Origin.*

religion, they postulated that it might possibly exist to *encourage tribe loyalty or reinforce kinship ties or the stability of a closely knit clan.*[182]

PHILOSOPHICAL AND PSYCHOLOGICAL DISPUTE AS TO THE DIVINE DESIGN OF WORSHIP

Throughout the centuries, scholars from every field and discipline have sought various means for accounting for the inner drive to worship that is acknowledged to reside with the human being. Two of the more famous of such accounts can be found in the works of Sigmund Freud and Karl Marx. While they held totally different viewpoints, their explanations are evident examples of man's effort to explain the undeniable urge to worship God.

Freud saw belief merely as a means of consolation. He taught that the human tendency is to project our own fear and loneliness onto the blank screen of the universe and bounce back a comforting fairytale that tells us we are not alone. While Marx's point of view was substantially different, he also viewed belief as a means of consolation. In Marx's view, it represented a temporary consolation for the miseries of life, cruelly manipulated by those in power to hold humanity in subjection.

The common thread of their postulations is that the origin of belief itself derives from the human sense of fear and loneliness. Their claims however remain without proof or evidence, since the origin of human faith and worship goes back to time immemorial. Both Freud and Marx imposed their own conclusions on all of human history and held them as valid explanation for something that transcended their generation. Richard Holloway writes in *Why Belief?*

---

182 Holtz, Robert Lee. Broadcast on BIC News, 31 October 1997, © Los Angeles Times 1997.

Nevertheless, the facts suggest that this primary trust or belief is an almost universal human instinct... the instinct to worship, to exclaim in awe, to praise, is the basic experience of faith. This is why worship together is the most characteristic activity of faith communities, whatever their conception of God is... the worshipping community is both a result of and a support for the individual's experience of God. If God is as we have experienced then the primary response is worship, giving due to God.[183]

THEOLOGICAL TESTIMONY TO THE DIVINE DESIGN OF WORSHIP

J.B. Phillips was born in London in 1906, ordained in 1930 and in 1940 he became Vicar of the Church of the Good Shepherd, London. He is noted for his work in the field of Biblical translation, the *J. B. Phillips New Testament*, and in particular for two books: *Letters to Young Churches* and *Your God is Too Small*. In *God our Contemporary*, he wrote,

All men naturally worship someone or something, but in the commonly assumed absence of God, this worship is given almost wholly to such things as success, sport, the heroes or heroines of the fantasy-world of the screen or stage, or to the mysteries of science. Such a superstition as astrology may flourish as a substitute-religion for the ignorant, while some fancy version of an Eastern religion may attract the intellectual agnostic. But perversions of the instinct to worship God do not in the long run rescue man either from his own solitariness or from the closed-system of materialism. The way out, paradoxically enough, lies in no form of uncommitted escapism, but in a closer commitment to life.

---

183   Holloway, Richard. *Why Belief?* http://www.christianevidencesociety.org.uk/uploads/Belief.pdf

Christianity shows the way of such closer commitment; it does not merely restore a man's faith in God but inevitably involves him in compassion and service... That is why only Christianity can fully satisfy the desire to worship and the desire to serve.[184]

BIBLICAL TESTIMONY TO THE DIVINE DESIGN OF WORSHIP

Clearly, as human beings, we are instinctively worshipping creatures. And, if we don't worship God, we will worship something else. The apostle Paul addresses this issue in the opening segment of his epistle to the saints in Rome. He points out that the Creator made His existence known in His gloriously created universe so that those who reject that evidence are without excuse.

Since what may be known about God is plain to them, because God has made it plain to them. For since the creation of the world God's invisible qualities—his eternal power and divine nature—have been clearly seen, being understood from what has been made, so that men are without excuse. For although they knew God, they neither glorified him as God nor gave thanks to him, but their thinking became futile and their foolish hearts were darkened. Although they claimed to be wise, they became fools and exchanged the glory of the immortal God for images made to look like mortal man and birds and animals and reptiles. Therefore God gave them over in the sinful desires of their hearts to sexual impurity for the degrading of their bodies with one another. They exchanged the truth of God for a lie, and worshiped and served created things rather than the Creator—who is forever praised. Amen (Romans 1:19-25 NIV).

---

184   Phillips, J.B. *God Our Contemporary.* New York, NY: The Macmillan Company, 1960.

Paul observed that when people refuse to glorify God they will engage in futile senseless acts of worship. They will experience a reversal in the divinely appointed order: instead of worshipping the Creator, they will resort to worship of the created. In exchanging worship of the Creator for worship of the created, they will fashion "gods" that resemble mortal man, birds, animals and reptiles. In the next passage he indicates that the reversal of order in worship may result in the reversal of order in sexual practices. He goes on to dramatically describe the resulting wrath of God that ensues as a result of these practices.

HISTORICAL AND ANTHROPOLOGICAL TESTIMONY TO THE DIVINE DESIGN OF WORSHIP

Evidence of such practices abounds in many religions. A prime example is within the Hindu religion, known for its worship of animals. While the phrase "sacred cow" derives from the better known custom that regarded cattle as sacred, other animals are also regarded as holy in the Hindu religion. A United Press International news story entitled *Indian Woman Marries Cobra for Love*, published on June 6, 2006, records this rather bizarre account:

> An Indian woman says she loves her new husband and knows he returns her feelings—even though he happens to be a snake. "More than 2,000 people turned out Wednesday to celebrate the wedding of Bimbala Das, 30, to a cobra that lived on an ant hill near her home in the village of Atala," the Times of India reported Friday. Das said she fell in love with the snake and knew it felt the same about her, even though they could not transmit their feelings in the usual manner. "Though snakes cannot speak nor under-stand, we communicate in a peculiar way," she explained to the

newspaper. Whenever I put milk near the ant hill where the cobra lives, it always comes out to drink." The woman's new husband was not actually at the Hindu wedding, however. "A brass replica of the cobra was used as a stand-in during the ritual and processional," the newspaper said.[185]

In his June 30 commentary on this story, Wayne Jackson, writing for Christian Courier Publications, said:

> It is very difficult not to see some humor in this, as indeed Isaiah did when he spoke of the man who cut down a tree, burned part of it in a fire, and with the residue made a god to worship (Isaiah 44:12-17). In reality, it reflects a most tragic circumstance. It illustrates, in a painful way, how very far away from God a culture can depart when knowledge of Creator is abandoned and the human worship-urge is satisfied on the basest level imaginable.[186]

When Paul preached to the Athenians in Acts 17, he encountered a culture so obsessed with a desire not to neglect any god, that among their altars they had erected an altar that they had designated to the unknown god.

> Paul then stood up in the meeting of the Areopagus and said: "Men of Athens! I see that in every way you are very religious. For as I walked around and looked carefully at your objects of worship, I even found an altar with this inscription: TO AN UNKNOWN GOD. Now what you worship as something unknown I am going to proclaim to you. The God who made the world and everything in it is the Lord of heaven and earth and does not live in temples built by hands. And he is not served by human hands, as if he needed anything, because he himself gives all men life and breath

---

185   © Copyright 2006 United Press International, Inc. All Rights Reserved
186   Jackson, Wayne. *My Husband Is a Snake.* © 2006 by Christian Courier Publications. All rights reserved.

and everything else. From one man he made every nation of men, that they should inhabit the whole earth; and he determined the times set for them and the exact places where they should live. God did this so that men would seek him and perhaps reach out for him and find him, though he is not far from each one of us. For in him we live and move and have our being." (Acts 17:22-28 NIV).

What Paul encountered in the first century in Athens is a snapshot of what exists all over the world, where people without knowledge of the one true God seek to express a worship that derives from an internal and eternal wellspring with the human spirit. This urge to worship takes on a multitude of forms and expressions, and sometimes is expressed to a multitude of "gods."

For example, Buddhists believe that there are thirty three million gods and demigods, a multitude of heavenly beings. However, unlike human beings they are incapable of gathering any merit while in the heavens but depend on the merit offered by humans accrued by way of performing numerous meritorious deeds. The gods avail of this merit to elevate themselves in their positions, which they enjoy in the heavens. Human beings in general appeal to these gods in their need for relief whenever they confront misfortune. Besides the unknown gods who have no direct association with human beings, there is a category of twelve gods believed to be constantly interven-ing in the affairs of humans who adore them, worship them and appeal for redress relating to their concerns in their life on earth and of this life alone. Buddhists believe that there is so much of goodness, sympathy and generosity dormant in the nature of these unseen gods that they need faithful appeals to kindle their benevolence. Man's natural instinct for subservience is evident in the worship of gods. In time of adversity the people seek help and protection from these self-created gods. As the gods are invisible and believed to be everywhere, fear and servility characterize the worship that is ignorantly directed towards them.[187]

In today's age of materialism, where wealth and prosperity are not only venerated, but also propagated by many preachers as the right and privilege of the believer, there is often perplexity as to why some cultures place little or no value on the accumulation of worldly possessions. For example, in many areas of the Pacific, rank and position is elevated far above material possessions, and it is the office that is worshipped and held in the highest regard. The following account, recorded in *A History of Fiji* by Dr. Alfred Goldsborough Mayer illuminates this practice:

> Hoarded wealth inspires no respect in the Pacific, and indeed, were it discovered, its possession would justify immediate confiscation. Yet man must raise idols to satisfy his instinct to worship things above his acquisition, and thus rank is the more reverenced because respect for property is low. Even today there is something god-like in the presence of the high chiefs, and none will cross the shadow of the king's house.[188]

We see parallels of this in our own culture, where while not regarded as *worship*, these attitudes closely approximate the practice of veneration of possessions, position, title, and rank. In his epistle, James warns against such subtleties of demonstrating deference, preference and favoritism when he writes:

> My brothers, as believers in our glorious Lord Jesus Christ, don't show favoritism. Suppose a man comes into your meeting wearing a gold ring and fine clothes, and a poor man in shabby clothes also comes in. If you show special attention to the man

---

187   ibid

188   Mayer, Dr. Alfred Goldsborough. *A History of Fiji.* https://www.amazon.com/History-Fiji-Alfred-G-Mayer/dp/1523496215

wearing fine clothes and say, "Here's a good seat for you," but say to the poor man, "You stand there" or "Sit on the floor by my feet," have you not discriminated among yourselves and become judges with evil thoughts? Listen, my dear brothers: Has not God chosen those who are poor in the eyes of the world to be rich in faith and to inherit the kingdom he promised those who love him? But you have insulted the poor. Is it not the rich who are exploiting you? Are they not the ones who are dragging you into court? Are they not the ones who are slandering the noble name of him to whom you belong? If you really keep the royal law found in Scripture, "Love your neighbor as yourself," you are doing right. But if you show favoritism, you sin and are convicted by the law as lawbreakers (James 2:1-8 NIV).

While the practices of worship that we see in cultures in far-flung corners of the earth that are so vastly different from our own may seem strange, futile, and even ridiculous, what they prove is the undeniable instinct of mankind everywhere to worship. One of the most common expressions of worship that can be found in anthropological studies of many races, cultures, and in different parts of the world is the worship of a sun-god. From the earliest of times, humankind recognized the sun as their source of life, light and heat. One of the more obscure references to such worship can be found in the history of the residents of the Isle of Mann, where to this day, the primary national festival day reaches back into primitive worship of the sun.

John Joseph Kneen addresses this in examining the origins of Tynwald, the chief national festival day on the Isle of Mann, and writes of a form of worship that goes back to ancient civilization long before the birth of Christianity.

A custom which had already existed from time immemorial, a custom almost coeval with the advent of man upon the earth, a custom which had through the ages evolved from a primitive human instinct to worship something, and the object which appealed mostly to their prehensile imaginations was the sun, the glorious Orb-of-Day, which gave them light and heat, caused their corn and fruits to grow, filled the rivers with fish, thus giving them a bountiful food supply and benefiting them in many and varied ways too difficult to enumerate.[189]

The tendency to worship nature was not, however, limited to those elements with which we are likely most familiar such as the sun, the moon and the stars. Another expression of worship that characterized antiquity was *well-worship,* worship that which embraced the worship of rivers, lakes, fountains and springs. Robert Charles Hope, wrote of this in the last decade of the19th century:

> From all parts of the globe a vast accumulation of legendary lore connected with this cult has from time to time been brought to light, taking us back to ages far anterior to Christianity, through days of darkness, when all traces of the one and only true religion, revealed to man by God, as recorded in Holy Scripture, had been forgotten, or had died out. The tower of Babel had caused the dispersion of nations, and the farther they receded from the common centre, the more corrupted became the forms of worship adopted, and gradually, in course of time, retained little, if any, of the truth at all… where all trace of the true religion had disappeared, the heathen, ever prone to obey a natural instinct to worship something, looked upon every object around him from which be derived personal benefits, as a physical iota like himself—the sun, which gave him warmth and light, hence fire-worship; the trees, that sheltered him, hence tree-worship; and, in an especial manner,

---

189   Kneen, John Joseph. http://www.isle-of-man.com/manxnotebook/mquart/mq25091.htm

the waters from above that moistened his soil, and those below which provided him with a very necessity of life… The Indians, Egyptians, Persians, and Greeks all had deities of fountains and streams.[190]

Plutarch, A Greek philosopher of the first century, served for many years as one of the two priests at the temple of Apollo at Delphi (the site of the famous Delphic Oracle) twenty miles from his home. By his writings and lectures Plutarch became a celebrity in the Roman Empire, yet he continued to reside where he was born, and actively participated in local affairs, even serving as mayor. At his country estate, guests from all over the empire congregated for serious conversation, presided over by Plutarch in his marble chair. Many of these dialogues were recorded and published, and the 78 essays and other works that have survived are now known collectively as the *Moralia*. He was a strong believer in God, and his argument against atheism is well worth quoting. He is recorded as having said,

> There has never been a state of atheists. You may travel over the world, and you may find cities without walls, without king, without mint, without theatre or gymnasium; but you will never find a city without God, without prayer, without oracle, without sacrifice. Sooner may a city stand without foundations, than a state without belief in the gods. This is the bond of all society and the pillar of all legislation.[191]

---

190 Hope, Robert Charles F.S.A., F.R.S.L., *The Legendary Lord of the Holy Wells of England Including Rivers, Fountains and Springs.* London: Elliot Stock, 1893. http://www.antipope.org/feorag/wells/hope/introduction.html

191 As recorded in The History of the Christian Church, Volume II: Ante-Nicene Christianity. A.D. 100-325., reference Adv. Colotem (an Epicurean), c. 31 (Moralia, ed. Tauchnitz, VI. 265).

MORE THEOLOGICAL TESTIMONY TO THE
DIVINE DESIGN OF WORSHIP

Nearly 1800 years after the writings of Plutarch, Milton Valentine was ordained to the Lutheran ministry by the synod of Maryland in 1853. He was professor of ecclesiastical history and church polity in the theological seminary at Gettysburg from 1866 to 1868, and president of Pennsylvania College from 1868 to 1884. In addition to his many articles that were published with wide circulation, he issued the *Natural Theology and Rational Theism* in 1885. He is recorded in *Christian Theology* in 1906 by The United Lutheran Publication House as having written:

> Beyond the idea of God, found to be so universal, there is the further principle of human nature that shows itself in religious feeling and acts of worship… Not only the intellect with its idea of God, but the heart with its feeling of dependence and impulse to worship… Man worships something everywhere; if he fails to reach a conception of the true God, he gives homage to imaginary divinities and seeks favor from them. This principle of worship appears to rise with the characteristics of an organic psychical instinct. Its persistence is even more impressive than its genesis. For it cannot be annihilated.[192]

A contemporary of Valentine, Episcopal priest George Washington Doane, earned his reputation as an educator, mission organizer and hymn writer. In 1823 he was ordained a priest and served in New York City, where he helped found St. Luke's Church, and taught and edited his denomination's magazine, the Episcopal Watchman. Between 1828 and 1832 he served in Boston and then, at the relatively young age of thirty-three, became bishop in the diocese of

---

192   Valentine, Milton D.D., LL.D, *Christian Theology.* Philadelphia, PA: The United Lutheran Publication House, Lutheran Publication Society © 19062

Newark, New Jersey. In his classic sermon, The Beauty of Holiness, preached at the consecration of Grace Church in Newark on October 5th, 1848, Bishop Doane said:

> Even the heathen show the instinct of the heart, to lay its powers all out, and work them to the last perfection, in results of consecrated beauty. Look at the Parthenon. Look at the Coliseum… What have we here, in every age, and every land; what shall we find in every form of worship, true or false, Jewish, Christian, or Heathen, but the use of consecrated beauty; in the height of its conceptions, and in the fullness of its consummation, for the service of religion! What is it all but comment upon comment, upon David's text, "Worship the Lord, in the beauty of holiness!" [193]

CONTEMPORARY THEOLOGICAL TESTIMONY TO THE DIVINE DESIGN OF WORSHIP

The last decade has witnessed a strong resurgence of interest in the subject of worship, with a proliferation of writings on the topic. In *Experiencing Worship, A Study of Biblical Worship,* Stephen M. Newman writes,

> The need or desire to worship is born in every person. It is not something that is taught or developed. It is created within us to do. Think if you will of every culture in the world. No explorer has ever found a tribe or culture that did not worship. Each culture worships something or someone. Some worship self or money, some idols, others false gods. Because we are born with a desire

---

[193]   Doane, Bishop George Washington. *The Beauty of Holiness.* Burlington: Samuel C. Atkinson, The Missionary Press, 1848.

and instinct to worship, the question is not do we worship, but whom do we worship.[194]

Many of the recent works on worship resonate with a return to the well-known statement from the Shorter Westminster Catechism, that "Man's chief end is to glorify God, and to enjoy him for ever."[195] That theme surfaces time and again in the titles of recent texts and worship, and is echoed in the thoughts of Ronald Byars who writes in *Christian Worship: Glorifying and Enjoying God,*

> Some vital instinct rises up to praise the One from who our lives—and all lives—have sprung. The majesty of the Divine evokes praise, much as a spectacular sunset moves even the atheist to a sense of awe. A deeply rooted human impulse urges us to bless the power that formed the universe and keeps it in motion. People worship because it comes as naturally as eating and drinking. We simply can't help it.[196]

LaMar Boschman is the Academic Dean of the International Worship Institute. As the author of numerous books and videos, his preaching and worship leading impacts churches and individuals around the world. In his book, *A True Heart for Worship*, he quotes Don McMinn as saying,

> Our entire being is fashioned as an instrument of praise. Just as a master violin maker designs an instrument to produce maximum aesthetic results, so God tailor-made our bodies, souls and spirits to work together in consonance to produce pleasing expressions of praise and worship. When we use body language to express praise, that which is internal becomes visible.[197]

194   Newman, Stephen M. *Experiencing Worship. A Study of Biblical Worship. http://www.experiencingworship.com/ articles/studies/2001-7-Experiencing-Worship-The-print.html*
195   http://www.asa3.org/gray/westminster_standards/shorter_catechism.html
196   Byars, Ronald *Christian Worship: Glorifying and Enjoying God.* Louisville, KY: Geneva Press, 2001.
197   McMinn, Don. quoted by Lamar Boschman. *A True Heart for Worship.* http://www.experiencingworship.com/ articles/reviews/-p5.html

Senator Mark Hatfield, served as governor of the State of Oregon from 1959 to 1967 before moving on the U.S. Senate. Known to never mince his words, and to be outspoken in his Christian witness, Hatfield said,

> Man will always have a god. In communist countries, where the death of God is made a tenet of government belief, the leaders and their dogma are deified so they can be worshipped. Man has an inherent instinct to worship; if God is not the source of his ultimate allegiance, he will then create his own gods. He will worship other people, or his country, or institutions, or money, or power or fame —and all of these are different ways of worshipping himself.[198]

We will worship… whether rightly or wrongly, the inward compulsion that resides within us by divine design must find expression. We were created thus by God. The drive to worship is central to our very existence. It is the core of our reason for being. We were created in God's image—to mirror and reflect his glory.

In *Coming Back to the Heart of Worship,* published in the April, 2004 edition of Christianity Today, Harold Best states:

> We can't not worship. But we can worship wrongly. We were created worshipping. Not created to worship—we were created worshipping. And when we fell, we didn't stop our worship, we exchanged gods. That explains why we have a world full of idolatries. When we come to Jesus, we don't start to worship again. Rather our worship—which is fallen and flawed and misdirected—is washed in the blood of Christ and turned right side out, and now we worship authentically in Christ.[199]

---

198 Hatfield, Mark O. *The Vulnerability of Leadership.* Carol Stream, IL Christianity Today, 6/22/73

199 https://www.christianitytoday.com/ct/2004/juneweb-only/6-14-42.0.html

In his book, *Worship: The missing Jewel of the Evangelical Church*, A.W. Tozer has written a chapter entitled, *Worship: The Normal Employment of Moral Beings*. In that chapter he declares:

Why did Christ come? Why was He Conceived? Why was He born? Why was He crucified? Why did He rise again? Why is He now at the right hand of the Father? The answer to all these questions is, in order that He might make worshippers out of rebels; in order that He might restore us again to the place of worship we knew when we were first created. Now because we were created to worship, worship is the normal employment of moral beings.[200]

Far too many Christians see the ultimate goal of living the Christian life as going to heaven when you die. To reduce salvation to constituting a fire escape from hell on the one hand and a free ticket to heaven on the other cheapens the gospel and God's redemptive plan and hurls an insult into the face of our Creator. Yet the reality of an eternity in heaven with our Lord is part of the glorious hope of the redeemed. It is in that light that we ask the question, "What is it that will make heaven *heaven*?" When we turn to the book of Revelation we will find the answer.

The twenty-four elders fall down before him who sits on the throne, and worship him who lives for ever and ever. They lay their crowns before the throne and say: "You are worthy, our Lord and God, to receive glory and honor and power, for you created all things, and by your will they were created and have their being" (Revelation 4:10-11 NIV)

The four living creatures said, "Amen," and the elders fell down and worshiped (Revelation 5:14 NIV).

---

200   Tozer, A. W. *Worship: The Missing Jewel of the Evangelical Church*. Camp Hill, PA: Christian Publications, 1961.

And they cried out in a loud voice: "Salvation belongs to our God, who sits on the throne, and to the Lamb." All the angels were standing around the throne and around the elders and the four living creatures. They fell down on their faces before the throne and worshiped God, saying: "Amen! Praise and glory and wisdom and thanks and honor and power and strength be to our God for ever and ever. Amen!" (Revelation 7:10-12).

"The kingdom of the world has become the kingdom of our Lord and of his Christ, and he will reign for ever and ever." And the twenty-four elders, who were seated on their thrones before God, fell on their faces and worshiped God, saying: "We give thanks to you, Lord God Almighty, the One who is and who was, because you have taken your great power and have begun to reign" (Revelation 11:15-17 NIV).

And sang the song of Moses the servant of God and the song of the Lamb: "Great and marvelous are your deeds, Lord God Almighty. Just and true are your ways, King of the ages. Who will not fear you, O Lord, and bring glory to your name? For you alone are holy. All nations will come and worship before you, for your righteous acts have been revealed" (Revelation 15:3-4 NIV).

The twenty-four elders and the four living creatures fell down and worshiped God, who was seated on the throne. And they cried: "Amen, Hallelujah!" (Revelation 19:4 NIV).

Clearly, the worship of God will be the eternal occupation of the redeemed. This is our divine destiny. This is our divine design. For this we were created. For this we were redeemed. In the words of Revelation 19:20 that are repeated in 22:9, "Worship God."

21

WORSHIP OR WARSHIP?

Warning: This chapter is not for the faint of heart!

*How I did weep, in Your Hymns and Canticles, touched
to the quick by the voices of your sweet-attuned Church!
The voices flowed into mine ears, and the truth distilled
into my heart, whence the affections of devotion overflowed
and tears ran down, and happy was I therein.*

—**Augustine**

*A congregation is just as responsible to sing the gospel
as the preachers are to preach it. These two acts
(singing and preaching) jointly taken to their fullest,
then reduce themselves to one common act.*

—**Harold Best**, *Through the Eyes of Faith*

Yet a time is coming and has now come when the true worshippers will worship the Father in spirit and in truth, for they are the kind of worshippers the Father seeks. God is spirit, and his worshippers must worship in spirit and in truth" (John 4:23-24 NIV).

As they listen, their secret thoughts will be laid bare, and they will fall down on their knees and worship God declaring, 'God is really here among you' (I Corinthians 14:22-25 NLT).

Sing psalms and hymns and spiritual songs to God with thankful hearts. (Colossians 3:16)

AN UNLIKELY BATTLEFIELD

A pastor friend that I've known for many years shared with me that one well-known church leader referred to the music department of the church as "The War Department,"[201] while another well-known preacher pinpointed the local church choir loft as the most probable location on planet earth for Satan's fall from heaven![202] In an article entitled *Peace in the War Room*, Pete Sanchez of Integrity Worship Institute proposed to broker a biblical cease-fire in the so-called "worship wars." When you read his pedigree, you are compelled to recognize that if anyone has the qualifications to do so, it would be him. He states, *"Perhaps honest, God-honoring, authentic dialogue will lead to renewed worship and less war."*

However, the worship wars are not a phenomena limited to the evangelical church of North America. Alan Philps wrote that a fight broke out in July 2002, at the Church of the Holy Sepulchre in Jerusalem about the placement of a chair used by an Egyptian monk near the entrance to the roof. It was a hot day and the chair was moved to the shade—against written policy derived in 1757—and, as such, violated the status quo. "The fracas involved monks from the Ethiopian Orthodox church and the Coptic church of Egypt,

---

201   Attributed to Charles Haddon Spurgeon (1834-92), and cited in numerous articles and websites.

202   Attributed to Dr. J. Vernon McGee, quoted by John A. White in an article entitled *Faith's Language* on the web page *Experiencing Worship.* http://www.experiencingworship.com/articles/general/2003-4-Faith-s-Language.html

who have been vying for control of the rooftop for centuries,"[203] said Philps. As a result, 11 monks were treated in a hospital for their injuries. At issue—the position of a chair. Before we shake our heads in shocked disbelief and bewilderment, let us reflect on our own lives as pastors and worship leaders. How often have we fought over the trivial, not wanting to be moved? Have you ever witnessed the indignation aroused when a lifelong church member enters the sanctuary to find a first time visitor occupying their favorite pew? In an article entitled *Relevance and Irrelevance in Worship*, Doug Goins writes,

> Increasingly across our country, worship is a controversial subject in the church of Jesus Christ. The Christian publishing market is flooded with books on the worship wars raging in our churches. There is tension between *emotional worship* and *intellectual* worship. There is conflict between *traditional* worship and *contemporary worship,* but even those categories are subdivided. There are *liturgical traditionalists* and *informal traditionalists*. Even among traditionalists, there is controversy over what kind of music is most fitting—hymns, classical music or gospel music.[204]

"Drums in worship; choir robes or regular clothes; hymnals versus projection screens, and the question of outdated organs; these are all tensions that can cause worship wars among church members," said Robert Wagoner, music events consultant for the Southern Baptist Convention. "Differing opinions about these decisions tend to hurt worship services," Wagoner told church leaders in a session entitled "How to Strengthen Your Worship without Starting a War."[205]

Both church leaders and lay people of my vintage lament the loss of the *style* of worship that they love. Sometimes their blatant

---

203   https://www.smh.com.au/world/middle-east/monks-hit-the-roof-in-holy-stoush-20020731-gdfi12.html
204   https://www.pbc.org/messages/relevance-and-irrelevance-in-worship/
205   http://bpnews.net/13741/tickytacky-worship-wars-divert-attention-from-god-consultant-says

decrying of anything other than the traditional church service in which they were raised reminds me of the resistance to any translation of the Bible other than the King James Version. I remember one sincere but unlearned believer saying, "If the King James Version was good enough for the Apostle Paul, it's good enough for me." While some might regard their longing for the "good old days" as nothing more than a "sentimental journey", we will discover that perhaps much has been lost with the replacement of the hymns of the faith by contemporary choruses.

And while my associations are mostly within the Pentecostal and Charismatic ranks, the phenomenon of "worship wars" is not restricted to our ranks. As with the franchise on tongues that Pentecostals thought they enjoyed exclusively until the advent of the Charismatic movement, so we have to move over and share the *worship warship* with other denominations as well. In fact, the phrase "worship wars" probably had its genesis more in mainline Protestantism than in the evangelical community, let alone the Pentecostal wing. In 2002, a Lutheran Church leader at the National Conference on Worship, Music and the Arts in Kenosha, Wisconsin, addressed the topic of "Lutheran Worship Wars."[206]

While my own theology leans toward Calvinism, I cannot conscientiously concur with everything that John Calvin wrote or said. The 16th-century pillar of the Protestant Reformation once wrote, "God disapproves of all modes of worship not expressly sanctioned by his word."[207] In this Calvinistic tradition, an alliance of churches in Reformed Protestantism has been formed as guardian of "the regulative principle of worship". This *regulative principle* holds that "God specifically commanded the elements he desired in worship, to which

---

206   http://www.christforus.org/Papers/Content/LutheranWorshipWars.html

207   http://www.piney.com/calvinworship.html

we may neither add nor take away".[208] This alliance bemoans the fact that it is not merely Pentecostal and nondenominational churches that have been adding and subtracting, but also those in the Presbyterian, Reformed and Baptist followings. This modern feud among the Reformed tradition has also been branded "the worship wars".

Michael Horton, a professor of apologetics and historical theology at Westminster Seminary, said "Typically, modern praise choruses don't focus on what God has done for us in Christ but on my response to all of that. 'I praise you... I serve you... I... I... I.' the music has shifted from rehearsing Christ's work in the history of redemption..."[209]

Professor Robert Webber serves as head of the Institute for Worship Studies at Northern Baptist Theological Seminary. He has written extensively on the subject of worship and has edited *The Complete Library of Christian Worship.* He is quoted by Jim Remsen in an article entitled *Urging a return to 'God-centered' worship* from *Inquirer Faith Life,* in the April 18, 2004 edition of *The Philadelphia Inquirer* as having said,

> Too much praise music is about 'my personal experience with God' and not reflective of what worship ought to be, which is God's mission to the world, to save and restore the whole creative order. It's an epistemological shift from the objective work of God to my subjective experience.[210]

In an article entitled *Worship Wars: Are We on the Right Battlefield,* Maureen Bradley of Christ Presbyterian Church, Richmond, Indiana, wrote,

---

208   Ibid.

209   Horton, Michael, quoted by Jim Remsen. *Worship Wars.* Grand Forks, NK: North Dakota Herald, April 24, 2004.

210   Remsen. Jim. *Urging a Return to 'God-Centered' Worship.* Philadelphia, PA: *Inquirer Faith Life, The Philadelphia Inquirer.* April 18, 2004.

> When churches begin to look at the congregation as consumers and the programs of the church as products, when worship services begin to resemble a well-staged Broadway show, then maybe, just maybe the church has taken a few steps into the wrong social structure. Is the church defeating herself by fraternizing with the enemy—by being on the wrong battlefield?[211]

Back in 1999, Michael S. Hamilton wrote a "worship wars" cover story for Christianity Today. Subtitled, *How Guitars Beat out the Organ in the Worship Wars,*[212] he describes a Methodist church near Birmingham, Alabama, that employs five different musical styles for six services as embodying "the new reality of congregational singing in America" as all over the country churches are customizing worship-music styles for particular demographic groups.

In the face of this reality, some church leaders believe that the newest demonstration of sectarianism concerns worship style rather than theology. Conflicts over worship in general and over musical style in particular have erupted in churches of nearly every denomination. The battle lines that were drawn decades ago round baptismal modes and dispensational doctrines have surrendered to the boundaries and barriers now erected by disparate views over music and worship.

The recent changes reflected in the worship life of the church are not unique to church life. The progeny of my baby boomer generation, often disparagingly referred to as Generation X, are also frequently described as the "me generation". This generation is marked by a strong focus on individual autonomy. It is only natural that a generation which rejects the traditions it has inherited will also dramatically change its approach to worshipping God. Music is a

---

211   May-June 2000 issue of Viewpoint. Carol Stream, IL: Reformation & Revival Ministries.

212   https://www.christianitytoday.com/ct/1999/july12/9t8028.html?ctlredirect=true

means by which a generation will tend to affirm is identity. What we are witnessing with "Generation X" and the "Millennial Generation" is similarly and simply a means by which each respective generation declares its own identity. It will follow then that the style of music that characterizes the worship of a given congregation will to some degree define the generation that it will attract.

Attempting to bridge the breach of worship divisions may be as futile as trying to span the gulf of doctrinal divisions over modes of baptism. Different expressions of Christianity are neither inherently nor implicitly bad in and of themselves. While Richard Niebuhr declared that, "Denominationalism represents the moral failure of Christianity,"[213] the fact remains that a clear advantage of multiple expressions of Christianity—whether they are based in doctrine or based in worship—is that there is an expression for everyone.

As I have read various positions on Christian worship in general and music in particular, I've noticed that while every complaint about worship music—no matter which style—claims to be rooted in theological principles, yet in every critique, the theology aligns perfectly with the critic's own musical taste. It may be more helpful to look at the *fruit* as well as the *root*. If we hold that the purpose of the church is to communicate the gospel of Christ and to invite people into a living relationship with God, then any worship music that aids a church in these tasks can be a channel of the Holy Spirit.

In his book, *Putting an End to Worship Wars*, Elmer Towns writes,

> When I said the new seeker worship services expressed biblical principles, I encouraged the young minister using this new worship format, but some older ones were not pleased with my opinion. Then I said the older Lutheran liturgy expressed biblical principles,

---

213   Niebuhr, H. Richard. *The Social Sources of Denominationalism*. New York: Meridian Books, 1957 Edition Reprint, originally published 1929, p. 25.

making the older ministers happy. I pointed out the new seeker services could be superficial and frothy, hence becoming unbiblical. Also, the old Lutheran liturgy could be dead and meaningless, also becoming unbiblical.[214]

Towns continues,

> This is not a prescriptive book that a leader follows to plan a worship service… it is a descriptive book that reflects the trends and tensions in our contemporary church over worship practices… this book is about worship wars. Does the pastor have the authority to change the worship style of the people, i.e. to take away the form of worship they have always followed in worshipping God? Do the people have the authority to rebel against their pastor who is attempting to revitalize an ineffective worship service?[215]

While Towns' balanced message on Biblical worship in 1996 heralded from Lynchburg, Virginia, home of Jerry Falwell's Bible Baptist fellowship, another speaker delivered a lecture series on Worship Wars three years later at the Christian Church (Disciples of Christ) Phillips Theological Seminary in Tulsa, Oklahoma. There, the theme, *Beyond the Worship Wars* focused on the turmoil in which many congregations are embroiled as some members cling to traditional worship forms while others press for contemporary variations. "Peace is possible in the worship wars some congregations are facing but it won't come fast and it probably won't be easy,"[216] said author O.I. Harrison, of Twin Falls, Idaho.

In another 1994 article simply entitled, *The Worship Wars,*[217] Keith Drury reiterated what my mentor and Bible College instructor

214 Towns, Elmer. *Putting an End to Worship Wars.* Nashville, TN: Broadman & Holman Publishers, 1996, p.2.
215 Ibid., p.3.
216 Disciples News Service, **Worship Wars Lecture Series,** September 29, 1999. Indianapolis, IN: Christian Church (Disciples of Christ).
217 http://www.drurywriting.com/keith/worship.htm

said when I asked his opinion on a tentative title for this book: war and worship do not fit together. This author claims to have survived a couple of worship wars and having experienced three worship styles in the process. I have experienced these same stages as I have witnessed an evolutionary shift in worship styles during my years of pastoral ministry. Keith Drury gave "voice" to my own experience, and while there are striking parallels, and the paragraphs that follow are enriched by his description, they reflect my own experience in this evolution.

1. *Camp Meeting Style of Worship* was predominant during my childhood and adolescent years—the 1950s and 1960s. This is the style of worship on which I was raised, and in which I can most easily participate. My first profession of faith in Christ was "walking the sawdust trail" in a camp meeting at Harvey Lake, New Brunswick. The singing was comprised of rousing renditions of upbeat gospel songs and choruses. We proudly (and piously) raised the rafters of the old tabernacle to the accompaniment of an old upright piano and pickup orchestra. The song leader urged people to "get out their ten stringed instruments" and join in by clapping their hands. Less than a decade after my first profession of faith, I led the camp meeting choir, and if we could get the congregation to spontaneously rise to their feet and join the singing, we had contributed to a "great service." Often people would shout, wave their handkerchiefs, move out into the aisles and dance, or do a "Jericho march" (walk around the aisles). I will always remember the entire congregation at one such camp meeting moving out into such a "Jericho march" as I led the choir in the Gaither favorite, "The King is Coming."[218] On those occasions when this sustained expression prevented the preacher from getting

---

218   Gaither, William J., Gloria Gaither, and Charles Milhuff. *The King is Coming.* ©1970.

to his sermon, you might hear someone say, "Great service tonight… no preaching!"

2. Semi-Formal Mainstream Worship superseded the *camp-meeting* genre as the complexion of our congregations became more middle class and professional during the 1970s. Having grown up in modest roots and in a narrow segment of the evangelical church, I finished my Th. B. and went on to pursue graduate studies. I suddenly found myself among a company of pastors who along with myself were increasingly embarrassed by the brand and breed of camp meeting worship expression that we now deemed more "primitive". The two churches that I served in the 1970s had already made the organ the primary instrument, and the choir marched onto the platform decked out in matching robes. Congregational prayer gave way to the "pastoral prayer" accompanied by an occasional muffled "Amen" from the pew. The Scripture in which we found refuge was "Do all things decently and in order" (I Corinthians 14:40).

3. Contemporary Worship soon succeeded the semi-dignified style that we had embraced in the 1970s. When I pioneered churches in Newfoundland, I led the singing with a guitar or accordion until I was able to purchase an upright piano and a Hammond Organ. But barely a decade alter, by the early 1980s, the very costly Allen organ in our beautiful sanctuary fell silent, and both it and the Steinway grand piano were superseded by a keyboard and worship band. We were blessed with highly talented musicians who made up the praise team. Several of them were recording artists in their own right, and I gladly stepped aside as they took the stage to lead the congregational singing. The burden of planning the service was no longer on my shoulders. My Minister of Music gave me a tightly scheduled cue sheet to follow—allowing me a half hour for preaching. This was both practical and necessary, since we ran duplicate Sunday morning services back to back. Long before this, in a previous pastorate, we had already replaced the classical Christmas *cantata* with the *Living Christmas Tree*. In this larger congregation with an auditorium that seated 2,000, we installed special lighting effects to augment dramatic productions that consistently attracted overflow crowds. Since the idea of selling tickets to these events in order to control the attendance always met with contention, we addressed this by donating the proceeds from ticket sales to local missions and charities. As we embraced a contemporary style, the natural evolution was to the "seeker sensitive" approach that many churches adapted or adopted.

Douglas LeBlanc on his website *Get Religion* describes how the battle lines that were once drawn over doctrine and other areas of faith and practice are now redrawn around conflicting values as they are reflected in styles of worship.

North American churches don't just fight about sexuality. Many of them—old-line Protestant, Catholic, mega-church evangelical, you name it—are also fighting about music and other forms of post-Matrix worship... As the old saying goes: "What's the difference between a terrorist and a liturgist? You can negotiate with a terrorist."[219]

He continues,

Of all the topics I write on year after year, the worship wars columns generate the most reader response. In addition, there are similar stories in Judaism and other faiths. Check out the 'flexidoxy' sub-plot in David Brook's *Bobos in Paradise*.[220] Or note that some of the wildest acts of doctrinal deconstructionism are taking place in some of the most conservative churches. Let me share a hint of

219   http://www.getreligion.org/?p=172

220   Brooks, David. *Bobos In Paradise: The New Upper Class and How They Got There.* New York, NY: Simon & Schuster, 2000.

this from five years ago: The worshippers may gather in a candle-lit sanctuary and follow a liturgy of ancient texts and solemn chants, while gazing at Byzantine icons. The singing, however, will be accompanied by waves of drums and electric guitars and the result often sounds like a cross between Pearl Jam and the Monks of Santo Domingo de Silos. The icons, meanwhile, are digital images downloaded from the World Wide Web and projected on screens. The people who are experimenting with these kinds of rites are not interested in the bouncy Baby Boomer-friendly mega-church praise services that have dominated American Protestantism for a generation. They want to appeal to teens and young adults who consider contemporary worship shallow and old-fashioned and out of touch with their darker, more ironic take on life. They are looking for what comes next.[221]

In *Bringing Peace to the Worship Wars*, Roger Clark, a minister with graduate degrees in music, educational administration, organization and leadership, said,

> I believe every one of us involved in the worship wars looks on the outward appearance—the form and style of the music... we prefer the musical styles that were popular during our initial spiritual formation... this is why worship wars can get ugly. We have strong emotional attachments to our style. If God looks on the heart rather than the outward appearance, the bitterness, anger, impatience, and selfishness that has fuelled the fires of many worship wars call for some spiritual heart surgery. There are no easy answers, only hard questions... You can win the war and still sustain casualties. At the root of worship wars are generational, regional, and philosophical differences.[222]

---

221 http://www.getreligion.org/?p=172

222 Clark, Roger, Executive Minister, Sherman Oaks Christian Church, Sherman Oaks, CA www.socc.org.

In an article entitled *Military Worship Wars*, Chaplain (LTC) Kenneth W. Bush writes,

> From the congregational to the denominational level, worship wars have divided the body of Christ into a variety of camps... While this debate has many complex undercurrents, much of the public conflict appears to be focused on musical styles and the purpose of worship... For the most part, military chapel communities have been on the periphery of these debates. In recent years, however, military congregations have also become a battleground for the debate over worship... witness to the gospel is hampered if these worship wars take on the same divisive nature that we have observed in many churches in the Christian community at large.[223]

In an article entitled *Worship Wars, Blenders, and "Ancient-Future" Faith*,[224] Chris Alford describes the outdated term *blended worship* as having once described the mixing of traditional elements, like hymns, with more contemporary ones, like choruses. He writes, "Most of us weren't blending—we were on one side of the musical fence or the other. The hope was that *blended worship* might help to end the raging worship wars." Alford goes on to state that "Robert Webber has replaced the term *blended worship* (which he coined) with the new term, *convergent worship*. As *blended worship* has given way to *convergent worship,* the idea is to bring traditions together and create something new. Interestingly, much of the "new" is really the "old" recycled as droves of post-modern worshipers—especially youth— are turning for inspiration to classic Christianity and learning to draw strength and spirituality from a deep well of time-tested truth

223 https://www.coursehero.com/file/p7mjk3m/
note-238-at-86-87-Kenneth-W-Bush-Military-Worship-Wars-Blended-Worship-as-a/

224 https://www.tandfonline.com/doi/abs/10.1080/04580630208599227

and tradition." In describing a retreat with a group of young people, Chris Alford said:

> What we experienced that week was powerful. It was more than blended, more than ancient, and more than contemporary: it was convergent. And it was simple. Here was a group of traditional Southern Baptists worshiping with the lifting of hands, bending of knees, using responses from the ancient church, and sitting in stillness and quiet contemplation! We were not trying to attract kids or get someone to make a public decision or even try to grow our numbers. We were trying to worship... Musical style does not win people to Christ, personal relationships do; musical style does not connect people to God, the Holy Spirit does; musical style does not grow our Christian character and discipleship, the Word does... A pastoral musician cannot design a service based on popular taste or consumer product. A pastoral musician cannot go to worship war.[225]

Alford then quotes from Dr. Connie Cherry who offers this insight,

> A pastoral musician is immersed in the scriptures more deeply, understands the liturgy, the church year, the theology of worship, the prominent role of music as servant to the Word, the need to approach people from a position of pastoral care, the dynamics of Christian leadership, and the importance of administering effectively.[226]

My dear friend, Barry Crane, who served with me as executive pastor at Westgate Chapel in Edmonds, Washington in the mid-eighties, has since planted a new church in that community. In describing the worship at North Sound Church, Barrie writes,

---

225 Ibid.
226 Ibid.

We are developing a style of worship that affirms the liturgical, Pentecostal and contemporary pieces. We believe it is helpful to connect with the rich liturgical history of the worship of the church. This year we are observing Lent, did an Ash Wednesday service, and are doing the Stations of the Cross on Good Friday. We are Pentecostal in terms of desiring the manifest presence of God. And we are contemporary in terms of overall feel. It is an interesting experiment![227]

During a worship seminar that he led in Forth Worth, Texas, Kyle Matthews, a composer and performer from Nashville, Tennessee, stated,

The praise and worship battle raging in churches is a silly war with dire consequences… The worship war is silly because it's unnecessary and damaging. If anybody wins, we all lose. Unfortunately, many churches are being torn apart over worship style. Worship conflict is creating career crises and church crises all over the country. It is a travesty that the church would allow itself to denigrate to such a place where style would become the conflict. However, the battle to win the worship war can't be won.[228]

Matthews refers to the research from religion researcher George Barna, who stated that culture "'reinvents itself' every three to five years."[229] Therefore, when a church or worship leader determines one style is best or most effective, it probably will be superseded or out of date before long.

One would think that if any branch of the Christian Church might be impervious to the influence of the *worship wars*, it would be the Seventh-day Adventists. After all, with their belief that we are in

---

227 E-mail message to Don Carmont from Barry Crane March 21, 2005.

228 http://www.baptiststandard.com/2002/8_5/pages/matthews.html

229 Barna, George. *The Second Coming of the Church.* Nashville, TN: W Publishing, 1998.

the final countdown to the great controversy between true and false worship, as described in book of Revelation, they would hardly fall prey to the influences that will lead the world into perverted forms of worship and promote the false worship of Babylon. Yet one Adventist leader laments,

> An increasing number of Adventist churches are joining the new "sectarianism of worship style." They accept uncritically the worship style of charismatic denominations, rather than developing a worship service that reflects the unique Adventist message and prophetic mission. This trend should cause us to ponder: is it possible that some Adventist churches today are being infiltrated by some forms of the false worship of Babylon that they have been called to warn the world against? The battle over worship, which is intensifying in our Adventist church, suggests the possibility that while we are trying to warn the world about the false creature-centered worship promoted by spiritual Babylon, we may allow some forms of this false worship in some of our churches.[230]

"Congregations across America may be grappling with traditional versus contemporary worship styles, but faithful followers don't have to choose between centuries-old hymns and the latest Christian chart-toppers,"[231] says the Rev. Tom Long of United Methodist-related Candler School of Theology. In his recent book, *Beyond the Worship Wars*, Long says he discovered a *third way* of worship that cannot be classified as traditional, contemporary or even *blended*.

> There are congregations who have discovered how to be faithful to the great liturgical traditions of the church, but do it in a way that is alert to the new cultural environment. These

---

230   http://www.anym.org/pdf/BP/BP_48_worship_wars.pdf

231   Adapted from book by Thomas G. Long, *Beyond the Worship Wars: Building Vital and Faithful Worship.* Herndon, VA: The Alban Institute, 2001.

churches have created a new thing in the earth, a form of worship that is authentically Christian, theologically rich and magnetic to a seeking, restless, individualistic, de-institutionalized culture.[232]

While much of the tension and conflict arises over taste and style, there is much in musical rendition passing for worship that bears little semblance to the worship that God intended—or to the praise in which He delights.

Much controversy revolves around what is *appropriate* expression of Christian worship in music. Tensions over this issue have resulted in churches actually splitting because they could not resolve their issues. Tempers flare as tensions mount, and what should be "worship" becomes "warship". It seems somewhat enigmatic that in the Body of Christ that is already divided over so many issues of doctrine, that we cannot at least harmonize our voices in how to sing praise to our Lord!

Clearly, the battle lines have been drawn in many sectors. And, just as clearly, any claim to bring peace to the worship wars would be preposterous and arrogant, and a call to laying down of arms would be fruitless and futile. And while the term "retreat" resonates with all the wrong implications when you are talking about "battle", it is to the Scriptures themselves that I will "advance" in my attempts to lay a Biblical foundation for worship that goes beyond style.

FASHION, STYLE AND CONSUMER CHRISTIANITY

While we recognize that disharmony in the church goes all the way back to early New Testament times, the current feud is fuelled over issues of style and taste in worship. This has replaced the splitting of doctrinal hairs, and has fractured and fragmented the Body of Christ

---

232   Ibid.

in the worship of our Lord. However, when we reflect a bit more somberly and seriously on this apparent paradox, it is less surprising than at first blush. After all, we live in an era that values style above substance. This is an age that chases fads and fashions. In this "me first" generation, contemporary Christianity has echoed the mantra of the age. We have embraced a "consumer" Christianity where the emphasis is more on what I get out of the experience rather than what God receives from my worship.

Furthermore, another way in which the spirit of the age has affected and infected the church, is apparent in how the Christian community has demonstrated no immunity to the marketing genius of the music industry. In the past two decades, we have moved from "mass marketing" to "target" or "niche" marketing in every major industry. We have gone from AM to FM to XM (satellite) radio, where every taste in music is matched and met by a dedicated channel or station. In the same way that the music of the world reflects this diversity and variety in its marketing, the religious music industry has commercially marched to the beat of the same drum. Radio stations have mastered the art of targeting specific audiences where listeners can tune in according to their particular taste or preference for *their* specific kind of music.

A major factor contributing to the divisive nature of music in our churches is that we have become accustomed to being entertained, rather than focusing on the worship of our Lord. Consequently, our own interests take precedence over everything else. It is human nature to want what is comfortable to *us*. Frankly, as a "boomer", I grew up with a certain style of music. The music style in the church followed closely on the heels of the contemporary music style in the world. We become comfortable with a particular style of music that suits our personality. We readily attribute the qualities of *spiritual* or *godly* to certain styles of music based entirely upon the emotional response we experience upon hearing it performed, or even when we participate in congregational singing.

Music tends to trigger associations, evoke memories, and awaken consciences. The specific associations that we make are based on the experiences we have had. When I hear a flourish of piano arpeggios, or the seventh and ninth chords blasting from the Leslie speaker of a Hammond B3 organ, this immediately takes me back to camp meeting memories, tent revivals, or even to crusades that I've conducted. Inevitably this evokes a warm emotional sensation that I can easily mistake as spiritual. Conversely, I find the harsh chords of modern guitar riffs unpleasant, and could easily judge them as "less spiritual." The simple truth is that I don't have the same recollection of warm memories or associations with that sound. The tendency to assign moral value to music even without accompanying words is so innately human that we assume it to be correct and appropriate.

How many times I heard while growing up, "That's the devil's music," in describing a particular beat or rhythm with no accompanying words. How interesting it was the next summer at camp meeting to hear the missionaries from Africa or South America playing the same beats and rhythms in accompaniment to songs of praise sung to God in languages I did not understand. We tragically mistake tradition with spirituality. In so doing, we fall into the trap of the Pharisees, whom Jesus chastened and chided, "In vain do you worship me, teaching for the commandments of God the doctrines of man" (Matthew 15:9).

TRADITION, TASTE AND FOREIGN FOODS

While I love many of the old hymns because of their theological richness, if I were absolutely honest, I would have to acknowledge that I also prefer them because I know them. When I go to church, I often sit or stand silently during most of the newer music. And while others reach for a hymnal on the older hymns, I know most of them by heart. And when I raise my voice to sing those old and familiar hymns and gospel songs, I experience an emotional sensation of warmth and resonance. It is far easier for me to confuse this with the "anointing" of God's Holy Spirit, than to acknowledge my all too human tendency to equate my sentimental attachment for the familiar as being some dimension of spirituality.

Additionally, some forms of music go against our training and upbringing. Our attitude toward styles of music that don't appeal to our palate merely reflects our natural resistance to anything that is contrary to our own culture and background. There are geographical influences as well as generational influences that inform our tastes in a multitude of areas.

I am deeply indebted to the brilliant work of Barry Liesch in chapter twelve of his book *The New Worship*[233] as well as material delivered in his excellent seminars on worship for suggesting the parallel between "music" and "food" in both the experience of Peter recorded in Acts 10, and the teachings of Paul in his epistles. Much of the material in the following paragraphs draws richly from his work, without attempting to directly quote or intending to plagiarize.

Pardon the play on the word "taste" but we could take a page from Peter's handbook of "lessons learned" on this one. God had to hit Peter over the head to convince him to take the gospel to the Non-Jewish world. And whoever said that God did not have a sense

---

233   Liesch, Barry. *The New Worship*. Grand Rapids: Baker Book House, 1996, Expanded 2001., pp.177-205.

of humor? God gives Peter a vision with a sheet let down from heaven on which there were various types of unclean animals that neither Peter nor any other Jew would ever eat. For Peter, this vision does not seem right. It did not meet with his "taste". It was totally foreign to Peter that God would command him to eat the very things that He had condemned. Yet, in order to get the message across to Peter, God required him to violate his conscience and contravene his training, upbringing and religious heritage.

If your experience is anything like mine, you will probably attest that some music may "taste" foreign or wrong and even violate your training and contravene your upbringing. Yet, there is no Biblical evidence to suggest that any melody, chord, or rhythm is—in and of itself—unclean. The judgments that we often make are based on our preferences, tastes and traditions. Seldom, if ever, do they have any actual grounding in the Word of God. (Frankly, I have often wished I could find some Scriptural basis to forbid those things contrary to my tastes and enforce those that I find palatable!) As I have traveled to various places around the world, I have learned to enjoy and appreciate the music of cultures dramatically different from my own. I have worshipped God to the salsa beats of Latin America and to the rhythmic cadence of drums in West Africa. I've had to learn to adjust my "musical" taste while I was learning to eat the foods native to the environs in which I found myself.

Barry Liesch invites us to consider what would happen if we were to substitute the word "music" for "meat" in Romans 14:22. It would read, "Listen to any musical style in the marketplace without raising questions of conscience. But if someone regards a music style as unclean, for him it is unclean. If he listens to it, he feels guilty." Remember, if we take that approach we must balance it with Romans 14:20, "It is wrong for a man to eat anything that causes someone else to stumble" and with I Corinthians 8:9, "Be careful… that the exercise of your freedom does not become a stumbling block to the weak". When musical style causes guilt or threatens spiritual progress, we should refrain for the benefit of our brother and not flaunt our stylistic freedom before our weaker brother (Romans 14:21).[234]

Some would argue that certain types of music are unacceptable because of the evil associations that have been made with them. While I enjoy jazz, I have less appreciation for hip hop or rap. Certainly, a case could be made for negative associations with both. If we follow Paul's argument, the evil association does not disqualify its usefulness. However, refrain for your brother's sake, if it causes offence. So while use or abuse does not in and of itself invalidate a form or make it taboo, there is a caution not to offend.

GOD'S TABLE IS A SMORGASBORD

While the sheet that Peter saw let down from heaven was a smorgasbord, it did not appeal to his taste buds. "It was about noon, and he was hungry. But while lunch was being prepared, he fell into a trance. He saw the sky open, and something like a large sheet was let down by its four corners. In the sheet were all sorts of animals, reptiles, and birds. Then a voice said to him, 'Get up Peter; kill and eat.' 'Never, Lord,' Peter declared. 'I have never in all my life eaten anything forbidden by our Jewish laws.' The voice spoke again, 'If God says something is acceptable, don't say it isn't'" (Acts 10:9-16 NLT).

I find this passage fascinating. Peter lost his appetite in a hurry. In some of my travels, I have been faced with a smorgasbord of food that did not appeal to me. I have yet to develop a taste or even

---

234   Liesch, Barry. *The New Worship.* Grand Rapids: Baker Book House, 1996, Expanded 2001. p.190.

tolerance for sushi. While living in Newfoundland, I greatly enjoyed the jig's dinner, but never could develop a taste for seal flipper pie. Any in many parts of the world that I have traveled, I have found the food not necessarily to my own taste buds. While pastoring a congregation in the Pacific Northwest, my Music Minister, of Scandinavian descent, often threatened to "treat" the pastoral team to a feast of lutefisk —and those on the pastoral team familiar with the dish in question were eternally grateful that he never kept his promise!

Yet, we encounter a God who has inscribed incredible variety into all of His creative works. When it comes to worship music in the Psalms, they are resplendent with stylistic diversity. The early church was encouraged to embrace musical variety. God forcefully told Peter that all foods were clean to eat. Paul goes so far as to say that even meat offered to idols is acceptable. I Corinthians 12 clearly establishes that God has a view for variety in His Body. This mirrors the creative work of God in the entire universe. Only a fool would suggest that God does not appreciate variety. This must also be true for God's design for worship within His Body, the Church. The arguments for variety in the Scriptures are legion.

Over my years in Christian ministry, I have been involved in various types of media. My first radio broadcasts were typical religious broadcasts, based on early versions of Billy Graham's *Hour of Decision*.[235] Before long, I changed the format, and used a musical format very similar to that of the secular station on which I broadcasted. When I began in television, it was a talk-variety format, not unlike the television talk show. While I hosted phone-in programs, I did not allow the use of that format by Howard Stern and others to convince me that it was wrong to use it for the gospel.

---

235   Billy Graham Evangelistic Association. *The Hour of Decision*. First broadcast, November 5, 1950.

Paul makes his case for adapting his style to the specific target audience that he is attempting to influence to Christ. Writing to Corinthian believers he states,

> When I am with the Jews, I become one of them so that I can bring them to Christ. When I am with those who follow the Jewish laws, I do the same, even though I am not subject to the law, so that I can bring them to Christ. When I am with the Gentiles who do not have the Jewish law, I fit in with them as much as I can. In this way, I gain their confidence and bring them to Christ. But I do not discard the law of God; I obey the law of Christ. When I am with those who are oppressed, I share their oppression so that I might bring them to Christ. Yes, I try to find common ground with everyone so that I might bring them to Christ. I do all this to spread the Good News, and doing so I enjoy its blessings (I Corinthians 9:20-23 NLT).

Following Paul's argument, we could say that whatever style of music communicates the gospel to a given people at a given time, in the context of individual taste, personal preference and cultural environment is both acceptable and appropriate. This may mean Mozart concertos for some and Country Western ballads for others.

THE DEVIL'S MUSIC VS. SACRED STYLE

Whenever I hear people say, "That rhythm is of the devil" or "that music is just too worldly," I recall an experience at camp meeting when I was a young teenager. Since I learned to play piano by ear at a young age, I was playing for camp meeting when I reached my teens. Since our version of camp meeting was big on "church" and short on "recreation" there was not much to do on the recesses between services. On one such recess, I was in the tabernacle on the platform, playing piano with my friend Brian Usher, who has become a very accomplished musician. Admittedly, we were doing some music of the "boogie" vein when we were accosted and reprimanded by a dear saint, her hair piled high upon her head. In response to her condemnation for playing worldly music, I replied, "Sister, don't you recognize that song?" When she said, "No," I quickly retorted, "Why, that's the 'Glory Land Boogie!'" She half apologized, and rushed off to engage in matters that were more spiritual.

It is simply not as simple as saying that a particular style of music is "of the devil" or even "worldly". The fact is that there is no style of music in existence that does not in some way conflict with the Christian message. When we attempt to build a case for a particular "style" and baptize it as "Christian" or even as "Biblical" we will find ourselves skating on thin theological ice. There is no style that is intrinsically "sacred". During my several trips to Israel, I always enjoyed listening to Jewish music, even though I couldn't understand the lyrics, nor could I personally relate to the particular style or rhythm. In fact, Old Testament Hebrew music had no scales as we know them, nor were they sung to what we would describe as harmony. Furthermore, they were without any type of rhythmic meter that we would recognize. Hebrew music differed greatly from anything we would recognize or appreciate. But most importantly, God accepted it.[236]

Furthermore, the Hebrews knew the styles of their neighboring countries, and borrowed liberally from those styles. While most evangelicals of my genre will shudder at the thought of this, as Gerhard von Rad points out in his *Old Testament Theology, Volume I*, "In the matter of her sacred song, Israel went to school with the Canaanites."[237] Sigmund Mowinckel confirms this in his comment

---

236 Liesch, Barry. *The New Worship.* Grand Rapids: Baker Book House, 1996, Expanded 2001. p.199.
237 von Rad, Gerhard. *Old Testament Theology,* vol 1. New York, NY: Harper, 1962. p. 24.

that Jewish temple music "can be traced back to Canaanite patterns."[238] It is no secret that Israel followed the styles of her neighbors. Rather *worldly* for a people called to be separate unto God! While the Psalter was the hymnbook of the early church, the Psalms were not a literary form unique to the people of God. "Harps were the guitars of the Old Testament, and Asaph, who wrote many of the Psalms, was a percussionist"[239] (Psalms 50 and 73-83).

If we disqualify certain styles of music and disallow their use as an acceptable vehicle of praise to God, we may find ourselves in a rather precarious theological quagmire. After all, Paul described his thorn in the flesh as a "messenger of Satan sent to buffet him" and simultaneously said that it was "given to keep him from becoming proud." Since pride is one of the devil's traps, we can only conclude that God sent the thorn in the flesh. So that we now have a "messenger of Satan" that was "sent from God" (I Corinthians 12:7).

We also read of Saul in the Old Testament, that he was sent "an evil spirit from the Lord." (I Samuel 1:10) Throughout the Scriptures, God uses both the diabolical strategies of men that are crafted with evil intent and the demonic design of Satan to bring glory to His name. A God that can communicate His Word through a donkey and make the works of men to praise Him can certainly harness any form of music to glorify Him.

To bolster the argument that music without words is neutral, we could appeal to the teachings of Christ when he encountered the Pharisees. When the Pharisees faulted the disciples for eating bread with unwashed hands, Jesus countered, "It is the thought-life that defiles you. For from within, out of a person's heart, come evil thoughts, sexual immorality, theft, murder, adultery, greed, wicked-

---

238   Mowinckel, Sigmund. *The Psalms in Israel's Worship*, vol 3. Oxford: Basil Blackwell, 1962. p.81.

239   Liesch, Barry. *The New Worship*. Grand Rapids: Baker Book House, 1996, Expanded 2001. p.203.

ness, deceit, eagerness for lustful pleasure, envy, slander, pride, and foolishness. All these vile things come from within; they are what defile you and make you unacceptable to God" (Mark 7:18, 20-23 NLT). Although it is not particularly hygienic to do so, eating food with dirty hands does not cause immoral thoughts. Nor can a musical style or sound cause adultery. It is not the style that is so evil—it is our hearts that are persistently sinful.

While very few people have expertise in music style, everybody can deal with words. While we might concede that music *without* words is neutral, we recognize that music *with* words can be more potentially dangerous. Words can and do communicate explicit ideas and some go so far as to advocate a sinful and destructive way of life. Common sense should prevail in those cases where lyrics associated with a particular melody are familiar and not honoring to God.[240]

In reflecting on the blending of so-called "worldly" melodies with Christian lyrics, two experiences stand out in my memory. While I was pastoring in the City of Halifax, I walked into the sanctuary one day to the smooth sound of a tenor voice praising God with what I recognized as a "secular" tune. This young man, Ralph Yarn, who had found his way into the church had recently reaffirmed his commitment to faith in Christ. He simply substituted the word "Lord" for the word "love" in a popular love song and by so doing raised the rafters in an anthem of praise that ascended to God as pure worship. "Lord, You are my song, my song of love…" he sang. As he began his "ministry in music" this young vocalist initially sang *only* secular songs that he had "Christianized" by slightly varying the words. Today Ralph Yarn pastors a church in that same metropolitan area. In an e-mail message, Ralph wrote.

---

240   See Dr. Barry Liesch's article *Is Music Morally Neutral? Is Any Music Style Appropriate for Worship?* http://www.worshipinfo.com/quicktakes/musicneut.htm

I am amazed that the song spoke to you like that... I believe that I still have the words to *Song of Love* and my first one, *True Love Story*, as well. I also remember *Back Home Again* which seemed to resonate with you. I think the chorus for *Song of Love* goes something like this:

> Lord, this is my song, This my song - my song of love to you
> You gave everything, All that I have I give to you
> I cannot reason why you loved me, I have no other way to thank you,
> So Lord, this is my song, This is my song - my song of love, Lord, to you[241]

I recall the second experience frequently when I am dining in my favorite Italian restaurant and hear the popular Italian melody, "O Sole Mio". As was common in the early days of the Pentecostal movement, secular tunes were Christianized, and this was no exception. An early Pentecostal songwriter, William Booth Clibborn, penned the words "Down from His Glory"[242] to the tune of "O Sole Mio"[243], arranged from Eduardo di Capua (1864-1917).

> *O how I love Him! How I adore Him! My breath, my sunshine, my all in all.*
> *The great Creator became my Savior, And all God's fullness dwelleth in Him.*
> *Down from His Glory, Ever living story,*
> *My God my Savior came, And Jesus was His name*
> *Born in a manger, To His own, a stranger*
> *A Man of sorrows, fears and agony*
> *Without reluctance, Flesh and blood His substance*
> *He took the form of man, Revealed the hidden plan*
> *Oh, glorious mystery, Sacrifice of Calvary*
> *And now I know Thou wert the great "I am"*
> *What condescension, Bringing us redemption;*
> *That in the dead of night, Not one faint hope in sight,*
> *God, gracious, tender, Laid aside His splendor,*
> *Stooping to woo, to win, to save my soul.*

---

241 E-mail message to Don Carmont from Ralph Yarn August 15, 2006, lyrics by Ralph Yarn.
242 Booth-Clibborn, William 1921.
243 di Capua, Eduardo. (1864-1917).

A traditional feature in the Pentecostal circle in which I was raised was the performance of vocal or instrumental solos. When I was asked to play a "piano special", this was one of my favorites. To this day, if I hear the tune while dining in an Italian restaurant, I will hear my heart singing, "Oh how I love Him; how I adore Him; my Breath my Sunshine, my All in All; the great Creator, became My Savior, and all God's fullness dwelleth in Him."

WORSHIP WARS FROM DAYS OF YORE

The "worship wars" currently being waged in modern churches, however, are not a new phenomenon. For centuries, issues of style have divided the church in her worship of a Holy God. For example, consider the matter of dance as an expression of worship. To worship God in dance is biblical. The Bible commends it (Psalm 149:3; 150:4). Scripture gives many references to the use of dance as a form of joyous celebration and of reverent worship. In the first five centuries of the Christian church dance was still acceptable because it was planted deep in the soil of the Judeo-Christian tradition. Christians were accustomed to celebrating in dance at worship and festivals because of the Hebrew tradition of dance.

Lucinda Coleman, a high school teacher and a dance coordinator at Gateway Baptist Church in Brisbane, Australia, conducted extensive research on "Dance in the Church" as part of her studies at the Queensland University of Technology. Her article entitled "Worship God in Dance" was adapted in an internet article referenced below.[244] It briefly traces the history of dance in worship.

---

244   Coleman, Lucinda. *Worship God in Dance.* https://renewaljournal.blog/2011/05/20/ worship-god-in-dance-by-lucinda-coleman/

While in the following paragraphs I have not quoted her verbatim, I have attempted to summarize some of the key points of her findings.

In the Hebrew tradition, dance functioned as a medium of prayer and praise, and as an expression of joy and reverence. This understanding of dance permeated the faith of the early Christian church. While this continued during the Middle Ages despite increasing pressure against its use, by the time of the Reformation both Catholic and Protestant churches had eliminated dance from worship.

In the early church dance was perceived as one of the heavenly joys and part of the adoration of the divinity by the angels and by the saved. This contrasted sharply with Roman society in which Christianity first appeared. As the religious life of Rome became debauched, their religious dances became occasions for unbridled licentiousness and sensuality.

In reaction to what the Christians perceived as moral decadence, the church sought to purify the dance by expunging all traces of paganism from the intention and expression of the movement. However, other leaders in the church began to voice their opposition to the use of dance. John Chrysostom (AD 345-407) commented, "Where dancing is, there is the evil one".[245] Augustine (AD 354-430) insisted on prayer, not dance.[246]

This conflict reflects the difficulties the Church Fathers were experiencing as the church grew in popularity. The increasing number of converts attempted to retain the dances of their own

---

245   Gagne, R., Kane, T. & Ver Eecke, R. *Dance in Christian Worship.* Washington: Pastoral, 1984.

246   Adams D. & Apostolos-Cappadona, D. eds. (1990) Dance as Religious Studies. New York: Crossroad.

pagan cults, so that by the beginning of the sixth century, dance came under severe condemnation in the church.[247]

This early conflict over the use of dance in worship prefigured the worship wars that would follow. With the Protestant Reformation of the sixteenth century came the thrust to involve all worshipers, not just the clergy, in the music of worship. However, there were differences among the Reformation movements over the type of music that should be used in worship. Richard Leonard writes in his Laudemont Ministries website in, *Singing the Psalms: A Brief History of Psalmody,* "The German-speaking Lutherans developed a tradition of hymnody, producing chorales with freely composed devotional texts. They also made greater use of instruments, especially the organ. The French-speaking Calvinists of Geneva held a stricter view of what was acceptable in worship, and limited their music to the biblical psalms, New Testament hymns and a few other portions of Scripture."[248]

In a website article entitled, *A Thumbnail Sketch of How We Arrived at Worship Choruses*, Dr. Barry Liesch writes "Calvin's ideas were exported to Britain where they became accepted practice. Since only the singing of Old Testament psalms was permitted in church services, for roughly two centuries, there were no songs about Christ in English churches."[249]

When Issac Watts rebelled against this state and wrote original hymns about Christ, the church fought hymnbooks until after his death. The hymns of Isaac Watts found acceptance in the renewal of singing in New England in the early decades of the eighteenth century. In his article, *Singing the Psalms: A Brief History of Psalmody,*

247 Coleman, Lucinda. *Worship God in Dance. https://renewaljournal.blog/2011/05/20/worship-god-in-dance-by-lucinda-coleman/*

248 Leonard, Richard C. *Singing the Psalms: A Brief History of Psalmody.* http://www.laudemont.org/index.html?MainFrame=http://www.laudemont.org/a-mawitb.htm

249 Liesch, Barry. *A Thumbnail Sketch of How We Arrived at Worship Choruses.* http://www.worshipinfo.com/quicktakes/thumbnail.htm 2001.

referenced above, Richard Leonard writes, "Still many churches maintained the distinction between psalms and hymns in public worship, and congregations were sharply divided over the use of anything other than 'close fitting' metrical psalms. The 'great psalmody controversy' echoed for more than a century, with the Presbyterians of the middle colonies retaining the exclusive use of metrical psalms well into the nineteenth century."[250] In the same article, Leonard continues,

> However, musical conventions had changed with the Renaissance, and people were now familiar with secular music marked off by measures instead of unmeasured chanting. To enable the congregation to join in the psalms, it was necessary to recast them into a singable metrical structure and to introduce rhyme. However, this conflicted with the Calvinist emphasis on the authority of the Word of God, rendering this practice problematic, for it required altering the biblical text, destroying the Hebrew parallelism. The nineteenth and early twentieth centuries saw the near eclipse of psalmody in most Protestant communions of North America. Popular taste encouraged the introduction of the devotional lyric and the gospel song into public worship. Often set to folk melodies, these compositions featured emotional and subjective expression of the faith.[251]

The worship wars continued, as many communions retained the belief in singing psalms only, while still others confined the use of the psalms in public worship to the spoken word. Leonard goes on to say,

> Early English psalmody, like the psalmody of plainchant, was almost exclusively vocal. Organs were found in only a few of the cathedrals and larger churches. Although many Reformed leaders

---

250 Leonard, Richard C. *Singing the Psalms: A Brief History of Psalmody.* http://www.laudemont.org/index.html?MainFrame=http://www.laudemont.org/a-mawitb.htm

251 Ibid.

were skilled in music, they believed that instruments were appropriate only for secular music or for personal devotion and not for public worship.[252]

BAN THE PIANO AND BASH THE ORGAN

What a difference a century can make. A little over a hundred years ago, the Pope banned the use of the piano in 1903[253], while the Puritans took axes to organs and destroyed them[254]. The battle over song and dance spread to the battleground of musical instruments in worship—and whether there is Biblical precedent and foundation for their utilization.

While clearly musical instruments were part and parcel of Old Testament worship, they are "conspicuously absent" in New Testament mention. Some have therefore supposed that if we are to be "New Testament" in our worship, we will not use musical instruments. In fact, some denominations have taken that as their official position. Years ago, when I negotiated the purchase of a small church building for a church plant that I was leading, it was from one such denomination. We had to modify the platform and altar area to accommodate the use of the piano and organ in our worship services.

The question therefore, remains, "Why were instruments not used for worship in the New Testament? Why are no instruments mentioned?" When we research the background to New Testament worship, we readily recognize that it closely followed the worship of the Jewish synagogue. Since the rabbis had banned instruments and they were not allowed in synagogue, the early Christian Jews banned instruments as well. They merely followed the contemporary practice

---

252 Ibid.

253 http://www.matthewhoffman.net/music/

254 https://www.revolvy.com/topic/Puritans&item_type=topic

of synagogue worship and did not use instruments. The following paraphrases Barry Liesch's insights offered in *The New Worship*.

Yet since instruments were used in the temple until about 70AD, one has to wonder as to why the rabbis banned them. The threat of the pervasive influence of Greek culture of the day—Greek instrument named for their use in Greek temples orgies—was adequate reason for the Rabbis to forbid their use. Further, panpipes were used to imitate serpent songs, and trumpets were used in calling people to war. This horrified the rabbis, and prompted them to ban the use of musical instruments of any kind.[255]

Church History reveals that some of the early church fathers also banned instruments. For example, Clement of Alexandria said, "One makes noise with cymbals and tympana, one rages and rants with instruments of frenzy… the flute belongs to those superstitious men who run to idolatry."[256] How quickly he forgot that the flute was highly regarded in Old Testament worship. The use of instruments would never have been questioned had they not become associated with pagan worship and debauchery.

HIGHBROW VS. FREE FLOW

For those who prefer what some call "highbrow" or "art music", the question is sometimes raised as to whether this form of music is acceptable in worship. I cannot help but chuckle when I reflect on where the lines are likely to be drawn around this issue. Those who are most likely to have disdain for "highbrow" art music are also those who are most likely to encourage and embrace the "free flow" of charismatic gifts in worship services, including loud, public

255   Liesch, Barry. *The New Worship*. Grand Rapids: Baker Book House, 1996, Expanded 2001. p.200.

256   www.earlychristianwritings.com/clement.html

expressions of tongues or "glossalalia". On the other hand, those most likely to promote "art music" are those most likely to frown on the "Pentecostal" outbursts and expressions of free flow praise and especially utterances in tongues. Interestingly, though, both groups have made the same error, and have contravened the same Biblical injunction. In I Corinthians 14:22-25, Paul clearly establishes that our public expressions of worship must be intelligible. "If I come… and speak in tongues, what good will it be to you, unless I bring you some revelation or knowledge? Unless you speak intelligible words, how will anyone know what you are saying?" By the same token, the same principle must apply to music: church music must be intelligible. Music that is not understandable by the average worshipper fails to communicate.

Around the time of the Protestant reformation (1520), many art composers wrote for the church. However, by 1850, church music adapted a more popular style and was now available both to and for the masses. By 1900, church music was popular in style with the rise of Gospel songs that held direct appeal to the average person. The new expectation was that everybody should understand church music and be able to share in it. For example, today's chorus singing is one of the most extreme forms of the development of this philosophy.[257]

LET'S GET BIBLICAL: PSALMS, HYMNS, AND SPIRITUAL SONGS

In our best efforts to be "Biblical" and "New Testament" in our worship, we often cite Colossians 3:16, or the parallel passage in Ephesians 5:19, "Let the word of Christ dwell in you richly as you

---

257   Adapted from a website article by Barry Liesch. *A Thumbnail Sketch of How We Arrived at Worship Choruses.* http://www.worshipinfo.com/quicktakes/thumbnail.htm 2001.

teach and admonish one another with all wisdom as you sing psalms, hymns, and spiritual songs with gratitude in your hearts to the Lord." The challenge before us is to determine that we have a "Biblical" definition for the meaning of psalms, hymns, and spiritual songs. In an on-line supplement to his book, *The New Worship,* Dr. Barry Liesch offers some insights. The following paragraphs summarize the essence of his thoughts.

One view of what is meant by "psalms, hymns, and spiritual songs" is that the three terms are interchangeable, and that it took all three terms to describe the full range. Apparently, Calvin took "hymns" to mean the Old Testament Psalms, because he allowed only those to be used in singing, with no texts about Jesus. As modern scholarship has uncovered Greek hymn fragments, I Timothy 3:16 seems to take on the form of Greek poetical style. This "hymn to Jesus" states that "He appeared in a body, was vindicated by the Spirit, was seen by angels, was preached among the nations, was believed on in the world, was taken up in glory."

A second view, the "Three Forms View" holds that Hymns were Greek, were metered, and addressed to the Son; Psalms were Hebrew, were unmetered, and addressed to the Father; while Spiritual Songs were improvised, inspired by the Holy Spirit, possibly even "songs on the breath", or singing in "tongues.

There can also be found support for the "Three Forms View" beyond the Scriptures themselves. For example, Cannanite and Hebrew music was unmetered and melismatic (a passage of several notes sung to one syllable of text, as in Gregorian chant). Ancient Greek popular music was metered and syllabic. Tertullian describes improvisation, while both Augustine and Jerome describe the jubilus ("alleluia"). Saint Jerome (c. 347-420) described it as neither "words nor syllables nor letters nor speech." Saint Augustine said, "It is a certain sound of joy without words... the expression of a mind poured forth with joy... with certain words which cannot be understood... sounds of exultation without words so that it seemeth that he cannot express in words the subject of that joy."[258]

However, all of these views overlook one of the most revealing facts from the Septuagint version of the Scriptures. In the Septuagint version of the Psalter, the various psalms were identified with headings that described them as *psalms, hymns or spiritual songs*. The book of Psalms is a fabric woven together from spiritual songs composed over the course of many centuries. The psalms were used for private, domestic, as well as for public worship, and we find them similarly employed in the New Testament.

In an article entitled, *Disputed Aspects of Worship*, on the Still Water Revival Books website, we read,

> In the Hebrew Old Testament, they are sometimes alluded to as psalms (mizmohr) in the titles affixed to them, while in other occasions, a psalm may be referred to as praise (t'hillah), since many of the psalms begin with the word Hallelujah in Hebrew, which means, "Praise the Lord." A psalm may also be called a song (sheer), by title, or as a description of its nature... in the Greek New Testament, there are several terms which correspond closely with the language of the Old Testament. While the word translated psalm (psalmos) is equivalent to its Old Testament counterpart, the word translated hymn (humnos) comes from a root word meaning praise. Similarly, there is another word for song (odee), from which we derive the English term ode. All three of these Greek terms are frequently found in the descriptive headings of

---

258 Liesch, Dr. Barry. *The New Worship: On-line Supplement Ch2: Teaching, the Spirit, & Our Congregational Songs.* http://www.worshipinfo.com/category/the-new-worship-powerpoints-chapter-lectures

the Psalms within the Septuagint. All three terms are used together in Ephesians 5:19 and Col. 3:16.

The singing of the 150 biblical psalms is a practice that Christ and the apostles conveyed into the New Testament. The Psalter is the divinely inspired songbook for worship, and it contains timeless expressions of praise to God. After Christ instituted the Lord's Supper, he and his disciples sang a hymn (a praise), before going to the Mount of Olives (Matt. 26:30; Mark 14:26). This singing was likely from the hallel, or praise psalms traditionally associated with the Jewish Passover.

In his first epistle to the Corinthians, Paul rebukes the church for its discord and chaos. In chapter 14, verse 26, he mentions a psalm as one of the elements of public worship. Whereas Paul chides the Corinthians for unseemliness in many aspects of their practice, he never questions the propriety of psalms in worship.

Both Ephesians 5:19 and Colossians 3:16 affirm the continued use of psalms in the New Testament. The words used are "psalms, hymns, and spiritual songs." These are different terms, previously used in scripture, referring to various portions of the Psalms. While some employ these passages as a rationale for introducing uninspired "hymns" into public worship, today's language lacks the precision of scripture, thus reading back into Paul's writings a meaning for the word hymn that is far from his original intentions.[259]

When Augustine referred to "words which cannot be understood" or songs "without words,"[260] he may have referred to ecstatic expression similar to that mentioned in the Old Testament (I Sam.

259   http://www.swrb.com/newslett/actualNLs/BibW_ch4.htm
260   Reese, Gustave. *Music in the Middle Ages, 64.Migne XXXVII, 1271; Nicene & Post-N, Ser. 1, VIII, 488.*

10:5-6; 16:13-14, 23) or "singing in the spirit" that occurred in the Corinthian church (I Corinthians 14:1-3).[261] "For if I pray in a tongue, my spirit prays, but my mind is unfruitful. So what shall I do? I will pray with my spirit, but I will also pray with my mind; I will sing with my spirit, but I will also sing with my mind" (I Corinthians 14:14-15). In his on-line supplement, Barry Liesch continues:

> A contemporary counterpart to this spontaneous praise is practiced today in both liturgical and non-liturgical evangelical churches. Occasional improvised praise may follow at the end of choruses for upwards to a minute, and sometimes sustained for a longer period. (One sometimes gets the feeling that the length of time for which you can sustain this exercise is to be equated with your level of spirituality) Many Pentecostal and Charismatic churches "sing in the spirit" for a few minutes as a regular part of their Sunday morning service. However, there is nothing necessarily "supernatural" or particularly "spiritual" about this expression of praise. Many simply improvise alleluias and other short phrases a cappella over a sustained instrumental chord. The total effect is often quite reverential and resembles the strumming of many harps.[262]

In all of this, we must reflect on the place of style versus substance in worship. The "style" of worship is not nearly as important as the substance. As Jerry Solomon of Probe Ministries wrote in a 1997 article simply entitled *Worship*, "In other words, if the people are called to worship God with integrity and concentration on Him, the style is secondary. However, when the style overshadows substance,

---

261   Liesch, Dr. Barry. *The New Worship: On-line Supplement Ch2: Teaching, the Spirit, & Our Congregational Songs.* http://www.worshipinfo.com/category/the-new-worship-powerpoints-chapter-lectures

262   Ibid.

true worship is thwarted. A wise church brings both style and substance together in a manner that pleases God.:[263]

The central clause of Colossians 3:16, "Let the word of Christ dwell in you richly…" would indicate in the passage that follows that richness in Christ is linked to worship, singing to the Lord, community with others, singing to one another and variety of form. If this passage is viewed as an accurate description of a worshipping congregation, it clearly indicates that the early church had musical variety, and that there may be precedence for singing in the spirit, even for singing in tongues. Certainly, it teaches that music is linked to teaching, admonishing and to spiritual growth. Early church worship was characterized by teaching through song, singing to God and one another with a variety of forms (psalms, hymns, spiritual songs).

TEMPORARY OR CONTEMPORARY: GOSPEL SONGS AND WORSHIP CHORUSES

The contemporary definition for *hymn* defines it as a lyric poem, designed to be sung expressing a worshipper's attitude to God. It is simple, metrical, emotional, literary in style, spiritual in quality and able to unify a congregation singing it.

How did we make the leap from "psalms, hymns, and spiritual songs" to the worship choruses that are so prevalent in churches today? In actuality, is it in fact a leap? Could it be that the worship choruses may be a closer approximation of what Paul had in mind? The following is a summary of Dr. Barry Liesch's comments on the evolution of Christian worship from psalms to gospel songs

---

263 http://www.leaderu.com/orgs/probe/docs/worship.html

and choruses, in his website article *A Thumbnail Sketch off How We Arrived at Worship Choruses:*

> During the early part of the Protestant Reformation, shortly after 1500 AD, Lutheran and Calvinistic churches took dramatically different directions with their music. While Luther engaged poets to write original works capturing Christian theology for congregational singing, Calvin permitted only Old Testament psalms without instrumental accompaniment. Luther's influence contributed to the flourishing of the arts in Germany. While Calvin's concepts made it to Britain, Luther's did not. For about two centuries in England, no songs about Christ were heard, since only the Psalms were permitted in church services. Consequently, no New Testament theology was put to music.[264]

It seems incomprehensible that for 200 years English Protestants sang only the 150 psalms from the Old Testament, with no songs about Jesus or the cross. After this two hundred year drought, Issac Watts began to rewrite the Old Testament psalms from a New Testament vantage. Liesch goes on to say

> (Watts) began to create original lyrics about Christ and New Testament theology. While his work was rejected for seventy-five years, gradually church leaders embraced singing original songs in church services. It was some time after his death that Isaac Watts' hymns became great favorites in Britain and North America. Gospel songs first appeared in the mid-nineteenth century. While they were initially used in evangelistic crusades, their popularity soon carried them into evangelical churches services. Fanny Crosby is one of the most famous gospel songwriters, well known for her "Blessed Assurance" and "To God be The Glory". One feature

---

264　Adapted from a website article by Barry Liesch. *A Thumbnail Sketch of How We Arrived at Worship Choruses.* http://www.worshipinfo.com/quicktakes/thumbnail.htm 2001.

that distinguished gospel songs from hymns was the chorus that was sung between the verses. They also were sung to more lilting rhythms than hymns. Hymns and gospel songs were the common musical language of churches until the "Jesus People" phenomenon of the 1960s.

Spawned from the Calvary Chapel[265] churches in Southern California, a new form of worship music emerged as these young people began to write music and to lead worship. As these worship songs and choruses began to be published, they gained popularity. As a sort of mini-poem, these worship songs and choruses lacked the multiple verses common to hymns and gospel songs. They were easier to memorize, and featured the melodies and rhythm patterns that were more acceptable to the new generation.[266]

While the evolution of worship music in the church is a fascinating story, and the modern worship songs and choruses have brought a breath of fresh air to the choir loft, there is a question that we need to confront in view of the fact that these have rapidly replaced hymns in modern churches. Can these worship songs and choruses stand the true test—the test of time? Will coming generations accept these worship songs and choruses? Moreover, will we be able to transfer to coming generations the legacy of truth that has been passed on to us? While a coming generation may know hundreds of worship songs and choruses, will they know any hymns?

I ask myself these questions week after week as I partially participate in Sunday worship services in my church. I witness the silent disengagement of an entire generation as those in the sunset years raise their voices to God in the great hymns of the faith and in the

---

265   www.calvarychapel.com

266   Adapted from a website article by Barry Liesch. *A Thumbnail Sketch of How We Arrived at Worship Choruses.* http://www.worshipinfo.com/quicktakes/thumbnail.htm   2001.

anthems of praise. Even the gospel songs are lost on today's generation. I then witness those same voices go silent as today's generation
comes alive with the modern choruses and worship songs.

DEATH OF A LEGACY AND DEARTH OF THEOLOGY

The tragic side to this whole story is the imminent and impending
death of the Protestant Hymnody. Forged through fires of reformation and revival, and developed over a 450-year period, it has been
all but trashed in the past 30-40 years, and now stands in jeopardy of
going the way of the horse and buggy. "Hymns are totally ignored
in many emerging churches: some report that they have not sung
a hymn in years. In addition, very little emphasis is given to cross-
generational worship."[267] The inevitable result is that churches are
actually splitting over worship music.

> The Hymnody of which we speak is uniquely Protestant; it
> is not part of the Catholic tradition nor can it be found in any
> other religious tradition. This collective enterprise consists of songs
> of, by, and for the people. They were composed and contributed
> by pastors, poets, musicians, and ordinary people across many
> denominations and eras. They find their origin in many countries
> with individuals from many races participating. This Hymnody
> represents our collective wisdom and experience developed over a
> period of 450 years.[268]

If the disappearance of the hymnal and its replacement with worship
choruses could be honestly traced to a new move of God, even then,
it would be difficult enough for most of the older generation to

---

267 Adapted and summarized from a PowerPoint supplement by Dr. Barry Liesch, copyright 1996, downloaded
      from his website at http://www.worshipinfo.com/materials/nwscpwdl.htm
268 Ibid.

accept. I believe that many of these worship songs and choruses are inspired by God and bring honor and glory to Him. I have to believe this since I have written more than a dozen such choruses myself! Be that as it may, when we look more closely we must confront another influence that is **not** inspired of God—that of the music industry that markets the music and makes merchandise of the new worship songs and choruses.

> The simple truth is that hymns represent reduced revenues for music industry since they are not subject to copyright or any other type of protection that guarantees residuals to the music publishers. Turn on your television and channel surf until you come across some music videos on MTV™ or Much Music™. You soon recognize that the music industry is designed for and dominated by the youth of our day. I am not saying that this is wrong: I am simply stating that it is. It is the youth who possess both the freedom and the money to make the purchases that dictate the shape of music. Once again, that which is true in the world at large is also paralleled in the church and the Christian sub-culture.[269]

I recently visited a church that I once pastored. The organ had been moved out of the sanctuary, and the grand piano was silent. The music was led from the platform where a keyboard, guitar and drums set the pace for the congregational singing. While I found that I could freely engage in some of the congregational singing, there were awkward moments for all participants. The worship leader made certain that several of the older hymns and gospel songs were showcased, and these were sung heartily by the older members of the congregation. However, the instrumental accompaniment for these hymns and gospel songs was weak and stilted. When the piano and

---

269 Ibid.

organ are replaced by guitars, the accompaniment is significantly weakened. Barry Liesch goes on to describe how and why this occurs:

> Guitarists tend to find hymns threatening since the chords change too fast—there may be as many as 3-4 chord changes per measure—whereas guitarists prefer only one chord per measure. Furthermore, hymnbooks are written for keyboard, usually in keys with several flats, whereas guitar players prefer playing in G, D, A or E: in one, two, three, or four sharps.[270]

During my years of ministry, I have had the privilege of pioneering churches, and pastoring in smaller as well as larger congregations. I vividly remember the days of leading congregational worship while playing the guitar or piano accordion. Since there were no other instrumentalists, I had the liberty of transposing the key signatures to whatever key I found comfortable. Fortunately, in those days, my baritone voice had not dropped in range as significantly as it has in later years, and I was able to modulate the keys from time to time in such a way as to enrich the congregational singing and worship.

When I read the incredible narratives behind some of the great hymns, the simple stories that gave genesis to songs I have written pale by comparison. Horatio Spafford penned "It Is Well with My Soul"[271] having just lost his son, and then his entire fortune to the Chicago fire of 1871. He then received a cable from his wife, who was en route to Britain to join evangelist D.L. Moody, that his four daughters had drowned as the ship in which they were sailing sank. Awareness of this tragic trial of his faith gives new meaning to the words, "When sorrows like sea billows roll."

In similar vein, the great hymn "Now Thank We All Our God"[272] was composed by Rinkart, a German pastor, when pestilence

---

270   Ibid.
271   Spafford, Horatio. *It Is Well with My Soul*. 1873. Music: Bliss, Philip. 1876
272   Rinkart, Martin 1663. *Now Thank We All Our God*. Music: Crüger, Johann. 1647.

struck in 1637. He conducted more than four thousand funerals, sometimes as many as forty in one day, often personally digging the graves. From this experience, he wrote these transcendent words of praise and thanksgiving, "And keep us in His grace, And guide us when perplexed, And free us from all ills, In this world and the next."

Whether it is through psalms, hymns, gospel songs, or worship choruses—music should glorify Christ. When it does, it will simultaneously edify believers. Moreover, that witness will speak to non-believers in a powerful way. Unquestionably, hymns and choruses edify worshippers differently. Hymns have stood the test of time—they provide stability and continuity of faith. Whereas choruses have gaps that may not adequately address the work of Christ on the cross, hymns teach theology and discipleship. "If Charles Wesley could contribute 7000 hymns to the posterity of the church, surely there is a place for some of those to be set to new tunes and rhythms."[273]

We have ample Biblical precedent for persevering and preserving the great hymns of the faith. The Psalms show respect for the past, recalling God's faithfulness to His people through Moses and during the time of David. Simultaneously, the Psalms repeatedly call for us to "Sing a new song unto the Lord" (Psalm 33:3, Psalm 96:1, Psalm 98:1, Psalm 144:9, Psalm 149:1). Additionally, we have the witness of "Paul and early church leaders who demonstrated respect for both temple and synagogue traditions."[274]

The injunction of the Psalmist to "Sing unto the Lord a new song" reminds us that many of the modern worship songs and choruses are based on scripture while creating contemporary appeal.

---

273   Adapted and summarized from a PowerPoint supplement by Dr. Barry Liesch, copyright 1996, downloaded from his website at http://www.worshipinfo.com/materials/nwscpwdl.htm

274   Liesch, Barry. *The New Worship*. Grand Rapids: Baker Book House, 1996, Expanded 2001. pp.161-175.

They often resonate with a freshness of faith and an expression of intimacy with God.

PURPOSE-DRIVEN MUSIC

While many church leaders today are calling for a "theology of church music" in the wake of the so-called "worship reformation", many music leaders agree that the realm of worship music suffers from lack of a theological foundation. The following summary, although not necessarily a verbatim quote, summarizes the work of Dr. Barry Liesch in Chapter Eleven of his book, *The New Worship*, where he skillfully describes that theological foundation.

Church music should be determined by the nature and purpose of the church. By examining three Greek words, we can discover the basic purposes of the church. From examining these three terms, then we can observe the following:

- *Kerygma* describes the "one-to-many" expression of preaching or proclamation

- *Koinonia* describes the "one-to-another" experience of fellowship and nurture

- *Leitourgia* describes the "many-to-one" expression of corporate worship to God

The first term, *kerygma* means proclamation and refers to the preaching of the good news (Mark 16:15, I Corinthians 1:22-23). A key feature of the *kerygma* is that it originates with God, and is a communication from one to many. The second term, *koinonia* means fellowship and refers to the nurture and encouragement within the community of Christ (Philippians 1:4-5, 2:1-2, I Corinthians 10:16). A key aspect of the communication is from one to another. The third term, *leitourgia* is used to describe worship or service. This term is used to describe priestly service, ministry, or presenting public face of worship. Its focus is the communication of many to one as when a large group worships God (Acts 13:2, Hebrews 8: 1-2, 5, 9:21).

On closer examination, there is also a divine order in the sequence of these three elements. The *kerygma* must be proclaimed, believed and received for believers to then experience *koinonia*. It follows then that corporate *leitourgia* can only be experienced on the basis of both *kerygma* and *koinonia*.

While the sequence is readily recognized, the question as to whether worship should be given priority over or parity with evangelism originates in a far too narrow view of worship. God is glorified in the *kerygma,* as surely as He is in *koinonia* and in *leitourgia.* In fact, a concert of worship breaks out in heaven when one sinner repents as a result of the *kerygma* (Luke 15:10). Further, when *koinonia* occurs, the Lord commands the blessing (Psalm 133:1-3).[275]

Since the first five of the Ten Commandments center on worship, we can appeal to the teaching of Christ in this regard to settle the argument once for all. "You must love the Lord your God with all your heart, all your soul, and all your mind. This is the first and greatest commandment. A second is equally important: 'Love your neighbor as yourself.' All the other commandments and all the demands of the prophets are based on these two commandments" (Matthew 22:37-40 NLT). In referring to the "two" commandments, Christ refers to the "two" tables of the law: the first half dealing with man's relationship with God, the second half dealing with man's relationship to fellow man.

To separate "worship" from "evangelism" has become a popular modus operandi in those churches that describe themselves as "seeker

---

275   Ibid.

sensitive". Who can argue with the results in converts that many of these churches boast, and who would want to debate the merits of their approach in reaching the un-churched? Not me! I am with Paul on this one, when he said, "The fact remains that the message about Christ is being preached, so I rejoice. And I will continue to rejoice" (Philippians 1:18-19 NLT).

I believe that the "seeker sensitive" philosophy has brought awareness to the church that we have espoused many traditions and rituals of our own that may not necessarily glorify God, and that may create barriers that hinder honest seekers from finding faith in Christ. Moreover, there is a sense in which God is worshipped through the *kerygma* as the gospel of Christ is presented and faith is awakened in the hearts of people.

In the "seeker sensitive" philosophy, the Sunday morning service exists primarily for the seeker, not the worshipper. The premise is that worship and evangelism do not mix, and that worship is incompatible with evangelism. Again, I would suggest, that this requires a far-too-narrow view of worship.

MULTI-SENSORY WORSHIP ENCOUNTERS
OF THE TRIUNE KIND

When we explore the scope of Biblical terms for worship, we are convinced that worship involves the total person. There is both the verbal and the physical as reflected in Philippians 2:10, "That at the name of Jesus every knee should bow... and every tongue confess that Jesus is Lord" and in Revelation 1:14, "When I saw him, I fell at his feet as though dead."

It would follow that the more senses involved in the worship experience, the more intense the worship. Since senses intensify meaning, meaning is more vital when received by several senses. This was certainly true for Isaiah when he saw the Lord high and lifted up. In Isaiah 6:1-9, the prophet's experience was multi-sensory:

- Isaiah *saw* the Lord high and lifted up and His train filled the temple

- Isaiah *heard* the seraphim sing "Holy, Holy, Holy"

- Isaiah *felt* the temple shake to its foundations

- Isaiah *smelt* smoke as it filled the temple

- Isaiah *spoke* out loud to verbalize his response

- Isaiah *felt* a burning coal touch his lips

- Isaiah *heard* the Lord speak to him

- Isaiah *spoke* to God and conversed with God

Since music is multi-sensory, this brings us to look more closely at music as a vital part of worship. Music tends to attach itself quickly to the part of our being that we commonly refer to as soul. Many times, I have found myself tapping my feet to the rhythm of a song on the radio, or humming along to a tune on the car radio without even thinking about it. Music appeals to the emotions, which then in turn open the mind.

Earlier in this chapter, we examined how *kerygma, koinonia,* and *leitourgia* blend together in three-part harmony as an anthem of worship to God. While we recognize the link of these three elements, church services typically tend to be dominated by one or other of these three elements.

For example, in a service that is more kerygma dominant, it may seem more like a like a concert where the people come to listen and receive with very little participation. This type of service can take on an air of entertainment where everything is done for people who sit as a passive audience, courteously applauding each element of the service. The choir sings, the musicians play, the soloists perform, the preacher preaches, and the "audience" sits and "enjoys" the performance.[276]

On the other hand, a service that is more koinonia dominant will be characterized by sharing in a family atmosphere with less formality. People may pray for and with each other, participate in congregational singing, respond to the preaching with an "Amen" or a "Hallelujah". Often there is small group prayer and a real interest in being "led of the Spirit". This type of service is marked by both the giving and receiving of ministry.

Thirdly, there is the leitourgia dominant service that includes both kerygma and koinonia. As the people come before God, their singing is to the Lord and not to one another. It may at times be characterized by reverence as the people wait on God. The music is directed to God in congregational response to His redemptive grace. The musicians support rather than supplant the congregational worship. God is the audience, and the worshippers are there to glorify Him.

All three of these models of worship are found in the Bible. The kerygma is more common to the Jewish synagogue, which became the prototype for the early church worship experience. The koinonia describes the kind of "body ministry" worship that Paul refers to in his writings to the Corinthians, Ephesians and Colossians. The leitourgia would be more descriptive of the Old

---

276   Adapted and summarized from a PowerPoint supplement by Dr. Barry Liesch, copyright 1996, downloaded from his website at http://www.worshipinfo.com/materials/nwscpwdl.htm

Testament worship of the Tabernacle in the wilderness, and the Temple of Solomon. It would also describe worship as we witness it in the book of Revelation.[277]

PERFORMANCE WORSHIP: EXCELLENCE FOR HIS EXCELLENCY

Another troublesome issue in contemporary worship has to do with the whole concept of *performance*, and whether *performance* can or should have any place in our worship expression and experience. Even those who protest that there is no room for performance in Christian worship will with slip of the tongue admit that they have been distracted by church music that was performed poorly.

While wearing my "pastor's" hat, I would contend that performance has no place in the congregation of the saints. (How holy is that?) And then, I would bounce from piano to organ to pulpit, and in every case render somewhat of a performance. I preferred to call it "delivering" the sermon, but if totally honest, would have to admit that there was a strong element of performance involved. I used the jokingly say that the Scripture I used to validate my multitasking and switching hats was "I can do *all* things through Christ who strengthens me" (Philippians 4:13).

As with all matters that relate to faith and worship, our final appeal must be to the Scriptures and what they say about performance. In the Bible, performance is connected with "obedience, artistic skill, serving and ministering."[278] And all of these terms occur in connection with each other. If you do a concordance search for the word

---

277 Ibid.
278 Ibid.

"performance" in the Scriptures, you may be surprised at how many times it occurs and how it is used.

1. Obedience: When the Scriptures record, "All that is to be done, they shall perform.. All their work, shall be performed at the command of Aaron and his sons" these words are preceded by the phrase, "And the Lord said to Moses" (Numbers 4:26-27).

2. Artistic Skill: Moses told the people in that God had chosen Bezalel, "See the Lord has called by name Bezalel… to make designs… in the cutting of stones… the carving of wood, so as to perform in every inventive work" (Exodus 35:30-33).

3. Serving: "Then the Lord said to Moses… they will serve Aaron and the whole community, performing their sacred duties in and around the tabernacle" (Numbers 3:7 NLT).

4. Serving and Ministering: "David assigned the following men to lead the music at the house of the Lord after he put the Ark there. They ministered with music there at the Tabernacle until Solomon built the Temple of the Lord in Jerusalem. Then they carried on their work there, following all the regulations handed down to them." (I Chronicles 6:31-32 NLT). We read again, "They are to come near my table to minister to me and perform my service" (Ezekiel 44:16).

The Scriptures abound with compelling evidence of the performance element in worship. Worship always involves action, as in Psalm 95:6, "Come let us worship and bow down; Let us kneel before the Lord our maker." An examination of both the Hebrew and Greek derivatives for worship reveals an insistence upon some type of action.

OLD TESTAMENT WORSHIP MUSIC: NOT A
NOT-FOR-PROPHET PROPOSITION

When we look at the Old Testament, we discover that both composing and performing of music was normative to the life of the Israelite prophets. Many of them were musicians. As we will discussed earlier in Chapter Eleven, Miriam the prophetess led the women in song and dance, celebrating the Lord's triumph over the Egyptians (Exodus 15:20-21).

Saul was met by a band of sanctuary prophets who prophesied to instrumental accompaniment (I Samuel 10:5). Isaiah composed music, including a song that celebrated the Lord's deliverance of those who trust in him (Isaiah 26:1-6). Ezekiel was publicly regarded as "one who has a beautiful voice and plays well on an instrument" (Ezekiel 33:32).

Notwithstanding the significance that others had in establishing music as worship, it is David with whom we are most familiar. He was a musician as well as a warrior, and he firmly established the place of music in the worship of the Lord. Prior to the sacrifices offered in moving the ark of the covenant to Jerusalem, he instructed the Levitical musicians to celebrate the ark's journey to Zion (I Chronicles 15:16-24), and appointed Asaph as chief musician in charge of continual thanksgiving and praise (I Chronicles 16:1-7).

HEBREW WORSHIP: SKILFUL AND TRAINED MUSICIANS

In *Music and Worship in the Bible*[279], Richard C. Leonard carefully traces the history and development of music in both the Old and

---

279   Leonard, Richard C. *Music and Worship in the Bible*. http://www.laudemont.org/index.
html?MainFrame=http://www.laudemont.org/a-mawitb.htm

New Testament records. The following paragraphs, although not a verbatim quote, summarize some of his reflections.

In temple worship, music was viewed as "sacrifice of praise," or as an offering of song to accompany the offering of sacrifice. The performance of music was regulated and standardized under the Judean rulers. The headings and titles of fifty-five of the Psalms refer to the music director, with instructions for performance on various instruments or using certain tunes. This continued to be a feature of Israelite and Jewish worship. After the exile, Ezra appointed more than two hundred Levites for service in the sanctuary (Ezra 8:18-20).

After the Babylonian exile, most Jews lived in areas outside of Palestine and could not participate in temple worship. This gave birth to the synagogue, which accommodated prayer and the study of the Scriptures. Here, the Psalms were sung along with other portions of the Scriptures, and prayers were chanted. It was this style of music that would have informed the worship of the early church.

The worship music of Israel was both vocal and instrumental. The instruments were of the same general classes with which we are familiar—percussion, winds (pipes) and strings. Horns, cymbals, harps, trumpets and lyres accompanied the journey of the ark to Mount Zion, and continued in use, as reflected by their mention in the Psalms. The sanctuary instruments sounded simultaneously to call the assembly to worship (Psalms 98:6). Strings and pipes probably played the tune in the psalm being sung. Horns, trumpets and cymbals added to the festive joy by creating a larger sound. Tambourines were usually played by women and are mentioned mostly in connection with dancing (Psalms 68:25). They were probably not used in the sanctuary since only men served as priests and musicians.

While we do not know exactly how the music of Israel's worship sounded, recent research has validated a similarity between Hebraic music and ancient forms of Christian chant. When you examine the elements and characteristics of Old Testament music, the aspect of skilled and complicated performance becomes patently obvious. While the main melody line was typically without harmony, instrumental accompaniment could create a primitive form of harmony. Ornamentation added enhancements suited to the skill of the performer. The rhythm was of a more complex pattern than the regular beat of modern Western music. The scale made some use of quartertone intervals as well as whole or half tones. The use of improvisation—the practice of composing the music in the process of performing it—required skills that had been acquired through a long period of training.

Another feature of Hebrew worship was antiphonal music, in which groups of performers answer one another in statement and response. Examples of this are found in the Psalms (24 and 118) and the "Holy, Holy, Holy" of Isaiah's seraphim (Isaiah 6:3). In all probability, this vision was influenced in its expression by the chanting of priestly choirs.

This last feature suggests that the congregation, as well as trained musicians, may have been involved in the musical responses of the service. In the Old Testament, the temple priest-musician, singers and dancers were thoroughly trained, serving five years of apprenticeship before being admitted to the regular chorus. The singing was accompanied by many kinds of instruments, including lyres, pipes, harps, trumpets and cymbals. Worship for Israel was serious business. It was not marked by irrelevant thoughts, fragmented elements, silly asides nor unconnected directions in purpose. Worship was not haphazard music done poorly or even great music as performance—worship was preparation and offering—they offered that which cost them something.[280]

PERFORMANCE WORSHIP FOR AN AUDIENCE OF ONE

Therefore, it can be readily confirmed that there was a strong element of performance in Old Testament worship. However, one distinct difference separates the performance of true Biblical worship from performance as it is commonly viewed today. The issue at stake has to do with the identity of the audience. In many modern worship services, the musicians perform and the audience listens. This is more than a moot point: it is the entire point. In Biblical worship, God is the audience, and the worshippers are the performers who render their sacrifices of praise and adoration to God. We do not perform for human applause. While I seldom sit in silent protest while those around me applaud the musical renditions in a worship service, I am always reminded of how far we have moved from the Biblical model. We dealt with the concept of singing *for* the Lord as well as *to* the Lord and *of* the Lord in our examination of the song of Moses in Chapter Eleven.

As Robert N. Schaper, Associate Professor of Practical Theology, and Dean of the Chapel at Fuller Theological Seminary, observes in his book, *In His Presence*:

Our culture richly radiates professional performance—the combination of aesthetic beauty and personal accomplishment. Whether on television or in the concert hall, we are treated to

---

280 Ibid.

an audible feast by capable artists who diligently prepare, where we simultaneously enjoy the music and appreciate the skill of the performer. The pleasure for us is an experience of excitement and beauty. For the performer it is the thrill of performance, the applause, and the reward. However, this contrasts dramatically with worship, where the ultimate concern is the glory of God. The church is neither a lecture hall for sermons nor a concert hall for performers. Too many services could be characterized as a "Christian Lawrence Welk Show.[281]

Søren Kierkegaard reminds us of this in *Purity of Heart Is to Will One Thing*[282] when he says that the people should be the performers and God the audience. In this context, the pastor and worship team become the prompters.

TUNING IN WITHOUT TURNING OFF

You do it at home, and you do it in your car. You channel surf while watching television and hit the "seek" or "scan" button on your car radio. There are not enough locations on the dial for all the voices seeking to be heard on radio, and three hundred channels can't accommodate all the streams of television broadcasting. Our generation has become very sophisticated in their tastes.

Frankly, I'm often embarrassed by the offering of many so-called Christian venues. On the one hand, I'm ashamed by those that buy airtime and showcase musical renditions that shouldn't be offered beyond a high school variety show. On the other hand, I'm also offended by those who have so imitated the latest fad in secular per-

---

281 Schaper, Robert N. *In His Presence: Appreciating Your Worship Tradition*. Nashville, TN: Thomas Nelson Publisher. 1984, pp. 187-188

282 Kierkegaard, Søren. *The Purity of Heart Is to Will One Thing*. New York: Harper and Row, 1938.

formance that it can't be distinguished in any way from its worldly counterpart.

In this media-maddened age of computer graphics and moving satellite pictures, television has raised the standards of our expectations for quality. While I am old enough to remember the first IBM Selectric typewriter and the advent of overhead projectors, I would not dream of using an overhead projector today. Similarly, the level of skill that might have once been acceptable for worship music has been eclipsed by new standards and expectations of a media-savvy congregation.

When I was a teenager, there were no music videos. And there was no real sacred music industry. I remember playing some old scratchy 78s on a record player and mimicking the nasal tones of southern gospel to the accompaniment of my acoustic guitar. There was no "Christian" music on the radio. The closest thing was Elvis singing, "Crying in the Chapel,"[283] and listening to George Beverly Shay sing, "How Great Thou Art"[284] on the Sunday broadcast of "The Hour of Decision"[285] with Billy Graham.

How different is our world today. Not only is Christian music played on secular radio stations, but also entire radio stations are dedicated to the business of so-called sacred music. And make no mistake about it, it is a business. The commercial aspect of this must be appreciated to understand how our world has changed. While my adolescent renditions of the genre of the day may have been acceptable in my day, today's generation, exposed to musical excellence at a more sophisticated level, demands a higher quality of performance.

283 Glenn, Arthur. *Crying in the Chapel,* 1953.

284 Boberg, Carl G. 1885. *How Great Thou Art.* Translated by Stuart Hine, 1899. © Manna Music, Pacific City, OR.

285 Billy Graham Evangelistic Association. *The Hour of Decision.* First broadcast, November 5, 1950.

The church should not become the last stand for those whose talents won't quite cut it in the "real world". God should be given our best, and we should present our best to Him and to those we want to reach in His name. It is a further necessity to immediately clarify "professional performance" as distinct from worship. This does not mean that professional ability cannot worship. Quite the contrary! Ability is an increase in the service of God. We are reminded that Paul the Apostle charged Timothy with the responsibility of "striving for the mastery" (II Timothy 2:5). Clearly, he encouraged him in the pursuit of excellence.

The body of Protestant Hymnody, developed over a 450-year period, presents music at a zenith of excellence. Similarly, the hymnbook of the early church, the Psalter, is rich with artistic excellence. The Psalms reveal technique, both in "acrostic form as well as in elaborate symmetry."[286] The Psalmist said, "My tongue is the pen of a skilful writer" (Psalm 45:1 NIV).

AN ETERNAL SONG—FROM EARTH TO GLORY

The gospel story begins with a hymn of praise by the heavenly host, "Glory to God in the highest" (Luke 2:14). Luke quotes several hymns in the beginning chapters of his Gospel, as we discussed in Chapter Eleven. Jesus and his disciples sang a hymn after the Last Supper (Matthew 26:30). Paul and Silas were singing hymns in prison at Philippi when an earthquake occurred (Acts 16:25). Paul quotes what may have been another song, "Awake, O sleeper," in Ephesians 5:14.

In John's vision in the Revelation, acts of praise before God's throne accompany the dramatic unfolding of events on earth. These

---

286   Adapted from a PowerPoint supplement by Dr. Barry Liesch, copyright 1996, downloaded from his website at http://www.worshipinfo.com/materials/nwscpwdl.htm

hymns glorify the Creator (4:11), proclaim the worth of the Lamb (5:9-10; 5:12), and extol both the Father and the Son (5:13; 7:10; 7:12).

I recently came across an article that resonates with my spirit and communicates my convictions more eloquently than I could ever dream of doing. In his address to the American Choral Directors Association at their National Convention in Chicago, Illinois, February 27, 1999, Dr. Harold Best, former dean of Wheaton Conservatory of Music and author of *Music Through the Eyes of Faith* delivered an address on *Authentic Worship and Faithful Music* to a diverse audience of professional musicians. He said:

> In this agitated, stirred up, divisive, less-than-creative present-day pottage we call sacred music, we must rediscover something that has very little to do with music. But once discovered, music— good music, bad music, music of diversity —finds its place, falls under judgment, and makes its way into the halls of praise. A thousand tongues, to paraphrase the Wesleys, who never dreamed of the world of music that we know—a thousand tongues, will never be enough... In these days of church growth by style change; in these times of prolonged, professionalized, and self-indulgent worship of worship, the near narcissism of big-time Gospel, the strut, the hype and swagger of consumerist Christianity, mega-this and media-that; what is it that finally counts: the size and scope of these things or the faith that proceeds with integrity, quietness, and authority? Only in recognition of these spiritual obesities and in repentance of them; only in a growing humility; only then, let the music come. Let it come in its corrected and rightful newness. Let it come in waves of excelling and bursts of newness and hilarity. Let it come, not to alert God to presence Himself with us. No! Let it come because He is now here, eternities before we can ever

bring tune to our instruments or pitch to our song. Let it come because we authentically worship and cannot wait to lift our tunes authentically and faithfully to the One who is Author and Finisher, Sin-bearer and Redeemer, Servant and Lord.[287]

LOOK WHO'S LEADING THE SINGING

The Book of Hebrews addresses the subject of worship more than any other New Testament book. Borrowing richly from Old Testament passages, it implores us to "Come boldly to the throne of our gracious God" (Hebrews 4:16 NLT). It is in the second chapter of Hebrews, however, that we are given insight into the cause of our celebration.

And it was only right that God—who made everything and for whom everything was made—should bring his many children into glory. Through the suffering of Jesus, God made him a perfect leader, one fit to bring them into their salvation. So now Jesus and the ones he makes holy have the same Father. That is why Jesus is not ashamed to call them his brothers and sisters. For he said to God, "I will declare the wonder of your name to my brothers and sisters. I will praise you among all your people." He also said, "I will put my trust in him." And in the same context he said, "Here I am—together with the children God has given me" (Hebrews 2:10-13 NLT).

In the KJV the text reads, "In the midst of the church I will sing praise to Thee!" How glorious the truth that we are brought into relationship with the Father through our Lord Jesus Christ. And that He calls us His brothers and sisters. And, that He is "leading the singing" of praise to God the Father! Let the redeemed of the Lord sing His praises!

---

287   Best, Harold. *Authentic Worship and Faithful Music.* Chicago, IL: The American Choral Directors Association National Convention, 1999.

SEEKER-SENSITIVE WORSHIP OF ANOTHER KIND

As I thought of the term "seeker-sensitive", it occurred to me that there is another "seeker" to whom we want to be sensitive as well. Jesus said, "Yet a time is coming and has now come when the true worshippers will worship the Father in spirit and in truth, for they are the kind of worshippers the Father seeks. God is Spirit, and His worshippers must worship in spirit and in truth" (John 4:23-24 NIV). I'm convinced that we can be sensitive to both the heart of the Seeker (God the Father) and the seeker (the hungry pre-Christian).

Worship can never be incompatible with evangelism since evangelism is one of the ways in which we worship God. Further, when a congregation is engaging in the kind of worship that Christ describes, the worship is vibrant, attractive, and an expression of real relationship with God. In fact, the corporate worship of the congregation can result in the conversion of a pre-Christian into a worshipper in one fell swoop.

Paul admonishes the pro-Pentecostal believers in Corinth,

So you see that speaking in tongues is a sign, not for believers, but for unbelievers; prophecy, however, is for the benefit of believers, not unbelievers. Even so, if unbelievers or people who don't understand these things come into your meeting and hear everyone talking in an unknown language, they will think you are crazy. But if all of you are prophesying, and unbelievers or people who don't understand these things come into your meeting, they will be convicted of sin, and they will be condemned by what you say. As they listen, their secret thoughts will be laid bare, and they will fall down on their knees and worship God, declaring, "God is really here among you" (I Corinthians 14:22-25 NLT).

While worship begins within the regenerated spirit of the believer, it will be expressed through the redeemed soul, and ultimately demonstrated through the dedicated body. The Hebrew word *shachad* is used 81 times and means to bow or bend low as in Psalm 95:6-7 "O come, let us worship and bow down; let us kneel before the Lord our maker." The Greek *proskuneo* is used 51 times and primarily means "to kiss the hand toward." It is often seen as the New Testament equivalent of the Old Testament *shachad*. The Hebrew word *abodah* is used 13 times and means to serve or work. In the New Testament, the Greek word latreuo is translated worship 6 times, and is rendered as service 20 times. One example is Romans 12:1, "Present your bodies a living and holy sacrifice, acceptable to God, which is your spiritual service of worship." As Barry Liesch points out, "To perform is to do... worship involves actions."[288]

In a BBC radio broadcast, later transcribed in the Anglican Digest, William Temple said that to worship is *to quicken the conscience by the holiness of God, to feed the mind with the truth of God, to purge the imagination with the beauty of God and to devote the will to the purposes of God.* [289] May we so worship our Lord!

---

288 Adapted from a PowerPoint supplement by Dr. Barry Liesch, copyright 1996, downloaded from his website at http://www.worshipinfo.com/materials/nwscpwdl.htm

289 Temple, William. *What Worship Is.* Eureka Springs, AR: The Anglican Digest 1944.

LEXICON OF HEBREW AND GREEK
DERIVATIVES FOR WORSHIP AND PRAISE

Derivative	Meaning and Usage
Hebrew שָׁחָה shachah (shaw-khaw') **Common usage:** *worship*	**Meaning**: to bow down, to prostrate oneself **Usage**: worship—99, bow—31, bow down—18, obeisance—9, reverence—5, fall down—3, stoop—1, crouch—1 Genesis 18:2, 19:1, 22:5, 23:7, 12, 24:26, 48, 52, 27:29, 33:3, 6, 7, 37:7, 9, 10, 42:6, 43:26, 28, 47:31, 48:12, 49:8, Exodus 4:31, 11:8, 12:27, 18:7
Hebrew שָׁבַח shabach (shaw-bakh')	**Meaning**: to soothe, still, stroke, to laud, praise, commend, praise (God), to commend, congratulate (the dead), to boast **Usage**: praise—5, still—2, keep it in—1, glory—1, triumph—1, commend—1 I Chronicles 16:35, Psalms 63:3, 65:7, 89:9, 106:47, 117:1, 145:4, 147:12, Proverbs 29:11, Ecclesiastes 4:2, 8:15
Hebrew יָדָה yadah (yaw-daw') **Common usage:** *praise*	**Meaning**: to bow down, to prostrate oneself **Usage:** praise—53, give thanks—32, confess—16, thank—5, make confession—2, thanksgiving—2, cast—1, cast out—1, shoot—1, thankful—1 Genesis 29:35, 49:8, II Samuel 22:50, I Chronicles 16:4, 35, 23:30, 25:3, 29:13, II Chronicles 5:13, 7:3, 6, 20:21, 31:2, Ezra 3:11, Nehemiah 12:24, 12:46, Psalms 7:17, 9:1, 18:49, 28:7, 30:9, 12, 33:2, 35:18, 42:5, 11, 43:4, 5, 44:8, 45:17, 49:18, 52:9, 54:6, 57:9, 67:3, 5, 71:22, 76:10, 79:13, 86:12, 88:10, 89:5, 92:1, 99:3, 100:4, 106:1, 47, 107:8, 15, 21, 31, 108:3, 109:30, 111:1, 118:19, 118:21, 28, 119:7, 138:1, 2, 4, 139:14, 142:7, 145:10, Isaiah 12:1, 4, 25:1, 38:18, 19, Jeremiah 33:11

| Hebrew לָלַהּ
halal (haw-lal')
Common usage: *praise* | **Meaning**: to shine, (figuratively, of God's favor); to flash forth light, to praise, boast, be boastful; to praise, to be praised, be made praiseworthy, be commended, be worthy of praise, to glory, to make a fool of, make into a fool, to act madly, act like a madman
Usage: praise—117, glory—14, boast—10, mad—8, shine—3, foolish—3, fools—2, commended—2, rage—2, celebrate—1, give—1, marriage—1, renowned—1
Genesis 12:15, Judges 16:24, I Samuel 21:13, II Samuel 14:25, 22:4, I Kings 20:11, I Chronicles 16:4, 10, 25, 16:36, 23:5, 30, 25:3, 29:13 II Chronicles 5:13, 7:6, 8:14, 20:19, 21, 23:12, 13, 29:30, 30:21, 31:2, Ezra 3:10, 11, Nehemiah 5:13, 12:24, Job 12:17, 29:3, 31:26, 41:18, Psalms 5:5, 10:3, 18:3, 22:22, 23, 26, 34:2, 35:18, 44:8, 48:1, 49:6, 52:1, 56:4, 10, 63:5, 11, 64:10, 69:30, 34, 73:3, 74:21, 75:4, 78:63, 84:4, 96:4, 97:7, 102:8, 18, 104:35, 105:3, 45, 106:1, 5, 48, 107:32, 109:30, 111:1, 112:1, 113:1, 3, 9, 115:17, 18, 116:19, 117:1, 2, 119:164, 175, 135:1, 3, 21, 145:2, 3, 146:1, 2, 10, 147:1, 12, 20, 148:1, 2, 3, 4, 5, 7, 13, 14, 149:1, 3, 9, 150:1, 2, 3, 4, 5, 6, Proverbs 12:8, 20:14, 25:14, 27:1, 2, 28:4, 31:28, 30, 31, Ecclesiastes 2:2, 7:7, Song of Solomon 6:9, Isaiah 13:10, 38:18, 41:16, 44:25, 45:25, 62:9, 64:11, Jeremiah 4:2, 9:23, 24, 20:13, 25:16, 31:7, 46:9, 49:4, 50:38, 51:7, 26:17, Joel 2:26, Nahum 2:4 |
| Hebrew רָמַז
zamar (zaw-mar')
Common usage: *praise* | **Meaning**: to sing, sing praise, make music; to play a musical instrument
Usage: praise—26, sing—16, sing psalms—2, sing forth—1
Judges 5:3, II Samuel 22:50, I Chronicles 16:9, Psalms 7:17, 9:2, 11, 18:49, 21:13, 27:6, 30:4, 12, 33:2, 47:6, 47:7, 57:7, 9, 59:17, 61:8, 66:2, 4, 68:4, 32, 71:22, 23, 75:9, 92:1, 98:4, 5, 101:1, 104:33, 105:2, 108:1, 3, 135:3, 138:1, 144:9, 146:2, 147:1, 7, 149:3, Isaiah 12:5 |

Hebrew מִלּוּלָה hilluwl (hil-lool') **Common usage:** *rejoicing, praise*	**Meaning**: rejoicing, praise **Usage:** praise—1, make merry—1 Leviticus 19:24, Judges 9:27
Hebrew הָלְהָת tahillah (teh-hil-law') **Common usage:** *praise*	**Meaning**: praise, song or hymn of praise, adoration, thanksgiving (paid to God), act of general or public praise, praise-song (as title), praise (demanded by qualities or deeds or attributes of God), renown, fame, glory **Usage:** praise—57 Exodus 15:11, Deuteronomy 10:21, 26:19, I Chronicles 16:35, II Chronicles 20:22, Nehemiah 9:5, 12:46, Psalms 9:1, 22:3, 25, 33:1, 34:1, 35:28, 40:3, 48:10, 51:15, 65:1, 66:2, 8, 71:6, 8, 14, 78:4, 79:13, 100:4, 102:21, 106:2, 12, 47, 109:1, 111:10, 119:171, 145:1, 21, 147:1, 148:14, 149:1, Isaiah 42:8, 10, 12, 43:21, 48:9, 60:6, 18, 61:3, 11, 62:7, 63:7, Jeremiah 13:11, 17:14, 33:9, 48:2, 49:25, 51:41, Habbakuk 3:3, Zephaniah 3:19, 20
Hebrew דָּרַב barak ({baw-rak') **Common usage:** *bless*	**Meaning**: to bless, kneel, to be blessed, be adored, to cause to kneel, to bless oneself, to praise, salute, curse **Usage:** bless—302, salute—5, curse—4, blaspheme—2, blessing—2, praised—2, kneel down—2, congratulate—1, kneel—1, make to kneel—1 Genesis 1:22, 28, 2:3, 5:2, 9:1, 26, 12:2, 3, 14:19, 20, 17:16, 20, 18:18, 22:17, 18, 24:1, 11, 27, 31, 35, 48, 60, 25:11, 26:3, 4 (and many more passages)
Hebrew הָדוֹת towdah (to-daw') **Common usage:** *bless*	**Meaning**: confession, praise, thanksgiving; give praise to God; thanksgiving in songs of liturgical worship, hymn of praise; thanksgiving choir or procession or line or company; thank-offering, sacrifice of thanksgiving; confession **Usage:** thanksgiving—18, praise—6, thanks—3, thank offerings—3, confession—2 Leviticus 7:12, 13, 15, 22:29, Joshua 7:19, II Chronicles 29:31, 33:16, Ezra 10:11, Nehemiah 12:27, 31, 38, 40, Psalm 26:7, 42:4, 50:14, 23, 56:12, 69:30, 95:2, 100:1, 4, 107:22, 116:17, 147:7, Isaiah 51:, 17:26, 30:19, 33:11, Amos 4:5, Jonah 2:9

Greek **προσκυνέω** proskuneo (pros-koo-neh'-o) **Common usage:** *worship*	**Meaning:** to kiss the hand to (towards) one, in token of reverence, by kneeling or prostration to make obeisance **Usage:** worship—60 Matthew 2:2, 8, 11, 4:9, 10, 8:2, 9:18, 14:33, 15:25, 18:26, 20:20, 28:9, 28:17, Mar 5:6, 15:19, Luke 4:7, 8, 24:52, John 4:20, 21, 22, 23, Acts 7:43, 8:27, 10:25, 24:11, I Corinthians 14:25, Heb 1:6, 11:21, Rev 3:9, 4:10, 5:14, 7:11, 9:20, 11:1, 16, 13:4, 8, 12, 15, 14:7, 9, 11, 15:4, 16:2, 19:4, 10, 20, 20:4, 22:8, 9
Greek **σέβω** sebomai (seb'-om-ahee)	**Meaning:** to revere, to worship; **Common usage:** *worship* **Usage:** worship—6, devout—3, religious—1 Matthew 15:9, Mark 7:7, Acts 16:14, 18:7, 13, 19:27
Greek **σεβάζομαι** sebazomai (seb-ad'-zom-ahee)	**Meaning:** to fear, to honor religiously, to worship; **Common usage:** *worship* **Usage:** worship—1 Romans 1:25
Greek **λατρεύω** latreuo (lat-ryoo'-o) **Common usage:** *worship* **Usage:** serve—16, worship—3, do the service—1, worshipper—1	**Meaning:** to serve, minister to, to render religious service or homage, to worship, to perform sacred services, to offer gifts, to worship God in the observance of the rites instituted for his worship; of priests: to officiate, to discharge the sacred office Matthew 4:10, Luke 1:74, 2:37, 4:8, Acts 7:7, 42, 24:14, 26:7, 27:23, Romans 1:9, 1:25, Philippians 3:3, II Timothy 1:3, Hebrews 8:5, 9:9,14, 10:2, 12:28, 13:10, Revelation 7:15, 22:3
Greek **εὐσεβέω** eusebeo (yoo-seb-eh'-o) **Common usage:** *worship*	**Meaning:** to act piously or reverently towards God, one's country, magistrates, relations, and all to whom dutiful regard or reverence is due **Usage:** worship—1, show piety—1 Acts 17:23, I Timothy 5:4
Greek **σέβασμα** sebasma (seb'-as-mah) **Common usage:** *what is worshipped*	**Meaning:** whatever is religiously honored, an object of worship, a) of temples, altars, statues, idolatrous images **Usage:** devotion—1, that is worshipped—1 Acts 17:23, II Thessalonians 2:4

Greek **ἐθελοθρησκία** ethelothreskeia (eth-el-oth-race-ki'-ah) **Common usage: *voluntary, arbitrary worship***	**Meaning:** voluntary, arbitrary worship; worship which one prescribes and devises for himself, contrary to the contents and nature of faith which ought to be directed to Christ **Usage:** will worship—1 Colossians 2:23
Greek **θρησκεία** threskeia (thrace-ki'-ah) **Common usage: *religious discipline, religion***	**Meaning:** religious worship, especially external, that which consists of ceremonies **Usage:** religion—3, worshipping—1 Acts 26:5, Colossians 2:18, James 1:26, 27
Greek **αἶνος** ainos (ah'-ee-nos) **Common usage: *praise***	**Meaning:** praise, laudatory discourse **Usage:** praise—2 Matthew 21:16, Luke 18:43
Greek **ἔπαινος** epainos (ep'-ahee-nos) **Common usage: *praise***	**Meaning:** approbation, commendation, praise **Usage:** praise—11 Romans 2:29, Rom 13:3, I Corinthians 4:5, II Corinthians 8:18, Ephesians 1:6, 12, 14, Philippians 1:11, 4:8, I Peter 1:7, 2:14
Greek **αἴνεσις** ainesis (ah'-ee-nes-is) **Common usage: *praise***	**Meaning:** praise, a thank offering **Usage:** praise—1 Hebrews 13:14
Greek **αἰνέω** aineo (ahee-neh'-o) **Common usage: *praise***	**Meaning:** to praise, extol, to sing praises in honor to God, to allow, recommend, to promise or vow **Usage:** praise—9 Luke 2:13, 20, 19:37, 24:53, Acts 2:47, 3:8, 9, Romans 15:11, Rev 19:5
Greek **ἐπαινέω** epaineo (ep-ahee-neh'-o) **Common usage: *praise***	**Meaning:** to approve, to praise **Usage:** praise—4, laud—1, commend—1 Luke 16:8, Romans 15:11, I Corinthians 11:2, 17, 22

Greek ὑμνέω	**Meaning:** to sing the praise of, sing hymns to, to sing a hymn, to sing
humneo (hoom-neh'-o) **Common usage:** *sing praise*	**Usage:** sing an hymn—2, sing praise—2 Luke 16:8, Romans 15:11, I Corinthians 11:2, 17, 22
Greek δόξ doxa (dox'-ah) **Common usage:** *sing praise*	**Meaning:** opinion, judgment, view; in the NT always a good opinion concerning one, resulting in praise, honor, and glory; splendor, brightness, magnificence, excellence, preeminence, dignity, grace, majesty; a thing belonging to God; the kingly majesty which belongs to him as supreme ruler, majesty in the sense of the absolute perfection of the deity; a thing belonging to Christ; the kingly majesty of the Messiah; the absolutely perfect inward or personal excellency of Christ; the majesty; a most glorious condition, most exalted state; of that condition with God the Father in heaven to which Christ was raised after he had achieved his work on earth; the glorious condition of blessedness into which is appointed and promised that true Christians shall enter after their Savior's return from heaven **Usage:** glory—145, glorious—10, honor—6, praise—4, dignity—2, worship—1 168 times including: Matthew 4:8, 6:13, 29, 16:27, 19:28, 24:30, 25:31, Mark 8:38, 10:37, 13:26, Luke 2:9, 14, 32, 4:6, 9:26, 31, 32, 12:27, 14:10, 17:18, 19:38, 21:27, 24:26, John 1:14, 2:11, 5:41, 44, 7:18, 8:50, 54, 9:24, 11:4, 40, 12:41, 43, 17:5, 22 , 24, Acts 7:2, 55, 12:23, 22:11, Romans 1:23, 2:7, 10, 3:7, 3:23, 4:20, 5:2, 6:4
Greek ψάλλω psallo (psal'-lo) **Common usage:** *sing*	**Meaning:** to pluck off, pull out , to cause to vibrate by touching, to twang, to touch or strike the chord, to twang the strings of a musical instrument so that they gently vibrate, to play on a stringed instrument, to play, the harp, etc. ; to sing to the music of the harp; in the NT to sing a hymn, to celebrate the praises of God in song **Usage:** sing—3, sing psalms—1, make melody—1 Romans 15:9, I Corinthians 14:15, Ephesians 5:19, James 5:13

Greek	Meaning: to confess, to profess; acknowledge openly and joyfully; to one's honor: to celebrate, give praise to; to profess that one will do something, to promise, agree, engage
ἐξομολογέω exomologeo (ex-om-ol-og-eh'-o) **Common usage:** *to confess*	**Usage:** confess—8, thank—2, promise—1 Matthew 3:6, 11:25, Mark 1:5, Luke 10:21, 22:6, Acts 19:18, Romans 14:11, 15:9, Philippians 2:11, James 5:16, Revelation 3:5

SELECTED QUOTES
ON WORSHIP

*To gather with God's people in united adoration of the
Father is as necessary to the Christian life as prayer.*

—**Martin Luther**

*A man can no more diminish God's glory by refusing
to worship Him than a lunatic can put out the sun by
scribbling the word, 'darkness' on the walls of his cell.*

—**C. S. Lewis**

*Worship is the dramatic celebration of God in his
supreme worth in such a manner that his "worthiness"
becomes the norm and inspiration of human living.*

—**Ralph Martin,** *The Worship of God*

*But this I know: when the Holy Spirit of God comes among
us with His anointing, we become a worshipping people.*

—**A.W. Tozer,** *Whatever Happened to Worship?*

*Worship is not passive, but it is participative.
Worship is not simply a mood; it is a response.
Worship is not just a feeling; it is a declaration.*

—**Ronald Allen and Gordon Borror,** *Worship:
Rediscovering the Missing Jewel*

To worship is to quicken the conscience by the holiness of God, to feed the mind with the truth of God, to purge the imagination with the beauty of God, to devote the will to the purpose of God.

—William Temple

Christian worship is the most momentous, the most urgent, the most glorious action that can take place in human life.

—Karl Barth

Worship is the loving ascription of praise to God for what he is in himself and in his providential dealings. It is the bowing of our innermost spirit before him in deepest humility and reverence.

—J. Oswald Sanders

Worship is the total adoring response of man to the one eternal God self revealed in time.

—Evelyn Underhill

Worship is God's enjoyment of us and our enjoyment of him. Worship is a response to the father/child relationship.

—Graham Kendrick

Worship involves awareness of God, awe in his presence, adoration of him because of his excellencies and acts, and affirmation in praise of all he is and does.

—Dr. Vernon Grounds

Worship is the believers response of all that he is—mind, emotion, will and body—to all that God is and says and does. This response has a mystical side in subjective experience, and it's practical side in objective obedience to God's revealed truth. It is a loving response that is balanced by the fear of the Lord, and it is a deepening response as the believer comes to know God better.

—Warren Wiersbe

Worship is the acknowledgement of God's supreme worth. Worship is prayer to and praise of the almighty God that fills us with joy at who he is and transforms us into a living fellowship with him in the very essence of life.

—Robert Bailey

Christian worship is man's loving response in personal faith to God's personal revelation of himself in Jesus Christ. Worship is man's communion with God in Christ, this conscious relationship being effected by the Holy Spirit in the spirit of the worshipper.

—Franklin Segler

Worship is adoring contemplation of God.

—Dr. R.A. Torrey

Worship is a personal meeting with God in which we honor, magnify and glorify him for his person and actions.

—Robert Webber

*Worship is an active response to God whereby we
declare his worth. To worship God is to ascribe to
him supreme worth for he alone is worthy.*

—Ronald Allen

*Worship is the honor and adoration which are
rendered to God by reason of what he is in himself,
and what he is for those who render it.*

—J.N. Darby

*Worship is to engage in Christ's praise, not our pleasure; his
purposes, not our plans; his redeeming life, not our fallen
experience; his eternal truth, not our temporal prosperity.*

—Duane Arnold

*Christian worship involves an encounter in which God speaks
to us and gives us the tokens of his love, and in which we offer
to him our praise and thanks, seek his forgiveness and renew our
commitment, ask for his help and entrust our future to him.*

—Geoffrey Wainwright

*Worship is the love making expression between the bride (body
of Christ) and the groom (Jesus Christ). Worship is love freely
given to God it is the expression of awe and respect to God.*

—John Wimber

*To worship God is to fall down before him and to serve
him. Worship is the act of declaring to God his worth,*

affirming who he is and what he has done, and responding to him in praise, adoration, thanksgiving and awe.

—Barry Liesch

Worship is the direct acknowledgment to God, of his nature, attributes, ways and claims, whether by the outgoing of the heart in praise and thanksgiving or by deed done in such acknowledgment.

—W.E. Vine

Worship is man's recognition of the 'worthship' of God. It is man's attempt to give to the Lord the glory due to him as creator and redeemer. Worship is an obligation, an activity and a response.

—Frank Colquhoun

Christian worship is not only offering all that we are to a Holy God. It is the intentional response of praise, thanksgiving, and adoration to The God, the One revealed in the Word, made known and accessible to us in Jesus Christ and witnessed in our hearts through the Holy Spirit. In real worship, we carry on an exchange of love with the God who is present, the God who speaks to us in the now, who has done and is doing marvelous things.

—Sally Morgenthaler

BIBLIOGRAPHY

Achtemeier, Paul J. *Harper's Bible Dictionary, 1st ed.* San Francisco: Harper and Row, 1985.

Aldridge, Marion D. *The Pastor's Guidebook: A Manual for Worship.* Nashville: Broadman Press, 1984.

Allen, Ronald, and Gordon Borror. *Worship: Rediscovering the Missing Jewel.* Portland OR: Multnomah Press, 1982.

Anderson, Leith. *A Church for the 21st Century.* Bloomington, MN: Bethany House, 1992.

Anderson, William M. Jr., comp. *Music in the Worship Experience.* Nashville: Convention Press, 1984.

Andrews, John S. *"Hymns"* in *The International Dictionary of the Christian Church, ed. J. D. Douglas.*

Grand Rapids: Zondervan, 1974.

Are, Thomas L. *Faithsong: A New Look at the Ministry of Music.* Philadelphia: The Westminster Press, 1981.

Augustine. *Confessions, Book One, Chapter One.* 397 A.D., http://www.ccel.org/a/augustine/confessions/confessions.html

A Select Library of the Nicene and Post-Nicene Fathers of the Christian Church, Volume VI, The Confessions and Letters of St. Augustine. Edited by Philip Schaff, D.D., L.L. D, Grand Rapids: Eerdmans Publishing Company.

A Select Library of the Nicene and Post-Nicene Fathers of the Christian Church, Volume IX, The Confessions and Letters of

St. Augustine. Edited by Philip Schaff, D.D., L.L. D, Grand Rapids: Eerdmans Publishing Company.

A Select Library of the Nicene and Post-Nicene Fathers of the Christian Church, Volume I, The Confessions and Letters of St. Augustine. Edited by Philip Schaff, D.D., L.L. D, Grand Rapids: Eerdmans Publishing Company.

Bailey, Robert W. *New Ways in Christian Worship.* Nashville: Broadman, 1981.

Barna, George. *The Second Coming of the Church.* Nashville, TN: W Publishing, 1998.

Barry, James C., and Jack Gulledge, comp. *Ideas for Effective Worship Services.* Nashville, TN: Convention Press, 1977.

Basden, Paul. *The Worship Maze.* Downers Grove, IL: Intervarsity Press, 1999.

Beasley-Murray, Paul. *Faith and Festivity.* London: Monarch, 1991.

Bernard of Clairvaux. *Commentary on the Song of Songs Sermon 3.*

http://glorifyhisname.com/sys-tmpl/b5/

Commentary on the Song of Songs by Sermon 4. http://glorifyhis-name.com/sys-tmpl/b6/

12th Century (Jesu dulcis memori); translated from Latin to English by Ray Palmer, 1858, in his Poetical Works (New York: 1876). *Hymns of the Christian Church. Vol. XLV, Part 2. The Harvard Classics.* New York: P.F. Collier & Son, 1909–14.

Best, Harold. *Music Through the Eyes of Faith.* New York, NY: HarperCollins, 1993.

Authentic Worship and Faithful Music. Chicago, IL: The American Choral Directors Association National Convention, 1999.

Blomberg, David. *Restoring Praise and Worship.* Merrimac, MA: Destiny, 1989.

Bounds, E.M. *Prayer and Praying Men.* Grand Rapids, MI: Christian Classics Ethereal Library, 2004.

Bowater, Chris. *Creative Worship.* Cambridge, UK: Marshall, 1986.

Brooks, David. *Bobos In Paradise: The New Upper Class and How They Got There.* New York, NY: Simon & Schuster, 2000.

Byars, Ronald. *Christian Worship: Glorifying and Enjoying God.* Louisville, KY: Geneva Press, 2001.

Cairns Earle E., and Graham, Billy. *V. Raymond Edman: In the Presence of the King.* Chicago, IL : Moody Press, 1972.

Calvin, John. *On the Necessity of Reforming the Church.* Dallas, TX: The Protestant Heritage Press, 1995. First published by The Calvin Translation Society,1844, 1995, .

Campolo, Tony. *Partly Right: Learning from the Critics of Christianity.* Dallas, TX: Word Publishing, 1985.

Carmont, Donald M. *Harnessed for Harvest: The Forgotten Force of the Laity.* Glendale, CA: California Graduate School of Theology, 1984.

Carson, D.A. *Worship by the Book.* Grand Rapids, MI: Zondervan, 2002.

Charnock, Stephen. *The Existence and Attributes of God.* Grand Rapids, MI: Baker Book House, 2000.

Christensen, James L. *Creative Ways to Worship*. Old Tappan, NJ: F. H. Revell Co., 1974.

Clines, David J. A. *Word Biblical Commentary: Job 1-20*. Dallas, TX: Word, Incorporated, 1989, 2002.

Coleman, Michael and Ed Lindquist. *Come and Worship*. Dallas, TX: Word Publishing, 1989.

Cornwall, Judson. *David Worshipped a Living God*. Merrimac, MA: Destiny,1989.

Elements of Worship. South Plainfield, NJ: Bridge, 1985.

Let us Worship. South Plainfield, NJ: Bridge, 1983.

Meeting God. Phoenix, AZ: Creation House, 1986.

Worship as David Lived it. Shippensburg, PA: Revival, 1990.

Worship as Jesus Taught it. Tulsa, OK: Victory, 1987.

Davies, J. G., ed. *A Dictionary of Liturgy and Worship*. New York: Macmillan, 1972.

Dawn, Marva J. *Reaching Out without Dumbing Down: A Theology of Worship for the Turn-of-the-Century Culture*. Grand Rapids MI: William B. Eerdmans Publishing Company, 1995.

Disciples News Service. *Worship Wars Lecture Series*. September 29, 1999. Indianapolis, IN: Christian Church (Disciples of Christ).

Doane, Bishop George Washington. *The Beauty of Holiness*. Burlington: Samuel C. Atkinson, The Missionary Press, 1848.

Dobson, Ed. *Starting a Seeker Sensitive Service*. Grand Rapids, MI: Zondervan, 1993.

Due, Noel. *Created for Worship: From Genesis to Revelation to You.* Scotland: Mentor Imprints, 2005, pp. 232-33. www.christian-focus.com

Eastman, Dick. *A Celebration of Praise.* Grand Rapids, MI: Baker, 1984.

Easton, M.G. *Easton's Bible Dictionary.* Oak Harbor, WA: Logos Research Systems, Inc., 1996, c1897.

Easum, William and Bandy, Thomas. *Growing Spiritual Redwoods.* Nashville, TN: Abingdon, 1997.

Edwards, David. *Living Christ's Character from the Inside Out.* West Monroe, LA: Howard Publishing, 2002.

Engle, Paul E. and Basden, Paul A. *Exploring the Worship Spectrum.* Grand Rapids, MI: Zondervan, 2004.

Fitch, David E. *The Great Giveaway: Reclaiming the Mission of the Church from Big Business,*

Parachurch Organizations, Psychotherapy, Consumer Capitalism, and Other Modern Maladies.

Grand Rapids, MI: Baker Books, ©2005.

Fitch, Peter. The Supreme Value of Worship. http://www.vineyard.ca/engine.cfm?i=47&e=10275&cid=100000460

Flynn, Leslie. *Worship: Together We Celebrate.* Wheaton: Victor Books. 1983.

Frame, John M. *Contemporary Worship Music.* Phillipsburg, NJ: Presbyterian and Reformed Publishing, 1997.

Furr, Gary A., and Milburn Price. *The Dialogue of Worship: Creating Space for Revelation and Response.* Macon GA: Smyth & Helwys Publishing, Inc., 1998.

Gaddy, C. Welton. *The Gift of Worship.* Nashville, TN: Broadman Press, 1992.

, and Don W. Nixon. *Worship: A Symphony for the Senses. Volume One: Resources.* Macon, GA: Smyth & Helwys, 1995.

Garmo, John. *Lifestyle Worship: How to Bring Worship into Your Daily Life.* Nashville, TN: Thomas Nelson Publishers, 1993.

Gentile, Ernest. *Worship God!* Portland, OR: Bible Temple, 1994.

Giglio, Louie. *The Air I Breathe: Worship as a Way of Life.* Sisters, OR: Multnomah, 2003.

Gray, Ronald. *Enter to Worship, Exit to Serve.* Shippensburg, PA: Revival, 1988.

Grenz, Stanley. *A Primer on Postmodernism.* Grand Rapids, MI: Eerdmans Publishing Co., 1996.

Guffey, Paul. *Live Out Loud.* www.worshipHim.com

Hardin, Grady. *The Leadership of Worship.* Nashville: Abingdon, 1980.

Hardy, Daniel W. and David F. Ford. *Praising and Knowing God.* Philadephia: Westminister Press, 1985.

Harper, John. *The Forms and Orders of Western Liturgy from the Tenth to the Eighteenth Century.* New York: Oxford University Press, 1991.

Hatfield, Mark O. *The Vulnerability of Leadership.* Carol Stream, IL Christianity Today, 6/22/73

Hayford, Jack W. *Worship His Majesty.* Ventura, CA: Regal Gospel Light, 2000.

Killinger, John, Stevenson, Howard. *Mastering Worship.* Sisters, Oregon: Multnomah, 1990.

Hendricks, William. *Exit Interviews.* Chicago: Moody, 1993.

Henry, Matthew. *Matthew Henry's Commentary on the Whole Bible.* Peabody, MA: Hendrickson, 1996.

Holloway, Richard. *Why Belief?* http://www.christianevidencesociety.org.uk/uploads/Belief.pdf

Hooper, John. *The Regulative Principle and Things Indifferent.* Found in Iain H. Murray, T*he Reformation of the Church* (Edinburgh: Banner of Truth, 1965), 55.

Hope, Robert Charles F.S.A., F.R.S.L., *The Legendary Lord of the Holy Wells of England Including Rivers, Fountains and Springs.* London: Elliot Stock, 1893. http://www.antipope.org/feorag/wells/hope/introduction.html

Horton, Michael S. *Beyond Style Wars: Recovering the Substance of Worship.* The Banner, June 9, 1997, quoted by Jim Remsen. *Worship Wars.* Grand Forks, NK: North Dakota Herald, April 24, 2004.

A Better Way: Rediscovering the Drama of God-Centered Worship. Grand Rapids, MI: Baker Books, 2002.

Houghton Mifflin Company. *The American Heritage® Dictionary of the English Language, Fourth Edition*, Boston, MA: Copyright © 2000 by.

Hughes, Selwyn. *Understanding the Presence of God.* Farnham, Surrey, UK: CWR Publishers, 1991.

Hurtado, Larry W. *At the Origins of Christian Worship.* Grand Rapids, William B. Eerdmans Publishing Company, 2000.

Hustad, Donald P. *Jubilate II: Church Music in Worship and Renewal.* Carol Stream IL: Hope Publishing Company, 1993.

True Worship: Reclaiming the Wonder & Majesty. Wheaton IL: Harold Shaw Publishers, 1998.

Jackson, Wayne. *My Husband Is a Snake.* © 2006 by Christian Courier Publications. All rights reserved.

Jacobsen, Wayne. *The Naked Church.* Oxnard, CA: Body Life Publishers, 1997.

Jakes, T. D. *Naked and Not Ashamed.* Shippensburg, PA: Destiny Image Publishers, 2001.

Julian, John. *Dictionary of Hymnology.* London: John Murray, 1892.

Kendall, R. T. *Worshipping God: Rediscovering the Full Dimension of Worship.* London: Hodder & Stoughton, 1999.

Kendrick, Graham. *Worship.* Eastbourne: Kingsway, 1984.

Ten Worshipping Churches. Essex: MARC, 1986.

Kennington, John D. http://www.theoed.org/

Kimball, Dan. *Emerging Worship.* Grand Rapids, MI: Zondervan, 2004.

Kierkegaard, Søren. *The Purity of Heart Is to Will One Thing.* New York: Harper and Row, 1938.

Kneen, John Joseph. http://www.isle-of-man.com/manxnotebook/mquart/mq25091.htm

Kraueter, Tom. *Developing an Effective Worship Ministry.* Hillsboro: Training Resources, 1993.

Keys to Becoming an Effective Worship Leader. Hillsboro: Training Resources, 1991.

Krejcir, Richard Joseph. *God's Pattern for Worship: The History of 'Doing Church' through the Centuries.* www.intothyword.com 2002.

Lang, Bernhard. *Sacred Games: A History of Christian Worship.* Y ale University Press, 1997.

Law, Terry. *The Power of Praise and Worship.* Phoenix, AZ: Victory House Publishers, 1985.

Lawrence, Brother (Nicholas Herman, c. 1605-1691) *The Practice of the Presence of God: The Best Rule of Holy Life.* London: Hodder, 1981.

Layton, Dian. *Soldiers with Little Feet.* Shippensburg, PA: Destiny, 1989.

Leisch, Barry. *People in the Presence of God.* Grand Rapids, MI: Zondervan, 1988.

The New Worship. Grand Rapids, MI: Baker Book House, 1996, Expanded 2001.

Long, Thomas G. *Beyond the Worship Wars: Building Vital and Faithful Worship.* Herndon, VA: The Alban Institute, 2001.

Lovelace Austin and William C. Rice, *Music and Worship in the Church.* Nashville, TN: Abingdon, 1976.

Lovette, Roger. *Come to Worship.* Nashville: Broadman, 1990.

Luther, Martin. *Preface to a musical collection by his friend Walther.* printed in 1538.

MacArthur, John, Jr. *True Worship.* Chicago, IL: Moody, 1985.

The MacArthur Study Bible. electronic ed. Nashville, TN: Word Pub., 1997.

MacDonald, Gordon. *Forging a Real World Faith.* Nashville, TN: Thomas Nelson, 1989.

MacDonald, William and Farstad, Arthur: *Believer's Bible Commentary: Old and New Testaments.* Nashville, TN: Thomas Nelson, 1997.

Mains, David. *The Sense of His Presence.* Texas: Word, 1988.

Malm, Richard. *Perfected Praise.* Shippensburg, PA: Destiny, 1988.

Marian, Jim. *Leading Your Students in Worship.* Wheaton, IL: Victor Books, 1993.

Marshall, Michael. *Renewal in Worship.* London: Marshalls, 1982.

Martin, Ralph P. *Worship in the Early Church.* London: Marshall, Morgan and Scott. 1964.

Mayer, Dr. Alfred Goldsborough. *A History of Fiji.* http://www.worldwideschool.org/library/books/hst/historyofotherareas/AHistoryOfFiji/Chap1.html

McGee, J. Vernon. *Thru the Bible Commentary. electronic ed.* Nashville, TN: Thomas Nelson, 1997.

McIntosh, Gary L. *One Size Doesn't Fit All.* Grand Rapids, MI: Revell, 1999.

McLaren, Brian. *Reinventing Your Church.* Grand Rapids, MI: Zondervan, 1998.

McKenna, David L. and Ogilvie, Lloyd J. *The Preacher's Commentary Series, Volume 12: Job.* Nashville, TN: Thomas Nelson Inc, 1986

McMinn, Don. quoted by Lamar Boschman. *A True Heart for Worship.* http://www.experiencingworship.com/articles/reviews/-p5.html

Menzies, Gavin. *1421: The Year China Discovered America.* New York, NY: William Morrow and Company, 2003.

Miller, Kim. *Handbook for Multi-Sensory Worship.* Nashville: Abingdon Press, 1999.

Moody, D. L. *Notes From My Bible.* Amsterdam, NL: Fredonia, 2002.

Morgenthaler, Sally. *Worship Evangelism.* Grand Rapids, MI: Zondervan, 1995.

Morrill, Bruce T., ed. *Bodies of Worship: Explorations in Theory and Practice.* Liturgical Press, 2000.

Mowinckel, Sigmund. *The Psalms in Israel's Worship.* Trans. D. R. Ap-Thomas. Nashville: Abingdon Press, 1962.

Mumford , Bob. *Entering and Enjoying Worship.* Florida: Manna Christian Outreach, 1975.

Murchison, Anne. *Praise and Worship.* Dallas, TX: Word, 1981.

Myers, Warren. *Praise: a Door for God's Presence.* Surrey: NavPress, 1987.

Newman, Stephen M. *Experiencing Worship: A Study of Biblical Worship.* http://www.experiencingworship.com/articles/studies/2001-7-Experiencing-Worship-The-print.html

Niebuhr, H. Richard. *The Social Sources of Denominationalism.* New York: Meridian Books, 1957 Edition Reprint, originally published 1929.

Nori, Don. *His Manifest Presence.* Shippensburg, PA: Destiny, 1988.

Nouwen, Henri J.M. *Intimacy.* San Francisco, CA: Harper, 1969.

Ortlund, Anne. *Up With Worship.* Nashville, TN: Broadman and Holman, 2001.

Owens, Ron. *Return to Worship: Letters to the Church.* Nashville: Broadman and Holman, 1999.

Packer, James I. *Knowing God.* Downers Grove, IL: Intervarsity Press, 1993.

Parrett, Gary A. *9.5 Theses on Worship.* Carol Stream, IL: Christianity Today, February 2005, Vol. 49, No. 2, Page 38.

Payton, Leonard R. *Reforming Our Worship Music.* Wheaton, IL: Crossway Books, 1999.

Peterson, David. *Engaging With God: A Biblical Theology of Worship.* Downers Grove, IL: InterVarsity Press, 2002.

Peterson, Eugene H. *The Message.* Colorado Springs, CO: Navpress 1993.

Phillips, J.B. *God Our Contemporary.* New York, NY: The Macmillan Company, 1960.

The J.B. Phillips New Testament. London: HarperCollins, 1958.

Pick, Bernard. *Luther as a Hymnist.* Philadelphia, 1875: Publisher Unknown, Public Domain.

Redman, Matt. *The Heart of Worship.* 1997 Kingsway's Thankyou Music.

and Beth Redman. *Blessed Be Your Name.* Ventura, CA: Regal Gospel Light, 2005.

and friends. *Inside Out Worship.* Ventura, CA: Regal Gospel Light, 2005.

Reese, Gustave. *Music in the Middle Ages, 64.Migne XXXVII, 1271; Nicene & Post-N, Ser. 1, VIII, 488.*

Rimmer, Harry. *Flying Worms.* Grand Rapids, MI: Wm. B. Eerdmans Publishing Co., 1943.

Saliers, Donald E. *Worship as Theology.* Nashville, TN: Abingon Press, 1994.

Worship Come to Its Senses. Nashville, TN: Abingon Press, 1996.

Sample, Tex. *The Spectacle of Worship in a Wired World: Electronic Culture and the Gathered People of God.* Nashville, TN: Abingdon Press, 1998.

Schaff, Philip. *The History of the Christian Church, Volume II: Ante-Nicene Christianity. A.D. 100-325., reference Adv. Colotem (an Epicurean), c. 31 (Moralia, ed. Tauchnitz, VI. 265).*

Segler, Franklin, *Christian Worship.* Nashville: Broadman, 1967.

Franklin M., and Randall C. Bradley. *Understanding, Preparing for, and Practicing Christian Worship.* 2nd Edition. Nashville: Broadman and Holman, 1996.

Slaughter, Michael. *Out on the Edge.* Nashville: Abingdon, 1998.

Unlearning Church. Loveland, CO: Group Publishing, 2002.

Sorge, Bob. *Exploring Worship.* New York: Sorge, 1987.

Spurgeon, Charles Haddon. *The Immutability of God.* January 7th, 1855, at New Park Street Chapel, Southwark. http://www.spurgeon.org/sermons/0001.htm

Stacker, Joe R., and Wesley Forbis. *Authentic Worship: Exalting God and Reaching People.* Nashville: Convention Press, 1990.

Stott, John R. W. *Between Two Worlds.* Grand Rapids, MI: Eerdmans Publishing Company, 1982.

Strawbridge, Gregg. *Worship & Worship Services, Biblical Studies in Worship & Worship Services.* http://www.wordmp3.com/gs/wws.htm

Sweet, Leonard. *Aqua Church.* Colorado: Group, 1999.

SoulTsunami. Grand Rapids, MI: Zondervan, 1999.

Taylor, Jack R. *The Hallelujah Factor.* Suffolk: Highland, 1987.

Temple, William. *What Worship Is.* Eureka Springs, AR: The Anglican Digest 1944.

Thielen, Martin. *Ancient-Modern Worship: A Practical Guide to Blending Worship Styles.* Nashville: Abingdon Press, 2000.

Thompson, Frank C. *The Thompson Chain-Reference Bible.* Dobbs Ferry, NY: 1908.

Tippit, Sammy. *Worthy of Worship.* Chicago: Moody, 1989.

Tittley, Mark. *The Worship Leaders Manual.* Sonlife Africa, 2003.

Torrance, James B. *Worship, Community and the Triune God of Grace.* Downers Grove, IL: InterVarsity Press, 1996.

Towns, Elmer. *Putting an End to Worship Wars.* Nashville, TN: Broadman & Holman Publishers, 1996.

Tozer, A.W. *Whatever Happened to Worship.* Eastbourne: Kingsway, UK: 1985.

The Pursuit of God. Camp Hill, PA: Christian Publications, 1993.

Worship: The Missing Jewel of the Evangelical Church. Camp Hill, PA: Christian Publications, 1961.

Underhill, Evelyn. *Worship.* Guildford, Surrey: Eagle, 1991 [originally published 1936].

Valentine, Milton D.D., LL.D, *Christian Theology.* Philadelphia, PA: The United Lutheran Publication House, Lutheran Publication Society © 19062

van Unnik, W.C. *Luke-Acts, a Strom Center in Contemporary Scholarship, Studies in Luke-Acts.* edited by L. Keck and J. Martyn; Philadelphia: Fortress, 1966.

VanDooren, G. *The Beauty of Reformed Liturgy.* Winnipeg, MB: Premier, 1980

Veith, Gene Edward, Jr. *Postmodern Times.* Wheaton, IL: Crossway Books, 1994.

Viewpoint. May-June 2000 issue. Carol Stream, IL: Reformation & Revival Ministries.

Wainwright, Geoffrey. *Doxology: The Praise of God in Worship, Doctrine and Life.* Oxford: Oxford University Press, 1984.

Warren, Rick ©2004. Reprinted from the website www.purpose-driven.com. Used by permission. All rights reserved.

The Purpose Driven Life. Grand Rapids, MI: Zondervan, 2002.

Webber, Robert E. *Worship is a Verb.* Nashville, TN: Star Song, 1992.

Blended Worship. Peabody, MA: Hendrickson Publishers, 1996.

Werner, Eric. *The Sacred Bridge.* New York: Schocken Books, 1970.

White, James F. *Christian Worship in Transition.* Nashville: Abingdon, 1976.

A Brief History of Christian Worship. Nashville: Abingdon Press, 1993.

White, L.J. *Origin.* http://www.revistainterforum.com/english/articles/origin1_en031801.html

Whitfield, Frederick. *Oh How I Love Jesus.* London: Primitive Methodist Publishing House, 1889.

Wiersbe, Warren W. *Be Patient.* Wheaton, IL: Victor Books, 1996.

Real Worship. Grand Rapids, MI: Baker Books, 2000.

Wiersbe's Expository Outlines on the Old Testament. Wheaton, IL: Victor Books, 1993.

Wilt, Dan. *You, You Are God.* http://www.verticalmusic.com/index.php?page=resources&cat=1

Winter, Miriam Therese. *Preparing the Way of the Lord.* Nashville: Abingdon, 1978.

Wright, Timothy. *A Community of Joy.* Nashville: Abingdon, 1994.

Yancey, Phiip. *Reaching for the Invisible God.* Grand Rapids, MI: Zondervan Publishers, 2000.

Youngblood, Ronald F., Bruce, F. F., Harrison, R. K. *Nelson's New Illustrated Bible Dictionary.* Nashville: TN: Thomas Nelson Publishers, 1995.

BIBLIOGRAPHIC WEBSITES

Unfortunately, many of the websites references in the footnotes throughout the text of this manuscript are no longer active. The following URLs were still working as of the latest edit of this manuscript.

https://www.asa3.org/gray/westminster_standards/shorter_catechism.html
https://www.christianitytoday.com/pastors/2005/december-online-only/beyond-sermons-and-songs-2-further-thoughts-on-worship-and.html
http://www.laudemont.org/index.html
www.earlychristianwritings.com/clement.html
www.gracecentered.com/worship_as_lifestyle.htm
http://www.piney.com/VineyardIntimacy.html
www.roadsideamerica.com/attract/NMLAKtortilla.html
www.songsandhymns.com/Brix?pageID=7130
http://ecclesia.org/truth/corrie.html
http://en.thinkexist.com/quotes/with/keyword/awesome/
http://en.wikipedia.org/wiki/Lex_orandi,_lex_credendi
www.apologeticsindex.org/b40.html
https://renewaljournal.blog/2011/05/19/worship-intimacy-with-god-by-john-carol-wimber/
http://www.ancientfutureworship.com
http://www.asa3.org/gray/westminster_standards/shorter_catechism.html
http://www.askmoses.com/article.html?h=107&o=148
http://www.catholic.org/featured/headline.php?ID=2367
http://www.christforus.org/Papers/Content/LutheranWorshipWars.html
http://www.ctlibrary.com/ct/1999/july12/9t8028.html
http://www.drurywriting.com/keith/worship.htm
http://www.getreligion.org/?p=172
http://www.tmatt.net/columns/2002/11/worship-for-sale-worship-for-sale
http://www.touchstonemag.com/archives/article.php?id=17-04-013-v
www.songsandhymns.com/Brix?pageID=7130
https://hymnary.org/person/Watts_Isaac
http://www.piney.com/calvinworship.html
http://www.subversiveinfluence.com/wordpress/?p=108

CPSIA information can be obtained
at www.ICGtesting.com
Printed in the USA
FFHW010812020519
52202798-57565FF

9 781642 250930